Teaching and Learning in the College Classroom

THIRD EDITION

Edited by

Michele M. Welkener
Alan Kalish
Heather M. Bandeen

ASHE Reader Series
Lenoar Foster, Washington State University
Jerlando Jackson, University of Wisconsin
Series Editors

Learning Solutions

New York Boston San Francisco
London Toronto Sydney Tokyo Singapore Madrid
Mexico City Munich Paris Cape Town Hong Kong Montreal

Cover Art: *Riverdance,* by Angela Sciaraffa

Pearson Learning Solutions, 501 Boylston Street, Suite 900, Boston, MA 02116
A Pearson Education Company
www.pearsoned.com

Printed in the United States of America

1 2 3 4 5 6 7 8 9 10 XXXX 14 13 12 11 10 09

2009220057

DC/JR

ISBN 10: 0-558-57549-8
ISBN 13: 978-0-558-57549-6

Contents

PART II STUDENTS: UNDERSTANDING OUR LEARNERS

PART III COURSE/CURRICULUM: DESIGNING FOR LEARNING

To Irene and John Welkener, who model lifelong learning,
Claudia Kalish, for constant support,
and Nancy and Roger Bandeen, with gratitude for their teaching.

Acknowledgments

We are privileged to have worked with so many talented individuals during the compilation of this third edition of *Teaching and Learning in the College Classroom.* The challenge of selecting texts led to many thoughtful questions and enlightening conversations as well as a renewed dedication to supporting faculty and students in their efforts to create classroom innovations. We are grateful to The Association for the Study of Higher Education (ASHE) for the opportunity to collaborate on the many aspects of this important endeavor.

Kenneth Feldman and Michael Paulsen, editors behind the first two editions, provided a solid foundation for continuing to explore the complex subjects of teaching and learning.

Thanks go to Karen Abney, a doctoral student at the University of Dayton, who helped us track down numerous sources via library and web searches. Irene Welkener dedicated valuable time to assisting us with organizing copies of the readings and proofreading drafts.

Our advisory panel, a collection of some of the greatest minds engaged in the current discourse on teaching and learning, made countless contributions to the following pages. Their rich expertise allowed us to frame teaching and learning through the research strands of higher education, the scholarship of teaching and learning, and educational development. Members of this group to whom we owe sincere thanks are

Ann E. Austin, Professor, Higher, Adult, and Lifelong Education (HALE) Program, Michigan State University

Marcia B. Baxter Magolda, Distinguished Professor, Educational Leadership, Miami University

Tuesday Cooper, Associate Dean, School of Education/Professional Studies and Graduate Division, Eastern Connecticut State University

Milt Cox, Director, Center for the Enhancement of Learning and Teaching at Miami University; Founder and Director, Lilly Conference on College Teaching; Editor-in-Chief of the Journal on Excellence in College Teaching

Suki Ekaratne, Senior Academic Staff Developer, University of Bath, UK

L. Dee Fink, Instructional Consultant; Founder of the Instructional Development Program, The University of Oklahoma

Susana Gonçalves, Adjunct Professor, Polytechnic Institute of Coimbra/College of Education; Researcher, CIE FCUL—Research Centre on Education of the University of Lisbon, Portugal

Pat Hutchings, Vice President, Carnegie Foundation for the Advancement of Teaching

George Kuh, Chancellor's Professor, Higher Education; Director, Center for Postsecondary Research, Indiana University

Joy Mighty, Director, Centre for Teaching and Learning; Professor, School of Business, Queen's University, Canada

Craig Nelson, Professor Emeritus, Indiana University; Former Carnegie Fellow

Laurie Richlin, Director, Office of Faculty Development, College of Medicine, Charles Drew University of Medicine and Science

Mary Deane Sorcinelli, Associate Provost for Faculty Development; Associate Professor of Educational Policy, Research, and Administration; Founder and Director, Center for Teaching, University of Massachusetts-Amherst

Christine Stanley, Executive Associate Dean, Faculty Affairs; Professor, Higher Education, College of Education and Human Development, Texas A&M University

John Zubizarreta, Director, Honors Program; Professor, Department of English, Columbia College

Heartfelt thanks to Karen Whitehouse from Pearson Publishing for her guidance and encouragement throughout the process of completing this project.

Lastly, we would like to express gratitude to the late Len Foster for his initial assistance as ASHE Reader Series Editor and his lifetime of dedication to the field.

Foreword

Anyone hoping to understand and improve teaching and learning quality in American higher education will benefit greatly from reading this new volume. Whether that reader is a teacher, academic administrator, faculty developer or policy maker—novice or expert—this new edition provides an invaluable, comprehensive guide to the most significant ideas, influential thinkers, and powerful trends of the past quarter century. This third edition is especially timely, since improving the quality and effectiveness of teaching and learning in colleges and universities has never been more critical to the future of the United States and the world, given the myriad of complex problems we confront.

The period covered by this new edition is also noteworthy. Over the past twenty-five years, teaching and learning in college and university classrooms have changed more and faster than in the previous three and a half centuries of American higher education's history. Between the mid-1980s and 2010, dramatic and widespread change occurred in both teaching contexts and technologies. This period spans the rapid introduction and infusion of personal computing, the Internet, the World Wide Web, learning management systems, and many related spin-off technologies into classrooms previously dominated by blackboards and overhead projectors. In 1985, online learning was still mainly a vision. By 2010, blended learning had become unremarkably commonplace. In 1985, "classroom" still denoted a real room with a class of students sitting in it. By 2010, the term had taken on a much broader, more fluid connotation.

Even more significant than these changes in technologies, however, have been fundamental shifts in the prevailing mental models of teaching and learning that shape and inform classroom practice—changes that have affected every aspect of the culture of American higher education.

Teaching and Learning in the College Classroom (3rd edition) is simply the best single history of those powerful shifts in the foundations and philosophies of teaching and learning, changes that Barr and Tagg (1995) presciently labelled "a new paradigm." This ongoing paradigm shift—more evolution than revolution—can be characterised as learning-centered, outcomes focused, evidence based, and scholarly. All four characteristics are well explored in this text. This edition is also the most concise single collection of writings which influenced and informed that paradigm shift. Included are key texts by a roll call of the remarkable intellectual leaders of that pivotal period in American higher education: Astin, Boyer, Brookfield, Chickering and Gamson, Cross, Huber and Hutchings, McKeachie and many others.

While this volume offers readers an impressive overview of the intellectual history of that period, it is also a very practical guide to the most effective, evidence-based approaches, strategies and techniques for curriculum design, assessment, faculty development, teaching, and the scholarship of teaching and learning.

In sum, the third edition of *Teaching and Learning in the College Classroom* represents a valuable, unique contribution to the now-considerable literature in this field. It will provide students and scholars of contemporary American higher education, as well as teachers and academic leaders, with information and inspiration for many years to come.

Tom Angelo
Professor of Higher Education
Pro Vice-Chancellor (Curriculum and Academic Planning) and
Director, Curriculum, Teaching and Learning Centre
La Trobe University
Melbourne, Australia

Introduction

This new edition of *Teaching and Learning in the College Classroom* is an attempt to extend the coverage of earlier editions, bringing this topic up to date and incorporating important strands of the current conversation that are not fully covered in other texts. We have tried to include a balance of seminal and contemporary literature on teaching and learning from the areas of 1) higher education research, 2) scholarship of teaching and learning (SoTL), and 3) educational development. These three areas each provide interesting and important insight into university pedagogy; however, it is our experience that they rarely intersect. We hope that this reader, by bringing work from these three areas together, will begin to braid these strands into a complex and more comprehensive whole, encouraging dialogue across and among the various discourses related to teaching and learning in higher education. Articles and chapters were chosen to represent theoretical, conceptual, and empirical work to comprise a practical college teaching guide that is grounded in theory and reflective of the latest inquiry in the field.

In surveying the literature, we discovered that there is an abundance of outstanding resources available. Our first list of selections was four or five times larger than the space available in this volume, requiring that we omit scores of articles or chapters that we would have liked to include. Another difficulty in making decisions for this collection arose from the variability in royalties required by some key publishers, making many important works too expensive to reprint. We have tried to ameliorate this by supplying additional recommended readings and web resources for each section. While we have chosen many substantive pieces, no one resource on teaching and learning could be considered exhaustive given the amount of work produced in this field across the globe.

The intended audience of this volume includes researchers, faculty, staff, and students involved in the three focus areas mentioned above. Scholars doing research on postsecondary education are, of course, a primary audience. College and university educators who are either consuming or producing SoTL, studies of their own students' learning, are also likely to be interested in this collection of texts. Another important audience is faculty/educational developers, those professionals whose mission is to support teaching in institutions of higher education. A potential contribution of this reader is that it provides exposure to foundational works across these areas and to these various groups.

There are many possible uses of this reader for current scholars, practitioners, and those aspiring to become involved in the field. With the emergence of College Teaching graduate courses, students who are seeking a career in the professoriate or are serving as graduate instructors can gain from exposure to this blend of theory and practice as they learn about the complexity found within the study of teaching and learning. Additionally, this collection of influential writings and innovative classroom techniques may provide a strong foundation for Faculty Learning Communities, promoting faculty members' reflection on their teaching and definition (and redefinition) of learning environments. Lastly, centers for teaching and learning across the country will benefit from having this set of articles and book chapters on their shelves. This reader can be used as a recommended text for faculty and academic departments seeking to emphasize and improve their teaching and understanding of students' learning.

Colleges and universities throughout the country are addressing teaching as a means to attract quality undergraduate students, gain state funding, and enhance professional development opportunities. From an increasing international emphasis represented by calls to globalize the curriculum, to the expansion of the learning environment through the introduction of technology, it has become apparent that the development of quality teaching and learning experiences remains paramount to the missions of colleges and universities. In this time of increasing accountability and assessment, resources that promote pedagogical understanding among faculty, academic administrators, and graduate students throughout the academic disciplines are needed. University administrators and leaders, and policy analysts in higher education, business, and government, can use this reader to inform their awareness of issues affecting teaching and learning in higher education in the United States.

This ASHE reader differs from other college teaching guides and anthologies in several ways. It provides a set of articles and book chapters that represent classic and current resources by well-known as well as emerging authors in the field. While there are many research monographs and compilations of teaching tips available in the field today, this collection is intended to blend theory and practice. The benefit of an edited volume is that a range of research paradigms, perspectives, and conclusions can be incorporated to supply a spectrum of possibilities. Each section foregrounds learning as the primary focus for the understanding and design of teaching. The appended lists of additional resources attempt to expand the range of coverage beyond what is possible in a single work.

The content and organization of this reader purposely mirror the basic steps of instructional design theory—understanding learners, setting goals/learning outcomes (which leads to effective assessment), and designing practice and educational environments. Each section will also integrate articles/chapters from the three strands—higher education research, scholarship of teaching and learning, and educational development.

PART I

FOUNDATIONS AND PHILOSOPHIES: SHAPING CONTEMPORARY IDEAS AND INQUIRY

Part I—Foundations and Philosophies: Shaping Contemporary Ideas and Inquiry

In Part I, we present some of the most prominent resources that have shaped the conversation about teaching and learning or illuminate how the conversation has evolved over a number of years, providing a context for today's perspectives. These pieces are organized by the three foci of the reader—higher education studies, scholarship of teaching and learning, and educational development.

Higher Education Studies

McKeachie's article traces the history of research on college teaching: eras and lessons learned that have informed the trajectories of current inquiry. He provides a review of findings on class size, lecture, discussion, peer teaching/learning, and the evaluation of teaching, leading into a brief but valuable analysis of the influence of technology and the field of psychology. McKeachie claims that progress made by scholars from early studies in the 1920s and 1930s to the work being done today has raised the status of inquiry in teaching and learning to a scientific field of its own.

Guidelines for practice grounded in research are the focus of the second reading by Chickering and Gamson. The "principles for good practice" they developed with a team of American Association of Higher Education scholars, based on 50 years of research and originally published over twenty years ago, remain strikingly relevant and useful today. These principles are intended to be a framework that faculty, staff, and students can employ to improve undergraduate education. In this article, each principle is accompanied by practical examples to aid the reader in application.

Barr and Tagg's (1995) charge to shift our attention in higher education from an instruction paradigm to a learning paradigm signaled a revolution in educational philosophy that is still taking hold and transforming how educators think about our work. This shift requires that faculty and administrators become designers of learning experiences rather than deliverers of content. Faculty, staff, *and* students share responsibility for learning, moving students from a passive role to an active one in the mission of the academy. This article has sparked countless conversations about the "center of gravity" in teaching and learning.

Scholarship of Teaching and Learning

Ernest Boyer's ideas in *Scholarship Reconsidered* set the stage for many subsequent explorations of the definitions and types of scholarship that faculty perform. He introduced the language "scholarship of discovery," "scholarship of integration," "scholarship of application," and the "scholarship of teaching" to address the priorities of faculty life and their interconnections. In a time of great change in higher education, Boyer's expanded notions of scholarship encourage dynamic, creative, inclusive, and multi-dimensional discussions about the roles and functions of faculty in the academy.

Bass, in his article titled "The Scholarship of Teaching: What's the Problem?" prompts readers to consider "problems" in teaching the way scholars do "problems" in research—inquiry that is shared and analyzed to provide better understanding. He encourages the "deliberate act" of exploring teaching through the lens of learning in order to locate the complex problems that faculty, as colleagues, can undertake together.

Huber and Hutchings share a similar, although perhaps even broader, perspective on classroom inquiry and call it "the teaching commons, an emergent conceptual space for exchange and community among faculty, students, administrators, and all others committed to learning as an essential activity of life in contemporary democratic society" (p. 1). They endorse "going public" with scholarship that explores teaching and learning to promote engagement with new ideas and expand traditional conceptions of research dissemination. In this chapter, the authors share four "defining features" of the scholarship of teaching and learning, a vital component of the teaching commons.

Educational Development

Finally, Sorcinelli, Austin, Eddy, and Beach detail the history of educational development as a field, shedding light on its foundations, purposes, research and unique features. In this important piece, the authors trace the "five ages of faculty development," ending with the most recent—the "age of the network." Faculty developer goals and practices are reflected in a diverse array of services designed to meet the changing needs of faculty and the institutions they serve. As the field continues to evolve, Sorcinelli, et al. identify a body of research that promotes quality teaching and learning across the United States and the world.

Cross' classic article adds to this rich history by sharing a thoughtful argument for college teaching becoming a profession of its own so that faculty can utilize knowledge from their disciplines as well as knowledge garnered from experts in teaching and learning to promote successful learning. This profession for which Cross advocates is a site where the best models are researched, implemented, and shared. She outlines classroom research as a consistent examination of teaching and learning over time that encourages faculty to identify relevant problems for further study.

CHAPTER 1

HIGHER EDUCATION STUDIES

Research on College Teaching: The Historical Background

Wilbert J. McKeachie

Experimental research on college teaching began with single variable studies of class size and lecture vs. discussion. During the 1930s, research on student ratings of teachers began, and following World War II, studies of college teaching and learning became more common. In the decades from then to the 1980s, research moved to concern with a broader range of variables, to analyses of interaction between student and classroom variables, and to attention to processes as well as products resulting from teaching. Research on college teaching clearly meets Conant's criteria for a scientific field: progress in theory, methods, and established knowledge. Moreover, we now have demonstrated that educational research can contribute to educational practice.

Has research on college teaching made progress? Conant (1947) argued that a field could be called scientific when knowledge has accumulated, progress is evident in the development of new conceptual schemes resulting from experiments and observations, and the conceptual schemes lead, in turn, to more research. He suggested that one of the tests of whether a field qualifies would be to imagine the reaction of the pioneers in the field if they were to be brought back to life and viewed the current status of the research and theory. Would they acknowledge that there had been progress?

What would Carl E. Seashore, Edward L. Thorndike, or J. B. Edmondson say if they were to examine the research on college teaching today? In this article, I will choose a few of the significant studies in major areas of research on college teaching to subject our field to Conant's (1947) test.

World War I gave American psychologists their first opportunity to demonstrate the usefulness of psychological methods on a large scale. By the end of the war, 1,700,000 soldiers had taken Army Alpha or Beta tests of intelligence. Psychologists came out of the war with a greater sense of competence and confidence that empirical methods could solve important practical problems such as college teaching (e.g., Jones, 1923). Although educators had written scholarly works about college teaching in prior years (Klapper, 1920; Seashore, Angell, Calkins, Sanford, and Whipple, 1910), it was in the decade of the 1920s that researchers began a sustained empirical attack on the problems of college teaching.

As in other areas, the focus of research on college teaching shifted from decade to decade; therefore, this article will not follow a strictly chronological order. Rather than lose the sense of continuity in research on a particular problem, I will follow selected topics from their beginnings to the present; the topics, which will be discussed in the order in which they first appeared on the research scene, include class size, lecture versus discussion, student-centered discussion, independent study and peer learning, evaluation of teaching, teaching and technology, and the impact of cognitive psychology.

Reprinted from *Journal of Educational Psychology* (1990), by permission of American Psychological Association.

In addition to summarizing the substantive results, I shall highlight methodological lessons to be learned. My background in social, personality, and cognitive psychology undoubtedly influences both the selection and the interpretation of the studies reported. I view effective teaching and learning as a function of teaching methods interacting with student, group, and subject matter variables. I place heavier value on the importance of motivation and mindfulness in learning than would be typical of college faculty members. My hope is that this brief history will give a sense both of the progress our field of research has made and of its continuing promise and that this article will provide a useful perspective for the articles in this special issue. It is not, however, intended to be a comprehensive "Psych. Bulletin type" research review. For such a review, see Dunkin and Barnes (1986), McKeachie, Pintrich, Lin, and Smith (1986), and the triennial reviews of instructional psychology in the *Annual Review of Psychology*. Also useful is Menges and Mathis's (1988) *Key Resources on Teaching, Learning, Curriculum, and Faculty Development*.

Class Size

Early Research

Are small classes more effective than large classes? This was probably the first major question that research on college teaching tried to answer. Size does not seem to be a conceptually exciting variable. Yet, as we shall see, psychologists have, as in other studies, developed a conceptual understanding that makes the size variable more psychologically interesting.

Among the first investigators of class size were Edmondson and Mulder (1924), who compared the performance of students enrolled in a 109-student class with that of students enrolled in a 43-student class of the same course in education. Achievement of the two groups was approximately equal; the small class had a slight edge on an essay and the midsemester tests, and the large class had a slight edge on quizzes and the final examination. Students reported a preference for small classes.

Edmondson and Mulder's (1924) results stimulated the Committee of Research at the University of Minnesota to begin a classic series of studies of class size. In 59 experiments that involved such widely varying subjects as psychology, physics, accounting, law, and education, the results of 46 favored the large classes for achievement measured largely by classroom examinations (Hudelson, 1928).

Support for small classes, however, came from studies in the teaching of French conducted by Cheydleur (1945) at the University of Wisconsin between 1919 and 1943. With hundreds of classes ranging in size from 9 to 33, Cheydleur found consistent superior performance on objective departmental examinations for small classes.

Post-World War II experiments were also favorable to small classes. Macomber and Siegel's (1957a, 1957b, 1960) experiments at Miami University are particularly important because, in addition to conventional achievement tests, they included measures of critical thinking and problem solving, scales measuring stereotypic attitudes, and tests of student attitudes toward instruction. Statistically significant differences favored the smaller classes (particularly for high-ability students). When retention of knowledge was measured 1–2 years after completion of the courses, small differences favored the smaller classes in eight of the nine courses compared (Siegel, Adams, and Macomber, 1960).

Few instructors are satisfied with the achievement of knowledge if it is not remembered, if the students are unable to use it in solving problems in which the knowledge is relevant, or if the students fail to relate the knowledge to relevant attitudes. If one takes these more basic outcomes of retention, problem solving, and attitude differentiations as criteria of learning, the weight of the evidence favors small classes, a conclusion consistent with Glass and Smith's (1979) classic but controversial meta-analysis of class size research at all educational levels.

What Did We Learn?

The methodological lesson for both researchers and teachers is to measure higher level outcomes as well as knowledge.

What about theory? The early researchers were simply interested in answering a practical question, but there are both practical and theoretical reasons why class size should make a difference. The larger the class, the less the sense of personal responsibility and activity, and the less the likelihood that the teacher can know each student personally and adapt instruction to the individual student. Nonetheless, it seems plausible that the effect of class size on learning depends on what the teacher does. We lack descriptive studies of teacher behavior in college classes of differing sizes, but it seems likely that in larger classes, faculty members typically require less written work and spend more time lecturing and less in discussion. Thus the effect of class size also depends on the relative effectiveness of lecture and discussion, and it is not surprising that shortly after the first research on class size, experiments comparing lecture and discussion began to appear.

Lecture Versus Discussion

Early Research

Only a year after Edmondson and Mudler's (1924) and Mueller's (1924) studies on class size, Bane (1925) published a comparison of lecture and discussion[1] teaching methods. Not only was Bane's research pioneering in studying teaching methods in college; he also introduced an important methodological advance by obtaining a measure of delayed recall after the course examination as well as the conventional final examination score. There was little difference between his groups on the immediate test, but there was significant superiority for discussion on the measure of delayed recall.

In a well-designed study of teachers of adult education courses, Solomon, Rosenberg, and Bezdek (1964) found that those who stressed lectures produced higher achievement on a factual test but were not as effective as other teachers on a test of comprehension. Other studies also supported the superiority of discussion for higher level outcomes (reviewed by McKeachie, 1984).

What Did We Learn?

In general, later research supported Bane's (1925) earliest findings: Lecture tends to be at least equal to, and often more effective than, discussion for immediate recall of factual knowledge on a course examination, but discussion tends to be superior for long-term retention. Current cognitive theory would explain this finding in terms of greater likelihood of elaboration or deep processing when students are actively engaged in discussion.

The method of testing delayed recall, such as Bane used, is all too seldom used. The typical use of final course examinations, for which students have crammed, as the primary outcome measure is a major reason for the small effects often found in research on college teaching.

Student-Centered Discussion

Early Research

Interest in discussion methods seems to be a cyclical function, peaking in even-numbered decades: the 1940s, 1960s, and 1980s. Although there were a number of experiments on lecture versus discussion in the 1930s, the next peak of interest occurred after World War II when two independent movements in psychology converged to produce a spate of experiments on nondirective, group-centered, or student-centered discussion methods. Carl Roger's nondirective approach to counseling and Kurt Lewin's "group dynamics" movement both spilled over into research on "student-centered" or "group-centered" teaching.

Both the Rogerian and the Lewinian position emphasized movement away from the teacher's role as expert and authority to a role of facilitating student responsibility for learning. Thus student-centered discussion went beyond conventional discussion methods in emphasizing (a) much more interaction between students and (b) student responsibility for decisions about goals and activities of the class. Accompanying this was a shift away from thinking of subject-matter knowledge as the only goal of education. Although cognitive goals were still recognized as being important, student-centered classes accepted the expression of feelings and development of group cohesion as important mechanisms for achieving "gut" learning: learning linked to motivation, attitudes and deeper understanding (McKeachie, DeValois, Dulany, Beardslee and Winerbottom, 1954).

A pioneering study of this genre preceded World War II. Zeleny (1940) found that a group-centered method was superior to a recitation method not only in cognitive outcomes but also in changes in self-confidence, leadership, and other personality variables.

Another early comparison of student-centered and instructor-centered instruction was that made by Faw (1949). A class was divided into three discussion groups; one group was taught by a student-centered method, one was taught by an instructor-centered method, and one alternated between the two methods. In comparison with the instructor-centered class, the student-centered class was characterized by more student participation, no correction by the instructor of inaccurate statements, lack of instructor direction, and more discussion of ideas related to personal experiences.

Scores on the objective course examination based on the textbook showed small but significant differences favoring the student-centered method. In the area of major interest, emotional growth, Faw's (1949) method of evaluation was to ask students to write anonymous comments about the class. In general, comments indicated that the students felt that they received greater social and emotional value from the student-centered discussion groups.

Following the model of Lewin, Lippitt, and White's study (1939) of authoritarian, democratic, and laissez faire group climates, the staff of the University of Michigan's general psychology course set up an experiment in 1947, using three styles of teaching: recitation, discussion, and group tutorial (Guetzkow, Kelly, and McKeachie, 1954; McKeachie, 1951). In comparison with discussion and tutorial methods, the more autocratic recitation method proved to produce not only better examination scores but also greater interest in psychology, as measured by the election of advanced courses in psychology. Furthermore, students liked the recitation method better than the other methods. The greater gains in knowledge produced by the recitation method fit in with the general principle that feedback aids learning, for students in the recitation sections had weekly or semiweekly quizzes.

Despite the immediate superiority of the recitation method, two motivational outcomes favored the discussion and tutorial methods: (a) The students in discussion sections were significantly more favorable than the other groups in attitude toward psychology, and (b) a follow-up of the students 3 years later revealed that 7 men each from the tutorial and discussion groups majored in psychology, whereas none of those in the recitation group did so. Women majoring in psychology came about equally from all three groups.

Wispe (1951) carried out an interesting variation of the student-centered versus instructor-centered experiment. Instead of attempting to control the instructor personality variable by forcing instructors to teach both instructor-centered and student-centered classes, Wispe selected instructors who were rated as naturally permissive or directive. He then compared their sections of the Harvard course in "Social Relations." He found no difference in final examination scores between students taught by different methods. Students preferred the directive method, and the poorer students gained more in directive classes.

Whereas scores on objective final examinations seem to be little affected by teaching method, there are, in addition to the positive changes in adjustment reported by Asch (1951), Faw (1949), Moore and Popham (1959), Slomowitz (1955), and Zeleny (1940), other indications that student behavior outside the usual testing situation may be influenced. Bovard (1951a, 1951b) and McKeachie (1954) found that student-centered classes showed greater insight (as rated by clinical psychologists) into problems of the young women depicted in the film "The Feeling of Rejection." As in the studies of class size and lecture discussion, we find that the favorable effects of student-centered teaching methods emerge in the more subtle, "higher level" outcomes rather than in factual knowledge. These results parallel those found by Giaconia and Hedges (1982) in their meta-analysis of recitation on open education.

Although most of these studies were carried out in the late 1940s, they were not published until the 1950s and were thus still in the current literature when a new impetus to student-centered learning came to the fore—independent study. This movement in the late 1950s, followed by the sensitivity training movement in the 1960s, maintained interest in student-centered teaching despite the post-Sputnik panic about out-of-date and ill-organized scientific content.

What Did We Learn?

The studies of student-centered classes carried methodology forward by pointing to a broader range of outcomes involving attitudes, motivation, and personality variables. In addition, Wispe's (1951) method of studying natural variation rather than manipulated differences in teaching led to greater use of this method in later studies.

One methodological feature was important for the field of psychology in general. These were among the first studies to look at attribute-treatment interactions (ATIs). Even before Cronbach's (1957) classic article, "The Two Disciplines of Scientific Psychology," Remmers (1933) had reported that more intelligent students achieved more with a higher proportion of class time in recitation, whereas less intelligent students profited more from a larger proportion of time in lecture.

Independent Study and Peer Learning

The World War II veterans bulge had barely passed when leaders in higher education began warning colleges and universities that they would face even greater strains on their facilities when the postwar "baby boomers" reached college age. The projected rapid increase in enrollments would not be matched by an increase in PhDs to teach; so mechanisms to handle more students with few faculty needed to be found. Advocates of television, teaching machines, and computers predicted enormous gains in efficiency if faculty conservatism could be overcome. The research on the effectiveness of technology, disappointingly, provided little support for these proposed panaceas.

One potential solution, however, went beyond the problem of teaching greater numbers to emphasize an important goal of education—training autonomous learners (students who would presumably be better equipped for lifelong learning because they experienced less teaching in college and practiced independent study). Thus the period spawned a number of studies of learning with reduced formal classroom instruction. Some of these sent individual learners off to study by themselves; others involved small-group, peer-learning experiences.

With the support of the Ford Foundation's Fund for Advancement of Education, a number of colleges experimented with large programs of independent study. As with other comparisons of teaching methods, few large differences were found between the achievement of students working independently and that of students taught in conventional classes. Moreover, the expected gains in independence also often failed to materialize. Students taught by independent study did not always seem to develop greater ability or motivation for learning independently. Nevertheless, a number of encouraging results emerged.

Favorable results on independent study were obtained in the experiments carried out at the University of Colorado by Gruber and Weitman (1960). In a course in freshman English in which the group met in class about 90% of the regularly scheduled hours and had little formal training in grammar, the self-directed study group was significantly superior to control groups on a test of grammar. In a course in physical optics, groups of students who attended class without the instructor learned fewer facts and simple applications but were superior to students in conventional classes in performing difficult applications and learning new material. Moreover, the areas of superiority were maintained in a retest 3 months later when the difference in factual knowledge had disappeared. In educational psychology, an experimental class meeting once a week with the instructor and twice a week in groups of 5 or 6 students without the instructor was equal to a conventional three-lecture-a-week class in mastery of content, but tended to be superior on measures of curiosity. In another experiment, students in self-directed study paid more constant attention to a lecture than did students in conventional classes.

Different kinds of learning may take place out of class than in class. The experiment reported by McKeachie, Lin, Forrin, and Teevan (1960) involved a fairly high degree of student-instructor contact. In this experiment, "tutorial" students normally met with the instructor in small groups only weekly or biweekly, but students were free to consult the instructor whenever they wished. The results of the experiment suggest that the "tutorial" students did not learn as much from the textbook as students taught in conventional lecture periods and discussion sections, but they did develop stronger motivation both for course work and for continued learning after the course. This was indicated not only by responses to a questionnaire administered at the end of the course but also by the number of advanced psychology courses later elected.

Webb and Grib (1967) reported six studies in which student-led discussions were compared with instructor-led discussions or lectures. In two of the six studies, significant differences in achievement tests favored the student-led discussions. In the other four, differences were not significant. Both students and instructors reported that the student-led discussions increased student motivation. Students reported that the sense of freedom to ask questions and express their own opinions is a major advantage of the student-led discussions. It makes theoretical sense that this opportunity to expose individual conceptions and misconceptions and compare one's ideas with those of others should contribute to learning if the group contains sufficient resources of knowledge and higher level thinking.

The Pyramid Plan

The most impressive findings on the results of student-led discussion come from the research on the Pyramid Plan at Pennsylvania State University (Carpenter, 1959; Davage, 1958, 1959). The basic plan may be represented by a description of their experiments in psychology. Each "Pyramid Group" of psychology majors consisted of 6 freshmen, 6 sophomores, 2 juniors (who were assistant leaders), and a senior (who was group leader). The group leaders were trained by a faculty supervisor. A control group received comparable special attention by being given a special program of lectures, films, and demonstrations equal to the time spent in discussion by the Pyramid Groups. The results on such measures as attitude toward psychology, knowledge of the field of psychology, scientific thinking, use of library for scholarly reading, intellectual orientation, and resourcefulness in problem solving were significantly favorable to the Pyramid Plan. Moreover, a follow-up study showed that more of the Pyramid students continued as majors in psychology. Unfortunately, this program was never widely publicized and apparently was not adopted on other campuses.

The independent study movement thus extended student-centered teaching to peer teaching and learning. The sensitivity training movement of the 1960s was also based on the underpinnings of student-centered teaching—Lewinian and Rogerian theories.

T-Groups

During the 1960s, sensitivity training (T-groups, encounter groups) became the fad for high-level business executives as well as for government workers, teachers, and students. Originating in the group dynamics theories and practice of Kurt Lewin and his followers, sensitivity training groups met the 1960s generation's desire for self-analysis, confrontation of stereotypes, and overthrowing norms restricting the expression of personal needs and feelings. Many universities developed courses involving sensitivity training, and many faculty members incorporated elements of sensitivity training in conventional courses.

A number of studies of T-group effectiveness were carried out, some in academic settings. In general, the results were favorable, particularly in participants' self-reports of gains in self-understanding and sensitivity to others' feelings and behavior (see review by P. B. Smith, 1975).

The College Classroom

The decade of the 1960s was a period when federal funding of educational research resulted in substantial progress in our understanding of teaching and learning. The study to which I most often refer dates from this period. Combining quantitative and qualitative approaches, using data from observations and questionnaires, focusing on feelings underlying verbal expressions, and yet concerned with the goal of productive educational "work," *The College Classroom* (Mann et al., 1970) provides an unequaled source of insights with respect to student characteristics, teacher roles, and the development of the class as a working group over the course of a semester. The book describes the development of four introductory psychology classes over a semester; that development began with a phase in which the teachers' behaviors emphasized the roles of "formal authority" and "facilitator" while the student "heroes" and "snipers" tested the teachers' tolerance for student autonomy. During the first 2 weeks, much of the teacher's effort was to socialize the students into the methods and viewpoints of the field.

In a second phase, the teachers became dissatisfied with the students' lack of work, the dependence of the "anxious-dependent" students, and the excessive irrelevance of the participation of the "attention getters." Teachers, who had previously been trying to facilitate independent, autonomous work, were likely to become more punitive and authoritarian. Nonetheless, during this second period, the students and teachers began to gain a better understanding of the kind of work and involvement that was needed, and in the third phase, coming after 4 to 5 weeks, anxious dependence diminished, the classes became more collegial and cooperative, and effective work occurred.

As the term continued, the teacher assumed more control but now moved more toward a situation in which the teacher was leading a joint exploration of the subject matter with contributions from both students and teacher. The last phase, "Separation," was characterized by warmth, yet also by the beginnings of withdrawal.

Although the phases described in *The College Classroom* are not likely to be precisely replicated in other classes, most teachers will recognize some resonance with their own experience. *The College Classroom* thus helps both teachers and students understand and think about the unique development of their own classes and the sort of interaction that can facilitate productive development.

Peer-Learning, Cooperative-Learning

The forces of cognitive revolution in psychology and education swept over the "touchy-feely" movement of the 1960s, but student-centered, peer-group learning survived and emerged in new cognitively oriented forms in the 1970s and 1980s as the most effective method for helping students to achieve cognitive goals.

One of the best-developed systems for helping pairs of students learn more effectively is the "Learning Cell" developed by Marcel Goldschmid of the Swiss Federal Institute of Technology in Lausanne (Goldschmid, 1971). The Learning Cell, or student dyad, refers to cooperative learning in pairs in which students alternate asking and answering questions on commonly read materials:

1. To prepare for the learning cell, students read an assignment and write questions dealing with the major points raised in the reading proper or other related materials.
2. At the beginning of each class meeting, students are randomly assigned to pairs, and one partner, *A*, begins by asking the first question.
3. After having answered and perhaps having been corrected or given additional information, the second student, *B*, puts a question to *A*, and so on.
4. During this time, the instructor goes from dyad to dyad, giving feedback and asking and answering questions.

A variation of this procedure has each student read (or prepare) different materials. In this case, *A* "teaches" *B* the essentials of his or her readings and then asks *B* prepared questions, whereupon they switch roles.

The effectiveness of the learning cell method was first explored in the large (250-student) psychology course (Goldschmid, 1970) in which four learning options were compared: seminar, discussion, independent study (essay), and learning cell. Students in the learning cell option performed significantly better on an unannounced experiment and rated their ongoing learning cell's effectiveness higher regardless of the size of the class, its level, or the age of the students (Schirmerhorn, Goldschmid, and Shore, 1975).

"Pay to be a tutor, not to be tutored" is the message from these studies of peer tutoring. For example, Annis (1983) compared learning under five conditions:

1. Students read a textbook passage.
2. Students read the passage and were taught by a peer.
3. Students did not read the passage but were taught by a peer.
4. Students read the passage and prepared to teach it to other students.
5. Students read the passage and taught it to another student.

The results demonstrated that teaching resulted in better learning than did being taught. In a similar study, Bargh and Schul (1980) also found positive results: the largest part of the gain in retention was attributable to students' deeper studying of material when preparing to teach. The research in higher education is congruent with research at other levels of education demonstrating the effectiveness of peer teaching and learning (Johnson, Maruyama, Johnson, Nelson, and Skon, 1981).

What Did We Learn?

These results fit well with contemporary theories of learning and memory. Preparing to teach, teaching, questioning, and explaining involve active thought, analysis, selection of main ideas, and processing the concepts into one's own thoughts and words. The greater freedom, found by Webb and Grib (1967), of students to admit confusion and ask questions in peer learning groups also fits with current cognitive-instructional theory stressing the importance of restructuring incorrect or inadequate cognitive structures or schemata. Motivational effects of peer learning and independent study also fit well with motivation theorists' emphasis on the importance of personal control of one's environment. The results of these studies complement those of peer tutoring in elementary and high school classes. In their meta-analysis, Cohen, Kulik, and Kulik (1982) found favorable effects on learning, attitudes, and self-concept.

Methodologically, the studies in this group extended even further the list of relevant outcome measures to include, in addition to factual learning, simple versus difficult applications of concepts, retention of knowledge months later, scientific thinking, resourcefulness in problem solving, intellectual orientation, attention to lectures, ability to learn independently, student acceptance of responsibility for learning, student motivation for continued learning (assessed by both questionnaires and election of advanced courses), choosing to major in the area of the course, use of the library for scholarly reading, curiosity, attitudes, self-understanding, sensitivity to others' feelings and behavior, and effectiveness as a leader or group member.

But the most important methodological advance evidenced in these studies was the move toward more detailed analysis of the processes responsible for outcomes. Whereas in earlier studies, such as McKeachie's (1951, 1958), researchers had used observers and student ratings to describe classroom processes involved in the experimental comparisons, the detailed inferential coding of every verbal act represented in *The College Classroom* study by Mann et al. (1970) carried the analysis of interaction between teacher and students to a new level. Similarly, the processes responsible for the success of peer learning were analyzed in the studies by Webb and Grib (1967), Gruber and Weitman (1960), and Bargh and Schul (1980). Thus these studies were early representatives of the process-product paradigm (Mitzel, 1960).

Evaluation of Teaching

Early Studies

Anyone who carries out research on teaching effectiveness quickly runs into the problem of evaluating the outcomes of teaching. Obviously, one first looks at student learning, and the studies cited above typically include measures of student achievement. But if one takes increased interest and motivation for learning as important outcomes, it is hard to come up with better measures than the students' own perceptions of their interest. Not only can students' provide data about the effects that instruction has had on them, but they also have an excellent opportunity to observe what the teacher does and what the course requires. Thus student reports of instruction have commonly been used as a source of data, not only for research, but also to improve teaching and to evaluate teaching for personnel decisions.

Once again we go back to the 1920s for the beginnings of this active field of research on college teaching. In 1927, Herman Remmers published the first of an impressive series of reports on his Purdue Rating Scale for Instructors. In that series, basic questions about validity and reliability were confronted and answered with a good deal of clarity. Unfortunately, even today many faculty raise questions that were well handled by Remmers and his students and by later research that reinforced and extended his conclusions (see Marsh, 1987):

1. Do students' judgments agree with those of peers or administrators? Yes.
2. Do students change their minds after they have been out of college long enough to appreciate the sterling qualities of teachers whom they failed to appreciate while enrolled? No.
3. Can the poorer students' judgments be disregarded? No. When a teacher is particularly effective with the poorer students, these students rate the teacher higher than do other students.
4. When several teachers are teaching sections of the same course, do the teachers whose students score highest on the achievement tests get the highest ratings? Yes, a result most convincingly demonstrated by Cohen's (1981) meta-analysis of 68 validity studies.

One might surmise that the area of research on students' rating of faculty would have been exhausted by the extensive series of research studies carried out in the past 60 years and comprehensively reviewed by Costin, Greenough, and Menges (1971), by Feldman (1978), and by Marsh (1984, 1987). However, two current lines of research seem particularly worthy of special mention.

One of these is the series of well-controlled laboratory studies involving videotaped presentations of teaching carried out by Raymond P. Perry and his associates at the University of Manitoba (Perry, Abrami, and Leventhal, 1979). Originally, the methodology was devised to investigate the "Dr. Fox effect"—named after the pseudonymous "Dr. Fox," an actor whose animation and expressiveness seduced an audience of professionals into giving high ratings to a lecture devoid of content. The Manitoba research group showed that expressiveness was positively related to learning with content held constant but that student ratings of an expressive teacher were perhaps overly generous. However, the basic findings turned out, as most research does, to reveal complex interactions. More recently the method has been turned to investigations of students' "learned helplessness"—a drop in performance following failure.

A second line of research investigates the relationship between instructor personality, instructor behavior, and teaching effectiveness. Erdle, Murray, and Rushton (1985) found two personality factors, "Achievement Orientation" and "Interpersonal Orientation," that relate to classroom behavior factors "Charisma" and "Organization." Research on student rating of instructors has often yielded somewhat similar factors (e.g., Cranton and Smith, 1990 [this issue]: Smalzreid and Remmers, 1943). Personality characteristics related to effective teaching vary, depending on the type of course (Murrah, Rushton, and Paunonen, 1990 [this issue]).

What Have We Learned?

Despite faculty doubts about the ability of students to appreciate good teaching, the research evidence indicates that students are generally good judges—surprisingly so, in view of the fact that most research on student evaluation has been carried out in introductory classes, in which one would expect the students to be less able to evaluate than in more advanced classes. Moreover, ratings are robust. Potentially contaminating variables, such as time of day, class size, or required versus elective classes, make a difference, but not a large enough difference to cause researchers to misclassify a good teacher as "poor." Although one should also get evidence from other sources if a teaching evaluation is to lead to an important personnel decision, student ratings are the best validated of all the practical sources of relevant data.

But, in addition to what we have learned about evaluating teaching, the student rating research has contributed to the broader field of research on college teaching. The student rating literature led the way in the substantive identification of classroom *processes* affecting learning outcomes. This area of research also made it clear that different students reacted differently to the same teacher. This truth was at first taken to be a telling blow against the validity of student ratings, but, as early as 1949, attribute-treatment interactions had been demonstrated in student learning, and these interactions paralleled the ATIs in student ratings (Elliot, 1949). Furthermore, the research indicated not only that there were general attributes of effective teaching, such as clarity of explanations and enthusiasm, but also that there are a variety of ways in which teachers can be effective.

Finally, an important methodological contribution was the use (by Raymond R. Perry and the University of Manitoba group) of films to enable researchers to manipulate variables in well-controlled laboratory experiments.

Teaching and Technology

From Films to Computers

Instructional films came into widespread use during World War II, and research on uses of film in instruction continued after World War II. Carpenter and Greenhill (1955, 1958), working at Pennsylvania State University, had produced a series of studies of instructional films, and so they were well positioned to take advantage of the interest of the Ford Foundation's Fund for the Advancement of Education in encouraging the use of television for college-level instruction. During the mid-1950s, television seemed to offer great promise for coping with the great hordes of students expected to arrive as a result of the baby boom. Although many faculty members decried the loss of face-to-face contact with students, others embraced the chance to be among the first to appear on television. (In fact, I was one such [McKeachie, 1952].) Grants by the Fund led to a large number of well-controlled studies of the effectiveness of television, particularly as an alternative to large lectures for semester-long courses.

The results of this research may be used either to exalt or to damn television. Essentially, they indicated that although students learn nearly as much information in courses taught by television as in courses taught conventionally, live classes tend to be superior (e.g., Schramm, 1962; Sullivan, Andrews, Hollinghurst, Maddigan, and Noseworthy, 1976). Most television students learned the information needed to pass examinations, and most did not object strongly to the televised classes, although they preferred live instruction.

A course adapted for television by the addition of supplementary visual aids proved to be no more effective than televised lecture-blackboard presentations. In fact, at both Pennsylvania State University (Carpenter and Greenhill, 1955, 1958) and New York University (Adams, Carter, and Smith, 1959), the "visual" productions tended to be less effective than "bare bones" television.

The bloom of hopes for educational television had hardly begun to fade when a new technology threatened to eliminate the need for television. Teaching machines were to revolutionize education, increasing the efficiency of teaching manyfold. Skinner (1954) wrote,

> We are on the threshold of an exciting and revolutionary period, in which the scientific study of man will be put to work in man's best interests. Education must play its part. It must accept the fact that a sweeping revision of educational practices is possible and inevitable. (p. 97)

Skinner further stated, "The technical problem of providing the necessary instrumental aid is not particularly difficult" (p. 95), and "If the teacher is to take advantage of recent advances in the study of learning, she [or he] must have the help of mechanical devices" (p. 95).

So persuasive were Skinner's writings that many of the major electronic and book companies moved quickly into the teaching machine movement. Programs for teaching were written in accordance with carefully specified behavioral objectives, and, in some of the early research, human beings simulated teaching machines to test the material. It soon became apparent that programmed learning material could be presented in text-like form as effectively as by machine. Programmed books and booklets were designed to permit students to learn without formal classroom instruction or, in some cases, to be used as an adjunct to other teaching materials.

The research on teaching machines and programmed learning failed to reveal the dramatic gains expected by Skinner and the corporations that invested in the field. Nonetheless, programmed learning was not as unsuccessful educationally as it was commercially. Students do learn from the programs, but learning is generally slower than with conventional printed materials (but faster than with lectures; N. H. Smith, 1962). Reviews by Kulik, Cohen, and Ebeling (1980), Lange (1972), Nash, Muczyk, and Vettori (1971), and Schramm (1964) show programmed instruction to be slightly superior to traditional instruction in about 40% of the over 100 research studies reported, equally effective in about half the studies, and seldom less effective.

Although programmed learning was not an enormous success, two related methods proved to be more effective. One of these was the Keller Plan, or Personalized System of Instruction, a self-paced, mastery oriented, modular system of instruction that produced not only superior end-of-course achievement but also superior retention (Kulik, Kulik, and Bangert-Drowns, 1988).

The other was Postlethwait's Audio-Tutorial method, which also involves a modularized self-instructional approach. Postlethwait developed slides, audiotapes, demonstration experiments, and other materials for modules of his introductory botany course (Postlethwait, Novak, and Murray, 1972). The results were so encouraging that the method was widely used in laboratory courses. A meta-analysis by Kulik, Kulik, and Cohen (1979) showed a significant positive effect on student achievement. It should be noted that there is little evidence of the value of conventional laboratory courses, although a few studies suggest that specific attention to scientific thinking does produce gains (see review by Hofstein and Lunetta, 1982).

The teaching machine revolution was quickly lost in the apparent brilliance of an even more glamorous technological competitor—the computer. By the early 1960s, the claims for teaching machines paled beside those made for the computer. Clearly, the flexibility offered by the computer could individualize learning much more than could the teaching machine. In fact, however, the first educational programs for computers differed little from the branching programs offered in many printed programmed-learning materials. Once again, manufacturers, research sponsors, and those interested in educational technology found that it is easier to envision the potential of educational technology than to develop the educational software that achieves this potential. By the early 1970s, it was apparent that the initial hopes had not been sustained. Nonetheless, some progress was made and, with the widespread use of microcomputers, the 1980s have seen a revival of optimism, with somewhat less grandiose visions of the role of the computer in education. In their meta-analysis of research on computer-based education, Kulik, Kulik, and Cohen (1980) found that computers made small but significant contributions to achievement. The greatest successes, however, were achieved with drill and practice programs—not the stuff of our dreams.

What Have We Learned?

Probably the most important thing we learned from the research on technology was to be skeptical about claims for revolutionary advances in education brought about by technology. We also learned that technology does not substitute for teachers; there is little likelihood that the classroom will be robotized. However, technological tools can facilitate student learning. How much learning takes place still depends on student activity and thought.

Technology has been methodologically useful in helping us examine the microprocesses of education, as exemplified in the research of Tobias (1988, in press).

Although "think-aloud" techniques and protocol analysis have less commonly been used in research on college student learning than in research with children, these methods, often used in connection with research with computers, provide an additional tool in our research kit, particularly as we move into cognitive approaches concerned not only with classroom processes but also with cognitive processes of students and teachers.

The Cognitive Era

Applications of Cognitive Psychology

The shift from behaviorism to cognitivism in psychology occurred gradually, even though it seemed to move with exciting speed during the decades of the 1960s and 1970s. Its impact on instructional research came in various forms, but one of the most striking effects was that deriving from research carried out at the University of Gothenburg by Ference Marton and his associates (Marton and Saljo, 1976a, 1976b; Svensson, 1976). Using a phenomenological-like approach that Marton calls *phenomenography,* the Swedish researchers described the differing ways in which students approach textbook assignments. "Surface processors" read the assignment straight through with little attempt to think about the purpose of the author or about the relationship between the assigned reading and their own previous knowledge; "deep processors," on the other hand, are more likely to look for cues to the organization and purpose of the reading and to relate it to previous chapters or other learning. Svensson (1976), in a study of student learning over the course of a semester, similarly found contrasts between those who approached study holistically and those who were characterized as atomists. Examinations in different disciplines differed in the extent to which a holistic approach was necessary, but atomistic students generally did less well. These studies represented well the move from a focus on instructional materials to a focus on the students.

The Gothenburg studies stimulated researchers in Great Britain, Australia, and the United States to devise questionnaires and develop remedial programs for students whose approaches to learning were rigid and ineffective. Thus the focus in research on instruction shifted from the teacher to the students. Diagnosis of deficiencies in study skills has shifted to a greater emphasis on deep processing (or elaboration) and on meta-cognition—the ability to think about one's own learning and thinking and to choose effective strategies for different learning situations (Biggs, 1976; Entwistle, Hanley, and Hounsell, 1979; Weinstein, Underwood, Wicker, and Cubberly, 1979). Courses designed to teach students how to be more effective learners have been devised (see McKeachie, Pintrich, and Lin, 1985; Weinstein, Goetz, and Alexander, 1985; Weinstein and Mayer, 1986). Traditional topics of research such as test anxiety have benefited from theoretical analysis based on cognitive psychology (McKeachie, 1984; Tobias, 1985). Research on college teaching has become more closely integrated with that at other levels of education (e.g., De Corte, Lodewijks, Parmentier, and Span, 1987; Goldschmid, 1971; Palincsar and Brown, 1984). Cognitive theory and research has spilled over into the areas of college classrooms so that "teaching thinking" has become a major theme of educational discussions in higher education, as well as in business and in other levels of education (McMillan, 1986).

What Have We Learned?

Cognitive theory has provided a conceptual base for understanding the results of the earlier studies and for providing guidance for instruction (e.g., Bjork, 1979). Small classes and discussion methods tend to be effective because students are actively processing material rather than passively listening and reading. Cognitive research, both in the laboratory and in the classroom, has given us a much more detailed account of how problem solving occurs in different disciplines, and this in turn is influencing textbooks and teachers. Motivation theory, too, is beginning to help us understand why some students fail to achieve up to capacity. We are now beginning to see the relationships between active deep processing and intrinsic motivation for continued learning as these relationships are affected by teaching methods that provide guidance and yet also provide opportunities for students to feel responsible and efficacious as learners.

What of the Future?

Recently someone asked me if we had made any progress in learning about college teaching since I began doing research in 1946. The answer is obvious, I hope, in the preceding pages. Moreover, the advances continue. But, as I told my questioner, the greater the advance, the greater the complexity ahead. The circle separating what we know from the unknown becomes even larger.

We now realize that the variables influencing learning are almost numberless. Because their interactions change from day to day, we need to move from pretest-posttest measures to studies of ongoing processes, from single-variable studies to individual students interacting in groups, and from studies of outcomes of learning to studies of what goes on in the thoughts, feelings, and desires of students. The frontier of knowledge about college teaching thus becomes even more challenging. And I suspect that the progress in the next decade will be even greater than in past decades. We have more researchers, better tools, and more comprehensive cognitive, motivation, and instructional theories. We have a clearer and more comprehensive grasp of the goals of education—the intertwining of intrinsic motivation for learning with elaboration, metacognition, and "mindful" learning.

We now know that we can teach thinking skills; in the next decade, we will gain a better understanding of how to go beyond discipline-specific skills to more broadly transferable intelligence.

We now know learning skills and strategies that generally help students to learn more effectively; in the next decade, we will better understand which strategies are most effective for which students with which material and which goals.

We now know that intrinsic motivation and a sense of self-efficacy have much to do with learning strategies and the mindfulness of student learning; in the next decade, we will gain a better understanding of the kinds of instructional methods that facilitate such motivation and that integrate learning with basic values.

We now know that peer-teaching is a very effective method of learning; in the next decade, we will gain a better understanding of how to structure peer-learning groups and when and where to use them.

We now know more about the processes leading toward educational outcomes; in the next decade, we will gain a better understanding of the way in which individual differences in motives and cognition interact with teaching methods and how the interactions change as courses develop, learners learn, and learning is assessed (see Covington and Omelich, 1988; Mann et al., 1970; Tobias, 1988).

We now know that students can evaluate teaching effectively; in the next decade, we will gain a better understanding of the validity of peer review of course materials, how various aspects of teaching contribute to learning outcomes, and how to teach students to evaluate their own gains in thinking and in knowledge.

We now know that faculty teaching can be improved with consultation; we will gain a better understanding of how consultation, training, and feedback can be combined to achieve greater effectiveness.

We now know that educational research can be of practical help to faculty members and institutions; in the next decade, we will better understand how to avoid the misuse of research and how to get more effective links to practice.

Do we meet Conant's (1947) criteria for a scientific field? I believe that if Edward L. Thorndike, Carl E. Seashore, J. B. Edmondson, and Herman Remmers could see us today, there would be a ringing chorus, "Yes"!

Note

1. *Recitation, discussion,* and *seminar* are sometimes used interchangeably. I think of recitation as involving student participation in which students answer fairly specific questions assessing their knowledge of the assigned lesson; discussion, on the other hand, is more likely to involve broader questions with openness to alternative points of view; a seminar typically involves a student presentation followed by discussion and usually implies a small group with advanced students.

References

Adams, J.C., Carter, C.R., and Smith, D. R. (Eds.) (1959). *College teaching by television.* Washington, DC: American Council on Education.

Annis, L.F. (1983). The processes and effects of peer tutoring. *Human Learning*, 2, 39–47.

Asch, M.J. (1951). Non-directive teaching in psychology: An experimental study. *Psychological Monographs, 65*(4).

Bane, C.L. (1925). The lecture vs. the class-discussion method of college teaching. *School and Society, 21,* 300–302.

Bargh, H.A., and Schul, Y. (1980). On the cognitive benefits of teaching. *Journal of Educational Psychology, 72,* 593–604.

Biggs, J.B. (1976). Dimensions of study behavior: Another look at ATI. *British Journal of Educational Psychology, 46,* 68–80.

Bjork, R.A. (1979). Information-processing analysis of college teaching. *Educational Psychologist, 14,* 15–23.

Bovard, E.W., Jr. (1951a). Group structure and perception. *Journal of Abnormal and Social Psychology, 46,* 398–405.

Bovard, E.W., Jr. (1951b). The experimental production of interpersonal affect. *Journal of Abnormal and Social Psychology, 46,* 521–528.

Carpenter, C.R. (1959, March). *The Penn State pyramid plan: Interdependent student work study grouping for increasing motivation for academic development.* Paper presented at the 14th National Conference on Higher Education, Chicago.

Carpenter, C.R., and Greenhill, L.P. (1955). *An investigation of closed-circuit television for teaching university courses* (Instructional Television Research Project No. 1). University Park: Pennsylvania State University.

Carpenter, C.R., and Greenhill, L.P. (1958). *An investigation of closed-circuit television for teaching university courses* (Instructional Television Research Project No. 2). University Park: Pennsylvania State University.

Cheydleur, F.D. (1945, August). Criteria of effective teaching in basic French courses. *Bulletin of the University of Wisconsin* (Monograph 2783).

Cohen, P.A. (1981). Student ratings of instruction and student achievement: A meta-analysis of multisection validity studies. *Review of Educational Research, 51,* 281–309.

Cohen, P.A., Kulik, J.A., and Kulik, C.-L.C. (1982). Educational outcomes of tutoring: A meta-analysis of findings. *American Educational Research Journal, 19,* 237–248.

Conant, J.B. (1947). *On understanding science.* New Haven: Yale University Press.

Costin, F., Greenough, W. T., and Menges, R. J. (1971). Student ratings of college teaching: Reliability, validity, and usefulness. *Review of Educational Research, 41,* 511–535.

Covington, M.V., and Omelich C.L. (1988). Achievement dynamics: The interaction of motives, cognitions, and emotions over time. *Anxiety Research, 1,* 165–183.

Cranton, P., and Smith, R.A. (1990). Reconsidering the unit of analysis: A model of student ratings of instruction. *Journal of Educational Psychology, 82,* 207–212.

Cronbach, L.J. (1957). The two disciplines of scientific psychology. *American Psychologist, 12,* 671–684.

Davage, R.H. (1958). *The pyramid plan for the systemic involvement of university students in teaching-learning functions.* Unpublished manuscript, Division of Academic Research and Services, Pennsylvania State University.

Davage, R.H. (1959). *Recent data on the pyramid project in psychology.* Unpublished manuscript, Division of Academic Research and Services, Pennsylvania State University.

De Corte, E., Lodewijks, H., Parmenteir, R., and Span, P. (Eds.) (1987). *Learning and instruction: European research in an international context* (Vol. I). Oxford, England: Pergamon/Leuven University Press.

Dunkin, M.J., and Barnes, J. (1986). Research on teaching in higher education. In M. C. Wittrock (Ed.), *Handbook of research on teaching* (3rd ed., pp. 754–777). New York: Macmillan.

Edmondson, J.B., and Mulder, F.J. (1924). Size of class as a factor in university instruction. *Journal of Educational Research, 9,* 1–12.

Elliot, D.N. (1949). *Characteristics and relationships of various criteria of teaching.* Unpublished doctorial dissertation, Purdue University.

Entwistle, N., Hanley, M., and Hounsell, D. (1979). Identifying distinctive approaches to studying. *Higher Education, 8,* 3655–3680.

Erdle, S., Murray, H.G., and Rushton, J.P. (1985). Personality, classroom behavior, and student ratings of college teaching effectiveness: A path analysis. *Journal of Educational Psychology, 77,* 394–407.

Faw, V.A. (1949). A psychotherapeutic method of teaching psychology. *American Psychologist, 4,* 104–109.

Feldman, K.A. (1978). Course characteristics and college students' ratings of their teachers: What we know and what we don't. *Research in Higher Education, 9,* 199–242.

Giaconia, R.M., and Hedges, L.V. (1982). Identifying features of effective open education. *Review of Educational Research, 52,* 579–602.

Glass, G.V., and Smith, M.L. (1979). Meta-analysis of research on class size and achievement. *Educational Evaluation and Policy Analysis, 1,* 2–16.

Goldschmid, M.L. (1970). Instructional options: Adapting the large university course to individual differences. *Learning and Development, 1,* 1–2.

Goldschmid, M.L. (1971). The learning cell: An instructional innovation. *Learning and Development, 2,* 1–6.

Gruber, H.E., and Weitman, M. (1960, April). *Cognitive processes in higher education: Curiosity and critical thinking.* Paper presented at the meeting of the Western Psychological Association, San Jose, CA.

Guetzkow, H.S., Kelly, E.L., and McKeachie, W. J. (1954). An experimental comparison of recitation, discussion, and tutorial methods in college teaching. *Journal of Educational Psychology, 45,* 193–209.

Hofstein, A., and Lunetta, V.N. (1982). The role of the laboratory in science teaching: Neglected aspects of research. *Review of Educational Research, 52,* 201–217.

Hudelson, E. (1928). *Class size at the college level.* Minneapolis: University of Minnesota Press.

Jones, H.E. (1923). Experimental studies of college teaching. The effect of examinations on permanence of learning. *Archives of Psychology, 10*(68), 5–70.

Johnson, D.W., Maruyama, G., Johnson, R., Nelson, D., and Skon, L. (1981). Effects of cooperative, competitive, and individualistic goal structures on achievement: A meta-analysis. *Psychological Bulletin, 89,* 47–62.

Klapper, P. (Ed.) (1920). *College teaching.* Yonkers-on-Hudson, NY: World Book Co.

Kulik, J.A., Cohen, P.A., and Ebeling, B.J. (1980). Effectiveness of programmed instruction in higher education: A meta-analysis of findings. *Educational Evaluation and Policy Analysis, 2,* 51–64.

Kulik, J.A., Kulik, C.-L.C., and Bangert-Drowns, R.L. (1988, May). *Effectiveness of mastery learning programs: A meta-analysis.* Ann Arbor: University of Michigan, Center for Research on Learning and Teaching.

Kulik, J.A., Kulik, C.-L.C., and Cohen, P.A. (1979). Research on audio-tutorial instruction: A meta-analysis of comparative studies. *Research on Higher Education, 11,* 321–341.

Kulik, J.A., Kulik, C.-L.C., and Cohen, P. (1980). Effectiveness of computer-based college teaching: A meta-analysis of findings. *Review of Educational Research, 50,* 525–544.

Lange, P.C. (1972). Today's education. *National Education Association, 61,* 59.

Lewin, K., Lippitt, R., and White, R.K. (1939). Patterns of aggressive behavior in experimentally created social climates. *Journal of Social Psychology, 10,* 271–299.

Macomber, F.G., and Siegel, L. (1957a). A study of large-group teaching procedures. *Educational Research, 38,* 220–229.

Macomber, F.G., and Siegel, L. (1957b). *Experimental study in instructional procedures* (Progress Report No. 2). Oxford, OH: Miami University.

Macomber, F.G., and Siegel, L. (1960). *Experimental study in instructional procedures* (Final Report). Oxford, OH: Miami University.

Mann, R.D., Arnold, S. M., Binder, J.L., Cytrynbaum, S., Newman, B. M., Ringwald, B. E. Ringwald, J. W., and Rosenwein, R. (1970). *The college classroom.* New York: Wiley.

Marsh, H.W. (1984). Student's evaluations of teaching: Dimensionality, reliability, validity, potential biases, and utility. *Journal of Educational Psychology, 76,* 707–754.

Marsh, H.W. (1987). *Student's evaluations of university teaching: Research findings, methodological issues and directions for future research.* Elmford, NY: Pergamon.

Marton, F., and Säljö, R. (1976a). On qualitative differences in learning: I. Outcome and process. *British Journal of Educational Psychology, 46,* 4–11.

Marton, F., and Säljö, R. (1976b). On qualitative differences in learning: II. Outcome and process. *British Journal of Educational Psychology, 46,* 115–127.

McKeachie, W.J. (1951). Anxiety in the college classroom. *Journal of Educational Research, 45,* 153–160.

McKeachie, W.J. (1952). Teaching psychology on television. *American Psychologist, 7,* 503–506.

McKeachie, W.J. (1954). Student-centered instruction versus instructor-centered instruction. *Journal of Educational Psychology, 45,* 143–150.

McKeachie, W.J. (1958). Students, groups, and teaching methods. *American Psychologist, 13,* 580–584.

McKeachie, W.J. (1984). Does anxiety disrupt information processing or does poor information processing lead to anxiety? *International Review of Applied Psychology, 33,* 187–203.

McKeachie, W.J., DeValois, R. L. Dulany, D. E., Jr., Beardslee, D. C., and Winterbottom, M. (1954). Objectives of the general psychology course. *American Psychologist, 9,* 140–142.

McKeachie, W.J., Lin, Y.-G., Forrin, B., and Teevan, R. (1960). Individualized teaching in elementary psychology. *Journal of Educational Psychology, 51,* 285–291.

McKeachie, W.J., Pintrich, P. R., and Lin, Y.-G. (1985). Learning to learn. In G. d'Ydewalle (Ed.), *Cognition, information processing and motivation.* (pp. 601–618). North Holland: Elsevier Science Publishers.

McKeachie, W.J., Pintrich, P. R., Lin, Y.-G., and Smith, D. A. F. (1986). *Teaching and learning in the college classroom: A review of the research literature.* Ann Arbor: University of Michigan, National Center for Research to Improve Post-Secondary Teaching and Learning.

McMillan, L. (1986, March 5). Many professors now start at the beginning by teaching their students how to think. *The Chronicle of Higher Education,* pp. 23–55.

Menges, R.J., and Mathis, B. C. (1988). *Key resources on teaching, learning, curriculum, and faculty development.* San Francisco: Jossey-Bass.

Mitzel, H.E. (1960). Teacher effectiveness. In C. W. Harris (Ed.), *Encyclopedia of educational research* (3rd ed., pp. 1481–1486). New York: Macmillan.

Moore, M.R., and Popham, W.J. (1959, December). *The role of extraclass student interviews in promoting student achievement.* Paper presented at the joint session of the American Association for the Advancement of Science and American Educational Research Association, Chicago.

Mueller, A.D. (1924). Class size as a factor in normal school instruction. *Education, 45,* 203–277.

Murray, H.G., Rushton, J.P., and Paunonen, S.V. (1990). Teacher personality traits and student instructional ratings in six types of university courses. *Journal of Educational Psychology, 82,* 250–261.

Nash, A.N., Muczyk, J. P., and Vettori, F.L. (1971). The relative practical effectiveness of programmed instruction. *Personnel Psychology, 24,* 297–418.

Palincsar, A.S., and Brown, A.L. (1984). Reciprocal teaching of comprehension-monitoring activities. *Cognition and Instruction, 1,* 117–175.

Perry, R.P., Abrami, P.C., and Leventhal, L. (1979). Educational seduction: The effect of instructor expressiveness and lecture content on student ratings and achievement. *Journal of Educational Psychology, 71,* 107–116.

Postlethwait, S.W., Novak, J., and Murray, H.T., Jr. (1972). *The audio-tutorial approach to learning.* Minneapolis, Burgess.

Remmers, H.H. (1933). Learning, effort, and attitudes as affected by three methods of instruction in elementary psychology. *Purdue University Studies in Higher Education* (Monograph No. 21).

Schirmerhorn, S., Goldschmid, M.L., and Shore, B.S. (1975). Learning basic principles of probability in student dyads: A cross-age comparison. *Journal of Educational Psychology, 67,* 551–557.

Schramm, W.L. (1962). Learning from instructional television. *Review of Educational Research, 32,* 156–167.

Schramm, W.L. (1964). *The research on programmed instruction.* Washington, DC: U.S. Government Printing Office.

Seashore, C.E., Angell, J. R., Calkins, M.W., Sanford, E.C., and Whipple G.M. (1910). Report of the committee on the American Psychological Association on the teaching of psychology. *Psychological Monographs, 12,* 1–93.

Siegel, L., Adams, J.F., and Macomber, F.G. (1980). Retention of subject matter as a function of large-group instructional procedures. *Journal of Educational Psychology, 51,* 9–13.

Skinner, B.F. (1954). The science of learning and the art of teaching. *Harvard Educational Review, 24,* 86–97.

Slomowitz, M. (1955). A comparison of personality changes and content achievement gains occurring in two modes of instruction (Doctoral dissertation, New York University, 1955). *Dissertation Abstracts, 15,* 1790.

Smalzreid, N.T., and Remmers, H.H. (1943). A factor analysis of the Purdue Rating Scale for Instructors. *Journal of Educational Psychology, 34,* 363–367.

Smith, N.H. (1962). The teaching of elementary statistics by the conventional classroom method vs. the method of programmed instruction. *Journal of Educational Research, 55,* 417–420.

Smith, P.B. (1975). Controlled studies of sensitivity training. *Psychological Bulletin, 82,* 597–622.

Solomon, D., Rosenberg, L., and Bezdek, W.E. (1964). Teacher behavior and student learning. *Journal of Educational Psychology, 55,* 23–30.

Sullivan, A.M., Andrews, E.A., Hollinghurst, F., Maddigan, R., and Noseworthy, C.M. (1976). The relative effectiveness of instructional television. *Interchange, 7*(1), 46–51.

Svensson, L. (1976). *Study skills and learning.* Goteberg, Sweden: Acta Universitates, Gothenburgensis.

Tobias, S. (1985). Test anxiety: Interference, defective skills, and cognitive capacity. *Educational Psychologist, 20,* 135–142.

Tobias, S. (1988, August). *Adapting instruction to student charaterization.* Presidential address of Division of Educational Psychology, American Psychological Association, Atlanta, GA.

Tobias, S. (in press). Teaching strategic text review by computer and interaction with student characteristics. *Computers in Human Behavior.*

Webb, N.J., and Grib, T.F. (1967). *Teaching process as a learning experience: The experimental use of student-led groups* (Final Report, No. HE-000-882). Washington, DC: U.S. Department of Health, Education, and Welfare.

Weinstein, C.E., Goetz, E.T., and Alexander, P.A. (Eds.) (1985). *Learning and study strategies: Issues in assessment, instruction, and evaluation.* San Diego, CA: Academic Press.

Weinstein, C.W., and Mayer, R.E. (1986). The teaching of learning strategies. In M. Wittrock (Ed.), *Handbook of research on teaching* (3rd ed., pp. 315–327). New York: Macmillan.

Weinstein, C.E., Underwood, V.L., Wicker, F.W., and Cubberly, W.E. (1979). Cognitive learning strategies: Verbal and imaginal elaboration. In H. F. O'Neill, Jr., and C. D. Spielberger (Eds.), *Cognitive and affective learning strategies* (pp. 45–75). New York: Academic Press.

Wispe, L.G. (1951). Evaluative section methods in the introductory course. *Journal of Educational Research, 45,* 161–168.

Zeleny, L.D. (1940). Experiment appraisal of a group learning plan. *Journal of Educational Research, 34*(1), 37–42.

SEVEN PRINCIPLES FOR GOOD PRACTICE IN UNDERGRADUATE EDUCATION

ARTHUR W. CHICKERING AND ZELDA F. GAMSON*

Apathetic students, illiterate graduates, incompetent teaching, impersonal campuses—so rolls the drumfire of criticism of higher education. More than two years of reports have spelled out the problems. States have been quick to respond by holding out carrots and beating with sticks.

There are neither enough carrots nor enough sticks to improve undergraduate education without the commitment and action of students and faculty members. They are the precious resources on whom the improvement of undergraduate education depends.

But how can students and faculty members improve undergraduate education? Many campuses around the country are asking this question. To provide a focus for their work, we offer seven principles based on research on good teaching and learning in colleges and universities.

Good practice in undergraduate education:

1. Encourages contacts between students and faculty.
2. Develops reciprocity and cooperation among students.
3. Uses active learning techniques.
4. Gives prompt feedback.
5. Emphasizes time on task.
6. Communicates high expectations.
7. Respects diverse talents and ways of learning.

We can do it ourselves—with a little bit of help. . . .

A Focus for Improvement

These seven principles are not ten commandments shrunk to a twentieth century attention span. They are intended as guidelines for faculty members, students, and administrators—with support from state agencies and trustees—to improve teaching and learning. These principles seem like good common sense, and they *are*—because many teachers and students have experienced them and because research supports them. They rest on 50 years of research and on the way teachers teach and students learn, how students work and play with one another, and how students and faculty talk to each other.

While each practice can stand on its own, when all are present their effects multiply. Together, they employ six powerful forces in education:

- Activity
- Cooperation

Reprinted from *AAHE Bulletin* (March 1987), American Association for Higher Education and Accreditation.

- Diversity
- Expectations
- Interaction
- Responsibility

Good practices hold as much meaning for professional programs as for the liberal arts. They work for many different kinds of students—white, black, Hispanic, Asian, rich, poor, older, younger, male, female, well-prepared, underprepared.

But the ways different institutions implement good practice depends very much on their students and their circumstances. In what follows, we describe several different approaches to good practice that have been used in different kinds of settings in the last few years. In addition, the powerful implications of these principles for the way states fund and govern higher education and for the way institutions are run are discussed briefly at the end.

As faculty members, academic administrators, and student personnel staff, we have spent most of our working lives trying to understand our students, our colleagues, our institutions, and ourselves. We have conducted research on higher education with dedicated colleagues in a wide range of schools in this country. We draw the implications of this research for practice, hoping to help us all do better.

We address the teacher's *how,* not the subject-matter *what,* of good practice in undergraduate education. We recognize that content and pedagogy interact in complex ways. We are also aware that there is much healthy ferment within and among the disciplines. What is taught, after all, is at least as important as how it is taught. In contrast to the long history of research in teaching and learning, there is little research on the college curriculum. We cannot, therefore, make responsible recommendations about the content of a good undergraduate education. That work is yet to be done.

This much we can say: An undergraduate education should prepare students to understand and deal intelligently with modern life. What better place to start but in the classroom and on our campuses? What better time than now?

Seven Principles of Good Practice

1. Encourages Contacts Between Students and Faculty

Frequent student-faculty contact in and out of classes is the most important factor in student motivation and involvement. Faculty concern helps students get through rough times and keep on working. Knowing a few faculty members well enhances students' intellectual commitment and encourages them to think about their own values and future plans.

Some examples: Freshman seminars on important topics, taught by senior faculty members, establish an early connection between students and faculty in many colleges and universities.

In the Saint Joseph's College core curriculum, faculty members who lead discussion groups in courses outside their fields of specialization model for students what it means to be a learner. In the Undergraduate Research Opportunities Program at the Massachusetts Institute of Technology, three out of four undergraduates have joined three-quarters of the faculty in recent years as junior research colleagues. At Sinclair Community College, students in the College Without Walls program have pursued studies through learning contracts. Each student has created a "resource group," which includes a faculty member, a student peer, and two "community resource" faculty members. This group then provides support and assures quality.

2. Develops Reciprocity and Cooperation Among Students

Learning is enhanced when it is more like a team effort than a solo race. Good learning, like good work, is collaborative and social, not competitive and isolated. Working with others often increases involvement in learning. Sharing one's own ideas and responding to others' reactions sharpens thinking and deepens understanding.

Some examples: Even in large lecture classes, students can learn from one another. Learning groups are a common practice. Students are assigned to a group of five to seven other students, who meet regularly during class throughout the term to solve problems set by the instructor. Many colleges use peer tutors for students who need special help.

Learning communities are another popular way of getting students to work together. Students involved in SUNY at Stony Brook's Federated Learning Communities can take several courses together. The courses, on topics related to a common theme like science, technology, and human values, are from different disciplines. Faculty teaching the courses coordinate their activities while another faculty member, called a "master learner," takes the courses with the students. Under the direction of the master learner, students run a seminar which helps them integrate ideas from the separate courses.

3. Uses Active Learning Techniques

Learning is not a spectator sport. Students do not learn much just by sitting in classes listening to teachers, memorizing pre-packaged assignments, and spitting out answers. They must talk about what they are learning, write about it, relate it to past experiences, apply it to their daily lives. They must make what they learn part of themselves.

Some examples: Active learning is encouraged in classes that use structured exercises, challenging discussions, team projects, and peer critiques. Active learning can also occur outside the classroom. There are thousands of internships, independent study, and cooperative job programs across the country in all kinds of colleges and universities, in all kinds of fields, for all kinds of students. Students also can help design and teach courses or parts of courses. At Brown University, faculty members and students have designed new courses on contemporary issues and universal themes; the students then help the professors as teaching assistants. At the State University of New York at Cortland, beginning students in a general chemistry lab have worked in small groups to design lab procedures rather than repeat prestructured exercises. At the University of Michigan's Residential College, teams of students periodically work with faculty members on a long-term original research project in the social sciences.

4. Gives Prompt Feedback

Knowing what you know and don't know focuses learning. Students need appropriate feedback on performance to benefit from courses. When getting started, students need help in assessing existing knowledge and competence. In classes, students need frequent opportunities to perform and receive suggestions for improvement. At various points during college, and at the end, students need chances to reflect on what they have learned, what they still need to know, and how to assess themselves.

Some examples: No feedback can occur without assessment. But assessment without timely feedback contributes little to learning.

Colleges assess students as they enter in order to guide them in planning their studies. In addition to the feedback they receive from course instructors, students in many colleges and universities receive counseling periodically on their progress and future plans. At Bronx Community College, students with poor academic preparation have been carefully tested and given special tutorials to prepare them to take introductory courses. They are then advised about the introductory courses to take, given the level of their academic skills.

Adults can receive assessment of their work and other life experiences at many colleges and universities through portfolios of their work or through standardized tests; these provide the basis for sessions with advisors.

Alverno College requires that students develop high levels of performance in eight general abilities such as analytic and communication skills. Performance is assessed and then discussed with students at each level for each ability in a variety of ways and by a variety of assessors.

In writing courses across the country, students are learning, through detailed feedback from instructors and fellow students, to revise and rewrite drafts. They learn, in the process, that feedback is central to learning and improving performance.

5. Emphasizes Time on Task

Time plus energy equals learning. There is no substitute for time on task. Learning to use one's time well is critical for students and professionals alike. Students need help in learning effective time management. Allocating realistic amounts of time means effective learning for students and effective teaching for faculty. How an institution defines time expectations for students, faculty, administrators, and other professional staff can establish the basis for high performance for all.

Some examples: Mastery learning, contract learning, and computer assisted instruction require that students spend adequate amounts of time on learning. Extended periods of preparation for college also give students more time on task. Maneo Ricci College is known for its efforts to guide high school students from the ninth grade to a B.A. in six years through a curriculum taught jointly by faculty at Seattle Preparatory School and Seattle University. Providing students with opportunities to integrate their studies into the rest of their lives helps them use time well.

Workshops, intensive residential programs, combinations of televised instruction, correspondence study, learning centers are all being used in a variety of institutions, especially those with many part-time students. Weekend colleges and summer residential programs, courses offered at work sites and community centers, clusters of courses on related topics taught in the same time block, and double-credit courses make more time for learning. At Empire State College, for example, students design degree programs organized in manageable time blocks; students may take courses at nearby institutions, pursue independent study, or work with faculty and other students at Empire State learning centers.

6. Communicates High Expectations

Expect more and you will get more. High expectations are important for everyone—for the poorly prepared, for those unwilling to exert themselves, and for the bright and well motivated. Expecting students to perform well becomes a self-fulfilling prophecy when teachers and institutions hold high expectations of themselves and make extra efforts.

Some examples: In many colleges and universities, students with poor past records or test scores do extraordinary work. Sometimes they outperform students with good preparation. The University of Wisconsin-Parkside has communicated high expectations for underprepared high school students by bringing them to the university for workshops in academic subjects, study skills, test taking, and time management. In order to reinforce high expectations, the program involves parents and high school counselors.

The University of California, Berkeley introduced an honors program in the sciences for underprepared minority students; a growing number of community colleges are establishing general honors programs for minorities. Special programs like these help. But most important are the day-to-day, week-in and week-out expectations students and faculty hold for themselves and for each other in all their classes.

7. Respects Diverse Talents and Ways of Learning

There are many roads to learning. People bring different talents and styles of learning to college. Brilliant students in the seminar room may be all thumbs in the lab or art studio. Students rich in hands-on experience may not do so well with theory. Students need the opportunity to show their talents and learn in ways that work for them. Then they can be pushed to learning in new ways that do not come so easily.

Some examples: Individualized degree programs recognize different interests. Personalized systems of instruction and mastery learning let students work at their own pace. Contract learning helps students define their own objectives, determine their learning activities, and define the criteria and methods of evaluation. At the College of Public and Community Service, a college for older working adults at the University of Massachusetts-Boston, incoming students have taken an orientation course that encourages them to reflect on their learning styles. Rockland Community College has offered a life-career-educational planned course. At the University of California, Irvine, introductory physics students may choose between a lecture-and-textbook course, a computer-based version of the lecture-and-textbook course, or a computer-based course based on notes developed by the faculty that allow students to program the computer. In both computer-based courses, students work on their own and must pass mastery exams.

Whose Responsibility Is It?

Teachers and students hold the main responsibility for improving undergraduate education. But they need a lot of help. College and university leaders, state and federal officials, and accrediting associations have the power to shape an environment that is favorable to good practice in higher education.

What qualities must this environment have?

- A strong sense of shared purposes.
- Concrete support from adminstrators and faculty leaders for those purposes.
- Adequate funding appropriate for the purposes.
- Policies and procedures consistent with the purposes.
- Continuing examination of how well the purposes are being achieved.

There is good evidence that such an environment can be created. When this happens, faculty members and administrators think of themselves as educators. Adequate resources are put into creating opportunities for faculty members, administrators, and students to celebrate and reflect on their shared purposes. Faculty members receive support and release time for appropriate professional development activities. Criteria for hiring and promoting faculty members, administrators, and staff support the institution's purposes. Advising is considered important. Departments, programs, and classes are small enough to allow faculty members and students to have a sense of community, to experience the value of their contributions, and to confront the consequences of their failures.

States, the federal government, and accrediting associations affect the kind of environment that can develop on campuses in a variety of ways. The most important is through the allocation of financial support. States also influence good practice by encouraging sound planning, setting priorities, mandating standards, and reviewing and approving programs. Regional and professional accrediting associations require self-study and peer review in making their judgments about programs and institutions.

These sources of support and influence can encourage environments for good practice in undergraduate education by:

- Setting policies that are consistent with good practice in undergraduate education.
- Holding high expectations for institutional performance.
- Keeping bureaucratic regulations to a minimum that is compatible with public accountability.
- Allocating adequate funds for new undergraduate programs and the professional development of faculty members, administrators, and staff.
- Encouraging employment of under-represented groups among administrators, faculty members, and student services professionals.
- Providing the support for programs, facilities, and financial aid necessary for good practice in undergraduate education.

Note

* Prepared with the assistance of Alexander W. Astin, Howard Bowen, Carol M. Boyer, K. Patricia Cross, Kenneth Ehle, Russell Edgerton, Jerry Gaff, Joseph Katz, C. Robert Pace, Marvin W. Peterson, and Richard C. Richardson, Jr.

This work was co-sponsored by the American Association for Higher Education and the Education Commission of the States. The Johnson Foundation supported the preparation of early drafts and a meeting for the authors at Wingspread in Racine, Wisconsin. William Boyd and Henry Halsted of the Johnson Foundation made useful contributions to the group's deliberations and to revisions.

References

Adelman, C. (1984). *Starting with students: Promising approaches in American higher education.* Washington, DC: National Institute of Education.

Astin, A.W. (1977). *Four critical years: Effects of college on beliefs, attitudes, and knowledge.* San Francisco: Jossey-Bass.

Astin, A.W. (1985). *Achieving educational excellence.* San Francisco: Jossey-Bass.

Bayer, A.E. (1975). Faculty composition, institutional structure, and students' college environment. *Journal of Higher Education,* 46(5), 549–555.

Beal, P.E., and Noel, L. (1980). *What works in student retention.* American College Testing Program.

Bouton, C., and Garth, R.Y. (1983). Learning in groups. *New Directions for Teaching and Learning,* 14. San Francisco: Jossey-Bass.

Bowen, H.R. (1977). *Investment in learning.* San Francisco: Jossey-Bass.

Boyer, C.M., and Ahlgren, A. (1987, July/August). Assessing undergraduates' patterns of credit distribution: Amount and specialization. *Journal of Higher Education,* 58(4), forthcoming.

Boyer, C.M., and Ewell, P.T., Finney, J.E., and Mingle, J.R. (1987). Assessment and outcomes measurement—A view from the states: Highlights of a new ECS survey. *AAHE Bulletin,* 39: 7, 8–12.

Chickering, A.W. (1969). *Education and identity.* San Francisco: Jossey-Bass.

Chickering, A.W., and McCormick, J. (1973). Personality development and the college experience. *Research in Higher Education,* 1, 43–70.

Chickering, A.W. (1974). *Commuting versus resident students: Overcoming the educational inequities of living off campus.* San Francisco: Jossey-Bass.

Chickering, A.W., and Associates (1981). *The modern American college: Responding to the new realities of diverse students and a changing society.* San Francisco: Jossey-Bass.

Claxton, C.S., and Ralston, Y. (1978). Learning styles: Their impacts on teaching and administration. *AAHE-ERIC/Higher Education, Research Report No. 10.* Washington, DC: American Association for Higher Education.

Cohen, E.G. (1986). *Designing groupwork: Strategies for the heterogeneous classroom.* New York: Teachers College Press.

Cross, K.P. (1986, March). Taking teaching seriously. Presentation at the Annual Meeting of the American Association for Higher Education.

Eble, K. (1976). *Craft of teaching.* San Francisco: Jossey-Bass.

Feldman, K.A., and Newcomb, T.M. (1969). *The impact of college on students.* San Francisco: Jossey-Bass.

Gamson, Z.F., and Associates. (1984). *Liberating education.* San Francisco: Jossey-Bass.

Gardner, H. (1983). *Frames of mind: A theory of multiple intelligence.* New York: Basic Books.

Heath, D. (1968). *Growing up in college.* San Francisco: Jossey-Bass.

Jacob, P.E. (1957). *Changing values in college.* New York: Harper.

Katz, J., and Associates. (1968). *No time for youth.* San Francisco: Jossey-Bass.

Keeton, M.T. (Ed.) (1976). *Experiential learning.* San Francisco: Jossey-Bass.

Kolb, D. (1984). *Experiential learning.* New Jersey: Prentice Hall.

Kulik, J.A. (1982). Individualized systems of instruction. In Harold E. Mitzel (Ed.), *Encyclopedia of educational research,* 2. New York: The Free Press.

Lowman, J. (1984). *Mastering the techniques of teaching.* San Francisco: Jossey-Bass.

McKeachie, W.J. (1985). *Improving undergraduate education through faculty development.* San Francisco: Jossey-Bass.

Messick, S., and Associates. (Ed.) (1976). *Individuality in learning.* San Francisco: Jossey-Bass.

Newcomb, T.M. (1943). *Personality and social change.* New York: Dryden Press.

Newcomb, T.M., and others. *Persistence and change: A college and its students after twenty-five years.* Huntington, NY: Krieger.

Pace, C.R. (1943). *Measuring outcomes of college: Fifty years of finding and recommending for future assessment.* San Francisco: Jossey-Bass.

Pascarella, E.T. (1980). Student-faculty informal contact and college outcomes. *Review of Educational Research,* 50, Winter, 545–595.

Pascarella, E.T., Terenzini, P.T., and Wolfe, L.M. (1986). Orientation to college and freshman year persistence/withdrawal decisions. *Journal of Higher Education,* 57, 155–175.

Perry, W.G., Jr. (1970). *Forms of intellectual and ethical development in the college years: A scheme.* New York: Holt, Rinehart and Winston.

Peterson, M.W., Jedamus, P., and Associates. (1981). *Improving academic management.* San Francisco: Jossey-Bass.

Richardson, R.C., Jr., Fisk, E.C., and Okun, M.A. (1983). *Literacy in the open access college.* San Francisco: Jossey-Bass.

Sanford, N. (Ed.) (1962). *The American college.* New York: John Wiley and Sons.

Wallace, W.L. (1966). *Student culture.* Chicago: Aldine.

Wilson, R.C., Gaff, J.G., Dienst, E.R., Wood, L., and Bavry, J.I. (1975). *College professors and their impact upon students.* New York: John Wiley and Sons.

Winter, D.G., McClelland, D.C., and Stewart, A.J. (1981). *A new case for the liberal arts.* San Francisco: Jossey-Bass.

From Teaching to Learning: A New Paradigm for Undergraduate Education

Robert B. Barr and John Tagg

The significant problems we face cannot be solved at the same level of thinking we were at when we created them

—Albert Einstein

A paradigm shift is taking hold in American higher education. In its briefest form, the paradigm that has governed our colleges is this: A college is an institution that exists *to provide instruction.* Subtly but profoundly we are shifting to a new paradigm: A college is an institution that exists *to produce learning.* This shift changes everything. It is both needed and wanted.

We call the traditional, dominant paradigm the "Instruction Paradigm." Under it, colleges have created complex structures to provide for the activity of teaching conceived primarily as delivering 50-minute lectures—the mission of a college is to deliver instruction.

Now, however, we are beginning to recognize that our dominant paradigm mistakes a means for an end. It takes the means or method—called "instruction" or "teaching"—and makes it the college's end or purpose. To say that the purpose of colleges is to provide instruction is like saying that General Motors' business is to operate assembly lines or that the purpose of medical care is to fill hospital beds. We now see that our mission is not instruction but rather that of producing *learning* with every student by *whatever* means work best.

The shift to a "Learning Paradigm" liberates institutions from a set of difficult constraints. Today it is virtually impossible for them to respond effectively to the challenge of stable or declining budgets while meeting the increasing demand for postsecondary education from increasingly diverse students. Under the logic of the Instruction Paradigm, colleges suffer from a serious design flaw: it is not possible to increase outputs without a corresponding increase in costs, because any attempt to increase outputs without increasing resources is a threat to quality. If a college attempts to increase its productivity by increasing either class sizes or faculty workloads, for example, academics will be quick to assume inexorable negative consequences for educational quality.

Just as importantly, the Instruction Paradigm rests on conceptions of teaching that are increasingly recognized as ineffective. As Alan Guskin pointed out in a September/October 1994 *Change* article premised on the shift from teaching to learning, "the primary learning environment for undergraduate students, the fairly passive lecture-discussion format where faculty talk and most students listen, is contrary to almost every principle of optimal settings for student learning." The Learning Paradigm ends the lecture's privileged position, honoring in its place whatever approaches serve best to prompt learning of particular knowledge by particular students.

The Learning Paradigm also opens up the truly inspiring goal that each graduating class learns more than the previous graduating class. In other words, the Learning Paradigm envisions the insti-

Reprinted from *Change Magazine* (November/December 1995), by permission of Taylor and Francis Group.

tution itself as a learner—over time, it continuously learns how to produce more learning with each graduating class, each entering student.

***

For many of us, the Learning Paradigm has always lived in our hearts. As teachers, we want above all else for our students to learn and succeed. But the heart's feeling has not lived clearly and powerfully in our heads. Now, as the elements of the Learning Paradigm permeate the air, our heads are beginning to understand what our hearts have known. However, none of us has yet put all the elements of the Learning Paradigm together in a conscious, integrated whole.

Lacking such a vision, we've witnessed reformers advocate many of the new paradigm's elements over the years, only to see few of them widely adopted. The reason is that they have been applied piecemeal within the structures of a dominant paradigm that rejects or distorts them. Indeed, for two decades the response to calls for reform from national commissions and task forces generally has been an attempt to address the issues *within the framework of the Instruction Paradigm*. The movements thus generated have most often failed, undone by the contradictions within the traditional paradigm. For example, if students are not learning to solve problems or think critically, the old logic says we must teach a class in thinking and make it a general education requirement. The logic is all too circular: What students are learning in the classroom doesn't address their needs or ours; therefore, we must bring them back into another classroom and instruct them some more. The result is never what we hope for because, as Richard Paul, director of the Center for Critical Thinking observes glumly, "critical thinking is taught in the same way that other courses have traditionally been taught, with an excess of lecture and insufficient time for practice."

To see what the Instruction Paradigm is we need only look at the structures and behaviors of our colleges and infer the governing principles and beliefs they reflect. But it is much more difficult to see the Learning Paradigm, which has yet to find complete expression in the structures and processes of any college. So we must imagine it. This is what we propose to do here. As we outline its principles and elements, we'll suggest some of their implications for colleges—but only some, because the expression of principles in concrete structures depends on circumstances. It will take decades to work out many of the Learning Paradigm's implications. But we hope here that by making it more explicit we will help colleagues to more fully recognize it and restructure our institutions in its image.

***

That such a restructuring is needed is beyond question: the gap between what we *say* we want of higher education and what its structures *provide* has never been wider. To use a distinction made by Chris Argyris and Donald Schön, the difference between our espoused theory and our theory-in-use is becoming distressingly noticeable. An "espoused theory," readers will recall, is the set of principles people offer to explain their behavior; the principles we can infer from how people or their organization actually behave is their "theory-in-use." Right now, the Instruction Paradigm is our theory-in-use, yet the *espoused* theories of most educators more closely resemble components of the Learning Paradigm. The more we discover about how the mind works and how students learn, the greater the disparity between what we say and what we do. Thus so many of us feel increasingly constrained by a system increasingly at variance with what we believe. To build the colleges we need for the 21st century—to put our minds where our hearts are, and rejoin acts with beliefs—we must consciously reject the Instruction Paradigm and restructure what we do on the basis of the Learning Paradigm.

The Paradigms

When comparing alternative paradigms, we must take care: the two will seldom be as neatly parallel as our summary chart suggests (see pages 33 and 34). A paradigm is like the rules of a game: one of the functions of the rules is to define the playing field and domain of possibilities on that field.

But a new paradigm may specify a game played on a larger or smaller field with a larger or smaller domain of legitimate possibilities. Indeed, the Learning Paradigm expands the playing field and domain of possibilities and it radically changes various aspects of the game. In the Instruction Paradigm, a specific methodology determines the boundary of what colleges can do; in the Learning Paradigm, student learning and success set the boundary. By the same token, not all elements of the new paradigm are contrary to corresponding elements of the old; the new includes many elements of the old within its larger domain of possibilities. The Learning Paradigm does not prohibit lecturing, for example. Lecturing becomes one of many possible methods, all evaluated on the basis of their ability to promote appropriate learning.

In describing the shift from an Instruction to a Learning Paradigm, we limit our address in this article to undergraduate education. Research and public service are important functions of colleges and universities but lie outside the scope of the present discussion. Here, as in our summary chart, we'll compare the two paradigms along six dimensions: mission and purposes, criteria for success, teaching/learning structures, learning theory, productivity and funding, and nature of roles.

Mission and Purposes

In the Instruction Paradigm, the mission of the college is to provide instruction, to teach. The method and the product are one and the same. The means is the end. In the Learning Paradigm, the mission of the college is to produce learning. The method and the product are separate. The end governs the means.

Some educators may be uncomfortable with the verb "produce." We use it because it so strongly connotes that the college takes *responsibility* for learning. The point of saying that colleges are to *produce* learning—not provide, not support, not encourage—is to say, unmistakably, that they are responsible for the degree to which students learn. The Learning Paradigm shifts what the institution takes responsibility for: from quality instruction (lecturing, talking) to student learning. Students, the co-producers of learning, can and must, of course, take responsibility for their own learning. Hence, responsibility is a win-win game wherein two agents take responsibility for the same outcome even though neither is in complete control of all the variables. When two agents take such responsibility, the resulting synergy produces powerful results.

The idea that colleges cannot be responsible for learning flows from a disempowering notion of responsibility. If we conceive of responsibility as a fixed quantity in a zero-sum game, then students must take responsibility for their own learning, and no one else can. This model generates a concept of responsibility capable of assigning blame but not of empowering the most productive action. The concept of responsibility as a framework for action is quite different: when one takes responsibility, one sets goals and then acts to achieve them, continuously modifying one's behavior to better achieve the goals. To take responsibility for achieving an outcome is not to guarantee the outcome, nor does it entail the complete control of all relevant variables; it is to make the achievement of the outcome the criterion by which one measures one's own efforts. In this sense, it is no contradiction to say that students, faculty, and the college as an institution can all take responsibility for student learning.

In the Learning Paradigm, colleges take responsibility for learning at two distinct levels. At the organizational level, a college takes responsibility for the aggregate of student learning and success. Did, for example, the graduating class's mastery of certain skills or knowledge meet our high, public standards for the award of the degree? The college also takes responsibility at the individual level, that is, for each individual student's learning. Did Mary Smith learn the chemistry we deem appropriate for a degree in that field? Thus, the institution takes responsibility for both its institutional outcomes and individual student outcomes.

Turning now to more specific purposes, in the Instruction Paradigm, a college aims to transfer or deliver knowledge from faculty to students; it offers courses and degree programs and seeks to maintain a high quality of instruction within them mostly by assuring that faculty stay current in their fields. If new knowledge or clients appear, so will new course work. The very purpose of the Instruction Paradigm is to offer courses.

In the Learning Paradigm, on the other hand, a college's purpose is not to transfer knowledge but to create environments and experiences that bring students to discover and construct knowledge for themselves, to make students members of communities of learners that make discoveries and solve problems. The college aims, in fact, to create a series of ever more powerful learning environments. The Learning Paradigm does not limit institutions to a single means for empowering students to learn; within its framework, effective learning technologies are continually identified, developed, tested, implemented, and assessed against one another. The aim in the Learning Paradigm is not so much to improve the quality of instruction—although that is not irrelevant—as it is to improve continuously the quality of learning for students individually and in the aggregate.

Under the older paradigm, colleges aimed to provide access to higher education, especially for historically underrepresented groups such as African-Americans and Hispanics. Too often, mere access hasn't served students well. Under the Learning Paradigm, the goal for underrepresented students (and *all* students) becomes not simply access but success. By "success" we mean the achievement of overall student educational objectives such as earning a degree, persisting in school, and learning the "right" things—the skills and knowledge that will help students to achieve their goals in work and life. A Learning Paradigm college, therefore, aims for ever-higher graduation rates while maintaining or even increasing learning standards.

CHART I

Comparing Educational Paradigms

The Instruction Paradigm	The Learning Paradigm
Mission and Purposes	
• Provide/deliver instruction	• Produce learning
• Transfer knowledge from faculty to students	• Elicit student discovery and construction of knowledge
• Offer courses and programs	• Create powerful learning environments
• Improve the quality of instruction	• Improve the quality of learning
• Achieve access for diverse students	• Achieve success for diverse students
Criteria for Success	
• Inputs, resources	• Learning and student-success outcomes
• Quality of entering students	• Quality of exiting students
• Curriculum development, expansion	• Learning technologies development, expansion
• Quantity and quality of resources	• Quality and quality of outcomes
• Enrollment, revenue growth	• Aggregate learning growth, efficiency
• Quality of faculty, instruction	• Quality of students, learning
Teaching/Learning Structures	
• Atomistic; parts prior to whole	• Holistic; whole prior to parts
• Time held constant, learning varies	• Learning held constant, time varies
• 50-minute lecture, 3-unit course	• Learning environments
• Classes start/end at same time	• Environment ready when student is
• One teacher, one classroom	• Whatever learning experience works
• Independent disciplines, departments	• Cross discipline/department collaboration
• Covering material	• Specified learning results
• End-of-course assessment	• Pre/during/post assessments
• Grading within classes by instructors	• External evaluations of learning
• Private assessment	• Public assessment
• Degree equals accumulated credit hours	• Degree equals demonstrated knowledge and skills

CHART I *(Continued)*

Learning Theory	
• Knowledge exists "out there"	• Knowledge exists in each person's mind and is shaped by individual experience
• Knowledge comes in "chunks" and "bits" delivered by instructors	• Knowledge is constructed, created, and "gotten"
• Learning is cumulative and linear	• Learning is a nesting and interacting of frameworks
• Fits the storehouse of knowledge metaphor	• Fits learning how to ride a bicycle metaphor
• Learning is teacher centered and controlled	• Learning is student centered and controlled
• "Live" teacher, "live" students required	• "Active" learner required, but not "live" teacher
• The classroom and learning are competitive and individualistic	• Learning environments and learning are cooperative, collaborative, and supportive
• Talent and ability are rare	• Talent and ability are abundant
Productivity/Funding	
• Definition of productivity: cost per hour of instruction per student	• Definition of productivity: cost per unit of learning per student
• Funding for hours of instruction	• Funding for learning outcomes
Nature of Roles	
• Faculty are primarily lecturers	• Faculty are primarily designers of learning methods and environments
• Faculty and students act independently and in isolation	• Faculty and student work in teams with each other and other staff
• Teachers classify and sort students	• Teachers develop every student's competencies and talents
• Staff serve/support faculty and the process of instruction	• All staff are educators who produce student learning and success
• Any expert can teach	• Empowering learning is challenging and complex
• Line governance; independent actors	• Shared governance; teamwork

By shifting the intended institutional outcome from teaching to learning, the Learning Paradigm makes possible a continuous improvement in productivity. Whereas under the Instruction Paradigm a primary institutional purpose was to optimize faculty well-being and success—including recognition for research and scholarship—in the Learning Paradigm a primary drive is to produce learning outcomes more efficiently. The philosophy of an Instruction Paradigm college reflects the belief that it cannot increase learning outputs without more resources, but a Learning Paradigm college expects to do so continuously. A Learning Paradigm college is concerned with learning productivity, not teaching productivity.

Criteria for Success

Under the Instruction Paradigm, we judge our colleges by comparing them to one another. The criteria for quality are defined in terms of inputs and process measures. Factors such as selectivity in student admissions, number of PhDs on the faculty, and research reputation are used to rate colleges and universities. Administrators and boards may look to enrollment and revenue growth and the expansion of courses and programs. As Guskin put it, "We are so wedded to a definition of quality based on resources that we find it extremely difficult to deal with the *results* of our work, namely student learning."

The Learning Paradigm necessarily incorporates the perspectives of the assessment movement. While this movement has been under way for at least a decade, under the dominant Instruction

Paradigm it has not penetrated very far into normal organizational practice. Only a few colleges across the country systematically assess student learning outcomes. Educators in California community colleges always seem to be surprised when they hear that 45 percent of first-time fall students do not return in the spring and that it takes an average of six years for a student to earn an associate's (AA) degree. The reason for this lack of outcomes knowledge is profoundly simple: under the Instruction Paradigm, student outcomes are simply irrelevant to the successful functioning and funding of a college.

Our faculty evaluation systems, for example, evaluate the performance of faculty in teaching terms, not learning terms. An instructor is typically evaluated by her peers or dean on the basis of whether her lectures are organized, whether she covers the appropriate material, whether she shows interest in and understanding of her subject matter, whether she is prepared for class, and whether she respects her students' questions and comments. All these factors evaluate the instructor's performance in teaching terms. They do not raise the issue of whether students are learning, let alone demand evidence of learning or provide for its reward.

Many institutions construe teaching almost entirely in terms of lecturing. A true story makes the point. A biology instructor was experimenting with collaborative methods of instruction in his beginning biology classes. One day his dean came for a site visit, slipping into the back of the room. The room was a hubbub of activity. Students were discussing material enthusiastically in small groups spread out across the room; the instructor would observe each group for a few minutes, sometimes making a comment, sometimes just nodding approval. After 15 minutes or so the dean approached the instructor and said, "I came today to do your evaluation. I'll come back another time when you're teaching."

In the Instruction Paradigm, teaching is judged on its own terms; in the Learning Paradigm, the power of an environment or approach is judged in terms of its impact on learning. If learning occurs, then the environment has power. If students learn more in environment A than in environment B, then A is more powerful than B. To know this in the Learning Paradigm we would assess student learning routinely and constantly.

Institutional outcomes assessment is analogous to classroom assessment, as described by K. Patricia Cross and Thomas Angelo. In our own experience of classroom-assessment training workshops, teachers share moving stories about how even limited use of these techniques has prompted them to make big changes in their teaching, sometimes despite years of investment in a previous practice. Mimi Steadmen, in a recent study of community college teachers using classroom assessment, found that "eighty-eight percent of faculty surveyed reported that they had made changes in their teaching behaviors as a result." This at first was startling to us. How could such small amounts of information produce such large changes in teaching behavior?

Upon reflection, it became clear. The information was feedback about learning, about results—something teachers rarely collect. Given information that their students were not learning, it was obvious to these teachers that something had to be done about the methods they had been using. Likewise, we think, feedback on learning results at the institutional level should have a correspondingly large impact on an institution's behavior and on the means it uses to produce learning.

Of course, some will argue, true education simply cannot be measured. You cannot measure, for example, true appreciation of the beauty of a work of art. Certainly some learning is difficult, even impossible to measure. But it does not follow that useful and meaningful assessment is impossible.

If we compare outcomes assessment with the input measures controlling policy in the Instruction Paradigm, we find that measures of outcome provide far more genuine information about learning than do measures of input. Learning outcomes include whatever students do as a result of a learning experience. Any measurement of students' products from an educational experience is a measure of a learning outcome. We could count the number of pages students write, the number of books they read, their number of hours at the computer, or the number of math problems they solve.

Of course, these would be silly methods to determine institutional incentives, and we do not recommend them. Any one of them, however, would produce more useful information on learning than the present method of measuring inputs and ignoring outcomes. It would make more sense to fund a college on the number of math problems students solve, for example, than to fund it on the number of students who sit in math classes. We suspect that *any* system of institutional incentives based on outcomes would lead to greater learning than any system of incentives based on inputs. But we need not settle for a system biased toward the trivial. Right now, today, we can construct a good assessment regime with the tools we have at hand.

The Learning Paradigm requires us to heed the advice of the Wingspread Group: "New forms of assessment should focus on establishing what college and university graduates have learned—the knowledge and skill levels they have achieved and their potential for further independent learning."

Teaching/Learning Structures

By structures we mean those features of an organization that are stable over time and that form the framework within which activities and processes occur and through which the purposes of the organization are achieved. Structure includes the organization cart, role and reward systems, technologies and methods, facilities and equipment, decision-making customs, communication channels, feed-back loops, financial arrangements, and funding streams.

Peter Senge, in *The Fifth Discipline*, a book about applying systems theory to organizational learning, observes that institutions and their leaders rarely focus their attention on systemic structures. They seldom think, he says, to alter basic structures in order to improve organizational performance, even though those structures generate the patterns of organizational action and determine which activities and results are possible. Perhaps the recent talk about restructuring, re-engineering, and reinvention in higher education reflects a change in focus and a heightened awareness of both the constraining and liberating power of organizational structures.

There is good reason to attend to structure. First, restructuring offers the greatest hope for increasing organizational efficiency and effectiveness. Structure is leverage. If you change the structure in which people work, you increase or decrease the leverage applied to their efforts. A change in structure can either increase productivity or change the nature of organizational outcomes. Second, structure is the concrete manifestation of the abstract principles of the organization's governing paradigm. Structures reflecting an old paradigm can frustrate the best ideas and innovations of new-paradigm thinkers. As the governing paradigm changes, so likewise must the organization's structures.

In this section, we focus on the main structures related to the teaching and learning process; funding and faculty role structures are discussed later under separate headings. The teaching and learning structure of the Instruction Paradigm college is atomistic. In its universe, the "atom" is the 50-minute lecture, and the "molecule" is the one-teacher, one-classroom, three-credit-hour course. From these basic units the physical architecture, the administrative structure, and the daily schedules of faculty and students are built. Dennis McGrath and Martin Spear, professors at the Community College of Philadelphia, note that "education proceeds everywhere through the vehicle of the three-credit course. Faculty members [and everyone else, we might add] have so internalized that constraint that they are long past noticing that it is a constraint, thinking it part of the natural order of things."

The resulting structure is powerful and rigid. It is, of course, perfectly suited to the Instruction Paradigm task of offering one-teacher, one-classroom courses. It is antithetical to creating almost any other kind of learning experience. A sense of this can be obtained by observing the effort, struggle, and rule-bending required to schedule even a slightly different kind of learning activity such as a team-taught course.

In the "educational atomism" of the Instruction Paradigm, the parts of the teaching and learning process are seen as discrete entities. The parts exist prior to and independent of any whole; the whole is no more than the sum of the parts, or even less. The college interacts with students only in discrete, isolated environments, cut off from one another because the parts—the classes—are prior to the whole. A "college education" is the sum the student's experience of a series of discrete, largely unrelated, three-credit classes.

In the Instruction Paradigm, the teaching and learning process is governed by the further rule that time will be held constant while learning varies. Although addressing public elementary and secondary education, the analysis of the National Commission of Time and Learning nonetheless applies to colleges:

> Time is learning's warden. Our time-bound mentality has fooled us all into believing that schools can educate all of the people all of the time in a school year of 180 six-hour days. . . . If experience, research, and common sense teach nothing else, they confirm the truism that people learn at different rates, and in different ways with different subjects. But we have put the cart before the horse: our schools . . . are captives of clock and calendar. The boundaries of student growth are defined by schedules . . . instead of standards for students and learning.

Under the rule of time, all classes start and stop at the same time and take the same number of calendar weeks. The rule of time and the priority of parts affect every instructional act of the college.

Thus it is, for example, that if students come into college classes "unprepared," it is not the job of the faculty who teach those classes to "prepare" them. Indeed, the structure of the one-semester, three-credit class makes it all but impossible to do so. The only solution, then, is to create new courses to prepare students for the existing courses; within the Instruction Paradigm, the response to educational problems is always to generate more atomized, discrete instructional units. If business students are lacking a sense of ethics, then offer and require a course in business ethics. If students have poor study skills, then offer a "master student" course to teach such skills.

Instruction Paradigm colleges atomistically organize courses and teachers into departments and programs that rarely communicate with one another. Academic departments, originally associated with coherent disciplines, are the structural home bases for accomplishing the essential work of the college: offering courses. "Departments have a life of their own," notes William D. Schaefer, professor of English and former executive vice chancellor at UCLA. They are "insular, defensive, self-governing, [and] compelled to protect their interests because the faculty positions as well as the courses that justify funding those positions are located therein."

Those globally applicable skills that are the foundation of meaningful engagement with the world—reading, writing, calculating, reasoning—find a true place in this structure only if they have their own independent bases: the English or math or reading departments. If students cannot reason or think well, the college creates a course on reasoning and thinking. This in turn produces pressure to create a corresponding department. "If we are not careful," warns Adam Sweeting, director of the Writing Program at the Massachusetts School of Law at Andover, "the teaching of critical thinking skills will become the responsibility of one university department, a prospect that is at odds with the very idea of a university."

Efforts to extend college-level reading, writing, and reasoning "across the curriculum" have largely failed. The good intentions produced few results because, under the Instruction Paradigm, the teacher's job is to "cover the material" as outlined in the disciplinary syllabus. The instructor charged with implementing writing or reading or critical thinking "across the curriculum" often must choose between doing her job or doing what will help students learn—between doing well, as it were, or doing good.

From the point of view of the Learning Paradigm, these Instruction Paradigm teaching and learning structures present immense barriers to improving student learning and success. They provide no space and support for redesigned learning environments or for experimenting with alternative learning technologies. They don't provide for, warrant, or reward assessing whether student learning has occurred or is improving.

In a Learning Paradigm college, the structure of courses and lectures becomes dispensable and negotiable. Semesters and quarters, lectures, labs, syllabi—indeed, classes themselves—become options rather than received structures or mandatory activities. The Learning Paradigm prescribes no one "answer" to the question of how to organize learning environments and experiences. It supports any learning method and structure that works, where "works" in defined in terms of learning outcomes, not as the degree of conformity to an ideal classroom archetype. In fact, the Learning

Paradigm requires a constant search for new structures and methods that work better for student learning and success, and expects even these to be redesigned continually and to evolve over time.

***

The transition from Instruction Paradigm to Learning Paradigm will not be instantaneous. It will be a process of gradual modification and experimentation through which we alter many organizational parts in light of a new vision for the whole. Under the Instruction Paradigm, structures are assumed to be fixed and immutable; there is no ready means for achieving the leverage needed to alter them. The first structural task of the Learning Paradigm, then, is to establish such leverage.

The key structure for changing the rest of the system is an institutionwide assessment and information system—an essential structure in the Learning Paradigm, and a key means for getting there. It would provide constant, useful feedback on institutional performance. It would track transfer, graduation, and other completion rates. It would track the flow of students through learning stages (such as the achievement of basic skills) and the development of in-depth knowledge in a discipline. It would measure the knowledge and skills of program completers and graduates. It would assess learning along many dimensions and in many places and stages in each student's college experience.

To be most effective, this assessment system would provide public institutional-level information. We are not talking about making public the status of individual students by name, but about making the year-to-year graduation rate—or the mean score of graduating seniors on a critical thinking assessment, for example—"public" in the sense that they are available to everyone in the college community. Moreover, in the Learning Paradigm college, such data are routinely talked about and acted upon by a community ever dedicated to improving its own performance.

The effectiveness of the assessment system for developing alternative learning environments depends in part upon its being *external* to learning programs and structures. While in the Instruction Paradigm students are assessed and graded within a class by the same instructor responsible for teaching them, in the Learning Paradigm much of the assessment would be independent of the learning experience and its designer, somewhat as football games are independent measures of what is learned in football practice. Course grades alone fail to tell us what students know and can do; average grades assigned by instructors are not reliable measures of whether the institution is improving learning.

Ideally an institution's assessment program would measure the "value-added" over the course of students' experience at the college. Student knowledge and skills would be measured upon entrance and again upon graduation, and at intermediate stages such as at the beginning and completion of major programs. Students could then be acknowledged and certified for what they have learned; the same data aggregated, could help shift judgments of institutional quality from inputs and resources to the value-added brought to student learning by the college.

The college devoted to learning first identifies the knowledge and skills it expects its graduates to possess, without regard to any particular curriculum or educational experiences. It then determines how to assess them reliably. It assesses graduating students, and the resulting information is then used to redesign and improve the processes and environments leading to such outcomes. In this manner, enhancing intellectual skills such as writing and problem solving and social skills such as effective team participation become the project of *all* learning programs and structured experience. The whole would govern the parts.

Information from a sophisticated assessment system will gradually lead to the transformation of the college's learning environments and supporting structures. Such a system seeks out "best practice" benchmarks against which improvements in institutional performance can be measured in learning terms. It is the foundation for creating an institutional capacity to develop ever more effective and efficient ways of empowering learning. It becomes the basis for generating revenue or funding according to learning results rather than hours of instruction. Most importantly, it is the key to the college's and its staff's taking responsibility for and enjoying the progress of each student's education.

Instead of fixing the means—such as lectures and courses—the Learning Paradigm fixes the ends, the learning results, allowing the means to vary in its constant search for the most effective and efficient paths to student learning. Learning outcomes and standards thus would be identified and held to for all students—or *raised* as learning environments became more powerful—while the time students took to achieve those standards would vary. This would reward skilled and advanced students with speedy progress while enabling less prepared students the time they needed to actually master the material. By "testing out," students could also avoid wasting their time being "taught" what they already know. Students would be given "credit" for degree-relevant knowledge and skills regardless of how or where or when they learned them.

In the Learning Paradigm, then, a college degree would represent not time spent and credit hours dutifully accumulated, but would certify that the student had demonstrably attained specified knowledge skills. Learning Paradigm institutions would develop and publish explicit exit standards for graduates and grant degrees and certificates only to students who met them. Thus colleges would move away from educational atomism and move toward treating holistically the knowledge and skills required for a degree.

Learning Theory

The Instruction Paradigm frames learning atomistically. In it, knowledge, by definition, consists of matter dispensed or delivered by an instructor. The chief agent in the process is the teacher who delivers knowledge; students are viewed as passive vessels, ingesting knowledge for recall on tests. Hence any expert can teach. Partly because the teacher knows which chunks of knowledge are most important, the teacher controls the learning activities. Learning is presumed to be cumulative because it amounts to ingesting more and more chunks. A degree is awarded when a student has received a specified amount of instruction.

The Learning Paradigm frames learning holistically, recognizing that the chief agent in the process is the learner. Thus, students must be active discoverers and constructors of their own knowledge. In the Learning Paradigm, knowledge consists of frameworks or wholes that are created or constructed by the learner. Knowledge is not seen as cumulative and linear, like a wall of bricks, but as a nesting and interacting of frameworks. Learning is revealed when those frameworks are used to understand and act. Seeing the whole of something—the forest rather than the trees, the image of the newspaper photo rather than its dots—gives meaning to its elements, and that whole becomes more than a sum of component parts. Wholes and frameworks can come in a moment—a flash of insight—often after much hard work with the pieces, as when one suddenly knows how to ride a bicycle.

In the Learning Paradigm, learning environments and activities are learner-centered and learner-controlled. They may even be "teacherless." While teachers will have designed the learning experiences and environments students use—often through teamwork with each other and other staff—they need not be present for or participate in every structured learning activity.

Many students come away from college with a false notion of what learning is and come to believe falsely that learning—at least for some subjects—is too difficult for them. Many students cruise through schools substituting an ersatz role-playing exercise for learning.

The first time I (Barr) studied calculus as a college freshman, I did well by conventional standards. However, while I could solve enough problems to get A's on exams, I really didn't feel that I understood the Limit Theorem, the derivative, or much else. But 15 years later, after having completed college and graduate school and having taught algebra and geometry in high school, I needed to relearn calculus so that I could tutor a friend. In only two, albeit intense, days, I relearned—or really learned for the first time, so it seemed—two semesters of calculus. During those days, I wondered how I ever thought that calculus was difficult and why I didn't see the Limit Theorem and derivative for the simple, obvious things they are.

What was the difference between my first learning of calculus and the second? It certainly wasn't a higher IQ. And I don't think it was because I learned or remembered much from the first time. I think it was that I brought some very powerful intellectual frameworks to the learning the second time that I didn't have the first time. Having taught algebra and geometry, I had learned their basic structure, that is, the nature of a mathematical system. I had learned the lay of the land, the whole. Through many years of schooling and study, I had also learned a number of other frameworks that were useful for learning calculus. Thus learning calculus the second time within these "advanced" frameworks was easy compared to learning, or trying to learn, calculus without them as I did as a freshman.

So much of this is because the "learning" that goes on in Instruction Paradigm colleges frequently involves only rudimentary, stimulus-response relationships whose cues may be coded into the context of a particular course but are not rooted in the student's everyday, functioning understanding.

The National Council on Vocational Educational summarizes the consequences in its 1991 report, *Solutions*: "The result is fractionation, or splitting into pieces: having to learn disconnected sub-routines, items, and sub-skills without an understanding of the larger context into which they fit and which gives them meaning." While such approaches are entirely consistent with educational atomism, they are at odds with the way we think and learn. The same report quotes Sylvia Farnham-Diggory's summary of contemporary research: "Fractionated instruction maximizes forgetting, inattention, and passivity. Both children and adults acquire knowledge from active participation in holistic, complex, meaningful environments organized around long-term goals. Today's school programs could hardly have been better designed to prevent a child's natural learning system from operating."

The result is that when the contextual cues provided by the class disappear at the end of the semester, so does the learning. Howard Gardner points out that "researchers at Johns Hopkins, MIT, and other well-regarded universities have documented that students who receive honor grades in college-level physics courses are frequently unable to solve basic problems and questions encountered in a form slightly different from that on which they have been formally instructed and tested."

The Learning Paradigm embraces the goal of promoting what Gardner calls "education for understanding"—"a sufficient grasp of concepts, principles, or skills so that one can bring them to bear on new problems and situations, deciding in which way one's present competencies can suffice and in which ways one may require new skills or knowledge." This involves the mastery of functional, knowledge-based intellectual frameworks rather than the short-term retention of fractionated, contextual cues.

The learning theory of the Instruction Paradigm reflects deeply rooted societal assumptions about talent, relationships, and accomplishment: that which is valuable is scarce; life is a win-lose proposition; and success is an individual achievement. The Learning Paradigm theory of learning reverses these assumptions.

Under the Instruction Paradigm, faculty classify and sort students, in the worst cases into those who are "college material" and those who cannot "cut it," since intelligence and ability are scarce. Under the Learning Paradigm, faculty—and everybody else in the institution—are unambiguously committed to each student's success. The faculty and the institution take an R. Buckminster Fuller view of students: human beings are born geniuses and designed for success. If they fail to display their genius or fail to succeed, it is because their design function is being thwarted. This perspective is founded not in wishful thinking but in the best evidence about the real capabilities of virtually all humans for learning. As the Wingspread Group points out, "There is growing research evidence that all students can learn to much higher standards than we now require." In the Learning Paradigm, faculty find ways to develop every student's vast talents and clear the way for every student's success.

Under the Instruction Paradigm, the classroom is competitive and individualistic, reflecting a view that life is a win-lose proposition. The requirement that the students must achieve individually and solely through their own efforts reflects the belief that success is an individual accomplishment. In the Learning Paradigm, learning environments—while challenging—are win-win environments that are cooperative, collaborative, and supportive. They are designed on the principle that accomplishment and success are the result of teamwork and group efforts, even when it appears one is working alone.

Productivity and Funding

Under the Instruction Paradigm, colleges suffer from a serious design flaw—they are structured in such a way that they cannot increase their productivity without diminishing the quality of their product. In the Instruction Paradigm, productivity is defined as cost per hour of instruction per student. In this view, the very quality of teaching and learning is threatened by any increase in the student-to-faculty ratio.

Under the Learning Paradigm, productivity is redefined as the cost per unit of learning per student. Not surprisingly, there is as yet no standard statistic that corresponds to this notion of productivity. Under this new definition, however, it is possible to increase outcomes without increasing costs. An abundance of research shows that alternatives to the traditional semester-length, classroom-based lecture method produce more learning. Some of these alternatives are less expensive; many produce more learning for the same cost. Under the Learning Paradigm, producing more with less becomes possible because the more that is being produced is learning and not hours of instruction. Productivity, in this sense, cannot even be measured in the Instruction Paradigm college. All that exists is a measure of exposure to instruction.

Given the Learning Paradigm's definition, increases in productivity pose no threat to the quality of education. Unlike the current definition, this new definition requires that colleges actually produce learning. Otherwise, there is no "product" to count in the productivity ratio.

But what should be the definition of "unit of learning" and how can it be measured? A single, permanent answer to that question does not and need not exist. We have argued above that learning, or at least the effects of learning, can be measured, certainly well enough to determine what students are learning and whether the institution is getting more effective and efficient at producing it.

***

The Instruction Paradigm wastes not only institutional resources but the time and energy of students. We waste our students' time with registration lines, bookstore lines, lock-step class scheduling, and redundant courses and requirements. We do not teach them to learn efficiently and effectively. We can do a lot, as D. Bruce Johnstone, former chancellor of SUNY, suggests, to reduce the false starts and aimless "drift" of students that slow their progress toward a degree. Now let's consider how colleges are funded. One of the absurdities of current funding formulas is that an institution could utterly fail its educational mission and yet its revenue would remain unaffected. For example, attendance at public colleges on the semester system is measured twice, once in the fall and again in the spring. Normally, at California community colleges, for example, about two-thirds of fall students return for the spring term. New students and returning stop-outs make up for the one-third of fall students who leave. Even if only half—or none at all—returned, as long as spring enrollments equal those of the fall, these institutions would suffer no loss of revenue.

There is no more powerful feedback than revenue. Nothing could facilitate a shift to the Learning Paradigm more swiftly than funding learning and learning-related institutional outcomes rather than hours of instruction. The initial response to the idea of outcomes-based funding is likely to be "That's not possible." But, of course, it is. As the new paradigm takes hold, forces and possibilities shift and the impossible becomes the rule.

Nature of Roles

With the shift to the Learning Paradigm comes a change in roles for virtually all college employees.

In the Instruction Paradigm, faculty are conceived primarily as disciplinary experts who impart knowledge by lecturing. They are the essential feature of the "instructional delivery system." The Learning Paradigm, on the other hand, conceives of faculty as primarily the designers of learning environments; they study and apply best methods for producing learning and student success.

If the Instruction Paradigm faculty member is an actor—a sage on a stage—then the Learning Paradigm faculty member is an inter-actor—a coach interacting with a team. If the model in the

Instruction Paradigm is that of delivering a lecture, then the model in the Learning Paradigm is that of designing and then playing a team game. A coach not only instructs football players, for example, but also designs football practices and the game plan; he participates in the game itself by sending in plays and making other decisions. The new faculty role goes a step further, however, in that faculty not only design game plans but also create new and better "games," ones that generate more and better learning.

Roles under the Learning Paradigm, then, begin to blur. Architects of campus buildings and payroll clerks alike will contribute to and shape the environments that empower student learning. As the role structures of colleges begin to loosen up and as accountability for results (learning) tightens up, organizational control and command structures will change. Teamwork and shared governance over time replace the line governance and independent work of the Instruction Paradigm's hierarchical and competitive organization.

In the Learning Paradigm, as colleges specify learning goals and focus on learning technologies, interdisciplinary (or nondisciplinary) task groups and design teams become a major operating mode. For example, faculty may form a design team to develop a learning experience in which students networked via computers learn to write about selected texts or on a particular theme.

After developing and testing its new learning module, the design team may even be able to let students proceed through it without direct faculty contact except at designated points. Design teams might include a variety of staff: disciplinary experts, information technology experts, a graphic designer, and an assessment professional. Likewise, faculty and staff might form functional teams responsible for a body of learning outcomes for a stated number of students. Such teams could have the freedom that no faculty member has in today's atomized framework, that to organize the learning environment in ways that maximize student learning.

Meeting the Challenge

Changing paradigms is hard. A paradigm gives a system integrity and allows it to function by identifying what counts as information within the infinite ocean of data in its environment. Data that solve problems that the paradigm identifies as important are information; data that are irrelevant to those problems are simply noise, static. Any system will provide both channels for transmitting information relevant to the system and filters to reduce noise.

Those who want to change the paradigm governing an institution are—from the institution's point of view—people who are listening to the noise and ignoring the information. They appear crazy or out of touch. The quartz watch was invented by the Swiss. But the great Swiss watchmakers responded to the idea of gearless timepieces in essentially the same way that the premiere audience responded to Stravinsky's *The Rite of Spring*. They threw tomatoes. They hooted it off the stage.

The principle also operates in the other direction. From the point of view of those who have adopted a new paradigm, the institution comes to sound like a cacophony-generating machine, a complex and refined device for producing more and louder noise. From the perspective of the governing paradigm, the advocates of the insurgent paradigm seem willing to sacrifice the institution itself for pie-in-the-sky nonsense. But from the perspective of the insurgents, the defenders of the present system are perpetuating a system that no longer works.

But paradigms do change. The Church admits Galileo was right. *The Rite of Spring* has become an old warhorse. Paradigms can even change quickly. Look at your watch.

***

Paradigms change when the ruling paradigm loses its capacity to solve problems and generate a positive vision of the future. This we very much see today. One early sign of a paradigm shift is an attempt to use the tools and ideas of a new paradigm within the framework provided by the old, or to convey information intelligible in the new paradigm through the channels of the old. This, too, is now happening.

In our experience, people will suffer the turbulence and uncertainty of change if it promises a better way to accomplish work they value. The shift to the Learning Paradigm represents such an opportunity.

The Learning Paradigm doesn't answer all the important questions, of course. What it does do is lead us to a set of new questions and a domain of possible responses. What knowledge, talents, and skills do college graduates need in order to live and work fully? What must they do to master such knowledge, talents, and skills? Are they doing those things? Do students find in our colleges a coherent body of experiences that help them to become competent, capable, and interesting people? Do they understand what they've memorized? Can they act on it? Has the experience of college made our students flexible and adaptable learners, able to thrive in a knowledge society?

How do you begin to move to the new paradigm? Ultimately, changing paradigms means doing everything differently. But we can suggest three areas where changes—even small ones—can create leverage for larger change in the future.

First, you begin by speaking. You begin to speak *within* the new paradigm. As we come to understand the Learning Paradigm, we must make our understanding public. Stop talking about the "quality of instruction" or the "instructional program." Instead, talk about what it takes to produce "quality learning" and refer to the college's "learning programs." Instead of speaking of "instructional delivery," speak about "learning outcomes."

The primary reason the Instruction Paradigm is so powerful is that it is invisible. Its incoherencies and deficiencies appear as inherent qualities of the world. If we come to see the Instruction Paradigm as a product of our own assumptions and not a force of nature, then we can change it. Only as you begin to experiment with the new language will you realize just how entrenched and invisible the old paradigm is. But as you and your colleagues begin to speak the new language, you will then also begin to think and act out of the new paradigm.

Second, if we begin to talk about the "learning outcomes" of existing programs, we'll experience frustration at our nearly complete ignorance of what those outcomes are—the Learning Paradigm's most important category of information is one about which we know very little now. The place to start the assessment of learning outcomes is in the conventional classroom; from there, let the practice grow to the program and institutional levels. In the Learning Paradigm, the key structure that provides the leverage to change the rest is a system for requiring the specification of learning outcomes and their assessment through processes external to instruction. The more we learn about the outcomes of existing programs, the more rapidly they will change.

Third, we should address the legally entrenched state funding mechanisms that fund institutions on the basis of hours of instruction. This powerful external force severely constrains the kinds of changes that an institution can make. It virtually limits them to changes within classrooms, leaving intact the atomistic one-teacher, one-classroom structure. We need to work to have state legislatures change the funding formulas of public colleges and universities to give institutions the latitude and incentives to develop new structures for learning. Persuading legislators and governors should not be hard; indeed, the idea of funding colleges for results rather than seat time has an inherent political attractiveness. It is hard to see why legislators would resist the concept that taxpayers should pay for what they get out of higher education, and get what they pay for.

Try this thought experiment. Take a team of faculty at any college—at your college—and select a group of students on some coherent principle, any group of students as long as they have something in common. Keep the ratio of faculty to students the same as it already is. Tell the faculty team, "We want you to create a program for these students so that they will improve significantly in the following knowledge and cognitive skills by the end of one year. We will assess them at the beginning and assess them at the end, and we will tell you how we are going to do so. Your task is to produce learning with these students. In doing so, you are not constrained by any of the rules or regulations you have grown accustomed to. You are free to organize the environment in any way you like. The only thing you are required to do is to produce the desired result—student learning."

We have suggested this thought experiment to many college faculty and asked them whether, if given this freedom, they could design a learning environment that would get better results than what they are doing now. So far, no one has answered that question in the negative. Why not do it?

The change that is required to address today's challenges is not vast or difficult or expensive. It is a small thing. But it is a small change that changes everything. Simply ask, how would we do things differently if we put learning first? Then do it.

Those who say it can't be done frequently assert that environments that actually produce learning are too expensive. But this is clearly not true. What we are doing now is too expensive by far. Today, learning is prohibitively expensive in higher education; we simply can't afford it for more and more of our students. The high cost of learning is an artifact of the Instruction Paradigm. It is simply false to say that we cannot afford to give our students the education they deserve. We can, but we will not as long as we allow the Instruction Paradigm to dominate our thinking. The problem is not insoluble. However, to paraphrase Albert Einstein, we cannot solve our problem with the same level of thinking that created it.

Buckminster Fuller used to say that you should never try to change the course of a great ship by applying force to the bow. You shouldn't even try it by applying force to the rudder. Rather you should apply force to the trim-tab. A trim-tab is a little rudder attached to the end of the rudder. A very small force will turn it left, thus moving the big rudder to the right, and the huge ship to the left. The shift to the Learning Paradigm is the trim-tab of the great ship of higher education. It is a shift that changes everything.

Chapter 2

Scholarship of Teaching and Learning

Scholarship Reconsidered: Priorities of the Professoriate

Ernest L. Boyer

Scholarship over Time

Several years ago, while completing our study of undergraduate education, it became increasingly clear that one of the most crucial issues—the one that goes to the core of academic life—relates to the meaning of scholarship itself. In *College: The Undergraduate Experience in America,* we said, "Scholarship is not an esoteric appendage; it is at the heart of what the profession is all about . . ." and "to weaken faculty commitment for scholarship . . . is to undermine the undergraduate experience, regardless of the academic setting." The challenge, as we saw it, was to define the work of faculty in ways that enrich, rather than restrict, the quality of campus life.

Today, on campuses across the nation, there is a recognition that the faculty reward system does not match the full range of academic functions and that professors are often caught between competing obligations. In response, there is a lively and growing discussion about how faculty should, in fact, spend their time. Recently, Stanford University president Donald Kennedy called for more contact between faculty and students, especially in the junior and senior years, a time when career decisions are more likely to be made. "It is time," Kennedy said, "for us to reaffirm that education—that is, teaching in all its forms—is the primary task" of higher education.

Several years ago, the University of California completed a study of undergraduate education, recommending that more weight be placed on teaching in faculty tenure decisions. In the East, the University of Pennsylvania, in its faculty handbook, now states that "the teaching of students at all levels is to be distributed among faculty members without regard to rank or seniority as such." In the Midwest, Robert Gavin, president of Macalester College, recently reaffirmed his institution's view of the liberal arts mission as including not only academic quality, but also internationalism, diversity, and service.

It is *this* issue—what it means to be a scholar—that is the central theme of our report. The time has come, we believe, to step back and reflect on the variety of functions academics are expected to perform. It's time to ask how priorities of the professoriate relate to the faculty reward system, as well as to the missions of America's higher learning institutions. Such an inquiry into the work of faculty is essential if students are to be well served, if the creativity of all faculty is to be fully tapped, and if the goals of every college and university are to be appropriately defined.

While we speak with pride about the great diversity of American higher education, the reality is that on many campuses standards of scholarship have become increasingly restrictive, and campus priorities frequently are more imitative than distinctive. In this climate, it seems appropriate to ask: How can each of the nation's colleges and universities define, with clarity, its own special purposes? Should expectations regarding faculty performance vary from one type of institution to another? Can we, in fact, have a higher education system in this country that includes multiple models of success?

Reprinted from *Scholarship Reconsidered: Priorities of the Professoriate* (1990), Princeton University Press.

Other issues within the academy must be candidly confronted. For example, the administrative structure has grown more and more complex, the disciplines have become increasingly divided, and academic departments frequently are disconnected from one another. The curriculum is fragmented, and the educational experience of students frequently lacks coherence. Many are now asking: How can the work of the nation's colleges and universities become more intellectually coherent? Is it possible for scholarship to be defined in ways that give more recognition to interpretative and integrative work?

According to the dominant view, to be a scholar is to be a researcher—and publication is the primary yardstick by which scholarly productivity is measured. At the same time, evidence abounds that many professors feel ambivalent about their roles. This conflict of academic functions demoralizes the professoriate, erodes the vitality of the institution, and cannot help but have a negative impact on students. Given these tensions, what is the balance to be struck between teaching and research? Should some members of the professoriate be thought of primarily as researchers, and others as teachers? And how can these various dimensions of faculty work be more appropriately evaluated and rewarded?

Beyond the campus, America's social and economic crises are growing—troubled schools, budget deficits, pollution, urban decay, and neglected children, to highlight problems that are most apparent. Other concerns such as acid rain, AIDS, dwindling energy supplies, and population shifts are truly global, transcending national boundaries. Given these realities, the conviction is growing that the vision of service that once so energized the nation's campuses must be given a new legitimacy. The challenge then is this: Can America's colleges and universities, with all the richness of their resources, be of greater service to the nation and the world? Can we define scholarship in ways that respond more adequately to the urgent new realities both within the academy and beyond?

Clearly, the educational and social issues now confronting the academy have changed profoundly since the first college was planted on this continent more than 350 years ago. Challenges on the campus and in society have grown, and there is a deepening conviction that the role of higher education, as well as the priorities of the professoriate, must be redefined to reflect new realities.

***

Looking back, one can see that scholarship in American higher education has moved through three distinct, yet overlapping phases. The colonial college, with its strong British roots, took a view of collegiate life that focused on the student—on building character and preparing new generations for civic and religious leadership. One of the first goals the English settlers of Massachusetts pursued, said the author of a description of the founding of Harvard College in 1636, was to "advance *Learning* and perpetuate it to Posterity." Harvard College, patterned after Emmanuel College of Cambridge, England, was founded to provide a continuous supply of learned clergy for "the city on the hill" that the Massachusetts Puritans hoped would bring redemptive light to all mankind.

The colonial college was expected to educate and morally uplift the coming generation. Teaching was viewed as a vocation—a sacred calling—an act of dedication honored as fully as the ministry. Indeed, what society expected of faculty was largely dictated by the religious purposes of the colleges that employed them. Students were entrusted to tutors responsible for their intellectual, moral, and spiritual development. According to historian Theodore Benditt, "professors were hired not for their scholarly ability or achievement but for their religious commitment. Scholarly achievement was not a high priority, either for professors or students."

This tradition, one that affirmed the centrality of teaching, persisted well into the nineteenth century. Young scholars continued to be the central focus of collegiate life, and faculty were employed with the understanding that they would be educational mentors, both in the classroom and beyond. In 1869, the image of the scholar as *teacher* was evoked by Charles W. Eliot, who, upon assuming the presidency of Harvard. College, declared that "the prime business of American professors . . . must be regular and assiduous class teaching."

***

But change was in the wind. A new country was being formed and higher education's focus began to shift from the shaping of young lives to the building of a nation. As historian Frederick Rudolf says of the new generation of educators: "All were touched by the American faith in tomorrow, in the unquestionable capacity of Americans to achieve a better world." It was in this climate that Rensselaer Polytechnic Institute in Troy, New York, one of the nation's first technical schools, was founded in 1824. RPI became, according to Rudolf, "a constant reminder that the United States needed railroad-builders, bridge-builders, builders of all kinds, and that the institute in Troy was prepared to create them even if the old institutions were not."

In 1846, Yale University authorized the creation of a professorship of "agricultural chemistry and animal and vegetable physiology." In the same decade, Harvard president Edward Everett stressed his institution's role in the service of business and economic prosperity. The college took Everett's message to heart. When historian Henry Adams asked his students why they had come to study at Cambridge, the answer he got was unambiguous: "The degree of Harvard College is worth money to me in Chicago."

The practical side of higher learning was remarkably enhanced by the Morrill Act of 1862, later called the Land Grant College Act. This historic piece of legislation gave federal land to each state, with proceeds from sale of the land to support both education in the liberal arts and training in the skills that ultimately would undergird the emerging agricultural and mechanical revolutions. The Hatch Act of 1887 added energy to the effort by providing federal funds to create university-sponsored agricultural experiment stations that brought learning to the farmer, and the idea of education as a democratic function to serve the common good was planted on the prairies.

Something of the excitement of this era was captured in Willa Cather's description of her fellow students and her teachers at the University of Nebraska in the 1890s: "[They] came straight from the cornfields with only summer's wages in their pockets, hung on through four years, shabby and underfed, and completed the course by really heroic self-sacrifice. Our instructors were oddly assorted: wandering pioneer school teachers, stranded ministers of the Gospel, a few enthusiastic young men just out of graduate school. There was an atmosphere of endeavor, of expectancy and bright hopefulness about the young college that had lifted its head from the prairie only a few years ago."

Thus, American higher education, once devoted primarily to the intellectual and moral development of students, added *service* as a mission, and both private and public universities took up the challenge. In 1903, David Starr Jordan, president of Stanford University, declared that the entire university movement in the twentieth century "is toward reality and practicality." By 1908, Harvard president Charles Eliot could claim: "At bottom most of the American institutions of higher education are filled with the modern democratic spirit of serviceableness. Teachers and students alike are profoundly moved by the desire to serve the democratic community. . . . All the colleges boast of the serviceable men they have trained, and regard the serviceable patriot as their ideal product. This is a thoroughly democratic conception of their function."

Skeptics looked with amusement, even contempt, at what they considered the excesses of utility and accommodation. They long resisted the idea of making the university itself a more democratic institution and viewed with disdain Ezra Cornell's soaring pledge in the 1860s to ". . . found an institution 'where any person can find instruction in any study.'" Some critics even viewed the agricultural experiment stations as a betrayal of higher education's mission. They ridiculed the "cow colleges," seeing in them a dilution of academic standards. Others recoiled from the idea that non-elite young people were going on to college.

Still, a host of academics flocked to land-grant colleges, confident they had both the expertise and the obligation to contribute to building a nation. They embodied the spirit of Emerson, who years before had spoken of the scholarship of "action" as "the raw material out of which the intellect moulds her splendid products." In this tradition, Governor Robert LaFollette forged, in Wisconsin, a powerful link between the campus and the state, one that became known nationally as the "Wisconsin Idea." After visiting Madison in 1909, social critic Lincoln Steffens observed: "In Wisconsin the university is as close to the intelligent farmer as his pig-pen or his tool-house; the university laboratories are part of the alert manufacturer's plant. . . ."

The idea that professors could spread knowledge that would improve agriculture and manufacturing gave momentum to what later became known as *applied* research. In the 1870s and 1880s, many agreed that education was, above all, to be considered useful. In commenting on the link between the campus and applied agricultural research, historian Margaret Rossiter presented this vivid illustration: "The chief activities of a professor of agriculture . . . were to run field tests with various fertilizers and to maintain a model farm, preferably, but rarely, without financial loss." Over the next thirty years, these agricultural sciences developed at a rapid pace, vastly increasing the knowledge that scholars could apply.

Service during this expansive period had a moral meaning, too. The goal was not only to *serve* society, but *reshape* it. Andrew White, the first president of Cornell University, saw graduates "pouring into the legislatures, staffing the newspapers, and penetrating the municipal and county boards of America. Corruption would come to an end; pure American ideals would prosper until one day they governed the entire world." Sociologist Edward Shils, in describing the spirit of the times, observed that "the concept of improvement was vague and comprehensive, signifying not only improvement of a practical sort but spiritual improvement as well."

This ideal—the conviction that higher education had a moral mission to fulfill—was especially important to those who organized the American Economic Association in 1885, under the leadership of Richard Ely. Soon after joining the newly formed faculty at Johns Hopkins University, Ely wrote to the president, Daniel Coit Gilman, that the fledgling association would help in the diffusion of "a sound Christian political economy." Most faculty were less zealous. Still, in this remarkable era marked by continued emphasis on liberal education and values, the faculty's role was energized by determined efforts to apply knowledge to practical problems.

***

Basic research, a third dimension of scholarly activity which can be traced to the first years of the Republic, also began to take hold. The earliest research effort was largely led by investigators *outside* the academy—people such as Thomas Jefferson; the mathematician Nathaniel Bowditch; the pioneer botanists John and William Bartram; and the intrepid astronomer Maria Mitchell, who set up an observatory on lonely Nantucket Island and, on one October night in 1847, discovered a new comet. When President Jefferson sought a scientific leader for the first of the great western explorations, he did not go to the colleges, where science was not yet well developed. Instead, he looked within government and selected his personal secretary, Meriwether Lewis, who was known to have a keen eye for the natural world. Before the expedition, Lewis was sent to Philadelphia, where he received careful training in astronomy, botany, and mineralogy from members of the American Philosophical Society.

Still, colleges themselves were not wholly devoid of scientific effort. As early as 1738, John Winthrop of Harvard, the first academic scientist, had a laboratory in which to conduct experiments. He later persuaded the lawmakers in Massachusetts to sponsor America's first astronomical expedition. These early scientists traveled to Newfoundland in 1761 to observe the transit of Venus. Moreover, George Ticknor and Edward Everett, who attended a German university in 1815, are believed to have been the first Americans to go abroad to pursue advanced scholarly studies. Upon their return, they called, even then, for the introduction at Harvard of the German approach to scholarship.

Yet, change came slowly. The new sciences were very much on the edges of academic life and expectations were modest. As Dael Wolfle wrote: "Professors were hired to teach the science that was already known—to add to that knowledge was not expected. . . ." Consider also that when Benjamin Silliman became the first chemistry professor at Yale in 1802, there were only twenty-one other full-time scientific faculty positions in the United States.

By the mid-nineteenth century, however, leading Atlantic seaboard colleges were giving more legitimacy to the authority of scientific effort and a few were beginning to transform themselves into research and graduate institutions. For example, Harvard's Lawrence Scientific School and Yale's Sheffield Scientific School were forerunners of the academy's deep commitment to the scholarship of science. Graduate courses in philosophy and the arts were established, and America's first Doctor of Philosophy was conferred at Yale in 1861. And the Massachusetts Institute of Technology, which opened its doors at the end of the Civil War, soon was recognized as a center of scientific investigation.

In the late nineteenth century, more Americans who, like Ticknor and Everett, had studied in Europe were profoundly influenced by the research orientation of the German university and wanted to develop a similar model here. G. Stanley Hall, first president of Clark University, wrote in 1891, "The German University is today the freest spot on earth. . . . Nowhere has the passion to push on to the frontier of human knowledge been so general." Some, it is true, resisted the German influences. The prominent American humanist Irving Babbitt argued that the Ph.D. degree led to a loss of balance. He complained about the "maiming and mutilation of the mind that comes from over-absorption in one subject," declaring that German doctoral dissertations gave him "a sort of intellectual nausea."

Still, research and graduate education increasingly formed the model for the modern university. Academics on both continents were moving inevitably from faith in authority to reliance on scientific rationality. And to men like Daniel Coit Gilman, this view of scholarship called for a new kind of university, one based on the conviction that knowledge was most attainable through research and experimentation. Acting on this conviction, Gilman founded Johns Hopkins University in 1876, a step described by Shils as "perhaps the single, most decisive event in the history of learning in the Western hemisphere."

In the 1870s, the universities of Pennsylvania, Harvard, Columbia, and Princeton, in that order, also began to offer programs leading to the Ph.D. degree, and the University of Chicago, founded in 1891, made the degree "the pinnacle of the academic program." By 1895 William Rainey Harper, president of this newly formed university, could require "each appointee to sign an agreement that his promotions in rank and salary would depend chiefly upon his research productivity."

By the late nineteenth century, the advancement of knowledge through *research* had taken firm root in American higher education, and colonial college values, which emphasized teaching undergraduates, began to lose ground to the new university that was emerging. Indeed, the founders of Johns Hopkins University considered restricting study on that campus to the graduate level only. In the end, some undergraduate education proved necessary, but the compromise was reluctantly made, and for many professors, class and lecture work became almost incidental. Service, too, was viewed as unimportant. Some even considered it a violation of the integrity of the university, since the prevailing Germanic model demanded that the professor view the everyday world from a distance.

It should be stressed, however, that throughout most of American higher education the emphasis on research and graduate education remained the exception rather than the rule. The principal mission at most of the nation's colleges and universities continued to be the education of undergraduates. And the land-grant colleges, especially, took pride in service.

***

But in the 1940s, as the Great Depression gave way to a devastating war, the stage was set for a dramatic transformation of academic life. At that historic moment, Vannevar Bush of M.I.T. and James Bryant Conant of Harvard volunteered the help of the universities in bringing victory to the nation. In 1940, Bush took the lead in establishing the National Defense Research Committee which, a year later, became the Office of Scientific Research and Development. Academics flocked to Washington to staff the new agencies and federal research grants began to flow. Universities and the nation had joined in common cause.

After the war, Vannevar Bush urged continuing federal support for research. In a 1945 report to the President entitled *Science: The Endless Frontier,* he declared: "Science, by itself, provides no panacea for individual, social, and economic ills. It can be effective in the national welfare only as a member of a team, whether the conditions be peace or war. But without scientific progress no amount of achievement in other directions can insure our health, prosperity, and security as a nation in the modern world." The case could not have been more clearly stated. Higher learning and government had, through scientific collaboration, changed the course of history—and the impact on the academy would be both consequential and enduring.

Soon, a veritable army of freshly minted Ph.D.s fanned out to campuses across the country. Inspired by their mentors, this new generation of faculty found themselves committed not only to their institutions, but also to their professions. Young scholars sought to replicate the research climate they themselves had recently experienced. Academic priorities that had for years been the inspiration of the few now became the imperative of the many. In the new climate, discipline-based departments became the foundation of faculty allegiance, and being a "scholar" was now virtually synonymous with being an academic professional. Christopher Jencks and David Riesman, capturing the spirit of that period, declared that an *academic revolution* had taken place.

In 1958, Theodore Caplow and Reece McGee defined this new reality when they observed that while young faculty were hired as *teachers,* they were evaluated primarily as *researchers.* This shift in expectations is vividly revealed in two national surveys conducted by The Carnegie Foundation for the Advancement of Teaching. Twenty-one percent of the faculty surveyed in 1969 strongly agreed that it is difficult to achieve tenure without publishing. By 1989, the number had doubled, to 42 percent (table 2.1). The change at comprehensive colleges—from 6 percent to 43 percent—is especially noteworthy since these institutions have virtually no doctoral programs and only limited resources for research. Even at liberal arts colleges, where teaching has always been highly prized, nearly one in four faculty strongly agreed in 1989 that it is difficult to get tenure without publishing.

Meanwhile, the nation's colleges and universities were experiencing another remarkable social transformation—the revolution of rising expectations. In 1947, Harry S Truman appointed a President's Commission on Higher Education and almost overnight the mission of higher education in the nation was dramatically redefined. In its landmark report, this panel of prominent citizens concluded that America's colleges and universities should no longer be "merely the instrument for producing an intellectual elite." Rather, the report stated, higher education must become "the means by which every citizen, youth, and adult, is enabled and encouraged to carry his education, formal and informal, as far as his native capacities permit."

In response to this expansive vision, the nation moved from an *elite* to a *mass* system of higher education, to use sociologist Martin Trow's helpful formulation. New colleges were built, new faculty hired, and the G.I. Bill of Rights, first authorized in 1944, changed the entire tradition of who should go to college. Almost eight million former servicemen and women benefited from the legislation. In the years to come, younger brothers and sisters, and eventually sons and daughters, followed in the footsteps of the veterans. Higher education, once viewed as a privilege, was now accepted as a right.

But even as the mission of American higher education was expanding, the standards used to measure academic prestige continued to be narrowed. Increasingly, professors were expected to

TABLE 2.1

In My Department It Is Difficult for a Person to Achieve Tenure If He or She Does Not Publish
(Percentage Saying "Strongly Agree")

	1969	1989
All Respondents	21%	42%
Research	44	83
Doctorate-granting	27	71
Comprehensive	6	43
Liberal Arts	6	24
Two-Year	3	4

Please see Appendix C for a definition of institution classifications.
Source: The Carnegie Foundation for the Advancement of Teaching, 1969 and 1989 National Surveys of Faculty.

conduct research and publish results. Promotion and tenure depended on such activity, and young professors seeking security and status found it more rewarding—in a quite literal sense—to deliver a paper at a national convention in New York or Chicago than teach undergraduates back home. Lip service still was being paid to maintaining a balance between *collegiate* responsibilities and *university* work, but on most campuses the latter had clearly won the day.

Research *per se* was not the problem. The problem was that the research mission, which was appropriate for *some* institutions, created a shadow over the entire higher learning enterprise—and the model of a "Berkeley" or an "Amherst" became the yardstick by which all institutions would be measured. Ernest Lynton, Commonwealth Professor at the University of Massachusetts, in commenting on the new priorities, concluded that developments after the Second World War "established too narrow a definition of scholarship and too limited a range of instruction." Ironically, at the very time America's higher education institutions were becoming more open and inclusive, the culture of the professoriate was becoming more hierarchical and restrictive.

Thus, in just a few decades, priorities in American higher education were significantly realigned. The emphasis on undergraduate education, which throughout the years had drawn its inspiration from the colonial college tradition, was being overshadowed by the European university tradition, with its emphasis on graduate education and research. Specifically, at many of the nation's four-year institutions, the focus had moved from the student to the professoriate, from general to specialized education, and from loyalty to the campus to loyalty to the profession.

We conclude that for America's colleges and universities to remain vital a new vision of scholarship is required. What we are faced with, today, is the need to clarify campus missions and relate the work of the academy more directly to the realities of contemporary life. We need especially to ask how institutional diversity can be strengthened and how the rich array of faculty talent in our colleges and universities might be more effectively used and continuously renewed. We proceed with the conviction that if the nation's higher learning institutions are to meet today's urgent academic and social mandates, their missions must be carefully redefined and the meaning of scholarship creatively reconsidered.

Enlarging the Perspective

Since colonial times, the American professoriate has responded to mandates both from within the academy and beyond. First came teaching, then service, and finally, the challenge of research. In more recent years, faculty have been asked to blend these three traditions, but despite this idealized expectation, a wide gap now exists between the myth and the reality of academic life. Almost all colleges pay lip service to the trilogy of teaching, research, and service, but when it comes to making judgments about professional performance, the three rarely are assigned equal merit.

Today, when we speak of being "scholarly," it usually means having academic rank in a college or university and being engaged in research and publication. But we should remind ourselves just how recently the word "research" actually entered the vocabulary of higher education. The term was first used in England in the 1870s by reformers who wished to make Cambridge and Oxford "not only a place of teaching, but a place of learning," and it was later introduced to American higher education in 1906 by Daniel Coit Gilman. But scholarship in earlier times referred to a variety of creative work carried on in a variety of places, and its integrity was measured by the ability to think, communicate, and learn.

What we now have is a more restricted view of scholarship, one that limits it to a hierarchy of functions. Basic research has come to be viewed as the first and most essential form of scholarly activity, with other functions flowing from it. Scholars are academics who conduct research, publish, and then perhaps convey their knowledge to students or apply what they have learned. The latter functions grow *out of* scholarship, they are not to be considered a part of it. But knowledge is not necessarily developed in such a linear manner. The arrow of causality can, and frequently does, point in *both* directions. Theory surely leads to practice. But practice also leads to theory. And teaching, at its best, shapes both research and practice. Viewed from this perspective, a more comprehensive, more dynamic understanding of scholarship can be considered, one in which the rigid categories of teaching, research, and service are broadened and more flexibly defined.

There is a readiness, we believe, to rethink what it means to be a scholar. Richard I. Miller, professor of higher education at Ohio University, recently surveyed academic vice presidents and deans at more than eight hundred colleges and universities to get their opinion about faculty functions. These administrators were asked if they thought it would be a good idea to view scholarship as more than research. The responses were overwhelmingly supportive of this proposition. The need to reconsider scholarship surely goes beyond opinion polls, but campus debates, news stories, and the themes of national conventions suggest that administrative leaders are rethinking the definitions of academic life. Moreover, faculty, themselves, appear to be increasingly dissatisfied with conflicting priorities on the campus.

***

How then should we proceed? Is it possible to define the work of faculty in ways that reflect more realistically the full range of academic and civic mandates? We believe the time has come to move beyond the tired old "teaching versus research" debate and give the familiar and honorable term "scholarship" a broader, more capacious meaning, one that brings legitimacy to the full scope of academic work. Surely, scholarship means engaging in original research. But the work of the scholar also means stepping back from one's investigation, looking for connections, building bridges between theory and practice, and communicating one's knowledge effectively to students. Specifically, we conclude that the work of the professoriate might be thought of as having four separate, yet overlapping, functions. These are: the scholarship of *discovery;* the scholarship of *integration;* the scholarship of *application;* and the scholarship of *teaching.*

The first and most familiar element in our model, the *scholarship of discovery,* comes closest to what is meant when academics speak of "research." No tenets in the academy are held in higher regard than the commitment to knowledge for its own sake, to freedom of inquiry and to following, in a disciplined fashion, an investigation wherever it may lead. Research is central to the work of higher learning, but our study here, which inquires into the meaning of scholarship, is rooted in the conviction that disciplined, investigative efforts within the academy should be strengthened, not diminished.

The *scholarship of discovery,* at its best, contributes not only to the stock of human knowledge but also to the intellectual climate of a college or university. Not just the outcomes, but the process, and especially the passion, give meaning to the effort. The advancement of knowledge can generate an almost palpable excitement in the life of an educational institution. As William Bowen, former president of Princeton University, said, scholarly research "reflects our pressing, irrepressible need as human beings to confront the unknown and to seek understanding for its own sake. It is tied inextricably to the freedom to think freshly, to see propositions of every kind in everchanging light. And it celebrates the special exhilaration that comes from a new idea."

The list of distinguished researchers who have added luster to the nation's intellectual life would surely include heroic figures of earlier days—Yale chemist Benjamin Silliman; Harvard naturalist Louis Agassiz; astronomer William Cranch Bond; and Columbia anthropologist Franz Boas. It would also include giants of our time—James Watson, who helped unlock the genetic code; political philosopher Hannah Arendt; anthropologist Ruth Benedict; historian John Hope Franklin; geneticist Barbara McClintock; and Noam Chomsky, who transformed the field of linguistics; among others.

When the research records of higher learning are compared, the United States is the pacesetter. If we take as our measure of accomplishment the number of Nobel Prizes awarded since 1945, United States scientists received 56 percent of the awards in physics, 42 percent in chemistry, and 60 percent in medicine. Prior to the outbreak of the Second World War, American scientists, including those who fled Hitler's Europe, had received only 18 of the 129 prizes in these three areas. With regard to physics, for example, a recent report by the National Research Council states: "Before World War II, physics was essentially a European activity, but by the war's end, the center of physics had moved to the United States." The Council goes on to review the advances in fields ranging from elementary particle physics to cosmology.

The research contribution of universities is particularly evident in medicine. Investigations in the late nineteenth century on bacteria and viruses paid off in the 1930s with the development of immunizations for diphtheria, tetanus, lobar pneumonia, and other bacterial infections. On the basis of painstaking research, a taxonomy of infectious diseases has emerged, making possible streptomycin and other antibiotics. In commenting on these breakthroughs, physician and medical writer Lewis Thomas observes: "It was basic science of a very high order, storing up a great mass of interesting knowledge for its own sake, creating, so to speak, a bank of information, ready for drawing on when the time for intelligent use arrived."

Thus, the probing mind of the researcher is an incalculably vital asset to the academy and the world. Scholarly investigation, in all the disciplines, is at the very heart of academic life, and the pursuit of knowledge must be assiduously cultivated and defended. The intellectual excitement fueled by this quest enlivens faculty and invigorates higher learning institutions, and in our complicated, vulnerable world, the discovery of new knowledge is absolutely crucial.

The Scholarship of Integration

In proposing the *scholarship of integration,* we underscore the need for scholars who give meaning to isolated facts, putting them in perspective. By integration, we mean making connections across the disciplines, placing the specialties in larger context, illuminating data in a revealing way, often educating non-specialists, too. In calling for a scholarship of integration, we do not suggest returning to the "gentleman scholar" of an earlier time, nor do we have in mind the dilettante. Rather, what we mean is serious, disciplined work that seeks to interpret, draw together, and bring new insight to bear on original research.

This more integrated view of knowledge was expressed eloquently by Mark Van Doren nearly thirty years ago when he wrote: "The connectedness of things is what the educator contemplates to the limit of his capacity. No human capacity is great enough to permit a vision of the world as simple, but if the educator does not aim at the vision no one else will, and the consequences are dire when no one does." It is through "connectedness" that research ultimately is made authentic.

The scholarship of integration is, of course, closely related to discovery. It involves, first, doing research at the boundaries where fields converge, and it reveals itself in what philosopher-physicist Michael Polanyi calls "overlapping [academic] neighborhoods." Such work is, in fact, increasingly important as traditional disciplinary categories prove confining, forcing new topologies of knowledge. Many of today's professors understand this. When we asked faculty to respond to the statement, "Multidisciplinary work is soft and should not be considered scholarship," only 8 percent agreed, 17 percent were neutral, while a striking 75 percent disagreed (table 2.2). This pattern of opinion, with only slight variation, was true for professors in all disciplines and across all types of institutions.

The scholarship of integration also means interpretation, fitting one's own research—or the research of others—into larger intellectual patterns. Such efforts are increasingly essential since specialization, without broader perspective, risks pedantry. The distinction we are drawing here between "discovery" and "integration" can be best understood, perhaps, by the questions posed. Those engaged in discovery ask, "What is to be known, what is yet to be found?" Those engaged in integration ask, "What do the findings *mean!* Is it possible to interpret what's been discovered in ways that provide a larger, more comprehensive understanding?" Questions such as these call for the power of critical analysis and interpretation. They have a legitimacy of their own and if carefully pursued can lead the scholar from information to knowledge and even, perhaps, to wisdom.

Today, more than at any time in recent memory, researchers feel the need to move beyond traditional disciplinary boundaries, communicate with colleagues in other fields, and discover patterns that connect. Anthropologist Clifford Geertz, of the Institute for Advanced Study in Princeton, has gone so far as to describe these shifts as a fundamental "refiguration, . . . a phenomenon general enough and distinctive enough to suggest that what we are seeing is not just another redrawing of the cultural map—the moving of a few disputed borders, the marking of some more picturesque

TABLE 2.2

Multidisciplinary Work Is Soft and Should Not Be Considered Scholarship

	Agree	Neutral	Disagree
All Respondents	8%	17%	75%
Research	7	9	84
Doctorate-granting	6	13	80
Comprehensive	8	14	78
Liberal Arts	8	16	77
Two Year	9	27	63

Source: The Carnegie Foundation for the Advancement of Teaching, 1989 National Survey of Faculty.

mountain lakes—but an alteration of the principles of mapping. Something is happening," Geertz says, "to the way we think about the way we think."

This is reflected, he observes, in:

> . . . philosophical inquiries looking like literary criticism (think of Stanley Cavell on Beckett or Thoreau, Sartre on Flaubert), scientific discussions looking like belles lettres *morceaux* (Lewis Thomas, Loren Eisley), baroque fantasies presented as deadpan empirical observations (Borges, Barthelme), histories that consist of equations and tables or law court testimony (Fogel and Engerman, Le Roi Ladurie), documentaries that read like true confessions (Mailer), parables posing as ethnographies (Castaneda), theoretical treatises set out as travelogues (Levi-Strauss), ideological arguments cast as historiographical inquiries (Edward Said), epistemological studies constructed like political tracts (Paul Feyerabend), methodological polemics got up as personal memoirs (James Watson).

These examples illustrate a variety of scholarly trends—*interdisciplinary, interpretive, integrative.* But we present them here as evidence that an intellectual sea change may be occurring, one that is perhaps as momentous as the nineteenth-century shift in the hierarchy of knowledge, when philosophy gave way more firmly to science. Today, interdisciplinary *and* integrative studies, long on the edges of academic life, are moving toward the center, responding both to new intellectual questions and to pressing human problems. As the boundaries of human knowledge are being dramatically reshaped, the academy surely must give increased attention to the *scholarship of integration.*

The Scholarship of Application

The first two kinds of scholarship—discovery and integration of knowledge—reflect the investigative and synthesizing traditions of academic life. The third element, the *application* of knowledge, moves toward engagement as the scholar asks, "How can knowledge be responsibly applied to consequential problems? How can it be helpful to individuals as well as institutions?" And further, "Can social problems *themselves* define an agenda for scholarly investigation?"

Reflecting the *Zeitgeist* of the nineteenth and early twentieth centuries, not only the land-grant colleges, but also institutions such as Rensselaer Polytechnic Institute and the University of Chicago were founded on the principle that higher education must serve the interests of the larger community. In 1906, an editor celebrating the leadership of William Rainey Harper at the new University of Chicago defined what he believed to be the essential character of the American scholar. Scholarship, he observed, was regarded by the British as "a means and measure of self-development," by the Germans as "an end in itself," but by Americans as "equipment for service." Self-serving though it may have been, this analysis had more than a grain of truth.

Given this tradition, one is struck by the gap between values in the academy and the needs of the larger world. Service is routinely praised, but accorded little attention—even in programs where it is most appropriate. Christopher Jencks and David Riesman, for example, have pointed out that when free-standing professional schools affiliated with universities, they lessened their commitment to applied work even though the original purpose of such schools was to connect theory and practice. Professional schools, they concluded, have oddly enough fostered "a more academic and less practical view of what their students need to know."

Colleges and universities have recently rejected service as serious scholarship, partly because its meaning is so vague and often disconnected from serious intellectual work. As used today, service in the academy covers an almost endless number of campus activities—sitting on committees, advising student clubs, or performing departmental chores. The definition blurs still more as activities beyond the campus are included—participation in town councils, youth clubs, and the like. It is not unusual for almost any worthy project to be dumped into the amorphous category called "service."

Clearly, a sharp distinction must be drawn between *citizenship* activities and projects that relate to scholarship itself. To be sure, there are meritorious social and civic functions to be performed, and faculty should be appropriately recognized for such work. But all too frequently, service means not doing scholarship but doing good. To be considered *scholarship,* service activities must be tied directly to one's special field of knowledge and relate to, and flow directly out of, this professional activity. Such service is serious, demanding work, requiring the rigor—and the accountability—traditionally associated with research activities.

The *scholarship of application,* as we define it here, is not a one-way street. Indeed, the term itself may be misleading if it suggests that knowledge is first "discovered" and then "applied." The process we have in mind is far more dynamic. New intellectual understandings can arise out of the very act of application—whether in medical diagnosis, serving clients in psychotherapy, shaping public policy, creating an architectural design, or working with the public schools. In activities such as these, theory and practice vitally interact, and one renews the other.

Such a view of scholarly service—one that both applies and contributes to human knowledge—is particularly needed in a world in which huge, almost intractable problems call for the skills and insights only the academy can provide. As Oscar Handlin observed, our troubled planet "can no longer afford the luxury of pursuits confined to an ivory tower. . . . [Scholarship has to prove its worth not on its own terms but by service to the nation and the world."

The Scholarship of Teaching

Finally, we come to the *scholarship of teaching.* The work of the professor becomes consequential only as it is understood by others. Yet, today, teaching is often viewed as a routine function, tacked on, something almost anyone can do. When defined as scholarship, however, teaching both educates and entices future scholars. Indeed, as Aristotle said, "Teaching is the highest form of understanding."

As a *scholarly* enterprise, teaching begins with what the teacher knows. Those who teach must, above all, be well informed, and steeped in the knowledge of their fields. Teaching can be well regarded only as professors are widely read and intellectually engaged. One reason legislators, trustees, and the general public often fail to understand why ten or twelve hours in the classroom each week can be a heavy load is their lack of awareness of the hard work and the serious study that undergirds good teaching.

Teaching is also a dynamic endeavor involving all the analogies, metaphors, and images that build bridges between the teacher's understanding and the student's learning. Pedagogical procedures must be carefully planned, continuously examined, and relate directly to the subject taught. Educator Parker Palmer strikes precisely the right note when he says knowing and learning are communal acts. With this vision, great teachers create a common ground of intellectual commitment. They stimulate active, not passive, learning and encourage students to be critical, creative thinkers, with the capacity to go on learning after their college days are over.

Further, good teaching means that faculty, as scholars, are also learners. All too often, teachers transmit information that students are expected to memorize and then, perhaps, recall. While well-prepared lectures surely have a place, teaching, at its best, means not only transmitting knowledge, but *transforming* and *extending* it as well. Through reading, through classroom discussion, and surely through comments and questions posed by students, professors themselves will be pushed in creative new directions.

In the end, inspired teaching keeps the flame of scholarship alive. Almost all successful academics give credit to creative teachers—those mentors who defined their work so compellingly that it became, for them, a lifetime challenge. Without the teaching function, the continuity of knowledge will be broken and the store of human knowledge dangerously diminished.

Physicist Robert Oppenheimer, in a lecture at the 200th anniversary of Columbia University in 1954, spoke elegantly of the teacher as mentor and placed teaching at the very heart of the scholarly endeavor: "The specialization of science is an inevitable accompaniment of progress; yet it is full of dangers, and it is cruelly wasteful, since so much that is beautiful and enlightening is cut off from most of the world. Thus it is proper to the role of the scientist that he not merely find the truth and communicate it to his fellows, but that he teach, that he try to bring the most honest and most intelligible account of new knowledge to all who will try to learn."

***

Here, then, is our conclusion. What we urgently need today is a more inclusive view of what it means to be a scholar—a recognition that knowledge is acquired through research, through synthesis, through practice, and through teaching. We acknowledge that these four categories—the scholarship of discovery, of integration, of application, and of teaching—divide intellectual functions that are tied inseparably to each other. Still, there is value, we believe, in analyzing the various kinds of academic work, while also acknowledging that they dynamically interact, forming an interdependent whole. Such a vision of scholarship, one that recognizes the great diversity of talent within the professoriate, also may prove especially useful to faculty as they reflect on the meaning and direction of their professional lives.

THE SCHOLARSHIP OF TEACHING: WHAT'S THE PROBLEM?

RANDY BASS (GEORGETOWN UNIVERSITY)

> We realized that if we could represent practice, then the possibilities for investigating and communicating about teaching and learning—by different communities—would be enhanced. Although others wanted to highlight our practice, what we needed to draw on was our knowledge of *investigative practice,* not our own evolving knowledge of practice itself.
>
> We understood this as a problem of representation and communication. How could the many complex layers of practice be represented? And how could practice be engaged and discussed by a wider range of people concerned with teaching and learning?
>
> —DEBORAH LOEWENBERG BALL AND MAGDALENE LAMPERT

One telling measure of how differently teaching is regarded from traditional scholarship or research within the academy is what a difference it makes to have a "problem" in one versus the other. In scholarship and research, having a "problem" is at the heart of the investigative process; it is the compound of the generative questions around which all creative and productive activity revolves. But in one's teaching, a "problem" is something you don't want to have, and if you have one, you probably want to fix it. Asking a colleague about a *problem* in his or her research is an invitation; asking about a problem in one's teaching would probably seem like an accusation. Changing the status of the *problem* in teaching from terminal remediation to ongoing investigation is precisely what the movement for a scholarship of teaching is all about. How might we make the problematization of teaching a matter of regular communal discourse? How might we think of teaching practice, and the evidence of student learning, as problems to be investigated, analyzed, represented, and debated?

Definitions

Two related challenges are implicit in this transformation. When Ball and Lampert ask above, "how could the many complex layers of practice be represented?" they are really asking two broad questions: what are some of the ways that we can investigate and analyze the complexities of teaching and learning? And, what are some of the ways that our investigations and analyses can be represented, communicated, and brought forward into professional conversation?

Reprinted from *Inventio: Creative Thinking About Learning and Teaching.*

These questions are at the core of the Carnegie project on the scholarship of teaching, and the culmination of nearly a decade of discussion that began with the 1990 publication of *Scholarship Reconsidered* (Boyer), and then refined later in *Scholarship Reassessed* (Glassick, Huber, Maeroff, 1997). Over this time, a "scholarship of teaching" has come to imply not merely the existence of a scholarly component in teaching, but a particular kind of activity, in which faculty engage, separate from the act of teaching, that can be considered scholarship itself. "For an activity to be designated as scholarship," argues Lee Shulman, the President of the Carnegie Foundation for the Advancement of Teaching, "it should manifest at least three key characteristics: It should be *public,* susceptible to *critical review and evaluation,* and accessible for *exchange and use* by other members of one's scholarly community." These are the core components of all forms of scholarship, and the features by which "scholarship properly communicated and critiqued serves as the building blocks for knowledge growth in a field" (5).

But in order to apply this model to one's "teaching," or to think it even possible to produce a scholarship of teaching, there first needs to be a fundamental shift in how one defines teaching as an activity and thus as an object of investigation. As Shulman puts it, "Too often teaching is identified only as the active interactions between teacher and students in a classroom setting (or even a tutorial session). I would argue that teaching, like other forms of scholarship, is an extended process that unfolds over time" (5). Shulman describes that process as embodied by at least five elements: vision, design, interactions, outcomes, and analysis. With these elements, the extended act of teaching becomes like the extended act of traditional scholarship or research. It includes a broad vision of disciplinary questions and methods; it includes the capacity to plan and design activities that implement the vision; it includes the interactions that require particular skills and result in both expected and unexpected results; it includes certain outcomes from that complex process, and those outcomes necessitate some kind of analysis. Like scholarship, teaching also involves what Daniel Bernstein calls a "transactional relation" between teaching practice and student performance. "Indeed such a transactional relation [between scholarly activity and the results of that activity] is a benchmark of excellence in scholarly practice" (77). There is then a tight connection between the shift to seeing teaching as an activity over time and a belief in the visibility and viability of teaching *problems* that can be investigated as scholarship, and not merely for the purpose of "fixing" them.

A Problem I Could Live With

My own engagement with the scholarship of teaching followed a similar trajectory from seeing my teaching as a problem (or failure) to seeing *in my teaching* a set of problems worth pursuing as an ongoing intellectual focus. As with many people, my heightened attention to teaching was occasioned by a crisis. Three years ago, after introducing a number of experimental "electronic literacy" components into my courses, my teaching evaluations plummeted. I now know that this is not too uncommon when teachers significantly revise their teaching, especially involving educational technology. As little solace as that fact is now, it probably would have meant even less to me at the time, occurring as it did the year prior to tenure. This was particularly perilous in my case, as I had dedicated my whole career to new technologies in the humanities, including the subject of technology and pedagogy. A "failed" semester proposed to deconstruct my entire portfolio. I felt an acute pressure to reconstruct my courses and teaching methods one element at a time, and to justify, track, and evaluate each component of that reconstruction.

Over the next year and a half I revised some courses and created others from the ground up, especially a new introductory American literature course, "American Literary Traditions," for which I've written an online course portfolio (Bass, 1998). In this process of reflection and redesign, I resolved to make every course component *intentional.* That is, I tried to articulate for myself the reasoning behind every aspect of the course, especially the connections between technology and discipline-based pedagogy. In doing so, I found myself asking questions about student learning I had never asked before. For a decade I had had good success as a teacher: positive feedback, strong evaluations, evidence (anecdotal and otherwise) that students learned something in my courses.

Yet, I now realized I knew very little about *why* certain students did better than others. Or, more generally, I knew very little about *how* students came to know the material I was teaching. Ever since graduate school I had taught mostly the way I had been taught, and tended to replicate the pedagogies that worked best—quite frankly—on *me* (or slight variations of me). Now that I was trying to change my teaching radically, those *naturalized* teaching methods and the assumptions behind them were exposed to be without any clear scaffolding or support by the evidence of learning, however sound or useful some of the approaches were.

Understanding and Mastery

This point was most driven home to me as I reflected on what I knew and didn't know about how students developed what Howard Gardner calls a "deep understanding" of my subject. Looking at my discipline through my own eyes only, I assumed that "understanding" was equivalent and coextensive with mastery. I assumed that students in a particular course achieved understanding (in the space of a semester) by replicating a partial and incomplete version of mastery (a mimicry of mastery) that was like the understanding that developed across a whole course of study. Upper division majors were just farther along in this journey of mastery, with the depth of their mimicry ever more convincing. Either way, I imagined that every student, freshman or senior, major or not, was engaged in some version of the mastery of knowledge model that in its completeness was designed primarily to produce English teachers.

It was only by "virtue" of my crisis that led to a reconstruction that I found myself looking critically at this model for the first time. For example, I realized I didn't know really if the better students in a course who demonstrated a real understanding of the material by the end of the semester were actually acquiring that understanding in my course, or were merely the percentage of students who entered the course with a high level of background and aptitude. Similarly, I realized I didn't really know if the students who I watched "improve" from their early work to later work were really understanding the material and the paradigm from which I was operating, or merely learning to perform their knowledge in ways that had adapted to my expectations. (Or, for that matter, I wasn't sure if there was any meaningful difference between understanding and *performing* understanding; or as Tom Hatch, a scholar at the Carnegie Foundation is always asking, I didn't know if "understanding" was the most important learning goal at all times anyway).

As the "crisis" part of this story resolved, I turned to the task of documenting what I had learned in a "course portfolio." When I focused on the process of recording and framing what was happening in my courses, I was struck by the thinness of resources on which I could draw for help in analyzing the nature of learning in my discipline. I realize now that the gaping quality of my questions was rooted in both the nature of teaching itself and the culture of the academy. Grant Wiggins puts it well in an essay, entitled "Embracing Accountability":

> Teaching, by nature, is an egocentric profession in the sense Piaget used the term: we find it difficult to see when our teaching isn't clear or adequate. We don't easily imagine how what is so obvious and important to us *cannot* be equally so to novices. Combined with our strong desire to cause learning and to find any evidence of success, we are prone to unending self-deception. How easily we hear what we want and need to hear in a student answer or question; how quickly we assume that if a few intelligent comments are made, all students get the point. This is the tragic flaw inherent in trying hard, and for the right reasons, to get people to understand and value what we understand and value. It then often doesn't occur to us that students are trying equally hard to *appear* knowledgeable (5).

My journey that had begun with a crisis had *progressed* to a problem, in fact a set of problems. The ending had become a new beginning where the broad set of questions that had been raised in the process of rethinking my courses were now coming into focus as clear lines of inquiry that I wanted to investigate over the next several years, in the context of my teaching. My objectives in this investigation do not replace my interest in teaching well (and better), and to make each semester's experience for students worthwhile; but I also want to look at a set of questions *over time,* both for my own professional development and as a contribution to the scholarship of teaching in my field.

The Inverted Pyramid

For me, the questions I have become most interested in pursuing as ongoing inquiry come back to the issues of teaching for *understanding* and the match between vision, practice, and outcomes. Let me briefly describe two dimensions here. The first is what I came to call in my own practice the "inverted pyramid." In reconstructing my courses, and in asking myself how students come to understand what they do, I was led to a set of subsidiary questions. I asked myself what specifically were the four or five learning goals that I had for students in a particular course (as opposed to purely teaching goals or content/coverage goals)? Then I asked myself:

- What did I really believe (and what did I know) about what percentage of students were achieving all of the goals, some of the goals, one or two of them?
- If I had to pick one of these learning goals or outcomes as the *one* thing that students would retain from this course after leaving it, what would it be?
- Thinking about that one goal, then, could I honestly say that I spent the most amount of time in the course teaching to the goal I valued most?

I think of this as the "inverted pyramid" because in the schematization of my own teaching I perceived that I had my process upside down. That is, I decided (without going into any of the specifics here) that I spent the least amount of time teaching *to* the kind of understanding I valued most. I was teaching a whole range of subsidiary goals on the assumption that they would "add up" to the kind of paradigmatic understanding that *I* brought to the subject (the goal of mastery that builds on a wide base and narrows to the destination of paradigmatic understanding). If this was the best way to teach prospective majors, or the students in a class most likely to take more courses in the subject, I had no *evidence* of that, other than my own education experience; nor did I have any evidence that it was the best way to teach *all* students, especially the novice learners being introduced to the subject, and those who might possibly never take another literature course again.

Benchmark Understanding

One focus of my ongoing inquiry is now on the problem of teaching more directly to the student learning goals I value most. For me, in my own subject and pedagogical practice, that entails (to state it briefly) a combination of constructivist pedagogies—including work with electronic archives and hypertext writing tools—that engage students more actively with the complexities of textual form and contextual meaning, even at the expense of more traditional kinds of coverage. The general problem of teaching for understanding has led me to wonder specifically about the extent to which students' *prior* understandings of a field—its deep structures and assumptions, not just its facts and principles—situate a person to acquire new knowledge.

Many years ago, I was teaching a Freshman Honors English course in American literature. We were reading a non-fiction travel narrative by the historian Francis Parkman, called the *Oregon Trail,* a story of his youthful excursions into "frontier" America in the mid 1840's. Parkman's book is not really literature in any traditional sense. The value in reading it in a literature course was for the exquisite insight the book gives into 19th-century scientism and ethnocentrism. In this way the book lays bare a set of 19th-century assumptions about romanticism, realism, culture, and truth that underlie much of the literature of the period. This was my rationale for teaching it, and it was my impression that these were the themes that the class and I were unpacking this particular semester in each of the first three class sessions on Parkman's text. Then, on the fourth day, as I was unpacking my backpack before class, I overheard one student (a really good student) say to another student in the front row: "I can't believe that Professor Bass thinks this is a great book."

I was stunned. I had to interrupt: "You think I think this is a great book? Not only don't I think it is a great work of literature, I don't even think it is a great book in terms of ideas. In fact I think it is a horrible book, full of arrogance and self-aggrandizement. But it is also full of insight into a particular way of seeing in the 19th century. That's why we're reading it. I don't think it is a great book. I think it is an *important* book."

At the time, I thought the problem was merely that I had not clearly communicated my intentions for teaching this book to the class. And indeed I hadn't. But I realize now that the problem was deeper than that. To me, the distinction between a "great" book and an "important" book was sufficiently rationalized in the context of my field. But it was a meaningless distinction to these freshmen. It was a distinction that they couldn't make based not only on a lack of disciplinary knowledge, but on a whole set of learned assumptions (perhaps "socializations") about what literature is supposed to be, about why you take literature in college, about what it should have meant to be in a "freshman honors English" course, and about what kind of knowledge you were supposed to take away from studying particular kinds of objects in particular contexts. I'm not saying that all their assumptions were wrong and had to be unlearned; I'm merely saying that I hadn't taken into account—nor endeavored to discover—what those assumptions were. And if my goal was to expand those assumptions—which in large part it was—then I needed to do much more to begin where the students were beginning.

Now, many years later, I find myself returning to questions about the relationship between student prior understanding and their capacity to acquire new understanding, as a problem worth pursuing for my own scholarship of teaching. In this line of inquiry I want to learn more not only about my students' entering knowledge, but how their self-awareness of learning might help them develop a deeper understanding of certain disciplinary principles more quickly and meaningfully. In fall 1998, while a visiting professor at George Mason University, I instituted for the first time an opening day reflective exercise that asked students to read and respond to a set of documents similar to those we would be working with throughout this interdisciplinary course on the culture and history of the 1890's. I had been using opening day inventories for years. In these I would ask questions about previous literature courses, what books students had read by the authors we would be reading, and how much experience they had working with new technologies (all valuable opening day data); this time I asked questions that attempted to elicit from students what they knew—and what they thought about what they knew—regarding the kind of work we would be doing. In this opening exercise I directed them to three different cultural/historical artifacts: a poem, a photograph, and a review of a stage play from the 1890's. I asked them to answer the following questions about each artifact:

1. What do you see here? Describe the document/artifact in terms of content, without being interpretive.
2. What do you think you know about this document based on reading it and any previous knowledge?
3. What do you think the document reveals about its era? What kinds of information can be learned from the document? (There might be more than one kind of information).
4. What don't you know about the document? What questions would you ask about it?
5. If you were going to do further research on this document on the World Wide Web or in the library, how would you go about it?
6. What knowledge or skills are you bringing to this course from other learning experiences you've had that help you make sense of these documents?

The exercise took a long time. I gave them more than hour. In fact it took the entire balance of the opening day after the general introduction to the course. It was an hour when I would normally have started presenting or introducing them to the subject. I suppose I could have had them do it outside of class, but it was important to me for them to complete the activity before I had started contextualizing the course. I wanted to know what they knew, and what they knew about what they knew, not what they were able to perform based on what they thought I wanted them to know.

What I learned was in part diagnostic. I learned which students had what kind of background (or background they remembered) in the period and in history and literature. But I learned much more than that. Their responses revealed a great deal about their assumptions of what it meant to look at and derive information from historical documents. For example, in their responses to #3

("What do you think the document reveals about its era") most students indicated in one form or another that there was a "right answer" that they did not yet have enough context to know. Or, in their responses to #6 ("What knowledge or skills are you bringing to this course from other learning experiences you've had that help you make sense of these documents"), most students said they either were or were not bringing specific *content* knowledge to make sense of them. Only two recognized that they might have *skills*, or ways of reading, (as opposed to positive content knowledge) that would help them make sense of the documents. This was really important. Since one of my stated goals of the course was to give students skills and methods that would enable them to encounter historical materials in other contexts more capably, the disjunction between content-knowledge and method-knowledge was critical for me (*and* them) to see at the outset. This all helped me immeasurably to adjust the course even more to approach the question of historical and documentary interpretation from the standpoint of process and complexity and to foreground these emphases in the course.

On the last day of class I handed back their opening day responses, asked them to look at the same three artifacts *and* to look at what they wrote on the first day. On this day I asked them how their response to these artifacts would be different now, what they had gained from the course that helped them read the documents more knowledgeably, and what they were taking away from the course that would help them in another course about culture and history. With this reflection, (again without going into any detail here) I was able to see a change in their rhetoric about the complexity of textual meaning, and in their perceptions about the components of the course that led to that change.

This meta-reflective dimension is a key piece of evidence in my ongoing inquiry into how students come to learn and understand complex ideas about culture and history. Of course as I assess the effectiveness of the course and its methods there are other places I would look for evidence of student learning, such as in their written work. But overall, what has been striking for me is the way in which my initial questions gave rise to particular problems. And, as with other kinds of scholarly and intellectual work, the more I pursue those problems as inquiry and the more I reflect on what I'm learning, the more complex those problems seem.

Against the Grain

It takes a deliberate act to look at teaching from the perspective of learning. Actually, it takes a set of acts—individually motivated and communally validated—to focus on questions and problems, gather data, interpret and share results. The range of questions may take many different forms. The nature of the data may be quantitative or qualitative; it may be based on interviews, formative assessment instruments, test performances, student evaluations, or peer review, or any combination by which the "multiples of evidence" may be obtained. The nature of the scholarly design could vary from tracking three students of ranging abilities from the beginning of the semester to the end, to studying group dynamics in videotape of student collaborative work, to comparing and contrasting content analysis of student written work across semesters. The object of analysis may range from the acquisition of basic skills to the development of personal values or the transformation of whole knowledge paradigms.

As with scholarship or research, you cannot investigate everything at once. Indeed it may be that you can't investigate more than one question at a time. What matters most is for teachers to investigate the problems that matter most to them. In this way, a scholarship of teaching does not imply a new set of elaborate accountability procedures tied onto the luggage rack of every teaching vehicle. The movement for a scholarship of teaching seeks first and foremost to legitimate a new set of questions as intellectual problems. Arriving there, the discourse surrounding the scholarship of teaching can begin to chart what is yet uncharted terrain, a landscape that will feature the convergence of disciplinary knowledge, pedagogical practice, evidence of learning, and theories of learning and cognition. Ultimately, it will be a discourse based on disciplinary protocols of investigative practice calibrated to the idioms of particular campus and institutional cultures.

I agree with Diana Laurillard's claim in her book, *Rethinking University Teaching,* that "teaching is not a normative science" (8). It can be done effectively or ineffectively. It can always be done better. But the widely held presumption that it can be done *right,* or that it need only be done competently, has strangulated the development of teaching as an intellectual enterprise and analytic subject. Laurillard puts it this way:

> The academic system must change. It works to some extent, but not well enough. And as higher education expands we cannot always rely on human ingenuity to overcome its inadequacies. It is always possible to defend the inspirational lecturer, the importance of academic individuality, the value of pressuring students to work independently, but we cannot defend a mode of operation that actively undermines a professional approach to teaching. Teachers need to know more than just their subject. They need to know the ways it can come to be understood, the ways it can be misunderstood, what counts as understanding: they need to know how individuals experience the subject. But they are neither required nor enabled to know these things. (6)

Enabling teachers not only "to know these things" but to share them in serious ways is what a scholarship of teaching is about. Ultimately, the measure of success for the scholarship of teaching movement will not be the degree to which it can—by focusing on the "many layers of practice" at the heart of teaching—discover *solutions* worth implementing, but the extent to which it is successful in discovering *problems* worth pursuing.

References and Acknowledgements

Many thanks to Tom Hatch, of the Carnegie Foundation for the Advancement of Teaching, for his comments on the revision of this article.

Ball, Deborah Loewenberg, and Magdalene Lampert. "Multiples of Evidence, Time, Perspective: Revising the Study of Teaching and Learning." Paper prepared for the Commission on Improving Educational Research, National Academy of Education: 1998.

Bass, Randall. *Hypertext Course Portfolio on 'American Literary Traditions*. Georgetown University: December 1998. (http://www.georgetown.edu/bassr/portfolio/amlit)

Bernstein, Daniel. "Putting the Focus on Student Learning." *The Course Portfolio: How Faculty Can Examine Their Teaching to Advance Practice and Improve Student Learning*. 77–83.

Hutchings, Pat, ed. *The Course Portfolio: How Faculty Can Examine Their Teaching to Advance Practice and Improve Student Learning*. American Association for Higher Education: 1998.

Laurillard, Diana. *Rethinking University Teaching: A Framework for the Effective Use of Educational Technology*. London: Routledge, 1993.

Shulman, Lee. "Course Anatomy: The Dissection and Analysis of Knowledge Through Teaching." *The Course Portfolio: How Faculty Can Examine Their Teaching to Advance Practice and Improve Student Learning*. 5–12.

Wiggins, Grant. "Embracing Accountability." *New Schools, New Communities* 12. 2 (Winter 1996): 4–10.

Defining Features

M.T. Huber and P. Hutchings

> Thinking about teaching begins where all intellectual inquiry begins, with questions about what is going on and how to explain, support, and replicate answers that satisfy us.[1]

How exactly to define the scholarship of teaching and learning has been the subject of much debate. Like other emergent fields of endeavor (think of biochemistry and women's studies in their formative years—or even snowboarding), the scholarship of teaching and learning does not come cut from whole cloth but builds on existing traditions and lines of work, some of them long-standing. Decades of work by faculty whose research has focused on the pedagogy of their field clearly feeds into today's scholarship of teaching and learning. The assessment movement, too, especially that aspect of assessment that focuses directly on the classroom, is an older cousin. Many campuses have centers for teaching and learning that have promoted scholarly work to improve instruction. And scholars of teaching and learning in higher education owe a debt to the K–12 teacher-research movement and to other disciplines and fields that have developed the methods and paradigms for action research.[2]

If the scholarship of teaching and learning is a phenomenon at the intersection of older lines of work, it is also a movement with new dimensions, new angles, new ambitions. Practices and insights borrowed from various traditions and communities are being adopted by a different and wider group of educators, and, as a consequence, adapted to new purposes and opportunities. Like other new areas of work, this one is a moving target,[3] still taking shape as a larger community of practice forms around it, and as conventions and standards develop around emerging interests and needs.

In this chapter, then, we propose a definition that reflects an evolving set of ideas and practices that can and should shape the work of all faculty as they bring their habits, methods, and commitments as scholars to their work as teachers—and to their students' learning. We do so by looking first at the need for the scholarship of teaching and learning, then at four features that define it, and finally at what it promises for the teaching commons.

Needs and Reasons

One of the best ways to understand the scholarship of teaching and learning is by looking at the need that prompts it. In a nutshell, that need is to capture the work of teaching and learning in ways that can be built upon—to *stop losing* "the intellectual work that is regularly being done," as Dan Bernstein has written, by creating "a community of teachers whose decisions about how to teach will be informed by the collective effectiveness of the work" (2001, pp. 228–229). To put it a bit differently, the problem the scholarship of teaching and learning aims to address is that teaching has, traditionally, had so few ways to improve itself.

Reprinted from *The advancement of learning: Building the teaching commons* (2005), Carnegie Foundation for the Advancement of Teaching.

As a profession, teaching has long been vexed by perceptions that make its advancement difficult. It's easy: anyone "off the street" can do it. It's magic: not something you learn to do but a gift you are born with. It's technique and tricks, not intellectually substantive. Carrying such baggage, teaching has developed few of the mechanisms that make improvement possible over time. *Individual* faculty work hard at their classroom craft, but the larger, collective enterprise of teaching does not move forward because the work of improvement is so often done in isolation, in the school of hard knocks, one might say, and by the seat of the pants. In contrast, the scholarship of teaching and learning offers the prospect of work in which teachers—to use Sir Isaac Newton's famous image—"stand on the shoulders of giants."[4]

Lee Shulman has written extensively about the need for this shift of perspective. It was as a newly minted faculty member, he recalls, that he felt the first sharp pangs of "pedagogical solitude," the fact that teaching, which might seem to be the most social of work, done in community with others, is much less public than research (1993, p. 6). In fact, teaching is private work for many faculty, taking place behind doors that are both metaphorically and physically closed. Not surprisingly, then, there are few habits or conventions for exploring what teachers do and how it affects their students, and for sharing what they do and know with colleagues who might benefit from it. "Unlike fields such as architecture (which preserves its creations in both plans and edifices), law (which builds a case literature of opinions and interpretations), medicine (with its records and case studies), and even unlike chess, bridge, or ballet (with their traditions of preserving both memorable games and choreographed performances through inventive forms of notation and recording), teaching is conducted without an audience of peers. It is devoid of a history of practice" (Shulman, 1987, pp. 11–12).

Moving teaching from a mostly private enterprise, where what teachers know and do disappears "like dry ice," as Shulman has written, to teaching as "community property," which is documented, shared, and built upon, is a central theme of the scholarship of teaching and learning (1993, p. 7). Such publicness is, after all, part of what is implied when something is called scholarship. One may think brilliant thoughts in the shower, or, for that matter, come to fascinating conclusions in the lab, but, unless new insights are captured in ways that can be shared with others, they are not properly called scholarship. This is not to say that everything that happens in the classroom needs to be made public. Just as not everything that is learned in the library or lab is shared, faculty must be able to make choices about what to document and when to share the work of teaching (see Hutchings, 1996). The confidentiality of student work—an important source of evidence in the scholarship of teaching and learning—must be protected, as well.[5] Faculty and students alike need a safe place to try out new ideas and to bring them to fruition. But that is the point: the fruits are too seldom brought to market. Ongoing improvement will only be possible when the intellectual work of teaching and learning is captured and represented in ways that others can build on.

The need for this shift toward publicness is greater now than ever, for two reasons. First, as described in the previous chapter, the classroom is shifting ground for many faculty today. Growing numbers of students are not prepared for college work. The disciplines are in transition. New technologies, and a whole host of new or newly discovered classroom approaches, bring exciting possibilities but also novel challenges. And ironically perhaps, the more that is known about the social and psychological processes of learning and the science of the brain, the more daunting the work of teaching may feel. Indeed, as our travels have taken us from campus to campus and brought us into conversation with teachers from diverse fields and institutions, we have been struck by a growing sense, perhaps especially among veteran teachers, that what used to work, pedagogically speaking, may not get the job done for today's students. As one former teacher of literature put it, "While I may have been an excellent teacher of British literature twenty years ago, I might not be in today's classroom. I might, but I don't know for certain" (Rhem, 2003, p. 3). The scholarship of teaching and learning is needed today because teaching now is harder than it used to be.

It is also needed because so much interesting pedagogical innovation is being prompted by the challenges of today's educational realities. As University of Pittsburgh English professor Mariolina Salvatori has written (she is referring to her students' learning but the point applies more generally), "moments of difficulty often contain the seeds of understanding" (2000, p. 81), and our work with the scholarship of teaching and learning has persuaded us that the difficulty of teaching is also a spur to real creativity for many faculty and campuses. In short, this is a time of incredible pedagogical ferment and invention, and higher education cannot afford *not* to learn from the innovations and experiments going on in today's classrooms.

Four Defining Features

What, then, does the scholarship of teaching and learning look like? What do faculty who embrace this work actually *do?*

One way to answer this question is to return to the example of Dennis Jacobs, the chemist at Notre Dame whose story introduces the previous chapter. Jacobs looked hard at his students' difficulties in introductory chemistry and saw questions and problems he needed to understand more deeply. He designed a variety of strategies for doing that, including a large-scale study tracking students through subsequent courses but also "up-close" qualitative work through videotaping small groups. As he did this work, and as new insights and evidence emerged, he brought his work to bear on the teaching of the course, applying his new ideas, trying them out, refining approaches as he came to understand them better. As the work progressed he shared what he was learning with colleagues, first in his own setting at Notre Dame but also beyond, for instance at a special forum of the American Chemical Society. His work draws on previous efforts by others, and it is now available for others to build on in turn. Indeed, the work has come full circle—as research generally does—bringing Jacobs to a next set of questions and problems to address.[6]

Certainly not every project in the scholarship of teaching and learning proceeds just as Dennis Jacobs's has. Nevertheless his work is a useful window into four core practices that make up the scholarship of teaching and learning: framing questions, gathering and exploring evidence, trying out and refining new insights in the classroom, and going public with what is learned in ways that others can build on. These practices provide an operational definition of the scholarship of teaching and learning, and we will take them one at a time—though recognizing that the work does not necessarily proceed in a step-by-step, linear way.

Questioning

In our work with scholars of teaching and learning, we have identified a variety of motivations that bring faculty to this work: they may be seeking colleagues who share their interests in pedagogy, they may be looking for ways to bring greater recognition and reward to their work as teachers, they may see themselves as reformers connecting with a national movement they believe has the potential to change higher education. But, as we learned through our recent survey of CASTL Scholars, the single most powerful motivation for becoming involved (identified by 97 percent as somewhat or very important) was having "questions about my students' learning that I wanted to explore" (Cox, Huber, and Hutchings, 2004; see Table 2.3). Indeed, finding and framing questions about student learning is the germ, the catalyst, the first step in the scholarship of teaching and learning.

Frequently the work begins with questions about whether a new classroom strategy or curricular model will promote certain kinds of learning better than a more traditional method. Not surprisingly, such "what works" questions often lead to others that are more open-ended, aimed at uncovering and more deeply understanding "what happens" under particular pedagogical conditions—the use of a simulation to teach about labor law (Corrada, 2001a, 2001b), for instance, or a new model for teaching abnormal psychology that focuses on resilience rather than pathologies (Duffy, 2000). Other questions have a more conceptual and theoretical bent, aiming to articulate new ways *to think about* learning and teaching, which in turn suggest additional questions.[7] In our next chapter we will look at several examples of the scholarship of teaching and learning that take a conceptual turn.

Whatever the thrust and focus of the question, it is, we have seen, the complex, "transactional relation" between teaching and learning that catalyzes this scholarship (Bernstein, 1998, p. 77). As one faculty member writes, the reason to get involved in the scholarship of teaching is not because it is the newest fad or because promotion and tenure guidelines include it but because there is "something you really care about, something you're really interested in learning about" (Cerbin,

TABLE 2.3

Reasons for Involvement in the Scholarship of Teaching and Learning

	Percent of Respondents		
	Not Important	Somewhat Important	Very Important
I had questions about my students' learning that I wanted to explore.	3	16	81
I wanted to expand the range of scholarly work in which I am involved.	26	35	39
I wanted to connect my interests in teaching and learning to a recognized body of research.	9	42	50
I wanted to participate in the movement to bring greater recognition and reward to the scholarly work of teaching.	10.5	34.5	54
I wanted to find new colleagues with whom to pursue my interests in teaching and learning.	6	42	52
I was urged to become involved by colleagues who knew about the scholarship of teaching and learning.	48	25.5	26.5

Source: *Cox, Huber, and Hutchings, CASTL Scholars Survey, 2004.*

2000, p. 19). Serious work on teaching begins, that is, where all scholarship begins, with curiosity and an urge to understand more clearly what is happening and why. And the "what" in question—the focus of inquiry and investigation—is student learning.

Faculty's questions about their students' experience as learners may focus on individual courses, on clusters of courses, or on whole programs; they may focus on particular kinds of learning (say, in interdisciplinary settings), or on particular groups of students (women in engineering or students for whom English is a second language). Some questions can be pursued by individual faculty investigating their own classrooms; others require teams of faculty looking across settings and working together to share data and deliberate about their conclusions—sometimes with support from an office of institutional research or assessment, or a center for teaching excellence.

For most faculty the most compelling and urgent questions emerge directly from their own practice. Take, for example, the burgeoning interest in technology. As faculty today employ new digital archives, as they require students to collaborate online, as they move whole courses onto the Web, they encounter (and sometimes are asked by colleagues or administrators) questions about the relative effectiveness of these approaches—especially because technology can entail significant investments of time and money. In this sense, technology is the camel's nose under the teaching tent; it is a small step from questions about the impact of Web-based teaching to questions about other instructional approaches and curricular innovations. Questions about the use of online class discussion in learning communities, for instance, may generate questions about the character of discussion more generally, or about the impact of linked courses on students' ability to integrate their learning across contexts.

To say that student learning raises stimulating questions is not, perhaps, new or startling. But it is worth remembering that teaching is not, for most academics, an arena in which they have developed (or received training to inculcate) habits and skills of inquiry.[8] Georgetown University professor Randy Bass notes the revealing contrast between teaching and research in this regard:

> One telling measure of how differently teaching is regarded from traditional scholarship or research within the academy is what a difference it makes to have a "problem" in one versus the other. In scholarship and research, having a "problem" is at the heart of the investigative process; it is the compound of the generative questions around which all creative and productive activity revolves. But in one's

> teaching, a "problem" is something you don't want to have, and if you have one, you probably want to fix it. Asking a colleague about a problem in his or her research is an invitation; asking about a problem in one's teaching would probably seem like an accusation. [1999b, p. 1]

Thinking of teaching as a source of interesting, consequential, intellectual problems and questions is a first, defining step in the scholarship of teaching and learning.

Gathering and Exploring Evidence

But asking questions is not enough. As faculty begin to think of teaching as a source of challenging intellectual questions, a second imperative emerges: to devise ways to explore those questions and shed light on them. The scholarship of teaching and learning is not simply a casual interlude of mulling and reflection. Though it may be of limited scope and scale, and therefore modest in one sense, it entails systematic, disciplined inquiry, and requires hard thinking about how to gather and analyze evidence. This process of exploration is, then, the second aspect of our definition.

Looking across the projects undertaken by CASTL Scholars over the past several years, we are struck by the rich array of possibilities that has emerged for gathering and analyzing evidence: course portfolios, the collection and systematic review of student work (sometimes by secondary readers, sometimes with newly devised rubrics that capture aspects of learning that were previously hard to discern), videotape, focus groups, ethnographic interviews, classroom observation, large-scale longitudinal tracking, questionnaires, surveys, and more. This methodological pluralism makes sense. Teaching and learning are complex processes, and no single source or type of evidence can provide a sufficient window into the difficult questions raised by student learning. Sometimes what is needed are data about groups of students, sometimes a "drill down" into the work of a single learner; sometimes numbers speak most clearly, sometimes more qualitative evidence, and often a combination of "counting and recounting" (Shulman, 2004a, p. 165). As in any research, the challenge is to employ the right set of methods and the best sources of evidence to explore the question in ways that will be credible and significant.

But of course, *credible* and *significant* are not adjectives about which everyone agrees. Indeed, it is around issues of method and evidence that disciplinary differences in the scholarship of teaching and learning often surface in ways that are both contested and fruitful. An anecdote from the CASTL program makes the point: A group of faculty from a mix of disciplines was discussing what kinds of work would qualify as scholarship of teaching and learning. How about an in-depth examination of the learning of one student over time? one person proposed. Although some members of the group concurred that such an approach might yield important insights about how learners engage with course material, a sociologist in the group (a past editor of the journal *Teaching Sociology*) objected strenuously. "An *n* of one!" he exclaimed. "That would never count as scholarship in my field" (see Huber, 2000).

He is not alone in this view, of course; many social scientists want to see data that meet their tests for sample size and generalizability, and faculty from the natural sciences and math often share this view. "Scientists are scientists and they know that the data do not lie," reported one scholar from chemistry (Huber, 2000, p. 25). But for scholars in the humanities, *data* (a word they are unlikely even to use) usually means close reading and analysis, not numbers. The experience of a historian contrasts with the comment by the sociologist. T. Mills Kelly began his scholarship of teaching and learning project by looking at the research literature on teaching and technology (his questions were about the impact of his "hybrid" course on students' understanding of world history) where he found himself face-to-face with "a methodology that I knew nothing about—a new language, a use of control groups, a scientific approach." It was not familiar or comfortable ground: "I'm not an educational researcher by training," he reminded us. "I'm an historian." Accordingly, he developed a course portfolio that allowed him to create a kind of history of the course, a genre he was more comfortable with and one that his colleagues in the field found familiar as well (2000, p. 55).

The point is not that the historian (or the sociologist) was right (or wrong) but that different disciplines bring different rules and assumptions about what constitutes credible evidence, and what kinds of methods yield "scholarly" results. Differences of opinion about these matters may make it hard for work to be valued across disciplinary borders. At the same time, it is clear that disciplines can borrow and learn from one another in matters methodological. Certainly this is true in more familiar kinds of research, where, for instance, one can find computer-based content analysis in literary studies and mathematical modeling in the work of historians. Similarly in the scholarship of teaching and learning, borrowing methods from other fields may enrich the process and make lessons learned from the work both deeper and more broadly significant. Thus, in the Carnegie program we have seen microbiologists using discourse analysis (Elmendorf, 2004) and American studies professors using focus group interviews (Linkon, 2000). The important thing is that the method and the question match. Whatever its form, systematic inquiry is central to the scholarship of teaching and learning.

Trying Out and Refining New Insights

Complicating the inquiry process is the fact that the scholarship of teaching and learning occurs in the highly dynamic environment of the classroom (or other learning context). For some faculty, this reality presents a challenge and even a frustration, placing the work in what Donald Schön calls "the swampy lowlands" of scholarship (as opposed to the "high, hard ground") where "problems are messy and confusing and incapable of technical solution" (1995, p. 28).[9] For example, William Cerbin, a psychologist, found himself unable to do the kind of design experiment that he believed his colleagues in psychology would find most credible: "In reality, I was teaching this class as I was experimenting with it and studying it, and under those conditions you sometimes have to change the script as you go because your best judgment tells you that a change would be an improvement for the students. But as a result, I didn't have control, in terms of introducing a certain kind of situation, controlling the variables, and then analyzing student performance" (2000, p. 16). But if this confounding of inquiry and intervention, research and practice, sometimes feels like a limitation, it is also a source of great appeal for many faculty. Those who become involved in systematic investigation of their classrooms almost universally report that the work leads to important changes. Thus, this process of trying out and refining new insights is the third of our four defining features of the scholarship of teaching and learning.

Among CASTL Scholars, for instance, 81 percent agree or strongly agree that the quality of their students' learning has been improved by their work as scholars of teaching and learning. Sixty-nine percent agree or strongly agree that "more of my students achieve high standards of work since I became involved in the scholarship of teaching and learning" (Cox, Huber, and Hutchings, 2004; see Table 2.4). Many also report that their questions about student learning led them to develop more demanding modes of assessment (see, for example, Bernstein, 2000, or Flannery, 2001a).

Sometimes trying out one's findings in practice is more a matter of changed expectations and ambitions than of implementing any particular innovation. Consider this statement from a faculty member in music who became deeply involved in the scholarship of teaching and learning: "[This work] has deeply and permanently changed the way I look at my teaching and my students' learning. The upside is that this has made that aspect of my career exciting. The downside is that I am never, ever satisfied. Once I was rather pleased and even a bit smug about my success as a teacher. Now I see how far I still need to go to truly make a difference in my students' learning, and it feels somewhat overwhelming" (Barkley, Response to CASTL Scholars Survey, 2004).

The point here is that the scholarship of teaching and learning brings with it an expectation that results will not be held at arm's length but rather tried out and used for improvement. As Schön's swamp metaphor suggests, such work is cousin to a wider universe of scholarship that has its center in professional practice and its perennial ambiguities. In short, the scholarship of teaching and learning is often messy rather than neatly linear, engaged rather than disinterested, and highly personal in its impact.

Going Public

The scholarship of teaching and learning is about more than individual improvement and development—it is about producing knowledge that is available for others to use and build on. This, it

TABLE 2.4

Consequences of Involvement in the Scholarship of Teaching and Learning

	Percent of Respondents			
Statement of Consequence	**Strongly Disagree**	**Disagree**	**Agree**	**Strongly Agree**
I have changed the design of my courses since becoming involved in the scholarship of teaching and learning.	0	6	35	58
I have changed the kinds of assessments I use in my courses as a result of my participation in the scholarship of teaching and learning.	0	8	40	52
My expectations for my students' learning have changed since participating in the scholarship of teaching and learning.	0	8	32	60
I have documented improvements in my students' learning since becoming involved in the scholarship of teaching and learning.	1	15	52	29
More of my students achieve high standards of work since I became involved in the scholarship of teaching and learning.	1	20	49	20

Source: *Cox, Huber, and Hutchings, CASTL Scholars Survey, 2004.*

should be said, is an ambitious goal, and one that distinguishes the scholarship of teaching and learning from many other approaches to classroom improvement.

For one thing, the scholarship of teaching and learning is not really finished until it has been captured in ways that others can see and examine. Toward this end, scholars of teaching and learning are inventing new genres, forms, and outlets for sharing their work. In addition to traditional journal articles and books, one sees, for instance, the emergence of course portfolios that trace the unfolding of teaching and learning from conception to outcomes (Hutchings, 1998). Many of these portfolios are now electronic, and multimedia technologies have become a powerful resource for revealing not only the final results of a scholarly investigation into teaching and learning but the particular setting, students, and pedagogy. Documentation that preserves these rich details makes it possible for others to ask the all-important question: "Is this work relevant to me and my circumstances?" (Shulman, 2002a, p. vi).

Because its purpose is not only to build new knowledge but to improve practice, the scholarship of teaching and learning lends itself to forms of representation and exchange that are more about engagement than dissemination. The workshop, for instance, has become a staple of campus-based faculty development and of conferences both discipline-based and cross-disciplinary. Or consider the teaching circle, the pedagogical colloquium, the assessment seminar, and the online listserv (like H-Teach, sponsored by the H-NET Humanities and Social Sciences On-Line initiative).[10] These forms of documentation and exchange become a seedbed for new ideas in very much the ways we take for granted in more traditional areas of research scholarship. Indeed, the leader of one national initiative on the scholarship of teaching and learning observes that the faculty he has worked with only fully understand the significance of their own questions and data when they start trying to explain them to others (Randy Bass, e-mail to the authors, November 27, 2004). Going public is not simply a final step in the process—a *t* to be crossed or an *i* to be dotted; instead, it creates new lenses and angles on the entire process and the significance of the work.

As in traditional scholarship, going public also presumes an audience, a community of scholars who will engage with what is captured, documented, and shared. This means thinking in advance about how it will be captured—the genre question, if you will—but also about the most relevant audiences for the work, the communities one seeks to influence, the conversation one seeks to enter and connect with. Many scholars of teaching and learning are interested in engaging colleagues who are close to home—fellow department members, for instance, who teach the same (or similar) students and whose own courses may be enriched by the work. Widening the circle, audiences may also include colleagues from other departments. Campus-based groups are particularly important for asking questions about the local curriculum or innovations aimed at outcomes the campus especially values. But communities need not always be face-to-face. There are larger, more diffuse colleague groups that connect online, read the same journals, and follow the same literature. Some of these focus on a particular pedagogy, like learning communities or service learning. Others are disciplinary. Whether discipline-based or more multi-disciplinary, whether close to home or far-ranging, building an audience for this work is an essential component of the scholarship of teaching and learning.

***

As noted earlier in this chapter, the four elements of the scholarship of teaching and learning need not, and often *do* not, march along in linear fashion. Although it is true that the entry point is often the framing of a question or problem for investigation, the work may also grow from an encounter with the efforts of others at a conference session or in published research, which, in turn, invites a rethinking of evidence that is already at hand (like the stack of student exams sitting on the desk). Or it may be that in testing out a new practice in class, the need to gather more data about students and their learning becomes evident. One of the telling moments in the CASTL summer residency comes when scholars announce, at the end of their fellowship year, after gathering lots of data and going public in all kinds of venues, that they have finally figured out what their project was *really* about. Indeed, like other complex intellectual endeavors (think of writing, for example) the scholarship of teaching and learning is an iterative, "looping" kind of work. And the fact that its four elements occur in all kinds of permutations and rhythms makes it an easier fit with the variable rhythms of faculty life itself.

Moreover, not everyone who ventures into these waters will leap in with both feet. Some begin with modest reflection on evidence they already have at hand (that stack of student exams), or with participation in conversations about teaching. In time, those activities may lead to more full-fledged enactments of the process described in this chapter. Though CASTL has used the language of "the project" to describe the work done by scholars of teaching and learning, it is perhaps better described as a set of habits and commitments that come into play in different combinations and levels of ambition throughout a faculty member's career.

This description, we are well aware, stretches the envelope of the scholarship of teaching and learning. And some readers will certainly object, concerned that such a broad view puts the status and dignity of the work at risk, reinforcing concerns about whether the work is "too soft" to be seen as real research, or, for that matter, to guide improvement efforts reliably. We understand these concerns. The place of this kind of scholarship in the reward system may well depend—especially in more research-oriented settings—on hewing to a narrower definition that closely parallels the features of traditional scholarship and leads to traditional forms of publication. Yet all serious scholarly enterprises have and *need* this range to be successful. That is, intellectual and professional habits, on the one hand, and more formal features of traditional scholarship and publication, on the other, necessarily underwrite and reinforce each other; an intellectual field or pursuit cannot flourish without both (or without the full range of engagement between these extremes).[11] Moreover, if the scholarship of teaching and learning is to be something more than a special area in the research of a few faculty, if it is to influence and improve the work in large numbers of classrooms, it needs, as we say in Chapter One, a big tent where there is space for small-scale efforts aimed mostly at local improvement as well as more ambitious, sustained work of larger scale. The key, in fact, is not the scale and scope but the care and thoughtfulness of the work, its capacity to change thought and practice, its generativity, even, perhaps, its power to surprise and delight. These are not, it should be said, soft standards but rigorous demands appropriate to the purposes and character of the work.

The Promise of the Teaching Commons

As we end this chapter, it is useful perhaps to reiterate that the scholarship of teaching and learning is not new. There have been groups of faculty who have made systematic work on pedagogy a central aspect of their careers for decades, and those who have come more recently to the work owe these earlier pioneers a debt of gratitude. What is *new* is the realization that scholars from across the full range of disciplines and professional fields can productively engage with pedagogical questions. Whereas educational research has traditionally been the province of faculty in schools or departments of education, or education specialists in some disciplines, the scholarship of teaching and learning invites involvement by faculty across the full spectrum of research specialties and fields.

This invitation is not without its challenges. Faculty in most disciplines have no formal training in the kind of work we are talking about. Indeed, they often have no training in teaching itself. For the scholarship of teaching and learning to deliver on its promises, campuses (and graduate schools) will need to become places that can nurture and support this work through appropriate programs, structures, and rewards. Scholarly and professional societies will need to develop top-notch journals, conferences, special events, and standards to advance it. As we will report in later chapters, there is still much to be done to meet these needs, but significant progress has been made.

In our view, some of the most important progress comes in the form of visions and images of what the future might look like if the scholarship of teaching and learning delivers fully on its promises. In an essay on teaching and scholarship in her field, sociologist Carla Howery ends with what she calls her "I have a dream speech." Imagine, she invites her readers, that discussants at professional meetings would routinely ask presenters: "What are the implications of this material for undergraduate education and how would you teach it?" Imagine "inspiring metrics for teaching excellence at *each* faculty rank," and that "national associations would be called on to recommend peer reviewers of teaching products" (Howery, 2002, pp. 155–156). Similarly, Stanford English professor Andrea Lunsford, writing to colleagues in a national initiative on the doctorate, imagines a world in which "graduate students are colleagues rather than acolytes, our partners in exploring major issues, in constructing new knowledge, and in sharing the wealth of our experiences, our learning, and our teaching." In such an atmosphere, she says, "a focus on pedagogy would be right and necessary," and graduate programs would develop "ongoing teaching/pedagogy circles that would include faculty, staff, and graduate students, again working collaboratively" (Lunsford, 2006).

Lunsford does not use the language of the scholarship of teaching and learning, but her vision captures, in miniature, the promise of a teaching commons to which such work can contribute and from which it can benefit. It is not, of course, a physical place but rather an intellectual space, characterized by what Corynne McSherry calls an "ethic of sharing" (2001, p. 17), where ideas, practices, products, and (to use the language now popular in educational technology circles) learning and teaching objects can be made available, known, and built on. In an important essay on course portfolios, Dan Bernstein muses about the difference such a space would make:

> To me the most important benefit of creating a community [around teaching and learning] is that we no longer lose a great deal of intellectual work that is regularly being done. Talented people find ingenious solutions to problems in learning every academic term, and traditionally most of that work is lost. When people know that there is a community of people who will look at their work, especially the cumulative intellectual work of several offerings of a course, they will be willing to take the modest extra steps of recording and reflecting on what they are already accomplishing as teachers. As a result there will be a large community of teachers whose decisions about how to teach will be informed by the collective effectiveness of the work. [Bernstein, 2001, pp. 228–229]

This powerful vision captures the possibilities of the scholarship of teaching and learning as it has evolved over recent years. The teaching commons that is now being built by growing numbers of faculty engaged in such work makes real breakthroughs in teaching and learning more likely than ever before. In such a space, conversation about teaching and learning—informed by evidence and grounded in practice—can become the norm rather than the exception. Disciplines can engage in active trading of ideas about pedagogy. Ways of sharing and citing one another's work will emerge and become commonplace. And faculty will stand on the shoulders of others who have gone before.

Notes

1. This epigraph is from "The Scholarship of Teaching and Learning," by Eileen Bender and Donald Gray (1999). Bender and Gray's piece introduces a collection of essays about scholars of teaching and learning at Indiana University. Indiana embraced the scholarship of teaching and learning early on, and has developed an extensive campus program that won the nationally competitive Hesburgh Award for faculty development in 2003.
2. Action research takes place in many sites, in each of which it has different roots and meanings. In K–12 settings, where it is variously known as *classroom action research, teacher research,* or *practitioner research,* it generally "involves the use of qualitative, interpretive modes of inquiry and data collection by teachers [often with help from academics] with a view to teachers' making judgments about how to improve their own practices" (Kemmis and McTaggart, 2000, p. 569). For a review of its recent past and future prospects in schools, professional development programs, and teacher education, see Cochran-Smith and Lytle, 1999. Often seen as a way to engage classroom teachers with academic discourse on teaching and learning, action research has generated much discussion about relationships between educators in the schools and in colleges and universities, and the different kinds of knowledge they generate, value, and use (see, for example, Coulter, 1999; Anderson and Herr, 1999; Ellis, 1997). The scholarship of teaching and learning in higher education may bear a family resemblance to action research, but its emphasis on faculty using their own disciplines and research styles to pursue classroom inquiry is different, as are its tensions and problems.
3. Numerous definitions have been floated out onto higher education's waters. Carnegie's own publications on the topic have, in fact, told an evolving story, moving from the very broad definition in the 1990 report *Scholarship Reconsidered* (see Chapter One of this volume), to more pointed ones in later statements. For instance, in a 1999 *Change* magazine article, Hutchings and Shulman propose distinctions among teaching well, scholarly teaching, and the scholarship of teaching and learning. Although these distinctions have been found useful by many, and we have built on them, we believe there is an argument to be made for a more inclusive view.
4. The image of standing on the shoulders of giants is usually traced to Newton, but its longer history is delightfully documented in Robert Merton's *On the Shoulders of Giants* (1993). For an additional spin on the idea, take a look at *The Rule of Four,* a novel whose main characters are writing senior theses at Princeton University. One of those characters, Paul, tells his roommate about the assistance he received from friends and mentors in solving the puzzle to a Renaissance text he has been writing about: "Only a man who sees giants," he says, "can ever stand upon their shoulders" (Caldwell and Thomason, 2004, p. 276). The point is nicely relevant to the themes of this volume as well, where knowing there are others "out there" doing significant intellectual work on teaching and learning is a prerequisite to serious engagement with the teaching commons.
5. Concerns about students as human subjects have been on the rise for several years now—part of a more general trend toward increased vigilance by institutional review boards (IRBs). An informal survey of CASTL Scholars in 2001 showed that on a majority of campuses it was "a given" that scholarship of teaching and learning projects should go through the IRB. For faculty from fields that do not usually encounter issues related to the protection of human subjects, this has meant an additional hurdle and learning curve, but the process can also be helpful in raising awareness about the role of students in the scholarship of teaching and learning. As documented in a 2002 Carnegie Foundation publication, *Ethics of Inquiry,* many faculty are involving their students as active participants and collaborators in the scholarship of teaching and learning. For further discussion, including case studies and commentary, see that publication (Hutchings, 2002).
6. For instance, Jacobs has been looking at the role of community-based (or service) learning in the chemistry curriculum. He has also worked with a colleague to develop "TextRev," an initiative examining how students use and value textbook resources. For more information, visit http://www.textrev.com.
7. For a "taxonomy of questions" in the scholarship of teaching and learning, see the introduction to *Opening Lines: Approaches to the Scholarship of Teaching and Learning* (Hutchings, 2000).
8. Stephen Ehrmann, director of a national project on technology and teaching, proposes that what is needed for the scholarship of teaching and learning is an embrace of "useful uncertainty" (Ehrmann, 2002). The point aligns nicely with Randy Bass's discussion of teaching "problems" as an entrée to such work.

9. It is worth quoting the fuller passage by Schön, which goes as follows: "There is a high, hard ground overlooking a swamp. On the high ground, manageable problems lend themselves to solution through the use of research-based theory and technique. In the swampy lowlands, problems are messy and confusing and incapable of technical solution. The irony of this situation is that the problems of the high ground tend to be relatively unimportant to individuals or to the society at large, however great their technical interest may be, while in the swamp lie the problems of greater human concern" (1995, p. 28).
10. See the H-Teach Web site at http://www.h-net.org/~teach/. These strategies are described in Hutchings's 1996 volume from the American Association for Higher Education, *Making Teaching Community Property*.
11. We are indebted to Randy Bass for this point about the symbiosis between different levels of engagement in all kinds of intellectual and scholarly work.

CHAPTER 3

EDUCATIONAL DEVELOPMENT

The Evolution of Faculty Development

Mary Deane Sorcinelli, Ann E. Austin,
Pamela L. Eddy, and Andrea L. Beach

Faculty development is not a new phenomenon in the history of higher education. The oldest support for faculty development, the sabbatical leave, began at Harvard University in 1810 (Eble & McKeachie, 1985) and has enjoyed a long tenure. In fact, sabbaticals, leaves, and other means of advancing scholarship remained almost the exclusive form of faculty development until the 1970s. Since that time, the field has expanded to include a much broader range of concerns. As early as 1976, faculty development was defined as "the total development of the faculty member—as a person, as a professional and as a member of an academic community" (Crow, Milton, Moomaw, & O'Connell, 1976, p. 3). But fulfilling the goal of "total development" has been an ongoing challenge as the field has worked to broaden its horizons and meet the expectations set for it.

In this chapter, we first review the general history of faculty development and its growth as a profession, then trace the evolution of the goals, practices, and structures that have characterized faculty development from its inception to the present day. Finally, we summarize the studies that have had a significant effect on the field. We divide the earlier history of faculty development into four ages: the Age of the Scholar, the Age of the Teacher, the Age of the Developer, and the Age of the Learner. As we enter the current age, which we call the Age of the Network, the emphases, interconnections, and contradictions among the four earlier ages will help us to envision the future of faculty development.

The Five Ages

From the mid-1950s well into the 1960s, American higher education grew rapidly in size and affluence. Equally striking was the prestige and status afforded to the academic profession. For example, between 1953 and 1962, the role of professor rose from seventh to third place in Gallup polls assessing the attractiveness of nine leading professions, a rank it would hold until 1973 (Rice, 1996). In describing this expansionist period, marked by new sources of funding for programs and the rising influence of the academic scholar, Rice noted that

> institutional responsibilities such as the teaching of undergraduates and committee work could be tolerated as long as time was made for doing one's own work and support was provided; a Faustian bargain was struck. Within a relatively short period, being a scholar became virtually synonymous with being an academic professional, and a powerful image of what this meant took hold. (p. 8)

This period, then, was the Age of the Scholar, and faculty development efforts were directed almost entirely toward improving and advancing scholarly competence.

By the late 1960s and throughout the 1970s the baby boomers were heading off to college; suddenly institutions of higher education found themselves serving a much larger and broader range of students. Student activism was not only political, but also academic and focused on teaching—

Reprinted from *Creating the future of faculty development: Learning from the past, understanding the present* (2006), John Wiley & Sons, Inc.

students demanded the right to exercise some control over the quality of their undergraduate learning experience, by such means as evaluating their teachers' performance in the classroom. At the same time, economic recession and the concomitant decline in faculty mobility and opportunities for renewal also contributed to new interest in faculty development and instructional improvement. These changes ushered in the Age of the Teacher. A seminal monograph, *Faculty Development in a Time of Retrenchment* (Astin, Comstock, Epperson, Greeley, Katz, & Kaufman, 1974), focused on teaching development as key to faculty vitality and renewal. Earlier interest in behavioristic research on college-level teaching was superseded by an interest in research and practice related to the development of teaching skills and competencies, as well as the design of teaching development and evaluation programs (Alstete, 2000).

The 1980s began the Age of the Developer; with an upsurge in faculty development programs, the profession came of age. Although this period was characterized by tight budgets and a concomitant decline in conditions of academic life (e.g., reduced travel, equipment, and personnel resources), a number of universities and colleges began new programs or rejuvenated existing ones (Eble & McKeachie, 1985; Erickson, 1986). Concerned about faculty vitality, foundations such as Bush, Ford, and Lilly assisted by making major investments in faculty development. Several national reports urging that more attention be paid to undergraduate education spurred further activity (Boyer, 1987; National Commission on Excellence in Education, 1983; Study Group on the Conditions of Excellence in American Higher Education, 1984). While some researchers continued to explore the question of who was participating in faculty development and what services were offered (Erickson, 1986), others began to study the usefulness and measurable outcomes of development activities (Clark, Corcoran, & Lewis, 1986; Eble & McKeachie, 1985; Young, 1987). The evaluation of faculty members, particularly as teachers, became a popular concept, indeed a buzzword, in the 1980s (Alstete, 2000).

The 1990s saw accelerated changes in academic work that had enormous implications for faculty development. As Austin (2002a) noted, it was a decade characterized by changing approaches to teaching and learning. Student learning rather than teaching took center stage—the teacher was no longer the "sage on the stage," pouring knowledge into empty vessels, but a "guide on the side," facilitating student learning. Student diversity, which became greater than at any other time in the history of higher education, also called for a greater range and variety in teaching and learning methods, skills, and sensitivities. If the 1970s were the Age of the Teacher, the 1990s were the Age of the Learner.

The role of new technologies, both in teaching and research, continued to evolve. There was a veritable explosion of technology use in college teaching, including presentation tools, web sites, classroom communication systems, and online courses (McKeachie, 2002). In addition, teaching and learning centers and entire campuses witnessed the growing phenomenon of assessment and performance measurement—from the individual faculty member in his or her classroom to the departmental, institutional, and state levels (Bourne, Gates, & Cofer, 2000; Ewell, 2001; Stassen & Sorcinelli, 2001).

Perhaps most dramatic was the change in faculty roles. Traditional faculty appointments became more demanding and expansive. Teaching, research, service, outreach, advising, grant-getting, and administrative duties were all part of the full-time faculty role at many universities and colleges (Rice, Sorcinelli, & Austin, 2000). At the same time, some faculty jobs became more circumscribed; these included, for example, teaching-intensive appointments in writing, foreign languages, and instructional technology, as well as clinical or extension appointments. The rise in new, nontenure-track, and part-time faculty demanded ever more attention to faculty needs as teachers and scholars (Finkelstein & Schuster, 2001).

Finally, greater competition, less funding, and the press to develop new revenues became pronounced as the 1990s ended. Particularly in public higher education, it became evident that major increases in funding would have to come from federal grants and the private sector. Both faculty and faculty developers were encouraged to do their part to raise money for their colleges and universities at a time when funding was becoming more difficult to secure and traditional sources of funding were declining.

With the new millennium faculty development has, we believe, entered a new age—the Age of the Network. Faculty, developers, and institutions alike are facing heightened expectations, and meeting these expectations will require a collaborative effort among all stakeholders in higher education. The roles of full-time tenure-track faculty are expanding and the variety of faculty appointments is increasing, as is the pressure on faculty to perform well in all roles. Institutional environments are changing both externally and internally; issues of funding and accountability can be expected to remain at the fore throughout the coming years. How faculty development can best grow and change to meet the needs of faculty and their institutions is the subject of this book. The number of developers is increasing, and research on faculty development continues to expand as well. In addition to the study on which this book is based, several other more recent studies are highlighted in the last section of this chapter. These projects, as well as the data reported in the subsequent chapters of this book, point to the variety of ways in which faculty developers and teaching and learning centers are being called on to help faculty members fulfill their many responsibilities.

Professional Organization and Recognition

As faculty development began to expand its goals and establish formal programs, it also took on a professional identity. Two national conferences were held in the early 1970s for practitioners and experts in the field, one at Kansas State University and the other at the University of Massachusetts Amherst (Blackburn, 1980). These early gatherings signaled a growing interest in faculty development as an area for study and professional focus. In 1974, the Professional and Organizational Development Network in Higher Education (POD Network) was formed. From its outset, the POD Network's purpose has been to support improvement in higher education through faculty, instructional, and organizational development activities. The POD Network has more than 1400 members—faculty and graduate student developers, faculty members, administrators, consultants, and others. It provides support and services for its members through publications and resources, grants and awards, conferences, consulting, and networking (http://www.podnetwork.org).

Three years later, in 1977, the National Council for Staff, Program, and Organizational Development (NCSPOD) was formed to provide support for community college faculty developers. Since its inception, NCSPOD has sponsored an annual conference on the "nuts and bolts" of practical solutions to development problems. Like POD, the goal of NCSPOD is to support its members via an annual conference, publications, retreats, and awards (http://www.ncspod.org).

At around the same time, a desire for a more formal structure for faculty development in Canada rose to the top of the agenda of a group of faculty development professionals. Developers from the Universities of Guelph, McMaster, Waterloo, and Western Ontario had met informally for several years to discuss teaching and learning issues. In 1981, they founded the Society for Teaching and Learning in Higher Education (STLHE) to bring together and support those individuals who were interested in the improvement of teaching and learning in higher education in Canada. STLHE sponsors an annual conference, a series of workshops and special interest groups, an electronic forum, 3M Teaching Fellowships, and a range of publications, including a newsletter (http://www.mcmaster.ca/stlhe).

During the 1980s faculty development solidified its professional base and expanded its activities. The 1990s saw a spike in interest among higher education associations and foundations in establishing programs that support the teaching roles of faculty, or faculty development. Sometimes they joined forces with centers for teaching and learning, such as in the Carnegie Academy for the Scholarship of Teaching and Learning, and sometimes they launched their own initiatives. For example, the American Association for Higher Education (AAHE), the American Association of Colleges and Universities, the American Council on Education (ACE), the Carnegie Academy for the Advancement of Teaching, the Council of Graduate Schools, the National Science Foundation, and the Woodrow Wilson Foundation have tackled issues related to faculty roles and rewards, the scholarship of teaching and learning, the preparation of graduate students and new faculty, diversity, technology, active learning, and assessment.

Similarly, the role of professional associations such as the American Historical Association and the American Assembly of Collegiate Schools of Business in supporting effective teaching and student learning increased during the 1990s. Work began at the level of academic disciplines to reconsider definitions of scholarly, creative, and intellectual contributions in order to further important work such as the development of courses and curricula, instructional software, and textbooks (Diamond & Adam, 1993).

The recognition of faculty development as a key to educational excellence was further strengthened by the Theodore M. Hesburgh Award, inaugurated in 1993. This award, sponsored by the Teachers Insurance and Annuity Association–College Retirement Equities Fund, recognizes exceptional faculty development programs that enhance undergraduate teaching and learning. The Hesburgh Award has brought national visibility to meritorious faculty development programs at a range of institutions and has encouraged programs to prove their success and impact through evidence of systemic change in teaching effectiveness and sustained faculty commitment, hard data objectively documenting improvements in teaching and learning outcomes, and results showing the program's impact on the academic community.

Finally, the 1990s marked the globalization of faculty development with the creation of several international faculty development organizations. Both the Staff and Educational Development Association (SEDA) and the International Consortium for Educational Development (ICED) were founded in England in 1993. SEDA's mission is to encourage the improvement of all aspects of learning and teaching in higher education through staff development. ICED was established to promote educational or academic development in higher education worldwide. Both organizations sponsor national and international conferences, publications, and networks. SEDA's specific aims and activities can be found at http://www.seda.ac.uk; ICED's services are detailed at a web site hosted by the University of Western Australia at http://www.osds.uwa.edu.au/about/activities/hosted_sites/iced.

In 1999 the Institute for Learning and Teaching in Higher Education (ILTHE) was launched in the United Kingdom and then transferred into a new Higher Education Academy (HEA) in 2004. Unlike the nonprofit faculty development associations typical in the United States, HEA receives direct funding from the Higher Education Funding Councils and the government. It serves as the authoritative national voice on teaching and learning issues and is designed to promote the professional development of staff through a range of services, to support the enhancement work of universities and colleges, and to stimulate and carry out research into learning and teaching. HEA news, events, publications and resources can be found on their website at http://www.heacacademy.ac.uk.

Goals

The general goals of faculty development have shifted considerably over the last five decades. In the Age of the Scholar, the emphasis on research as the central professional endeavor of academic life meant that the definition and purpose of faculty development was fairly narrow—to provide opportunities for improvement and advancement in scholarship. Eble and McKeachie (1985), Rice (1996), and others noted that academics long tended to be professionals in their discipline but not necessarily professionals in teaching. Hence the key goal of professional development was to help faculty maintain currency in their disciplines and to enhance their content expertise, a goal tied to the dominant belief system about content mastery as the means for development. Tiberius (2002) characterized this belief system as one in which little could be done to improve the teaching of professors: "Teachers were expected to be the masters of their specialty and needed not be a master of teaching" (p. 22).

The emergence of faculty development programs during the Age of the Teacher reflected a realization that faculty should not only be better prepared in their disciplines, but also better able to teach. Thus the goals of improving educational quality and of sustaining the vitality of faculty members as scholars expanded to emphasize the improvement of faculty as teachers. While the faculty member as teacher was a dominant consideration of many programs, some explored other approaches such as instructional development, focused on courses and curriculum, and organizational development, focused on institutional structure and process (Diamond, 2002).

Gaff and Simpson (1994) argue that the 1980s were characterized by centers that "aimed more at meeting the multidimensional and ever-changing needs of the total faculty" rather than earlier centers that tended to "reflect a singularity of purpose" (p. 170). Indeed, Eble and McKeachie (1985) found an amazing diversity of 37 different types of faculty development programs proposed and conducted by a range of institutions supported by the Bush Foundation. If measured by participation, activities such as teaching and learning workshops and seminars were greeted with more enthusiasm than in the 1970s. During the Age of the Developer, the faculty development movement also broadened its scope to include programs responding to the career span of academic life (e.g., mid-career renewal, retirement planning programs, career counseling, and wellness programs). As Lewis (1998) notes, "faculty development moved into more holistic development activities" (p. 29). Regardless of purpose, faculty development programs were increasingly supported by institutional as well as foundation funds, received much stronger support for instruction from central administration, and were guided by the needs of faculty rather than those of a president or provost (Gaff & Simpson, 1994).

During the 1990s, the number of faculty development centers continued to grow, not only at research universities, but also at comprehensive campuses, small liberal arts colleges, and community colleges. Many centers continued to focus on teaching and learning goals and agendas—assisting instructors in understanding underlying theories of teaching and learning and in expanding their repertoire of skills and strategies in order to adapt to the educational needs of students. At the same time, the goals and priorities of centers in the 1990s reflected the new developments, fast-moving fields, and the complex, ever-changing dynamics of college teaching in the Age of the Learner. Faculty development programs were asked to anticipate and provide support for new priorities driven by increasing opportunities and challenges, such as technology, multiculturalism, and assessment. In addition, faculty development centers, national-level foundations, disciplinary organizations, and other higher education associations all encouraged a focus on rewarding good teaching and promoting best practices. These goals will continue in the Age of the Network, and how best to prioritize them will be one of the major challenges of the new century.

Practices

During the Age of the Scholar, both institutions and foundations supported the press for research and scholarly capability as the keys to professionalism and the belief in content mastery as the key to teaching. Faculty development was individual development as well. Faculty were given funding for such activities as sabbatical leaves, attending the meetings of professional associations, and completing advanced degrees. They were given paid leaves of absence for advanced study and load adjustments for research and writing. Faculty themselves perceived such conventional support for scholarship as the best means of furthering their professional development (Eble & McKeachie, 1985). One major exception was the Associates Program, established by the Danforth Foundation in 1941. It sought to improve the quality of human relations in colleges and universities by recognizing talented teachers and their spouses through grants to support individual educational projects (Mathis, 1982).

The 1970s offered a broader range of suggested activities for faculty development work, guided by the seminal frameworks outlined by Bergquist and Phillips (1975) and Gaff (1975). Bergquist and Phillips posited that effective faculty development must become an interactive process along three dimensions: organizational, instructional, and personal. *Organizational development* includes programs that create an effective institutional environment for teaching and learning, with such activities as administrative development for chairs, deans, and other academic leaders, and the establishment of policies that incorporate the evaluation and recognition of teaching into the reward structure. *Instructional development* is focused on the process of education and includes evaluating course organization, presentation skills, and effectiveness through such means as class visits, videotaping, and student feedback. Programs might address the identification of course goals and teaching methods, broader curriculum development, and media design components. *Personal development* includes programs to promote personal growth, life planning, and interpersonal skills.

Gaff's model (1975), based on an analysis of about 200 institutions, was similar, emphasizing *faculty development*, focused on the improvement of classroom teaching and learning over the career span; *instructional development*, focused on the design of courses; and *organizational development*, focused on the institutional environment that creates the context for faculty work. These models and others (Toombs, 1975) initiated a major paradigm shift to a more multifaceted view of faculty development. But while Gaff observed that the most successful programs needed to include elements of all three approaches in some kind of comprehensive plan, the agenda of many programs in the Age of the Teacher placed a primary emphasis on the improvement of teaching through whatever institutional strengths and resources—staffing, budget, programs—were available. Improving teaching was perhaps perceived as an easier starting point than changing an institutional environment.

While individual consultations, workshops, and grants remained key services during the Age of the Developer, some teaching and learning centers or programs also began to bring groups of faculty together to work on achieving common goals for instructional development and curricular change within and across disciplines. A specific faculty development program that was highly successful in creating and sustaining intensive, collaborative teaching and learning forums was the Lilly Teaching Fellows Program, sponsored by the Lilly Endowment. This program encouraged cohorts of early career faculty in research-intensive institutions to work together and with mentors over an academic year to share ideas on teaching and offer one another collegial support, a model sustained to this day (Austin, 1992; Cox, 1995; Cox & Richlin, 2004; Simpson & Jackson, 1990; Sorcinelli & Austin, 1992).

Another impetus for collaborative ventures was the series of academic challenges that arose around the curriculum—challenges that could not be addressed by individual faculty members. These included improving general education, strengthening and assessing academic majors, attending to issues of gender, race, and class, and enhancing learning skills, such as writing and critical thinking, across the curriculum (Gaff & Simpson, 1994). Indeed, teaching and learning communities like the Lilly Teaching Fellowship were expanded throughout the 1980s and 1990s to tackle issues such as diversity, technology, assessment, and general education (Cox, 2001; Ouellett & Sorcinelli, 1995; Shih & Sorcinelli, 2000). Writing across the curriculum, course development, and curricular change projects were highlighted in the Bush Foundation study as particularly effective, not only in terms of helping faculty to develop particular skills such as establishing course goals and teaching writing, but also in facilitating interaction and cooperation across disciplinary boundaries (Eble & McKeachie, 1985). As Gaff and Simpson (1994) concluded, "For each of these agendas, faculty development became the means to the end of curriculum change. Faculty development for curriculum change required groups of faculty to work together to see their own individual interest within the context of the department or institution" (p. 170).

The 1990s pressed both instructors and faculty developers to learn an incredible range of new skills for facilitating teaching and student learning, thus expanding the demands on a number of teaching and learning centers. Perhaps the fastest-moving change in the Age of the Learner was in instructional technology. Faculty moved from using overheads and VCRs to using PowerPoint, streaming video, web-based course management systems such as WebCT and Blackboard, and distance-learning systems. Centers were increasingly called upon to support these instructional tools through teaching technology staff and services (Zhu & Kaplan, 2002).

Scholarly research began to document the value of student diversity to individual students, institutions, and society (Hurtado, 1996; Regents of the University of Michigan 1997–2005) and, in response, some teaching and learning centers made considerable efforts to infuse diversity awareness into their orientations, workshops, publications, and other teaching development activities (Cook & Sorcinelli, 1999). Furthermore, as the value of learner-centered teaching (Barr & Tagg, 1995) was increasingly emphasized, faculty developers played a key role in supporting faculty efforts to explore the effective use of "traditional" active-learning activities such reading, writing, and listening, as well as newer cooperative, collaborative, problem-based, and inquiry-based learning strategies (McKeachie, 2002).

Interest in the assessment of student learning filtered down from institutional approaches in the 1980s (Ewell, 1985) to classroom and course-based assessment in the 1990s (Angelo & Cross, 1993;

Walvoord & Anderson, 1998). Here again, teaching and learning centers were instrumental in helping faculty systematically collect and analyze information to assess student learning and their teaching. The boundaries between teaching development and evaluation became more fluid, with collaborations among centers for teaching and learning and offices of assessment more common (Stassen & Sorcinelli, 2001).

In a related vein, Ernest Boyer's book *Scholarship Reconsidered* (1990) stimulated discussion throughout higher education about the nature of scholarship. Boyer and his colleague, Gene Rice, suggested that teachers who devise better ways to help students learn, or who do research on teaching and student learning, are engaged in scholarly work. The outgrowth of this notion was a Scholarship of Teaching and Learning (SOTL) movement initiated through the Carnegie Foundation for the Advancement of Teaching and AAHE. Now, a national network of institutions participate in SOTL. It has engaged colleges, universities, and teaching and learning centers in supporting classroom research, peer review of teaching, the use of course and teaching portfolios, and publications presenting the scholarship of teaching and learning (Hutchings, 2000).

Finally, the continued need to support faculty across the career span was recognized and responded to, both inside and outside of teaching and learning centers. Widespread criticism of the underpreparation of graduate students for teaching careers and broader faculty roles led to new initiatives such as training programs for teaching assistants (Lambert & Tice, 1993), Preparing Future Faculty initiatives (Gaff, Pruitt-Logan, Weibel, & Associates, 2000; Pruitt-Logan & Gaff, 2004), Re-envisioning the Ph.D. (Nyquist, Woodford, & Rogers, 2004), the Carnegie Initiative on the Doctorate (Hutchings & Clarke, 2004), and the Toward the Responsive Ph.D. Initiative (Weisbuch, 2004). In *Paths to the Professoriate,* Wulff and Austin (2004) offer a compendium of recent research and initiatives. In addition, there were more programs and practices to support new and early career faculty, such as new faculty orientations, tenure preparation seminars, and mentoring programs (Rice, Sorcinelli, & Austin, 2000; Sorcinelli, 2000). And while mid-career and senior faculty traditionally received less support than newcomers, some teaching and learning centers created faculty development programs for senior faculty (Cox, 2001; Shih & Sorcinelli, 2000; Stassen & Sorcinelli, 2001) and tenured faculty undergoing post-tenure review (e.g., http://www.umass.edu/cft/teaching_development.htm).

Our review of faculty development program web sites at the cusp of the Age of the Network illuminated the result of these increasing demands on the teaching and learning front. We found that even modest-sized faculty development programs often offer a "cafeteria" of services, and, as a backdrop to our findings, it seems useful to provide a brief review of what services are typically offered. Prior studies of the feld have reported a fair degree of consistency in the kinds of resources offered by faculty development programs (Centra, 1976; Erickson, 1986). More recent surveys (Gullatt & Weaver, 1997; Wright, 2002) have continued to find similar services regardless of the size or mission of the institution. These services include:

- *Consultations for individual instructors.* The consultation process may include several phases: clarification of instructional goals; assessment of teaching (e.g., review of course materials, feedback from students, classroom observation, videotaping); analysis of information gathered; establishment of improvement efforts; and review of progress. Consultants often suggest classroom assessment techniques and mid-semester student feedback so that instructors can better understand the learning process and the impact of their teaching on students.
- *University-wide orientations.* Many centers offer orientation programs for new faculty and, separately, for new teaching assistants, both domestic and international. They may include keynote speakers, workshops with tips on "getting started" in teaching, graduate school, and faculty careers. Experienced teaching assistants and faculty often lead training workshops and share their approaches to teaching.
- *University-wide workshops.* Centers and programs also present, on an ongoing basis, a variety of workshops for full-time faculty, teaching assistants, and/or part-time faculty. Subject matter ranges from interactive lecturing to building web pages to infusing multiculturalism into a course and the teaching of it. Workshop leaders vary from in-house and campus facilitators

to external experts. Individual academic departments and schools may request customized programs to address instructional questions or problems identified by the unit.

- *Intensive programs.* Some programs offer intensive seminars (from a weeklong institute to yearlong learning communities) for faculty at different career stages or those interested in a particular teaching and learning topic. Signature aspects of yearlong seminars (e.g., the Lilly Teaching Fellowship) include an immersion retreat at the outset, a monthly seminar on teaching and learning, individual consultations, mentoring, and a teaching development project. Other intensive programs include teaching and learning institutes, faculty learning communities, book clubs, special-interest communities, and regular meetings of groups in a breakfast or luncheon format.
- *Grants and awards for individuals and departments.* Programs often offer grant competitions to encourage exploration of new and improved instructional approaches, for conference presentations of successful teaching methods, or for reporting on research findings. Grant amounts range widely depending on available resources. Some programs select faculty associates who receive funding to enrich the activities offered by the center. Programs may also engage in the selection process for campus teaching awards and in the preparation of nominees for external awards such as the Hesburgh Award, the U.S. Professor of the Year Award, or the Robert Foster Cherry Award for Great Teaching.
- *Resources and publications.* Faculty development programs often have a resource room that offers books, videotapes, CD-ROMs, and other instructional materials. Many centers offer on their web sites a range of resources that can be viewed or downloaded, including handbooks, annotated bibliographies, articles, teaching tips, newsletters, and links to other web-based resources.
- *Other services.* Some programs offer specialized services related to instruction, such as student evaluation of teaching instruments, computerized examination and test scoring, programs to assess student learning outcomes, resources in instructional technology, classroom/audio-visual, and distance-learning services.

These are the basic practice models that faculty developers will build upon in the coming years.

Structures

The structured faculty development activities, programs, and policies of the 1950s and 1960s were largely focused on improving scholarly and creative performance. Structures tended to be informal and uncoordinated—an academic chair, dean, or other campus administrator provided the necessary funding for development. At the end of the 1960s, the Project to Improve College Teaching, supported by the American Association of University Professors and ACE, sponsored a series of conferences that included faculty members at some 150 colleges and universities throughout the United States. A key goal of the project was to identify the extent of institutional support for faculty development in teaching. Findings indicated that about 60% of faculty respondents reported specific institutional support for research and only about 10% reported specific support for teaching (Eble, 1972). Thus Eble's study confirmed that faculty development in the Age of the Scholar was focused on research rather than on the improvement of teaching.

A few faculty development units were introduced in the United States during this time. The first was the Center for Research on Learning and Teaching at the University of Michigan, which opened its doors in 1962. The Clinic to Improve University Teaching at the University of Massachusetts Amherst was established soon thereafter. Directors of early units were often outstanding teachers who came out of academic departments (e.g., English, history, psychology) or faculty members with research interests in the teaching and learning process (e.g., psychology, education). These units concentrated primarily on assisting faculty in solving instructional problems or in generating and disseminating research knowledge and information about teaching and learning (Tiberius, 2002).

At the same time that authors and researchers were conceptualizing models for faculty development, campuses were already moving toward practice. Beginning in the 1970s, colleges and universities started to formalize faculty development programs, and centers for teaching and learning began to open on campuses around the country. A series of competitive grant programs for improving teaching fueled their growth (Gaff & Simpson, 1994). Credit is due to private foundations and federally funded agencies, such as the Danforth, W. K. Kellogg, Andrew Mellon, Exxon Education, and National Science Foundations, the Lilly Endowment, the National Endowment for the Humanities, and the Fund for the Improvement of Postsecondary Education, for providing funds for early innovations in teaching and learning.

As the Age of the Developer began, institutional commitment and resources increased, leading to a new emphasis on organizational issues: establishing faculty development priorities, obtaining a wider range of staff expertise, deciding the location of the office—both physically and within the organizational hierarchy—and locating sources of funding (Alstete, 2000). Centers for teaching and learning were often uncoupled from the unit that handled student evaluations of teaching. In fact, many centers developed or confirmed guiding principles that made sure the program was voluntary, confidential, and developmental rather than evaluative, and built a firewall between teaching development work and personnel decision-making processes (Sorcinelli, 2002). At the same time, centers for teaching and learning often collaborated with undergraduate deans, graduate deans, and writing program directors on faculty development initiatives, such as teaching assistant training, or curricular initiatives, such as general education, writing across the curriculum and freshman seminars.

At the end of the 1980s, faculty developers, as well as faculty and administrators interested in promoting and sustaining faculty development programs in their institutions, were further guided by the POD Network, which developed *A Handbook for New Practitioners* (Wadsworth, 1988). This book served as a fundamental resource for both new and seasoned faculty developers and offered practical information on faculty development topics such as setting up a faculty development program, assessing teaching practices, offering a range of programs and services, and reaching specific audiences. In 2002, Gillespie, Hilsen, and Wadsworth edited a second book, *A Guide to Faculty Development*, to provide more up-to-date advice, examples, and resources for developers and their institutions.

The 1990s saw continued growth in faculty development programs, despite the much publicized closing of a prominent teaching and learning center at a large research university. Critical to the success of many centers was a high-quality staff of instructional developers who may or may not have come from faculty ranks but typically had Ph.D.s in a variety of fields, college teaching experience, and experience working with colleagues on teaching improvements. Some had specialized expertise in instructional technology, evaluation research, course and program assessment, and multicultural education to promote inclusivity. The community of developers in the POD Network became increasingly well connected through their annual meeting, several journals and newsletters, and an active listserv. This network of professionals expanded annually as more new teaching centers were established (Cook & Sorcinelli, 2002). Many centers continued to collaborate with other campus offices (e.g., graduate school, academic computing, library, community service-learning) on institutional priorities, but still relied on institutional funds and private foundations to support their work.

Since their inception, programs for faculty development have shared a common theme: improving the quality of education by working with faculty. There has, however, been considerable variety in program types, depending on institutional leadership, community, faculty, age and historical evolution, and available resources (Wright, 2002). Structural variations among programs occur in how they are organized and where they are located in the institution. The current range of structures includes:

- A *centralized unit* with dedicated staff that is budgeted by the institution to offer a range of faculty development programs. It serves the entire institution, or a substantial segment of it, in a variety of ways.
- An office that serves as a *clearinghouse* for programs and offerings that are sponsored across the institution, but offers few programs itself.
- A *committee* charged with supporting faculty development, usually made up of unpaid volunteer faculty who oversee faculty development offerings.

- *Single individual programs* often run by an administrator responsible for faculty matters or a faculty member with a part-time assignment for development activities.
- *Other programs* such as multicampus, cooperative programs, and special-purpose centers.

Other structural variations can he found in Wright (2002) and at the POD web site (http://www.podnetwork.org). Which type of program will most effectively serve a given institution will remain an important question for developers in the coming years.

Studies

Early appraisals of the effectiveness of faculty development focused primarily on traditional measures of enhanced or renewed scholarly productivity: a completed degree, an increase in scholarly presentations, books, or articles, or the winning of external grants or fellowships. While benefits might accrue to students in terms of their learning or to broader institutional goals such as development of curriculum in the major or student advising, such benefits were assumed rather than measured.

The Project on College Teaching, directed by Kenneth Eble (1972), produced one of the first reports on faculty development efforts. The project reported on career development in college teaching and on the evaluation and recognition of good teaching. Eble concluded that policies and practices in many institutions did not encourage faculty members to improve teaching and argued that paying attention to teaching played a role in institutional vitality and quality. This early study provided a stimulus for interest in faculty development activities to improve teaching and a prototype for reports about the results of grants given for faculty development.

The first large-scale study of faculty development was conducted by Centra in 1976, in a survey to which 756 U.S. colleges and universities responded. His goals were to identify faculty development activities, to evaluate their effectiveness, to determine funding sources, and to identify various organizational structures for faculty development programs. More than 40% of the institutions had a unit or a person that coordinated the faculty or instructional development activities on their campus. The majority of units had one full- or part-time person who served as director or coordinator. Interestingly, 25% of institutions were part of a consortium or regional group (e.g., Great Lakes Colleges Consortium) that concentrated on faculty development. Cooperative arrangements were found most often in four-year liberal arts colleges, enabling such schools to share expertise and activities at lower cost to each institution.

Perhaps the most valuable aspect of the study was the identification of groups of services and activities that institutions used and considered particularly effective in promoting faculty development. These included traditional practices (e.g., sabbaticals, leaves, summer grants), instructional assistance (e.g., use of teaching consultants to assist individual faculty in developing teaching skills), workshops (e.g., on specific instructional or advising strategies), grants and travel funds, and assessment techniques (e.g., ratings of instruction by students). In terms of measuring the outcomes of faculty development programs, Centra found that only 14% of faculty development programs were evaluated, with an additional 33% reporting some partial evaluation. Suggested reasons for not documenting faculty development outcomes included limitations in staff, funding, and knowledge of assessment practices (Centra, 1976).

The 1970s also provided a closer look at faculty development in community colleges and liberal arts colleges. At community colleges, faculty renewal programs looked much like the required, in-service training conducted by public school systems (Lewis, 1998). A 1970 survey by the American Association of Junior Colleges indicated that most faculty development programs involved workshops and short courses on education, curriculum, and learning theories (O'Banion, 1972).

The 1970s concluded with the first evaluation of faculty development programs at undergraduate liberal arts institutions, funded by the Association of American Colleges and the Andrew Mellon Foundation (Nelsen & Siegel, 1980). The project directors visited 20 colleges, and interviewers engaged more than 500 faculty, administrators, and students about a wide range of faculty development activities and their impact. The results of the evaluation suggested that the most frequent and successful activities, as viewed by liberal arts college participants, involved individual professional development options such as study leaves and support for attendance at professional meetings. Projects that focused on discussions and innovations in the curriculum were also viewed quite favorably. Instructional development efforts, especially workshops, were greeted with less enthusiasm unless they were organized to provide specific, usable skills (e.g., lecturing skills, grading practices). Organizational development, with its focus on the institutional environment that creates the context for faculty work, was found to be the most neglected area of faculty development. Interestingly, effective management was identified as the tie that binds the most successful faculty development programs. Important components included the presence of a unit—a committee or group of administrators—with a clear charge and structure, some linkage of faculty development activities to the reward structure of the college, and flexibility in terms of supporting various approaches to faculty development.

The field of faculty development "spawned] a literature throughout the 1970s rich in diagnoses and prescriptions" (Schuster, Wheeler, & Associates, 1990, p. 3), but it was not until the 1980s that the literature was enriched with more evidence of the systematic evaluation of programs. In 1986, Erickson, on behalf of the POD Network, conducted a survey of faculty development practices, adapted from Centra's (1976) survey a decade earlier. Erickson received responses from some 630 faculty development coordinators, directors, committee chairs, and administrators. He found that "50% or more of our four-year colleges, universities and professional schools offer some formal faculty development, instructional development, or teaching improvement services" (p. 196), up from about 40% a decade earlier. A committee or an administrator—typically a dean whose primary responsibilities lay elsewhere—most often coordinated these activities. While documenting a steady growth in faculty development services, Erickson noted that only 14% of institutions had dedicated centers and another 14% had coordinators or directors of faculty development.

The survey also assessed availability of the following services: workshops and seminars; assessment practices; individual consultation; grants, leaves, and exchanges; and other practices. Erickson (1986), similar to Centra (1976), found that "traditional" practices like grants, awards, leaves, and exchanges were the most frequently offered services. Individual consultation services were available at the fewest numbers of institutions. Not surprisingly, larger institutions offered a greater variety of services than smaller ones. He also discovered that 95% of the campuses made available student ratings of instruction, although less than half provided faculty with individual help from consultants trained to interpret such ratings.

During this decade, there were several other key scholarly studies that either evaluated faculty development programs or investigated the connections among faculty development, faculty career stages, and institutional missions. For example, Baldwin and Blackburn (1981) researched the distinguishing characteristics of faculty members at successive ages and in different career stages and advocated mapping faculty development activities with career stages. Clark, Corcoran, and Lewis's (1986) study of faculty vitality proposed an approach to faculty development that emphasized linking faculty work to institutional missions and needs.

Eble and McKeachie (1985) analyzed a wide variety of faculty development programs in 24 different institutions—public and private, small liberal arts colleges to research universities—supported by the Bush Foundation. Their overall message was positive. They found that while traditional practices such as leaves and grants were still valued by faculty, instructional development activities and projects involving course development and curricular change were both popular and highly effective. They also argued that faculty development programs "were rallying points for renewed interest in teaching during a time of considerable need at virtually all of the participating institutions" (p. 158) and could make a difference in faculty vitality. Finally, they identified key factors influencing faculty development program success, including faculty ownership, administrative support, use of local expertise, sustained or follow-up activities, and programs involving faculty members working together to achieve common objectives.

Two works reviewed the literature on faculty development, providing easily accessible sources of information for researchers and practitioners. Bland and Schmitz (1988) conducted a systematic analysis of faculty development literature from 1965 to 1985. They concluded that the literature base had grown considerably in the early 1980s, suggesting increased interest in the field. They also found that strategies and recommendations for faculty development had become more multidimensional—drawn from individual, departmental, and institutional perspectives. Menges and Mathis (1988) developed a comprehensive guide to more than 600 books and articles on teaching, learning, curriculum, and faculty development in colleges and universities. The authors offered a critical evaluation of the most significant theory and research on these four essential topics and illuminated the role each has had in shaping and advancing theory and practice in higher education.

Alstete (2000) conducted a search of faculty development literature from 1989–1997, which showed an initial increase in the early 1990s and a slightly upward trend in the amount of faculty development literature as the decade progressed. He concluded that while interest in and descriptive literature about how institutions have engaged in effective faculty development programs have grown, there is more work to he done to build and articulate "a clearly defined supporting theory underlying faculty development" (p. 28).

During the 1990s, there were no large-scale studies of the field to follow up the research of Centra (1976) and Erickson (1986). There were, however, a number of studies and reviews that explored various aspects of faculty development practices. Hellyer and Boschmann (1993) reviewed information on faculty development programs gathered from 94 institutions of higher education, drawn in part from a description of programs compiled by members of the POD Network. Their goal was to identify common practices. As in earlier studies, the authors found great variance in the depth and breadth of programs. The authors reported that for the most part the creation of faculty development centers had been relatively recent. While one program began in the 1940s and a few in the 1960s, 50% of the institutions surveyed started their programs in the 1980s. By far the most common faculty development practices were workshops and discussions (93%). Other activities included individual consultations (63%), new faculty orientations and teaching assistant training (60%), research on teaching (51%), and teaching grants (34%). The authors concluded from the materials they surveyed that faculty strongly support the existence of faculty development offices.

Wright and O'Neil (1995) surveyed an international community of faculty developers in Canada, the United States, the United Kingdom, and Australasia. Data from 331 respondents suggested "what works" within the wide range of practices for the support of teaching and learning. Findings pointed to the critical role of academic deans and department chairs, of employment practices that recognize and reward good teaching, and of institutionalized teaching centers that offer development opportunities such as mentoring programs for new teachers, grants, and workshops.

Crawley (1995) surveyed 104 research universities to learn about faculty development programs available to senior faculty. The findings revealed a high level of support for traditional approaches to faculty development (e.g., sabbaticals, unpaid leaves, grants), but suggested that faculty development approaches that expanded employment options or created new roles and responsibilities for senior faculty were more limited.

Chism and Szabo (1996) surveyed a random sample of 100 institutions drawn from the POD Network to determine who used faculty development services. In part, the study was a response to the common perception that "good" teachers use faculty development services, while "bad" teachers eschew them (Angelo & Cross, 1993; Boice, 1984; Centra, 1976). Again, because faculty development programs varied so greatly in mission, composition of potential clients, and range of services offered, it was difficult for the authors to aggregate data and provide simple answers on the extent of faculty use. They found, however, that most faculty development programs kept records on who used what services. For the 70% of programs with data on usage, the survey determined that the average program reached 82% of users through publications, 47% through events, 11% through consultation, and 8% through mentoring programs. Overall, use of services was fairly distributed across faculty ranks, with assistant professors accounting for a somewhat higher percentage of use. Females used faculty development services at somewhat higher rates than males, and only slight differences among the disciplines were reported. The authors also found "some support for the claim that faculty are motivated both by interest in teaching and by difficulties" (p. 126). Murray (2002) reviewed faculty development literature and practices in community colleges, turning up few national or regional studies and finding some serious methodological questions in many of the single-institution studies. Still, some consistent themes emerged from the literature. In many community colleges, faculty development programs lacked goals—especially goals tied to the college's mission. Few programs attempted to evaluate their work, and faculty participation was low. Successful programs tended to have conditions that mirrored the results of earlier researchers and practitioners (Eble & McKeachie, 1985; Sorcinelli, 2002): administrative support that encourages faculty development; a formal, structured, goal-directed program; connections between faculty development and the reward structure; faculty ownership; and collegial support for investment in teaching. These principles of good practice in faculty development seem to have held true across a range of institutions and throughout the decades.

Most recently, in addition to the study that forms the basis of this book, two electronic surveys of POD Network members have been conducted. One surveyed 27 previous presidents of the POD Network and opinion leaders in higher education (Sell, 2002) and the other surveyed 109 directors of teaching and learning centers (Frantz, Beebe, Horvath, Canales, & Swee, 2005). Key themes in these studies include accountability practices of faculty development centers, best practices, resources and services provided by teaching and learning centers, and future strategies for faculty development.

Conclusion

The history of faculty development, then, is one of both challenge and opportunity. Since its inception, faculty development has proven its capacity to anticipate and respond to changes and to act as a lever of change in higher education. It has evolved from individual to collective development, from singular to multidimensional purposes, from largely uncoordinated activities to centralized units, from "soft" funding to foundation, association, government, and institutional support, and from a small network of developers in the United States to a global faculty development profession. Its measurable impact has increased along with these changes.

We believe that in the Age of the Network the changes facing institutions will continue to accelerate. Colleges and universities committed to high productivity and quality will be well advised to situate faculty development at the center of their institutional planning. The future of faculty development may depend on our collective ability to fashion guiding principles and practices for the field that acknowledge new responsibilities while sustaining core values, and to articulate their significance to higher education. The next three chapters illustrate some of the opportunities and challenges currently engaging faculty developers, faculty members, and their institutions. What goals and practices will best serve faculty developers in the coming years is the subject of last three chapters of this book.

Chapter highlights

- In the Age of the Scholar (1950s and early 1960s) the term *faculty development* referred primarily to practices for improving scholarly competence. Few colleges and universities had formal programs and there were few studies of faculty development efforts.
- In the Age of the Teacher (mid 1960s through 1970s), the field expanded to include faculty, instructional, and organizational development, but primarily focused attention on improving teaching. Foundation support spurred campuses to create faculty development programs. Faculty development secured a professional identity through the founding of two associations in the United States.
- In the Age of the Developer (1980s), faculty development broadened to address curricular issues, faculty needs at different career stages, and collective as well as individual faculty growth. Programs were increasingly supported by institutional and external funds, creating heightened interest in measuring the outcomes of teaching and faculty development efforts. Canada created its own society for teaching, learning, and faculty development.
- In the Age of the Learner (1990s) the number of teaching and learning centers continued to increase; the number of issues, their level of complexity, and the scope of activities expanded.

Multiple venues for faculty development proposals and recognition were created within educational associations, foundations, professional societies, and international consortia.

- In the current Age of the Network, faculty development programs continue to grow in breadth and use. Developers will be called upon to preserve, clarify, and enhance the purposes of faculty development, and to network with faculty and institutional leaders to respond to institutional problems and propose constructive solutions as we meet the challenges of the new century.

Teaching to Improve Learning

K. Patricia Cross

University of California, Berkeley

Most of us have been in classrooms a good share of our lives, both as students and teachers. I figure that by the time we finish our doctorates, we have had roughly 90 different teachers, an opportunity to observe them for thousands of hours and to make some assessment of the impact of their teaching on at least our own learning, and usually plenty of hearsay about their impact on the learning of our classmates. That database would be an incredible luxury to any educational researcher. To my knowledge, not one of my colleagues doing research on teaching has ever received a grant that would permit such close observation of such a wide variety of teachers over such a long period of time. Yet despite extensive opportunities to observe teaching and learning, most of us embark upon our teaching careers knowing very little about teaching and learning.

It occurred to me as I walked home in the dark the other night that I look at the heavens every night, or at least am aware of—and sometimes in awe of—stars, moon, and changing patterns in the sky. Yet I know almost nothing about astronomy. I am a naive observer of the heavens, just as most of us are naive observers of teaching. Were I a trained observer or an astronomer, I would find things of fascination that the untrained eye fails to see. I would know what to look for, and I would grow in understanding and knowledge. My walk home would do more than take me to my destination. It would be a new experience each evening, a source of energy, an opportunity for growth.

The analogy could be carried to listening to a symphony orchestra or watching the ocean. Most of us appreciate a good symphony when we hear one, but the trained musician hears the nuances that distinguish outstanding performance from the average and takes delight in hearing the subtleties of subthemes and supporting chords. The trained musician has a sophisticated ear that hears things the rest of us don't hear and permits growth in ability to appreciate the fine tuning that makes for excellence. Similarly, when I look at the ocean, I see tides, waves, changing color, and certainly anything that moves, such as a boat or a seal. But I don't see the infinite complexity that is apparent to the oceanographer, nor do I take delight in learning and constantly adding to my knowledge and appreciation. I am a naive observer, even if on occasion a delighted one.

Most of us are naive observers of teaching and naive practitioners of the art and science of teaching as well. We don't know enough about the intricate processes of teaching and learning to be able to learn from our constant exposure to the classroom. We see the big things. We can spot a dozing student, one lost in some other world, or an eager hand waver. We know some things that are not supposed to happen. We don't want embarrassing silences when we ask a question; certainly we don't want hostility or obvious inattention. If these things happen, we may actively seek to learn their causes. But we are not trained to observe the more subtle measures of learning.

This article is based on an address given at the First Annual Lilly Conference on College Teaching-West, March 17–19, 1989, University of California Conference Center, Lake Arrowhead, California.

Reprinted by permission from *Journal on Excellence in College Teaching*, vol. 1 (1990).

Indeed, we are not even trained to question our assumptions. We assume that what we say is heard accurately and retained by students, despite consistent evidence to the contrary. We assume that students can connect thoughts and write or communicate ideas and knowledge, and we are perpetually shocked at the consistency with which this turns out not to be true. But as naive observers, we don't question what we don't understand. Were we astronomers or oceanographers, we would pursue with great interest something that challenged our expectations or predictions. Are we curious about why students don't learn, why they come up with distorted ideas about what we thought was perfectly clear, why they fail to hear or follow the simplest directions? Well, maybe, fleetingly. But by and large, we don't set out to investigate these common departures from what we know should happen in class. We are soon on to other things, and the opportunity to learn from the experience is lost.

I must admit, of course, that even academics don't have to make everything into a learning experience. There are times when we want simply to relax without feeling an obligation to analyze, to understand, or to improve ourselves or others. I can probably afford to be a naive observer of the nighttime sky, despite my recognition that some knowledge of astronomy would almost certainly add to my enjoyment.

But the college classroom is not the place for relaxed naivete for either students or faculty. The experience would be far richer and more enjoyable if both teachers and students were more curious and more sophisticated about the effect of teaching on learning. But even more important, as educators, we have an obligation to understand the teaching/learning process well enough to improve it.

Teaching as art or science or voodoo is in an essentially primitive state of development. We are not standing on the shoulders of giants in advancing knowledge and improving practice with each generation of teachers. It is a fairly good guess that teachers coming out of graduate schools today are not teaching any better than those who graduated 50 years ago. That is not to say that their fields of study haven't made advances; it is simply to recognize that each young teacher starts from the beginning to learn how to teach. Education has become too important to human survival and progress to continue such an inefficient and ineffective approach to classroom instruction.

It is time to make college teaching a profession, one that grows and improves over the decades while offering the potential for continuous self-renewal for individual teachers. To do that, we will have to join knowledge of subject matter and knowledge of teaching. I think that union will have to come about in the graduate schools of this country. Graduate students preparing for life in academe will have to know their subject matter and how to teach it to undergraduates.

What I am suggesting is that training the next generation of teachers is primarily the responsibility of disciplinary specialists, in consultation with teaching and learning specialists. College teachers at every level need to know how to teach, not in an amateur way, in which some classes go well and others bomb, and we don't know why, or worse yet, in a way that leaves us uncertain whether our goals as teachers have been accomplished. We need to know how to teach in an expert way, with the ability to diagnose, analyze, evaluate, prescribe, and most important, improve the quality of teaching and learning in college classrooms.

The optimal mixture of teaching expertise and subject matter expertise will vary with the type of institution and level of instruction. Community college teachers need to be *experts* in teaching. Their teaching assignment is especially difficult, involving not only more students with learning problems and poor past histories of learning than any other segment of higher education, but also with unprecedented diversity in learning skills. It takes an expert to teach students ranging in reading ability from the 4th to the 16th grade level.

The teaching assignment of the graduate-level instructor is far easier. Students are more homogeneous in ability, and learning problems have been weeded out. But the complexity of subject matter has increased exponentially. These differences in emphases do not, however, excuse the community college teacher from keeping up with advances in the discipline or the graduate school instructor from developing expertise in teaching. Indeed, graduate teachers bear a huge responsibility for training the next generation of college teachers. Most of us teach as we were taught. Despite the fact that we are not very astute observers of the impact of teaching on our own learning, general patterns of classroom practices are picked up and perpetuated generation after generation without much question or evaluation of their effectiveness.

If we are serious about educational reform—and I think in statehouses and on most campuses, the desire to demonstrate improved student learning is sincere—then classroom teachers are going to have to play a more active role in assessing what students are learning. Teachers must use the results of that assessment to experiment with improving the learning of the students in their own classrooms.

Three years ago, I proposed in an address to the Annual Meeting of the American Association for Higher Education that it was time to take teaching seriously and that college teachers should become knowledgeable professionals in their chosen career of teaching. I suggested further that teachers should become Classroom Researchers, by which I mean careful and sophisticated observers of the process of teaching and learning as it takes place every day in their classrooms. Classrooms are invaluable laboratories in which to investigate the effect of teaching on learning. College teachers who know their disciplines and are charged with teaching them to others ought to be interested in determining how much of what they are teaching is learned by students, and they should be interested in experimenting to see if they can improve learning in their classrooms.

Classroom Research is different in concept, procedures, and purpose from educational research. I am using the word research in the simple dictionary definition of the term to mean, "careful, systematic, patient study and investigation . . ." The primary purpose of Classroom Research is to get feedback from students on what they are learning while the learning is in progress. It is not to seek generalizations about teaching and learning, but to answer the very specific question, What are my students learning in my classroom as a result of my instruction? Knowledge of sampling theory and the statistics of significant differences, the old standbys of social science research, are not required for Classroom Research, because classroom researchers are not trying to select a sample and generalize to the population at large. Although the results of Classroom Research will almost certainly enhance the knowledge of the instructor, they may or may not advance knowledge in general on contribute to learning theory; they may or may not be publishable; they may or may not utilize standard social science research techniques and designs.

Let me give an example of Classroom Research to make the concept concrete. One of our first activities in the Classroom Research Project was to develop some simple classroom assessment techniques that could be used by faculty members in any discipline to get feedback from students on what they were learning.

After a search of the literature and some modifications and inventions of our own, we came up with 30 classroom assessment techniques that we published in a handbook for faculty (Cross & Angelo, 1988). For example, one very simple classroom assessment technique is called "Minute Papers" and was developed by a physics professor at the University of California, Berkeley.

It was later revised and adapted for his purposes by a distinguished professor of statistics at Harvard (Wilson, 1986; Mosteller, 1989). A few minutes before the end of the class period, the instructor asks students to write the answers to two questions: (a) What was the most important thing you learned today?, and (b) What questions remain uppermost in your mind as we conclude this session?

I have used Minute Papers in my own graduate classes at Harvard and at Berkeley, and I must say that this quick and easy feedback device tells me more about my own teaching than anything I have ever used. It is more specific and timely than term papers, and it is more open-ended and subject to student selection of important points than a quiz or exam. An added advantage is that it forces students to think about the high points and to summarize and synthesize the day's lesson. Moreover, it implies that they should be actively thinking about new questions.

Minute Papers is an extremely simple classroom assessment technique. The 30 techniques that Tom Angelo and I have described in our handbook are generic, that is, they can be used to assess students' learning across a variety of disciplines. Assessment techniques in the handbook are organized into categories related to teaching goals. For example, a teacher might wish to assess critical thinking, or creativity, or students'awareness of themselves as learners. Or teachers might wish to get feedback about the effect of their teaching methods or assignments on students' learning.

The present handbook contains descriptions of feedback devices on topics such as these that are generic across the disciplines. But we are now in the process of preparing *Handbook II,* which will contain a second generation of classroom assessment techniques that are discipline-specific. We are working with college teachers in the San Francisco Bay Area to develop and field test in their classrooms assessment techniques appropriate to their disciplines.

In our experience so far, we have found it hard to get teachers to keep their questions for investigation simple. Many teachers initially propose studies patterned after the research they have seen or read about-experimental studies of the relative effectiveness of lecture versus discussion, for example, or an investigation into intellectual development, or studies of cognitive styles. The problem with this interpretation of Classroom Research is that most faculty lack the technical skills, time, and resources to conduct basic educational research and also the background that comes from extensive reading of the state of existing knowledge in the field. Thus, they are likely to reinvent the wheel and to face discouragement over their lack of technical and research skills in conducting credible social science research.

In making these observations, I do not intend to mystify research by contending that classroom teachers can't do it, or to discourage serious inquiry into learning issues that interest teachers. Some faculty are sufficiently interested in these broader questions about teaching and learning to inform themselves and to develop adequate skills for investigation. Indeed, some of our early participants in the Bay Area project have become sufficiently interested in learning that they are eager to equip themselves for investigation into more complex problems.

Our goal in Classroom Research, however, is not to *add* research projects to teaching loads, but to integrate research into everyday teaching. A well-designed Classroom Research project should teach as well as provide feedback about the effectiveness of that teaching. A study of critical thinking in the classroom, for example, might begin with the assignment of a task that requires critical thinking and permits systematic observations about how students approach the task and how well they perform. The Classroom Researcher would then experiment with modifications in the design of the task and its presentation, followed by an evaluation of the effectiveness of the changes.

Classroom Research is more a continuous, ongoing study of teaching and learning in the everyday classroom than a single investigation of a question, collection of data, and publication of the results. It is this ongoing, self-renewing feature that gives it its distinction as a faculty development activity capable of generating high interest and improved performance.

Now that you know roughly what Classroom Research is, I'd like to place it in the larger context of the educational reform movement of the 1980s. Nationally, we have attempted to use three levers to bring about improvements in the quality of undergraduate education. Those levers fall in the domains of politics, policy, and research.

The educational reform movement started in the *political arena* with the report of the Secretary of Education's National Commission on Excellence in Education (1983). The report, entitled *A Nation at Risk,* was a serious indictment of American education, making memorable such phrases as "the rising tide of mediocrity" and "unilateral educational disarmament." That report spawned statewide commissions and task forces in virtually every state in the union and eventually resulted in state-mandated assessments, with varying degrees of freedom for colleges to design their own institutional assessments.

One wing of the assessment movement is primarily interested in "assessment for accountability." The report with the no-nonsense title, *Time for Results,* issued by the National Governors' Association, is indicative of the promise of politicians to the public to assess the quality of education, and by implication, to do whatever is necessary to improve it. The other wing of the assessment movement emphasizes "assessment for improvement." It is represented by educators and politicians alike, and its purpose is to assess *in order* to improve.

While "assessment for improvement" seems the more constructive approach, we should probably raise questions now about the potential of even that logical approach to bring about significant improvements in students' learning.

Assessment, as it is usually conceived and carried out, is conducted at statewide and institution-wide levels, far from the classrooms where teaching and learning actually take place. Statewide assessments tend to slip into comparative assessments that tell which institutions are doing the best job of educating students. I'm not sure, nor I think is anyone else, how those comparisons will eventually lead to improvement in students' learning.

While institutional assessment is closer to the scene of the action, the criteria are usually still comparisons with state and national norms, and responsibility for improvement is hard to pinpoint. Faculty, it turns out, don't necessarily feel personally responsible for implementing the goals found in the mission statements of their college catalogs. In fact, most faculty members, even in relatively small, homogeneous liberal arts colleges, have rather specific, discipline-related concepts of their responsibility for the education of students.

As part of our Classroom Research project, we collected data from nearly 2,000 faculty members from two- and four-year colleges about their teaching goals, that is, what they wanted students to learn. It turns out, to no one's surprise, that science teachers have different goals from English teachers. Despite all of the recent emphasis on "writing across the curriculum," for example, our data show that faculty still perceive the development of students' writing skills to be primarily the responsibility of the English department. Whereas 68% of our respondents in the humanities divisions of four-year colleges rated the development of students' writing skills an "essential" goal of their teaching, only 13% of those teaching science considered it equally important. When teachers were asked to rate the importance of the presumably universal educational goal of "Developing respect for others, including persons of different backgrounds," 46% of those teaching career-related courses, for example, those in education, allied health, or communications, considered it an essential teaching goal, compared to 1% of those in the sciences. Teaching goals in the disciplines are visibly and legitimately different. What and how well students learn bears some relationship, we hope, to what teachers think it is important to teach. If teachers from the different disciplines have different teaching goals, then a variety of measures must be used to assess teaching effectiveness. Even more important, teachers themselves must be able to assess how well they are accomplishing their own discipline-related goals.

Fortunately for the "community" of academe, college teachers share some teaching goals. Our data show that the single most commonly accepted teaching goal today is the "development of analytic skills," considered essential by a majority of faculty across most of the disciplines. Presumably, then, most teachers would accept some responsibility if a college-wide assessment showed that students were failing to develop analytic skills, but many would shrug off data showing poor writing skills or failure to develop respect for persons of different backgrounds as "not my job."

Using the results of institutional assessment to improve learning is not going to be simple. I suppose that the outcome of most college-wide assessments will be revisions in the curriculum. Colleges will consider adding course requirements in areas where students are weak. But education, properly understood, is not so much additive as transformational. New learning transforms the old into new interpretations, and more subject matter or more courses may not be as valuable to students as the deeper understandings that might result from more skillful teaching.

I am not arguing that institutional assessments are not valuable. I think they are. What I am suggesting is that if the goal of the 1980s reforms is the improvement of students' learning, then how something is taught is every bit as important as what is taught. Classroom Research, as part of the assessment movement, is complementary to institutional assessment. It provides information that is timely, because it takes place during the semester while there is still time to make corrections. It provides credible information that has direct implications for change, since the teacher designs the assessment to provide information that he or she finds important and useful for improvement.

The second lever that we are using to implement reform is *educational policy.* Most policy is determined by state and campus administrators, but their responsibility for the improvement of learning is necessarily indirect. That is, they are not in the classroom and must try in whatever ways they can to influence the behavior of those who are in a position to affect teaching and learning directly. The further removed they are from the scene of the action, the more they must depend on manipulating reward and punishment to bring about the desired ends. Most of the rewards all along the line are monetary: budget, allocation, and salary. States determine budgets for institutions, campus administrators allocate funds for departments, and departments determine promotion and salary rewards for teachers.

The problem, according to research on faculty motivation, is that the extrinsic rewards that administrators and policy makers depend on are not very effective in changing faculty behavior. Most faculty members work hard and put in long hours without any supervision or work rules. Motivation in these autonomous situations is far more complex, it appears, than the simple reward/punishment views that prevail in determining incentives.

We have all witnessed the situation in which a faculty member is not working very hard and, as a consequence, receives low salary increases for several years. Does such a policy result in changing the inadequate performance that has been punished? Usually not. It is more likely that the faculty member will feel resentment and lack of appreciation, and the result will be less motivation for work rather than more. In an article entitled, "Financial Incentives are Ineffective for Faculty," McKeachie (1979) argues that policies that depend on extrinsic rewards will not do much to improve college teaching. What then should we do to develop more effective policy?

Rewards for teaching can be grouped in three categories. First are the external rewards that are used most often by administrators to effect change, such as salary, promotion, and tenure. Research demonstrates that these rewards frequently do not work as they are supposed to (McKeachie, 1979). For one thing, reward is in the eye of the beholder. Other things being equal, incentives such as salary, promotion, and tenure are probably more effective for a young faculty member than for an older one. We are facing a situation now in which tenure as an incentive has already been rendered ineffective for more than two thirds of the faculty.

A second group of rewards involve satisfactions that come as a byproduct of an activity. One may, for example, gain respect from colleagues and students for excellence in teaching, but the reward is the respect rather than the satisfactions derived from the activity of teaching. Teaching awards, although a nice recognition for teaching and outstanding teachers, have not been shown to improve the teaching performance of the faculty in general or even of the person recognized. In fact, if the individual really was motivated by the reward itself, what happens when the reward has been acquired? Even if you're the greatest teacher on the faculty, it is not very likely that you will receive the "Best Teacher Award" year after year. Teaching awards are more recognition for past performance than incentives for improving teaching.

The third type of reward is intrinsic. A person gives time and energy to teaching because of the intellectual stimulation to be found in preparing and delivering a lecture, for example, or the satisfaction of seeing students learn, or to satisfy one's intellectual curiosity about how students deal with an interesting concept in a stimulating class discussion. When faculty are asked about the major sources of work satisfaction, intrinsic satisfactions are almost always reported to be much more important than extrinsic rewards (McKeachie, 1979, p. 7).

Most policy makers don't give much attention to intrinsic rewards, figuring that policy can do little to enhance them. But such is not the case, and the research suggests that college faculty members are more likely than people who have chosen other careers to respond to intrinsic motivators.

Research into the characteristics of college faculty show them to be achievement oriented, intellectually curious, and autonomous. I therefore assume that most teachers want to be really good teachers, that they enjoy the intellectual challenge of discovering how to teach for maximum effect, and that they are self-motivated and self-renewing once started on the path of addressing a challenge to their intellectual curiosity and love of problem solving.

Why shouldn't faculty be involved directly in the assessment of the learning of the students in their classrooms? Wouldn't their predilections for problem solving and high achievement lead them to experimentation to see whether they could boost the learning of their students? Wouldn't this be one way to increase the intrinsic rewards for excellence in teaching? More important wouldn't engagement in research on teaching and learning in their own classrooms provide an opportunity for continuous growth and self-renewal?

A basic assumption underlying Classroom Research is that accurate and credible feedback about the impact of teaching on learning carries a built, in challenge to teachers to see if they can increase learning through experimentation with more effective teaching methods. The best way for teachers to get feedback that has high validity for them is to design the assessment measures themselves. In simplest terms, the feedback loop in Classroom Research involves stating in assessable terms what students should be learning in the class, designing feedback measures to assess the extent to which they are learning those things, and then experimenting with ways to improve learning.

Earlier, I suggested that Classroom Research should not replace institutional assessment, but rather be complementary to it. Similarly, my point here is not to suggest that intrinsic rewards replace extrinsic incentives in policy making, but that ways to increase intrinsic rewards have heretofore been ignored by policy makers, and it is now time to correct that oversight. I think improving the intellectual challenge to teaching through Classroom Research is potentially powerful way to do that.

Finally, *research* on teaching and learning has been, and continues to be an important activity in educational reform. But educational research has not as yet made much impact on teaching. There are three possible reasons foe the glacial pace of change in teaching: (a) It doesn't need changing, (b) It can't be changed, or (c) We don't know how to change it. There is a fourth, I guess, which is that it would be immoral to change it. Since I reject all of these as legitimate reasons for the present situation in which generation after generation continues to teach as they were taught, I want to take a brief look at what we know from research about effective teachers and effective teaching.

In higher education, most of what we know about effective teaching comes from the perceptions of college students. From hundreds of studies, most of them conducted in the last decade, we know quite a lot about what college students think constitutes good teaching. While students are, for the most part, naive observers of teaching, they do have maximum opportunity to set teachers throughout the semester, on good days and on bad, and they should know better than anyone else how the teaching affects their learning.

Ben Bloom, of the University of Chicago, distinguishes between "alterable" and "unalterable" variables in educational research (1980). Age, experience academic rank, gender, race, etc., are unalterable variables; there is not much that we can do to change them. Fortunately, none of these unalterable characteristics show any very consistent or significant relationship to teaching effectiveness, with the exception of experience. In one important study, teachers with 3 to 12 years of experience were rated somewhat higher than those with either less or more teaching experience (Centra & Creech, 1976), leaving us pondering the question of what to do to remotivate an aging faculty. The general conclusion, after years of research on the relationship between teacher characteristics and student learning (not just students' perceptions of learning), hovers around .20 (Bloom, 1980) hardly sufficient to endorse the old saw, "Teachers are born, not made."

The characteristics of teaching, as opposed to teachers, however, do show significant correlations with students' perceptions of teacher effectiveness. One conscientious researcher reviewed nearly 60 studies of students' descriptions of effective teaching and found eight characteristics that appeared related to high student ratings in almost all of the studies: knowledge of subject matter, enthusiasm, concern for students, preparation, stimulation of interest, availability, encouragement of discussion, and ability to explain clearly (Feldman, 1976). There is nothing very surprising about that list. I suspect most of us would recognize those characteristics as associated with the good teachers that we know. Fortunately, those characteristics are alterable, i.e., subject to change by teachers, although not always very easily. While it is pretty clear what teachers should do to improve their knowledge of subject matter or to be better prepared for class, it may not be self-evident what they should do to stimulate interest or to improve their ability to explain clearly.

A smaller set of studies have attempted to relate classroom *behaviors* to teaching effectiveness. Behaviors that have been shown related to high student ratings are: stressing important points, giving multiple examples, signaling the transition to a new point, and establishing rapport or encouraging student participation by asking questions, addressing students by name, and showing concern for student progress (Murray, 1985). Such behaviors, in addition to being specific, have the further advantages of being alterable and observable. If observation can inform a teacher of weaknesses, then it may be possible to alter the classroom behaviors responsible.

That, briefly, is what we know about teachers as seen through the eyes of what I would call naive but sincere observers (Cross, 1988). The question haunting that research, of course, is, How good are students at evaluating the effectiveness of teaching? That question, or at least one piece of it, has been studied almost to the point of exhaustion. Unfortunately, the studies have been largely defensive, focusing more on investigations into why we should not use students to evaluate teaching than on what we could do to make them better evaluators.

Almost everything that anyone can reasonably propose as a biasing condition in student ratings has been studied. For example, are student ratings of their teachers related to grade or expected grade in the course, academic ability, reason for taking the course, whether it is required or elective, gender match between student and teacher, and a host of other variables that might bias students to give undeservedly low or high ratings. The general conclusion from all of this research is that there are not consistent or significant biases related to student characteristics. Students are, for the most part, both consistent and objective in the ratings that are routinely collected by most colleges today (Cross, 1988).

There is, however, evidence of small but consistent relationships between student ratings and course characteristics, most notably class size and whether a course is required or elective. Small classes (fewer than 12 students) and electives receive somewhat higher ratings (Centra, 1977), but the relationships are so small that neither required classes nor large classes can serve as an excuse for poor ratings (Gleason, 1986).

My conclusion, from the literally hundreds of studies that have been done on student perceptions of teaching effectiveness, is that its potential contribution for improving classroom teaching has been positive, but its effect minimal. On the positive side, there is evidence that teachers do change in response to student evaluations, and that they do so in as little as 6 weeks (Centra, 1973; Murray, 1985). Moreover, it is teachers who rate themselves higher than students rate them who are most likely to change.

Even more positive are findings from a meta-analysis of 22 research studies that showed that if teachers consult with a faculty development specialist about their student evaluations, the average teacher moves to the 74th percentile (in the judgment of students) by the end of the semester (Cohen, 1980). If colleges could raise the performance of the average teacher from the 50th to the 74th percentile in a semester by using student evaluation augmented by consultation, the result would be a tremendous improvement in the quality of instruction nationwide, and by inference, in students' learning.

It is important to remember, however, that most of the research I have described equates teaching effectiveness with student perceptions of effectiveness. What we have shown is that teachers can and do respond to student evaluations. If serious attention were given to designing student evaluations to help teachers improve, rather than primarily or solely for use in administrative decisions, and if students were given training in observing the effect of teaching on their learning, the results might be truly astounding.

Most of the studies in higher education on teacher effectiveness shed considerable light on generic behaviors—qualities that make for good teaching generally—but they don't distinguish between differences in fields of study A very good physics teacher may behave quite differently from a very good English teacher. In fact, we found from our administration of the Teaching Goals Inventory (TGI) that teachers vary enormously in what they say they, are trying to accomplish. To my amazement, every one of the 48 items in the TGI received the full range of responses. A goal that one teacher said was "essential" to the teaching of his or her class was rated "irrelevant" by someone else. Teaching goals also showed significant differences by age, gender and, most dramatically, by discipline. Almost all of the 48 items in the TGI showed statistically significant differences among disciplines. Math and science teachers are especially interested in helping students develop analytic skills; teachers in the humanities are more interested than teachers in other fields of study in developing openness to new ideas and a lifelong love of learning. Teachers in the visual and performing arts are, as a group, far more interested than teachers in other departments in developing creativity.

There are interesting differences too in the values and goals of teachers classified by age or gender. Faculty members over the age of 56 are more interested than younger faculty in George Bush's "kinder, gentler nation." They are more likely than their younger colleagues to say that goals such as these are essential to their teaching: the development of academic honesty, respect for others, and a lifelong love of learning. Younger faculty, under the age of 36, are more interested in the academic reforms that we hear so much about today: developing analytic and problem-solving skills and helping students demonstrate creativity. Increasing the number of women on the faculty will preserve, to some extent, the values of the older retiring faculty; women are significantly more interested than men in helping students develop a sense of personal responsibility, respect for others of different backgrounds, listening skills, and the ability to work collaboratively with others.

Our data from the TGI constitutes an excellent argument for maintaining or aiming for diversity on the faculty. But it also argues for faculty taking more interest in assessing what is important to them as teachers in their classrooms. I see little hope for constructive improvement in the education of undergraduates without the full participation of the teaching faculty, not just as members of curriculum committees and consultants on institutionwide assessment, but as individuals who must be able to assess whether students are learning what they think it is important to teach.

Classroom Research is one way to get college teachers involved in the intellectual challenges of teaching. My hope is that it will make teachers and students more sophisticated participants in teaching and learning as it takes place daily in classrooms across the nation.

Let me close by quickly summarizing what I believe are the unique contributions of Classroom Research to the reforms called for in the 1980s:

- Involves faculty members directly and professionally in their own continuing development as teachers.
- Joins pedagogy and subject matter knowledge to acknowledge discipline-based differences in the goals of teachers.
- Reduces the gap between research and practice. Relevance and credibility are enhanced when practitioners become researchers, looking into the problems that are relevant to them.
- Provides an intellectual challenge to teaching, which enhances the intrinsic rewards.
- Takes assessment into the classroom, where teaching and learning are actually taking place.

References

Bloom, B. S. (19801. The new direction in educational research: Alterable variables. *Phi Delta Kappan, 61,* 382–385.

Centra, J. A. (1973). Effectiveness of student feedback in modifying college instruction. *Journal of Educational Psychology, 65,* 395–401.

Centra, J. A. (1977). Student ratings of instruction and their relationship to student learning. *American Educational Research Journal, 14,* 17–24.

Centra, J. A., & Creech, F. R. (1976). *The relationship between student, teacher, and course characteristics and student ratings of teacher effectiveness* (*PR*76-1). Princeton, NJ: Educational Testing Service.

Cohen, P. A. (1980). Effectiveness of student-rating feedback for improving college instruction: A meta-analysis of findings. *Research in Higher Education, 13(4).*

Cross, K. P. (1988). *Feedback in the classroom: Making assessment matter.* Washington, DC: American Association for Higher Education.

Cross, K. P., & Angelo, T. A. (1988). *Classroom assessment techniques: A handbook for faculty.* Ann Arbor, MI: University of Michigan, National Center for Research on the Improvement of Postsecondary Teaching and Learning.

Feldman, K. A. (1976). The superior college teacher from the students' view. *Research in Higher Education,* 5, 43–88.

Gleason, M. (1986, February). Getting a perspective on student evaluations. *AAHE Bulletin,* pp. 10–13.

McKeachie, W. J. (1979). Perspectives from psychology: Financial incentives are ineffective for faculty. In D. R. Lewis & W. E. Becker, Jr. (Eds.), *Academic Rewards in Higher Education* (pp. 3–20). Cambridge, MA: Ballinger.

Mosteller, F. (1989). The "muddiest point in the lecture" as a feedback device. *Journal of the Harvard Danforth Center on Teaching & Learning, 3,* 1021.

Murray, H. G. (1985). Classroom teaching behaviors related to college teaching effectiveness. *New directions for teaching and learning, 23.* San Francisco: Jossey-Bass.

National Commission on Excellence in Education. (1983). *A nation at risk,* Washington, DC: U.S. Department of Education.

Wilson, R. C. (1986). Improving faculty teaching: Effective use of student evaluations and consultants. *Journal of Higher Education,* 57, 196–211.

PART I—FOUNDATIONS AND PHILOSOPHIES: SHAPING CONTEMPORARY IDEAS AND INQUIRY

Recommended Readings

A National Dialogue: The Secretary of Education's Commission on the Future of Higher Education (2006). United States Department of Education. http://www.ed.gov/about/bdscomm/list/hiedfuture/reports/final-report.pdf

Angelo, T. (2000). Doing academic development as though we value learning most: Transformative guidelines from research and practice. In R. James, J. Milton and R. Gabb (Eds.), *Research and development in higher education, 22: Cornerstones of Higher Education* (pp. 111–122). Melbourne, Victoria: HERDSA.

Angelo, T. (2000). Turning departments into productive, scholarly learning communities: guidelines from research and practice. In A. Lucas (Ed.), *Leading academic change: Essential roles for department chairs* (pp.74–89). San Francisco, CA: Jossey Bass.

Asmar, C. (2002). Strategies to enhance learning and teaching in a research intensive university. *The International Journal for Academic Development, 7*(1), 18–29.

Atkinson, M. P. (2001). The scholarship of teaching and learning: Re-conceptualizing scholarship and transforming the academy. *Social Forces, 79,* 1217–1230.

Babb, M., & Hutchings, P. (2002). The scholarship of teaching and learning: Idea and impact. *HERDSA News, 24,* 7–9.

Badley, G. (2003). Improving the scholarship of teaching and learning. *Innovations in Education and Teaching International, 40,* 303–309.

Barnett, R. (Ed.). (2005). *Re-shaping the university: new relationships between research, scholarship and teaching.* Maidenhead, UK: McGraw-Hill/Open University Press/SRHE.

Becker, W. E., & Andrew, M. L. (Eds.). (2004). *The scholarship of teaching and learning in higher education: Contributions of research universities.* Bloomington, IN: Indiana University Press.

Bender, E. T. (2005, Sept/Oct). CASTLs in the air: The SoTL movement in mid-flight. *Change, 37*(5), 40–50.

Bender, E. T., & Gray, D. (1999). The Scholarship of teaching. *Research & Creative Activity, XXII,* 1.

Benjamin, J. (2000). The scholarship of teaching in teams: What does it look like in practice? *Higher Education Research and Development, 19,* 191–204.

Bernstein, D., & Bass, R. (2005). The scholarship of teaching and learning. *Academe, 91* (4), 37–43.

Booth, A. (2004). Rethinking the scholarly: Developing the scholarship of teaching in history. *Arts and Humanities in Higher Education, 3,* 247–66.

Bok, D. (2006). *Our underachieving colleges: A candid look at how much students learn and why they should be learning more.* Princeton, NJ: Princeton University Press.

Boyd, J. (2004). Scholarship of teaching and learning. *Communication Education, 53,* 340–347.

Boyer Commission on Educating Undergraduates in the Research University, Shirley Strum Kenny (Chair) (1998). *Reinventing undergraduate education: A blueprint for America's research universities.* Stony Brook, NY: SUNY.

Brew, A., & Sachs, J. (Eds.). (2007). *Transforming a university: The scholarship of teaching and learning in practice.* Sydney: Sydney University Press.

Brookfield, S. D. (1995). *Becoming a critically reflective teacher.* San Francisco, CA: Jossey-Bass.

Cambridge, B. L. (2000). The scholarship of teaching and learning: A national initiative. In K. and D. Lieberman, (Eds.), *To Improve the Academy: Vol. 18. Resources for Faculty, Instructional, and Organizational Development* (pp. 56–68). Bolton, MA: Anker.

Cambridge, B. L. (2001). Fostering the scholarship of teaching and learning: Communities of practice. In D. Lieberman & C. Wehlburg (Eds.), *To Improve the Academy: Vol. 19. Resources for Faculty, Instructional, and Organizational Development* (pp. 3–16). Bolton, MA: Anker.

Cambridge, B. L. (2002). Linking change initiatives: The Carnegie Academy for the Scholarship of Teaching and Learning in the company of other national projects. In D. Lieberman & C. Wehlburg, (Eds.), *To Improve the Academy: Vol. 20, Resources for Faculty, Instructional, and Organizational Development* (pp. 38–48). Bolton, MA: Anker.

Cambridge, B. L., & American Association for Higher Education. (2004). *Campus progress: Supporting the scholarship of teaching and learning.* Washington, DC: American Association for Higher Education.

Chanock, K. (2005). Scholarship of teaching and learning: Investigating patterns and possibilities in an academic oral genre. *Communication Education, 54,* 92–99.

Chism, N. (1998). The role of educational developers in institutional change: From the basement office to the front office. *To Improve the Academy: Vol. 17, Resources for Faculty, Instructional, and Organizational Development* (pp. 141–153). San Francisco, CA: Jossey-Bass.

Connolly, M. R., Bouwma-Gearhart, J. L., & Clifford, M. A. (2007). The birth of a notion: the windfalls and pitfalls of tailoring a SoTL-like concept to scientists, mathematicians, and engineers. *Innovative Higher Education, 32*(1), 19–34.

Cook, C. E., & Marincovich, M. (2009). Effective practices in the context of research universities. In K. H. Gillespie & D. R. Robertson (Eds.). *A guide to faculty development.* San Francisco, CA: Jossey-Bass.

Cottrell, S. A., & Jones, E. A. (2003). Researching the scholarship of teaching and learning: An analysis of current curriculum practices. *Innovative Higher Education, 27,* 169–181.

Cox, M. D. (2007). Fostering the scholarship of teaching and learning through faculty learning communities. *Journal on Excellence in College Teaching, 14*(2/3), 161–198.

Cross, K. P., & Steadman, M. H. (1996). *Classroom research: Implementing the scholarship of teaching.* San Francisco, CA: Jossey-Bass.

Cummins, L., Adu Poku, S., & Theall, M. (2008). Promoting the scholarship of teaching and learning in a faculty-staff learning community. *The Journal of Faculty Development, 22*(1), 40–51.

Diamond, R. M., & Adams, B. E. (Eds.). (1995). *The disciplines speak: Rewarding the scholarly, professional, and creative work of faculty.* Washington, DC: American Association for Higher Education.

Diamond, R. M., & Adams, B. E. (Eds.). (2000). *The disciplines speak II: More statements on rewarding the scholarly, professional, and creative work of faculty.* Washington, DC: American Association for Higher Education.

Eggins, H., & Macdonald, R. (Eds.). (2003). *The scholarship of academic development.* Buckingham: Open University Press/SRHE.

Elton, L. (2001). Research and teaching: what are the real relationships? *Teaching in Higher Education, 6*(1), 43–56.

Elton, L. (2008, January). Recognition and acceptance of the scholarship of teaching and learning. *International Journal for the Scholarship of Teaching and Learning, 2*(1). http://academics.georgiasouthern.edu/ijsotl

Elvidge, L. (Ed.). (2004). *Exploring academic development in higher education: Issues of engagement.* Cambridge, UK: Jill Roger Associates.

Fiddler, M. B., McGury, S., & Marienau, C. (1996). Broadening the scope of scholarship: A suggested framework. *Innovative Higher Education, 21,* 127–39.

Fisher, R. (2006). The scholarship of college teaching: Research opportunities in the new millennium. *Journal of Teaching and Learning, 4*(1), 57–71.

Frantz, A. C., Beebe, S. A., Horvath, V. S., Canales, J., Swee, D. E. (2005). The roles of teaching and learning centers. In S. Chadwick-Blossey (Ed.), *To Improve the Academy: Vol. 23, Resources for Faculty, Instructional, and Organizational Development* (pp. 72–90). Bolton, MA: Anker.

Gale, R. A. (2008). Inquiry unplugged: a scholarship of teaching and learning for open understanding. In T. Iiyoshi and M. S. Vijay Kumar (Eds.), *Opening up education: The collective advancement of education through open technology, open content, and open knowledge* (pp. 289–302). Cambridge, MA: MIT Press.

Gerhard, G., & Mayer-Smith, J. (2008). Casting a wider net: deepening scholarship by changing theories. *International Journal for the Scholarship of Teaching and Learning, 2* (1). http://academics.georgiasouthern.edu/ijsotl

Gilpin, L., & Liston, D. (2009, July). Transformative education in the scholarship of teaching and learning: An analysis of SoTL literature. *International Journal for the Scholarship of Teaching and Learning, 3*(2), 1–8. http://academics.georgiasouthern.edu/ijsotl/

Gittens, W. (2007). Shifting discourse in college teaching. *International Journal of the Scholarship of Teaching and Learning, 1*(1). http://academics.georgiasouthern.edu/ijsotl

Glassick, C. E., Huber, M. T., & Maeroff, G. I. (1997). *Scholarship assessed: Evaluation of the professoriate.* San Francisco, CA: Jossey-Bass.

Gordon, G., D'Andrea, V., Gosling, D., & Stefani, L. (2003). *Building capacity for change: research on the scholarship of teaching.* Bristol, UK: HEFCE and Centre for Higher Education Practice, Open University. http://www.hefce.ac.uk/pubs/rdreports/2003/rd02_03/

Halpern, D. F., & M. D. Hakel (Eds.). (2002). *New Directions for Teaching and Learning: No. 89, Applying the science of learning to university teaching and beyond.* San Francisco, CA: Jossey-Bass.

Hatch, T. (2005). *Into the classroom: Developing the scholarship of teaching and learning.* San Francisco, CA: Jossey-Bass.

Healey, M. (2000). Developing the scholarship of teaching in higher education: A discipline-based approach. *Higher Education Research and Development, 19,* 169–89.

Healey, M. (2003). The scholarship of teaching: Issues around an evolving concept. *Journal on Excellence in College Teaching, 14,* 5–16.

Healey, M. (2005). Linking research and teaching exploring disciplinary spaces and the role of inquiry-based learning. In R. Barnett (Ed.), *Reshaping the university: New relationships between research, scholarship and teaching* (pp. 67–78). Maidenhead, England; New York, NY: Society for Research into Higher Education/Open University Press.

Healey, M. (2005). Linking research and teaching to benefit student learning. *Journal of Geography in Higher Education,* 29 (2), 183–201.

Healey, M. (2006). SoTL in the UK: Some unsung developments. *The International Commons, 1*(1), 1 & 8. http://www.issotl.org/newsletter.html

Healey, M. (2008). Discipline-based approaches to SoTL. *The International Commons, 3* (1), 2–3. http://www.issotl.org/newsletter.html

Healey, M., & Jenkins, A. (2003). Discipline-based educational development. In R. Macdonald & H. Eggins (Eds.), *The scholarship of academic development* (pp. 47–57). Buckingham: Open University Press/SRHE.

Healey, M., & Jenkins, A. (2006). Strengthening the teaching-research linkage in undergraduate courses and programmes. *New Directions in Teaching and Learning: No. 107, Exploring research-based teaching* (pp. 43–53). San Francisco, CA: Jossey-Bass.

Henderson, B. B., & Buchanan, H. E. (2007). The scholarship of teaching and learning: A special niche for faculty at comprehensive universities? *Research in Higher Education, 48*(5), 523–543.

Henry, R. J. (2006). *Faculty development for student achievement: The QUE project.* Bolton, MA: Anker.

Hinchliffe, L. J. (2001). The scholarship of teaching and learning. *Research Strategies, 18,* 1–2.

Huber, M. T. (2004). *Balancing acts: The scholarship of teaching and learning in academic careers.* Washington, DC: American Association for Higher Education.

Huber, M. T., & Hutchings, P. (2006). Building the teaching commons. *Change, 38*(3), 24–31.

Huber, M. T., & Morreale, S. P. (Eds.). (2002). *Disciplinary styles in the scholarship of teaching and learning: Exploring common ground.* Washington, DC: American Association for Higher Education and The Carnegie Foundation for the Advancement of Teaching.

Hutchings, P. (2000). *Opening lines: Approaches to the scholarship of teaching and learning.* Menlo Park, CA: The Carnegie Foundation for the Advancement of Teaching.

Hutchings, P. (2002). *Ethics of inquiry: Issues in the scholarship of teaching and learning.* Menlo Park, CA: The Carnegie Foundation for the Advancement in Teaching.

Hutchings, P. (2003). Competing goods: Ethical issues in the scholarship of teaching and learning. *Change, 35*(5), 26–33.

Hutchings, P., & Shulman, L. S. (1999). The scholarship of teaching: New elaborations, new developments. *Change, 31*(5), 11–15.

Hutchings, P., & Huber, M. T. (Eds.). (2008). The scholarship of teaching and learning in the humanities: The place—and problem—of theory. *Arts and Humanities in Higher Education, 7,* 227–228.

Johnston, R. (1998). The university of the future: Boyer revisited. *Higher Education, 36,* 253–272.

Kalish, A., & Stockly, D. (2009, July). Building scholarly communities: Supporting the scholarship of teaching & learning with learning communities. *Transformative Dialogues: Teaching & Learning Journal,* 3(1). http://www.kwantlen.ca/TD.html

Kaplan, M. L., & Miller, A. T. (Eds.). (2007, Fall). *New Directions for Teaching and Learning: No. 111, The scholarship of multicultural teaching and learning.* San Francisco, CA: Jossey-Bass.

Koch, L. C., Holland, L. A., Price, D., Gonzalez, G. L., Lieske, P., Butler, A., Wilson, K., & Holly, M. L. (2002). Engaging new faculty in the scholarship of teaching. *Innovative Higher Education, 27*(2), 83–94.

Kreber, C. (Ed.). (2001). *New Directions for Teaching and Learning: No. 86, Scholarship revisited: Perspectives on the scholarship of teaching.* San Francisco, CA: Jossey-Bass.

Kreber, C. (2002). Controversy and consensus on the scholarship of teaching. *Studies in Higher Education, 27,* 151–167.

Kreber, C. (2002). Teaching excellence, teaching expertise, and the scholarship of teaching. *Innovative Higher Education, 27,* 5–23.

Kreber, C. (2003). Challenging the dogma: Toward a more inclusive view of the scholarship of teaching. *Journal on Excellence in College Teaching,* 14, 27–43.

Kreber, C. (2005). Reflection on teaching and the scholarship of teaching. *Higher Education, 50,* 323–359.

Kreber, C. (2006). Developing the scholarship of teaching and learning through transformational learning. *Journal of the Scholarship of Teaching and Learning, 6,* 88–109.

Kreber, C. (2007). What's it really all about? The scholarship of teaching and learning as an authentic practice. *International Journal of the Scholarship of Teaching and Learning, 1*(1). http://academics.georgiasouthern.edu/ijsotl

Kreber, C., & Cranton, P. A. (2000). Exploring the scholarship of teaching. *The Journal of Higher Education, 71*(4), 476–495.

Lee, V. S. (2009). Program types and prototypes. In K. H. Gillespie & D. R. Robertson (Eds.), *A guide to faculty development.* San Francisco, CA: Jossey-Bass.

Lieberman, D. A., & Guskin, A. E. (2003). The essential role of faculty development in new higher education models. In C. Wehlburg & S. Chadwick-Blossey (Eds.), *To Improve the Academy: Vol. 21, Resources for Faculty, Instructional, and Organizational Development* (pp. 257–272). Bolton, MA: Anker.

McKinney, K. (2001). Getting SoTL articles published: A few tips. *The National Teaching and Learning Forum, 10*(5), 1.

McKinney, K. (2003, August/September). Applying the scholarship of teaching and learning: How can we do better? *The Teaching Professor, 1*(5), 8.

McKinney, K. (2004). The scholarship of teaching and learning: Past lessons, current challenges, and future visions. In C. Wehlburg & S. Chadwick-Blossey (Eds.), *To Improve the Academy: Vol. 22, Resources for Faculty, Instructional, and Organizational Development* (pp. 3–19). Bolton, MA: Anker

McKinney, K. (2007). *Enhancing learning through the scholarship of teaching and learning.* San Francisco, CA: Jossey-Bass.

McKinney, K., & Jarvis, P. (2009, January). Beyond lines on the CV: Faculty applications of their scholarship of teaching and learning research. *International Journal for the Scholarship of Teaching and Learning, 3*(1). http://academics.georgiasouthern.edu/ijsotl

Mertler, C. A. (2006). *Action research: Teachers as researchers in the classroom.* Thousand Oaks, CA: Sage.

Myers, C. B. (2008). College faculty and the scholarship of teaching: Gender differences across four key activities. *Journal of the Scholarship of Teaching and Learning, 8*(2), 38–51.

Neal, E., & Peed-Neal, I. (2009). Experiential lessons in the practice of faculty development. In L. B. Nilson and J. E. Miller (Eds.), *To Improve the Academy: Vol. 27, Resources for Faculty, Instructional, and Organizational Development* (pp. 14–31). Bolton, MA: Anker.

Nelson, C. (2003). Doing it: Examples of several of the different genres of the scholarship of teaching and learning. *Journal on Excellence in College Teaching,* 14(2), 85–94.

Nicholls, G. (2001). *Professional development in higher education.* London, UK: Kogan Page.

Nicholls, G. (2004). Scholarship in teaching as a core professional value: What does this mean to the academic? *Teaching in Higher Education, 9,* 29–42.

Nicholls, G. (2005). *The challenge of scholarship: rethinking learning, teaching, and research.* London, UK: Routledge.

NSF Division of Undergraduate Education. (1996). Shaping the future: New expectations for undergraduate education in Science, Mathematics, Engineering, and Technology.

Ouellett, M. L. (2004). Faculty development and universal instructional design. *Equity & Excellence in Education, 37,* 135–144.

Paulsen, M. B. (2001). The relation between research and the scholarship of teaching. In C. Kreber (Ed.), *New Directions for Teaching and Learning: No. 86, Scholarship revisited: Perspectives on the scholarship of teaching* (pp. 19–29). San Francisco, CA: Jossey-Bass.

Paulsen, M. B., & Feldman, K. A. (2003). The scholarship of teaching as an action system. *Journal on Excellence in College Teaching, 14,* 45–68.

Perkins, D. (2004). Scholarship of teaching and learning, Assessment, and the Journal of Geoscience Education. *Journal of Geoscience Education, 52,* 113–4.

Perry, R., & Smart, J. (2007). *The scholarship of teaching and learning in higher education: An evidence-based perspective.* New York, NY: Springer.

Poole, G., Taylor, L., & Thompson, J. (2007, July). Using the scholarship of teaching and learning at disciplinary, national and institutional levels to strategically improve the quality of post-secondary education. *International Journal for the Scholarship of Teaching and Learning, 1*(2). http://academics.georgiasouthern.edu/ijsotl

Prosser, M., Martin, E., Trigwell, K., Ramsden, P. & Middleton, H. (2008). University academics' experience of research and its relationship to their experience of teaching. *Instructional Science, 36*(1), 3–16.

Prosser, M., & Trigwell, K. (1999). *Understanding learning and teaching: the experience of higher education.* Buckingham: Society for Research into Higher Education and Open University Press.

Prosser, M., & Trigwell, K. (2009). The international commons. *Newsletter of the International Society for the Scholarship of Teaching and Learning, 4*(1).

Ramsden, P. (2003). *Learning to teach in higher education* (2nd ed.). London, UK: Routledge.

Richlin, L. (2001). Scholarly teaching and the scholarship of teaching. In C. Kreber (Ed.), *New Directions for Teaching and Learning: No. 86, Scholarship revisited: Perspectives on the scholarship of teaching and learning* (pp. 57–68). San Francisco, CA: Jossey-Bass.

Richlin, L. (2003). Understanding, promoting and operationalizing the scholarship of teaching and learning: A message from the editor. *Journal on Excellence in College Teaching, 14,* 1–4.

Richlin, L., & Cox, M. (2004). Developing scholarly teaching and the scholarship of teaching and learning through faculty learning communities. In M. D. Cox and L. Richlin (Eds.), *New directions for teaching and learning: No. 97, Building faculty learning communities* (pp. 127–136). San Francisco, CA: Jossey-Bass.

Robinson, J., & Nelson, C. (2003). Institutionalizing and diversifying a vision of the scholarship of teaching and learning. *Journal on Excellence in College Teaching, 14,* 95–118.

Roxa, T., Olsson, T., & Martensson, K. (2008). Appropriate use of theory in the scholarship of teaching and learning as a strategy for institutional development. *Arts and Humanities in Higher Education, 7*(3), 276–294. http://dx.doi.org/DOI10.1177/1474022208094412

Salvatori, M. R. (2002). The scholarship of teaching: Beyond the anecdotal. *Pedagogy, 2,* 297–310.

Savory, P., Nelson Burnett, A., & Goodburn, A. (2007). *Inquiry into the college classroom: Journey toward scholarly teaching.* San Francisco, CA: Jossey-Bass/Anker.

Saylor, C., & Harper, V. (2003). The scholarship of teaching and learning: A faculty development project. *Journal on Excellence in College Teaching, 14,* 149–60.

Seldin, P., & Associates. (1995). *Improving college teaching.* Bolton, MA: Anker Publishing.

Shapiro, H. N. (2006). Promotion & tenure & the scholarship of teaching & learning. *Change, 38*(2), 38–43.

Shulman, L. S. (1993). Teaching as community property: Putting an end to pedagogical solitude. *Change, 25*(6), 6–7.

Shulman. L. S. (2000). From Minsk to Pinsk: Why a scholarship of teaching and learning? *The Journal of the Scholarship of Teaching and Learning, 1,* 48–52.

Shulman, L. S. (2004). Visions of the possible: Models for campus support of the scholarship of teaching and learning. In W. E. Becker & M. L. Andrews (Eds.), *The scholarship of teaching and learning in higher education* (pp. 9–23). Bloomington, IN: Indiana University Press.

Simpson, R. D. (2001). From adequacy to excellence: Honoring the scholarship of learning and teaching. *Innovative Higher Education, 26,* 83–86.

Skelton, A. (Ed). (2007). *International perspectives on teaching excellence in higher education.* London, UK: Routledge.

Sorcinelli, M. D. (2002). New conceptions of scholarship for a new generation of faculty members. In K. Zahorski (Ed.), *Scholarship in the postmodern era: New venues, new values, new visions* (pp. 41–48). San Francisco, CA: Jossey-Bass.

Sorcinelli, M. D., & Austin, A. E. (2006). Developing faculty for new roles and changing expectations. *Effective Practices for Academic Leaders, 1*(11), 1–16.

Sperling, C. (2003). How community colleges understand the scholarship of teaching and learning. *Community College Journal of Research and Practice, 27,* 593–601.

Tagg, J. (2003). *The learning paradigm college.* Bolton, MA: Anker.

Theall, M., & Centra, J. (2001). Assessing the scholarship of teaching: Valid decisions from valid evidence. In C. Kreber (Ed.), *New Directions for Teaching and Learning: No. 86, Revisiting scholarship: Perspectives on the scholarship of teaching* (pp. 31–45). San Francisco, CA: Jossey-Bass.

Thompson, S. (2001). Lessons learned in implementing the scholarship of teaching and learning. *The National Teaching & Learning Forum, 10*(5), 8–10.

Thompson, S. (2003). From two box lunches to buffets: Fulfilling the promise of the scholarship of teaching and learning. *Journal on Excellence in College Teaching, 14,* 119–134.

Tiberius, R. G. (2002). A brief history of educational development:nt: Implications for teachers and developers. In D. Lieberman (Ed.), *To Improve the Academy: Vol. 20, Resources for Faculty, Instructional, and Organizational Development* (pp. 20–37). Bolton, MA: Anker.

Trigwell, K., Martin, E., Benjamin, J., & Prosser, M. (2000). Scholarship of teaching: A model. *Higher Education Research and Development, 19,* 155–68.

Trigwell, K., & Shale, S. (2004). Student learning and the scholarship of university teaching. *Studies in Higher Education, 29,* 523–536.

Weimer, M. E. (2006). *Enhancing scholarly work on teaching and learning: Professional literature that makes a difference.* San Francisco, CA: Jossey-Bass.

Weimer, M. E. (2007). Intriguing connections but not with the past. *International Journal for Academic Development, 12*(1), 5–8.

Weimer, M. E. (2008). Positioning scholarly work on teaching and learning. *International Journal for the Scholarship of Teaching and Learning, 2*(1). http://academics.georgiasouthern.edu/ijsotl

Werder, C., & Otis, M. (2009). *Engaging student voices in the study of teaching and learning.* Sterling, VA: Stylus.

Witman, P., & Richlin, L. (2007). The status of the scholarship of teaching and learning in the disciplines. *International Journal of the Scholarship of Teaching and Learning, 1*(1), 1–17. http://academics.georgiasouthern.edu/ijsotl

Yakura, E., & Bennett, C. (2003). Finding common ground: Collaboration across the disciplines in the scholarship of teaching. *Journal on Excellence in College Teaching, 14,* 135–147.

Web Resources

Association of American Colleges and Universities (AAC&U)
http://www.aacu.org/

American Association for Higher Education and Accreditation, Inc.
http://www.aahea.org/

American Council on Education (ACE)
http://www.acenet.edu/

American Educational Research Association (AERA)
http://www.aera.net/

Association for the Study of Higher Education (ASHE)
http://www.ashe.ws/

The Carnegie Foundation
http://www.carnegiefoundation.org/

CASTL: Carnegie Academy for the Scholarship of Teaching and Learning
http://www.carnegiefoundation.org/programs/index.asp?key=21

The Chronicle of Higher Education
http://chronicle.com/section/Home/5

Council on Adult and Experiential Learning (CAEL)
http://www.cael.org/

International Council for Adult Education (ICAE)
http://www.icae2.org/

International Journal for the Scholarship of Teaching and Learning
http://academics.georgiasouthern.edu/ijsotl/index.htm

International Journal for Teaching and Learning in Higher Education (IJTLHE)
http://www.isetl.org/ijtlhe/

International Scholarship of Teaching and Learning Network (ISoTL)
http://www.tag.ubc.ca/about/institute/ISoTLNetwork.php

Journal of the Scholarship of Teaching and Learning
http://www.iupui.edu/~josotl/

Learning and Teaching in Higher Education (LATHE)
http://resources.glos.ac.uk/tli/lets/journals/lathe/index.cfm

National Institute of Adult Continuing Education (NIACE) (England and Wales)
http://www.niace.org.uk/

NCSPOD: North American Council for Staff, Program, and Organizational Development
http://www.ncspod.org/

POD: Professional and Organizational Network in Higher Education
http://www.podnetwork.org/

SoTL Commons: A Conference for the Scholarship of Teaching and Learning
http://academics.georgiasouthern.edu/ijsotl/conference/2010/

The Teaching Professor
http://www.teachingprofessor.com/

Tomorrow's Professor
http://cgi.stanford.edu/~dept-ctl/cgi-bin/tomprof/postings.php

University Continuing Education Association (UCEA)
http://www.ucea.edu/

PART II

STUDENTS: UNDERSTANDING OUR LEARNERS

Part II—Students: Understanding Our Learners

In order to create conditions for effective teaching and learning, educators must know who they are serving—students. As the population participating in higher education grows more complex and diverse, this understanding becomes even more essential. We should know something about how learning occurs, how students develop their systems of making meaning, and how students' multiple identities and learning styles may impact their learning and growth. Selections in Part II aim to address these issues.

How Students Learn

First, in a chapter from *How People Learn,* the authors juxtapose examples of expert and novice knowledge from research in various disciplines and share implications for teaching and learning. Bransford, Brown, and Cocking contend that experts have developed their existing knowledge base to reflect the complexity of a given discipline, whereas novices tend to have difficulty differentiating between significant knowledge and extraneous details. Their "six principles of expertise" explain the importance of experts' ability to find patterns; organize, apply, contextualize, and retrieve information; and monitor one's own learning.

James Zull, a biologist, is the author of the second reading selected for this section. He presents the parallels he discovered between Kolb's "learning cycle" and functions of the brain involved in learning from a structural point of view. He ends the chapter with prompts to promote consideration of how these theories from learning and biological sciences might be brought to bear on how we go about teaching for more effective learning.

Learners' Multiple Identities and Perspectives

Student Development Theory, a body of knowledge aimed at understanding college students' intellectual, interpersonal, and identity development, can greatly inform our work in the classroom. Marcia Baxter Magolda is one of the most prolific and well-known current scholars in this area and is the author of the third and fourth readings in this section. In the article from *Change,* she provides an overview of the literature on intellectual development, including the major theories and theorists and their contributions. The second work by Baxter Magolda focuses on lessons learned about students' perspectives from her longitudinal study of over twenty years; starting with students in their first year of college and continuing through their thirties. She traces their development toward "self authorship," what she describes as "the capacity to internally define one's beliefs, identity and social relations" (p. 143). Baxter Magolda also shares elements of the "learning partnerships" model derived from her longitudinal study to help educators think about ways to appropriately challenge and support students in their journey toward increasingly complex ways of making meaning.

While it would be impossible to include the number of readings necessary to adequately address the many identities that college students hold and how these identities play a role in their development, Pizzolato, Chaudhari, Murrell, Podobnik, and Schaeffer attend to the intersections they found between ethnic identity, intellectual development, and academic achievement.

Learning Styles

The last reading in this section, by Felder and Brent, is an ambitious piece aimed at recognizing the differences between learning style, approaches to learning, and intellectual development, what they call the "three facets of student diversity" (p. 57). While this piece was originally written for an audience of engineering educators, the concepts related to teaching and learning have great potential for transferability to any discipline in higher education.

CHAPTER 4

HOW STUDENTS LEARN

How Experts Differ from Novices

J.D. Bransford, A.L. Brown, and R.R. Cocking

People who have developed expertise in particular areas are, by definition, able to think effectively about problems in those areas. Understanding expertise is important because it provides insights into the nature of thinking and problem solving. Research shows that it is not simply general abilities, such as memory or intelligence, nor the use of general strategies that differentiate experts from novices. Instead, experts have acquired extensive knowledge that affects what they notice and how they organize, represent, and interpret information in their environment. This, in turn, affects their abilities to remember, reason, and solve problems.

This chapter illustrates key scientific findings that have come from the study of people who have developed expertise in areas such as chess, physics, mathematics, electronics, and history. We discuss these examples *not* because all school children are expected to become experts in these or any other areas, but because the study of expertise shows what the results of successful learning look like. In later chapters we explore what is known about processes of learning that can eventually lead to the development of expertise.

We consider several key principles of experts' knowledge and their potential implications for learning and instruction:

1. Experts notice features and meaningful patterns of information that are not noticed by novices.
2. Experts have acquired a great deal of content knowledge that is organized in ways that reflect a deep understanding of their subject matter.
3. Experts' knowledge cannot be reduced to sets of isolated facts or propositions but, instead, reflects contexts of applicability: that is, the knowledge is "conditionalized" on a set of circumstances.
4. Experts are able to flexibly retrieve important aspects of their knowledge with little attentional effort.
5. Though experts know their disciplines thoroughly, this does not guarantee that they are able to teach others.
6. Experts have varying levels of flexibility in their approach to new situations.

Meaningful Patterns of Information

One of the earliest studies of expertise demonstrated that the same stimulus is perceived and understood differently, depending on the knowledge that a person brings to the situation. DeGroot (1965) was interested in understanding how world-class chess masters are consistently able to out-think their opponents. Chess masters and less experienced but still extremely good players were shown examples of chess games and asked to think aloud as they decided on the move they would make if they were one of the players; see Box 4.1. DeGroot's hypothesis was that the chess masters would be

Reprinted from *National Research Council* (1999), by permission of the National Academies Press.

more likely than the nonmasters to (a) think through all the possibilities before making a move (greater breadth of search) and (b) think through all the possible countermoves of the opponent for every move considered (greater depth of search). In this pioneering research, the chess masters did exhibit considerable breadth and depth to their searches, but so did the lesser ranked chess players. And none of them conducted searches that covered all the possibilities. Somehow, the chess masters considered possibilities for moves that were of higher quality than those considered by the lesser experienced players. Something other than differences in general strategies seemed to be responsible for differences in expertise.

DeGroot concluded that the knowledge acquired over tens of thousands of hours of chess playing enabled chess masters to out-play their opponents. Specifically, masters were more likely to recognize meaningful chess configurations and realize the strategic implications of these situations; this recognition allowed them to consider sets of possible moves that were superior to others. The meaningful patterns seemed readily apparent to the masters, leading deGroot (1965:33-34) to note:

> We know that increasing experience and knowledge in a specific field (chess, for instance) has the effect that things (properties, etc.) which, at earlier stages, had to be abstracted, or even inferred are apt to be immediately perceived at later stages. To a rather large extent, abstraction is replaced by perception, but we do not know much about how this works, nor where the borderline lies. As an effect of this replacement, a so-called 'given' problem situation is not really given since it is seen differently by an expert than it is perceived by an inexperienced person. . . .

DeGroot's think-aloud method provided for a very careful analysis of the conditions of specialized learning and the kinds of conclusions one can draw from them (see Ericsson and Simon, 1993). Hypotheses generated from think-aloud protocols are usually cross-validated through the use of other methodologies.

The superior recall ability of experts, illustrated in the example in the box, has been explained in terms of how they "chunk" various elements of a configuration that are related by an underlying function or strategy. Since there are limits on the amount of information that people can hold in short-term memory, short-term memory is enhanced when people are able to chunk information into familiar patterns (Miller, 1956). Chess masters perceive chunks of meaningful information, which affects their memory for what they see. Chess masters are able to chunk together several chess pieces in a configuration that is governed by some strategic component of the game. Lacking a hierarchical, highly organized structure for the domain, novices cannot use this chunking strategy. It is noteworthy that people do not have to be world-class experts to benefit from their abilities to encode meaningful chunks of information: 10- and 11-year-olds who are experienced in chess are able to remember more chess pieces than college students who are not chess players. In contrast, when the college students were presented with other stimuli, such as strings of numbers, they were able to remember more (Chi, 1978; Schneider et al., 1993); see Figure 4.3.

Skills similar to those of master chess players have been demonstrated for experts in other domains, including electronic circuitry (Egan and Schwartz, 1979), radiology (Lesgold, 1988), and computer programming (Ehrlich and Soloway, 1984). In each case, expertise in a domain helps people develop a sensitivity to patterns of meaningful information that are not available to novices. For example, electronics technicians were able to reproduce large portions of complex circuit diagrams after only a few seconds of viewing; novices could not. The expert circuit technicians chunked several individual circuit elements (e.g., resistors and capacitors) that performed the function of an amplifier. By remembering the structure and function of a typical amplifier, experts were able to recall the arrangement of many of the individual circuit elements comprising the "amplifier chunk."

Mathematics experts are also able to quickly recognize patterns of information, such as particular problem types that involve specific classes of mathematical solutions (Hinsley et al., 1977; Robinson and Hayes, 1978). For example, physicists recognize problems of river currents and problems of headwinds and tailwinds in airplanes as involving similar mathematical principles, such as relative velocities. The expert knowledge that underlies the ability to recognize problem types has been characterized as involving the development of organized conceptual structures, or schemas, that guide how problems are represented and understood (e.g., Glaser and Chi, 1988).

Expert teachers, too, have been shown to have schemas similar to those found in chess and mathematics. Expert and novice teachers were shown a videotaped classroom lesson (Sabers et al., 1991). The experimental set-up involved three screens that showed simultaneous events occurring throughout the classroom (the left, center, and right). During part of the session, the expert and novice teachers were asked to talk aloud about what they were seeing. Later, they were asked ques-

Box 4.1
What Experts See

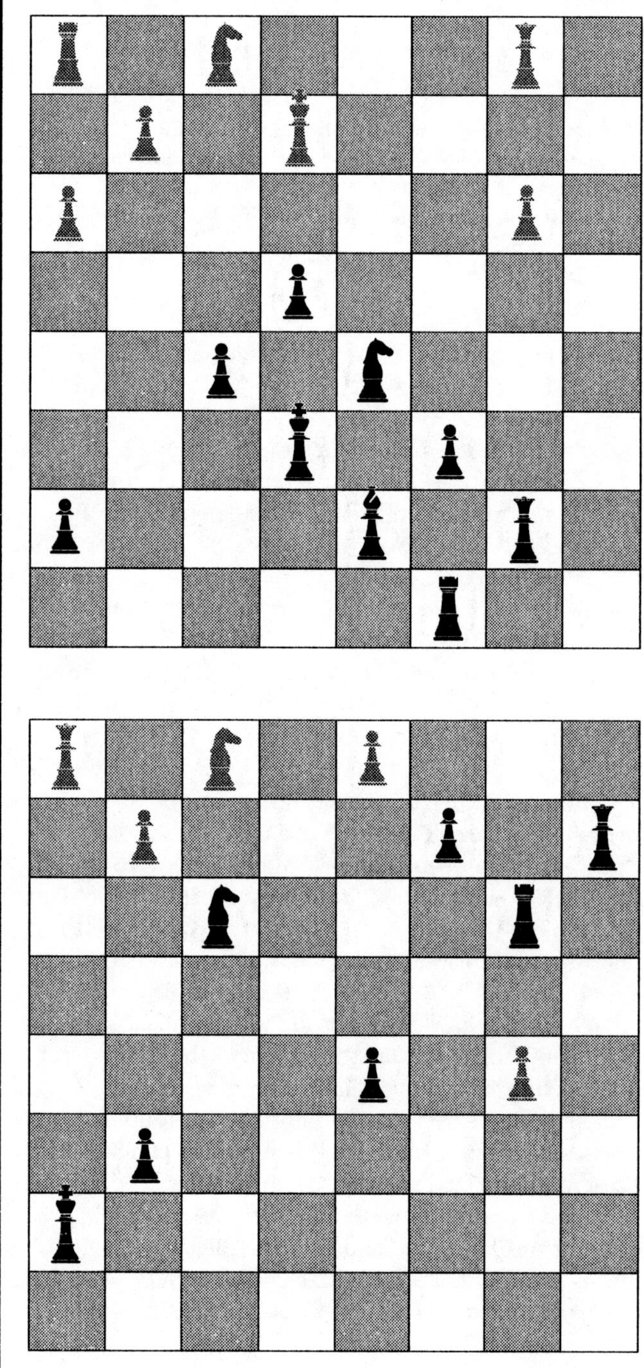

Figure 4.1
Chess board positions used in memory experiments.
SOURCE: Adapted from Chase and Simon (1973).

tions about classroom events. Overall, the expert teachers had very different understandings of the events they were watching than did the novice teachers: see examples in Box 4.2.

The idea that experts recognize features and patterns that are not noticed by novices is potentially important for improving instruction. When viewing instructional texts, slides, and videotapes, for example, the information noticed by novices can he quite different from what is noticed by experts (e.g., Sabers et al., 1991: Bransford et al., 1988). One dimension of acquiring greater competence appears to be the increased ability to segment the perceptual field (learning how to see).

In one study, a chess master, a Class A player (good but not a master), and a novice were given 5 seconds to view a chess board position from the middle of a chess game; see Figure 4.1. After 5 seconds the board was covered, and each participant attempted to reconstruct the board position on another board. This procedure was repeated for multiple trials until everyone received a perfect score. On the first trial, the master player correctly placed many more pieces than the Class A player, who in turn placed more than the novice: 16, 8, and 4, respectively.

However, these results occurred only when the chess pieces were arranged in configurations that conformed to meaningful games of chess. When chess pieces were randomized and presented for 5 seconds, the recall of the chess master and Class A player were the same as the novice—they placed from 2 to 3 positions correctly. Data over trials for valid and random middle games are shown in Figure 4.2.

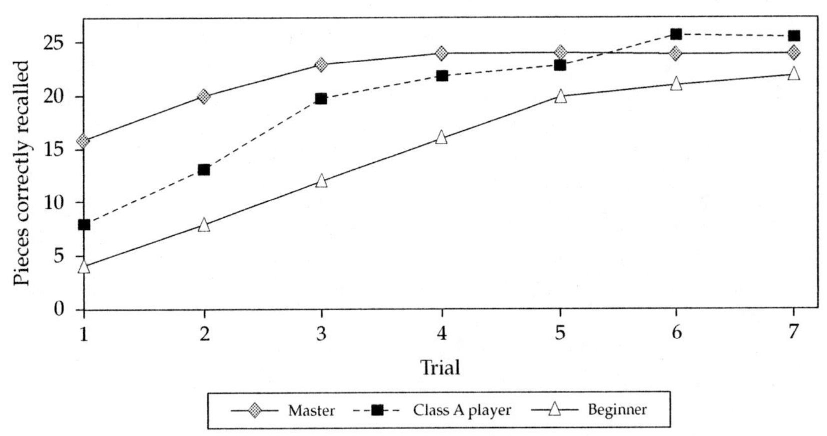

Figure 4.2
Recall by chess players by level of expertise.

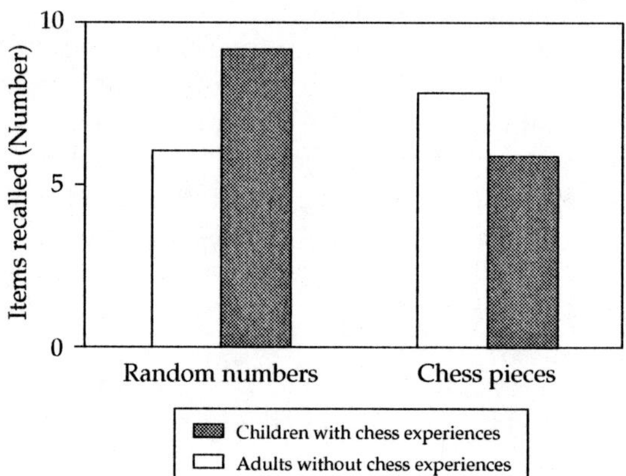

Figure 4.3
Recall for numbers and chess pieces.
SOURCE: Adapted from Chi (1978).

Research on expertise suggests the importance of providing students with learning experiences that specifically enhance their abilities to recognize meaningful patterns of information (e.g., Simon, 1980; Bransford et al., 1989).

Organization of Knowledge

We turn now to the question of how experts' knowledge is organized and how this affects their abilities to understand and represent problems. Their knowledge is not simply a list of facts and formu-

Box 4.2
What Expert and Novice Teachers Notice

Expert and novice teachers notice very different things when viewing a videotape of a classroom lesson.

Expert 6: On the left monitor, the students' note taking indicates that they have seen sheets like this and have had presentations like this before; it's fairly efficient at this point because they're used to the format they are using.

Expert 7: I don't understand why the students can't be finding out this information on their own rather than listening to someone tell them because if you watch the faces of most of them, they start out for about the first 2 or 3 minutes sort of paying attention to what's going on and then just drift off.

Expert 2: . . . I haven't heard a bell, but the students are already at their desks and seem to be doing purposeful activity, and this is about the time that I decide they must be an accelerated group because they came into the room and started something rather than just sitting down and socializing.

Novice 1: . . . I can't tell what they are doing. They're getting ready for class, but I can't tell what they're doing.

Novice 3: She's trying to communicate with them here about something, but I sure couldn't tell what it was.

Another novice: It's a lot to watch.

las that are relevant to their domain; instead, their knowledge is organized around core concepts or "big ideas" that guide their thinking about their domains.

In an example from physics, experts and competent beginners (college students) were asked to describe verbally the approach they would use to solve physics problems. Experts usually mentioned the major principle(s) or law(s) that were applicable to the problem, together with a rationale for why those laws applied to the problem and how one could apply them (Chi et al., 1981). In contrast, competent beginners rarely referred to major principles and laws in physics; instead, they typically described which equations they would use and how those equations would be manipulated (Larkin, 1981, 1983).

Experts' thinking seems to be organized around big ideas in physics, such as Newton's second law and how it would apply, while novices tend to perceive problem solving in physics as memorizing, recalling, and manipulating equations to get answers. When solving problems, experts in physics often pause to draw a simple qualitative diagram—they do not simply attempt to plug numbers into a formula. The diagram is often elaborated as the expert seeks to find a workable solution path (e.g., see Larkin et al., 1980; Larkin and Simon, 1987; Simon and Simon, 1978).

Differences in how physics experts and novices approach problems can also be seen when they are asked to sort problems, written on index cards, according to the approach that could be used to solve them (Chi et al., 1981). Experts' problem piles are arranged on the basis of the principles that can be applied to solve the problems; novices' piles are arranged on the basis of the problems' surface attributes. For example, in the physics subfield of mechanics, an expert's pile might consist of problems that can be solved by conservation of energy, while a novice's pile might consist of problems that contain inclined planes; see Figure 4.4. Responding to the surface characteristics of problems is not very useful, since two problems that share the same objects and look very similar may actually be solved by entirely different approaches.

Some studies of experts and novices in physics have explored the organization of the knowledge structures that are available to these different groups of individuals (Chi et al., 1982); see Figure 4.5. In representing a schema for an incline plane, the novice's schema contains primarily surface features of the incline plane. In contrast, the expert's schema immediately connects the notion of an incline plane with the laws of physics and the conditions under which laws are applicable.

Pause times have also been used to infer the structure of expert knowledge in domains such as chess and physics. Physics experts appear to evoke sets of related equations, with the recall of one equation activating related equations that are retrieved rapidly (Larkin, 1979). Novices, in contrast, retrieve equations more equally spaced in time, suggesting a sequential search in memory. Experts appear to possess an efficient organization of knowledge with meaningful relations among related elements clustered into related units that are governed by underlying concepts and principles; see Box 4.3. Within this picture of expertise, "knowing more" means having more conceptual chunks in memory, more relations or features defining each chunk, more interrelations among the chunks, and efficient methods for retrieving related chunks and procedures for applying these informational units in problem-solving contexts (Chi et al., 1981).

Differences between how experts and nonexperts organize knowledge has also been demonstrated in such fields as history (Wineburg, 1991). A group of history experts and a group of gifted, high-achieving high school seniors enrolled in an advanced placement course in history were first given a test of facts about the American Revolution. The historians with backgrounds in American history knew most of the items. However, many of the historians had specialties that lay elsewhere and they knew only one-third of the facts on the tests. Several of the students outscored several of the historians on the factual test. The study then compared how the historians and students made sense of historical documents; the result revealed dramatic differences on virtually any criterion. The historians excelled in the elaborateness of understandings they developed in their ability to pose alternative explanations for events and in their use of corroborating evidence. This depth of understanding was as true for the Asian specialists and the medievalists as it was for the Americanists.

When the two groups were asked to select one of three pictures that best reflect their understanding of the battle of Lexington, historians and students displayed the greatest differences. Historians carefully navigated back and forth between the corpus of written documents and the three images of

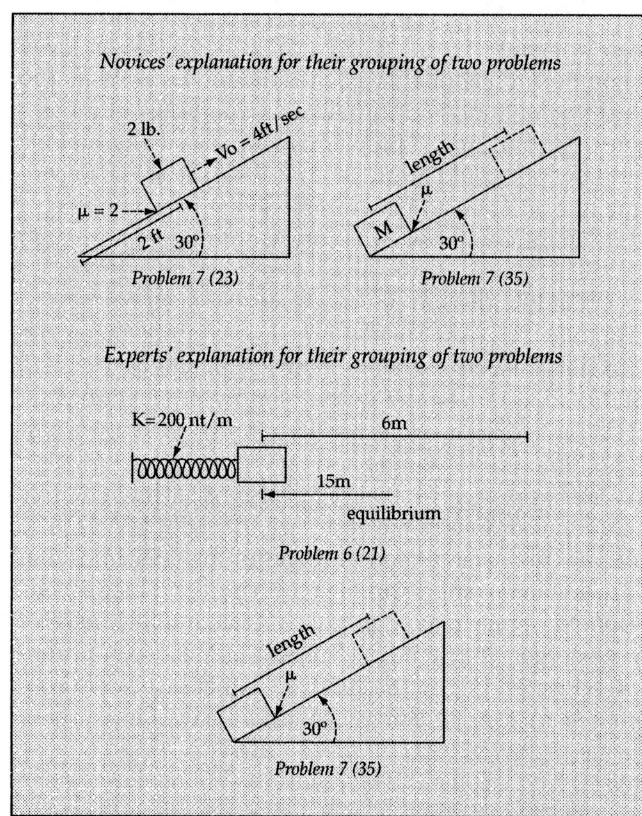

Explanations

Novice 1: These deal with blocks on an incline plane.

Novice 5: Incline plane problems, coefficient of friction.

Novice 6: Blocks on inclined planes with angles.

Explanations

Expert 2: Conservation of energy.

Expert 3: Work-theory theorem. They are all straight-forward problems.

Expert 4: These can be done from energy considerations. Either you should know the principle of conservation of energy, or work is lost somewhere.

Figure 4.4
An example of sortings of physics problems made by novices and experts. Each picture above represents a diagram that can be drawn from the storyline of a physics problem taken from an introductory physics textbook. The novices and experts in this study were asked to categorize many such problems based on similarity of solution. The two pairs show a marked contrast in the experts' and novices' categorization schemes. Novices tend to categorize physics problems as being solved similarly if they "look the same" (that is, share the same surface features), whereas experts categorize according to the major principle that could be applied to solve the problems. SOURCE: Adapted from Chi et al., (1981).

the battlefield. For them, the picture selection task was the quint essential epistemological exercise, a task that explored the limits of historical knowledge. They knew that no single document or picture could tell the story of history; hence, they thought very hard about their choices. In contrast, the students generally just looked at the pictures and made a selection without regard or qualification. For students, the process was similar to finding the correct answer on a multiple choice test.

In sum, although the students scored very well on facts about history, they were largely unacquainted with modes of inquiry with real historical thinking. They had no systematic way of making sense of contradictory claims. Thrust into a set of historical documents that demanded that they sort out competing claims and formulate a reasoned interpretation, the students, on the whole, were stymied. They lacked the experts' deep understanding of how to formulate reasoned interpretations of sets of historical documents. Experts in other social sciences also organize their problem solving around big ideas (see, e.g., Voss et al., 1984).

The fact that experts' knowledge is organized around important ideas or concepts suggests that curricula should also be organized in ways that lead to conceptual understanding. Many approaches to curriculum design make it difficult for students to organize knowledge meaningfully.

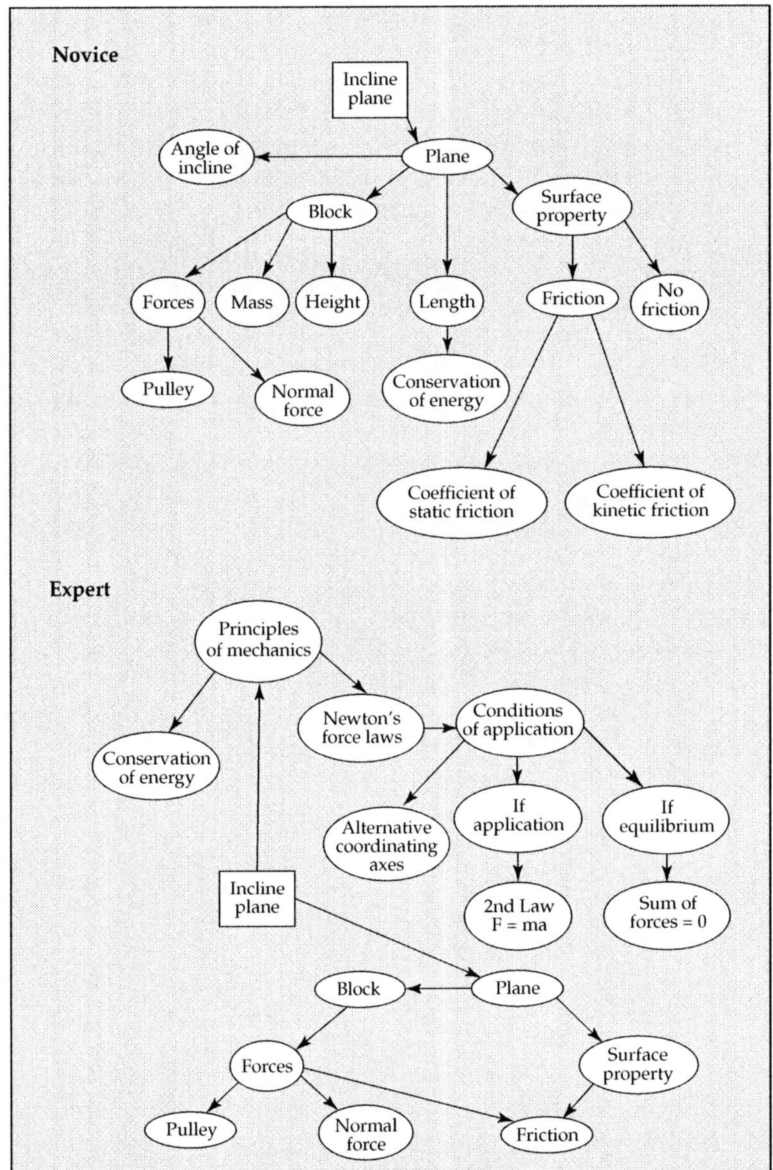

Figure 4.5
Network representations of incline plane schema of novices and experts. SOURCE: Chi et al. (1982:58). Used with permission of Lawrence Erlbaum Associates.
Copyright © 1988 by Michelene T.H. Chi, R. Glaser and M. Farr / Taylor and Francis.

Often there is only superficial coverage of facts before moving on to the next topic; there is little time to develop important, organizing ideas. History texts sometimes emphasize facts without providing support for understanding (e.g., Beck et al., 1989, 1991). Many ways of teaching science also overemphasize facts (American Association for the Advancement of Science, 1989; National Research Council, 1996).

The Third International Mathematics and Science Survey (TIMSS) (Schmidt et al., 1997) criticized curricula that were "a mile wide and an inch deep" and argued that this is much more of a problem in America than in most other countries. Research on expertise suggests that a superficial coverage of many topics in the domain may be a poor way to help students develop the competencies that will prepare them for future learning and work. The idea of helping students organize their knowledge also suggests that novices might benefit from models of how experts approach problem solving—especially if they then receive coaching in using similar strategies (e.g., Brown et al., 1989).

Box 4.3
Understanding and Problem Solving

In mathematics, experts are more likely than novices to first try to understand problems, rather than simply attempt to plug numbers into formulas. Experts and students in one study (Paige and Simon, 1966) were asked to solve algebra word problems, such as:

> A board was sawed into two pieces. One piece was two-thirds as long as the whole board and was exceeded in length by the second piece by four feet. How long was the board before it was cut?

The experts quickly realize that the problem as stated is logically impossible. Although some students also come to this realization, others simply apply equations, which results in the answer of a negative length.

A similar example comes from a study of adults and children (Reusser, 1993), who were asked:

> There are 26 sheep and 10 goats on a ship. How old is the captain?

Most adults have enough expertise to realize that this problem is unsolvable, but many school children didn't realize this at all. More than three-quarters of the children in one study attempted to provide a numerical answer to the problems. They asked themselves whether to add, subtract, multiply, or divide, rather than whether the problem made sense. As one fifth-grade child explained, after giving the answer of 36: "Well, you need to add or subtract or multiply in problems like this, and this one seemed to work best if I add" (Bransford and Stein, 1993:196).

Context and Access to Knowledge

Experts have a vast repertoire of knowledge that is relevant to their domain or discipline, but only a subset of that knowledge is relevant to any particular problem. Experts do not have to search through everything they know in order to find what is relevant; such an approach would overwhelm their working memory (Miller, 1956). For example, the chess masters described above considered only a subset of possible chess moves, but those moves were generally superior to the ones considered by the lesser ranked players. Experts have not only acquired knowledge, but are also good at retrieving the knowledge that is relevant to a particular task. In the language of cognitive scientists, experts' knowledge is "conditionalized"—it includes a specification of the contexts in which it is useful (Simon, 1980; Glaser, 1992). Knowledge that is not conditionalized is often "inert" because it is not activated, even though it is relevant (Whitehead, 1929).

The concept of conditionalized knowledge has implications for the design of curriculum, instruction, and assessment practices that promote effective learning. Many forms of curricula and instruction do not help students conditionalize their knowledge: "Textbooks are much more explicit in enunciating the laws of mathematics or of nature than in saying anything about when these laws may be useful in solving problems" (Simon, 1980:92). It is left largely to students to generate the condition-action pairs required for solving novel problems.

One way to help students learn about conditions of applicability is to assign word problems that require students to use appropriate concepts and formulas (Lesgold, 1984, 1988; Simon, 1980). If well designed, these problems can help students learn when, where, and why to use the knowledge they are learning. Sometimes, however, students can solve sets of practice problems but fail to conditionalize their knowledge because they know which chapter the problems came from and so automatically use this information to decide which concepts and formulas are relevant. Practice problems that are organized into very structured worksheets can also cause this problem. Sometimes students who have done well on such assignments—and believe that they are learning—are unpleasantly surprised when they take tests in which problems from the entire course are randomly presented so there are no clues about where they appeared in a text (Bransford, 1979).

The concept of conditionalized knowledge also has important implications for assessment practices that provide feedback about learning. Many types of tests fail to help teachers and students assess the degree to which the students' knowledge is conditionalized. For example, students might be asked whether the formula that quantifies the relationship between mass and energy is $E = MC$, $E = MC^2$, or $E = MC^3$. A correct answer requires no knowledge of the conditions under which it is appropriate to use the formula. Similarly, students in a literature class might be asked to explain the meaning of familiar proverbs, such as "he who hesitates is lost" or "too many cooks spoil the broth." The ability to explain the meaning of each proverb provides no guarantee that students will know the conditions under which either proverb is useful. Such knowledge is important because, when viewed solely as propositions, proverbs often contradict one another. To use them effectively, people need to know when and why it is appropriate to apply the maxim "too many cooks spoil the broth" versus "many hands make light work" or "he who hesitates is lost" versus "haste makes waste" (see Bransford and Stein, 1993).

Fluent Retrieval

People's abilities to retrieve relevant knowledge can vary from being "effortful" to "relatively effortless" (fluent) to "automatic" (Schneider and Shiffrin, 1977). Automatic and fluent retrieval are important characteristics of expertise.

Fluent retrieval does not mean that experts always perform a task faster than novices. Because experts attempt to understand problems rather than to jump immediately to solution strategies, they sometimes take more time than novices (e.g., Getzels and Csikszentmihalyi, 1976). But within the overall process of problem solving there are a number of subprocesses that, for experts, vary from fluent to automatic. Fluency is important because effortless processing places fewer demands on conscious attention. Since the amount of information a person can attend to at any one time is limited (Miller, 1956), ease of processing some aspects of a task gives a person more capacity to attend to other aspects of the task (LaBerge and Samuels, 1974; Schneider and Shiffrin, 1985; Anderson, 1981, 1982; Lesgold et al., 1988).

Learning to drive a car provides a good example of fluency and automaticity. When first learning, novices cannot drive and simultaneously carry on a conversation. With experience, it becomes easy to do so. Similarly, novice readers whose ability to decode words is not yet fluent are unable to devote attention to the task of understanding what they are reading (LaBerge and Samuels, 1974). Issues of fluency are very important for understanding learning and instruction. Many instructional environments stop short of helping all students develop the fluency needed to successfully perform cognitive tasks (Beck et al., 1989; Case, 1978; Hasselbring et al., 1987; LaBerge and Samuels, 1974).

An important aspect of learning is to become fluent at recognizing problem types in particular domains—such as problems involving Newton's second law or concepts of rate and functions—so that appropriate solutions can be easily retrieved from memory. The use of instructional procedures that speed pattern recognition are promising in this regard (e.g., Simon, 1980).

Experts and Teaching

Expertise in a particular domain does not guarantee that one is good at helping others learn it. In fact, expertise can sometimes hurt teaching because many experts forget what is easy and what is difficult for students. Recognizing this fact, some groups who design educational materials pair content area experts with "accomplished novices" whose area of expertise lies elsewhere: their task is to continually challenge the experts until the experts' ideas for instruction begin to make sense to them (Cognition and Technology Group at Vanderbilt, 1997).

The content knowledge necessary for expertise in a discipline needs to be differentiated from the pedagogical content knowledge that underlies effective teaching (Redish, 1996; Shulman, 1986,

1987). The latter includes information about typical difficulties that students encounter as they attempt to learn about a set of topics; typical paths students must traverse in order to achieve understanding; and sets of potential strategies for helping students overcome the difficulties that they encounter. Shulman (1986, 1987) argues that pedagogical content knowledge is not equivalent to knowledge of a content domain plus a generic set of teaching strategies; instead, teaching strategies differ across disciplines. Expert teachers know the kinds of difficulties that students are likely to face; they know how to tap into students' existing knowledge in order to make new information meaningful; and they know how to assess their students' progress. Expert teachers have acquired pedagogical content knowledge as well as content knowledge; see Box 4.4. In the absence of pedagogical content knowledge, teachers often rely on textbook publishers for decisions about how to best organize subjects for students. They are therefore forced to rely on the "prescriptions of absentee curriculum developers" (Brophy, 1983), who know nothing about the particular students in each teacher's classroom. Pedagogical content knowledge is an extremely important part of what teachers need to learn to be more effective. (This topic is discussed more fully in Chapter 7.)

Adaptive Expertise

An important question for educators is whether some ways of organizing knowledge are better at helping people remain flexible and adaptive to new situations than others. For example, contrast two types of Japanese sushi experts (Hatano and Inagaki, 1986): one excels at following a fixed recipe; the other has "adaptive expertise" and is able to prepare sushi quite creatively. These appear to be examples of two very different types of expertise, one that is relatively routinized and one that is flexible and more adaptable to external demands: experts have been characterized as being "merely skilled" versus "highly competent" or more colorfully as "artisans" versus "virtuosos" (Miller, 1978). These differences apparently exist across a wide range of jobs.

One analysis looked at these differences in terms of information systems design (Miller, 1978). Information systems designers typically work with clients who specify what they want. The goal of the designer is to construct systems that allow people to efficiently store and access relevant information (usually through computers). Artisan experts seek to identify the functions that their clients want automated; they tend to accept the problem and its limits as stated by the clients. They approach new problems as opportunities to use their existing expertise to do familiar tasks more efficiently. It is important to emphasize that artisans' skills are often extensive and should not be underestimated. In contrast, however, the virtuoso experts treat the client's statement of the problem with respect, but consider it "a point for departure and exploration" (Miller, 1978). They view assignments as opportunities to explore and expand their current levels of expertise. Miller also observes that, in his experience, virtuosos exhibit their positive characteristics *despite* their training, which is usually restricted solely to technical skills.

The concept of adaptive expertise has also been explored in a study of history experts (Wineburg, 1998). Two history experts and a group of future teachers were asked to read and interpret a set of documents about Abraham Lincoln and his view of slavery. This is a complex issue that, for Lincoln, involved conflicts between enacted law (the Constitution), natural law (as encoded in the Declaration of Independence), and divine law (assumptions about basic rights). One of the historians was an expert on Lincoln; the second historian's expertise lay elsewhere. The Lincoln expert brought detailed content knowledge to the documents and easily interpreted them; the other historian was familiar with some of the broad themes in the documents but quickly became confused in the details. In fact, at the beginning of the task, the second historian reacted no differently than a group of future high school teachers who were faced with the same task (Wineburg and Fournier, 1994): attempting to harmonize discrepant information about Lincoln's position, they both appealed to an array of present social forms and institutions—such as speech writers, press conferences, and "spin doctors"—to explain why things seemed discrepant. Unlike the future teachers, however, the second historian did not stop with his initial analysis. He instead adopted a working hypothesis that assumed that the apparent contradictions might be rooted less in Lincoln's duplicity than in his own ignorance of the nineteenth century. The expert stepped back from his own initial interpretation and

Box 4.4
Teaching *Hamlet*

Two new English teachers, Jake and Steven, with similar subject-matter backgrounds from elite private universities, set out to teach *Hamlet* in high school (Grossman, 1990).

In his teaching, Jake spent 7 weeks leading his students through a word-by-word *explication du texte,* focusing on notions of "linguistic reflexivity," and issues of modernism. His assignments included in-depth analyses of soliloquies, memorization of long passages, and a final paper on the importance of language in *Hamlet.* Jake's model for this instruction was his own undergraduate coursework; there was little transformation of his knowledge, except to parcel it out in chunks that fit into the 50-minute containers of the school day. Jake's image for how students would respond was his own responses as a student who loved Shakespeare and delighted in close textual analysis. Consequently, when students responded in less than enthusiastic ways, Jake was ill-equipped to understand their confusion: "The biggest problem I have with teaching by far is trying to get into the mind-set of a ninth grader . . ."

Steven began his unit on *Hamlet* without ever mentioning the name of the play. To help his students grasp the initial outline of the themes and issues of the play, he asked them to imagine that their parents had recently divorced and that their mothers had taken up with a new man. This new man had replaced their father at work, and "there's some talk that he had something to do with the ousting of your dad" (Grossman, 1990:24). Steven then asked students to think about the circumstances that might drive them so mad that they would contemplate murdering another human being. Only then, after students had contemplated these issues and done some writing on them, did Steven introduce the play they would be reading.

searched for a deeper understanding of the issues. As he read texts from this perspective, his understanding deepened, and he learned from the experience. After considerable work, the second historian was able to piece together an interpretive structure that brought him by the task's end to where his more knowledgeable colleague had begun. The future history teachers, in contrast, never moved beyond their initial interpretations of events.

An important characteristic exhibited by the history expert involves what is known as "metacognition"—the ability to monitor one's current level of understanding and decide when it is not adequate. The concept of metacognition was originally introduced in the context of studying young children (e.g., Brown, 1980; Flavell, 1985, 1991). For example, young children often erroneously believe that they can remember information and hence fail to use effective strategies, such as rehearsal. The ability to recognize the limits of one's current knowledge, then take steps to remedy the situation, is extremely important for learners at all ages. The history expert who was not a specialist in Lincoln was metacognitive in the sense that he successfully recognized the insufficiency of his initial attempts to explain Lincoln's position. As a consequence, he adopted the working hypothesis that he needed to learn more about the context of Lincoln's times before coming to a reasoned conclusion.

Beliefs about what it means to be an expert can affect the degree to which people explicitly search for what they don't know and take steps to improve the situation. In a study of researchers and veteran teachers, a common assumption was that "an expert is someone who knows all the answers" (Cognition and Technology Group at Vanderbilt, 1997). This assumption had been implicit rather than explicit and had never been questioned and discussed. But when the researchers and teachers discussed this concept, they discovered that it placed severe constraints on new learning because the tendency was to worry about looking competent rather than publicly acknowledging the need for help in certain areas (see Dweck, 1989, for similar findings with students). The researchers and the teachers found it useful to replace their previous model of "answer-filled experts" with the model of "accomplished novices." Accomplished novices are skilled in many areas and proud of their accomplishments, but they realize that what they know is minuscule compared to all that is potentially knowable. This model helps free people to continue to learn even though they may have spent 10 to 20 years as an "expert" in their field.

The concept of adaptive expertise (Hatano and Inagaki, 1986) provides an important model of successful learning. Adaptive experts are able to approach new situations flexibly and to learn throughout their lifetimes. They not only use what they have learned, they are metacognitive and continually question their current levels of expertise and attempt to move beyond them. They don't simply attempt to do the same things more efficiently; they attempt to do things better. A major challenge for theories of learning is to understand how particular kinds of learning experiences develop adaptive expertise or "virtuosos."

Conclusion

Experts' abilities to reason and solve problems depend on well-organized knowledge that affects what they notice and how they represent problems. Experts are not simply "general problem solvers" who have learned a set of strategies that operate across all domains. The fact that experts are more likely than novices to recognize meaningful patterns of information applies in all domains, whether chess, electronics, mathematics, or classroom teaching. In deGroot's (1965) words, a "given" problem situation is not really a given. Because of their ability to see patterns of meaningful information, experts begin problem solving at "a higher place" (deGroot, 1965). An emphasis on the patterns perceived by experts suggests that pattern recognition is an important strategy for helping students develop confidence and competence. These patterns provide triggering conditions for accessing knowledge that is relevant to a task.

Studies in areas such as physics, mathematics, and history also demonstrate that experts first seek to develop an understanding of problems, and this often involves thinking in terms of core concepts or big ideas, such as Newton's second law in physics. Novices' knowledge is much less likely to be organized around big ideas; they are more likely to approach problems by searching for correct formulas and pat answers that fit their everyday intuitions.

Curricula that emphasize breadth of knowledge may prevent effective organization of knowledge because there is not enough time to learn anything in depth. Instruction that enables students to see models of how experts organize and solve problems may be helpful. However, as discussed in more detail in later chapters, the level of complexity of the models must be tailored to the learners' current levels of knowledge and skills.

While experts possess a vast repertoire of knowledge, only a subset of it is relevant to any particular problem. Experts do not conduct an exhaustive search of everything they know; this would overwhelm their working memory (Miller, 1956). Instead, information that is relevant to a task tends to be selectively retrieved (e.g., Ericsson and Staszewski, 1989; deGroot, 1965).

The issue of retrieving relevant information provides clues about the nature of usable knowledge. Knowledge must be "conditionalized" in order to be retrieved when it is needed; otherwise, it remains inert (Whitehead, 1929). Many designs for curriculum instruction and assessment practices fail to emphasize the importance of conditionalized knowledge. For example, texts often present facts and formulas with little attention to helping students learn the conditions under which they are most useful. Many assessments measure only propositional (factual) knowledge and never ask whether students know when, where, and why to use that knowledge.

Another important characteristic of expertise is the ability to retrieve relevant knowledge in a manner that is relatively "effortless." This fluent retrieval does not mean that experts always accomplish tasks in less time than novices; often they take more time in order to fully understand a problem. But their ability to retrieve information effortlessly is extremely important because fluency places fewer demands on conscious attention, which is limited in capacity (Schneider and Shiffrin, 1977, 1985). Effortful retrieval, by contrast, places many demands on a learner's attention: attentional effort is being expended on remembering instead of learning. Instruction that focuses solely on accuracy does not necessarily help students develop fluency (e.g., Beck et al., 1989; Hasselbring et al., 1987; LaBerge and Samuels, 1974).

Expertise in an area does not guarantee that one can effectively teach others about that area. Expert teachers know the kinds of difficulties that students are likely to face, and they know how to tap into their students' existing knowledge in order to make new information meaningful plus assess their students' progress. In Shulman's (1986, 1987) terms, expert teachers have acquired pedagogical content knowledge and not just content knowledge. (This concept is explored more fully in Chapter 7.)

The concept of adaptive expertise raises the question of whether some ways of organizing knowledge lead to greater flexibility in problem solving than others (Hatano and Inagaki, 1986; Spiro et al., 1991). Differences between the "merely skilled" (artisans) and the "highly competent" (virtuosos) can be seen in fields as disparate as sushi making and information design. Virtuosos not only apply expertise to a given problem, they also consider whether the problem as presented is the best way to begin.

The ability to monitor one's approach to problem solving—to be metacognitive—is an important aspect of the expert's competence. Experts step back from their first, oversimplistic interpretation of a problem or situation and question their own knowledge that is relevant. People's mental models of what it means to be an expert can affect the degree to which they learn throughout their lifetimes. A model that assumes that experts know all the answers is very different from a model of the accomplished novice, who is proud of his or her achievements and yet also realizes that there is much more to learn.

We close this chapter with two important cautionary notes. First, the six principles of expertise need to be considered simultaneously, as parts of an overall system. We divided our discussion into six points in order to facilitate explanation, but each point interacts with the others; this interrelationship has important educational implications. For example, the idea of promoting fluent access to knowledge (principle 4) must be approached with an eye toward helping students develop an understanding of the subject matter (principle 2), learn when, where and why to use information (principle 3), and learn to recognize meaningful patterns of information (principle 1). Furthermore, all these need to be approached from the perspective of helping students develop adaptive expertise (principle 6), which includes helping them become metacognitive about their learning so that they can assess their own progress and continually identify and pursue new learning goals. An example in mathematics is getting students to recognize when a proof is needed. Metacognition can help students develop personally relevant pedagogical content knowledge, analogous to the pedagogical content knowledge available to effective teachers (principle 5). In short, students need to develop the ability to teach themselves.

The second cautionary note is that although the study of experts provides important information about learning and instruction, it can be misleading if applied inappropriately. For example, it would be a mistake simply to expose novices to expert models and assume that the novices will learn effectively; what they will learn depends on how much they know already. Discussions in the next chapters (3 and 4) show that effective instruction begins with the knowledge and skills that learners bring to the learning task.

Where We Ought To Be:
The Natural Relationship Between Brain Structure and Learning

J.E. Zull

'tis a gift to come down where we ought to be.
—Amish hymn

It was so pretty, it had to be true.
—James Watson on discovering the double helix

Being director of a teaching center had some terrific perks. One of the best was that I was expected to learn about learning. You might not consider this a perk, but I did. It was a luxury for me to read and study about how people learn. I never had time before.

So I looked for new reading. What I wanted wasn't in biology or psychology books I had seen. I needed to get beyond synapses, stimulus/response, habituation, and Pavlov's dogs. My hope was to understand understanding. What must a brain do to comprehend?

It was then that I discovered David Kolb's book, *Experiential Learning.*[1] It wasn't particularly about biology, but still it came closer to what interested me, so in I plunged.

Kolb began by talking about people I had heard of, but never read before, people like Dewey, Piaget, and Lewin. Combining their ideas about development and learning, he described a new "learning cycle." He said deep learning, learning for real comprehension, comes through a sequence of experience, reflection, abstraction, and active testing. These four cycle 'round and 'round as we learn.

I was skeptical of this idea at first. Surely there were many other ways to explain learning. It seemed too simple, too arbitrary.

But I gave it a chance. And, without warning, as I sat in my office on one warm spring afternoon, it all came together. I still remember taking that slow, deep breath, holding it for a second, and then releasing it with a sound somewhere between a laugh and a sigh.

I stood up and began to pace and talk to myself. "It is biological! Of course, it has to be. Everything is in the right place! It's too pretty not to be true!"

I surprised myself. I turned from skeptic to believer on that day. Things just came down where they ought to be.

***

Reprinted from *The art of changing the brain: Enriching the practice of teaching by exploring the biology of learning* (2002), Stylus Publishing.

In biology, the way things work depends on their structure—their physical structure. Genetic inheritance depends on the structure of DNA. Digestion depends on the structure of the gut. Any function found in any living organism must depend on some structure of some part of that organism.

This was my habit of thinking, and so it seemed that if the function we are interested in is learning, we should look for the structure that produces it, and the place we should look is in the brain. Ultimately, the structure of the brain should explain learning. It's only natural.

That is what I saw on that warm spring afternoon. What I knew about the brain told me that the learning cycle should work, and it told me why. For the first time I saw a structure designed for human learning, for understanding and comprehension.

First Look

In this chapter I will give you my proposal for this natural connection between brain structure and learning. We don't need to know much about the brain to do this. Neurons and synapses can wait until later, as can the complicated structures that lie deep in the brain. For now we can simply look at the outside of the brain and talk a little bit about what different parts do.

In the illustration shown below you can see a view of the left side of what is called the *cerebral cortex.* The *cerebrum* is the large part of the human brain that is thought to be responsible for much of the thinking and learning we do, and the *cortex* is the layer of tissue that coats the cerebrum, like the bark of a tree; hence the name *cerebral cortex.*

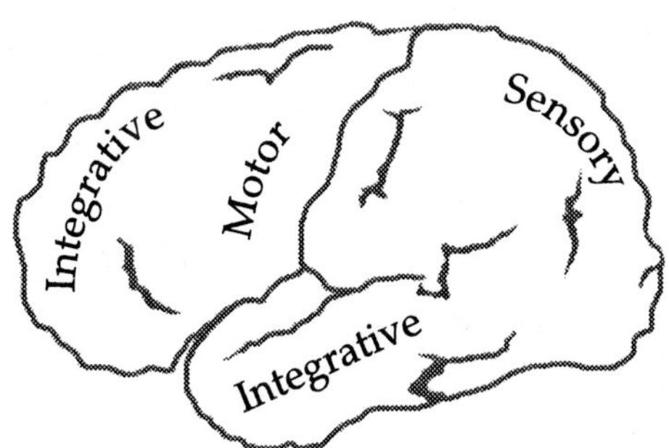

This illustration shows three functions of the cerebral cortex, and roughly which parts of the cortex are engaged in each. The functions are *sensing, integrating,* and *motor* (which means moving). Notice that there are two integrating regions of cortex; we will discuss the difference between them later in this chapter.

These three functions of the cortex are not an accident. They do the key things that are essential for all nervous systems. They sense the environment, add up (or integrate) what they sense, and generate appropriate movements (actions):

Sense → Integrate → Act

These three functions are seen in nervous systems ranging from those in simple animals to the human brain. In the paragraphs that follow I expand on this somewhat and describe more about these three brain functions.

The sensing function refers to the receipt of signals from the outside world. In people, these signals are picked up by the sense organs; eyes, ears, skin, mouth, and nose.[2] They are then sent on to special regions of the brain for each of the senses. These signals come in small bits and have no meaning in their raw form. They are just little individual pulses of electrical energy coming in from the sense organs.

Integration means that these individual signals get added up so that whatever is being sensed is recognized in the sum of all these signals. The small bits merge into bigger patterns that become meaningful things like images or language. In the human brain these meanings are then integrated in new ways that become ideas, thoughts, and plans. At their most basic, these integrated meanings become plans for actions. For example, they get added up in ways that generate a plan for *what* action is needed and *where* the action is needed.

Finally, the motor function is the execution of those plans and ideas by the body. Ultimately, motor signals are sent to the muscles that contract and relax in coordinated ways to create sophisticated movements. Importantly, we should realize that even *speaking* and *writing* fit in here because they involve some of the most sophisticated patterns of muscle contractions that the body carries out.

Brain Connections: An Overview

This transfer of signals from sensory input through the brain to motor output is a general pattern for all nervous systems, including the human brain. The most direct and simplest route for signaling in the brain, then, would be as shown in the illustration below. Sensory input could come from the outside world or from our own body, but once those signals have entered the sensory part of the cortex, they flow first through the integrative part of the brain nearest the sensory part, then through the integrative part nearest the motor brain, and then to the motor brain itself. Once action has been initiated, that action is detected by the sensory brain, so the output of the brain becomes new sensory input.

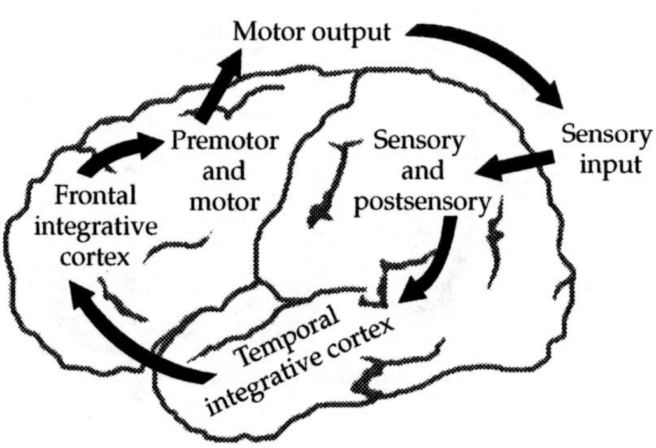

I want to stress that this picture is highly oversimplified. Later we will see that there are many other links, including parallel links and connections where signals go in both directions. What I have shown you is probably the simplest way to look at what the brain does.

Looking for Learning

Our objective is to get ideas about learning from the structure of the brain. We are looking for a structure that generates comprehension and understanding in people, something more than pure memory of facts or physical skills. It isn't necessarily obvious how this type of learning can come from the structure we have been talking about. Somehow deep learning should emerge from sensing, integrating, and acting.

But this is where biology takes us, so we have to keep looking.

The Learning Cycle

The learning cycle explained in Kolb's book is a key part of this search for learning, and this is the point where we can bring it into the story.

The cycle is shown below, in a simplified form.[3] It relies heavily on the ideas of Dewey and Piaget, among others, and you may recognize some of the terminology as originating from these giants in the study of human learning.

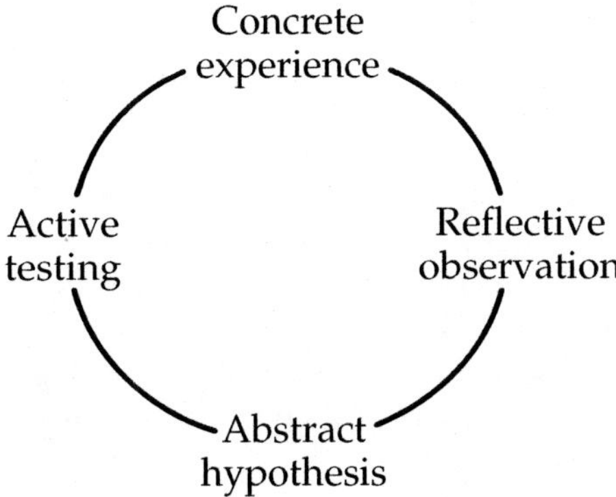

The cycle is based on the proposal that learning originates in concrete experience; hence the term *experiential learning*. But experience is *not* the whole thing.[4] In fact, it is just the beginning. Learning depends on experience, but it also *requires* reflection, developing abstractions, and active testing of our abstractions.

As you reflect on the learning cycle, remember that this is just the basic idea and that its implications are important and complex. I can't do it justice at this point, but I will expand on it in later chapters.

Natural Learning

Let me remind you that when I first saw the learning cycle, I was skeptical. It seemed arbitrary. Why does the cycle stress these particular four things? Why are they placed in this sequence? Why is there any sequence at all? And what about other things like memory, feedback, or trial and error?

I might still be struggling with these and other questions if I had not seen the natural link with biology. You may have seen it already, but if not, the idea is illustrated below.

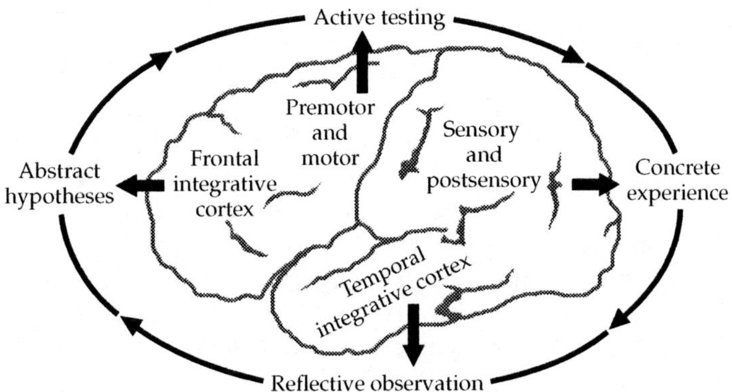

Put into words, the figure illustrates that concrete experience comes through the sensory cortex, reflective observation involves the integrative cortex at the back, creating new abstract concepts occurs in the frontal integrative cortex, and active testing involves the motor brain.[5] In other words, the learning cycle arises naturally from the structure of the brain. This *is* a pretty idea!

Is This about Teaching?

I will explain more about this connection between the learning cycle and the way brains are put together shortly. But I am worried that you may be wondering how this connects with teaching. Maybe you think that I am so enamored by my pretty idea that I have forgotten what the book is supposed to be about.

So I want to take a short break and talk about a teaching connection that comes up immediately if we accept the brain cycle that I propose in my model. Let's start with a story.

***

Lilly Conferences on college teaching were a discovery I had made when I became director of our teaching center. They were always interesting and energizing, and I was looking forward to the session on this particular morning. The title was something like "Improving Teaching in Large Classes."

I was surprised when the presenters began by discussing the record-keeping problems with large classes. How can you avoid making mistakes when you have a class of 1,000?

I agreed that this is important, but I began to get bored as the session went on. My real interest was in learning.

Finally, my frustration got the best of me, and I blurted out my question. "This is useful, but before we finish could you talk a little about learning? What is your experience with improving learning in large classes?"

She looked blank for a moment and then replied, "Well, this session isn't really about learning; it is more about teaching!"

This startled me, but I persisted, "But how can you separate teaching from learning?"

In all sincerity, she replied, "You can teach well, do all the right things, without any learning. Learning is up to the student. If I am teaching right, I am doing my part!"

The Teaching Trap

Is this right? Can we teach without anyone learning?

It does seem true in some ways. You may have experienced something similar yourself. You may have tried your best to help someone learn, but discovered that it just didn't work. You were there, you taught, but learning just didn't happen.

Or did it? Just because your learner didn't understand what you hoped he would, does that mean he learned nothing?

This is where our model comes in. If indeed learning begins through sensory experience, then the teacher is in a trap. *Anything* she does can produce learning, because it is sensory experience.

It happens in school all the time. A student may not learn history in our history class, but he may learn that his teacher thinks history is interesting. Or he may learn that his teacher dislikes students, or that he is just overwhelmed. The student has an experience of some sort. His brain processes that experience, and ultimately he acts on it in some way. His action may be to close the book and look out the window, but that is because his experience has taught him that he doesn't need to listen, or that he doesn't care to listen.

You can plug in your own examples. You may remember when your "teaching" was wasted on an employee, a child, or a parent. It was wasted because your "student" didn't learn what you hoped he would. But he did have an experience; he did have sensory input. And his brain did something with that experience.

The more we understand learning, the more we will realize this. We can't separate teaching from learning. The brain won't let us off the hook that easily.

Rationale for Natural Learning

The brain cycle, then, provokes us to think about the sensory input that students get in our classes. But it doesn't end there. It also suggests that we should look at its implications for other parts of learning.

However, before we can do that, we need more details about what happens in the four parts of the cerebral cortex we have identified and how these functions match up with the learning cycle.

I have tried to summarize this match by lining things up in the two lists below. On the left side, I have listed a few things that our four parts of the cortex are known to do, and on the right side I have tried to show how a particular stage of the learning cycle seems to fit the capabilities of its matched region of cortex.[5]

Important functions of each part of cortex	Match with each stage of the learning cycle
The sensory cortex receives first input from the outside world in form of vision, hearing, touch, position, smells, and taste.	This matches with the common definition of concrete experience, with its reliance on direct physical information from the world.
The back integrative cortex is engaged in memory formation and reassembly, language comprehension, developing spatial relationship, and identifying objects, faces, and motion. In short, it integrates sensory information to create images and meaning.	These functions match well with what happens during reflection, for example, remembering relevant information, daydreaming and free association, developing insights and associations, mentally rerunning experiences, and analyzing experiences.
The frontal integrative cortex is responsible for short-term memory, problem solving, making decisions, assembling plans for action, assembly of language, making judgments and evaluations, directing the action of the rest of the brain (including memory recall), and organizing actions and activities of the entire body.	This matches well with the generation of abstractions, which requires manipulation of images and language to create new (mental) arrangements, developing plans for future action, comparing and choosing options, directing recall of past experience, creating symbolic representations, and replacing and manipulating items held in short-term memory.
The motor cortex directly triggers all coordinated and voluntary muscle contractions by the body, producing movement. It carries out the plans and ideas originating from the front integrative cortex, including the actual production of language through speech and writing.	This matches with the necessity for action in completion of the learning cycle. Active testing of abstractions requires conversion of ideas into physical action, or movements of parts of the body. This includes intellectual activities such as writing, deriving relationships, doing experiments, and talking in debate or conversation.

The point of the list above is to point out that the four parts of the cortex do things that are qualitatively different from each other. When we look at those things, we see the many ways they fit the four parts of the learning cycle.[6]

Example: Learning a New Word Through the Learning Cycle

Let's go through a specific example of how the learning cycle meshes with the functions of these different parts of the brain. Then we will examine actual brain imaging studies that seem to support this proposal directly.

Suppose my task is to learn a new word from another person who knows its definition. Let's say the word is *flabmonk.* When I see or hear *flabmonk,* I have concrete experience. This is a visual and/or auditory sensory event for my brain. When I reflect on the word *flabmonk,* I remember other words and images that seem related or similar. I may recall that flab suggests fat, monk could be a religious person, or it could be an animal. This is the reflective brain at work; it primarily involves memory. As various possibilities come to me, I begin to develop an abstract idea for the meaning of *flabmonk.* I may think, for example, that a *flabmonk* is a new species of animal, or it may be a fat religious person, or a pompous fundamentalist. This is my abstracting brain at work. It is converting past images into new images, and then into new words—new symbols for the real thing. Finally, I test my hypothesis. To do this I must act; I must speak or write. So I ask, "A pompous fundamentalist?" This requires activity by my motor brain. Instantly, my teacher responds. "Yes!" she says and laughs out loud! I have tested my idea.

Or he says, "Sorry, good guess! Try again." I have tested and my test failed, but now my sensory brain has new input and the cycle can start again.

Here is a summary of this example:

1. Hear words or see words = concrete experience
2. Remember related words, images, or ideas = reflection
3. Generate new words or ideas = abstraction
4. Speak or write new words or ideas = active testing
5. Hear or see new words and teacher's response = new concrete experience

Our hypothesis about the brain would say that number 1 involves the sensory cortex, number 2 involves the back integrative cortex, number 3 involves the frontal integrative cortex, number 4 involves the motor cortex, and number 5 reengages the sensory cortex.

Brain Imaging Studies

One of the most important developments in neuroscience over the past few decades is the creation of methods for examining what parts of the brain are most active when we are doing different things. These brain imaging tools have opened the way to much deeper understanding of how brains think and what parts are most strongly engaged for specific tasks. A brief description of two of these methods is included in the notes for this chapter.[7]

Many brain imaging studies support the suggestions I made for learning a new word. Let's look at one of them.

The experiments illustrated in this chapter are related to brain processing of words. Each image shows the areas of the brain that are most active when we are seeing and hearing words, mentally creating a verb, and speaking words.

We can clearly see the activation of specific parts of the cortex in the sensory events of seeing and hearing. (And, by the way, it also is our first demonstration of the actual location of the visual cortex and auditory cortex.) Experiments like this have been done for many visual and auditory processes, and these regions are well established.

The mental generation of verbs, which involves comprehending meaning (activating the back integrative region of the brain) and preparing to speak the verb (which activates the lower region of the frontal lobe), is shown in the lower right panel of this illustration.[8]

Actually speaking the words activates the motor cortex region responsible for driving the muscle contractions needed in speech, which is shown in the lower left panel.

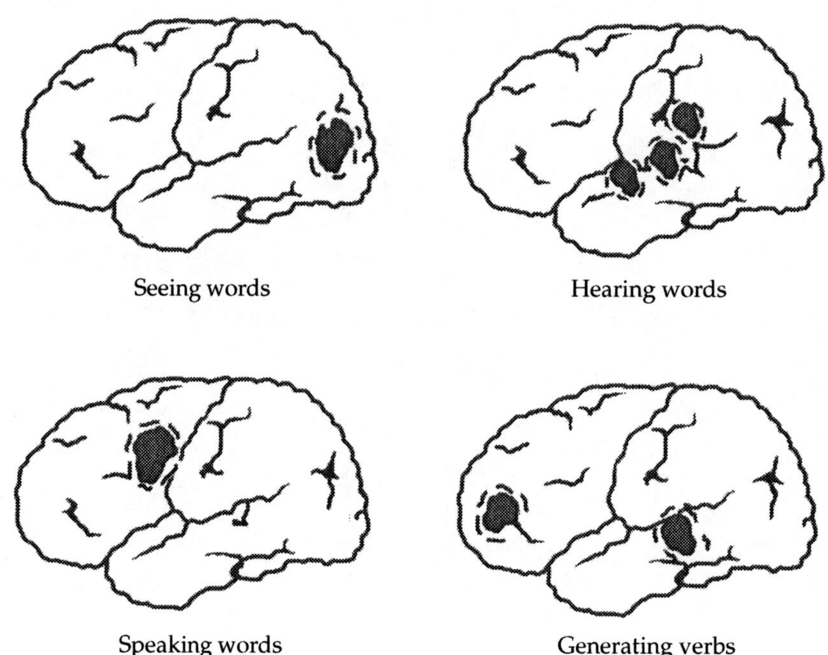

Together, then, these results demonstrate the separation of the experience, reflecting, abstracting, and active testing parts of the learning cycle in different parts of the brain.[9]

How Long Does a Learning Cycle Take?

You may be bothered by this example because it happens rather quickly. You might have gone through the whole cycle in a few seconds. But it wasn't instantaneous. You did need a second or two to reflect on *flabmonk* and make a guess about its meaning. It could have taken much longer, of course. If the word were a French word and you had taken French in high school, without a dictionary you might have thought for days, developing and testing several different ideas about a definition in that time. Only if you already knew the word could the process be instantaneous.

You also might have tried to speed things up by using a dictionary. But you would still be using the learning cycle. After reflection you would develop the hypothesis that you won't be able to recall the word, or at least not in a reasonable time, so you act on that hypothesis by turning to a dictionary.

This may seem like cheating, somehow, but my point is that we always seem to go through the four steps in one form or another. It could even be that we reflect on an experience for years, eventually arrive at an abstract understanding, and finally we confirm our understanding through some action. For example, we change our behavior as a test of our new hypotheses about how to live. Eventually we attain wisdom and regulate our lives by use of the learning cycle.

Our brain has the capacity to reflect, develop ideas, and take actions continually. We are always in the middle of a multitude of learning cycles, getting new sensory information, thinking about different experiences, getting new ideas about their meaning, and testing those ideas. This is the story of our day-to-day lives.

Potential Confusions

Drawing the learning cycle the way we have is a little misleading. We can get the idea that the cycle goes just in one direction all the time. That is true in the sense that a cycle can't be completed until all steps have occurred, but the structure of the brain tells us that the communication between the different regions of the brain can go both ways. Signals can bounce back and forth between different parts.

In fact, the reverberation of signals between meaning and hypothesis reminds us of what seems to happen anytime we think hard about something. We conceive meanings that have implications, and when we put those implications into a hypothesis, we are reminded of other, possibly conflicting, meanings that imply something else or add complexity to the implications. As a result we create a new hypothesis or modify our old one. So it goes until we decide to act on our hypothesis, and then we find out how well we have done our thinking!

There are also shortcuts that make it possible to skip over one part or another. It is important that you realize here that we are not talking about a simple merry-go-round.

Of course, the same is true of learning. We bounce back and forth between reflection and ideas all the time as we think about our experiences and try to make sense of them. Often we will almost skip reflection completely and try a shortcut directly to an idea or even an action. Trial-and-error learning in its least complex forms can be considered simply use of the sensory and motor brain, omitting the integrating brain completely. We try (act) and we fail (sense).

As we would expect, the way the brain is put together and the way learning goes overlap each other in these more complex ways as well as in the simple linear path suggested by our drawings.

Questions for Teachers

The idea that the learning cycle is the natural result of the structure of the brain should encourage us to think about how we might use it to help people learn. We will examine that approach more extensively later in the book, but in the mean time here are some questions that may lead to a few interesting ideas.

- What if we view our "teaching" simply as sensory input? Could we use knowledge of the sensory brain to guide us in our practice? Would this change how we plan our teaching and how we present information?
- What if the assignments we give were intentionally designed to integrate experience and memory through reflection? Could we use our knowledge of the integrative brain to guide us? Would assignments be different? Assessments?
- Could we insist that students develop their *own* abstract ideas and explanations—that is, use their integrative frontal cortex?
- How would we bring the motor brain into our teaching? How can we insist that students actively demonstrate their ideas—not our ideas, but theirs?
- How can we challenge students to use their sensory brains to *observe their own active testing of ideas.* How can we make them aware of their own learning?
- When we try to help people learn, can we find ways to encourage them to use all parts of the learning cycle?
- Why not say that all learning is experiential, school learning included? The structure of the brain does not change when we enter a school, so why should we think school learning is different? Aren't classes experiences? Won't students reflect on that experience? Won't they generate their own ideas about what the experience means? Won't their actions come from these ideas? In fact, isn't that the way it has always been?

As I have indicated, we will address some of these questions later in the book, but that doesn't mean you can't begin to think of your own answers now!

Starting a Foundation for Learning

This chapter is the first step in creating a foundation for learning. The building blocks for our foundation are the sensory, reflective, abstracting, and acting brain. We use those parts of our brain through experience, reflection, hypothesizing, and active testing. Everything I say from here on can be supported by these ideas.

Without biology, the learning cycle is theoretical. But with biology, it seems that we are closer to fact. The brain is actually constructed this way. We can build our ideas about teaching on a solid and secure foundation.

In the next chapter we may find ourselves feeling even more secure. As we look deeper into the structure of the brain, we will get a strong sense of the need for proportion in our foundation. And of greatest interest, we will begin to see that if we get the proportions right, our foundation becomes something more than a support. It becomes an agent of change in the learner.

Notes

1. D. A. Kolb, *Experiential Learning:* Experience as the source of learning and development, Prentice Hall, Englewood Cliffs, NJ (1984).
2. The chemical senses, taste and smell, are located in regions of the cortex that are not visible in this illustration.
3. This brief description does not show the deep conceptual foundation on which the cycle rests. This cycle combines experience, perception, cognition, and behavior into one learning theory. Each of these represents a major field of psychology/biology.
4. *Experiential learning* is often thought of as simply giving people experience. But I stress that little true learning takes place from experience alone. There must be a conscious effort to build understanding from the experience, which requires reflection, abstraction, and resting of abstractions.
5. It is important not to overinterpret these illustrations. They are not meant to be precise or anatomically accurate, but to help convey these general the ideas. Here are a few potential misunderstandings: (1) The connections do not directly follow the pathway shown by the lines or arrows. For example, the connections sometimes follow the folds of the cortex and sometimes pass through other, deeper brain

structures on the way. (2) The connections simply mean that the process *can* occur. There are no physical, lock-step mechanisms implied. Also, there is no implication that these are the only connections one could draw. (3) The brain illustrations are not exact. For example, in the sensory brain we have not really labeled the exact cortical sections for visual, audio, or touch. I will be more precise about this in later chapters. (4) The drawings showing sensory input and motor output do not imply direct entry or exit of information and actions to or from the cortex. This requires connections with the sensory organs such as the eye or the skin and connections with the muscles of the body through the spinal cord.

6. The reader should not take these lists of function as rigid or absolute. Different functions dominate different anatomical parts of the brain, but some of these functions also involve multiple areas. This is true in general about cognitive activities, which are complex and undoubtedly involve interactions between different brain regions.
7. The two imaging methods that I will mention are called PET and fMRI. In PET a small amount of radioactivity is injected into the subject, and when parts of the brain become active, they take up more of that radioactivity. Uptake is measured by sensitive detectors that send the information to a computer to produce the image. PET images are quite diffuse and tend to exaggerate size of the brain area that is affected. In fMRI no radioactivity is needed. Instead, a large magnet detects changes in the amount of oxygenated hemoglobin in the bloodstream that supplies specific areas of the brain. When such areas of the brain are more active than others, their oxygen requirements increase, which is detected and imaged by a computer. fMRI images show changes in smaller areas of the brain than those seen in PET images; they sometimes appear confusing because of the scattered appearance of these small areas. All PET and fMRI studies are averages of several subjects and require careful controls so that the background signals can be subtracted.
8. The area of the brain engaged in comprehension of language was identified by Wernike long before imaging techniques had been developed. Likewise, the frontal region required for assembly of language has been known for over half a century (Broca's area). In fact, all four of the imaging results shown in this illustration are merely confirmatory of the functions of these regions of cortex, whose functions have been previously known.
9. With permission; illustration modeled after M. I. Posner and M. E. Raichle, *Images of Mind* (New York: Scientific American Library, 1997), p. 115.

CHAPTER 5

LEARNERS' MULTIPLE IDENTITIES AND PERSPECTIVES

Intellectual Development in The College Years

Marcia B. Baxter Magolda

College educators share a common goal: to guide college students as they develop mature ways of making informed judgments. But moving away from uncritical acceptance of knowledge to critically constructing one's own perspective is more complex than learning a skill set. It is a transformation in how we think—a change in our assumptions about the certainty, sources, and limits of knowledge. The evolution from viewing knowledge as certain and possessed by authorities to seeing it as context-dependent judgment based on relevant evidence is what researchers call intellectual or epistemological development.

Many students enter college assuming that there are right answers to most questions, that authorities possess this information, and their role as students is to acquire it. Awareness that students use these assumptions to guide their learning helps educators understand the basis for students' persistent efforts to find out the "right" answer, the "right" length of a paper, the "right" concepts to study for a test, or the "right" major. Relinquishing these ways of thinking and learning to evaluate evidence in an effort to make an informed, responsible judgment are big challenges. Understanding these challenges helps educators build scaffolding to support students' transformation.

This review identifies sources of information to help college educators learn how this developmental trajectory mediates learning and how to design and assess educational practices to help students achieve the outcomes most colleges advocate—critical thinking, intercultural competence, and productive citizenship, to name a few. The resources address four topics: 1) multiple approaches to conceptualizing students' intellectual development, 2) theoretical models of college students' intellectual development, 3) educational practices that promote intellectual development, and 4) the assessment of intellectual development.

Multiple Conceptualizations of Intellectual Development

Four sources in Resource Box I illustrate the multiple approaches researchers have used to explore college students' intellectual development. Barbara Hofer's introduction to *Personal Epistemology* and "Introduction: Paradigmatic Approaches to Personal Epistemology" both summarize these approaches. They have in common a focus on students' assumptions about knowledge but differ on whether those assumptions evolve in an integrated developmental progression, develop independently at different times, or emerge as cognitive resources in contexts that call for them. I focus in this Resource Review on the developmental progression approach because it is based on extensive longitudinal studies yielding theoretical models that can be translated to higher education practice.

The developmental progression approach is articulated through constructive-developmental theories. 'Constructive' refers to the notion that people construct, or organize, meaning; 'developmental' refers to the notion that how we organize meaning develops over time. Thus, constructive-developmental theories focus on the development of our construction of meaning.

Reprinted from *Change* (2006), by permission of Taylor and Francis Group.

Resource Box I

Overview of Approaches

Publications

- Hofer, B.K., & Pintrich, PR. (2002). *Personal epistemology: The psychology of beliefs about knowledge and knowing*. Mahwah, NJ: L. Erlbaum Associates, 430 pages, $125 ($55 paperback).
- Hofer, B.K. (2004). Introduction: Paradigmatic approaches to personal epistemology. *Educational Psychologist*, 39(1), 1–3.
- King, PM., & Baxter Magolda, M.B. (2005). A developmental model of intercultural maturity. *Journal of College Student Development*, 46(6), 571–592.
- West, E.J. (2004). Perry's Legacy: Models of epistemological development. *Journal of Adult Development*, 11(2), 61–70.

Resource Box II

Theoretical Models

Web Sites

- Perry Network Web site: **http//www.PerryNetwork.org**
- Reflective Judgment Web site: **http//www.umich.edu/~refjudg/**

Publications

- Abes, E.S., & Jones, S.R. (2004). Meaning-making capacity and the dynamics of lesbian college students' multiple dimensions of identity. *Journal of College Student Development*, 45(6), 612–632.
- Baxter Magolda, M.B. (1992). *Knowing and reasoning in college: Gender-related patterns in students' intellectual development.* San Francisco: Jossey-Bass, 446 pp, $45.
- Baxter Magolda, M.B. (2002). Epistemological reflection: The evolution of epistemological assumptions from age 18 to 30. In B.K. Hofer & P.R. Pintrich (Eds.), *Personal epistemology: The psychology of beliefs about knowledge and knowing* (pp. 89–102). Mahwah, NJ: Lawrence Erlbaum, $125 ($55 paperback).
- Baxter Magolda, M.B. (2001). *Making their own way: Narratives for transforming higher education to promote self-development.* Sterling, VA: Stylus, 356 pp, $22.50 paperback.
- Baxter Magolda, M.B. (2004). Evolution of a constructivist conceptualization of epistemological reflection. *Educational Psychologist*, 39(1), 31–42.
- Belenky, M., Clinchy, B.M., Goldberger, N., & Tarule, J. (1986). *Women's ways of knowing: The development of self, voice, and mind.* New York: Basic Books, 256 pp, $19 paperback.
- Clinchy, B.M. (2002). Revisiting women's ways of knowing. In B.K. Hofer & P.R. Pintrich (Eds.), *Personal epistemology: The psychology of beliefs about knowledge and knowing* (pp. 63–87). Mahwah, NJ: Lawrence Erlbaum, $125 ($55 paperback).

Resource Box II (*Continued*)

- Goldberger, N., Tarule, J., Clinchy, B., & Belenky, M. (Eds.). (1996). *Knowledge, difference, and power: Essays inspired by* Women's Ways of Knowing. New York: Basic Books, 478pp, 256 pp, $24 paperback.
- Kegan, R. (1994). *In over our heads: The mental demands of modern life.* Cambridge, MA: Harvard University Press, 396 pp., $32.50 ($22.95 paperback).
- Kegan, R. (2000). What "form" transforms? A constructive-developmental approach to transformative learning. In J. Mezirow (Ed.), *Learning as transformation: Critical perspectives on a theory in progress* (pp. 35–69). San Francisco: Jossey-Bass, 371 pp, $43.
- King, P.M., & Kitchener, K.S. (1994). *Developing Reflective Judgment: Understanding and promoting intellectual growth and critical thinking in adolescents and adults.* San Francisco: Jossey-Bass, 323 pp, $45.
- King, P.M., & Kitchener, K.S. (2002). The Reflective Judgment Model: Twenty years of research on epistemic cognition. In B.K. Hofer & P.R. Pintrich (Eds.), *Personal epistemology: The psychology of beliefs about knowledge and knowing* (pp. 37–61). Mahwah, NJ: Erlbaum, $125 ($55 paperback).
- King, PM., & Kitchener, K.S. (2004). Reflective Judgment: Theory and research on the development of epistemic assumptions through adulthood. *Educational Psychologist,* 39(1), 5–18.
- Moore, W.S. (2002). Understanding learning in a postmodem world: Reconsidering the Perry scheme of intellectual and ethical development In B.K. Hofer & PR. Pintrich (Eds.), *Personal epistemology: The psychology of beliefs about knowledge and knowing* (pp. 17–36). Mahwah, NJ: Lawrence Erlbaum, $125 ($55 paperback).
- Palmer, B., & Marra, R.M. (2004). College student epistemological perspectives across knowledge domains: A proposed grounded theory. *Higher Education, 47, 311–335.*
- Perry, W.G. (1970). *Forms of intellectual and ethical development in the college years: A scheme.* Troy, MO: Holt, Rinehart, & Winston. Reprinted 1998, Jossey-Bass, 336 pp, $32 paperback.
- Pizzolato, J.E. (2003). Developing self-authorship: Exploring the experiences of high-risk college students. *Journal of College Student Development, 44(6), 797–S12.*
- Pizzolato, J.E. (2004). Coping with conflict: Self-authorship, coping, and adaptation to college in first-year, high-risk students. *Journal of College Student Development,* 45(4), 425–442.
- Pizzolato, J.E. (2005). Creating crossroads for self-authorship: Investigating the provocative moment. *Journal of College Student Development,* 46(6), 624–641.
- Torres, V., & Baxter Magolda, M.B. (2004). Reconstructing Latino identity: The influence of cognitive development on the ethnic identity process of Latino students. *Journal of College Student Development,* 45(3), 333–347.

Elise West synthesizes four of these theories in "Perry's Legacy: Models of Epistemological Development." She further links the constructive-developmental perspective with skill-complexity theory; the latter addresses the intellectual skills (for instance, reorganizing simple elements into abstractions) that must be developed in concert with more complex epistemic assumptions. In "A Developmental Model of Intercultural Maturity," Patricia King and Marcia Baxter Magolda describe how assumptions about knowledge evolve as students gain intercultural maturity; the writers also integrate this evolution with the development of identity and the relationship dimensions of maturation to arrive at a holistic view of college students' development. These four resources collectively portray the broad landscape of literature on college student intellectual development.

Theoretical Models

Resource Box II contains both seminal and contemporary theoretical models.

• ***The Perry Scheme.*** William Perry's 1970 *Forms of Intellectual and Ethical Development in the College Years* is widely regarded as the seminal work from which much of the constructivist-developmental literature flows. Perry's rich longitudinal interviews, recounted in depth in the book, offered the first portrait of how students give up dualistic, right/wrong thinking in favor of multiple perspectives and eventually learn to evaluate perspectives in a relativistic world. William Moore's "Understanding Learning in a Postmodern World: Reconsidering the Perry Scheme of Intellectual and Ethical Development" describes extensions of Perry's model, its relationship to recent scholarship on learning, and efforts to assess it. The Perry Network Web site **(http//www.PerryNetwork.org)** contains a bibliography of works (up to 1999) based on the Perry scheme.

• ***Women's Ways of Knowing.*** Perry's scheme was based on a predominantly male sample of Harvard undergraduates. Interest in providing more effective higher education for women led Mary Belenky, Blythe Clinchy, Jill Tarule, and Nancy Goldberger to study women's intellectual development. In *Women's Ways of Knowing* they trace a diverse group of college women from the point at which they receive knowledge without question, to believing all knowledge is subjective and personal, to deciding what to believe and constructing knowledge in context.

This research confirmed the over-arching trajectory of Perry's scheme and introduced a new pattern of knowing. Called connected knowing, this new pattern reflected a personal and intimate approach to knowledge acquisition: stepping into what one is trying to know rather than the impersonal, detached stepping back from it evident in Perry's scheme. They offer an update of this work in *Knowledge, Difference, and Power,* including multiple authors' work on cultural dynamics in the application of the model. Blythe Clinchy's "Revisiting *Women's Ways of Knowing*" is a recent summary of their model.

• ***Reflective Judgment.*** The reflective judgment model represents another major line of research inspired by Perry's scheme. Patricia King and Karen Kitchener's 20-year longitudinal study of epistemic cognition (assumptions about the nature, limits, and certainty of knowledge) in the context of solving ill-structured problems is best articulated in *Developing Reflective Judgment.*

This line of research makes more specific our understanding of the process of knowing and how knowledge is acquired. Their model describes three major ways of knowing: prereflective thinkers who assume knowledge is certain, quasi-reflective thinkers who tend to view judgments as idiosyncratic, and reflective thinkers who make reasonable judgments based on evaluating available evidence. King and Kitchener's "The Reflective Judgment Model: Twenty Years of Research on Epistemic Cognition" and "Reflective Judgment: Theory and Research on the Development of Epistemic Assumptions through Adulthood" summarize this model. The *Reflective Judgment* Web site, **http//www.umich.edu/~refjudg/** contains a bibliography of publications about the model.

• ***Holistic Development.*** Contemporary research places college students' intellectual development in the context of their holistic development. Robert Kegan first articulated this integration of intellectual, identity, and relationship development in *In Over Our Heads.* He portrayed how assumptions about knowledge evolve in concert with assumptions about identity and relationships in the transformation to self-authorship, or the internal capacity to define one's belief, values, identity, and relationships. This internal capacity is central to critical thinking. In "What 'Form' Transforms? A Constructive-Developmental Approach to Transformative Learning," Kegan summarizes the internal logic of how assumptions evolve from self-centered to other-centered to self-authorship and links this constructive-developmental view to transformative learning.

Inspired by Perry's and Kegan's work, Baxter Magolda's 20-year longitudinal study initially explored the role of gender in intellectual development and in later years, the intersections of intellectual, identity, and relational development in young adulthood. Her 1992 *Knowing and Reasoning in College* captures the gender-related patterns that emerged during college. These patterns confirm that separate and connected knowing are equally complex styles that appear across the trajectory and converge in complex ways of knowing. Baxter Magolda's 2001 *Making Their Own Way* traces the continued development of this group through their 20s and reveals the intersections of intellectual, identity, and relational development in students' transformation from following extemal formulas for knowing to self-authorship.

• ***Racial, Ethnic, Social-Class and Sexual-Orientation Dynamics.*** Recent research on college students' intellectual development and self-authorship extends and refines these overarching trajectories by identifying contextual variations on them. Vasti Torres' four-year longitudinal study of Hispanic students reveals that increased complexity in assumptions about knowledge positively influence students' ethnic identity development (see Torres and Baxter Magolda's "Reconstructing Latino Identity: The Influence of Cognitive Development on the Ethnic Identity Process of Latino Students," 2004).

Jane Pizzolato explores how dissonance prompts high-risk students to develop self-authorship prior to college ("Developing Self-Authorship: Exploring the Experiences of High-Risk College Students," 2003), how they cope with continued dissonance during the first year of college ("Coping with Conflict: Self-Authorship, Coping, and Adaptation to College in First-Year, High-Risk Students," 2004), and how provocation during college affects movement toward self-authorship ("Creating Crossroads for Self-Authorship: Investigating the Provocative Moment," 2005). In "Meaning-Making Capacity and the Dynamics of Lesbian College Students' Multiple Dimensions of Identity," Elisa Abes and Susan Jones report that lesbian students' meaning-making structures affect their identity development. Collectively these lines of research inform how multiple identities intersect with assumptions about knowledge. Betsy Palmer and Rose Marra's 2004 "College Student Epistemological Perspectives across Knowledge Domains: A Proposed Grounded Theory" articulates how science and engineering students' epistemologies vary across knowledge domains.

Educational Practice that Promotes Intellectual Development

Resource Box III contains contemporary perspectives on organizing educational practice to promote holistic development. Many of the theorists described earlier culled insights from their longitudinal research to describe conditions that promote advanced development. Others conducted additional empirical research in multiple contexts, both in the curriculum and co-curriculum, in order to guide educators in constructing practice to promote transformation during college. *Learning Partnerships* (Baxter Magolda & King, 2004) describes the comprehensive learning partnerships model that emerged from Baxter Magolda's longitudinal study of college, professional, graduate-school, and employment settings. This model challenges learners to consider knowledge as complex and their own role in constructing it as critical, as well as to share authority with educators. In order to support students whose epistemic assumptions conflict with these challenges, educators need to validate their ability to know, situate learning in their experience, and define learning as mutually constructing meaning. Chapters by practitioners demonstrate how the model promotes self-authorship in multiple curricular and co-curricular settings. A brief overview of the model is available in Baxter Magolda's 2002 "Helping Students Make their Way into Adulthood: Good Company for the Journey."

In "Self-Authorship and Women's Career Decision Making," Elizabeth Creamer and Anne Laughlin propose learning partnerships to assist educators in career advising for women in science, technology, engineering, and mathematics. Peggy Meszaros and Anne Laughlin coordinated the production of the *Power of Partners* video to assist parents and guidance counselors who are helping young women develop the epistemological capacities to make their own informed career decisions. Meszaros' research team is currently developing a facilitators guide to accompany the video; both it and the video are available on the *Women in Technology* Web site, **http://www.womenintechnology.org/**

In their 2002 "The Reflective Judgment Model: Twenty Years of Research on Epistemic Cognition" (see Resource Box II), Patricia King and Karen Kitchener offer suggestions for helping learners address ill-structured problems. Marc Schwartz's and Kurt Fischer's 2006 "Useful Metaphors for Tackling Problems in Teaching and Learning" outlines how educators can understand how students

Resource Box III

Developmentally Based Practice

Publications

- Baxter Magolda, M.B. (2002). Helping students make their way into adulthood: Good company for the journey. *About Campus: Enhancing the Student Learning Experience,* 6(6), 2–9.
- Baxter Magolda, M.B., & King, PM. (Eds.). (2004). *Learning partnerships: Theory & models of practice to educate for self-authorship.* Sterling, VA: Stylus, 342 pp, $69.95 ($24.95 paperback).
- Creamer, E.G., & Laughlin, A. (2005). Self-Authorship and women's career decision making. *Journal of College Student Development,* 46(1), 13–27.
- Hill, L. (2004). Changing minds: Developmental education for conceptual change. *Journal of Adult Development,* 11(1), 29–40.
- Ilacqua, J.A., & Prescott, M.E. (2003). Knowing economic theory: Applying the Reflective Judgment Model in introductory economics. *Education,* 124(2), 368–375.
- King, P.M., & VanHecke, J. (2006). Making connections: Using skill theory to recognize how students build—and rebuild—understanding. *About Campus: Enhancing the Student Learning Experience,* 11(1).
- Meszaros, P. (executive producer) & Laughlin, A. (associate producer). (2006). *The power of partners: Helping females find their way to high tech careers.* [DVD]. National Science Foundation: Washington, DC (available at no cost from **www.witvideo.org.vt.edu).**
- Mezirow, J. (2003). Transformative learning as discourse. *Journal of Transformative Education,* 1(1), 58–63.
- Schwartz, M.S., & Fischer, K.W. (2006). Useful metaphors for tackling problems in teaching and learning. *About Campus: Enhancing the Student Learning Experience,* 11(1).
- Wise, J.C, Lee, S.H., Litzinger, T., Marra, R.M., & Palmer, B. (2004). A report on a four-year longitudinal study of intellectual development of engineering undergraduates. *Journal of Adult Development,* 11(2), 103–110.

make sense of problems in particular disciplines and use skill theory to help them make better sense. Patricia King and Jones VanHecke's "Making Connections: Using Skill Theory to Recognize How Students Build—and Rebuild—Understanding" shows how educators can use skill theory in student-affairs contexts to promote intellectual development.

Jack Mezirow demonstrates in "Transformative Learning as Discourse" how dialogue involving the assessment of beliefs, feelings, and values promotes epistemological development and transformative learning. John Wise and colleagues' 2004 "A Report on a Four-Year Longitudinal Study of Intellectual Development of Engineering Undergraduates" demonstrates that active learning promotes intellectual development. But as Joseph Ilacqua and Mary Prescott report in "Knowing Economic Theory: Applying the Reflective Judgment Model in Introductory Economics," students with advanced reflective judgment capacities were better able to engage in collaborative learning than those with less developed capacities, who needed more support. Lola Hill's 2004 "Changing Minds: Developmental Education for Conceptual Change" further supports the contention that developmental approaches to instruction, in this case with preservice teachers, promote intellectual development.

Resource Box IV

Assessing Intellectual Development

Web Sites

- Perry Network Web site: **http//www.PerryNetwork.org**
- Reflective Judgment Web site: **http//www.umich.edu/~refjudg/**

Publications

- Dawson, T. (2004). Assessing intellectual development: Three approaches, one sequence. *Journal of Adult Development*, 11(2), 71–85.

Assessment of Intellectual Development

Because the constructive-developmental approach to intellectual development is about how students make meaning of knowledge, forms of assessment in which respondents are asked to make meaning (for instance, open-ended interviews or written instruments) are a better reflection of intellectual development than instruments that require only choosing a response from among those provided. Resource Box IV highlights sources that address the construction, quality, and limitations of current assessment measures.

The Perry Network Web site **(http// www.PerryNetwork.org)** contains information on various measures of tbe Perry scheme and issues related to their use. The reflective judgment Web site **(http//www.umich. edu/~refjudg/)** describes measures of Reflective Judgment and contains an excellent discussion of the merits of open-ended versus recognition measures. Theo Dawson's 2004 "Assessing Intellectual Development: Three Approaches, One Sequence" advocates an objective computerized system to interpret interview texts. Interview protocols and related production instruments are described in all tbe seminal works noted earlier.

Intellectual Development and 21st Century Higher Education

Responsible citizenship on campus and beyond requires complex intellectual development and self-authorship. This line of research can be used to design inclusive educational environments that promote and enable us to assess these learning outcomes for diverse students. Future research in this area will undoubtedly focus on new theoretical models for diverse populations, integration of multiple dimensions of development, new practices to aid students' transformation toward self-authorship, and refining assessment measures.

Educating Students for Self-Authorship: Learning Partnerships to Achieve Complex Outcomes

Marcia B. Baxter Magolda
Miami University

Educators in the United States and the United Kingdom share a common concern—graduates' ability to successfully use their academic knowledge in their post college work and personal lives. Graduates must be able to translate their academic learning to the "capacity and understanding for working with many different sorts of knowledge in order to engage with complex emergent problems for which there may be a range of possible solutions" (Jackson & Ward, 2004, p. 427). UK scholars frame this challenge as learners making the transition from disciplinary to transdisciplinary learning (Gibbons et al. as cited in Jackson & Ward, 2004). Personal Development Planning, the process being used in the UK for helping learners reflect on their learning and achievement and plan for their own educational, academic and career development, aims to develop learners' metacognition and self-regulatory capacities to make this transition. Similarly, US educators are advocating "intentional learning," as the authors of *Greater Expectations: A New Vision for Learning as a Nation Goes to College* wrote:

> In a turbulent and complex world, every college student will need to be purposeful and self-directed in multiple ways. Purpose implies clear goals, an understanding of process, and appropriate action. Further, purpose implies intention in one's actions. Becoming such an intentional learner means developing self-awareness about the reason for study, the learning process itself, and how education is used. Intentional learners are integrative thinkers who can see connections in seemingly disparate information and draw on a wide range of knowledge to make decisions. They adapt the skills learned in one situation to problems encountered in another: in a classroom, the workplace, their communities, or their personal lives. As a result, intentional learners succeed even when instability is the only constant.
>
> (Association of American Colleges & Universities, 2002, pp. 21–22)

The complexities young adults face in transdisciplinary contexts after college, as well as the complexities inherent in disciplinary learning during college, require something beyond skill acquisition and application. They require a transformation from authority dependence to self-authorship, or the capacity to internally define one's beliefs, identity and social relations (Baxter Magolda, 2001; Kegan, 1994). In this chapter I summarize the learning outcomes advocated both in the UK and US, offer a perspective on the developmental capacities these outcomes require, present possibilities about the developmental capacities learners possess and describe how to construct learning partnerships that help learners achieve the capacities required. Guiding learners through the transformation from authority dependence to self-authorship is a primary challenge for twenty-first century higher education.

Reprinted from *The University and its disciplines: Teaching and learning within and beyond disciplinary boundaries*, edited by C. Kreber (2008), by permission of Routledge.

Higher Education Learning Outcomes

Recent national reports in both the UK and US paint a similar picture of the desired outcomes of higher education despite using slightly different language to convey these ideas. US reports (e.g., American College Personnel Association, 1994; Association of American Colleges and Universities, 1995, 2002; Keeling, 2004) emphasize higher education's goal as fostering intentional learning and effective citizenship. Becoming informed, active, responsible global citizens is the first of eight key concepts the UK report *Putting the World into World-Class Education* (Department for Education and Skills, 2004) notes as necessary for living in a global society. Integrating numerous reports US national associations have published in recent years yields a model of contemporary US college learning outcomes that overlaps considerably with the key concepts advocated in *Putting the World into World-Class Education.*

Desired college learning outcomes in the US cluster into three distinct categories (Baxter Magolda, 2004b). *Cognitive maturity* includes the ability to discern the value of multiple perspectives through evaluating relevant evidence, problem solving in context, and making wise decisions based on complex analysis. These outcomes are typically in the forefront of disciplinary learning. A second cluster of outcomes, which I refer to as *integrated identity,* is necessary to enable cognitive maturity. Integrated identity includes understanding one's own history, confidence, the ability to act both autonomously and collaboratively, and integrity. A third category—*mature relationships*—is crucial to cognitive maturity and integrated identity. Mature relationships include respect for one's own and others' identities and cultures to enable productive collaboration to integrate multiple perspectives. As I have argued previously:

> Maturity in these three areas combines to enable effective citizenship—coherent, ethical action for the good of both the individual and the larger community. Effective citizenship requires the ability to evaluate possible actions, interpret contexts and consequences, and make wise choices—all characteristics of cognitive maturity. For these choices to be coherent and ethical requires an internal belief system and an internal identity that together guide action. Ethical action for the good of the individual and larger community requires the capacity for mutuality and interdependence characteristic of mature relationships: it requires understanding of and commitment to one's own interests in interaction with understanding and commitment to the interests of others. To act ethically as a citizen requires intercultural maturity, or the ability to use multiple cultural frames, engage in relationships with diverse others grounded in appreciation of difference, and consideration of social identities in a global and national context (King & Baxter Magolda, 2003).
>
> (Baxter Magolda, 2004b, p. 6)

These three categories resonate with Barnett's (2000a) constructs of epistemology (knowing), ontology (self-identity), and praxis (action). Organizing the Department for Education and Skills' (2004) eight concepts accordingly, similarities emerge with the model of US college learning outcomes. Understanding the key concepts of social justice, sustainable development, and human rights resonates with cognitive maturity. The key concept of values and perceptions, defined in the report as "developing a critical evaluation of images of other parts of the world and an appreciation of the effect these have on people's attitudes and values," recognizes the role of identity in effective citizenship. The key concepts of respecting diversity, interdependence, and conflict resolution interconnect with the category of mature relationships. Thus UK and US scholars offer a powerful, shared vision of the core outcomes of higher education. This vision includes what Robert Kegan (2000) calls informational learning (i.e., fund of knowledge and skills) yet extends further to include transformational learning—the remaking of how we make meaning. Both forms are crucial to prepare learners for success in the complex twenty-first-century society they will inhabit and lead.

Developmental Foundations of Learning Outcomes

Achieving these learning outcomes extends beyond informational learning to epistemological (i.e., knowing), intrapersonal (i.e., identity) and interpersonal (i.e., relationships) developmental capacities that support transformational learning. Here again, UK and US scholars concur. The idea that developmental capacities underlie learning outcomes is illustrated in the following exchange, taken from a course observation study (Baxter Magolda, 1999). Interviewed at the outset of his zoology course, Chris Snowden shared these aspirations for his students:

> I want them [students in Winter Biology] to appreciate the breadth of zoology and its connections to other disciplines. How do we put together disparate ideas? I'll use my research as examples of how one approaches problems. I want them to understand how information is gained. I want them to appreciate what facts really mean. Tentative facts. That's what all of science is. Subject to change and revision.
>
> (Baxter Magolda, 1999, p. 3)

Chris included this vision for learning on the course syllabus. Ann, a senior in the course, shared her reaction in an interview conducted at the conclusion of the course:

> I take sociology as my minor. It is all opinions, not hard-core facts where you are wrong [like Winter Biology]. I know he tried to play it off like there is still a lot of research, that it is a really new concept I guess, but still there is some stuff that is [fact]—like freezing cells. I understand what he was trying to do. He was trying to give examples to show what happened. But if he had just said cryoprotectants whatever, just said the point, I would believe him because he is the teacher. I don't need the proof, it's not like I'm going to argue with him about it.
>
> (Baxter Magolda, 1999, p. 3)

Clearly a disconnect exists. Ann seems to have heard Chris's words because she conveys that she knew what Chris was trying to do. As a senior Ann has succeeded thus far in a rigorous curriculum. Chris was very articulate in explaining his expectations and the course content. Yet Ann does not demonstrate an appreciation for how information is gained. How can this be?

The disconnect between Chris and Ann stems from the frameworks each uses to understand learning and knowledge. Ann views the nature of science as "hard core facts." From this vantage point she interpreted Chris's examples as attempts to prove to her what happened, did not understand his portrayal of cryobiology (the study of life at cold temperatures) as an evolving field, and preferred that he just tell her the facts that she is sure exist. Chris, in contrast, views science as tentative facts, subject to revision. Operating from this vantage point, he attempts to get Ann and her peers to appreciate how information is gained, unaware that Ann's views about science versus sociology affect her learning in his course. Ann uses her current understanding about knowledge and how it is acquired to make sense of Chris's portrayal of cryobiology as an evolving field and facts as tentative.

For Ann to really understand knowledge the way Chris does, she needs particular epistemological, intrapersonal and interpersonal meaning-making capacities. She would need to understand that knowledge is uncertain and created by experts in particular contexts using relevant evidence. She would need to be aware that multiple perspectives derive from how particular people construct knowledge claims based on particular evidence. These epistemological capacities would allow her to understand how science could be viewed as subject to revision. In order to apply these epistemological capacities, however, Ann would also need corresponding intrapersonal or identity capacities. She would need to have a sense of herself as a person capable of participating in this knowledge construction process. She would need to be able to reflect on, explore and choose her values to form a coherent sense of herself, or an integrated identity. This integrated identity would then serve as the foundation for her to interpret her experience and act on it. These intrapersonal capacities would enable her to envision joining Chris in knowledge construction rather than her present "don't argue with the teacher" perspective. Finally, Ann would need interpersonal capacities to meet Chris's expectations. She would need to be able to use others' thinking along with her own without being overly influenced by what authorities tell her. Thus she would need to achieve interdependence—the blend of her own integrated identity, openness to other perspectives, and the ability to critically analyze existing knowledge and other perspectives without fear of disapproval. If Ann had all these capacities, she would be capable of self-authorship, or the ability to internally define her beliefs, identity, and relations with others. As a college senior, she did not have these capacities and she is not alone.

Robert Kegan (1994) argues that much of what contemporary society (including education) expects of students and young adults is "over their heads;" that is to say, the expectations require ways of making meaning beyond those students currently hold. This is Ann's situation; it is likely the situation of many college students in both the US and UK. Helping college students acquire more complex ways of making meaning is essential in light of the demands they face as college students and adults. In articulating what he calls the mental demands of modern life, Kegan (1994) highlights the need for adults to be self-initiating, self-correcting, self-evaluating, responsible for their actions, open to diverse perspectives, and able to connect to partners and children while setting appropriate boundaries, to name just a few. He interprets these everyday demands as requiring integrating epistemological, intrapersonal and interpersonal capacities in a complex way of making meaning. Specifically, he describes this as:

> . . . an ideology, an internal identity, a *self-authorship* that can coordinate, integrate, act upon, or invent values, beliefs, convictions, generalizations, ideals, abstractions, interpersonal loyalties, and intrapersonal states. It is no longer *authored* by them, it *authors them* and thereby achieves a personal authority.
>
> (p. 185, italics in original)

Self-authorship offers a foundation upon which to function in what Ronald Barnett (2000b) calls a supercomplex world. Arguing that higher education is responsible for preparing students to survive in and contribute to this supercomplex world, Barnett explains:

> It is a world where nothing can be taken for granted, where no frame of understanding or of action can be entertained with any security. It is a world in which we are conceptually challenged, and continually so. A complex world is one in which we are assailed by more facts, data, evidence, tasks and arguments than we can easily handle within the frameworks in which we have our being. By contrast, a supercomplex world is one in which the very frameworks by which we orient ourselves to the world are themselves contested. Supercomplexity denotes a fragile world but it is a fragility brought on not merely by social and technological change; it is a fragility in the way that we understand the world, in the way in which we understand ourselves and in the ways in which we feel secure about acting in the world.
>
> (2000b, p. 3)

Barnett emphasizes that supercomplexity is "a matter of handling multiple frames of understanding, of action and of self-identity" (2000a, p. 6). Although he does not use the term self-authorship, his three dimensions resonate with the epistemological, intrapersonal and interpersonal dimensions of self-authorship.

My longitudinal study of young adult development and learning (Baxter Magolda, 2001), in which I have followed participants from age 18 to 38, provides empirical support for the argument that adult life requires complexity in how we know, how we see ourselves, and how we construct our relations with others. This study, originally designed to explore gender differences based on the work of Perry (1970) and Belenky, Clinchy, Goldberger, and Tarule (1986), began with 101 traditional age students (51 women and 50 men) when they entered college in 1986 at a state institution in the US with a liberal arts focus. Admission is competitive and the 70% of the entering class of which the participants were a part ranked in the top 20% of their high school class. Their majors included all six divisions within the institution (i.e., arts and sciences, education, fine arts, interdisciplinary studies, business, engineering and applied sciences), and cocurricular involvement in college was high.

Of the 70 participants continuing in the post college phase of the study, 21 pursued additional academic preparation after college graduation, including law school, seminary, medical school, and various graduate degrees. Their occupations included business, education, social service, ministry, and government work. Attrition over the last fifteen years resulted in 36 participants by year twenty. The annual interview began with a summary of the focus of the project, which was to continue to explore how participants learn and come to know. The participant was then asked to think about important learning experiences that took place since the previous interview. The participant volunteered those experiences, described them, and described their impact on her or his thinking. I asked questions to pursue why these experiences were important, factors that influenced the experiences, and how the learner was affected. The interview became more informal as the study progressed and addressed what life had been like for participants since we talked last. These conversations included discussion of the dimensions of life they felt were most relevant, the demands of adult life they were experiencing, how they made meaning of these dimensions and demands, their sense of themselves, and how they decided what to believe. Inherent in these dimensions was their sense of themselves in relation to others and their involvement in significant relationships. Interviews were conducted in person during college and by telephone after college; they ranged from 60 to 90 minutes (see Baxter Magolda, 1992; 2001 for more in-depth methodological details).

Most of my participants made little progress toward self-authorship during college, leaving college relying on externally derived formulas for what to believe, how to be and how to relate to others. They found these formulas wanting as they entered the workforce and adult relationships, contexts in which they were asked to define, express and act on internal constructions of their beliefs, identities, and interactions with others. Their stories offer a perspective on how self-authorship evolves and the kind of educational experiences that assist young people in achieving more complex ways of making meaning.

Journeys toward Self-Authorship

I offer one version of the developmental journey toward self-authorship based on my twenty-year longitudinal study. During the college phase of the study participants relied heavily on external sources of authority. In over 500 interviews in the fifteen years since these participants' college graduation I have heard how self-authorship evolved through their professional and personal lives. These stories are consistent with those told by the collective student development research done in the US.[1] Yet the stories shared here tell only one version of how assumptions evolve from external sources of definition to internal ones. As you read, consider these stories carefully to determine if this version resonates with your students in your educational context and how these stories inform the transitions your students are trying to navigate.

Following External Formulas

Ann's reaction to her zoology course reflects the early part of the developmental journey in which students rely on external formulas for what to believe, how to define their identities, and how to relate to others. Most of my longitudinal participants used this perspective when they entered college and maintained it through their early twenties. Mark's account of how he approached law school reveals the essence of this way of making meaning:

> I came here and I tried to figure out what the legal culture figures is success. I knew [that] a Supreme Court clerkship was, so one of my goals was to aim towards that. So I got here to law school and I figured out, "Okay, well, to be a success here you have to get to know some professors who are influential with judges to get a good clerkship, to get in the pipeline, get in the star system here. Also get on *Law Review.* Write a paper here that you can publish." I thought, "Okay, this is kind of the plan then, step by step." The ultimate plan for success in the legal culture, I mean, go to [this] Law School and do these things, then you've got it made. . . . I would be in the *ultimate* position to do whatever I want to do because I will have done *everything* possible, and then I'd be in a position to make a choice that reflected exactly who I was, or at least more clearly.
>
> (Baxter Magolda, 2001, p. 41, italics in original)

Mark was still following external formulas when he started law school despite a successful college career. As a college senior he understood knowledge as contextual and articulated the process of weighing evidence to decide what to believe. However, he had not yet developed an internal sense of self to bring to this decision-making process. He still assumed that doing all the right things would yield a choice that matched his identity. Like many of his peers, he discovered that to be a faulty assumption.

[1]For a summary of this research, see Hofer, B. K., & Pintrich, P. R. (2002). *Personal epistemology: the psychology of beliefs about knowledge and knowing.* Mahwah, NJ: Lawrence Erlbaum Associates.

Crossroads

At various points in their mid-twenties most of my participants encountered the shortcomings of external formulas. The formulas often did not serve them well in complex work roles where they were asked to construct new knowledge and be flexible in light of changing information and ambiguity. Participants' own emerging interests and values often conflicted with the formula. They realized the need to extract themselves from dependence on the external and to develop their own visions, beliefs and identities. Doing so, however, was a challenge as Kurt so clearly describes:

> I'm the kind of person who is motivated by being wanted, I think. I've gone to a couple of workshops and, either fortunately or unfortunately, I'm the kind of person who gets my self-worth [through] whether or not other people accept me for what I do or other people appreciate what I'm doing. . . . I'm coming from a position where I get my worth and my value from other people, which is, I think, wrong for me to do. But that's where I am right now. I feel like whether or not I choose to be happy is dependent upon me and only me. If I say, "You made me mad," or the converse, "You made me happy," then I'm giving all of the power that I have to you. The power of choice is mine, I have a choice of how I want to perceive each and every situation in my life. . . . Obviously I'm not to that point yet because I choose to make myself happy and make myself sad on what other people are thinking. But I think I'd like to someday get to a point where I can say, "Okay, that's your perception. I am not dependent on you for my happiness or my sadness." And I think that would be a very strong, very spiritual place to be.
>
> (Baxter Magolda, 2001, pp. 98–9)

Kurt shared this perspective in his mid-twenties and later reported, "I spent the entire decade of my twenties getting in touch with who I was and what is important to me" (Baxter Magolda, 2004b, p. 24). His story underscores the struggle to develop an internal sense of self upon which to ground one's identity and relationships. This internal sense of self is also needed to define one's beliefs internally. Like Kurt, most of my participants devoted a considerable part of their twenties to working through the crossroads.

Becoming the Author of One's Life

Successfully navigating the crossroads yielded an internal self-definition that transformed all three developmental dimensions. Dawn described this transformation as resulting from the self-discovery she experienced in theatre. She explained:

> The more you discover about yourself, the more you can become secure with it. And that obviously leads to greater self-confidence because you become comfortable with who you really are. My confidence level is so much better than it ever has been. I'm more willing to express my ideas and take chances expressing my ideas. "Who cares what people think?" sort of thing. When you're not as self-confident, you're afraid that people are going to laugh at what you think or you're afraid that they're going to think you're stupid—it's all those petty, little things that inhibit us. Whereas when you're confident, you are more willing to say, "This is my opinion; this is why I hold this opinion. You may agree with it or not, but this is what—with my mind—I have formulated this opinion and that's how I think and feel." I'm not as afraid to be willing to say that because of what I am this is how I feel. I try not to step on people's toes with my opinions, be offensive about it, but if someone asks me for my opinion or advice or how I think and feel about something, I will definitely tell them. And I think self-awareness too, because you realize that it doesn't really matter if other people agree with you or not. You can think and formulate ideas for yourself and ultimately that's what's important. You have a mind and you can use it. That's probably the most important thing, regardless of the content of what your thoughts and opinions are. I suppose it's very idealistic to think that everybody can see that. It's the fact that you can form an opinion that's more important than the opinion itself. But I don't think that happens. So it's kind of a self-confidence and self-awareness thing.
>
> (Baxter Magolda, 2001, pp. 152–3)

You can hear in Dawn's story how her internal self came into being, how it in turn changed her perception and fear of others' appraisals of her, which in turn allowed her to express her own thinking.

Thus the epistemological insight that she has a mind and can use it to develop her own opinions was made possible by advances in the intrapersonal and interpersonal dimensions of her development. I turn next to the characteristics of contexts in which participants' journeys toward self-authorship occurred.

Learning Partnerships Model

Listening to my longitudinal participants' experiences in multiple settings (e.g., college, employment, graduate and professional school, community involvement, personal life) revealed many characteristics that promote learning and self-authorship. From those stories I developed the Learning Partnerships Model (Baxter Magolda, 2004a) to promote self-authorship while simultaneously supporting learners' current meaning-making. Kegan emphasized the necessity of providing support when our expectations extend beyond students' current meaning making. He advocates creating:

> a holding environment that provides both welcoming acknowledgement to exactly who the person is right now as he or she is, and fosters the person's psychological evolution. As such, a holding environment is a tricky, transitional culture, an evolutionary bridge, a context for crossing over.
>
> (1994, p. 43)

The Learning Partnerships Model (LPM) creates an evolutionary bridge by merging three supportive components with three challenges in the learning environment.

Support is offered through *three principles*: validating learners' ability to know, situating learning in learners' experience, and defining learning as mutually constructing meaning. Participants reported greater willingness to take responsibility for constructing knowledge and their own beliefs when educators validated their potential to do so. Using their experience offered a foundation for learning and provided support in this challenging process. Having learning defined as mutual construction made it acceptable to participate in the process. These supports assist learners in engaging in the *three challenges* of learning environments that promote self-authorship: knowledge is complex and socially constructed, self is central to knowledge construction, and authority and expertise are shared among knowledgeable peers. Explicit portrayal of knowledge as complex and socially constructed challenged learners to move toward epistemological complexity. Emphasis on the role of

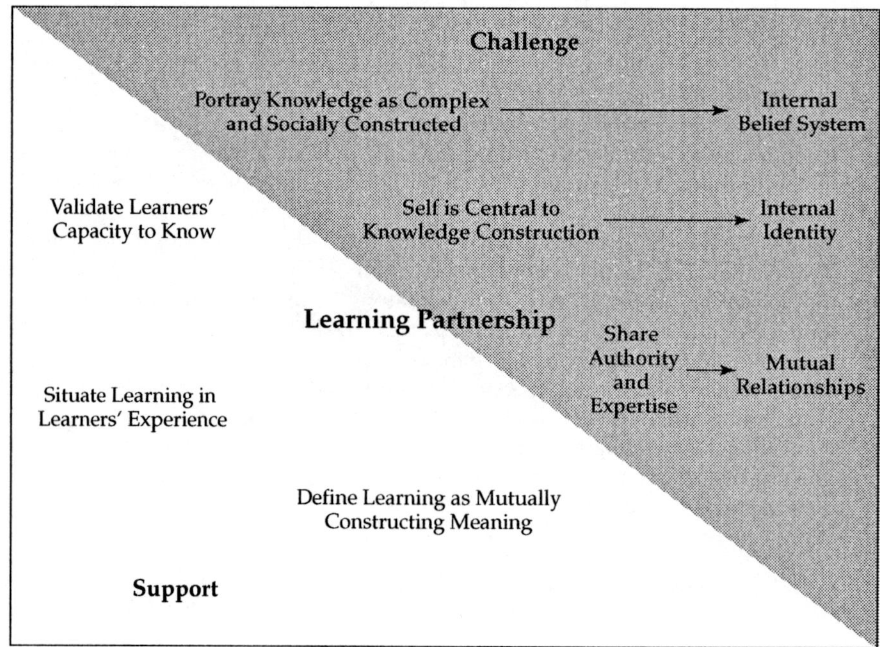

Figure 5.1
Learning Partnerships Model

the self in knowledge construction challenged them to bring their identity into learning thus moving them toward construction of an internal identity. Sharing of expertise and authority in the learning process engaged learners in mutually constructing knowledge and helped them develop more mature relationships. These six components connect to all phases of the journey because the educator is mutually constructing the educational process with the learner. The partnership adjusts as the learner adopts more complex ways of making meaning.

Exemplars

The three supportive principles of the LPM emerged first from my longitudinal participants' college narratives. The three challenges emerged more clearly in the post-college interviews. All six components were visible in an observation study in which I observed three semester-length courses: Chris Snowden's zoology course (mentioned earlier in this chapter), a mathematics course, and a large education course (Baxter Magolda, 1999). Student interviews at the end of the zoology course illustrate how Chris Snowden modeled the LPM in his teaching. Rich explained:

> The whole focus of most of my classes in college have been just regurgitating the facts, with the exceptions of a few like Winter Biology where the base facts were given to you on the ground level and where the actual learning was coming in above and beyond that. The learning was coming in where he would ask what do you think about this, and you couldn't just look on your notes, you couldn't just remember what he said. It is not just blatant memorization; learning comes into it when you are utilizing the ideas towards something new that hasn't been done. That kind of set-up seems to stimulate me more than just being like a computer and storing this information to really do nothing with. This class gave more interest into the applications, what is going on right now, ideas of it, theories on what they don't know. The other classes it was "here is what we know and you have to know it too." There wasn't any fairly mutual exchange between the instructor and the class, no formulations of ideas beyond.
>
> (Baxter Magolda, 1999, p. 122)

The challenge to create new formulations to extend existing knowledge put knowledge as complex in the foreground of learning. Rich appreciated being invited into the learning process with the question "what do you think about this?" Although Rich does not describe the mutual exchange between instructor and class, I observed it regularly. Chris routinely invited students to share their thinking, engaged the class in processing their ideas, and helped them work through the validity of various knowledge claims. Erica offered a perspective on how Chris supported students in facing these challenges:

> He takes the approach that he wants you to do it on your own. He will help you plot through your ideas and he will help you sort out what you are thinking and help direct you and he still encourages you to work independently. He just makes his office setting very comfortable. He'll ask "what are you confused about?" and he will ask your opinion on the matter rather than telling you what you should do. He will ask you exactly what is happening and what you need help with and try to direct you from there rather than presenting himself in a way that is kind of intimidating. . . . I think the way I see it is that he wants you to feel that you are at the same level as him, not in as far as the same knowledge, he wants the atmosphere to be such that you feel comfortable asking him or talking to him in any way.
>
> (Baxter Magolda, 1999, pp. 133–134)

Erica's description of her interactions with Chris reveals that he validated her ability to think and work independently. By asking her to direct the discussion and offer her opinion, he situated learning in her experience. He helped her plot through her ideas, simultaneously directing her and encouraging her to work independently, thus demonstrating mutual knowledge construction. By using the components of the LPM Chris helped his students learn both the content and the thinking processes of the discipline. In doing so he also promoted their development toward the complex ways of making meaning required to view science as "tentative facts, subject to change and revision."

Longitudinal participants' stories reinforce the notion that graduates must be able to translate their disciplinary learning into supercomplex, transdisciplinary contexts. This was most evident in employment contexts in which the three challenges took the foreground. Andrew's description of his work environment conveys these challenges:

> I'm trying to think how to word it, but I guess the true responsibility they give you, I mean, the freedom of work. Sometimes you may just have a manager who hands you stuff and then you do it. Or you're given a responsibility and then you can define your job from there. You take more initiative, rather than it being dictated to you. They kind of give you the ball and then tell you to go play with it rather than tell you how to shoot hoops. We joke at work, we call it the "dump and run," because sometimes it seems like they don't have a very formal training procedure. But by the same token I think it's good because it allows you to find your niche and do your thing. They take the approach if somebody comes in new, looks at the thing, they may find a better way to do it. So they don't like to say, "This is the way it should be done always." They're not afraid to let people reinvent the wheel, especially if it means they come out with a better wheel.
>
> (Baxter Magolda, 2001, p. 253)

Clearly Andrew's management team conveyed that there were multiple ways to approach work, that Andrew could bring his own approach to it, and management and employees shared authority. The opportunity to take initiative to define his work validated Andrew's ability to know. Doing his own thing situated learning in his experience. He did clarify that he and his colleagues were not without direction:

> When push comes to shove they give us the direction we need. But for the most part I completely do not feel like I have management looking over me. I feel that I'm making more of an effort to let my management know what I'm doing so they're kept abreast rather than them coming to me and saying, "Well, what are you doing?" And I think that makes just a big difference in the way you feel. Management never really checks up on you; you're given complete trust. Now if you don't perform, I'm sure things would be said.
>
> (Baxter Magolda, 2001, p. 253)

Direction provided when needed conveys that mutual construction took place when management or employees felt the need for it but otherwise employees were trusted to perform effectively until they proved otherwise. This balance of challenge and support helped Andrew develop more complex ways of approaching his work.

Another longitudinal participant explained more specifically how sharing expertise and authority in a learning partnership works. Gavin described how his boss helped him learn to think for himself in the insurance business:

> It's really nice to know that I can just say, "Mr. Smith, I'm having trouble with—I don't understand this." He doesn't always give me the answer. A lot of times he'll throw back questions like, "Well, what do you think about it?" He always tries to get you to answer it yourself. And if he feels differently, he'll tell you. . . . His method of getting people to learn is he always thinks that if you're a bright enough person you really do know the answer or it's easy enough for you to find out. If we disagree, then he says, "Well, if that's the way you see it, do it your way and if it works out let me know." . . . It gives me the impression that if my mindset is that I'm going to do it my way, I can do it that way. If it doesn't work, I'll tell him. And a lot of times he'll say, "Well, you'll feel a lot better with yourself because you tried it." So it's a very, very relaxed atmosphere with very, very professional people. They just know how to—it's like they're being a mentor. It's neat.
>
> (Baxter Magolda, 2001, p. 265)

Mr. Smith encouraged Gavin to reflect on his own ideas and expertise to think through his work. When Gavin needed help, his boss provided it without making Gavin feel incompetent. He supported Gavin trying things his way, even if he disagreed. Mr. Smith encouraged Gavin to try out his own thinking in order "to feel better about himself" even when it led to mistakes. This model of supervision balanced the risk associated with employees learning how to work effectively with the long-term benefit of their professional and personal growth.

The Learning Partnerships Model has been intentionally used in multiple settings to design educational practice to promote learning and self-authorship. For example, it is the foundation of the four-year writing curriculum in the Miami University School of Interdisciplinary Studies (SIS). To build an evolutionary bridge from external formulas to self-authorship, the academic staff "created a plan where students would progress from engagement with expressive modes to an increasingly critical awareness of and proficiency in disciplinary forms to the development of interdisciplinary scholarly inquiry" (Haynes, 2004, pp. 67, 70). The SIS academic staff organized this progression into seven increasingly complex stages spread out over the four years of the curriculum. Similarly, the LPM is the basis for a four-semester Earth Sustainability Project in which content is structured around developmental goals to promote increased cognitive complexity and the ability to use disciplinary knowledge beyond disciplinary boundaries (Bekken & Marie, 2007). The LPM is also the pedagogical foundation of Miami's College Student Personnel Master of Science program that prepares graduate students for professional roles in college and university administration (Rogers, Magolda, Baxter Magolda, & Knight-Abowitz, 2004). Systematic attention to the challenges and supports of the LPM help students self-author their professional and personal identity to become effective citizens in the complex world of higher education.

The LPM is a central feature of two experiential learning programs. The Casa de Solidaridad offers students a semester of study and cultural immersion in El Salvador. The Casa, co-sponsored by Santa Clara University and the University of Central America, is open to students from all over the US; the participants are primarily from Jesuit institutions. The LPM guides the pedagogy of the coursework, supervision of work in the Salvadorian community, and the community living component of the Casa to meet the Casa objectives of education for transformation, global citizenship, self-authorship, and institutional solidarity (Yonkers-Talz, 2004). The Urban Leadership Internship Program uses the LPM to supervise ten-week summer internships in urban contexts. Program coordinators note that, "With the support of the Learning Partnerships Model, students can be guided to self-authorship through the challenges of experiential learning—challenges that promote the transformation of other-directed students to self-directed citizens who are engaged in their communities" (Egart and Healy, 2004, p. 149). Detailed discussions of these and other uses of the LPM can be found in *Learning Partnerships* (Baxter Magolda & King, 2004) and *Self-Authorship: Advancing Students' Intellectual Growth* (Meszaros, 2007).

Designing Learning Partnerships

The LPM's use in the US offers hope that educators can design learning environments that simultaneously promote disciplinary and transdisciplinary learning. Table 5.1 provides an overview of the process for designing learning partnerships.

Designing learning partnerships involves consideration of the developmental capacities that underlie most learning goals. Once learning goals have been established for a particular learning context (step two), it is crucial to identify what those learning goals demand of students, to what degree those demands might be beyond their current meaning making, and how we might organize learning to create a transformational bridge from external formula to self-authorship. Analyzing the ways of constructing knowledge, oneself and relationships that particular learning goals require (step three) gives educators a sense of the epistemological, intrapersonal, and interpersonal capacities needed for achieving those goals. Assessing the degree to which learners possess those developmental capacities (step four) reveals the discrepancies between what is demanded and how learners currently make meaning. This enables educators to identify the developmental goals—the capacities students need to develop to be able to meet the learning goals (step five). The design phase begins with translating the learning and developmental goals into a reasonable "curriculum," or process that welcomes learners' current meaning making and gradually invites them into more complex meaning making (step six). This might take the form of a formal curriculum as in the case of the writing curriculum mentioned earlier or the form of a particular course. The LPM's three challenging assumptions (step seven) and three supportive principles (step eight) help educators intentionally devise pedagogical relations that respect learners' current meaning making yet invite learners to reconstruct their beliefs, values and relationships in the more complex terms required by college learning outcomes.[2]

[2]For a detailed discussion of this design process and examples, see King, P. M., & Baxter Magolda, M. B. (2004). Creating learning partnerships in higher education: Modeling the shape, shaping the model. In M. B. Baxter Magolda & P. M. King (Eds.), *Learning partnerships: Theory and models of practice to educate for self-authorship* (pp. 303–332). Sterling, VA: Stylus.

TABLE 5.1

Designing Learning Partnerships

Phase One – Assessing Learning Goals and Learners' Capacities for Self-Authorship	
Step 1	Select a context in which to develop a learning partnership.
Step 2	Identify the learning goals for this context—what should learners know and be able to do as a result of this educational experience?
Step 3	Identify the developmental capacities the learning goals require—what ways of understanding knowledge, oneself and relationships are required to achieve these learning goals?
Step 4	Identify the developmental capacities the learners in this context currently possess—what ways of understanding knowledge, oneself, and relationships do learners exhibit?
Step 5	Identify consistencies and discrepancies between learning goals and learner capacities; craft developmental goals that will help bridge the distance between current and required capacities.
Phase Two – Designing the "Evolutionary Bridge"	
Step 6	Outline the developmental "curriculum"—how can the learning and developmental goals be translated into cumulative steps over time?
Step 7	Address the three LPM challenging assumptions—to what extent are they currently in place and in what ways could they be more explicit in this context?
Step 8	Address the three LPM supportive principles—to what extent are they currently in place and in what ways could they be more explicit in this context?
Step 9	Review the consistencies and discrepancies between learning goals and learner capacities that exist in this newly designed learning partnership.
Step 10	Develop a plan to evaluate the effectiveness of the new learning partnership.

Adapted from *Learning Partnerships: Theory and Models of Practice to Educate for Self-Authorship,* edited by Marcia B. Baxter Magolda and Patricia M. King (Sterling, VA: Stylus Publishing, LLC) with permission of the publisher.

Numerous dilemmas are inherent in designing learning partnerships. Nearly every aspect of the higher education enterprise is designed in opposition to learning partnerships. As Terry Wildman wrote in his analysis of using the LPM in curricular reform at Virginia Tech,

> One of the first things we discover in our attempts to introduce new practices in institutional settings is that the *old designs run deep.* Indeed they are embodied in the classrooms where knowledge is *delivered,* in the curriculum practices where requirements are *checked off,* in the space utilization policies where time is *parsed out* in small manageable chunks, in the textbooks where knowledge is carefully *scripted and de-contextualized,* and even in the organizational structures where disciplines can be *isolated* and protected within their own departments.
>
> (2004, pp. 250–251, italics in original)

These structural barriers, deeply embedded in the fabric of our institutions, work against constructing learning partnerships. Similarly, the recent proficiency testing movement, aimed at ensuring that students possess basic knowledge and skills, often leads to greater rigidity in the curriculum rather than to mutually constructing knowledge with learners. Students' and their parents' expectations for vocational training that leads to successful employment is another source of pressure to tell students what they need to know rather than engage them in learning how to think and function in complex ways.

These pressures are exacerbated by the ways in which both students and educators have been socialized. Students are often socialized in pre-college education to rely on authorities and not take initiative for their own learning. They are disconcerted when these familiar ways of learning are challenged and their learned behavior does not yield success. Educators are often socialized to function as authorities with minimal expectation to share authority with learners. They are disconcerted when their familiar ways of teaching are challenged and they fear that sharing authority with students will not produce effective learning.

These institutional and human dynamics combine to sustain what Wildman called the "old designs"—those that frame learning as the passive acquisition of knowledge. These old designs have not produced the kind of complex meaning making necessary for success in twenty-first-century adult life. Conceptualizing educational practice that promotes the transdisciplinary, intentional learning required for success in contemporary adult life requires transforming learners' and educators' assumptions about the role of learners and educators in knowledge construction. As difficult as this may be, preliminary evidence suggests that it is possible. Wildman (2004) and his colleagues report substantial success with faculty learning communities in which sustained discussion of new frames has enabled implementation of the learning partnerships model. Similarly, Rebecca Mills and Karen Strong (2004) describe reframing their entire Division of Student Life organization to promote self-authorship. Divisions of Student Life in US colleges and universities include functions related to the cocurriculum (e.g., admission, orientation, programming for first-year students, residential life, career services, student activities, leadership, learning assistance, programming for special student populations). These units are staffed by professional educators with advanced degrees and headed by a Vice President. These large-scale efforts show that educators can create new designs for the higher education enterprise that model and engage students in the complex ways of making meaning inherent in self-authorship. To help learners achieve the complex learning outcomes I summarized at the outset of this chapter, educators will need to re-conceptualize the educator-learner relationship. The Learning Partnerships Model offers one vision for engaging students in the ways of making meaning their disciplinary knowledge communities require and simultaneously help them gain the developmental capacity to engage successfully in transdisciplinary communities.

References

American College Personnel Association (1994). *The Student Learning Imperative.* Alexandria, VA: Author.

Association of American Colleges and Universities (1995). *American pluralism and the college curriculum: Higher education in a diverse democracy.* Washington, DC: Author.

Association of American Colleges and Universities (2002). *Greater expectations: A new vision of learning as a nation goes to college.* Washington DC: Author.

Barnett, R. (2000a). *Realizing the University in an age of supercomplexity.* Buckingham: The Society for Research into Higher Education and Open University Press.

Barnett, R. (2000b). Supercomplexity and the curriculum. *Studies in Higher Education,* 25(3), 255–265.

Baxter Magolda, M. B. (1992). *Knowing and reasoning in college: Gender-related patterns in students' intellectual development* San Francisco, CA: Jossey-Bass.

Baxter Magolda, M. B. (1999). *Creating contexts for learning and self-authorship: constructive-developmental pedagogy* Nashville, TN: Vanderbilt University Press.

Baxter Magolda, M. B. (2001). *Making their own way: Narratives for transforming higher education to promote self-development* Sterling, VA: Stylus.

Baxter Magolda, M. B. (2004a). Learning Partnerships Model: A framework for promoting self-authorship. In M. B. Baxter Magolda & P. M. King (Eds.), *Learning partnerships: Theory and models of practice to educate for self-authorship* (pp. 37–62). Sterling, VA: Stylus.

Baxter Magolda, M. B. (2004b). Self-authorship as the common goal of 21st century education. In M. B. Baxter Magolda & P. M. King (Eds.), *Learning partnerships: Theory and models of practice to educate for self-authorship* (pp. 1–35). Sterling, VA: Stylus.

Baxter Magolda, M. B., & King, P. M. (Eds.) (2004). *Learning partnerships: Theory & models of practice to educate for self authorship.* Sterling, VA: Stylus.

Bekken, B. M., & Marie, J. (2007). Making self-authorship a goal of core curricula: The Earth Sustainability Pilot Project. In P. S. Meszaros (Ed.), *Self-Authorship: Advancing students' intellectual growth, New Directions for Teaching and Learning* (Vol. 109, pp. 53–67). San Francisco, CA: Jossey-Bass.

Belenky, M., Clinchy, B. M., Goldberger, N., & Tarule, J. (1986). *Women's ways of knowing: The development of self, voice, and mind.* New York: Basic Books.

Department of Education & Skills (DfES) (2004). Putting the world into world-class education: An international strategy for education, skills and children's services. Retrieved June 5, 2005, from http//www.planning .ed.ac.uk/Pub/Documents/DfESIntStrat.pdf

Egart, K., & Healy, M. (2004). An Urban Leadership Internship Program: Implementing Learning Partnerships "Unplugged" from Campus Structures. In M. B. Baxter Magolda & P. M. King (Eds.), *Learning partnerships: Theory and models of practice to educate for self-authorship* (pp. 125–149). Sterling, VA: Stylus.

Haynes, C. (2004). Promoting self-authorship through an interdisciplinary writing curriculum. In M. B. Baxter Magolda & P. M. King (Eds.), *Learning partnerships: Theory and models of practice to educate for self-authorship* (pp. 63–90). Sterling. VA: Stylus.

Jackson, N. and Ward, R. (2004). A fresh perspective on progress files – a way of representing complex learning and achievement in higher education. *Assessment & Evaluation in Higher Education,* 29 (4), 423–449.

Kegan, R. (1994). *In over our heads: The mental demands of modern life.* Cambridge, MA: Harvard University Press.

Kegan, R. (2000). What "form" transforms? A constructive-developmental approach to transformative learning. In J. Mezirow (Ed.), *Learning as transformation: Critical perspectives on a theory in progress* (pp. 35–69). San Francisco, CA: Jossey-Bass.

Keeling, R. P. (Ed.) (2004). *Learning reconsidered: A campus-wide focus on the student experience.* Washington DC: National Association of Student Personnel Administrators, American College Personnel Association.

Meszaros, P. S. (Ed.) (2007). *Self-Authorship: Advancing students' intellectual growth. New Directions for Teaching and Learning* (Vol. 109). San Francisco, CA: Jossey-Bass.

Mills, R., & Strong, K. L. (2004). Organizing for learning in a division of student affairs. In M. B. Baxter Magolda & P. M. King (Eds.), *Learning partnerships: Theory and models of practice to educator for self-authorship* (pp. 269–302). Sterling, VA: Stylus.

Perry, W. G. (1970). *Forms of intellectual and ethical development in the college years: A scheme.* Troy, MO: Holt, Rinehart, & Winston.

Rogers, J. L., Magolda, P. M., Baxter Magolda, M. B., & Knight-Abowitz, K. (2004). A community of scholars: Enacting the Learning Partnerships Model in graduate education. In M. B. Baxter Magolda & P. M. King (Eds.), *Learning partnerships: Theory and models of practice to educate for self-authorship* (pp. 213–244). Sterling, VA: Stylus.

Wildman, T. M. (2004). The Learning Partnerships Model: Framing faculty and institutional development. In M. B. Baxter Magolda & P. M. King (Eds.), *Learning partnerships: Theory and models of practice to educate for self-authorship* (pp. 245–268). Sterling, VA: Stylus.

Yonkers-Talz, K. (2004). A learning partnership: U.S. college students and the poor in El Salvador. In M. B. Baxter Magolda & P. M. King (Eds.), *Learning partnerships: Theory and models to educate for self-authorship* (pp. 151–184). Sterling. VA: Stylus.

Ethnic Identity, Epistemological Development, and Academic Achievement in Underrepresented Students

Jane Elizabeth Pizzolato
Prema Chaudhari
Ennad Dyana Murrell
Sharon Podobnik
Zachary Schaeffer

Through 2 related studies, we investigated the relation between ethnic identity, epistemological development, and achievement among students of color. Findings suggest that the three variables are related, with ethnic identity and epistemological development together contributing to explaining variance in college GPA almost as well as a combination of SAT score and high school grade point average. Findings regarding the two developmental processes are summarized.

Investigations into the achievement gap between students of color and White students typically have been focused on why the gap exists. Although conducted from a deficit perspective, a large body of research has pointed toward three key issues in understanding lower levels of achievement among college students of color. First, many college students of color are also first-generation students and/or students from low-income backgrounds. Consequently students of color are also less likely to have families who can support them procedurally and financially while in college (Choy, 2002; Horn & Chen, 1998; Terenzini, Cabrera, & Bernal, 2001; Yeh, 2002). The lack of financial support leads to heavier workloads, which students take on to finance their education, and which may then interfere with the time they have to study for their classes. And the lack of procedural knowledge—knowledge about how to navigate the college environment—puts students at a disadvantage when figuring out how to find resources and support systems to enhance their achievement. The second key issue is that because students of color are more likely than their White peers to also be first-generation and/or low-income students, they are also more likely to be poorly prepared for collegiate academics, making the challenge of college coursework that much greater (Choy; Horn & Chen; Terenzini et al.; Yeh). The third key issue is that students of color are also more likely to lack the types of cultural capital (e.g., styles of discourse and cultural knowledge) valued in school systems than their White peers, making the terrain that much more unfamiliar (Choy; Lopez, Ehly, & Garcia-Vazquez, 2002; Ogbu, 1997; Rendón, Jalomo, & Nora, 2000; Yeh).

These factors combine to decrease the ease with which students of color collectively can achieve. Identification of factors that inhibit achievement potential is important to understanding the obstacles that students must contend with as they work to achieve in college contexts, but not all students

Reprinted from *Journal of College Student Development* (2008).

of color are from low-income families, nor are they all the first in their families to go to college. Too often the "students of color" category is considered synonymous with "at-risk students," when a large portion of students of color in higher education are from economically comfortable families who value education. Coupled with the fact that there is still an achievement gap between students of color and White students, it seems important to examine other factors that may account for this achievement gap.

Ethnic Identity

In explaining why some students of color thrive in collegiate settings whereas others do not, ethnic identity development has been discussed as an effective buffer. Here we consider ethnic identity a dynamic, developmental, and contextual construct that can be described as one's affiliation and membership with a particular ethnic group that is based on one's conception of knowledge, attitudes, and feelings for that group (Bernal & Knight, 1993; Gloria, Kurpius, Hamilton, & Willson, 1999; Keefe, 1992; Phinney, 1989, 1993; Rotheram & Phinney, 1987).

One way to combat negative messages is to help students of color construct ethnic identities that include achievement as not only a desirable characteristic of the ethnic group, but an achievable characteristic as well (Ford, 1996; Johnson & Arbona, 2006; Oyserman, Gant, & Ager, 1995; Oyserman, Harrison, & Bybee, 2001; Oyserman, Terry, & Bybee, 2002). Through development of ethnic identities that include achievement goals, students of color develop a strong sense of self that helps them ignore threats to the viability of their academic self.

This observation makes sense theoretically given the trajectory for ethnic identity development. According to Phinney (1989), ethnic identity development can be conceptualized as an exploratory process of one's ethnic and cultural issues in relation to the self. Through a 3-stage process, individuals consider and construct a sense of self in relation to the values of their ethnic and cultural group.

Ethnic identity development then shapes individual consideration of just how to interpret and adapt values. As individuals explore their ethnic identity, the exploration process allows for investigation into whether and how one can be both a committed member of their ethnic group and espouse values that are seen as controversial within factions of their ethnic group, or which conflict with misplaced expectations of others based on their demographics. For students of color then, the ethnic identity exploration process should help them develop an internally and ethnically grounded reason for aspiring toward academic success despite negative messages.

When looking at college students specifically, however, the function of ethnic identity development in achievement becomes more complex. As Parham (1989) noted, after reaching achieved ethnic identity—the pinnacle of ethnic identity development (Phinney, 1989), individuals can reevaluate and reconfigure their ethnic identities, and are still prone to experience earlier developmental phases as they have new experiences. As students of color enter college and begin to think concretely about their career goals, they often reexamine the role that their ethnicity plays in their new environment (Johnson & Arbona, 2006). Establishing an achieved ethnic identity may be an important step for students of color. Here an achieved ethnic identity means that students construct personalized ethnic identities that equip them with the ability to make sense of internal and external challenges to their sense of themselves as ethnic beings, and their sense of themselves in other contexts based on their ethnicity. Harboring an achieved ethnic identity in turn should promote overall psychosocial well-being—which itself is important for coping with the challenges presented by the collegiate environment (Louis & Liem, 2005; Phinney, 1992; Phinney & Alipuria, 1990).

Ethnic Identity and Epistemological Development

Investigations into how and why ethnic identity is related to psychosocial well-being reveal that reasoning abilities may be one factor that develops as ethnic identity develops, and that increasingly more complex reasoning skills (i.e., the cognitive ability to think abstractly) in turn promote healthy psychosocial development. In Mexican American and Anglo American adolescents, for example, Karcher and Fischer (2004) demonstrated such a connection between reasoning and ethnic identity.

The degree to which adolescents previously explored their own ethnic identities influenced their ability to reason complexly—reason abstractly about experiences and concepts related to ethnicity—about both their own ethnic identity and those people of other ethnicities might hold. Across degrees of ethnic identity exploration, adolescents demonstrated increasingly complex levels of reasoning about ethnicity if they were scaffolded by a researcher (e.g., prompted to clarify, elaborate on, and provide relevant examples in their responses). In line with existing theory about ranges in reasoning skills from functional (what people can do on their own) to optimal (what people can do with support) based on levels of support (Fischer, 1980; Fischer & Lamborn, 1988; King & Kitchener, 2004), it appears that reasoning development related to identity parallels reasoning development about abstract concepts and purely cognitive processes (e.g., solution of ill-structured problems). This finding coupled with the previous one—that ethnic identity exploration is positively related to reasoning complexity—is important because they collectively suggest a strong relation between ethnic identity and cognitive development.

Although Karcher and Fischer (2004) provided empirical evidence of the relation between ethnic identity and reasoning, their results were limited to reasoning about ethnicity issues. Reasoning in other contexts was not examined. Furthermore, how and why the two developmental constructs were related, even in this limited context, remained unclear. As Torres and Baxter Magolda (2004) noted, "Existing ethnic identity theories seldom incorporate the interrelationship among the multiple dimensions of development" (p. 333), where "multiple dimensions" refers to other major developmental trajectories (e.g., cognitive development, moral development). In other words, the relation between ethnic identity development and other developmental trajectories is hazy. Into this gap came their exploratory, qualitative work on the influence of epistemological development on ethnic identity development. In their research they found that when their participants entered college, they tended to view authorities as omniscient. As the participants subsequently encountered situations where their closely held ideas and experiences were called into question, the participants began to see that they would need to negotiate between authorities' claims and their own views of themselves. In practicing wise restraint in evaluating these dissonant experiences college students began to see knowledge as socially constructed.

For the participants in Torres and Baxter Magolda's (2004) study, this change in understanding knowledge construction and their role in it then led to a second change—ethnic identity development. In the process, students appeared to transfer their new knowledge construction skills to exploring and further clarifying how they understood their own ethnic identities. For example, Angelica, a participant in Torres and Baxter Magolda's study, began to question socialization choices her family made regarding her Latina identity, as she also began to think about her own values and beliefs about being a phenotypically White Latina. Seeing herself as able to question parental authority, and as able to construct her own ethnic identity, Angelica could then revise her own ethnic identity. In short, where Karcher and Fischer (2004) found relations between ethnic identity and reasoning, Torres and Baxter Magolda's findings gestured toward a sequence of events where changes in reasoning gave way to further development of ethnic identity. Epistemological development appeared to precede ethnic identity development because the former seemed to qualitatively change the way college students could engage in exploration of the latter.

Torres and Baxter Magolda (2004) claimed that their participants' development evidenced movement from formula following (i.e., exclusively using information and guidelines from external authorities in knowledge construction) to Crossroads moments (i.e., abandonment of formula following because of a recognition of a need to internally define values and beliefs as part of the knowledge construction process). As students experienced these Crossroads moments, and began to reshape their epistemological orientations and ethnic identities, Torres and Baxter Magolda claimed these connected processes were part of each participant's "becoming the author of one's life" (p. 354). These terms, "formula following," "Crossroads," and "becoming the author of one's own life," are all key terms in the self-authorship development process (Baxter Magolda, 2001). So beyond examining how ethnic identity and epistemological development are related, Torres and Baxter Magolda showed that for their participants, ethnic identity development was inextricably linked to self-authorship development—a specific type of epistemology where such knowers recognize the contextual nature of knowledge and use internally developed goals, values, and beliefs to navigate the relativism that accompanies contextuality in knowing (Baxter Magolda, 2001; Kegan, 1994).

Although descriptive of how ethnic identity and epistemological development may relate, the proposed relation between the two types of development is based on only 28 Latina and Latino students. The Torres and Baxter Magolda (2004) study is a rich description, firmly grounded in theory, and built on multiple interviews with participants across multiple years, but what does this developmental relation look like for a more diverse population? And how do these forms of development impact academic achievement? Examining how ethnic identity and epistemological development relate may help explain achievement in college students of color. There have been investigations into how ethnic identity and epistemology develop independently (Baxter Magolda, 1992, 2001; Belenky, Clinchy, Goldberger, & Tarule, 1986; Inkelas, 2004; King & Baxter Magolda, 2004; Perry, 1968; Renn, 2000), with conjectures made regarding their impact on each other (e.g., Torres & Baxter Magolda) and on achievement (e.g., Wawrzynski & Pizzolato, 2006). There has also been empirical work on the relation between achievement and epistemology (Buehl & Alexander, 2001, 2005; Schommer, 1994). But how the three are related to each other, and specifically whether and how ethnic identity and epistemological development function together to influence achievement has yet to be investigated. For this project we investigated this triadic relation in college students of color.

Research Design

To understand the relation between ethnic identity, epistemological development, and achievement, we conducted two studies. In the first study we qualitatively explored the relation between ethnic identity and epistemological development in high-achieving students of color. In the second study we quantitatively explored how the relation between ethnic identity development, epistemological development, and achievement works. Because the triadic relation itself is not well documented, a two-study investigation seemed most appropriate to build and then test a model grounded in the actual experiences of the population in question. Each study is described separately on the following pages, and then a common discussion links the two.

Conducting two related studies seemed appropriate because the relation between ethnic identity, epistemological development, and achievement has not been empirically investigated. The first step in this process was examining the relation between ethnic identity and epistemological development. Although a positive relation between the two has been demonstrated for Latin students, questioning the degree to which this relation holds up across racial and ethnic categories was necessary so that a model of how ethnic identity, epistemological development, and academic achievement are related is grounded in data from a diverse group of students. Following this exploratory qualitative study, adding the achievement variable, and testing the triadic relation in a larger sample of students should allow for an empirical understanding of not just if and what type of relation exists, but also how this relation works after controlling for other variables that would be difficult to control for in a qualitative study (e.g., prior academic achievement).

In light of these research goals, we recruited participants from two large public universities in the Eastern United States. Participants were recruited from student organizations through announcements at organization meetings, and e-mailed announcements through group electronic mailing lists. Ultimately 726 students volunteered to participate. Of these 726 students, 307 students were students of color. From this group of 307, 67 students volunteered to participate in the qualitative interview portion of the study. Study 1 reports on this qualitative data. Study 2 then tests the emergent model from Study 1 using the whole sample of 307 students.

Study 1

Method

Participants ($N = 67$) represented a diverse array of racial and ethnic categories: African American or Black (35), Asian or Pacific Islander (7), Latino or Latina (12), multiethnic or multiracial students

(13). The majority of the students were first-year students (30), with the rest of the participants distributed across the three remaining years: sophomores (11), juniors (12), seniors (14). To be eligible for the study reported here, students needed to demonstrate a high level of academic achievement based on meeting one of two criteria: (a) students maintained a cumulative GPA of greater than 3.0, or (b) students had a semester GPA of greater than 3.0. The latter criteria was included because it allowed for participants to show signs of significant improvement and commitment to high achievement if they had previously had a semester where their performance had not been as high.

Data were collected via semistructured interviews. Each student participated in one 60- to 90-minute interview with a member of the research team. The interviews were semistructured to ensure all students were asked the same main questions, but flexibility was allowed so individual experiences could be explored in sufficient depth (Miles & Huberman, 1994). Each participant selected a pseudonym. Then the first goal of the interviews was to gain a sense of the students' ethnic identity by asking the students how they identified themselves, and then probing for reasons why, the stability of this identification, the ways they demonstrated this ethnic identity, and the way(s) in which they arrived at this particular ethnic sense of self. The second goal was to understand the types of experiences these students had during college (e.g., "I'd like you to tell me a story about an important experience you've had while in college"), with probes about the ways in which they processed these experiences and solved problems (i.e., "How did you make that decision?). The interview centered around students' stories about experiences they identified as important. Throughout each interview, the interviewer consistently posed her or his interpretations as questions to the participant (e.g., "So what I hear you saying is ____. Is this correct?"). In this way, participants were given repeated opportunities to help the interviewer construct an accurate understanding of the data being gathered.

All interviews were audiotaped and transcribed verbatim. Patterns, themes, and ultimately codes were constructed through constant comparative analyses of the interview transcripts (Glaser & Strauss, 1967; Strauss & Corbin, 1994). Constant comparative analyses seemed appropriate for code building (Boyatzis, 1998) because the relation between ethnic identity and subcomponents of epistemological development is a relatively new area of study in the college student development literature, so preexisting codes did not exist. Paying attention to patterns and themes in this triadic relation seemed important, and so coding efforts were focused on emerging patterns related to ethnic identity and epistemological development.

Constant comparative analyses led to repeated questioning of the codes generated from the data, and in so doing ensured that codes were not derived from only a small subset of the data, but instead were representative of the voices of all 67 participants. Furthermore, data were coded by two coders. Any disagreements in coding were discussed and mutually resolved, with any necessary code clarification taking place at that time, and then leading to rechecking of previously coded data. Additionally, an outside coder was brought in to review codes for bias.

Findings

Based on our analysis of 67 interview transcripts, two key findings emerged:

1. College students are exploring and reconsidering their ethnic identities, and as they explore the content and meaning of their ethnic identities based on their new/collegiate experiences, they engage in related epistemological development processes.
2. As the participants explored their ethnic identities, the types of epistemological development induced appeared to lead to a transitional period in epistemological development.

During this period, participants were considering and testing out new ways of knowing, but were not yet able to fully enact their new ways of knowing; there appeared to be difference in their reasoning abilities (their epistemologies) and their actions. Each of these two findings is discussed in an individual subsection below. Whenever a participant is first introduced, her or his class year is placed in parentheses.

Reconsidering Ethnic Identity. Although many of the participants ($n = 54$) believed they had firm, healthy ethnic identities prior to college, the college environment provided new opportunities for exploration, new information for them to consider, and new reactions of others to them. Together these new experiences in their collegiate environments led participants to question whether and why they were comfortable with their entering ethnic identities. For example, Emmanuel (junior) described the switch from a predominantly Black home environment to a predominantly White institution as "shocking," and Rachel (sophomore) described coming to college as being demographically "eye-opening." The actual content of participants' experiences ranged in intensity, but the common denominator was that these experiences led participants to question their ethnic identities (see Table 5.2).

Across these experiences, participants demonstrated both that events were occurring that spotlighted their ethnic identities, and that these experiences were not necessarily ones participants could easily ignore. In response to these experiences, participants began to reexplore their ethnic identities. These new explorations pushed students to consider not only what they thought, but also how some of their new beliefs or ideas conflicted with both their own previous ethnic identities, and the values of their families and friends. Dion (first year) captured this need for reexploration when he described his unsettling experiences and reactions to them.

> Things can work out, and I can't say that I got above those other people, but I can say I'm better than them. I'd still like to be above them, but at least I got my pride, and you know that's an accomplishment. It's hard to maintain your pride when you can't do nothing but be positive when everyone is being so negative about you. But you have to keep being positive or else you can't get to that better place, so you have to stop thinking like the other people, and start thinking about what you're really about and why you're going to keep on being positive even though you just don't want to anymore, even though it'd be easier to say, "Yeah. I agree," to the haters. But you gotta protect your pride, so you gotta figure out what you're about and be true to that.

Dion was not unique in his recognition of a need to reflect on his identity. For example, Callie (sophomore) said, "People focused on my ethnicity. It made me really self-conscious. . . . but for me

TABLE 5.2

Examples of Participants' Ethnic Identity Experiences

Participant	Participant Ethnicity	Quotation
Hailey	Mixed	I'm too Black for the White folks, too White for the Black folks . . . I'm stuck in the middle . . . people act all like you arrived when you get accepted to college, but arrived where?—stuck in the middle of nowhere is where . . . and pretty much this sucks.
Ashley	Black	I was really upset, because I felt like they only really wanted me because I'm Black . . . and that was *so* aggravating . . . and it's really not just about that organization, it's really about adjusting to this whole college thing and figuring myself out.
Los	Latino	[In high school] while everybody else was hanging out I was inside studying. I didn't have friends really, but all those people with friends didn't really have futures, but now that I'm here I'm not sure I have a future either. I'm so far behind most of the other kids, and from Day 1 the teacher I have for [Composition] acted like I was an idiot just because I speak with an accent.
Ron	Asian	I feel like a foreigner on campus, and I grew up in this town but you have no idea how often people talk to me slowly and loudly like I'm some sort of foreign national.

I realized finally that I didn't need to be ultra-Asian just because other people noticed I was Asian. I could be as Asian as I wanted to be—or not be." That said, not all students were able to rush into the task of self-reflection and reevaluation in the way Dion and Callie were.

Initially the notion of engaging in this type of self-work seemed like a daunting task, and many students (*n* = 42) questioned whether they could or should purposefully move forward with the identity development task at hand. Their questions about the appropriateness of a commitment to the identity development process seemed to lie in whether they felt they could effectively do the self-work and relationship negotiation that came as part of exploration and reconsideration of their ethnic identities. After encountering a myriad of challenges in college related to his status as a low-income, first-generation, Black student, Jonah (junior) deeply questioned not only whether he belonged in college, but also whether he had access to any useful support systems in the process.

> I can't really have an intelligent conversation with [my foster dad] about college and what's going on, because he doesn't—he hasn't been. I mean he's old. He hasn't been. I mean the dude never even got to finish high school . . . and I can't relate to my friends in college now . . . they're from all White towns and went to high school with friends and friends' parents who'd been to college.

Depending on whether these students felt like they could move forward with their ethnic identity development, their connection to their ethnic group varied. In Jonah's case, because he did not know how to move forward, he expressed a growing sense of distance from his home community and from his ethnic group, "If I'm in a rough situation I can't go to them." Michelle (first year) said she decided she needed "space from my Black friends, because I'm mixed and they want me to focus only on my Black side." And in response to her growing frustration with her Lebanese family and community Nadia (junior) claimed that she began by "going it alone," and that she needed "a break" from her ethnic community. To use Phinney's (1992) terms, these students' sense of affirmation, belonging, and commitment to their ethnic identity group decreased—one of two key components of ethnic identity.

Looking more closely at participants' descriptions of their reactions to ethnic identity challenges is telling of one reason why they collectively struggled to effectively reexplore their ethnic identities—their epistemological development. In Baxter Magolda's (1992) terms, these participants demonstrated clear signs of an early epistemological position in her scheme—absolute knowledge. From this perspective our participants were able to see that there multiple perspectives existed relative to their ethnic identity and its signifiers (e.g., associated characteristics and stereotypes). Although they were able to recognize this diversity in perspective, they believed the existence of this multiplicity was improper. Said otherwise, they felt that the multiplicity they were experiencing was a result of the majority of perspectives being wrong. Furthermore, if only an authority figure would point them and everyone else to the right view on their ethnic identity, all would be resolved in the singular, correct way. Jonah clearly depicted this position in his departure from his ethnic identity exploration because he lacked an authority figure to tell him what to do.

> If I just get upset about something, and start thinking about stuff, then I get upset that I don't have no support for figuring anything out, and then I get discouraged and quit trying. I feel like I still need someone to tell me what to do, because otherwise I just get it all wrong!

Without others to help them make sense of their challenging experiences, these participants felt discouraged and disengaged because they had yet to develop epistemological orientations that allowed for complex reasoning processes necessary for more effective coping alternatives.

Although a number of students (*n* = 42) seemed to prematurely depart from the ethnic identity development process, because they coped with the challenges in ways that made them feel like they could not or did not want to progress, other students (*n* = 25) made more progress. The participants in this latter category continued to explore and revise their ethnic identities as they sought to make sense of competing messages. For example, Cosette (first year) said,

> I guess another step is processing and identifying myself, because after you take away high school, and all those norms, who are you? . . . And I thought I had that figured out, but I guess I have a long way to go.

And Hollis (first year) described how he needed to "go to other cats to get some advice" on ways he could "survive being a multitalented Black dude on campus." Unlike their counterparts who saw a need to reexplore their ethnic identities, but then almost immediately got stuck, these students who were able to start to reexplore their ethnic identities saw not only a need to reexplore, but also a belief that such exploration was possible.

What seemed to separate students into these two categories was not that one group was more committed to reexploration of ethnic identity, but rather that these two groups possessed distinctly different epistemological orientations. Where the first group of participants was constrained by their epistemological orientations, those espoused by the second group of participants helped them begin to engage in the ethnic identity reexploration process. This group of participants saw that there were multiple perspectives on the issue of ethnic identity, and they saw that the goal was not being told which was the "right" perspective, but rather that they needed to figure out what they thought was right for them.

For example, Cosette acknowledged the ways in which new contexts influence identity development, and that what counts as complete in one situation is not even close to complete in another situation, because the rules change as the context shifts. And unlike participants who departed from the ethnic identity process once they recognized multiplicity, these students attempted to engage in working through the diversity of views as all potentially viable ways of thinking. The trick here, however, is that these participants still placed bounds on the degree to which they saw this type of thinking as legitimate. For these participants, such exploration of multiplicity was grounded in a deep belief that this is what they were supposed to do. As T (first year) said, "You've got to figure this stuff out if you think you're going to make it in [college]." Engaging with the multiplicity was a requirement—not imposed by these students themselves, but perceived by them as a requirement set out by external forces.

Despite whether or not students chose to continue with the ethnic identity development process, as all participants made this decision, their decisions affected their beliefs regarding their own ethnic identity. For students who disengaged from the process, their sense of dissatisfaction with their current ethnic identities, coupled with their lack of movement forward with their ethnic identity search led them to feel uncomfortable in their own skin. On the other hand, students who remained engaged in the exploration process were not fully satisfied either—in large part because they were still reconfiguring their ethnic identities. Across participants then, being in such a state of flux was certainly not comfortable, but figuring out how to move forward with their identity exploration required more than mere commitment to such a process.

Transitional Identities and Epistemologies. Even when they were committed to engaging in exploration of their ethnic identities, all our participants eventually got stuck. The absolute knower participants were stuck early in the process because they were constrained by their epistemological orientation. The other group also eventually ran into a wall when they could not reason in any more complex ways. Qiana (first year), for example, initially recognized the importance of exploration and began this process of considering competing claims about ethnicity and its signifiers. But as she proceeded with her exploration she became more and more frustrated.

> I want people to know how hard it is to fit in when you're not normal to anyone. I feel like I walk around with a big sticker on my head saying, "I'm one of those poor kids from [name of city]. I'm here because you people want to pretend you think diversity is important, not because I'm smart enough to be here on my own," because people treat me like I'm less than them just because I'm Black and because I'm from [name of city]. It's ridiculous! And I AM smart I think. I get good grades, but all this stuff, these stereotypes and the looks people give me when I talk in class, it makes me question myself more than I should. But I can't stop questioning. I mean, am I really good enough to be here? Am I really smart enough, or am I just delusional? And I hate that I have to even wonder. I just feel like an outcast. . . . It's like everyone is always looking down on me . . . and now sometimes when I look down on myself I'm not as sure of my own self, and that's what I really hate—more than the other people—the fact that I am not sure of my own self anymore.

Recognizing the persistence of the disconnect between others' and her own conception of herself as an academically talented Black student, Qiana questioned why she engaged in a process requiring that she acknowledge multiple perspectives as she defined herself.

Moreover, her questioning represented the tense space in which she found herself epistemologically. Her feelings of having to prove herself imply that she sees as necessary the reconciliation of her internally defined ethnic identity with that which is externally imposed based on her appearance as a Black student. Furthermore, this work is not for herself, but to show others who she is, and how they are supposed to view her. These goals and drives in her ethnic identity exploration process suggest that like other relativism subordinate knowers, Qiana sees multiple perspectives as a means to acknowledge different views with the goal of narrowing down to the singular right view. Consequently her inability to move herself and others beyond the inconsistencies she is experiencing is frustrating, because this stagnation means that she is not making forward progress. Without an ability to see her personal goal as not winning an ethnic identity or winning others to her side, the only way out of the vicious cycle of attempting to explain herself and being boxed in again is to stop putting up with the inconsistencies. In other words, the only option for getting out of the situation was to exit the exploration process.

Regardless of our participants' epistemologies, they inevitably came to a point where they could not figure out how to cope with challenges to their ethnic identity that also allowed them to continue their ethnic identity exploration. In short, participants' epistemological orientations appeared to constrain their ethnic identity development.

In response to this sense of futile struggle, the majority of our participants (n = 54) sought out others to help them make sense of the new experiences and questions they had related to their ethnic identity. These others included family members, professional counselors, peers, academic advisors, and trusted faculty members. Through conversation with others, participants gained tools for and developed new ways of making sense of their experiences. Cristina (first year) said:

> I've learned words I didn't know before, like "ethnocentrism," and "privilege," and "social reproduction." I knew what those words meant before I ever heard of them because me and my family have experienced the consequences of those words every day. So it's cool to learn that there are words for my experiences, and it helps me talk more about my experiences and what needs to change.

Elaborating on what she meant by "talk more," Cristina explained that learning about these concepts helped her "have another way to think about what's going on and feel like everything that is happening is not my fault. It's like now I can step outside my experiences to make sense of them." Learning about the broader picture of race, ethnicity, and society allowed to her to understand why she was being stereotyped, and her ability and responsibility to make change.

Similarly, Qiana found, "The hard part is remembering that I'm not delusional about the ways people are actually treating me, but that all that doesn't mean that I've got myself wrong." Ashley (first year) found,

> Just because there are inconsistencies [between how I think about myself and how others think about me] doesn't mean I'm wrong about myself; the inconsistencies might say more about the people questioning me. My job is to figure out what I want to believe about myself even though there are inconsistencies.

Johnny (senior) said that he learned from his brother that, "just because people look at us like we're so different doesn't mean that I have to be all isolated. I don't have a disease. I have a race, and I have to figure out what it means to me." And Hollis (first year) talked of how his therapist helped him, "get back on track. . . . because I'm learning to trust that I might know something about myself rather than just believing what people tell me about myself."

These participants and the majority of those who sought help from others (n = 54) showed signs of testing out new epistemological orientations. They began to experiment with ways of knowing that are driven by an internal sense of self. From this position, participants saw that what counted as right or wrong depended on context and perspective, and that their goal in meaning making was to resolve the dissonance they experienced in ways that worked for them. In their description of this space, participants talked about a process of coming to know; they were "learning" or "figuring out." This emphasis on process is reminiscent of Baxter Magolda's (2001) Crossroads—the epistemological place where people question the legitimacy of formulas and externally imposed ideas, and so they begin to search for meaning driven by an internal source. This new way of knowing helped participants make forward progress with their ethnic identity exploration because it allowed them to acknowledge but not be crushed under the weight of others' expectations and stereotypes.

It is important to note here, however, that participants were not necessarily adopting these new epistemological orientations, but instead were still in a transitional space with their new epistemologies. Although participants were reasoning in more complex ways relative to their ethnic identities, this complex reasoning did not always translate into behavior representative of similar levels of complexity. For example, Maija (first year) described how despite the fact that she could reason complexly about her mixed ethnic identity and what it signified about her, when it came to interacting with others, she did not know how to bring her reasoning into her interactions.

> I used to be very talkative about issues of race, but now I don't say much, or I don't start talking first. I wait to hear what other people have to say first so that I don't give them another reason to exclude me.

Maija was not the only participant to evidence such a split between her reasoning and actions. Nadia claimed that, "I've thought this through and through. I know what I want and who I want to be as a Lebanese American, but I can't bring myself to fully break away from [my parents'] ways." And Kasper (sophomore) said:

> I know I'm Indian enough even though I don't speak Bengali or any other language. Still, when I'm around my Indian friends, I pretend like I wish I did and that I want to learn words from them. . . . it's just easier than being all conflictual.

Collectively these participants illustrate a split between, on one hand, how they have made sense of and/or how they reason about their ethnic identities and, on the other hand, how they act.

All these participants were able to reason in ways suggestive of more complex epistemological orientation than those they began their college career with. This complexity, however, gave way when participants had to actually act on their reasoning. The participants were stuck in figuring out how to translate the thinking into behaviors. Los (first year) illustrated this when he described the way he was struggling to enact his ethnic identity.

> I started having trouble with [a Latino Student Group], because they want to tell me I'm giving them the shaft, and that means that I'm also ditching my Latino self—like I'm not Latino enough even though I actually speak Spanish and I am actually from Mexico. Now I'm starting to figure that I have Latin culture running through me, and the ways in which it is important to me. It's like I don't have to be in a group to be Mexican, and it's not on me to prove I'm Latin enough. But when they corner me about it I can't ever talk as smooth as I want; I just walk the other way to avoid having to talk about it.

Attributable in part to their transitional epistemologies—epistemologies that are still developing—although students were just developing new epistemologies they could bring to meaning-making about their ethnic identities, they were still figuring out how to translate this meaning-making into action. In all, the findings of this study implied that ethnic identity and epistemological development were positively related; as participants grappled with revising their ethnic identities, they were compelled to reconsider their epistemologies, and the resulting epistemological development influenced ethnic identity development.

Study 2

Given that Study 1 suggested that ethnic identity and epistemological development were related, but that action corresponding with reasoning capacity lagged behind reasoning development, we were able to then investigate how these two developmental processes related to achievement. Presumably progress along ethnic identity and epistemological development trajectories should give rise to reasoning skills useful in academic work. In Study 2 we investigated the degree to which students' GPAs are explained by ethnic identity search and epistemological development for students of color.

Method

Sample. The Study 2 sample included 307 students, among them those 67 students from Study 1. For this sample the students identified their racial and ethnic categorization as follows: African American or Black (112); American Indian or Alaskan Native (24); Asian or Pacific Islander (from underrepresented Asian groups such as Hmong, Samoan, 81); Hispanic, Latino, or Latina (68); more than one category (where at least one category was from an underrepresented group, 39).

Data Collection Procedures. Data were collected via survey. Surveys were administered in large group settings, and students were given 20 minutes to complete the survey packets. These packets included three measures: (a) a demographic survey, (b) the Multigroup Ethnic Identity Measure (Phinney, 1992), and (c) the Self-Authorship Survey (Pizzolato, 2005). The demographic survey asked students for information on their sex, ethnicity, age, SAT score, college GPA, and class year.

The Multigroup Ethnic Identity Measure (MEIM) is a 15-item scale where the first 12 items are 4-point, Likert-type items, and the remaining items are forced choice items about the participants' ethnic group, and those of their parents. The measure has strong reliability across ethnic groups and participant ages ($\alpha = .80$). There are two subscales: Ethnic Identity Search (i.e., the degree to and ways in which an individual has actively worked to construct an ethnic identity), and Affirmation, Belonging, and Commitment (i.e., the psychic and social comfort the individual experiences in relation to her or his ethnic identity; Phinney, 1992). The MEIM was included because it assesses ethnic identity along two key dimensions for college students: (a) searching for an ethnic identity/attempting to construct an ethnic identity, and (b) a sense of belonging within one's ethnic identity group.

The Self-Authorship Survey (SAS) is a 29-item, 5-point Likert-type measure of self-authorship (For additional information on the survey and scale development see Pizzolato, 2007). The SAS is comprised of four subscales: Capacity for Autonomous Action (CAA), Problem Solving Orientation (PSO), Perceptions of Volitional Competence (PVC), and Self-Regulation in Challenging Situations (SRC). It has been shown to have good to excellent internal consistency ($\alpha = .88$), test-retest reliability (.87, $p < .01$), and convergent validity ($\rho = .70$, $p < .01$; Pizzolato, 2007; Wawrzynski & Pizzolato, 2006). The SAS was selected to measure epistemological development because it is the only short form quantitative measure of epistemological development that assesses this construct in ways consistent with college student developmentalists' conceptions of epistemological development (Baxter Magolda, 1992, 2001; Belenky et al., 1986; King & Kitchener, 1994; Perry, 1968). Additionally, the SAS has been used in a previous study of epistemological development that attempted to examine its relation to demographic variables and academic patterns (Wawrzynski & Pizzolato, 2006).

For the purpose of this study, we used only the PSO and CAA subscales, as they focused on reporting reasoning and action pieces of epistemological development—two pieces of epistemological development that appeared to develop asynchronously during the Crossroads in Study 1. Table 5.3 shows an overview of the measures, including the means and standard deviations, and internal reliabilities for each measure.

TABLE 5.3

Means, Standard Deviations, and Reliability

Measure	*M*	*SD*	α
Ethnic Identity Search	2.51	.76	.91
Affirmation, Belonging, & Commitment	3.05	.70	.86
Problem Solving Orientation	3.56	.64	.89
Capacity for Autonomous Action	2.94	.75	.85

Results

We conducted a hierarchical regression analysis to examine the degree to which students' achievement (i.e., college GPA) could be explained by students' ethnic identity and epistemological development scores after controlling for high school GPA and SAT score. High school GPA and SAT score were entered at Step 1. At Step 2 students' SAS scores and MEIM subscale scores were entered. The MEIM subscale scores were entered rather than the total scale score because the subscales measure two different and important pieces of ethnic identity—the degree to which one is searching, which seems potentially related to epistemological development—and affirmation—the degree to which one feels comfortable and connected to one's ethnic group. Similarly PSO and CAA scores were entered individually.

Results of this analysis showed that the model as a whole was significant (F (306) = 8.93, $p <$ .001); the model explained 22.5% of the variance in college GPA among students of color. High school GPA and SAT score together explained 12.6% of the total variance, and ethnic identity and epistemological development added an additional 9.9% of explanation. Looking more closely at the contributions of each variable, the two that emerged as important predictor variables were SAT score and CAA (see Table 5.4).

Although this model predicted only 22.5% of the total college GPA variance, the fact that there was such a small difference in variance predicted between SAT and high school GPA, and the two developmental processes (ethnic identity and epistemology), these results seem important to note, as the former set of predictors are traditionally considered strong predictors of college achievement. Furthermore, the fact that capacity for autonomous action was one of the only two variables to significantly and uniquely contribute to explaining college GPA variance suggests that this may be an effective focal area for programs aimed to improve achievement.

Discussion

The findings of these two studies contribute to collective understanding of factors involved in the achievement gap, as well as build on existing early work investigating the relation between epistemological development and ethnic identity development. The findings from the present studies suggest that the two developmental processes are related, but how remains under study. Our work builds on the research of Torres and Baxter Magolda (2004) by gesturing toward a more bidirectional relation between epistemological development and ethnic identity. Additionally, the results point toward the importance of understanding these developmental processes in explaining academic achievement among college students of color.

As Torres and Baxter Magolda (2004) documented among Latina and Latino students, there did appear to be a similar sequence of events for our more diverse sample of students of color. College introduced new ethnic challenges into the lives of our participants, such that they were forced to question the degree to which they understood what it meant to be of their ethnicity and/or how their ethnic features determined the degree of belonging and success they could experience in college. These experiences catalyzed student reconsideration of their ethnic identities, but as students reconsidered their ethnic identities they ran into difficulty. This difficulty stemmed from their still-developing epistemological development; to effectively cope with the ethnic identity challenges that they were experiencing, they needed more complex methods of meaning making than they had already developed. Through supportive others these students then worked to develop sufficiently complex methods of meaning making to support their continued exploration of their ethnic identities. As they worked to develop these meaning making skills they were increasingly able to cope with ethnic identity issues and reconfigure their own ethnic identities. However, coping with these issues internally differed from coping with these issues in public arenas or interpersonal relationships.

Theoretically speaking then, our findings support existing research that suggests that ethnic identity and epistemological development appear related (Karcher & Fischer, 2004; Torres & Baxter Magolda, 2004). More than just supporting this contention, a closer look at our findings suggests that the relation between these two developmental constructs is bidirectional. Where past studies were focused on how the meaning making or cognitive dimension of epistemological development influenced ethnic identity development (Karcher & Fischer; Torres & Baxter Magolda), we took a more holistic view of epistemological development. According to Kegan (1994) and Baxter Magolda (2001), epistemological development includes three dimensions: cognitive (methods and processes for meaning making), intrapersonal (developed sense of self/identity), and interpersonal (abilities and practices of engaging in and beliefs regarding the nature of relationships). Data from our participants showed that epistemological development along the cognitive dimension first influenced the degree to which the participants' were able to effectively engage in reexploring and reconfiguring their ethnic identities. Then as their ethnic identities were being reconfigured, the degree to which participants were able to enact their ethnic identities was bound by the still limited degree of development along the interpersonal dimension. This finding is important because it highlights the interrelatedness of developmental processes in college students.

Practically, these findings are important because coupled with the results from Study 2, these two psychological development processes seem to impact academic achievement. Where many researchers of both identity development and epistemological development have helped to clarify and deepen understanding of the mechanisms of these development processes, researchers have undertaken significantly fewer studies to examine the ways in which such development relates to other desirable outcomes of participation in higher education such as academic achievement. Examination of such relations seems important both to understanding why institutions of higher education should be invested in psychological development and to continue to attempt to identify ways in which achievement can be enhanced—especially traditionally underperforming populations. The results of Study 2 show that together, an arguably objective aptitude test (the SAT) and prior achievement (high school GPA), contribute to explaining college GPA variance in students of color only marginally better than assessments of epistemological and ethnic identity development. Although still only explaining a small portion of college GPA variance, this is an important finding because it supports existing contentions that variables other than aptitude and achievement should be considered in predicting achievement—especially among students of color. Furthermore, where others (e.g., Sedlacek, 2004) have contended that noncognitive variables should be a focal area in predicting the success of students of color, our findings suggest that although noncognitive variables may be important, cognitive variables like epistemological development, which are related to meaning making but do not rely on formal academic knowledge, may be equally worth considering in predicting and working to promote achievement among students of color.

Limitations & Areas for Future Research

Because this was an exploratory study with a small sample of students there are a number of important limitations to note. First, inclusion of students from all racial or ethnic categories in a qualitative study would be useful for early investigations into whether there are categorical differences in how

TABLE 5.4

Results from Regression analysis

Variable	B	β	Sig.
SAT Score	.001	.310	.001
High School GPA	.002	.030	.510
Ethnic Identity Search	–.110	–.320	.750
Affirmation, Belonging, & Commitment	–.290	–.420	.290
Problem Solving orientation	.030	.040	.590
Capacity for autonomous action	.120	.160	.030

and why the relations between ethnic identity and epistemological development play out. Additionally, our sample included only high-achieving students of color; including students who are academically struggling would be useful in examining if and how differences in the ethnic identityepistemological development relation emerge by achievement level.

The sample for Study 1, although adequate for the analyses performed, included participants were drawn from two public, research universities in the Eastern United States. Drawing participants from other types of institutions (e.g., Historically Black Colleges and Universities, Hispanic Serving Institutions, and Tribal Colleges), as well as other regions of the United States would important in understanding the generalizability of the findings of this study. Because of regional differences in racial climate, as well as differences in ethnic experience of students at institutions that are not predominantly White institutions, a study drawing participants from these diverse areas would add much to collective understanding. Additionally, a larger sample with more equal numbers of participants in each racial and ethnic category would allow for investigation into differences by racial or ethnic category.

Conclusion

By bringing an understanding of epistemological development that includes three dimensions (cognitive, intrapersonal, and interpersonal) to a study of how such development is related to ethnic identity development, through this study we clarified the relation between these two processes in students of color. Furthermore, given the ethnic diversity of the sample, we were able to examine this relation in a more diverse sample than in previous research. Additionally, our findings point toward a model of the relation between ethnic identity and epistemological development that outlines the ways in which components of both developmental processes interact to produce greater development along both developmental trajectories. And finally, because of the collection of achievement measures, we were not only able to see how two psychological processes relate in college students of color, but also to investigate the ways in which this development may contribute to academic achievement among students of color.

References

Baxter Magolda, M. B. (1992). *Knowing and reasoning in college.* San Francisco: Jossey Bass.

Baxter Magolda, M. B. (2001). *Making their own way: Narratives for transforming higher education to promote self-authorship.* Sterling, VA: Stylus.

Belenky, M. F., Clinchy, B. M., Goldberger, N. R., & Tarule, J. M. (1986). *Women's ways of knowing: The development of self, voice, and mind.* New York: Basic Books.

Bernal, M., & Knight, G. (Eds.). (1993). *Ethnic identity: Formation and transmission among Hispanics and other minorities.* Albany: SUNY Press.

Boyatzis, R. E. (1998). *Transforming qualitative information: Thematic analysis and code development.* New York: Sage.

Buehl, M. M., & Alexander, P. A. (2001). Beliefs about academic knowledge. *Educational Psychological Review, 13,* 385–418.

Buehl, M. M., & Alexander, P. A. (2005). Motivation and performance differences in students' domain-specific epistemological belief profiles. *American Educational Research Journal, 42*(4), 697–726.

Choy, S. P. (2002). *Access and persistence: Findings from 10 years of longitudinal research on students* (Report No. EDO-HE-200202). Washington, DC: American Council on Education (ERIC Document Reproduction Service No. ED466105).

Fischer, K. W. (1980). A theory of cognitive development: The control and construction of hierarchies of skills. *Psychological Review, 87,* 477–531.

Fischer, K. W., & Lamborn, S. (1988). Optimal and functional levels in cognitive development: The individual's developmental range. *International Society for the Study of Behavioural Development Newsletter, 2*(14), 1–4.

Ford, C. A. (1996). Factors that contribute to resilience in urban "at-risk" African American male college students. *Challenge: A Journal of Research on African American Men, 7*(3), 17–29.

Glaser, B., & Strauss, A. L. (1967). *The discovery of grounded theory: Strategies for qualitative research.* Chicago: Aldine.

Gloria, A. M., Kurpius, S. E. R., Hamilton, K. D., & Willson, M. S. (1999). African American students' persistence at a predominantly White university: Influences of social support, university comfort, and self-beliefs. *Journal of College Student Development, 40,* 257–268.

Horn, L. J., & Chen, X. (1998). *Toward resiliency: At-risk students who make it to college.* (Report No. PLLI-98-8056). Washington, DC: National Institute on Postsecondary Education, Libraries, and Lifelong Learning (ERIC Document Reproduction Service No. ED419463).

Inkelas, K. K. (2004). Does participation in ethnic cocurricular activities facilitate a sense of ethnic awareness and understanding? A study of Asian Pacific American undergraduates. *Journal of College Student Development, 45,* 285–302.

Johnson, S. C., & Arbona, C. (2006). The relation of ethnic identity, racial identity, and race-related stress among African American college students. *Journal of College Student Development, 47*(5), 495–507.

Karcher, M. J., & Fischer, K. W. (2004). A developmental sequence of skills in adolescents' intergroup understanding. *Applied Developmental Psychology, 25,* 259–282.

Keefe, S. (1992). Ethnic identity: The domain of perceptions of and attachment to ethnic groups and cultures. *Human Organizations, 51,* 35–43.

Kegan, R. (1994). *In over our heads: The mental demands of modern life.* Cambridge, MA: Harvard University Press.

King, P. M., & Baxter Magolda, M. B. (2005). A developmental model of intercultural maturity. *Journal of College Student Development, 46*(6), 571–592.

King, P. M., & Kitchener, K. S. (1994). *Developing reflective judgment.* San Francisco: Jossey Bass.

Lopez, E. J., Ehly, S., & Garcia-Vazquez, E. (2002). Acculturation, social support, and academic achievement of Mexican and Mexican American high school students: An exploratory study. *Psychology in the Schools, 39*(3) 245–257.

Miles, M. B., & Huberman, A. M. (1994). *Qualitative data analysis: An expanded sourcebook* (2nd Ed.). Thousand Oaks, CA: Sage.

Ogbu, J. (1997). Understanding the school performance of urban Blacks: Some essential background knowledge. In H. Walberg & R. Weissberg (Eds.), *Children and youth: Interdisciplinary perspectives* (pp. 190–222). Thousand Oaks, CA: Sage.

Oyserman, D., Gant, L., & Ager, J. (1995). A socially contextualized model of African American identity: Possible selves and school persistence. *Journal of Personality and Social Psychology, 69,* 1216–1232.

Oyserman, D., Harrison, K., & Bybee, D. (2001). Can racial identity be promotive of academic efficacy in adolescence? *International Journal of Behavioral Development, 25*(4), 379–385.

Oyserman, D., Terry, K., Bybee, D. (2002). A possible selves intervention to enhance school involvement. *Journal of Adolescence, 25,* 313–326.

Parham, T. (1989). Cycles of psychological Nigrescence. *The Counseling Psychologist, 17,* 187–226.

Perry, W. G. (1968). *Forms of intellectual and ethnical development in the college years: A scheme.* New York: Holt, Rinehart, & Winston.

Phinney, J. S. (1989). Stages of ethnic identity development in minority group adolescents. *Journal of Early Adolescence, 9,* 34–49.

Phinney, J. S. (1992). The Multigroup Ethnic Identity Measure: A new scale for use with diverse groups. *Journal of Adolescent Research, 7,* 156–176.

Phinney, J. S. (1993). A three-stage model of ethnic identity development in adolescence. In M. Bernal & G. Knight (Eds.). *Ethnic identity: Formation and transmission among Hispanics and other minorities* (pp. 61–79). New York: SUNY Press.

Phinney, J. S., & Alipuria, L. (1990). Ethnic identity in college students from four ethnic groups. *Journal of Adolescence, 13,* 171–184.

Pizzolato, J. E. (2005). Creating crossroads for self-authorship: Investigating the provocative moment. *Journal of College Student Development, 46,* 624–641.

Pizzolato, J. E. (2007). Assessing selfauthorship. In P.M. Meszaros (Ed.). Self-authorship: Advancing students intellectual growth. *New Directions of Teaching and Learning,* no 109, 31–42.

Rendon, L. I., Jalomo, R. E., & Nora, A. (2000). Theoretical considerations in the study of minority student retention in higher education. In J. M. Braxton (Ed.), *Reworking the student departure puzzle* (pp. 127–156). Nashville, TN: Vanderbilt University Press.

Renn, K. R. (2000). Patterns of situational identity among biracial and multiracial college students. *The Review of Higher Education, 23*(4), 399–420.

Rotheram, M. J., & Phinney, J. S. (1987). Introduction: Definitions and perspectives in the study of children's ethnic socialization. In J. S. Phinney & M. J. Rotheram (Eds.), *Children's ethnic socialization* (pp. 10–28). Newbury Park, CA: Sage.

Schommer, M. (1994). An emerging conceptualization of epistemological beliefs and their role in learning. In R. Garner & P. A. Alexander (Eds.), *Beliefs about text and instruction with text* (pp. 25–40). Hillsdale, NJ: Erlbaum.

Sedlacek, W. E. (2004). *Beyond the big test: Noncognitive assessment in higher education.* San Francisco: Jossey Bass.

St. Louis, G. R. St., & Liem, J. H. (2005). Ego identity, ethnic identity, and the psychosocial wellbeing of ethnic minority and majority college students. *Identity: An International Journal of Theory and Research, 5*(3), 227–246.

Strauss, A., & Corbin, J. (1994). Grounded theory methodology: An overview. In N. K. Denzin & Y. S. Lincoln, (Eds.), *Handbook of qualitative research* (pp. 273–285). Thousand Oaks, CA: Sage.

Terenzini, P. T., Cabrera, A. F., & Bernal, E. M. (2001). *Swimming against the tide: The poor in American higher education* (Report No. 2001–01). New York: The College Entrance Examination Board.

Torres, V., & Baxter Magolda, M. B. (2004). Reconstructing Latino identity: The influence of cognitive development on the ethnic identity process of Latino students. *Journal of College Student Development, 45,* 333–347.

Wawrzynski, M. R., & Pizzolato, J. E. (2006). Predicting needs: A longitudinal investigation of the relation between student characteristics, academic paths, and self-authorship. *Journal of College Student Research, 47*(6), 677–692.

Yeh, T. L. (2002). *Asian Americans college students who are educationally at risk* (New Directions for Student Services, No. 97, pp. 61–71). San Francisco: Jossey Bass.

CHAPTER 6

LEARNING STYLES

UNDERSTANDING STUDENT DIFFERENCES

RICHARD M. FELDER
DEPARTMENT OF CHEMICAL ENGINEERING
NORTH CAROLINA STATE UNIVERSITY

REBECCA BRENT
EDUCATION DESIGNS, INC.

Abstract Students have different levels of motivation, different attitudes about teaching and learning, and different responses to specific classroom environments and instructional practices. The more thoroughly instructors understand the differences, the better chance they have of meeting the diverse learning needs of all of their students. Three categories of diversity that have been shown to have important implications for teaching and learning are differences in students' learning styles (characteristic ways of taking in and processing information), approaches to learning (surface, deep, and strategic), and intellectual development levels (attitudes about the nature of knowledge and how it should be acquired and evaluated). This article reviews models that have been developed for each of these categories, outlines their pedagogical implications, and suggests areas for further study.

Keywords: learning styles, approaches to learning, intellectual development

Instruction begins when you, the teacher, learn from the learner. Put yourself in his place so that you may understand what he learns and the way he understands it. (Kierkegaard)

I. Three Facets of Student Diversity

Declining interest in engineering among high school students in recent years has led to steep enrollment decreases in many engineering programs. Although the problem has been exacerbated by high student dropout rates that have characterized engineering curricula for decades, many engineering faculty members continue to view the attrition positively, believing the dropouts are mainly weak students who are unqualified to become engineers. This belief is wrong. In their classic study *Talking about Leaving* [1], Seymour and Hewitt showed that grade distributions of students who leave technical curricula are essentially the same as the distributions of those who stay in. While many of those who drop out do so because of academic difficulties, many others are good students who leave because of dissatisfaction with their instruction, a fact made graphically clear in comments quoted by Seymour and Hewitt.

Faculty complaints about students who remain in engineering through graduation are also commonly heard, with many of the complaints being variations of "They can memorize and plug numbers into formulas but they don't know how to think!" And yet, most engineering departments

Reprinted from *Journal of Engineering Education* (2005), by permission of American Society of Engineering Education.

have one or more faculty members who manage to get many of those same students to perform at remarkably high levels, displaying first-rate problem-solving and critical and creative thinking skills. Skill deficiencies observed in engineering graduates must therefore also be attributable in part to what instructors are doing or failing to do.

An implication of these observations is that to reduce enrollment attrition and improve the thinking and problem-solving skills of engineering graduates, engineering schools should attempt to improve the quality of their teaching, which in turn requires understanding the learning needs of today's engineering students and designing instruction to meet those needs. The problem is that no two students are alike. They have different backgrounds, strengths and weaknesses, interests, ambitions, senses of responsibility, levels of motivation, and approaches to studying. Teaching methods also vary. Some instructors mainly lecture, while others spend more time on demonstrations or activities; some focus on principles and others on applications; some emphasize memory and others understanding. How much a given student learns in a class is governed in part by that student's native ability and prior preparation but also by the compatibility of the student's attributes as a learner and the instructor's teaching style.

This is not to say that instructors should determine their students' individual learning attributes and teach each student exclusively in the manner best suited to those attributes. It is not possible to discover everything that affects what a student learns in a class, and even if instructors could, they would not be able to figure out the optimum teaching style for that student—the task would be far too complex. Moreover, even if a teacher knew the optimum teaching styles for all students in a class, it would be impossible to implement them simultaneously in a class of more than two students.

If it is pointless to consider tailoring instruction to each individual student, it is equally misguided to imagine that a single one-size-fits-all approach to teaching can meet the needs of every student. Unfortunately, a single approach has dominated engineering education since its inception: the professor lectures and the students attempt to absorb the lecture content and reproduce it in examinations. That particular size fits almost nobody: it violates virtually every principle of effective instruction established by modern cognitive science and educational psychology [2–5]. Any other approach that targets only one type of student would probably be more effective, but it would still fail to address the needs of most students. It follows that if completely individualized instruction is impractical and one-size-fits-all is ineffective for most students, a more balanced approach that attempts to accommodate the diverse needs of the students in a class at least some of the time is the best an instructor can do.

Diversity in education usually refers to the effects of gender and ethnicity on student performance. Those effects are important and are considered elsewhere in this journal issue [6]. This article examines three other important aspects of student diversity:

- **Learning Styles.** Learning styles are "characteristic cognitive, affective, and psychological behaviors that serve as relatively stable indicators of how learners perceive, interact with, and respond to the learning environment" [7]. The concept of learning styles has been applied to a wide variety of student attributes and differences. Some students are comfortable with theories and abstractions; others feel much more at home with facts and observable phenomena; some prefer active learning and others lean toward introspection; some prefer visual presentation of information and others prefer verbal explanations. One learning style is neither preferable nor inferior to another, but is simply different, with different characteristic strengths and weaknesses. A goal of instruction should be to equip students with the skills associated with every learning style category, regardless of the students' personal preferences, since they will need all of those skills to function effectively as professionals.
- **Approaches to Learning and Orientations to Studying.** Students may be inclined to approach their courses in one of three ways [8]. Those with a *reproducing orientation* tend to take a *surface approach* to learning, relying on rote memorization and mechanical formula substitution and making little or no effort to understand the material being taught. Those with a *meaning orientation* tend to adopt a *deep approach,* probing and questioning and exploring the limits of applicability of new material. Those with an *achieving orientation* tend to use a *strate-*

gic approach, doing whatever is necessary to get the highest grade they can, taking a surface approach if that suffices and a deep approach when necessary. A goal of instruction should be to induce students to adopt a deep approach to subjects that are important for their professional or personal development.

- **Intellectual Development.** Most students undergo a developmental progression from a belief in the certainty of knowledge and the omniscience of authorities to an acknowledgment of the uncertainty and contextual nature of knowledge, acceptance of personal responsibility for determining truth, inclination and ability to gather supporting evidence for judgments, and openness to change if new evidence is forthcoming. At the highest developmental level normally seen in college students (but not in many of them), individuals display thinking patterns resembling those of expert scientists and engineers. A goal of instruction should be to advance students to that level by the time they graduate.

In this article, we outline models of student learning style preferences, orientations to studying, and levels of intellectual development; review the implications of the models for engineering education; and suggest promising avenues for future study. Before doing so, we briefly discuss the topic of assessment instrument validation, a research issue central to all three of these diversity domains.

II. A Note on Validation

Much of this paper describes assessments of various student attributes and inferences that have been drawn from the data. Before too much stock is placed in such inferences, the instrument used to collect the data should be shown to be *reliable* (consistent results are obtained in repeated assessments) and *valid* (the instrument measures what it is intended to measure).

In another paper in this issue, Olds, Moskal, and Miller [9] offer a good introduction to reliability and validity analysis. Some of the measures of reliability and validity they discuss that are applicable to instruments of the types we will describe are these:

- *Test-retest reliability:* the extent to which test results for an individual are stable over time.
- *Internal consistency reliability:* the homogeneity of items intended to measure the same quantity—that is, the extent to which responses to the items are correlated.
- *Scale orthogonality:* the extent to which the different scales of the instrument (if there are two or more scales) are independent.
- *Construct validity:* the extent to which an instrument actually measures the attribute it purports to measure. The instrument scores are said to have *convergent* validity if they correlate with quantities with which they should correlate and *divergent* or *discriminant* validity if they fail to correlate with quantities with which there is no reason to expect correlation.

Reliability and validity data of these types are readily obtainable for some of the instruments to be discussed, while for others (notably several of the learning style assessment instruments) they are difficult or impossible to find. At the end of each of sections III (Learning Styles), IV (Approaches to Learning), and V (Levels of Intellectual Development), we offer lists of potential research questions. To each list might be added the following two-part question: *If an assessment instrument is used to study any of the preceding questions, what reliability and validity data support its use (a) in general, and (b) for the population studied?*

III. Learning Styles

Students are characterized by different *learning* styles, preferentially focusing on different types of information and tending to operate on perceived information in different ways [10, 11]. To reduce attrition and improve skill development in engineering, instruction should be designed to meet the needs of students whose learning styles are neglected by traditional engineering pedagogy [12–14].

Several dozen learning style models have been developed, five of which have been the subject of studies in the engineering education literature. The best known of these models is Jung's Theory of Psychological Type as operationalized by the Myers-Briggs Type Indicator (MBTI). Strictly speaking, the MBTI assesses personality types, but MBTI profiles are known to have strong learning style implications [14–16]. This instrument was the basis for a multi-campus study of engineering students in the 1970s and 1980s and a number of other engineering-related studies since then [17–24]. Other models that have been applied extensively to engineering are those of Kolb [12, 14, 25–31], and Felder and Silverman [13, 14, 32–40]. We discuss these three models in the sections that follow. Two other models that have been used in engineering are those of Herrmann [14, 41–43], and Dunn and Dunn [44–46]. Relatively little assessment has been performed on the applicability of these models to instructional design in engineering, and we do not discuss the models further in this paper. For information about them, see the cited references.

Before we look at specific models, we should note that the concept of learning styles is not universally accepted. The simple mention of the term arouses strong emotional reactions in many members of the academic community (notably but not exclusively the psychologists), who argue that learning style models have no sound theoretical basis and that the instruments used to assess learning styles have not been appropriately validated. On the other hand, the studies summarized in the sections that follow paint a clear and consistent picture of learning style differences and their effects on student performance and attitudes. Additionally, instruction designed to address a broad spectrum of learning styles has consistently proved to be more effective than traditional instruction, which focuses on a narrow range of styles. We therefore propose taking an engineering approach to learning styles, regarding them as useful heuristics for understanding students and designing effective instruction, and continuing to use them until demonstrably better heuristics appear.

A. The Myers-Briggs Type Indicator

People are classified on the Myers-Briggs Type Indicator® (MBTI) according to their preferences on four scales derived from Jung's Theory of Psychological Types [15]:

- *extraverts* (try things out, focus on the outer world of people) or *introverts* (think things through, focus on the inner world of ideas).
- *sensors* (practical, detail-oriented, focus on facts and procedures) or *intuitors* (imaginative, concept-oriented, focus on meanings and possibilities).
- *thinkers* (skeptical, tend to make decisions based on logic and rules) or *feelers* (appreciative, tend to make decisions based on personal and humanistic considerations).
- *judgers* (set and follow agendas, seek closure even with incomplete data) or *perceivers* (adapt to changing circumstances, postpone reaching closure to obtain more data).

Lawrence [15] characterizes the preferences, strengths, and weaknesses of each of the 16 MBTI types in many areas of student functioning and offers numerous suggestions for addressing the learning needs of students of all types, and Pittenger [16] reviews research based on the MBTI.

Most engineering instruction is oriented toward introverts (lecturing and individual assignments rather than active class involvement and cooperative learning), intuitors (emphasis on science and math fundamentals rather than engineering applications and operations), thinkers (emphasis on objective analysis rather than interpersonal considerations in decision-making), and judgers (emphasis on following the syllabus and meeting assignment deadlines rather than on exploration of ideas and creative problem solving). In 1980, a consortium of eight universities and the Center for Applications of Psychological Type was formed to study the role of personality type in engineering education. Predictably, introverts, intuitors, thinkers, and judgers generally outperformed extraverts, sensors, feelers, and perceivers in the population studied [19, 21]. In work done as part of this study, Godleski [20] reported on grades in four sections of the introductory chemical engineering course at Cleveland State University taught by three different instructors. The emphasis in this course is on setting up and solving a wide variety of problems of increasing complexity, with memory and rote substitution in formulas playing a relatively small role. Intuitors would be expected to be at an advantage in this course, and the average grade for the intuitors in all sections was indeed higher than that for sensors. Godleski obtained similar results for other courses that emphasized intuitive skills, while in the few "solid sensing" courses in the curriculum (such as engineering economics, which tends to be formula-driven) the sensors scored higher.

In a longitudinal study carried out at the University of Western Ontario by Rosati [22, 23], male introverts, intuitors, thinkers, and judgers at the low end of the academic spectrum were found to be more likely to succeed in the first year of the engineering curriculum than were their extraverted, sensing, feeling, and perceiving counterparts. Rosati also observed that the introverts, thinkers, and judgers in the low-performance male population were more likely than the extraverts, feelers, and perceivers to graduate in engineering after four years, although the sensors were more likely than the intuitors to do so. No statistically significant type differences were found for academically strong male students or for female students.

As part of another longitudinal study, Felder [24] administered the MBTI to a group of 116 students taking the introductory chemical engineering course at North Carolina State University. That course and four subsequent chemical engineering courses were taught in a manner that emphasized active and cooperative learning, and type differences in various academic performance measures and attitudes were noted as the students progressed through the curriculum. The results were remarkably consistent with expectations based on type theory:

- Intuitors performed significantly better than sensors in courses with a high level of abstract content, and the converse was observed in courses of a more practical nature. Thinkers consistently outperformed feelers in the relatively impersonal environment of the engineering curriculum, and feelers were more likely to drop out of the curriculum even if they were doing well academically. Faced with the heavy time demands of the curriculum and the corresponding need to manage their time carefully, judgers consistently outperformed perceivers.
- Extraverts reacted more positively than introverts when first confronted with the requirement that they work in groups on homework. (By the end of the study, both groups almost unanimously favored group work.)
- The balanced instruction provided in the experimental course sequence appeared to reduce or eliminate the performance differences previously noted between sensors and intuitors and between extraverts and introverts.
- Intuitors were three times more likely than sensors to give themselves top ratings for creative problem-solving ability and to place a high value on doing creative work in their careers.
- The majority of sensors intended to work as engineers in large corporations, while a much higher percentage of intuitors planned to work for small companies or to go to graduate school and work in research. Feelers placed a higher value on doing socially important or beneficial work in their careers than thinkers did.

Very few results failed to confirm expectations from type theory, and most of the failures involved type differences that might have been expected to be significant but were not. The conclusion was that the MBTI effectively characterizes differences in the ways engineering students approach learning tasks, respond to different forms of instruction and classroom environments, and formulate career goals.

B. Kolb's Experiential Learning Model

In Kolb's model, students are classified as having a preference for (a) *concrete experience or abstract conceptualization* (how they take information in) and (b) *active experimentation or reflective observation* (how they process information) [12, 25]. The four types of learners in this classification scheme are:

- *Type 1* (concrete, reflective)—*the diverger.* Type 1 learners respond well to explanations of how course material relates to their experience, interests, and future careers. Their characteristic question is "*Why?*" To be effective with Type 1 students, the instructor should function as a *motivator.*

- *Type 2* (abstract, reflective)—the *assimilator.* Type 2 learners respond to information presented in an organized, logical fashion and benefit if they are given time for reflection. Their characteristic question is "*What?*" To be effective, the instructor should function as an *expert.*
- *Type 3* (abstract, active)—the *converger.* Type 3 learners respond to having opportunities to work actively on well-defined tasks and to learn by trial-and-error in an environment that allows them to fail safely. Their characteristic question is "*How?*" To be effective, the instructor should function as a *coach,* providing guided practice and feedback in the methods being taught.
- *Type 4* (concrete, active)—the *accommodator.* Type 4 learners like applying course material in new situations to solve real problems. Their characteristic question is "*What if?*" To be effective, the instructor should pose open-ended questions and then get out of the way, maximizing opportunities for the students to discover things for themselves. Problem-based learning is an ideal pedagogical strategy for these students.

Preferences on this scale are assessed with the ***Learning*** Style Inventory® (McBer and Company, Boston) or the ***Learning Type Measure*** ® (About Learning Inc., Wauconda, Ill.). Most studies of engineering students based on the Kolb model find that the majority of the subjects are Types 2 and 3. For example, Sharp [26] reports that of 1,013 engineering students she tested, 40 percent were Type 3, 39 percent Type 2, 13 percent Type 4, and 8 percent Type 1. Bernold et al. [27] found that of the 350 students in their study, 55 percent were Type 3, 22 percent Type 2, 13 percent Type 4, and 10 percent Type 1.

Traditional science and engineering instruction focuses almost exclusively on lecturing, a style comfortable for only Type 2 learners. Effective instruction involves *teaching around the cycle*—motivating each new topic (Type 1), presenting the basic information and methods associated with the topic (Type 2), providing opportunities for practice in the methods (Type 3), and encouraging exploration of applications (Type 4).

A faculty training program based on the Kolb learning style model was initiated at Brigham Young University in 1989 [28]. About a third of the engineering faculty was trained in teaching around the cycle. The volunteers implemented the approach in their courses, reviewed videotapes of their teaching, and discussed their successes and problems in focus groups. Many courses were redesigned; instructors—including a number who did not participate in the original training—used a variety of teaching methods in addition to formal lecturing; discussions about teaching became a regular part of department faculty meetings; and several faculty members presented and published education-related papers. Articles describing the program do not indicate the extent to which the modified instruction led to improved learning.

Bernold et al. [27] describe an experiment at North Carolina State University in which one group of students was subjected to teaching around the cycle (in their term, "holistic instruction"), another was taught traditionally, and the course grades earned by the two groups were compared. Although the results were not conclusive, they appeared to indicate that Types 1 and 4 students were more likely to get low grades than the more numerous Types 2 and 3 students when teaching was traditional, and that holistic instruction may have helped a more diverse group of students to succeed. Spurlin et al. [29] report on an ongoing study comparing freshman engineering students of the four Kolb types. Their preliminary results also show Types 2 and 3 students doing better academically, and they are conducting further studies intended to pinpoint reasons for the relatively poor performance and high risk of attrition of the Types 1 and 4 students.

Julie Sharp of Vanderbilt University has used the Kolb model in several ways as the basis for instructional design. Her work includes the development of a variety of "writing to learn" assignments that should be effective for each of the four Kolb types [30] and applications of the model to instruction in communications and teamwork [26, 31].

C. The Felder-Silverman Model

1) Model Categories. According to a model developed by Felder and Silverman [13, 32], a student's learning style may be defined by the answers to four questions:

1. What type of information does the student preferentially perceive: *sensory* (sights, sounds, physical sensations) or *intuitive* (memories, thoughts, insights)? Sensing learners tend to be concrete, practical, methodical, and oriented toward facts and hands-on procedures. Intuitive learners are more comfortable with abstractions (theories, mathematical models) and are more likely to be rapid and innovative problem solvers [47]. This scale is identical to the sensing-intuitive scale of the Myers-Briggs Type Indicator.
2. What type of sensory information is most effectively perceived: *visual* (pictures, diagrams, flow charts, demonstrations) or *verbal* (written and spoken explanations)?
3. How does the student prefer to process information: *actively* (through engagement in physical activity or discussion) or *reflectively* (through introspection)? This scale is identical to the active-reflective scale of the Kolb model and is related to the extravert-introvert scale of the MBTI.
4. How does the student characteristically progress toward understanding: *sequentially* (in a logical progression of incremental steps) or *globally* (in large "big picture" jumps)? Sequential learners tend to think in a linear manner and are able to function with only partial understanding of material they have been taught. Global learners think in a systems-oriented manner, and may have trouble applying new material until they fully understand it and see how it relates to material they already know about and understand. Once they grasp the big picture, however, their holistic perspective enables them to see innovative solutions to problems that sequential learners might take much longer to reach, if they get there at all [48].

More detailed descriptions of the attributes of the different model categories and the nature and consequences of learning and teaching style mismatches are given by Felder and Silverman [13] and Felder [32]. Zywno and Waalen [36] report on the development and successful implementation of hypermedia instruction designed to address the learning needs of styles less favored by traditional instruction, and Sharp [40] describes an instructional module based on the Felder-Silverman model that makes students aware of differences in learning styles and how they may affect personal interactions, teamwork, interactions with professors, and learning difficulties and successes.

2) The Index of Learning Styles. The Index of Learning Styles® (ILS) is a forty-four-item forced-choice instrument developed in 1991 by Richard Felder and Barbara Soloman to assess preferences on the four scales of the Felder-Silverman model. In 1994 several hundred sets of responses to the initial twenty-eight-item version of the instrument were collected and subjected to factor analysis. Items that did not load significantly on single factors were discarded and replaced by new items to create the current version, which was put on the World Wide Web in 1997 [49]. The ILS is available at no cost to individuals who wish to assess their own preferences and to instructors or students who wish to use it for classroom instruction or research, and it may be licensed by non-educational organizations.

Learning style preferences of numerous students and faculty members have been determined using the Index of Learning Styles, with results summarized in Table 6.1 [50]. Unless otherwise indicated, the population samples shown in Table 6.1 are undergraduates. Thus, for example, of the 129 undergraduate engineering students who completed the ILS in a study conducted at Iowa State University, 63 percent were classified as active (A) learners (and by implication 37 percent were classified as reflective learners), 67 percent were sensing (S) learners (33 percent intuitive learners), 85 percent were visual (Vs) learners (15 percent verbal), and 58 percent were sequential (Sq) learners (42 percent global).

Table 6.1 illustrates several of the mismatches described by Felder and Silverman [13] between learning styles of most engineering undergraduates and traditional teaching styles in engineering education. Sixty-three percent of the undergraduates were sensors, while traditional engineering instruction tends to be heavily oriented toward intuitors, emphasizing theory and mathematical modeling over experimentation and practical applications in most courses; 82 percent of the undergraduates were visual learners, while most engineering instruction is overwhelmingly verbal, emphasizing written explanations and mathematical formulations of physical phenomena over

TABLE 6.1

Reported learning style preferences

POPULATION[a]	A	S	Vs	Sq	N	Reference
Iowa State, Materials Engr.	**63%**	**67%**	**85%**	**58%**	**129**	**Constant [51]**
Michigan Tech, Env. Engr.	**56%**	**63%**	**74%**	**53%**	**83**	**Paterson [52]**
Oxford Brookes Univ., Business	64%	70%	68%	64%	63	**De Vita [53]**
British students	**85%**	**86%**	**52%**	**76%**	**21**	
International students	52%	62%	76%	52%	42	
Ryerson Univ., Elec. Engr.						
Students (2000)	**53%**	**66%**	**86%**	**72%**	**87**	**Zywno & Waalen [36]**
Students (2001)	**60%**	**66%**	**89%**	**59%**	**119**	**Zywno [38]**
Students (2002)	**63%**	**63%**	**89%**	**58%**	**132**	**Zywno [54]**
Faculty	**38%**	**42%**	**94%**	**35%**	**48**	"
Tulane, Engr.						
Second-Year Students	**62%**	**60%**	**88%**	**48%**	**245**	**Livesay *et al.* [37]**
First-Year Students	**56%**	**46%**	**83%**	**56%**	**192**	***Dee et al.* [39]**
Universities in Belo Horizonte (Brazil)[b]						Lopes [55]
Sciences	65%	81%	79%	67%	214	
Humanities	52%	62%	39%	62%	235	
Univ. of Limerick, Mfg. Engr.	**70%**	**78%**	**91%**	**58%**	**167**	**Seery *et al.* [56]**
Univ. of Michigan, Chem. Engr.	**67%**	**57%**	**69%**	**71%**	**143**	**Montgomery [57]**
Univ. of Puerto Rico-Mayaguez						
Biology (Semester 1)	65%	77%	74%	83%	39	Buxeda & Moore [58]
Biology (Semester 2)	51%	69%	66%	85%	37	"
Biology (Semester 3)	56%	78%	77%	74%	32	"
Elect. & Comp. Engr.	47%	61%	82%	67%	?	Buxeda *et al.* [59]
Univ. of São Paulo, Engr.[b]	60%	74%	79%	50%	351	Kuri & Truzzi[60]
Civil Engr.	69%	86%	76%	54%	110	
Elec. Engr.	57%	68%	80%	51%	91	
Mech. Engr.	53%	67%	84%	45%	94	
Indust. Engr.	66%	70%	73%	50%	56	
Univ. of Technology Kingston, Jamaica	**55%**	**60%**	**70%**	**55%**	**?**	**Smith *et al.* [61]**
Univ. of Western Ontario, Engr.[c]	69%	59%	80%	67%	858	Rosati [35]
First year engr	66%	59%	78%	69%	499	Rosati [34]
Fourth year engr.	72%	58%	81%	63%	359	"
Engr. faculty	51%	40%	94%	53%	53	"
Engineering Student Average	**64%**	**63%**	**82%**	**60%**	**2506**	
Engineering Faculty Average	**45%**	**41%**	**94%**	**44%**	**101**	

[a] Rows in boldface denote studies using the current version of the Index of Learning Styles with native English speakers.
[b] Portuguese translation of the ILS used.
[c] Data collected with Version 1 of the ILS (All other studies used Version 2.)

demonstrations and visual illustrations; and 64 percent of the students were active, while most engineering courses other than laboratories rely almost exclusively on lectures and readings as the principal vehicles for transmitting information.

Table 6.1 also shows that 60 percent of the students assessed were sequential and traditional engineering education is heavily sequential, so this dimension does not involve the same type of mismatch observed for the others. Global students constitute a strong and important minority, however. They are the multidisciplinary thinkers, whose broad vision may enable them to become, for example, skilled researchers or chief executive officers of corporations. Unfortunately, traditional engineering education does little to provide students with the systemic perspective on individual subjects they need to function effectively, and the ones who take too long to get it by themselves are at risk academically.

Section II briefly discussed the issue of instrument validation. The Index of Learning Styles is one of the few instruments mentioned in this paper for which reliability and validity data have been collected for engineering student populations [37,50,54]. We will not provide details of the reliability analyses here; suffice it to say that all three of the studies just cited conclude that the ILS meets or exceeds accepted reliability standards for an instrument of its type. Felder and Spurlin [50] summarize results from several studies that provide evidence of both convergent and divergent construct validity. Profiles of engineering students at different institutions show a high degree of consistency with one another and differ substantially and in a predictable manner from profiles for engineering faculty and humanities students (see Table 6.1). Another indication of convergent validity is that preferences for sensing and active learning measured on the ILS were found to correlate with preferences for sensing and extraversion measured on the Myers-Briggs Type Indicator [33].

As noted previously, the conventional lecture-based teaching approach in engineering education favors intuitive, verbal, reflective, and sequential learners. In yet another demonstration of the construct validity of the ILS, Zywno and Waalen [36] found that on average the performance in conventionally taught courses of each of the favored types was superior to that of the less favored types, and they also found that the use of supplemental hypermedia instruction designed to address the needs of all types decreased the performance disparities. Felder and Spurlin [50], Livesay et al. [37], and Zywno [54] conclude that the ILS may be considered reliable and valid for assessing learning styles, although all three papers recommend continuing research on the instrument.

D. Pedagogical Implications and Potential Misuses of Learning Styles

Studies have shown that greater learning may occur when teaching styles match learning styles than when they are mismatched [11, 13, 62, 63], but the point of identifying learning styles is not to label individual students and tailor instruction to fit their preferences. To function effectively as engineers or members of any other profession, students will need skills characteristic of each type of learner: the powers of observation and attention to detail of the sensor and the imagination and abstract thinking ability of the intuitor; the abilities to comprehend information presented both visually and verbally, the systematic analysis skills of the sequential learner and the multidisciplinary synthesis skills of the global learner, and so on. If instruction is heavily biased toward one category of a learning style dimension, mismatched students may be too uncomfortable to learn effectively, while the students whose learning styles match the teaching style will not be helped to develop critical skills in their less preferred learning style categories [13, 14]. The optimal teaching style is a balanced one that sometimes matches students' preferences, so their discomfort level is not too great for them to learn effectively, and sometimes goes against their preferences, forcing them to stretch and grow in directions they might be inclined to avoid if given the option.

The preceding paragraph suggests what we believe to be the most important application of learning styles, which is to help instructors design a balanced teaching approach that addresses the learning needs of all of their students. Designing such an approach does not require assessing the students' learning style preferences: it is enough for instructors to select a model and attempt to address all of its categories (in Kolb model terms, to teach around the cycle), knowing that every class probably contains students with every preference [14]. Assessing the learning style profile of a class with an instrument such as the Myers-Briggs Type Indicator, the Kolb Learning Style Inventory, or the Index of Learning Styles—without being overly concerned about which students have which preferences—can provide additional support for effective instructional design. For example, knowing that a large majority of students in a class are sensing and visual learners can—and should—motivate the instructor to find concrete and visual ways to supplement the presentation of material that might normally be presented entirely abstractly and verbally. Many specific suggestions for designing instruction to address the full spectrum of learning styles are given by Felder and Silverman [13] and Lawrence [15].

What about identifying individual students' learning styles and sharing the results with them? Doing so can provide them with valuable clues about their possible strengths and weaknesses and indications of ways they might improve their academic performance. Precautions should be taken if students are told their learning styles, however. The instructor should emphasize that no learning style instrument is infallible, and if the students' perceptions of how they learn best differ from what the instrument says, they should not discount their own judgment. They should also be assured that their learning style preferences are not reliable indicators of what they are and are not capable of doing, and that people with every possible learning style can succeed in any profession or endeavor. If a student is assessed as, say, a sensing learner, it says nothing about his or her intuitive skills (or sensing skills, for that matter); it does not mean that he or she is unsuited to be an engineer or scientist or mathematician; and it does not excuse the low grade he or she made on the last exam. Instructors or advisers who use learning styles as a basis for recommending curriculum or career choices are misusing the concept and could be doing serious disservices to their students and advisees.

E. Questions for Further Study

As previously noted, learning styles are controversial, with questions commonly being raised regarding their meaning and even their existence. Much work needs to be done to resolve these questions and also to determine the validity of different learning style models for engineering students and to confirm or refute claims regarding the effectiveness of a balanced teaching approach. The following questions merit investigation:

1. Does an assessed learning style preference indicate (a) the type of instruction a student is most comfortable with or (b) the type of instruction most likely to lead to more effective learning? To what extent are the two coincident?
2. Do any learning style preferences depend on students' ethnic and cultural backgrounds? Which preferences, and what are the nature and extent of the dependences?
3. To what extent does teaching exclusively to a student's learning style preference lead to (a) greater student satisfaction, (b) improvement in skills associated with that preference, (c) lack of improvement in skills associated with the opposite preference?
4. Does a curriculum heavily biased toward a particular learning style increase the incidence of dropouts of students with conflicting styles? To what extent does more balanced instruction reduce attrition and improve academic performance of those students?
5. Is the provision of choice over learning tasks an effective strategy for accommodating different learning style preferences? How much choice should be provided and what kind?
6. How effective is instructional technology that provides alternative pathways through a body of material, with the pathways being designed to appeal to different learning style preferences?
7. How should learning style preferences be incorporated in advising? How effective are interventions that take learning style into account?
8. Does mixing learning styles when forming project teams lead to better team products? Does it lead to increased interpersonal conflict? If the answer to each question is "yes," do the improved products compensate for the greater conflict risk? Does making team members aware of their learning style differences lower the potential for conflict?

9. How helpful to students is discussion of learning styles in class?
10. To what extent are preferences on comparable scales of different instruments correlated?
11. To what extent do the answers to any of the preceding questions depend on the strength of students' learning style preferences?

IV. Approaches to Learning and Orientations to Studying

A. Definitions and Assessment

Marton and Säljö [64] define three different approaches to learning—a *surface approach, a deep approach,* and a *strategic approach.*

Students who adopt a surface approach to learning memorize facts but do not try to fit them into a larger context, and they follow routine solution procedures without trying to understand their origins and limitations. These students commonly exhibit an extrinsic motivation to learn (*I've got to learn this to pass the course, to graduate, to get a good job*) and an unquestioning acceptance of everything in the textbook and in lectures. To them, studying means scouring their texts for worked-out examples that look like the homework problems so they can simply copy the solutions. They either ignore the text outside of the examples or they scan through it with a highlighter, looking for factual information that the instructor might consider important, which they will attempt to memorize before the exam.

Students who take a deep approach do not simply rely on memorization of course material but focus instead on understanding it. They have an intrinsic motivation to learn, with intellectual curiosity rather than the possibility of external reward driving their efforts. They cast a critical eye on each statement or formula or analytical procedure they encounter in class or in the text and do whatever they think might help them understand it, such as restating text passages in their own words and trying to relate the new material to things they have previously learned or to everyday experience. Once the information makes sense, they try to fit it into a coherent body of knowledge.

Students who adopt a strategic approach do whatever it takes to get the top grade. They are well organized and efficient in their studying. They carefully assess the level of effort they need to exert to achieve their ambition, and if they can do it by staying superficial they will do so, but if the instructor's assignments and tests demand a deep approach they will respond to the demand.

A student may adopt different approaches to learning in different courses and even for different topics within a single course. An *orientation to studying* is a tendency to adopt one of the approaches in a broad range of situations and learning environments [5, 8]. Students who habitually adopt a surface approach have a *reproducing orientation;* those who usually adopt a deep approach have a *meaning orientation;* and those inclined to take a strategic approach have an *achieving orientation.* The Lancaster Approaches to Studying Questionnaire (LASQ) [65] is a sixty-four-item questionnaire that involves twelve subscales relevant to the three orientations and four additional subscales. Shorter forms of the LASQ that provide less detailed information are referenced by Woods et al. [66], and an alternative to the LASQ is the Study Process Questionnaire developed by Biggs [67].

Woods et al. [66] report on a study in which one of the short forms of the LASQ was administered to 1,387 engineering students. The strongest inclination of the students was toward a strategic approach, followed in order by a surface approach and a deep approach. Bertrand and Knapper [68] report LASQ results for students in other disciplines. Chemistry and psychology students went from a preference for strategic learning in their second year to a preference for deep learning in their fourth year, with both groups displaying consistently low inclinations toward a surface approach.

Bertrand and Knapper [68] also report on three groups of students in two multidisciplinary curricula—students in the second and fourth years of a project-based environmental resource studies program and students in a problem-based program on the impact of new materials. All three groups showed relatively strong inclinations toward a deep approach. There was little difference in the profiles of the second- and fourth-year students, suggesting that the results might reflect the orientations of the students selecting into the programs more than the influence of the programs.

There are similarities between orientations to studying and learning styles. Both represent tendencies that are situationally dependent, as opposed to fixed traits like gender or handedness that always characterize an individual. Just as a student who is a strong intuitor may function like a sensor in certain situations and vice versa, a student with a pronounced meaning orientation may under some circumstances adopt a surface approach to learning, and a strongly reproducing student may sometimes be motivated to dig deep. Similarly, just as students may be reasonably balanced in a learning style preference, frequently functioning in ways characteristic of, say, both sensors and intuitors, some students may be almost equally likely to adopt deep and surface approaches in different courses and possibly within a given course. We will shortly say more about instructional conditions that influence the choice.

B. Effects of a Deep Approach on Learning Outcomes

Researchers have assessed student approaches to learning and correlated the results with various learning outcomes [3, 5, 69]. In studies cited by Ramsden [5], students who took a deep approach to reading created comprehensive and integrated summaries of material they had read, interpreting the information rather than simply repeating it, while those who took a surface approach were more likely to recite fragments of the reading content almost randomly. The deep approach also led to longer retention of information—presumably because the information was learned in context rather than by rote memorization—and to consistently higher grades on examinations and in courses.

For example, Prosser and Millar [70] examined first-year physics students' understanding of force concepts before and after their introductory mechanics course. Eight out of nine students who took a deep approach and only two of twenty-three who used a surface approach showed significant progress in understanding force concepts, moving away from Aristotle and toward Newton. Meyer et al. [71] found that engineering students who adopted a deep approach in a course were very likely to pass the course (in fact, none of their subjects in this category failed), while students who adopted a surface approach were very likely to fail. The students who adopted a deep approach also generally expressed greater satisfaction with their instruction.

C. Motivating a Deep Approach to Learning

The approach a student might adopt in a particular situation depends on a complex array of factors. Some are intrinsic to the student (e.g., possession of prerequisite knowledge and skills and motivation to learn the subject), while others are determined more by the instructional environment (e.g., the content and clarity of the instructor's expectations and the nature and quality of the instruction and assessment).

Biggs [3] proposes that achieving desired learning outcomes requires *constructive alignment* of the elements just listed. *Alignment* means that the factors under the instructor's control are all consistent with the goal: the desired outcomes are clearly communicated to the students as expectations, instructional methods known to favor the outcomes are employed and methods that work against them are avoided, and learning assessments (homework, projects, tests, etc.) are explicitly directed toward the outcomes. *Constructive* means that the instructional design adheres to the principle of constructivism, which holds that knowledge is constructed by the learner, as opposed to being simply transmitted by a teacher and absorbed. The teacher's job is to create conditions that lead students to construct accurate representations of the concepts being studied, first abandoning prior misconceptions if any exist.

Certain features of classroom instruction have been found to be constructively aligned with the adoption of a deep approach to learning, while other features have the opposite effect [3, 5, 69]:

1. Interest in and background knowledge of the subject encourage a deep approach; lack of interest and inadequate background discourage it.
2. Clearly stated expectations and clear feedback on progress encourage a deep approach; poor or absent feedback discourages it.

3. Assessment methods that emphasize conceptual understanding encourage a deep approach; methods that emphasize recall or the application of routine procedural knowledge discourage it.
4. Teaching methods that foster active and long-term engagement with learning tasks encourage a deep approach.
5. Opportunities to exercise responsible choice in the content and method of study encourage a deep approach.
6. Stimulating and caring teaching encourages a deep approach; apathetic or inconsiderate teaching discourages it. A corollary is that students who perceive that teaching is good are more likely to adopt a deep approach than students with the opposite perception.
7. An excessive amount of material in the curriculum and an unreasonable workload discourage a deep approach.
8. Previous experiences with educational settings that encouraged deep approaches further encourage deep approaches. A similar statement can be made regarding surface approaches.

Well-established instructional strategies can be used to achieve these conditions. Inductive teaching methods such as *problem-based* and *project-based learning* [72–77] can motivate students by helping to make the subject matter relevant to their prior ex-perience and interests (addressing item #1 above) and they al-so emphasize conceptual understanding and de-emphasize rote memorization (item #3). An excellent way to make expectations clear (item #2) is to articulate them in the form of instructional *objectives* [78–80]—statements of observable actions students should be able to do (define, explain, calculate, derive, model, design) once they have completed a section of a course.

Several student-centered teaching approaches accomplish the goal of actively involving students in learning tasks (item #4), notably *active learning* (engaging students in class activities other than listening to lectures) and *cooperative learning* (getting students to work in small teams on projects or homework under conditions that hold all team members accountable for the learning objectives associated with the assignment) [81–84]. Trigwell et al. [85, 86] found a positive correlation between an instructor's use of such instructional methods and students' adoption of a deep approach to learning. Other references provide numerous examples of teaching in a stimulating caring manner (item #6), providing clear feedback by, among other ways, designing appropriate tests (item #2), and providing choice in learning tasks (item #5) [4, 87–91]. Several of the references cited in this paragraph and the preceding one also summarize research connecting the instructional methods mentioned with a variety of positive learning outcomes [72, 82, 84].

D. Questions for Further Study

Of the three diversity domains discussed in this paper, approaches to learning may be the one with the most solid research base [3, 5, 69, 92]. However, little has been done thus far to apply and extend the research to engineering. Following are some of the questions that might profitably be studied:

1. What percentages of students in traditional engineering curricula are characterized by reproducing, meaning, and achieving orientations to studying?
2. Do approaches to learning and orientations to studying depend on students' ethnic and cultural backgrounds? What are the nature and extent of the dependences?
3. Does the adoption of a deep approach to learning in an engineering course lead to improved learning as it has been shown to do in other disciplines? If so, for which learning outcomes can improvements be demonstrated?
4. Do the instructional conditions and methods (e.g., active learning, cooperative learning, and problem-based learning) that purportedly motivate the adoption of a deep approach do so in engineering? How and to what extent can students with a reproducing orientation be motivated to adopt a deep approach?

5. Would one need to reduce the content or extend the length of the engineering curriculum to reduce the heavy time demands on students that have been shown to discourage the adoption of a deep approach?
6. How do students with meaning, reproducing, and achieving orientations to learning compare in high-level thinking skills, such as critical thinking and creative thinking?
7. Might discussing approaches to learning with students promote their adoption of a deep approach?

V. Levels of Intellectual Development

Many students enter college in what Kroll [93] refers to as a state of "ignorant certainty," believing that knowledge is certain, beliefs are either right or wrong, the authorities (e.g., their professors and the authors of their textbooks) have the answers, and their job is to memorize those answers and repeat them on tests. As they gain experience, most gradually progress toward a state of (again in Kroll's terminology) "intelligent confusion," in which they recognize that all knowledge is contextual, take responsibility for making their own judgments on the basis of evidence rather than relying on the word of authorities, and become relatively sophisticated at gathering and interpreting evidence from a wide range of sources. In other words, those who attain that state (which relatively few do by the time they graduate) come to think like expert scientists and engineers. This progression has been referred to as *intellectual* (or *cognitive* or *epistemological*) development.

Different levels of intellectual development constitute the third category of student diversity to be discussed here. In this section we review several models of intellectual development, discuss their applicability to engineering education, survey existing applications, and suggest areas for further exploration. Much of the material presented is drawn from a pair of articles recently published in this journal [94, 95].

A. Models of Intellectual Development

Four models of intellectual development are described in the literature. The first, Perry's Model of Intellectual Development [96,97], is the only one that has had widespread application in engineering education [98–106]. The low and intermediate levels of Perry's model are almost identical to the low and intermediate levels of the King-Kitchener Model of Reflective Judgment [97, 107, 108], which may be the most widely used and validated of the four models outside engineering education. (The two models diverge at their highest levels, which are rarely attained by college students.) In *Women's Ways of Knowing,* Belenky et al. [109] suggest that Perry's model largely characterizes men (its formulation was based almost entirely on interviews with male students) and propose an alternative progression of stages intended to characterize women's development. Baxter Magolda's Model of Epistemological Development [97, 110] integrates the preceding models by defining alternative patterns for all levels but the highest one, with one pattern characterizing more men than women and the other more women than men. Table 6.2 shows the levels and patterns of the Baxter Magolda model and the correspondences between that model and the other three. The paragraphs that follow discuss primarily the models of Baxter Magolda and Perry.

The developmental pattern described by all four models has the following general form. Students at the lowest levels (Baxter Magolda's *absolute knowing* and Perry's *dualism*) believe that every intellectual and moral question has one correct answer and their professors (at least the competent ones) know what it is. As the students confront challenges to their belief systems in their courses and through interactions with peers, they gradually come to believe in the validity of multiple viewpoints and concurrently decrease their reliance on the word of authorities (Baxter Magolda's *transitional* and *independent knowing* and Perry's *multiplicity*). Baxter Magolda's highest level, *contextual knowing,* which parallels Perry's *contextual relativism* (Level 5) and the early stages of *commitment in the face of uncertainty* (Level 6 and perhaps Level 7), is characterized by final rejection of the notions of the certainty of knowledge and the omniscience of authorities. Contextual knowers take responsibility for constructing knowledge for themselves, relying on both objective analysis and intuition

TABLE 6.2

Models of intellectual development [94]

Baxter Magolda	Absolute Knowing[a]		Transitional Knowing[b]		Independent Knowing[c]		Contextual Knowing[d]
	Mastery Pattern	Receiving Pattern	Impersonal Pattern	Interpersonal Pattern	Individual Pattern	Interindividual Pattern	
Perry	2 Late Dualism		3 Multiplicity Subordinate		4 Multiplicity		5-7 Contextual Relativism Preliminary Commitment
Belenky (Women's Ways of Knowing)		Received Knowledge		Subjective Knowledge	Procedural Knowledge: Separate Pattern	Procedural Knowledge: Connected Pattern	Constructed Knowledge
King-Kitchener	Early Prereflective Thinking		Late Prereflective Thinking		Quasi-Reflective Thinking		Reflective Thinking

[a]**Absolute knowing.** All knowledge that matters is certain; all positions are either right or wrong. Authorities have The Truth and the responsibility to communicate it, and the students' job is to memorize and repeat it.*Mastery pattern* (more men than women): Students raise questions to make sure their information is correct and challenge deviations from their view of the truth. *Receiving pattern* (more women than men); Students take in and record information passively, without questioning or challenging it.
[b]**Transitional knowing.** Some knowledge is certain and some is not. Authorities have the responsibility to communicate the certainties, and the students are responsible for making their own judgments regarding the uncertainties. *Impersonal pattern* (more men than women): Make judgments using a logical procedure prescribed by authorities. Full credit is deserved for following the right procedure, regardless of the clarity of the reasoning and the quality of the supporting evidence. *Interpersonal pattern* (more women than men): Base judgments on intuition and personal feelings; distrust logical analysis and abstract reasoning.
[c]**Independent knowing.** Most knowledge is uncertain. Students take their responsibility for own learning rather than relying heavily on authorities or personal feelings. They collect and use evidence to support judgments, but often superficially, and believe that when knowledge is uncertain all conclusions regarding it are equally good if the right procedure is used to reach them. *Individual pattern* (more men than women): Rely on objective logic, critical thinking, and challenging their own and others' positions to establish truth and make moral judgments, *Interindividual pattern* (more women than men): Rely on caring, empathy, and understanding of others' positions as bases for judgments.
[d]**Contextual knowing.** All truths are contextual. Students take responsibility for making judgments, acknowledging the need to do so in the face of uncertainty and ambiguity. They use all possible sources of evidence in the process—objective analysis and intuition, their own thoughts and feelings and ideas of others whose expertise they acknowledge—and they remain open to changing their decisions if new evidence is forthcoming.

and taking into account (but not accepting without question) the ideas of others whose expertise they acknowledge. They move away from the idea commonly held by independent knowers (Level 4 on the Perry scale) that all opinions are equally valid as long as the right method is used to arrive at them, and they acknowledge the need to base judgments on the best available evidence within the given context, even in the face of uncertainty and ambiguity.

B. Assessment of Development

In the method traditionally used to assess developmental levels, trained interviewers conduct structured open-ended interviews, the interviews are transcribed, and trained raters analyze the transcripts and assign levels to the interviewees. While this method is universally considered the most valid and reliable approach to assessment, the cost of implementing it has motivated the design of pencil-and-paper instruments that can be more easily administered and scored. The Measure of Intellectual Development (MID) for the Perry model [111] and the Measure of Epistemological Reflection (MER) for the Baxter Magolda model [112, 113] call for students to write essays on topics derived from the interview protocols, and the essays are rated in the same manner as the interview transcripts. The Learning Environment Preferences (LEP) questionnaire [114] and Reflective Thinking Appraisal [115] are Likert-scale instruments for assessing levels on the Perry and King-Kitchener models, respectively.

While pencil-and-paper instruments are easier and faster to administer than interviews, the ratings obtained tend to be one to two positions lower than ratings obtained with interviews and correlate moderately at best with interview ratings [100, 104]. To improve the correlation, Pavelich, Miller, and Olds [104] developed an online tool called Cogito, which asks questions about scenarios related to four controversial issues, asks follow-up questions based on the responses, and uses a neural net to identify response patterns and assign levels to them. The neural net is trained on a set of responses submitted by individuals with known levels on the Reflective Judgment and Perry models (based on structured interviews). In initial tests, the maximum correlation coefficient of about 0.5 between the interview-based levels and the Cogito-assigned levels was indeed higher than the best values obtained for the pencil-and-paper instruments, but was still well below the desired minimum value of 0.8. The authors speculated that 0.5–0.6 might be an upper bound to the correlation coefficient between ratings obtained using interviews and objectively-scored instruments.

C. Levels of Development of Engineering Students

Table 6.3 summarizes results of two studies in which the Perry levels of beginning and advanced engineering undergraduates were measured. Pavelich's study [102] was carried out to assess the effect on intellectual development of the strong experiential learning environment at the Colorado School of Mines. The study by Wise et al. [106] was intended to determine the effect of a first-year project-based design course at Penn State. The studies are remarkably consistent in their assessments of the initial and final average levels of the subjects. Most of the entering students were near Perry Level 3, only beginning to recognize that not all knowledge is certain and still relying heavily on authorities as sources of truth. The average change after four years of college was one level, with most of the change occurring in the last year. Neither instructional approach met its goal of elevating a significant number of students to Level 5. As discouraging as these results might seem, one could speculate that a curriculum lacking such features as the experiential learning environment at Mines or the project-based first-year experience at Penn State (in Wankat's term, a "dualistic curriculum" [91]) would lead to even less growth than was observed in the two studies in question.

Wise et al. [106] also report Perry ratings of eight male engineering students and eight female engineering students who completed the first-year project-based design course. There was initially no appreciable difference between the two groups in average Perry rating or SAT scores. At the end of the first year, the average Perry rating was 3.50 for the men and 3.16 for the women; at the end of the third year the ratings were 3.50 (men) and 3.00 (women); and at the end of the fourth year the ratings were 4.00 (men) and 4.50 (women). None of the differences were statistically significant although the differences for the third year came close ($p = 0.054$). The lack of significance could be an artifact of the small sample size. To the extent that the observed differences are real, they support the contentions of Belenky et al.[109] and Baxter Magolda [110] that men and women exhibit different patterns of development.

TABLE 6.3

Perry levels of engineering students

Year (n)	Average Perry level (SD)	% at Level 5	Reference
1(45)	3.27 (0.44)		
2(34)	3.71 (0.53)		Pavelich & Moore [102]
4(46)	4.28 (0.70)	25%	
1(21)	3.27 (0.40)	0%	
3(21)	3.33 (0.35)	0%	Wise et al. [106]
4(21)	4.21 (0.50)	33%	

D. Promoting Intellectual Development

A necessary condition for students' intellectual growth is *challenge* to the beliefs that characterize their current developmental levels. An absolute knower who is never confronted with open-ended questions that have multiple solutions cannot be expected to accept the reality of multiplicity and move to transitional knowing spontaneously. Similarly, an independent knower who is not challenged for inadequate use of evidence in making judgments is not likely to make the shift to contextual knowing.

The challenge cannot be too great, however. If students are confronted with tasks that call for thinking too far above their current developmental level (in Vygotsky's term, outside their Zone of Proximal Development [116]), they may not be capable of understanding what is being required of them. Moreover, challenge alone—even at an appropriate level—may not be sufficient to move students to higher levels of development. Students confronted with challenges to their fundamental beliefs may feel threatened and either persist at their current developmental levels or retreat to even lower levels. To avoid these outcomes, instructors should provide appropriate *support* to help their students meet the challenges.

Felder and Brent [95] propose five instructional conditions that should provide the balance of challenge and support needed to promote intellectual growth and suggest numerous ways to establish the conditions. The conditions are listed in Table 6.4. Most of the methods suggested in [95] are supported by extensively cited references on teaching and learning [2, 3, 5, 87, 88, 90, 91], and the student-centered approaches of Condition D have repeatedly been shown to have positive effects on a wide variety of learning outcomes [119–123]. However, until a researcher implements the recommendations and assesses the intellectual development of the subjects (ideally comparing their growth with that of a control group that goes through a traditionally taught curriculum), the effectiveness of the conditions in Table 6.4 at promoting growth will remain speculative.

TABLE 6.4

Instructional conditions that facilitate intellectual growth [95]

A. *Variety and choice of learning tasks*
1. Varied problem types
2. Varied levels of assignment definition and structure
3. Choice on assignments, tests, and grading policies
B. *Explicit communication and explanation of expectations*
1. Instructional objectives covering high-level tasks
2. Study guides and tests based on the objectives
C. *Modeling, practice, and constructive feedback on high-level tasks*
1. Assignment of relevant tasks and modeling of required procedures
2. Practice in assignments followed by inclusion of similar tasks on tcsts
D. *A student-centered instructional environment*
1. Inductive learning (problem/project based learning, guided inquiry)
2. Active and cooperative learning
3. Measures to defuse resistance to student-centered instruction
E. *Respect for students at all levels of development*
1. A sense of caring about students

E. Questions for Further Study

The study of the intellectual development of engineering students is still in a preliminary stage, with many basic questions as yet unaddressed. Several of the questions follow.

1. What intellectual development level distributions characterize most engineering students at different stages of the curriculum? Are there differences between students at different types of schools? Do levels vary with demographic or sociological factors or academic predictors such as SAT scores, and if so, how? Do levels correlate with course grades? Are the contrasting gender-related patterns of Baxter Magolda's model observed for engineering students? What levels and patterns characterize engineering faculty?
2. To what extent do levels on the different models of intellectual development actually correspond in the manner shown in Table 6.2? (Those correspondences are based entirely on the descriptions of the levels and not on comparative data.)
3. To what extent do the instructional conditions listed in Table 6.4 promote intellectual development? What other instructional conditions or methods do so, and to what extent?
4. Is Vygotsky's Zone of Proximal Development a reality in the context of intellectual development? In other words, are assertions that students cannot cope with instruction more than (say) one Perry level above their current developmental level valid, or can suitable support enable them to bridge broader cognitive gaps?
5. What are the effects of introducing students to the concept of intellectual development? For example, would being able to identify their own attitudes in the context of developmental levels promote their intellectual growth, or might explicit description of the different stages of development lead to resentment and increased resistance from students at lower levels?

VI. Teaching to Address All Three Forms of Diversity

Teaching strategies have been recommended to help instructors meet the needs of the full spectrum of learning styles [13, 15, 26], induce students to adopt a deep approach to learning [3, 5, 69], and promote students' intellectual development [95]. The prospect of implementing three different teaching approaches simultaneously to achieve all three goals could be intimidating to instructors, but commonalities among the three diversity domains and the instructional methods that address them make the task manageable. The basis of the discussion that follows is the set of recommendations for promoting intellectual development presented in Table 6.4.

Assigning a variety of learning tasks (part of Condition A of Table 6.4) is foremost among the methods that have been recommended to address learning goals in all three diversity domains. Variation enables instructors both to challenge the beliefs about knowledge and its acquisition that characterize different developmental levels and to ensure that students are confronted with some assignments that require a deep approach to learning. Variety in assignments is also a cornerstone of recommendations for addressing the full spectrum of learning styles, with some problems emphasizing practical considerations and requiring careful attention to details (sensing strengths) and others calling for theoretical interpretation and mathematical modeling (intuitive strengths), some involving individual efforts (reflective) and others requiring teamwork (active), and so on.

A clear similarity exists between the characteristics of a deep approach to learning and the defining attributes of Baxter Magolda's contextual knowledge level of intellectual development (Perry Level 5 and above). Both a deep approach and contextual knowing involve taking responsibility for one's own learning, questioning authorities rather than accepting their statements at face value, and attempting to understand new knowledge in the context of prior knowledge and experience. A reasonable assumption is that conditions known to promote a deep approach should also promote intellectual growth. As we noted in section IV-C, Conditions A3, B, C, D1, D2, and E1 of Table 6.4 have been shown to encourage a deep approach.

Inductive instructional approaches such as problem-based learning (Condition D of Table 6.4) should also be effective for addressing the learning goals associated with all three domains. Open-ended problems that do not have unique well-defined solutions pose a serious challenge to students' low-level beliefs in the certainty of knowledge and the role of instructors as providers of knowledge. Such problems by their very nature also require a deep approach to learning (rote memorization and simple algorithmic substitution being clearly inadequate strategies for them), and solving them eventually requires skills associated with different learning styles: the imagination and capacity for abstract thinking of the intuitor and the attention to detail of the sensor; the holistic vision of the global learner and the systematic analytical approach of the sequential learner.

Requiring students to modify their fundamental beliefs about the nature of knowledge can be unsettling or threatening, as can calling on them to adopt a deep approach to learning when they are inclined to a surface approach or to complete assignments that call for abilities not normally associated with their learning style preferences. It is reasonable to speculate that the conditions in Table 6.4 involving support for students should help students respond successfully to these types of challenges. Offering a choice of learning tasks (part of Condition A of Table 6.4), explicitly communicating expectations (Condition B), modeling and providing practice and feedback on high-level tasks (Condition C), and showing respect for students at all levels of development (Condition E) are all ways to provide support.

While these linkages among the domains may appear logical, they must be considered speculative in the absence of rigorous confirmatory analysis. Here, then, is our final list of suggested questions to explore.

1. How strong is the hypothesized link between orientation to studying and level of intellectual development? Put another way, to what extent does a student's level of intellectual development correlate with his or her tendency to adopt a deep approach to learning?
2. What correlations exist between learning styles and approaches to learning and/or levels of intellectual development? For example, are intuitors more likely than sensors and global learners more likely than sequential learners to adopt a deep approach? Are there developmental level differences between students with different learning style preferences?
3. Are there gender-related patterns in learning style preferences or orientations to studying comparable to the patterns in Baxter Magolda's Model of Epistemological Development? Are there cultural differences in any of the three diversity categories?
4. To what extent do each of the conditions listed in Table 6.4—including the use of student-centered instructional models such as cooperative learning and problem/project-based learning—promote intellectual growth, the adoption of a deep approach, and the development of skills associated with different learning styles in engineering students? Are there instructional methods or conditions not covered in Table 6.4 that would achieve the same goals?

VII. Summary

Students differ from one another in a wide variety of ways, including the types of instruction to which they respond best (learning styles), the ways they approach their studies (orientations to studying and approaches to learning), and their attitudes about the nature of knowledge and their role in constructing it (levels of intellectual development). While much has been written about all three categories of diversity in the general education literature, relatively little solid research specific to engineering education has been performed. We have suggested a number of promising areas for study:

- *Validating instruments used to assess learning styles, orientations to study, and levels of intellectual development of engineering students.* Most of the instruments listed in this paper have been subjected to reliability and validity analysis, but few of the validation studies involved engineering student populations. While results obtained with an instrument that has not been rigorously validated may be informative (especially if they are consistently replicated in independent studies), conclusions can be made and generalized with much greater confidence if the instrument has been shown to be reliable and valid for the population being studied.

- *Characterizing students.* Learning style profiles, orientations to study, and levels of intellectual development of engineering students should be assessed and analyzed. Differences in any of the three should be identified among (a) students at different levels of a single engineering curriculum, (b) students in different branches of engineering, (c) students at different types of schools (research-intensive and teaching-intensive, public and private, small and large), (d) engineering students and students in other disciplines, and (e) students and faculty.
- *Establishing correlations among the three diversity domains.* Correlations among learning styles, orientations to study, and levels of intellectual development should be identified. Correlations could be useful for instructional design—so that, for example, if the anticipated correlation between a meaning orientation to study and a contextual knowing level of development on Baxter Magolda's scale (Perry Level 5) is verified, instructors wishing to promote the intellectual development of their students could feel more confident in using methods known to promote a deep approach to learning. Moreover, confirming the existence of anticipated correlations would support the construct validity of the instruments used to assess the positions or preferences being compared.
- *Evaluating the effectiveness of instructional methods and programs.* Most engineering faculty would agree that to be effective, instruction should address the needs of students across the full spectrum of learning styles, promote adoption of a deep approach to learning, and help students advance to higher levels of intellectual development. Many authors have proposed instructional methods for achieving one or more of those goals. What is needed is solid evidence that either supports or refutes claims of the effectiveness of those methods in achieving the desired outcomes.

We began this paper with an admonition by Kierkegaard that true instruction begins when instructors understand their students. An important component of that understanding is awareness of the different attitudes students have toward learning, the different ways they approach it, and how instructors can influence both their attitudes and approaches. The research summarized in this paper and the research that remains to be done can help instructors gain that awareness. The more successful they are in doing so, the more effectively they can design instruction that benefits all of their students. In turn, the better students understand the strengths and weaknesses associated with their attitudes and preferences, the more likely they will be to learn effectively while they are in school and throughout their careers.

Acknowledgments

The authors are grateful to Mike Prince, Kenny and Gary Felder, and the *Journal of Engineering Education* reviewers for their insightful comments on preliminary versions of this paper.

References

[1] Seymour, E., and Hewitt, H., *Talking about Leaving: Why Undergraduates Leave the Sciences,* Boulder, Colo.,: Westview Press, 1997.

[2] Bransford, J.D., Brown, A.L., and Cocking, R.R., eds., *How People Learn: Brain, Mind, Experience, and School,* Washington, D.C.: National Academy Press, 2000. Online at *http://books.nap.edu/catalog/ 9853.html./*

[3] Biggs, J., *Teaching for Quality Learning at University,* 2nd ed., Buckingham: The Society for Research into Higher Education and Open University Press, 2003.

[4] McKeachie, W.J., *McKeachie's Teaching Tips: Strategies, Research, and Theory for College and University Teachers,* 11th ed., Boston, Mass.: Houghton Mifflin, 2002.

[5] Ramsden, P., *Learning to Teach in Higher Education,* 2nd ed., London: Taylor and Francis, Inc., 2003.

[6] Chubin, D.E., May, G.S., and Babco, E.L., "Diversifying the Engineering Workforce," *Journal of Engineering Education,* Vol. 94, No. 1, 2005, pp. ***-***.

[7] Keefe, J.W., "Learning Style: An Overview," in Keefe, J.W., ed., *Student Learning Styles: Diagnosing and Prescribing Programs,* Reston, Va.: National Association of Secondary School Principals, 1979.

[8] Entwistle, N., "Motivational Factors in Students' Approaches to Learning," in Schmeck, R.R., ed., *Learning Strategies and Learning Styles,* Ch. 2, New York, N.Y.: Plenum Press, 1988.

[9] Olds, B.M., Moskal, B.M., and Miller, R.L., "Assessment in Engineering Education: Evolution, Approaches, and Future Collaborations," *Journal of Engineering Education,* Vol. 94, No. 1, 2005, pp. ***-***.

[10] Corno, L., and Snow, R.E., "Adapting Teaching to Individual Differences Among Learners," in M. C. Wittrock, ed., *Handbook of Research on Teaching,* 3rd ed., New York, N.Y.: Macmillan and Co., 1986.

[11] Schmeck, R.R., ed., *Learning Strategies and Learning Styles,* New York, N.Y.: Plenum Press, 1988.

[12] Stice, J.E., "Using Kolb's Learning Cycle to Improve Student Learning," *Engineering Education,* Vol. 77, No. 5, 1987, pp. 291–296.

[13] Felder, R.M., and Silverman, L.K., "Learning and Teaching Styles in Engineering Education," *Engineering Education,* Vol. 78, No. 7, 1988, pp. 674–681. Online at *http://www.ncsu.edu/felder-public/Papers/LS1988.pdf.*

[14] Felder, R.M., "Matters of Style," ASEE Prism, Vol. 6, No. 4, 1996, pp. 18–23. Online at *www.ncsu.edu/felder-public/Papers/LSPrism.htm.*

[15] Lawrence, G., *People Types and Tiger Stripes: A Practical Guide to Learning Styles,* 3rd ed., Gainesville, Fla.: Center for Applications of Psychological Type, 1993.

[16] Pittenger, D.J., "The Utility of the Myers-Briggs Type Indicator," *Review of Educational Research,* Vol. 63, 1993, pp. 467–488.

[17] McCaulley, M.H., "Psychological Types of Engineering Students—Implications for Teaching," *Engineering Education,* Vol. 66, No. 7, 1976, pp. 729–736.

[18] Yokomoto, C.E., and Ware, J.R., "Improving Problem Solving Performance Using the MBTI," *Proceedings, 1982 ASEE Conference and Exposition,* Washington, D.C.: American Society for Engineering Education.

[19] McCaulley, M.H., Godleski, E.S., Yokomoto, C.F., Harrisberger, L., and Sloan, E.D., "Applications of Psychological Type in Engineering Education," *Engineering Education,* Vol. 73, No. 5, 1983, pp. 394–400.

[20] Godleski, E.S., "Learning Style Compatibility of Engineering Students and Faculty," *Proceedings, 1984 Frontiers in Education Conference,* Washington, D.C.: ASEE/IEEE.

[21] McCaulley, M.H., Macdaid, G.P., and Granade, J.G., "ASEEMBTI Engineering Consortium: Report of the First Five Years," *Proceedings, 1985 ASEE Annual Conference,* Washington, D.C.: American Society for Engineering Education.

[22] Rosati, P.A., "Student Retention from First-Year Engineering Related to Personality Type," *Proceedings, 1993 Frontiers in Education Conference,* Washington, D.C.: ASEE/IEEE.

[23] Rosati, P.A., "Psychological Types of Canadian Engineering Students," *Journal of Psychological Type,* Vol. 41, 1997, pp. 33–37.

[24] Felder, R.M., Felder, G.N., and Dietz, E.J., "The Effects of Personality Type on Engineering Student Performance and Attitudes," *Journal of Engineering Education,* Vol. 91, No. 1, 2002, pp. 3–17. Online at *http://www.ncsu.edu/felder-public/Papers/longmbti.pdf.*

[25] Kolb, D.A., *Experiential Learning: Experience as the Source of Learning and Development,* Englewood Cliffs, N.J.: Prentice-Hall, 1984.

[26] Sharp, J.E., "Teaching Teamwork Communication with Kolb Learning Style Theory," *Proceedings, 2001 Frontiers in Education Conference,* Washington, D.C.: ASEE/IEEE.

[27] Bernold, L.E., Bingham, W.L., McDonald, P.H., and Attia, T.M., "Impact of Holistic and Learning-Oriented Teaching on Academic Success," *Journal of Engineering Education,* Vol. 89, No. 2, 2000, pp. 191–199.

[28] Harb, J.N., Durrant, S.O., and Terry, R.E., "Use of the Kolb Learning Cycle and the 4MAT System in Engineering Education," *Journal of Engineering Education,* Vol. 82, No. 2, 1993, pp. 70–77.

[29] Spurlin, J.E., Bernold, L.E., Crossland, C.L., and Anson, C.M., "Understanding How Freshman Engineering Students Think They Learn," *Proceedings, 2003 ASEE Conference and Exposition,* Washington, D.C.: American Society for Engineering Education.

[30] Sharp, J.E., Harb, J.N., and Terry, R.E., "Combining Kolb Learning Styles and Writing to Learn in Engineering Classes," *Journal of Engineering Education,* Vol. 86, No. 2, 1997, pp. 93–101.

[31] Sharp, J.E., "Learning Styles and Technical Communication: Improving Communication and Teamwork Skills," *Proceedings, 1998 Frontiers in Education Conference,* Washington, D.C.: ASEE/IEEE.

[32] Felder, R.M., "Reaching the Second Tier: Learning and Teaching Styles in College Science Education," *Journal of College Science Teaching,* Vol. 23, No. 5, 1993, pp. 286–290. Online at *www.ncsu.edu/felderpublic/Papers/Secondtier.html.*

[33] Rosati, P.A., and Felder, R.M., "Engineering Student Responses to an Index of Learning Styles," *Proceedings, 1995 ASEE Conference Exposition,* Washington, D.C.: American Society for Engineering Education.

[34] Rosati, P.A., "Comparisons of Learning Preferences in an Engineering Program," *Proceedings, 1996 Frontiers in Education Conference,* Washington, D.C.: ASEE/IEEE.

[35] Rosati, P.A., "Specific Differences and Similarities in the Learning Preferences of Engineering Students," *Proceedings, 1999 Frontiers in Education Conference,* Washington, D.C.: ASEE/IEEE.

[36] Zywno, M.S., and Waalen, J.K., "The Effect of Hypermedia Instruction on Achievement and Attitudes of Students with Different Learning Styles," *Proceedings, 2001 ASEE Conference and Exposition,* Washington, D.C.: American Society for Engineering Education.

[37] Livesay, G.A., Dee, K.C., Nauman, E.A., and Hites, Jr., L.S., "Engineering Student Learning Styles: A Statistical Analysis Using Felder's *Index of Learning Styles,*" Presented at the *2002 ASEE Conference and Exposition,* Montreal, Quebec, June 2002.

[38] Zywno, M.S., "Instructional Technology, Learning Styles, and Academic Achievement," *Proceedings, 2002 ASEE Conference and Exposition,* Washington, D.C.: American Society for Engineering Education.

[39] Dee, K.C., Livesay, G.A., and Nauman, E.A., "Learning Styles of First- and Second-Year Engineering Students," *Proceedings, 2003 ASEE/WFEO International Colloquium,* Washington, D.C.: American Society for Engineering Education.

[40] Sharp, J.E., "A Resource for Teaching a Learning Styles/Teamwork Module with the Soloman-Felder Index of Learning Styles," *Proceedings, 2003 Frontiers in Education Conference,* Washington, D.C.: ASEE/IEEE.

[41] Herrmann, N., *The Creative Brain,* Lake Lure, N.C.: Brain Books, 1990.

[42] Lumsdaine, E., and Voitle, J., "Introducing Creativity and Design into Traditional Engineering Design Courses," *Proceedings, 1993 ASEE Conference and Exposition,* Washington, D.C.: American Society for Engineering Education.

[43] Lumsdaine, M., and Lumsdaine, E., "Thinking Preferences of Engineering Students: Implications for Curriculum Restructuring," *Journal of Engineering Education,* Vol. 84, No. 2, 1995, pp. 193–204.

[44] Dunn, R., Beaudry, J.S., and Klavas, A., "Survey of Research on Learning Styles," *Educational Leadership,* Vol. 46, No. 6, 1989, pp. 50–58.

[45] Dunn, R., "Understanding the Dunn and Dunn Learning Styles Model and the Need for Individual Diagnosis and Prescription," *Reading, Writing, and Learning Disabilities,* Vol. 6, 1990, pp. 223–247.

[46] Hein, T.L., and Budny, D.D., "Teaching to Students' Learning Styles: Approaches That Work," *Proceedings, 1999 Frontiers in Education Conference,* Washington, D.C.: ASEE/IEEE.

[47] Felder, R.M., "Meet Your Students. 1. Stan and Nathan," *Chemical Engineering Education,* Vol. 23, No. 2, 1989, pp. 68–69. Online at *www.ncsu.edu/felder-public/Columns/Stannathan.html.*

[48] Felder, R.M., "Meet Your Students. 2. Susan and Glenda," *Chemical Engineering Education,* Vol. 24, No. 1, 1990, pp. 7–8. Online at *www.ncsu.edu/felder-public/Columns/Susanglenda.html.*

[49] Felder, R.M., and Soloman, B.A., *Index of Learning Styles, http://www.ncsu.edu/felder-public/ILSpage.html.*

[50] Felder, R.M., and Spurlin, J., "Applications, Reliability, and Validity of the Index of Learning Styles," *International Journal of Engineering Education,* in press.

[51] Constant, K.P., "Using Multimedia Techniques to Address Diverse Learning Styles in Materials Education," *Journal of Materials Education,* Vol. 19, 1997, pp. 1–8.

[52] Paterson, K.G., "Student Perceptions of Internet-Based Learning Tools in Environmental Engineering Education," *Journal of Engineering Education,* Vol. 88, No. 3, 1999, pp. 295–304.

[53] De Vita, G., "Learning Styles, Culture and Inclusive Instruction in the Multicultural Classroom: A Business and Management Perspective," *Innovations in Education and Teaching International,* Vol. 38, No. 2, 2001, pp. 165–174.

[54] Zywno, M.S., "A Contribution of Validation of Score Meaning for Felder-Soloman's *Index of Learning Styles,*" *Proceedings, 2003 ASEE Conference and Exposition,* Washington, D.C.: American Society for Engineering Education.

[55] Lopes, W.M.G., *ILS—Inventário de Estilos de Aprendizagem de Felder-Soloman: Investigação de sua Validade em Estudantes Universitários de Belo Horizonte,* Masters Thesis, Universidade Federal de Santa Ca-terina,Brazil, 2002.

[56] Seery, N., Gaughran, W.F., and Waldmann, T., "Multi-Modal Learning in Engineering Education," *Proceedings, 2003 ASEE Conference and Exposition,* Washington, D.C.: American Society for Engineering Education.

[57] Montgomery, S., "Addressing Diverse Student Learning Styles through the Use of Multimedia," *Proceedings, 1995 Frontiers in Education Conference,* Washington, D.C.: ASEE/IEEE.

[58] Buxeda, R., and Moore, D.A., "Using Learning Styles Data to Design a Microbiology Course," *Journal of College Science Teaching,* Vol. 29, 1999, pp. 159–164.

[59] Buxeda, R., Jimenez, L., and Morell, L., "Transforming an Engineering Course to Enhance Student Learning," *Proceedings. 2001 International Conference on Engineering Education,* Arlington, Va.: International Network for Engineering Education and Research.

[60] Kuri, N.P., and Truzzi, O.M.S., "Learning Styles of Freshmen Engineering Students," *Proceedings, 2002 International Conference on Engineering Education,* Arlington, Va.: International Network for Engineering Education and Research.

[61] Smith, N.G., Bridge, J., and Clarke, E., "An Evaluation of Students' Performance Based on Their Preferred Learning Styles," in Pudlowski, Z.L., ed., *Proceedings, 3rd Annual Conference of the UNESCO International Centre for Engineering Education,* Melbourne, Australia: UICEE, 2002.

[62] Hayes, J., and Allinson, C.W., "Matching Learning Style and Instructional Strategy: An Application of the Person-Environment Interaction Paradigm," *Perceptual and Motor Skills,* Vol. 76, 1993, pp. 63–79.

[63] Hayes, J., and Allinson, C.W., "The Implications of Learning Styles for Training and Development: A Discussion of the Matching Hypothesis," *British Journal of Management,* Vol. 7, 1996, pp. 63–73.

[64] Marton, F., and Säljö, R., "Approaches to Learning," in Marton et al. [92].

[65] Ramsden, P., *The Lancaster Approaches to Studying and Course Perceptions Questionnaire: Lecturer's Handbook,* Oxford: Educational Methods Unit, Oxford Polytechnic, 1983.

[66] Woods, D.R., Hrymak, A.N., and Wright, H.M., "Approaches to Learning and Learning Environments in Problem-based vs. Lecture-based Learning," *Proceedings, 2000 ASEE Conference and Exposition,* Washington, D.C.: American Society for Engineering Education.

[67] Biggs, J.B., *Study Process Questionnaire,* Australia: University of Newcastle, 1979.

[68] Bertrand, D., and Knapper, C.K., "Contextual Influences on Students' Approaches to Learning in Three Academic Departments," Unpublished honors thesis, Psychology Department, University of Waterloo, Waterloo, ON, Canada, 1991 (cited by Woods et al., [66]).

[69] Prosser, M., and Trigwell, K., *Understanding Learning and Teaching,* Buckingham: The Society for Research into Higher Education and Open University Press, 1999.

[70] Prosser, M., and Millar, R., "The 'How' and 'Why' of Learning Physics," *European Journal of Psychology of Education,* Vol. 4, 1989, pp. 513–528.

[71] Meyer, J.H.F., Parsons, P., and Dunne, T.T., "Individual Study Orchestrations and their Association with Learning Outcome," *Higher Education,* Vol. 20, 1990, pp. 67–89.

[72] Dochy, F., Segers, M., Van den Bossche, P., and Gijbels, D., "Effects of Problem-Based Learning: A Meta-Analysis," *Learning and Instruction,* Vol. 13, 2003, pp. 533–568.

[73] Duch, B.J., Groh, S.E., and Allen, D.E., eds., *The Power of Problem-Based Learning,* Sterling, Va.: Stylus, 2001.

[74] de Graaf, E. and Kolmos, A., "Characteristics of Problem-Based Learning," *International Journal of Engineering Education,* Vol. 19, No. 5, 2003, pp. 657–662.

[75] Kolmos, A., Fink, F.K., and Krogh, L., eds., *The Aalborg PBL Model: Progress, Diversity, and Challenges,* Aalborg, Denmark: Aalborg University Press, 2004.

[76] McMaster University Problem-Based Learning Web Site, *http://www.chemeng.mcmaster.ca/pbl/ PBL.HTM.*

[77] University of Delaware Problem-Based Learning Web Site, *http://www.udel.edu/pbl.*

[78] Gronlund, N.E., *How to Write and Use Instructional Objectives,* 5th ed., New York, N.Y.: Macmillan, 1994.

[79] Mager, R.F., *Preparing Instructional Objectives,* 3rd ed., Atlanta, Ga.: Center for Effective Performance, 1997.

[80] Felder, R.M., and Brent, R., "Designing and Teaching Courses to Satisfy the ABET Engineering Criteria," *Journal of Engineering Education,* Vol. 92, No. 1, 2003, pp. 7–25. Online at *http://www.ncsu.edu/felder-public/Papers/ABET_Paper_(JEE).pdf.*

[81] Felder, R.M., and Brent, R., "Learning by Doing," *Chemical Engineering Education,* Vol. 37, No. 4, 2003, pp. 282–283. Online at *http://www.ncsu.edu/felder-public/Columns/Active.pdf.*

[82] Prince, M., "Does Active Learning Work? A Review of the Research," *Journal of Engineering Education,* Vol. 93, No. 3, 2004, pp. 223–231.

[83] Johnson, D.W., Johnson, R.T., and Smith, K.A., *Active Learning: Cooperation in the College Classroom,* 2nd ed., Edina. Minn.: Interaction Book Co, 1998.

[84] Smith, K.A., Johnson, D.W., Johnson, R.W., and Sheppard, S.D., "Pedagogies of Engagement: Classroom-Based Practices," *Journal of Engineering Education,* Vol. 94, No. 1, 2005, pp. ***–***.

[85] Trigwell, K., Prosser, M., Ramsden, P., and Martin, E., "Improving Student Learning through a Focus on the Teaching Context," in Gibbs, G., ed., *Improving Student Learning,* Oxford: Oxford Centre for Staff Development, 1998.

[86] Trigwell, K., Prosser, M., and Waterhouse, F., "Relations between Teachers' Approaches to Teaching and Students' Approaches to Learning," *Higher Education,* Vol. 37, 1999, pp. 57–70.

[87] Chickering, A.W., and Gamson, Z.F., *Applying the Seven Principles for Good Practice in Undergraduate Education,* New Directions for Teaching and Learning, No. 47, San Francisco, Cal.: Jossey-Bass, 1991.

[88] Eble, K.E., *The Craft of Teaching,* 2nd ed., San Francisco, Cal.: Jossey-Bass, 1988.

[89] Felder, R.M., "Designing Tests to Maximize Learning," *Journal of Professional Issues in Engineering Education and Practice,* Vol. 128, No. 1, 2002, pp. 1–3. Online at *http://www.ncsu.edu/felder-public/Papers/ TestingTips.htm.*

[90] Lowman, J., *Mastering the Techniques of Teaching,* 2nd ed., San Francisco, Cal.: Jossey-Bass, 1995.

[91] Wankat, P., *The Effective, Efficient Professor: Teaching, Scholarship, and Service,* Boston, Mass.: Allyn and Bacon, 2002.

[92] Marton, F., Hounsell, D., and Entwistle, N., eds., *The Experience of Learning,* 2nd ed., Edinburgh: Scottish Academic Press, 1997.

[93] Kroll, B.M., *Teaching Hearts and Minds: College Students Reflect on the Vietnam War in Literature,* Carbondale, Ill.: Southern Illinois University Press, 1992.

[94] Felder, R.M., and Brent, R., "The Intellectual Development of Science and Engineering Students. 1. Models and Challenges," *Journal of Engineering Education,* Vol. 93, No. 4, 2004, pp. 269–277.

[95] Felder, R.M., and Brent, R., "The Intellectual Development of Science and Engineering Students. 2. Teaching to Promote Growth," *Journal of Engineering Education,* Vol. 93, No. 4, 2004, pp. 279–291.

[96] Perry, W.G., *Forms of Intellectual and Ethical Development in the College Years: A Scheme,* San Francisco, Cal.: Jossey-Bass, 1988. (An updated reprint of the original 1970 work.)

[97] Love, P.G., and Guthrie, V.L., *Understanding and Applying Intellectual Development Theory,* New Directions for Student Services, No. 88, San Francisco, Cal.: Jossey-Bass, 1999.

[98] Culver, R.S., and Hackos, J.T., "Perry's Model of Intellectual Development," *Engineering Education,* Vol. 72, 1982, pp. 221–226.

[99] Fitch, P., and Culver, R.S., "Educational Activities to Stimulate Intellectual Development in Perry's Scheme," *Proceedings, 1984 ASEE Conference and Exposition,* Washington, D.C.: American Society for Engineering Education.

[100] Pavelich, M.J., and Fitch, P., "Measuring Students' Development Using the Perry Model," *Proceedings, 1988 ASEE Conference and Exposition,* Washington, D.C.: American Society for Engineering Education.

[101] Pavelich, M.J., "Helping Students Develop Higher-Level Thinking: Use of the Perry Model," *Proceedings, 1996 Frontiers in Education Conference,* Washington, D.C.: ASEE/IEEE.

[102] Pavelich, M.J., and Moore, W.S., "Measuring the Effect of Experiential Education Using the Perry Model," *Journal of Engineering Education,* Vol. 85, No. 4, 1996, pp. 287–292.

[103] Felder, R.M., "Meet Your Students. 7. Dave, Martha, and Roberto," *Chemical Engineering Education,* Vol. 31, No. 2, 1997, pp. 106–107. Online at *http://www.ncsu.edu/felder-public/Columns/ Perry.html.*

[104] Pavelich, M.J., Miller, R.L., and Olds, B.M., "Software for Measuring the Intellectual Development of Students: Advantages and Limitations," *Proceedings, 2002 ASEE Conference and Exposition,* Washington, D.C.: American Society for Engineering Education.

[105] Marra, R., and Palmer, B., "Encouraging Intellectual Growth: Senior College Student Profiles," *Journal of Adult Development,* Vol. 11, No. 2, 2004, pp. 111–122.

[106] Wise, J., Lee, S.H., Litzinger, T.A., Marra, R.M., and Palmer, B., "A Report on a Four-Year Longitudinal Study of Intellectual Development of Engineering Undergraduates," *Journal of Adult Development,* Vol. 11, No. 2, 2004, pp. 103–110.

[107] King, P.M., and Kitchener, K.S., *Developing Reflective Judgment: Understanding and Promoting Intellectual Growth and Critical Thinking in Adolescents and Adults,* San Francisco, Cal.: Jossey Bass, 1994.

[108] King, P.M., and Kitchener, K.S., "The Reflective Judgment Model: Twenty Years of Research on Epistemic Cognition," in Hofer, B.K. and Pintrich, P.R., eds., *Personal Epistemology: The Psychology of Beliefs about Knowledge and Knowing,* Mahwah, N.J.: Lawrence Erlbaum Associates, 2001.

[109] Belenky, M.F., Clinchy, B.M., Goldberger, N.R., and Tarule, J.M., *Women's Ways of Knowing: The Development of Self, Voice, and Mind,* New York, N.Y.: Basic Books, 1986 (reissued 1997).

[110] Baxter Magolda, M.B., *Knowing and Reasoning in College.* San Francisco, Cal.: Jossey-Bass, 1992.

[111] Moore, W.S., *The Measure of Intellectual Development: An Instrument Manual,* Olympia, Wash.: Center for the Study of Intellectual Development, 1988.

[112] Baxter Magolda, M.B., and Porterfield, W.D., *Assessing Intellectual Development: The Link between Theory and Practice,* Alexandria, Va.: American College Personnel Association, 1988.

[113] Baxter Magolda, M.B., "A Constructivist Revision of the Measure of Epistemological Reflection," *Journal of College Student Development,* Vol. 42, No. 6, 2001, pp. 520–534.

[114] Moore, W.S., "The Learning Environment Preferences: Exploring the Construct Validity of an Objective Measure of the Perry Scheme," *Journal of College Student Development,* Vol. 30, 1989, pp. 504–514.

[115] Wood, P.K., King, P.M., Kitchener, K.S., and Lynch, C.L., *Technical Manual for the Reflective Thinking Appraisal,* Columbia, Mo.: University of Missouri, 1994.

[116] Vygotsky, L.S., *Mind in Society: The Development of Higher Psychological Processes,* Cambridge, Mass: Harvard University Press, 1978.

[117] Woods, D.R., et al., "Developing Problem-Solving Skills: The McMaster Problem Solving Program," *Journal of Engineering Education,* Vol. 86, No. 2, 1997, pp. 75–92.

[118] Marra, R.M., Palmer, B., and Litzinger, T.A., "The Effects of a First-Year Design Course on Student Intellectual Development as Measured by the Perry Scheme," *Journal of Engineering Education,* Vol. 89, No. 1, 2000, pp. 39–45.

[119] Hake, R.R., "Interactive Engagement vs. Traditional Methods: A Six-thousand Student Survey of Mechanics Test Data for Introductory Physics Courses," *American Journal of Physics,* Vol. 66, 1998, pp. 64–74.

[120] Springer, L., Stanne, M.E., and Donovan, S., *Effects of Small-Group Learning on Undergraduates in Science, Mathematics, Engineering, and Technology: A Meta-Analysis,* 1998, *http://www.wcer.wisc.edu/nise/CL1/CL/resource/R2.htm.*

[121] Johnson, D.W., Johnson, R.T., and Stanne, M.B., "Cooperative Learning Methods: A Meta-Analysis," May 2000, *http://www.cooperation.org/pages/cl-methods.html.*

[122] Terenzini, P.T., Cabrera, A.F., Colbeck, C.L., Parente, J.M., and Bjorklund, S.A., "Collaborative Learning vs. Lecture/Discussion: Students' Reported Learning Gains," *Journal of Engineering Education,* Vol. 90, No. 1, 2001, pp. 123–130.

[123] Fagen, A.P., Crouch, C.H., and Mazur, E., "Peer Instruction: Results from a Range of Classrooms," *The Physics Teacher,* Vol. 40, 2002, pp. 206–209. Online at *http://mazur-www.harvard.edu/publications/ Pub_286.pdf.*

Authors' Biographies

Richard M. Felder, Ph.D., is Hoechst Celanese Professor Emeritus of chemical engineering at North Carolina State University. He is co-author of the text *Elementary Principles of Chemical Processes* (3rd Ed., Wiley, 2000), co-director of the ASEE National Effective Teaching Institute, and a fellow of the ASEE.

Address: Dept. of Chemical Engineering, N.C. State University, Raleigh, NC 27695—7905; e-mail: rmfelder@mindspring.com.

Rebecca Brent, Ed.D., is president of Education Designs, Inc., a consulting firm specializing in university and college faculty development and assessment of pre-college and college teaching. She is co-director of the ASEE National Effective Teaching Institute.

Address: Education Designs, Inc., 101 Lochside Drive, Cary, NC, 27511; e-mail: rbrent@mindspring .com.

Part II—Students: Understanding Our Learners

Recommended Readings

Anderson, J. A., & Adams, M. (1992). Acknowledging the learning styles of diverse student populations: Implications for instructional design. In N. Chism and L. Border (Eds.), *Teaching for diversity* (pp. 19–33). San Francisco, CA: Jossey-Bass.

Anderson, L. W., & Krathwohl, D. R. (2001). *A taxonomy for learning, teaching, and assessing: A revision of Bloom's taxonomy of educational objectives.* New York, NY: Longman.

Astin, A. (1998). The changing American college student: Thirty-year trends 1966–1996. *Review of Higher Education, 21*(2).

Baxter Magolda, M. B. (1992). *Knowing and reasoning in college: Gender-related patterns in students' intellectual development.* San Francisco, CA: Jossey-Bass.

Baxter Magolda, M.B. (2001). *Making their own way: Narratives for transforming higher education to promote self-development.* Sterling, VA: Stylus.

Baxter Magolda, M. B. (2009). *Authoring your life: Developing an internal voice to navigate life's challenges.* Sterling, VA: Stylus.

Belenky, M.F., Clinchy, B.M., Goldberger, N.R., & Tarule, J.M. (1986). *Women's ways of knowing.* New York: Basic Books.

Cassidy, S. (2004). Learning styles: an overview of theories, models, and measures, *Educational Psychology, 24,* 419–444.

Chickering, A.W. & Reisser, L. (1993). *Education and Identity (Second Ed.).* San Francisco: Jossey-Bass.

Coffield, F., Moseley, D., Hall, E., & Ecclestone, K. (2004). *Learning styles and pedagogy in post-16 learning.* London, UK: Learning and Skills Research Centre.

Cuthbert, P. (2005). The student learning process: learning styles or learning approaches, *Teaching in Higher Education, 10*(2), 235–249.

Davidson, C. I., & Ambrose, S. A. (1994). Characteristics of student learning. In C. I. Davidson and S. A. Ambrose (Eds.), *The new professors handbook: A guide to teaching and researching in engineering and science.* Bolton, MA: Anker Publishing.

Erickson, B. L., Peters, C. B. & Strommer, D. W. (2006). *Teaching first-year college students.* San Francisco: Wiley.

Evans, N. J., Forney, D., & Guido-DiBrito, F. (1998). *Student development in college.* San Francisco: Jossey-Bass.

Gilligan, Carol. (1993). *In a different voice: Psychological theory and women's development.* Cambridge, MA: Harvard University Press.

Goldberger, N., Tarule, J., Clinchy, B., & Belenky, M. (1996). *Knowledge, difference, and power: Essays inspired by Women's Ways of Knowing.* New York, NY: BasicBooks.

Grasha, A. F. (1996). *Teaching with style: A practical guide to enhancing learning by understanding teaching and learning styles.* Pittsburgh, PA: Alliance Publishers.

Handelsman J., Ebert-May, D., Beichner R., Bruns P., Chang A., DeHaan R., Gentile J., Lauffer S., Stewart J., Tilghman S. M., & Wood, W. B. (2004). Scientific Teaching. *Science, 304,* 521–522.

Hawk, T. F., & Shah, A. J. (2007). Using learning style instruments to enhance student learning. *Decision Sciences Journal of Innovative Education, 5*(1), 1–19.

Healey M., & Jenkins, A. (2000). Learning cycles and learning styles: the application of Kolb's experiential learning model in higher education. *Journal of Geography, 99,* 185–195.

Josselson, R. (1996). *Revising herself: The story of women's identity from college to midlife.* New York: Oxford University Press.

Kegan, R. (1994). *In over our heads: The mental demands of modern life.* Cambridge, MA: Harvard University.

Kegan, R. (2009). What "form" transforms?: A constructive-developmental approach to transformative learning. In K. Illeris (Ed.), *Contemporary theories of learning* (pp. 35–52). New York, NY: Routledge.

King, P. M., & Kitchener, K.S. (1994). *Developing reflective judgment: Understanding and promoting intellectual growth and critical thinking in adolescents and adults.* San Francisco, CA: Jossey-Bass.

Kneale, P., Bradbeer, J., & Healey, M. (2006). Learning styles, disciplines and enhancing learning in higher education. In R. Simms and S. Simms (Eds.), *Learning styles and learning: A key to meeting the accountability demands in education.* Hauppauge, NY: Nova Science Publishers.

Knowles, M. S., Holton, E., & Swanson, A. (2005). *The adult learner* (6th ed.). Boston, MA: Elsevier Butterworth Heinemann.

Kohlberg, L. (1981). *Essays on moral development:* Vol. 1, *The philosophy of moral development.* San Francisco: Harper and Row.

Kohlberg, L. (1984). *Essays on moral development:* Vol. 2, *The psychology of moral development.* San Francisco: Harper and Row.

Kolb, D. A. (1981). Learning styles and disciplinary differences. In A. W. Chickering (Ed.), *The modern American college.* San Francisco, CA: Jossey-Bass.

Love, P. G., & Guthrie, V. L. (1999). *Understanding and applying cognitive development theory. New Directions for Student Services,* No. 88. San Francisco, CA: Jossey-Bass.

McKeachie, W. (1995). Learning styles can be learning strategies. *The National Teaching and Learning Forum,* 4(6),1–3. http://www.ntlf.com/html/pi/9511/v4n6.pdf

Mezirow, J. (Ed.). (2000). *Learning as transformation: Critical perspectives on a theory in progress.* San Francisco, CA: Jossey-Bass.

Murphy, P. K., & Alexander, P. A. (2006). *Understanding how students learn: A guide for instructional leaders.* Thousand Oaks, CA: Corwin Press.

Myers, I. B., & McCaulley, M. H. (1986). *Manual: A guide to the development and use of the Myers-Briggs type indicator* (2nd ed.). Palo Alto, CA: Consulting Psychologists Press.

Pascarella, E. T., Wolniak, G. C., Pierson, C. T., & Terenzini, P. T. (2003). Experiences and outcomes of first-generation students in community colleges. *Journal of College Student Development, 44*(3), 420–429.

Perry, W.G., Jr. (1968). *Forms of intellectual and ethical development in the college years: A scheme.* New York: Holt, Rinehart, and Winston.

Ponterotto, J. G., Casas, J. M., Suzuki, L. A., & Alexander, C. M. (1995). *Handbook of multicultural counseling.* Thousand Oaks, CA: Sage.

Reid, G. (2005). *Learning styles and inclusion.* Thousand Oaks, CA: PCP/Sage Publications.

Rose, M. (1989/2005). *Lives on the boundary: A moving account of the struggles and achievements of America's educational underclass.* New York, NY: Penguin Books.

Sarasin, L. C. (1998). *Learning styles perspectives: Impact in the classroom.* Madison, WI: Atwood.

Schroeder, C. C. (1993, September/October). New students—New learning styles. *Change, 25,* 21–26.

Simms, R. R., & Sims, S. J. (2005). *Learning styles and learning: A key to meeting the accountability demands in education.* Hauppauge, NY: Nova Science Publishers.

Skipper, T. L. (2005). *Student development in the first college year: A primer for college educators.* Columbia, SC: University of South Carolina, National Resource Center for the First-Year Experience and Students in Transition.

Sousa, D. A. (2000). *How the brain learns: A classroom teacher's guide.* Thousand Oaks, CA: Corwin Press.

Sternberg, R. J. (1990, January). Thinking styles: Keys to understanding student performance. *Phi Delta Kappan,* 336–71.

Strauss, W., & Howe, N. (2007). *Millennials go to college.* Great Falls, VA: Lifecourse Associates.

Sutherland, P. (1997). *Adult learning: A reader.* London, UK: Kogan Page.

Tatum, B.D. (1997). *Why are all the black kids sitting together in the cafeteria?* New York, NY: Basic Books.

Torres, V., Howard-Hamilton, M. & Cooper, D. (2003). *Identity development of diverse populations.* (pp. 33–66) ASHE/ERIC Higher Education Report, Wiley.

Weinstein, C., & Meyer, D. (1991). Cognitive learning strategies and college teaching. *New Directions for Teaching and Learning: No. 45, College teaching: From theory to practice* (pp. 15–26). San Francisco, CA: Jossey-Bass.

Whitt, E., Edison, M., Pascarella, E., Terenzini, P., & Nora, A. (2001). Influences on students' openness to diversity and challenge in the second and third years of college. *Journal of Higher Education, 72*(2), 172–204.

Wilson, L. H. (2006). *How students really learn: Instructional strategies that work.* Lanham, MD: Rowman & Littlefield Education.

Web Resources

American College Personnel Association (ACPA)—*Journal of College Student Development, About Campus*
http://www2.myacpa.org/

The Index of Learning Styles, by Richard M. Felder and Barbara A. Soloman of North Carolina State University
http://www4.ncsu.edu/unity/lockers/users/f/felder/public/ILSpage.html

National Resource Center for the First-Year Experience and Students in Transition
http://www.sc.edu/fye/

PART III

COURSE/CURRICULUM: DESIGNING FOR LEARNING

PART III—COURSE/CURRICULUM: DESIGNING FOR LEARNING

Part III is reflective of its content about effective design steps and considerations involved in the teaching and learning process—creating learning outcomes, bearing in mind learner needs, and using assessment of student learning and feedback on teaching to make continuous improvements.

Introduction to Design/Backward Design

The first reading of this section introduces the notion of "backward design." As Wiggins and McTighe describe it, the challenge of backward design is "to focus first on the desired learnings from which appropriate teaching will logically follow" (p. 14). A simple idea, and yet how often is educators' inclination to determine *how* they will teach something before considering *what* they will teach, or more importantly, what students should learn? Backward design, by starting with final learning goals, not only will lead to more appropriate choices for method, but naturally flows into assessment. Wiggins and McTighe share the philosophical underpinnings of this approach, as well as some practical examples of what it can "look like."

Learning Outcomes

Creating effective learning outcomes is a skill—one that we may not necessarily cultivate without some guidance, even as experts in our fields. In addition to the guidance provided in the first reading in this section, the second reading, a chapter from *Learner-Centered Assessment on College Campuses* by Huba and Freed, provides direction on the development of intended learning outcomes. The authors offer helpful questions to stimulate our thinking about learning outcomes by asking what students should know, understand, and be able to do. They also include numerous institutional examples and opportunities for readers to reflect on their professional work to create alignment at the course, program, and institutional levels.

Our colleagues across the Atlantic have found the notion of "alignment," popularized in John Biggs' "constructive alignment model," to be helpful in a similar way. In the article we include here, Biggs summarizes a systems approach with "four major steps to alignment" where teaching is framed as a catalyst for learning. He argues that "the key is that the components in the teaching system, especially the teaching methods used and the assessment tasks, are *aligned* with the learning activities assumed in the intended outcomes" (p. 2).

Considerations of Design for Different Learning Contexts and Learners

Good design necessitates knowing your learners and the cultures and contexts from which they forged their expectations of learning. Irvine and York review the literature on learning style related to students from various cultures in their chapter from the *Handbook of Multicultural Education.* While they propose that there are some learning-related patterns within cultural frameworks that can inform our work with multicultural students, they also caution the reader about the dangers of making generalizations. According to the authors, learning styles research can engender complex questions to explore the cultural contexts of teaching and learning, the social interactions implicit within teaching processes, and the progression toward making learning accessible for all students.

Assessing Student Learning

In addition to the earlier works on learning outcomes, which inevitably segue into assessment, in this section we provide three readings that specifically address formative and summative assessment strategies. In the first of these three, Tom Angelo, known for his work with Patricia Cross in this area, distinguishes between formative assessment (classroom assessment techniques, or CATs) and the type of assessment most recognized in higher education, summative assessment (tests, essays, etc.). He uses feedback from faculty who have used CATs over a number of years to proffer benefits for students and faculty, and suggests "seven guidelines for success."

The second reading specific to assessment comes from a project of The Higher Education Academy in York, England. The authors, who are educational developers, outline the research that has been done on formative feedback and provide principles for practice. Their seven principles establish strategies to integrate systemic assessment with effective instruction. As a useful accompaniment, several case studies are included to demonstrate how the principles may be implemented across diverse contexts.

Finally, Susan Brookhart, in an ASHE-ERIC Higher Education Report, communicates various forms and approaches often used in summative assessment and how to ensure the design of these assessments aligns with desired goals. She tackles the intricacies of assessment as both an art and science to address the complicated work of determining what students understand within a given discipline. The author provides an overview of the assessment research and literature since 1985, acknowledging the emerging influence of standards.

Evaluating Teaching

Part III concludes with resources on evaluating teaching, an important component of improving the design and delivery of any course, and thus the learning of students. On the heels of Barr and Tagg's (1995) seminal piece on shifting the paradigm "from teaching to learning" (shared in Part I of this reader), Barbara Cambridge published this piece on "examining the quality of teaching through assessment of student learning" in *Innovative Higher Education.* She posits that the exchange of student portfolios, teacher portfolios, major (disciplinary) portfolios, and the like can inform and transform the ways in which we think about teacher and student performance, most notably, the learning taking place.

The last reading in Part III is by Peter Seldin, a prominent scholar in the area of faculty evaluation. In this piece entitled "Evaluating College Teaching: Myth and Reality," Seldin confronts "five common assumptions" about the evaluation of teaching, connecting each assumption to research and perspectives from faculty development. He observes that methods for evaluating college teaching transform as external forces encourage systematic measurement and competition. The concept of evaluation is broadening beyond relying on student ratings as a singular measure to include faculty self-evaluation, feedback from faculty peers, and analysis of course design.

CHAPTER 7

INTRODUCTION TO DESIGN/BACKWARD DESIGN

Backward Design

G. Wiggins and J. McTighe

Design, v.,—To have purposes and intentions; to plan and execute
—*Oxford English Dictionary*

The complexity of design work is often underestimated. Many people believe they know a good deal about design. What they do not realize is how much more they need to know to do design well, with distinction, refinement, and grace.
—John McClean, "20 Considerations That Help a Project Run Smoothly," 2003

Teachers are designers. An essential act of our profession is the crafting of curriculum and learning experiences to meet specified purposes. We are also designers of assessments to diagnose student needs to guide our teaching and to enable us, our students, and others (parents and administrators) to determine whether we have achieved our goals.

Like people in other design professions, such as architecture, engineering, or graphic arts, designers in education must be mindful of their audiences. Professionals in these fields are strongly client-centered. The effectiveness of their designs corresponds to whether they have accomplished explicit goals for specific end-users. Clearly, students are our primary clients, given that the effectiveness of curriculum, assessment, and instructional designs is ultimately determined by their achievement of desired learnings. We can think of our designs, then, as software. Our courseware is designed to make learning more effective, just as computer software is intended to make its users more productive.

As in all the design professions, standards inform and shape our work. The software developer works to maximize user-friendliness and to reduce bugs that impede results. The architect is guided by building codes, customer budget, and neighborhood aesthetics. The teacher as designer is similarly constrained. We are not free to teach any topic we choose by any means. Rather, we are guided by national, state, district, or institutional standards that specify what students should know and be able to do. These standards provide a useful framework to help us identify teaching and learning priorities and guide our design of curriculum and assessments. In addition to external standards, we must also factor in the needs of our many and varied students when designing learning experiences. For example, diverse student interests, developmental levels, large classes, and previous achievements must always shape our thinking about the learning activities, assignments, and assessments.

Yet, as the old adage reminds us, in the best designs form follows function. In other words, all the methods and materials we use are shaped by a clear conception of the vision of desired results. That means that we must be able to state with clarity what the student should understand and be able to do as a result of any plan and irrespective of any constraints we face.

Reprinted from *Association for Supervision and Curriculum Development* (2005).

You probably know the saying, "If you don't know exactly where you are headed, then any road will get you there." Alas, the point is a serious one in education. We are quick to say what things *we* like to teach, what activities *we* will do, and what kinds of resources *we* will use; but without clarifying the desired results of our teaching, how will we ever know whether our designs are appropriate or arbitrary? How will we distinguish merely interesting learning from *effective* learning? More pointedly, how will we ever meet content standards or arrive at hard-won student understandings unless we think through what those goals imply for the learner's activities and achievements?

Good design, then, is not so much about gaining a few new technical skills as it is about learning to be more thoughtful and specific about our purposes and what they imply.

Why "backward" is best

How do these general design considerations apply to curriculum planning? Deliberate and focused instructional design requires us as teachers and curriculum writers to make an important shift in our thinking about the nature of our job. The shift involves thinking a great deal, first, about the specific learnings sought, and the evidence of such learnings, before thinking about what we, as the teacher, will do or provide in teaching and learning activities. Though considerations about what to teach and how to teach it may dominate our thinking as a matter of habit, the challenge is to focus first on the desired learnings from which appropriate teaching will logically follow.

Our lessons, units, and courses should be logically inferred from the results sought, not derived from the methods, books, and activities with which we are most comfortable. Curriculum should lay out the most effective ways of achieving specific results. It is analogous to travel planning. Our frameworks should provide a set of itineraries deliberately designed to meet cultural goals rather than a purposeless tour of all the major sites in a foreign country. In short, the best designs derive backward from the learnings sought.

The appropriateness of this approach becomes clearer when we consider the educational purpose that is the focus of this book: understanding. We cannot say *how* to teach for understanding or *which* material and activities to use until we are quite clear about which specific understandings we are after and what such understandings look like in practice. We can best decide, as guides, what "sites" to have our student "tourists" visit and what specific "culture" they should experience in their brief time there only if we are clear about the particular understandings about the culture we want them to take home. Only by having specified the desired results can we focus on the content, methods, and activities most likely to achieve those results.

But many teachers begin with and remain focused on textbooks, favored lessons, and time-honored activities—the inputs—rather than deriving those means from what is implied in the desired results—the output. To put it in an odd way, too many teachers focus on the *teaching* and not the *learning*. They spend most of their time thinking, first, about what they will do, what materials they will use, and what they will ask students to do rather than first considering what the learner will need in order to accomplish the learning goals.

Consider a typical episode of what might be called *content*-focused design instead of *results*-focused design. The teacher might base a lesson on a particular topic (e.g., racial prejudice), select a resource (e.g., *To Kill a Mockingbird*), choose specific instructional methods based on the resource and topic (e.g., Socratic seminar to discuss the book and cooperative groups to analyze stereotypical images in films and on television), and hope thereby to cause learning (and meet a few English/language arts standards). Finally, the teacher might think up a few essay questions and quizzes for assessing student understanding of the book.

This approach is so common that we may well be tempted to reply, What could be wrong with such an approach? The short answer lies in the basic questions of purpose: Why are we asking students to read this particular novel—in other words, what *learnings* will we seek from their having read it? Do the students grasp why and how the purpose should influence their studying? What should students be expected to understand and do upon reading the book, related to our goals beyond the book? Unless we begin our design work with a clear insight into larger purposes—whereby the book is properly thought of as a means to an educational end, not an end unto itself—

Design Tip

Consider these questions that arise in the minds of all readers, the answers to which will frame the priorities of coached learning: How should I read the book? What am I looking for? What will we discuss? How should I prepare for those discussions? How do I know if my reading and discussions are effective? Toward what performance goals do this reading and these discussions head, so that I might focus and prioritize my studies and note taking? What big ideas, linked to other readings, are in play here? These are the students' proper questions about the learning, not the teaching, and any good educational design answers them from the start and throughout a course of study with the use of tools and strategies such as graphic organizers and written guidelines.

it is unlikely that all students will *understand* the book (and their performance obligations). Without being self-conscious of the specific understandings about prejudice we seek, and how reading and discussing the book will help develop such insights, the goal is far too vague: The approach is more "by hope" than "by design." Such an approach ends up unwittingly being one that could be described like this: Throw some content and activities against the wall and hope some of it sticks.

Answering the "why?" and "so what?" questions that older students always ask (or want to), and doing so in concrete terms as the focus of curriculum planning, is thus the essence of understanding by design. What is difficult for many teachers to see (but easier for students to feel!) is that, without such explicit and transparent priorities, many students find day-to-day work confusing and frustrating.

The twin sins of traditional design

More generally, weak educational design involves two kinds of purposelessness, visible throughout the educational world from kindergarten through graduate school, as noted in the Introduction. We call these the "twin sins" of traditional design. The error of activity-oriented design might be called "hands-on without being minds-on"—engaging experiences that lead only accidentally, if at all, to insight or achievement. The activities, though fun and interesting, do not lead anywhere intellectually. As typified by the apples vignette in the Introduction, such activity-oriented curricula lack an explicit focus on important ideas and appropriate evidence of learning, especially in the minds of the learners. They think their job is merely to engage; they are led to think the learning *is* the activity instead of seeing that the learning comes from being asked to consider the *meaning* of the activity.

A second form of aimlessness goes by the name of "coverage," an approach in which students march through a textbook, page by page (or teachers through lecture notes) in a valiant attempt to traverse all the factual material within a prescribed time (as in the world history vignette in the Introduction). Coverage is thus like a whirlwind tour of Europe, perfectly summarized by the old movie title *If It's Tuesday, This Must Be Belgium*, which properly suggests that no overarching goals inform the tour.

As a broad generalization, the activity focus is more typical at the elementary and lower middle school levels, whereas coverage is a prevalent secondary school and college problem. Yet, though the apples and world history classrooms look quite different with lots of physical activity and chatter in the former versus lecturing and quiet note taking in the latter, the design result is the same in both cases: No guiding intellectual purpose or clear priorities frame the learning experience. In neither case can students see and answer such questions as these: What's the point? What's the big idea here? What does this help us understand or be able to do? To what does this relate? Why should we learn this? Hence, the students try to engage and follow as best they can, hoping that meaning will emerge.

Students will be unable to give satisfactory responses when the design does not provide them with clear purposes and explicit performance goals highlighted throughout their work. Similarly,

Misconception Alert!

Coverage is not the same as *purposeful survey*. Providing students with an overview of a discipline or a field of study is not inherently wrong. The question has to do with the transparency of purpose. *Coverage* is a negative term (whereas *introduction* or *survey* is not) because when content is "covered" the student is led through unending facts, ideas, and readings with little or no sense of the overarching ideas, issues, and learning goals that might inform study.

Design Tip

To test the merits of our claims about purposelessness, we encourage you to sidle up to a student in the middle of any class and ask the following questions:

What are you doing?

Why are you being asked to do it?

What will it help you do?

How does it fit with what you have previously done?

How will you show that you have learned it?

teachers with an activity or coverage orientation are less likely to have acceptable answers to the key design questions: What should students understand as a result of the activities or the content covered? What should the experiences or lectures equip them to do? How, then, should the activities or class discussions be shaped and processed to achieve the desired results? What would be evidence that learners are en route to the desired abilities and insights? How, then, should all activities and resources be chosen and used to ensure that the learning goals are met and the most appropriate evidence produced? How, in other words, will students be helped to see *by design* the purpose of the activity or resource and its helpfulness in meeting specific performance goals?

We are advocating the reverse of common practice, then. We ask designers to start with a much more careful statement of the desired results—the priority *learnings*—and to derive the curriculum from the performances called for or implied in the goals. Then, contrary to much common practice, we ask designers to consider the following questions after framing the goals: What would count as evidence of such achievement? What does it look like to meet these goals? What, then, are the implied *performances* that should make up the assessment, toward which all teaching and learning should point? Only after answering these questions can we logically derive the appropriate teaching and learning experiences so that students might perform successfully to meet the standard. The shift, therefore, is away from starting with such questions as "What book will we read?" or "What activities will we do?" or "What will we discuss?" to "What should they walk out the door able to understand, regardless of what activities or texts we use?" and "What is evidence of such ability?" and, therefore, "What texts, activities, and methods will best enable such a result?" In teaching students for understanding, we must grasp the key idea that *we are coaches of their ability to play the "game" of performing with understanding, not tellers of our understanding to them on the sidelines.*

The three stages of backward design

We call this three-stage approach to planning "backward design." Figure 7.1 depicts the three stages in the simplest terms.

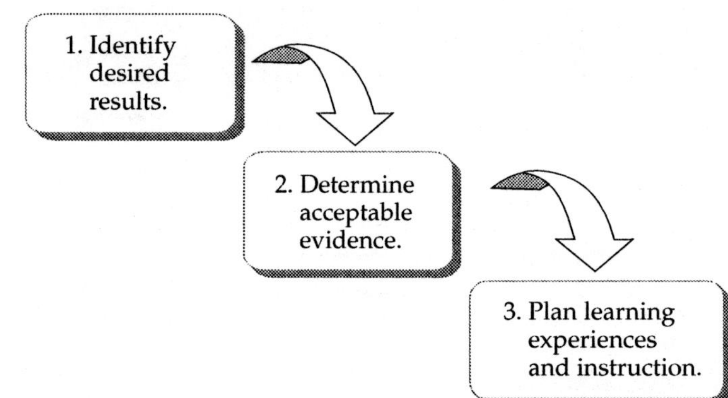

Figure 7.1
UbD: Stages of Backward Design

Stage 1: Identify desired results

What should students know, understand, and be able to do? What content is worthy of understanding? What *enduring* understandings are desired?

In Stage 1 we consider our goals, examine established content standards (national, state, district), and review curriculum expectations. Because typically we have more content than we can reasonably address within the available time, we must make choices. This first stage in the design process calls for clarity about priorities.

Stage 2: Determine acceptable evidence

How will we know if students have achieved the desired results? What will we accept as evidence of student understanding and proficiency? The backward design orientation suggests that we think about a unit or course in terms of the collected assessment evidence needed to document and validate that the desired learning has been achieved, not simply as content to be covered or as a series of learning activities. This approach encourages teachers and curriculum planners to first "think like an assessor" before designing specific units and lessons, and thus to consider up front how they will determine if students have attained the desired understandings.

Stage 3: Plan learning experiences and instruction

With clearly identified results and appropriate evidence of understanding in mind, it is now the time to fully think through the most appropriate instructional activities. Several key questions must be considered at this stage of backward design: What enabling knowledge (facts, concepts, principles) and skills (processes, procedures, strategies) will students need in order to perform effectively and achieve desired results? What activities will equip students with the needed knowledge and skills? What will need to be taught and coached, and how should it best be taught, in light of performance goals? What materials and resources are best suited to accomplish these goals?

Note that the specifics of instructional planning—choices about teaching methods, sequence of lessons, and resource materials—can be successfully completed only after we identify desired results and assessments and consider what they imply. Teaching is a means to an end. Having a clear goal helps to focus our planning and guide purposeful action toward the intended results.

Backward design may be thought of, in other words, as purposeful task analysis: Given a worthy task to be accomplished, how do we best get everyone equipped? Or we might think of it as building a wise itinerary, using a map: Given a destination, what's the most effective and efficient route? Or we might think of it as planning for coaching, as suggested earlier: What must learners master if they are to effectively perform? What will count as evidence *on the field,* not merely in drills, that they really get it and are ready to *perform with understanding, knowledge, and skill* on their own? How will the learning be designed so that learners' capacities are developed through use and feedback?

Misconception Alert!

When we speak of evidence of desired results, we are referring to evidence gathered through a variety of formal and informal assessments during a unit of study or a course. We are not alluding only to end-of-teaching tests or culminating tasks. Rather, the collected evidence we seek may well include traditional quizzes and tests, performance tasks and projects, observations and dialogues, as well as students' self-assessments gathered over time.

This is all quite logical when you come to understand it, but "backward" from the perspective of much habit and tradition in our field. A major change from common practice occurs as designers must begin to think about assessment *before* deciding what and how they will teach. Rather than creating assessments near the conclusion of a unit of study (or relying on the tests provided by textbook publishers, which may not completely or appropriately assess our standards and goals), backward design calls for us to make our goals or standards specific and concrete, in terms of assessment evidence, as we begin to plan a unit or course.

The logic of backward design applies regardless of the learning goals. For example, when starting from a state content standard, curriculum designers need to determine the appropriate assessment evidence stated or implied in the standard. Likewise, a staff developer should determine what evidence will indicate that the adults have learned the intended knowledge or skill before planning the various workshop activities.

The rubber meets the road with assessment. Three different teachers may all be working toward the same content standards, but if their assessments vary considerably, how are we to know which students have achieved what? Agreement on needed evidence of learning leads to greater curricular coherence and more reliable evaluation by teachers. Equally important is the long-term gain in teacher, student, and parent insight about what does and does not count as evidence of meeting complex standards.

This view of focusing intently on the desired learning is hardly radical or new. Tyler (1949) described the logic of backward design clearly and succinctly more than 50 years ago:

> Educational objectives become the criteria by which materials are selected, content is outlined, instructional procedures are developed, and tests and examinations are prepared. . . .
>
> The purpose of a statement of objectives is to indicate the kinds of changes in the student to be brought about so that instructional activities can be planned and developed in a way likely to attain these objectives, (pp. 1, 45)

And in his famous book, *How to Solve It,* originally published in 1945, Polya specifically discusses "thinking backward" as a strategy in problem solving going back to the Greeks:

> There is a certain psychological difficulty in turning around, in going away from the goal, in working backwards. . . . Yet, it does not take a genius to solve a concrete problem working backwards; anyone can do it with a little common sense. We concentrate on the desired end, we visualize the final position in which we would like to be from what foregoing position could we get there? (p. 230)

These remarks are old. What is perhaps new is that we offer herein a helpful process, a template, a set of tools, and design standards to make the plan and resultant student performance more likely to be successful by design than by good fortune. As a 4th grade teacher from Alberta, Canada, put it, "Once I had a way of clearly defining the end in mind, the rest of the unit 'fell into place.'"

The twin sins of activity-based and coverage-based design reflect a failure to think through purpose in this backward-design way. With this in mind, let's revisit the two fictitious vignettes from the Introduction. In the apples vignette, the unit seems to focus on a particular theme (harvest time), through a specific and familiar object (apples). But as the depiction reveals, the unit has no real depth because there is no enduring learning for the students to derive. The work is *hands-on* without being *minds-on,* because students do not need to (and are not really challenged to) extract sophisticated ideas or connections. They don't have to work at understanding; they need only engage in the activity. (Alas, it is common to reward students for mere engagement as opposed to understanding; engagement is necessary, but not sufficient, as an end result.)

Moreover, when you examine the apples unit it becomes clear that it has no overt priorities—the activities appear to be of equal value. The students' role is merely to participate in mostly enjoyable activities, without having to demonstrate that they understand any big ideas at the core of the subject (excuse the pun). All activity-based—as opposed to results-based—teaching shares the weakness of the apples unit: Little in the design asks students to derive intellectual fruit from the unit (sorry!). One might characterize this activity-oriented approach as "faith in learning by osmosis." Is it likely that individual students will learn a few interesting things about apples? Of course, But, in the absence of a learning plan with clear goals, how likely is it that students will develop shared understandings on which future lessons might build? Not very.

In the world history vignette, the teacher covers vast amounts of content during the last quarter of the year. However, in his harried march to get through a textbook, he apparently does not consider what the students will understand and apply from the material. What kind of intellectual scaffolding is provided to guide students through the important ideas? How are students expected to use those ideas to make meaning of the many facts? What performance goals would help students know how to take notes for maximal effective use by the course's end? Coverage-based instruction amounts to the teacher merely talking, checking off topics, and moving on, irrespective of whether students understand or are confused. This approach might be termed "teaching by mentioning it." Coverage-oriented teaching typically relies on a textbook, allowing it to define the content and sequence of instruction. In contrast, we propose that results-oriented teaching employ the textbook as a resource but not the syllabus.

A backward design template

Having described the backward design process, we now put it together in a useful format—a template for teachers to use in the design of units that focus on understanding.

Many educators have observed that backward design is common sense. Yet when they first start to apply it, they discover that it feels unnatural. Working this way may seem a bit awkward and time-consuming until you get the hang of it. But the effort is worth it—just as the learning curve on good software is worth it. We think of Understanding by Design as software, in fact: a set of tools for making you ultimately more productive. Thus, a practical cornerstone of Understanding by Design is a design template that is meant to reinforce the appropriate habits of mind needed to complete designs for student understanding and to avoid the habits that are at the heart of the twin sins of activity-based and coverage-based design.

Figure 7.2 provides a preliminary look at the UbD Template in the form of a one-page version with key planning questions included in the various fields. This format guides the teacher to the various UbD elements while visually conveying the idea of backward design. Later chapters present a more complete account of the template and each of its fields.

Although this one-page version of the template does not allow for great detail, it has several virtues. First, it provides a *gestalt,* an overall view of backward design, without appearing overwhelming. Second, it enables a quick check of alignment—the extent to which the assessments (Stage 2) and learning activities (Stage 3) align with identified goals (Stage 1). Third, the template can be used to review existing units that teachers or districts have developed. Finally, the one-page template provides an initial design frame. We also have a multipage version that allows for more detailed planning, including, for example, a Performance Task Blueprint and a day-by-day calendar for listing and sequencing key learning events. The *Understanding by Design Professional Development Workbook* (McTighe & Wiggins, 2004, pp. 46–51) includes a six-page template that allows for more detailed planning.

We regularly observe that teachers begin to internalize the backward design process as they work with the UbD Template. Stage 1 asks designers to consider what they want students to under-

Figure 7.2
1-Page Template with Design Questions for Teachers

Stage 1—Desired Results

Established Goals:

- What relevant goals (e.g., content standards, course or program objectives, learning outcomes) will this design address?

Understandings:

Students will understand that . . .

- What are the big ideas?
- What specific understandings about them are desired?
- What misunderstandings are predictable?

Essential Questions: 

- What provocative questions will foster inquiry, understanding, and transfer of learning?

Students will know . . . 

- What key knowledge and skills will students acquire as a result of this unit?
- What should they eventually be able to do as a result of such knowledge and skills?

Students will be able to . . . 

Stage 2—Assessment Evidence

Performance Tasks: 

- Through what authentic performance tasks will students demonstrate the desired understandings?
- By what criteria will performances of understanding be judged?

Other Evidence: 

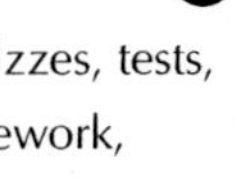

- Through what other evidence (e.g., quizzes, tests, academic prompts, observations, homework, journals) will students demonstrate achievement of the desired results?
- How will students reflect upon and self-assess their learning?

Stage 3—Learning Plan

Learning Activities: 

What learning experiences and instruction will enable students to achieve the desired results? How will the design

W = Help the students know Where the unit is going and What is expected? Help the teacher know Where the students are coming from (prior knowledge, interests)?

H = Hook all students and Hold their interest?

E = Equip students, help them Experience the key ideas and Explore the Issues?

R = Provide opportunities to Rethink and Revise their understandings and work?

E = Allow students to Evaluate their work and its implications?

T = Be Tailored (personalized) to the different needs, interests, and abilities of learners?

O = Be Organized to maximize initial and sustained engagement as well as effective learning?

stand and then to frame those understandings in terms of questions. In completing the top two sections of the Stage 1 portion of the template, users are prompted to identify the Understandings and Essential Questions to establish a larger context into which a particular unit is nested.

Stage 2 prompts the designer to consider a variety of assessment methods for gathering evidence of the desired Understandings. The two-box graphic organizer then provides spaces for specifying the particular assessments to be used during the unit. Designers need to think in terms of collected evidence, not a single test or performance task.

Stage 3 calls for a listing of the major learning activities and lessons. When it is filled in, the designer (and others) should be able to discern what we call the "WHERETO" elements.

The *form* of the template offers a means to succinctly present the design unit; its *function* is to guide the design process. When completed, the template can be used for self-assessment, peer review, and sharing of the completed unit design with others.

To better understand the template's benefits for the teacher-designer, let's take a look at a completed template. Figure 7.3 shows a completed three-page version of the template for a unit on nutrition.

Notice that the template in Figure 7.3 supports backward design thinking by making the longer-term goals far more explicit than is typical in lesson planning, and we can follow those goals through Stages 2 and 3 to ensure that the design is coherent. The focus on big ideas in Stage 1 is transparent, without sacrificing the more discrete elements of knowledge and skill. Finally, by calling for appropriately different types of assessment, the template reminds us that we typically need varied evidence and assessments grounded in performance to show transfer, if understanding is our aim.

Design standards

Accompanying the UbD Template is a set of Design Standards corresponding to each stage of backward design. The standards offer criteria to use during development and for quality control of completed unit designs. Framed as questions, the UbD Design Standards serve curriculum designers in the same way that a scoring rubric serves students. When presented to students before they begin their work, the rubric provides them with a performance target by identifying the important qualities toward which they should strive. Similarly, the Design Standards specify the qualities of effective units according to the Understanding by Design framework. Figure 7.4 (p. 222) presents the four UbD Design Standards with accompanying indicators.

The standards contribute to design work in three ways:

- *As a reference point during design*—Teachers can periodically check to see, for example, if the identified understandings are truly big and enduring, or if the assessment evidence is sufficient. Like a rubric, the questions serve as reminders of important design elements to include, such as a focus on Essential Questions.
- *For use in self-assessment and peer reviews of draft designs*—Teachers and peers can use the criteria to examine their draft units to identify needed refinements, such as using the facets to dig deeper into an abstract idea.
- *For quality control of completed designs*—The standards can then be applied by independent reviewers (e.g., curriculum committees) to validate the designs before their distribution to other teachers.

Our profession rarely subjects teacher-designed units and assessments to this level of critical review. Nonetheless, we have found structured peer reviews, guided by design standards, to be enormously beneficial—both to teachers and their designs (Wiggins, 1996, 1997). Participants in peer review sessions regularly comment on the value of sharing and discussing curriculum and assessment designs with colleagues. We believe that such sessions are a powerful approach to professional development, because the conversations focus on the heart of teaching and learning.

We cannot stress enough the importance of using design standards to regularly review curriculum—existing units and courses as well as new ones being developed. It is often difficult for

Figure 7.3
3-Page Nutrition Example

Established Goals:

Standard 6—Students will understand essential concepts about nutrition and diet.

6a—Students will use an understanding of nutrition to plan appropriate diets for themselves and others.

6c—Students will understand their own individual eating patterns and ways in which those patterns may be improved.

What essential questions will be considered?

- What is healthful eating?
- Are you a healthful eater? How would you know?
- How could a healthy diet for one person be unhealthy for another?
- Why are there so many health problems in the United States caused by poor nutrition despite all the available information?

What understandings are desired?

Students will understand that . . .

- A balanced diet contributes to physical and mental health.
- The USDA food pyramid presents relative guidelines for nutrition.
- Dietary requirements vary for individuals based on age, activity level, weight, and overall health.
- Healthful living requires an individual to act on available information about good nutrition even if it means breaking comfortable habits.

What key knowledge and skills will students acquire as a result of this unit?

Students will know . . .

- Key terms—protein, fat, calorie, carbohydrate, cholesterol.
- Types of foods in each food group and their nutritional values.
- The USDA food pyramid guidelines.
- Variables influencing nutritional needs.
- General health problems caused by poor nutrition.

Students will be able to . . .

- Read and interpret nutrition information on food labels.
- Analyze diets for nutritional value.
- Plan balanced diets for themselves and others.

Figure 7.3 (*continued*)
3-Page Nutrition Example

What evidence will show that students understand?

Performance Tasks:

You Are What You Eat—Students create an illustrated brochure to teach younger children about the importance of good nutrition for healthful living. They offer younger students ideas for breaking bad eating habits.

Chow Down—Students develop a three-day menu for meals and snacks for an upcoming Outdoor Education camp experience. They write a letter to the camp director to explain why their menu should be selected (by showing that it meets the USDA food pyramid recommendations, yet it is tasty enough for the students). They include at least one modification for a specific dietary condition (diabetic or vegetarian) or religious consideration.

What other evidence needs to be collected in light of Stage 1 Desired Results?

Other Evidence:

(e.g., tests, quizzes, prompts, work samples, observations)

Quiz—The food groups and the USDA food pyramid

Prompt—Describe two health problems that could arise as a result of poor nutrition and explain how these could be avoided.

Skill Check—interpret nutritional information on food labels.

Student Self-Assessment and Reflection:

1. Self-assess the brochure. You Are What You Eat.
2. Self-assess the camp menu, Chow Down.
3. Reflect on the extent to which you eat healthfully at the end of unit (compared with the beginning).

Figure 7.3 (*continued*)
3-Page Nutrition Example

Stage 3—Plan Learning Experiences

What sequence of teaching and learning experiences will equip students to engage with, develop, and demonstrate the desired understandings? Use the following sheet to list the key teaching and learning activities in sequence. Code each entry with the appropriate initials of the WHERETO elements.

1. Begin with an entry question (Can the foods you eat cause zits?) to hook students into considering the effects of nutrition on their lives. **H**
2. Introduce the Essential Questions and discuss the culminating unit performance tasks (Chow Down and Eating Action Plan). **W**
3. Note: Key vocabulary terms are introduced as needed by the various learning activities and performance tasks. Students read and discuss relevant selections from the Health textbook to support the learning activities and tasks. As an ongoing activity, students keep a chart of their daily eating and drinking for later review and evaluation. **E**
4. Present concept attainment lesson on the food groups. Then have students practice categorizing pictures of foods accordingly. **E**
5. Introduce the Food Pyramid and identify foods in each group. Students work in groups to develop a poster of the Food Pyramid containing cut-out pictures of foods in each group. Display the posters in the classroom or hallway. **E**
6. Give quiz on the food groups and Food Pyramid (matching format). **E**
7. Review and discuss the nutrition brochure from the USDA. Discussion question: Must everyone follow the same diet to be healthy? **R**
8. Working in cooperative groups, students analyze a hypothetical family's diet (deliberately unbalanced) and make recommendations for improved nutrition. Teacher observes and coaches students as they work. **E-2**
9. Have groups share their diet analyses and discuss as a class. **E, E-2** (Note: Teacher collects and reviews the diet analyses to look for misunderstandings needing instructional attention.)
10. Each student designs an illustrated nutrition brochure to teach younger children about the importance of good nutrition for healthy living and the problems associated with poor eating. This activity is completed outside of class. **E, T**
11. Students exchange brochures with members of their group for a peer assessment based on a criteria list. Allow students to make revisions based on feedback. **R, E-2**
12. Show and discuss the video, "Nutrition and You." Discuss the health problems linked to poor eating. **E**
13. Students listen to, and question, a guest speaker (nutritionist from the local hospital) about health problems caused by poor nutrition. **E**
14. Students respond to written prompt: Describe two health problems that could arise as a result of poor nutrition and explain what changes in eating could help to avoid them. (These are collected and graded by teacher.) **E-2**
15. Teacher models how to read and interpret food label information on nutritional values. Then have students practice using donated boxes, cans, and bottles (empty!). **E**
16. Students work independently to develop the three-day camp menu. Evaluate and give feedback on the camp menu project. Students self- and peer-assess their projects using rubrics. **E-2, T**
17. At the conclusion of the unit, students review their completed daily eating chart and self-assess the healthfulness of their eating. Have they noticed changes? Improvements? Do they notice changes in how they feel and their appearance? **E-2**
18. Students develop a personal "eating action plan" for healthful eating. These are saved and presented at upcoming student-involved parent conferences. **E-2, T**
19. Conclude the unit with student self-evaluation regarding their personal eating habits. Have each student develop a personal action plan for their "healthful eating" goal. **E-2, T**

Figure 7.4
UbD Design Standards

Stage 1—To what extent does the design focus on the big ideas of targeted content?

Consider: Are . . .

- The targeted understandings enduring, based on transferable, big ideas at the heart of the discipline and in need of uncoverage?
- The targeted understandings framed by questions that spark meaningful connections, provoke genuine inquiry and deep thought, and encourage transfer?
- The essential questions provocative, arguable, and likely to generate inquiry around the central ideas (rather than a "pat" answer)?
- Appropriate goals (e.g., content standards, benchmarks, curriculum objectives) identified?
- Valid and unit-relevant knowledge and skills identified?

Stage 2—To what extent do the assessments provide fair, valid, reliable, and sufficient measures of the desired results?

Consider: Are . . .

- Students asked to exhibit their understanding through authentic performance tasks?
- Appropriate criterion-based scoring tools used to evaluate student products and performances?
- Various appropriate assessment formats used to provide additional evidence of learning?
- The assessments used as feedback for students and teachers, as well as for evaluation?
- Students encouraged to self-assess?

Stage 3—To what extent is the learning plan effective and engaging?

Consider: Will the students . . .

- Know where they're going (the learning goals), why the material is important (reason for learning the content), and what is required of them (unit goal, performance requirements, and evaluative criteria)?
- Be hooked—engaged in digging into the big ideas (e.g., through inquiry, research, problem solving, and experimentation)?
- Have adequate opportunities to explore and experience big ideas and receive instruction to equip them for the required performances?
- Have sufficient opportunities to rethink, rehearse, revise, and refine their work based upon timely feedback?
- Have an opportunity to evaluate their work, reflect on their learning, and set goals?

Consider: Is the learning plan . . .

- Tailored and flexible to address the interests and learning styles of all students?
- Organized and sequenced to maximize engagement and effectiveness?

Overall Design—To what extent is the entire unit coherent, with the elements of all three stages aligned?

educators, both novice and veteran, to get in the habit of self-assessing their designs against appropriate criteria. A prevailing norm in our profession seems to be. "If I work hard on planning, it must be good." The UbD Design Standards help to break that norm by providing a means for quality control. They help us validate our curriculum's strengths, while revealing aspects that need improvement.

In addition to using the UbD Design Standards for self-assessment, the quality of the curriculum product (unit plan, performance assessment, course design) is invariably enhanced when teachers participate in a structured peer review in which they examine one another's unit designs and share feedback and suggestions for improvement. Such "critical friend" reviews provide feedback to designers, help teachers internalize the qualities of good design, and offer opportunities to see alternate design models. ("Gee, I never thought about beginning a unit with a problem. I think I'll try that in my next unit.")

Design tools

In addition to the design standards, we have developed and refined a comprehensive set of design tools to support teachers and curriculum developers. This is hard work! We have found that an array of scaffolds—prompts, organizers, idea sheets, and examples—help educators produce higher-quality designs. A full set of these resources is available in the *UbD Professional Development Workbook.*

We think that a good template serves as an intelligent tool. It provides more than a place to write in ideas. It focuses and guides the designer's thinking throughout the design process to make high-quality work more likely. In practice, curriculum designers work from a copy of the template, supported by specific design tools and numerous filled-in examples of good unit designs. In this way, we practice what we preach with students; models and design standards are provided up front to focus designer performance from the start.[1]

But why do we refer to the template, design standards, and corresponding design tools as "intelligent"? Just as a physical tool (e.g., a telescope, an automobile, or a hearing aid) extends human capabilities, an intelligent tool enhances performance on cognitive tasks, such as the design of learning units. For example, an effective graphic organizer, such as a story map, helps students internalize the elements of a story in ways that enhance their reading and writing of stories. Likewise, by routinely using the template and design tools, users will likely develop a mental template of the key ideas presented in this book: the logic of backward design, thinking like an assessor, the facets of understanding, WHERETO, and design standards.

By embodying the Understanding by Design elements in tangible forms (i.e., the template and design tools), we seek to support educators in learning and applying these ideas. Thus, the design tools are like training wheels, providing a steadying influence during those periods of disequilibrium brought on by new ideas that may challenge established and comfortable habits. Once the key ideas of Understanding by Design are internalized, however, and regularly applied, the explicit use of the tools becomes unnecessary, just as the young bicycle rider sheds the training wheels after achieving balance and confidence.

Misconception Alert!

Though the three stages present a logic of design, it does not follow that this is a step-by-step process in actuality. As we argue in Chapter 11, don't confuse the logic of the final product with the messy process of design work. It doesn't matter exactly where you start or how you proceed, *as long as you end up with a coherent design* reflecting the logic of the three stages. The final outline of a smoothly flowing college lecture rarely reflects the back-and-forth (iterative) thought process that went into its creation.

Backward design in action with Bob James

Setting: *We are inside the head of Bob James, a 6th grade teacher at Newtown Middle School, as he begins to design a three-week unit on nutrition. His ultimate design will be the unit provided above in Figure 7.3. But Bob is new to UbD, so his design will unfold and be revised over time. Throughout the book we'll show his thinking—and rethinking—as he considers the full meaning of the template elements.*

Stage 1: Identify desired results

The template asks me to highlight the goals of the unit, and for me that means drawing upon our state standards. In reviewing our standards in health, I found three content standards on nutrition that are benchmarked to this age level:

- Students will understand essential concepts about nutrition.
- Students will understand elements of a balanced diet.
- Students will understand their own eating patterns and ways in which these patterns may be improved.

Using these standards as the starting point, I need to decide what I want my students to take away from the unit. Knowledge and skill are what I have always focused on: knowledge of the food pyramid, the ability to read labels in the store and at home, and so on. Although I've never deliberately thought about *understandings,* per se, I like the concept and think that it will help me focus my teaching and limited class time on the truly important aspects of this unit.

As I think about it, I guess what I'm really after has something to do with an understanding of the elements of good nutrition so students can plan a balanced diet for themselves and others. The big ideas have to do with nutrition and planning meals in a feasible way. Then, the important questions are, So, what is good for you? What isn't? How do you know? What makes it difficult to know and to eat right? (The good taste of junk food makes it difficult!)

This idea is clearly important, because planning nutritious menus is an authentic, lifelong need and a way to apply this knowledge. I'm still a little unclear about what "an understanding" means, though, in this context. I'll need to reflect further on what an understanding is and how it goes beyond specific knowledge and its use. The basic concepts of nutrition are fairly straightforward, after all, as are the skills of menu planning. Does anything in the unit require, then, any in-depth and deliberate *uncoverage*? Are there typical misunderstandings, for example, that I should more deliberately focus on?

Well, as I think about it, I have found that many students harbor the two misconceptions that if food is good for you, it must taste bad; and if it is sold in famous and popular places, it must be okay. One of my goals in this unit is to dispel these myths so that the students won't have an automatic aversion to healthy food and unwittingly eat too much unhealthy stuff. In terms of the potential for engagement—no problem there. Anything having to do with food is a winner with 10- and 11-year-olds. And there are some points to menu planning (such as balancing cost, variety, taste, and dietary needs) that are not at all obvious. This way of thinking about the unit will enable me to better focus on these points.

Stage 2: Determine acceptable evidence

This will be a bit of a stretch for me. Typically in a three- or four-week unit like this one, I give one or two quizzes; have a project, which I grade; and conclude with a unit test (generally multiple choice or matching). Even though this approach to assessment makes grading and justifying the grades fairly easy, I have always felt a bit uneasy that these assessments don't reflect the point of the unit and that the project grade sometimes has less to do with the key ideas and more to do with effort. I think I tend to test what is easy to test instead of assessing for my deeper goals, above and beyond nutritional facts. In fact, one thing that has always disturbed me is that the kids tend to focus on their grades rather than on their learning. Perhaps the way I've used the assessments—more for grading purposes than to help shape and document learning—has contributed somewhat to their attitude.

Now I need to think about what would serve as evidence of the ideas I'm focusing on. After reviewing some examples of performance tasks and discussing "application" ideas with my colleagues, I have decided tentatively on the following task:

> Because we have been learning about nutrition, the camp director at the outdoor education center has asked as to propose a nutritionally balanced menu for our three-day trip to the center later this year. Using the food pyramid guidelines and the nutrition facts on food labels, design a plan for three days, including three meals and three snacks (a.m., p.m., and campfire). Your goal: a tasty and nutritionally balanced menu.

I'm excited about this idea because it asks students to demonstrate what I really want them to take away from the unit. This task also links well with one of our unit projects: to analyze a hypothetical family's diet for a week and propose ways to improve their nutrition. With this task and project in mind, I can now use my quizzes to check students' knowledge of the food groups and food pyramid recommendations, and a lengthier test to check for their understanding of how a nutritionally deficient diet contributes to health problems. Hey! This is one of the better assessment plans I have designed for a unit, and I think that the task will motivate students as well as provide evidence of their understanding.

Stage 3: Plan learning experiences and instruction

This is my favorite part of planning—deciding what activities the students will do during the unit and what resources and materials we'll need for those activities. But according to what I'm learning about backward design, I'll need to think first about what essential knowledge and skills my students will need if they're going to be able to demonstrate in performance the understandings I'm after.

Well, they'll need to know about the different food groups and the types of foods found in each group so that they'll understand the USDA food pyramid recommendations. They'll also need to know about human nutritional needs for carbohydrates, protein, sugar, fat, salt, vitamins, and minerals, and about the various foods that provide them. They'll have to learn about the minimum daily requirements for these nutritional elements and about various health problems that arise from poor nutrition. In terms of skills, they'll have to learn how to read and interpret the nutrition-fact labels on foods and how to scale a recipe up or down, because these skills are necessary for their culminating project—planning healthy menus for camp.

Now for the learning experiences. I'll use resources that I've collected during the past several years—a pamphlet from the USDA on the food groups and the food pyramid recommendations; a wonderful video, "Nutrition for You"; and, of course, our health textbook (which I now plan to use selectively). As I have for the past three years, I'll invite the nutritionist from the local hospital to talk about diet and health and how to plan healthy menus. I've noticed that the kids really pay attention to a real-life user of information they're learning.

My teaching methods will follow my basic pattern—a blend of direct instruction, inductive methods, cooperative-learning group work, and individual activities.

Planning backward to produce this new draft has been helpful. I now can more clearly see and state what knowledge and skills are essential, given my goals for the unit. I'll be able to concentrate on the more important aspects of the topic (and relieve some guilt that I'm not covering everything). It's also interesting to realize that even though some sections of the textbook chapters on nutrition will be especially useful (for instance, the descriptions of health problems arising from poor nutrition), other sections are not as informative as other resources I'll now use (the brochure and the video). In terms of assessment, I now know more clearly what I need to assess using traditional quizzes and tests, and why the performance task and project are needed—to have students demonstrate their understanding. I'm getting a feel for backward design.

Comments on the design process

Notice that the process of developing this draft nutrition unit reveals four key aspects of backward design:

1. The assessments—the performance tasks and related sources of evidence—are thought through prior to the lessons being fully developed. The assessments serve as teaching targets for sharpening the focus of instruction and editing the past lesson plans, because they define in very specific terms what we want students to understand and be able to do. The teaching is then thought of as *enabling* performance. These assessments also guide decisions about what content needs to be emphasized versus that which is not really essential.
2. It is likely that familiar and favorite activities and projects will have to be further modified in light of the evidence needed for assessing targeted standards. For instance, if the apples unit described in the Introduction were planned using this backward design process, we would expect to see revisions in some of the activities to better support the desired results.
3. The teaching methods and resource materials are chosen last, with the teacher keeping in mind the work that students must produce to meet the standards. For example, rather than focusing on cooperative learning because it's a popular strategy, the question from a backward-design perspective becomes, What instructional strategies will be most effective in helping us reach our targets? Cooperative learning may or may not be the best approach, given the particular students and standards.
4. The role of the textbook may shift from being the primary resource to being a support. Indeed, the 6th grade teacher planning the nutrition unit realized the limitations of relying on the text if he is to meet his goals. Given other valuable resources (the USDA materials, the video, and the nutritionist), he no longer felt compelled to cover the book word for word.

This introductory look is intended to present a preliminary sketch of the big picture of a design approach. Bob James will be refining his unit plan (and changing his thinking a few times) as he gains greater insight into understanding, essential questions, valid assessment, and the related learning activities.

A preview

Figure 7.5 presents the key elements of the UbD approach and thus an outline of points to come in the book. In the following chapters we "uncover" this design process, examining its implications for the development and use of assessments, the planning and organization of curriculum, and the selection of powerful methods of teaching. But a few explanatory points about each column in Figure 7.5 are appropriate to prepare you for what is to come throughout the book.

The chart is best read from left to right, one row at a time, to see how the three stages of design might look in practice. An outline of the three-stage design process for each of the three basic elements (the desired results, the assessment evidence, and the learning plan) is highlighted in the column headings. Begin with a key design question; ponder how to narrow the possibilities through intelligent priorities (Design Considerations); self-assess, self-adjust, and finally critique each element of design against appropriate criteria (Filters); and end up with a product that meets appropriate design standards in light of the achievement target (What the Final Design Accomplishes).

In summary, backward design yields greater coherence among desired results, key performances, and teaching and learning experiences, resulting in better student performance—the purpose of design.

Figure 7.5
The UbD Design Matrix

Key Design Questions	Chapters of the Book	Design Considerations	Filters (Design Criteria)	What the Final Design Accomplishes
Stage 1 • What are worthy and appropriate results? • What are the key desired learnings? • What should students come away understanding, knowing, and able to do? • What big ideas can frame all these objectives?	• Chapter 3—Gaining Clarity • Chapter 4—The Six Facets of Understanding • Chapter 5—Essential Questions: Doorways to Understanding • Chapter 6—Crafting Understandings	• National standards • State standards • Local standards • Regional topic opportunities • Teacher expertise and interest	• Focused on big ideas and core challenges	• Unit framed around enduring understandings and essential questions, in relation to clear goals and standards
Stage 2 • What is evidence of the desired results? • In particular, what is appropriate evidence of the desired understanding?	• Chapter 7—Thinking like an Assessor • Chapter 8—Criteria and Validity	• Six facets of understanding • Continuum of assessment types	• Valid • Reliable • Sufficient	• Unit anchored in credible and useful evidence of the desired results
Stage 3 • What learning activities and teaching promote understanding, knowledge, skill, student interest, and excellence?	• Chapter 9—Planning for Learning • Chapter 10—Teaching for Understanding	• Research-based repertoire of learning and teaching strategies • Appropriate and enabling knowledge and skill	Engaging and effective, using the elements of WHERETO: • Where is it going? • Hook the students • Explore and equip • Rethink and revise • Exhibit and evaluate • Tailor to student needs, interests, and styles • Organize for maximum engagement and effectiveness	• Coherent learning activities and teaching that will evoke and develop the desired understandings, knowledge, and skill; promote interest; and make excellent performance more likely

CHAPTER 8

LEARNING OUTCOMES

SETTING DIRECTION WITH INTENDED LEARNING OUTCOMES

MARY E. HUBA AND JANN E. FREED

Badly needed . . . is a set of agreements on what self-regulation in higher education ought to be fundamentally *about* . . . One is the community's own assurance of academic quality. This means first and foremost a predominant focus on the assessment of outcomes and results . . . Focusing on outcomes as the centerpiece of recognition also forces us to address (and eventually develop a satisfactory answer to) legitimate questions about the common meaning of academic awards given in common. What the baccalaureate really is supposed to *mean* in terms of knowledge, skills, or other attributes is a question increasingly asked by both society and ourselves. It is a question that deserves an answer and it is one that in the long run we cannot duck (Ewell, 1994, p. 29).

Making Connections

As you begin to read the chapter, think about the ideas and experiences you've already had that are related to intended learning outcomes . . .

- What are the *essential features* of your *institution* and how do they help shape the ideas, values, and attitudes of your students?
- What are the *essential features* of your *academic program* and how do they help shape the ideas, values, and attitudes of your students?
- What is *unique* about your *institution* and how are your graduates different because of that uniqueness?
- What is *unique* about your *academic program* and, as a result, what unique qualities do your graduates possess?
- What should graduates of your academic program know, understand, and be able to do when they leave the institution?
- How do you as a faculty member contribute to the development of the skills and abilities of your program's graduates?

What else do you know about intended learning outcomes?

What questions do you have about intended learning outcomes?

Reprinted from *Learner-Centered Assessment on College Campuses: Shifting the Focus from Teaching to Learning* (2000), Allyn and Bacon.

Answering the questions in Making Connections is the first step in creating the type of learner-centered environment discussed in Chapters 1 through 3. It is also the first step in helping an institution fulfill its teaching mission effectively. Students change in many ways during their college years. Their ability to think and reason is affected by the college experience (Baxter Magolda, 1996, King & Kitchener, 1994), as are their attitudes, values, aspirations, and self-concepts (Astin, 1993). Considerable research indicates that a variety of environmental factors influence the type of change that occurs, including factors associated with the curriculum, pedagogy, peer group interactions, and faculty attitudes toward students (Astin, 1993). Being clear about the desired outcomes of college can help faculty structure experiences that will lead to those outcomes.

Intended Learning Outcomes

Focusing on student learning requires that we specify the goals or intended outcomes of the experiences students have at our institutions. Intended learning outcomes can be written at a variety of levels, for example, for

- a course,
- an academic program, or
- an entire institution.

Intended learning outcomes describe the kinds of things that students know or can do after instruction that they didn't know or couldn't do before. Formulating such outcomes may require a change of mindset.

For example, if asked, "How would you describe your current teaching goals?" most of us would offer responses similar to the following:

- to provide the best course I can
- to provide a stimulating environment for learning
- to provide opportunities for students to experience the central ideas of my field.

Notice the focus of these goals. Who is the implied key player? Who will provide the best course, the stimulating environment, and the opportunities to experience central ideas? The professor. That's logical in one sense because our goals are important and worth pursuing. However, in learner-centered instruction, we also need to focus on learners in goal-setting. In other words, we need to ask, "If I provide the best possible course for students, creating a stimulating environment for learning with opportunities to explore central ideas,

- What will my students know?
- What will they understand?
- What will they be able to do with their knowledge at the end of the course?"

Our answers to these questions constitute our intended learning outcomes.

Learning outcomes for a course are typically developed by the professor or professors teaching the course. Developing learning outcomes for an institution or an academic program is a task for faculty to complete collectively, and it is a task that takes time and deliberation.

We may use a variety of strategies to develop learning outcomes. For example, as we work together with our colleagues to develop outcomes for an academic program, we may find it helpful to examine existing course descriptions and syllabi in order to review what is currently being taught in our program. Searches of the literature and the World Wide Web can provide us with the learning outcomes of programs at other institutions [e.g., see the University of Colorado outcomes at http://www.colorado.edu/outcomes/ or a list of other internet resources at http://www2.acs.ncsu.edu/UPA/survey/resource.htm. (Schechter, 1999)]. Rogers (1991) suggests that reports from national commissions and professional associations in various disciplines may include desirable learner outcomes. Or we can simply brainstorm about our own ideas and values about student learning.

Reflections

As you create your own meaning from the ideas in this section, begin to think about . . .

- How familiar am I with the concept of intended learning outcomes? How comfortable am I with this concept?
- What are my intended learning outcomes? Have I written them down or are they just in my head?
- What are some of the desired learning outcomes that I want students in my program or my courses to achieve?
- Under what circumstances have I discussed learning outcomes with my colleagues?
- What learning outcomes are considered important in my discipline?

Benefits of Formulating Intended Learning Outcomes

Three benefits of formulating intended learning outcomes are shown in Figure 8.1. Each is discussed below.

Intended learning outcomes form the basis of assessment at the course, program, and institutional levels

Assessment refers to our efforts to evaluate the learning component of all academic and nonacademic programs on campus. We defined assessment as the "process of gathering and discussing information from multiple and diverse sources in order to develop a deep understanding of what students know, understand, and can do with their knowledge as a result of their educational experiences; the process culminates when assessment results are used to improve subsequent learning."

The fundamental question that drives a clearly focused assessment program is a simple one: "Have our graduates learned what we intend them to learn?" This is a learner-centered question, which implies the following:

- As program faculty, we have intentions about what students in the program should learn.
- As program faculty, we develop collective expressions of our intentions in statements of intended learning outcomes.
- As program faculty, we develop curricula and instructional experiences in order to ensure that students have opportunities to learn what we intend.
- Students have experienced learner-centered instruction throughout their years at the institution.

Figure 8.1
Benefits of Formulating Intended Learning Outcomes

Intended learning outcomes

- form the basis of assessment at the course, program, and institutional levels.
- provide direction for all instructional activity.
- inform students about the intentions of the faculty.

To the extent that our instruction is learner-centered, we can assess students in our courses in ways that help students learn while they are being assessed. Well-designed course assessments provide feedback on our important intended outcomes at every step along the way. If the intended outcome of a program is that students critically analyze and interpret information, then during the program, students must participate in assessments that require the critical analysis and interpretation of information. If the intended outcome is that students understand and are able to apply fundamental principles of the discipline, then students must participate in assessments that require the application of those principles.

For example, Julian (1996) describes the way in which eight intended learning outcomes were used in the Speech Communications Department at the University of Tennessee, Knoxville, to design a comprehensive assessment approach in a newly designed capstone course for majors. Faculty developed a matrix in which they mapped eight learning outcomes (write clearly, effectively; speak effectively, intelligently; work constructively in groups; make reasoned decisions; use the library effectively; critically evaluate what is read; sketch rhetorical history and theories; understand theories and perspectives) onto six different assessments (a symposium speech, abstracts, an annotated bibliography, a final paper, an oral critique, and midterm/final exams). All but two of the outcomes were assessed by two or more assessments. This approach gave a clear focus to both the course and the assessment process.

The feedback students receive from assessments should deal directly with the learning to be acquired, whether it be knowledge or skills. In this way, assessments will result in feedback that learners can use, not only to know how well they are doing, but also to improve their performance. If students receive constant feedback that they can use throughout the program, they should perform well on both course and program assessments.

This may be a new view of assessment for many of us because our institutions make minimal demands on us in the area of assessment. Faculty members are required only to submit a final grade for each student. Grades are needed for bureaucratic reasons only—to certify a student's completion of a course and to indicate a student's general level of achievement in the course. In other words, the assessment represented in the grade is used to *monitor* students' levels of achievement. Although the administration undoubtedly assumes that grades are based on the collection of assessment data throughout a course, the collection of data itself is not really required by the institution.

In this book, we contend that the bureaucratic or monitoring aspects of assessment should be secondary to the instructional, diagnostic aspects. For learning to occur in a program, assessments must be employed primarily to give students feedback they can use to improve their performance. The individual professor's intended learning outcomes outline the knowledge, abilities, and skills on which assessments should be based. When assessments measure intended outcomes, students learn better, particularly when they know what the outcomes are.

The benefits of basing assessments on the individual professor's learning outcomes can extend well beyond the individual student. When the professor's goals reflect the intended outcomes developed collectively by faculty at the academic program and institutional levels, assessment that takes place within a course can enhance the effectiveness of the program and of the institution in fulfilling their teaching missions. The teaching function of the institution becomes an effective system of interrelated parts in which the nature and quality of each faculty member's assessment techniques affect the nature and quality of student learning, whether it is assessed at the course, program, or institutional levels.

Intended learning outcomes provide direction for all instructional activity

Because intended learning outcomes form the basis for ongoing assessment, they also form the basis for planning and implementing instruction each time a course meets. Knowing the characteristics that an institution's faculty desire in all graduates *of the institution* helps program faculty know, in part, what students in their program should be like when they complete it. Knowing what students are expected to achieve *at the end of their program* helps individual faculty members decide, in part, what students should achieve at the end of each course. In turn, knowing what students are expected to achieve at the end of a course helps us decide what students should achieve at the end of each section of the course, or indeed, at the end of each class period.

In other words, a learner-centered approach to teaching helps us develop a new mindset as we think about and plan our courses. No longer do we prepare courses or lessons by asking, "What material do I want to cover?" Rather, the organizing question becomes, "What do I want students to learn in the course?" or "What do I want students to learn today (or this week)?"

Answering these questions leads us to consider what content should be covered during a particular time period. It also prompts us to consider the ways in which students should be able to *use* the content. This in turn leads to a consideration of the kind of experiences students must have in the course or during the class period in order to be able to know and do what we expect.

Intended learning outcomes inform students about the intentions of the faculty

Perhaps the most important role of intended outcomes is to reveal to students the intentions of the faculty. When students know the goals of an institution, an academic program, or a course, they are able to make more informed decisions about whether the institution, program, or course will meet their needs. They are also in a better position to profit from the experiences they have in the settings they choose.

King (1999) points out that, for students, attending college is like putting together the pieces of a jigsaw puzzle without having the picture on the box to guide them. In her metaphor, the puzzle pieces are students' many collegiate experiences, both in and outside courses. The picture on the box is the kind of person we hope our students become as revealed in our intended learning outcomes.

> Clearly, for both educational and ethical reasons, we need to share this picture with our students and explicitly communicate the knowledge, skills, and attitudes we hope they will acquire as a result of the collegiate experiences. And as we go along, we need to ask them to look at this picture from different angles, in different lights, and from among different groups of people. We should also prepare them to revisit the question of the type of person they wish to become and the type of life they wish to lead (p. 3).

Thus, it is important for students to know our intended learning outcomes, and it is important for us to know theirs. In a learner-centered environment, we should seek to know students' goals so that we can help them achieve them within the context of the course or program.

The intended learning outcomes of the institution or program can be revealed to students in documents such as the catalog or other admissions material. The intended outcomes of a course should always be included in course syllabi that are distributed to students at the beginning of the course. Sharing outcomes helps students develop a sense of direction as they participate in class, study, and complete assignments. Learning outcomes can also serve as a basis for ongoing self-assessment as the course develops. Students can review the outcomes, asking themselves whether or not they have achieved them.

Reflections

As you create your own meaning from the ideas in this section, begin to think about . . .

- What would I have to do differently if intended learning outcomes formed the basis of assessment in my courses?
- What would I have to do differently if intended learning outcomes formed the basis of all instructional activity in my courses?
- How would my students react if I shared with them a list of my intended learning outcomes?
- How would my students react if I asked what they hoped to learn from the course?

Characteristics of Effective Intended Learning Outcomes

Figure 8.2 summarizes the characteristics of effective learning outcomes. Each of them is discussed in a following section.

Intended learning outcomes are student-focused rather than professor-focused

"What will my students know? What will they understand? What will they be able to do with their knowledge at the end of the course?" When we answer these questions with sentences that begin, "Students should be able to . . . ," we have formulated intended learning outcomes. With those in hand, we can intentionally go about the business of helping students achieve them. Intended learning outcomes provide direction for both us and for our students. They establish the basis for assessment.

The following intended outcomes, taken from a variety of major disciplines, are examples of goals that have been formulated to focus on student learning. They describe what students should know, understand, or be able to do with their knowledge at the end of a course or program.

Students will

- organize ideas in a way that increases the effectiveness of a message.
- analyze and interpret qualitative and quantitative social science research data.
- work effectively on problem-solving teams.
- make decisions consistent with moral and ethical principles.
- develop interior design solutions using creative problem-solving techniques.
- develop an erosion control policy based on plant, soil, water, and climate principles.

Intended learning outcomes focus on the learning resulting from an activity rather than on the activity itself

A learning outcome that reads, "Students will study at least one non-literary genre of art," describes a curricular experience that students will have, rather than the learning outcome that will result. We should ask, "If students study at least one non-literary genre of art, what will they know, what will they understand, and what will they be able to do with their knowledge?" Possible responses that would be appropriate can be found in two of the intended outcomes for the general education program at The College of St. Scholastica (The College of St. Scholastica, 1999).

Figure 8.2
Characteristics of Effective Intended Learning Outcomes

Effective statements of intended learning outcomes

- are student-focused rather than professor-focused.
- focus on the learning resulting from an activity rather than on the activity itself.
- reflect the institution's mission and the values it represents.
- are in alignment at the course, academic program, and institutional levels.
- focus on important, non-trivial aspects of learning that are credible to the public.
- focus on skills and abilities central to the discipline and based on professional standards of excellence.
- are general enough to capture important learning but clear and specific enough to be measurable.
- focus on aspects of learning that will develop and endure but that can be assessed in some form now.

Reflections

As you create your own meaning from the ideas in these sections, begin to think about . . .

- How can my colleagues and I make the intended learning outcomes of our *program* more focused on student learning?
- How can I make the intended learning outcomes of my *courses* more focused on student learning?
- What are the most effective activities that I use in my courses?
- What do I expect students to learn from each of them?

- The student will arrive at an analytical and reasoned appreciation of a specific art form.
- The student will be able to communicate the appreciation to others either in written or verbal form or in the artistic medium itself.

Intended learning outcomes reflect the institution's mission and the values it represents

Intended outcomes that we develop at the course, program, or institutional level should reflect our institutional mission. This assertion may seem surprising. Mission statements used to be tired documents, stored in file cabinets, pulled out and dusted off periodically for special occasions such as accreditation reviews. They were largely irrelevant to daily life at the institution, and as faculty, none of us would ever view our activities as being in any way circumscribed by the institutional mission.

Today, however, as the population of available students declines, institutions are struggling to attract students to their programs and to operate with declining resources. At virtually all institutions, this situation has forced a discussion about the institution's "competitive edge," what makes it unique, what makes it special. An increased emphasis on developing a clear and focused mission has resulted. Those things that the institution professes to achieve within its unique environment and with the particular resources it has available have important implications for educational programs and for the intended outcomes that faculty develop.

For example, the missions of The College of St. Scholastica, Babson College, Rutgers University, and Southern West Virginia Community and Technical College are shown in Figures 8.3, 8.4, 8.5, and 8.6, respectively. A review of the missions reveals that the institutions differ somewhat in focus. The College of St. Scholastica is a Catholic liberal arts institution, Babson College is an institution that prepares leaders for the business world, Rutgers is a state-sponsored land-grant research institution, and Southern West Virginia Community and Technical College is a two-year institution that provides vocational/technical programs. Although all these institutions focus on common aspects of students' intellectual development (e.g., communication skills, critical thinking), their missions reveal differences in educational values, and these differences are reflected in their learning outcomes.

For example, The College of St. Scholastica purports to stress "intellectual and moral preparation for responsible living and meaningful work. . . . The entire College is committed to . . . requiring students to meet rigorous academic standards, to broaden the scope of their knowledge, and to be accountable to both self and society." The general education outcomes of The College of St. Scholastica address learning in seven areas: problem solving, value-based decision making, social responsibility, effective communication, disciplinary understanding, the aesthetic response, and living with diversity. Some of these areas are those that all baccalaureate degree-granting institutions have in common (e.g., problem solving and communication). However, other areas in the general education outcomes (e.g., value-based decision making and social responsibility) focus on aspects of personal development related to morality and responsibility. Figure 8.3 presents the college's learning outcomes in the areas of problem solving, value-based decision making, and social responsibility.

Figure 8.3
The College of St. Scholastica Mission and General Education Outcomes

Mission

The College of St. Scholastica is an independent, coeducational comprehensive college with programs in the liberal arts and sciences and professional career fields. Founded in the Catholic intellectual tradition and shaped by the Benedictine heritage, the College stresses intellectual and moral preparation for responsible living and meaningful work. The curriculum serves the Mission of the College by providing undergraduate and graduate education that is grounded in the liberal arts and sciences. The entire College is committed to an educational process requiring students to meet rigorous academic standards, to broaden the scope of their knowledge, and to be accountable to both self and society. The College has a special commitment to bring its Mission to the people in the region through programs and services.

General Education

The General Education program at the College seeks to broaden students' grasp of the accumulated wisdom of the past so that the challenges of the present—racism, global conflict, injustice, dehumanization, spiritual emptiness—may be met with wisdom, faith and imagination. Integrated with their professional studies, General Education courses remind students that their professional lives will be touched, complicated, even shaped by these larger issues. The mission of General Education at The College of St. Scholastica is to help students envision the connection between the practice of their profession and the practice of their humanity.

General Education Outcomes

1. Outcome: Problem solving

   Problem solving is a process that incorporates the ability to analyze a situation; select, find, and evaluate appropriate information; and create one or more possible solutions to improve/correct the situation. It requires observation, information gathering, critical thinking, and communication skills, Problem solving is required in all academic disciplines and employment situations a student will face. A general education will provide students the opportunity to analyze and improve their problem solving skills.

   The student will:

   A. analyze a situation (either real or hypothetical) to identify a problem;

   B. use multiple resources to gain additional information regarding the problem;

   C. develop a procedure to solve the problem using a sufficient knowledge base;

   D. propose and critique a viable solution to the problem;

   E. communicate the problem statement, the solution steps and the eventual outcomes.

2. Outcome: Value-based decision making

   Broadly conceived, values have to do with ideas, motives, and standards that a society considers good and essential for sustaining life. Making decisions based on values involves developing analytical skills and moral reasoning, understanding the sources of our personal and community value assumptions, and fostering the disposition and capacity to learn from the insights and experiences of others who perceive the world differently. Ultimately it involves making decisions to act based on values which are well suited to achieving well-being for the individual and the community and the environments on which they depend.

   The student will:

   A. understand his/her own value system and how these values have been influenced by his/her personal experiences and decisions;

Figure 8.3 (*Continued*)
The College of St. Scholastica Mission and General Education Outcomes

B. differentiate between his/her own personal values and the value systems of others;

C. appraise personal and communal values in the light of new knowledge, recent experience, and insight;

D. defend value-based decisions as ultimately serving the common good.

3. Outcome: Social responsibility

   As a Catholic and Benedictine institution, the college has a particular obligation to share with students why it believes in the worth and dignity of all persons, why it places importance on exhibiting hospitality toward those in need, and why it works for peace and justice. Equally important is helping students to be better informed citizens who take the responsibility of citizenship seriously, for a democratic society is dependent upon the active participation of all of its people.

   The student will:

   A. identify specific issues that call for social responsibility;

   B. evaluate the complexity of social justice issues;

   C. evaluate differing points of view on social responsibility;

   D. evaluate the moral and social obligations to respond to injustice and to work for social change;

   E. understand the responsibilities of citizenship;

   F. demonstrate a beginning commitment to active citizenship.

4. Outcome: Effective Communication . . .
5. Outcome: Disciplinary Understanding . . .
6. Outcome: The Aesthetic Response . . .
7. Outcome: Living with Diversity . . .

(The College of St. Scholastica, 1999)

Alternatively, Babson College (Figure 8.4) focuses on leadership development in a changing world with a particular emphasis on "entrepreneurial initiative." As a result, Babson College's competency areas include leadership, teamwork, and creativity.

Rutgers (Figure 8.5) seeks to prepare students to be responsible citizens and productive contributors to society. Because it is a comprehensive, multi-campus, state university with a wide variety of majors, the institution has adopted learning outcomes that are broadly stated goals defining "common curricular ground" uniting the university. They are grouped in three areas: intellectual and communication skills; understanding human behavior, society, and the natural environment; and responsibilities of the individual in society.

Finally, Southern West Virginia Community and Technical College prepares students for further education or for work and career experiences. Its general education goals are similar to those of the baccalaureate degree-granting institutions above. However, in each of its divisions, the general education goals are interpreted as intended student learning outcomes that reflect the emphasis of the division. As Figure 8.6 shows, students enrolled in the Allied Health Division in programs like Nursing, Medical Laboratory Technology, or Radiologic Technology are expected to be able to communicate effectively with fellow health professionals and with patients and their families. They are expected to apply their inquiry and critical-thinking skills as they use technology in their field. They are also expected to develop a commitment to the continuing education that will be a fundamental component of their professional lives.

Figure 8.4
Babson College Mission and Competencies

Mission

Babson's mission is to educate innovative leaders capable of anticipating, initiating, and managing change. The undergraduate program carries out this mission by developing responsible and effective professionals who are broadly educated, think creatively and analytically, and take entrepreneurial initiative.

(Babson College, 1998, p. 23)

Competencies

- **Rhetoric**—The ability to communicate effectively in speech and writing is essential in the business world.
- **Numeracy**—Effectiveness in quantitative work is vital in nearly all areas of business, and helps improve the ability to think creatively and analytically.
- **Ethics and social responsibility**—Awareness and development of ethics is a foundation for a successful business career. Volunteer work and giving back to the community are key to personal development.
- **International and multicultural perspectives**—Exposure to different cultures is important in an increasingly global world of business and personal relationships.
- **Leadership/teamwork/creativity**—Learning to lead within the structure of a team is a crucial element of success in business today, as is creative entrepreneurial thinking.

(Babson College, 1998, p. 4)

Figure 8.5
Rutgers University Mission and University-Wide Learning Goals

Mission

As the sole comprehensive public research university in the New Jersey system of higher education and the state's land-grant institution. Rutgers University has the mission of instruction, research, and service. Among the principles the university recognizes in carrying out this three-fold mission are the following:

- Rutgers has the prime responsibility in the state to conduct fundamental and applied research; to train scholars, researchers, and professionals; and to make knowledge available to students, scholars, and the general public.
- Rutgers should maintain its traditional strength in the arts and sciences, while at the same time developing such new professional and career-oriented programs as are warranted by public interest, social need, and employment opportunities.
- Rutgers will continually seek to make its educational programs accessible to an appropriately broad student body.
- Rutgers is committed to extending its resources and knowledge to a variety of publics, and bringing special expertise and competence to bear on the solution of public problems.

(Rutgers University, 1998, p. 1.10)

Figure 8.5 (*Continued*)
Rutgers University Mission and University-Wide Learning Goals

University-Wide Learning Goals

The goals define the common curricular ground that unites the university. They are purposefully broad so that the various campuses, colleges, and schools can continue to develop their unique identities through varying ways in which the goals are met, given the mission of the academic unit. They allow for the multiple creative implementation methods that can be tailored to different types of student and faculty strengths and interests.

The goals define the skills and knowledge that all Rutgers students will acquire to support their development as responsible citizens and as productive contributors to society in their workplaces and in their intellectual, cultural, and social endeavors. The goals are grouped in three areas. Intellectual and communication skills are the basic skills necessary for acquisition, analysis, and communication of information. These skills include critical thinking, communication skills, mathematical reasoning analysis, scientific inquiry, and information and computer literacy. Goals in the area of understanding human behavior, society, and the natural environment focus on the major areas of knowledge necessary to function effectively in our society. These include historical understanding, multicultural and international understanding, understanding of literary and artistic expression, understanding the bases of individual and social behavior, and understanding of the physical and biological world. Goals in the area of responsibilities of the individual in society address the skills and knowledge essential to effective citizenship in a democratic society and to ethical social functioning. These include citizenship education and social and ethical awareness.

(Rutgers University, 1998, p. 3.9)

Figure 8.6
Southern West Virginia Community and Technical College Mission and Learning Outcomes

Mission

Southern West Virginia Community and Technical College is a comprehensive community college located in a rural environment. The College strives to fulfill current and future higher educational and vocational/technical needs of southern West Virginia, its service area, and beyond. Our College emphasizes student-oriented, transferable learning, enabling students to achieve work, career, and personal success.

Our College provides high quality, affordable, student-friendly, and easily accessible educational services. We are highly effective and flexible in responding to state and community demands, and in adapting to a global socio-economic system.

(Southern West Virginia Community and Technical College, 1998a)

General Education Goals

Southern West Virginia Community and Technical College is committed to providing a general education program that helps students develop the qualities and skills associated with college-educated adults. Southern's general education program promotes the development of independent, critical and conceptual thinking skills and those skills necessary for the effective communication of one's thoughts. Southern's general education program provides students with an integrated view of knowledge and prepares them for their role as productive and responsible members of society.

Figure 8.6 (*Continued*)
Southern West Virginia Community and Technical College Mission and Learning Outcomes

Students who have completed the general education requirements of an associate degree will gain the competencies to understand, be effective, aware and have sufficient knowledge in the following:

Critical Thinking Skills
Oral and Written Communication Skills
Mathematical Skills/Competencies
Informational Access/Literacy Skills
Scientific Inquiry and Research Skills
A Cultural, Artistic and Global Perspective

(Southern West Virginia Community and Technical College, 1998b, p. 4)

Intended Student Learning Outcomes in the Division of Allied Health

The Division of Allied Health is committed to delivering the highest quality education using state of the art technology to all students enrolled in allied health programs. Students pursuing an associate degree or certificate will maintain the high standards set forth by their chosen profession. Primary to the success of the student is the ability to think critically and apply decision making skills appropriately. Analysis, synthesis, and evaluation of knowledge obtained in specific allied health programs is a vital link in the future success of the student.

All students enrolled in allied health courses will be required to possess excellent communication skills, both written and oral. Students will be able to effectively communicate with peers, faculty, members of the health care community, patients and their families. Additionally, communication and research through the use of modem technology is essential to success in a global society. Scientific inquiry and research skills are integral components of all allied health professions.

Students will be cognizant of diverse cultures and populations both locally and abroad . . .

A strong belief in life-long education will be instilled in the student from the first class throughout the program. Qualities of the allied health professional include staying abreast of current trends and changes through continued education.

(Southern West Virginia Community and Technical College, 1998b, pp. 10–11)

Reflections

As you create your own meaning from the ideas in this section, begin to think about . . .

- When was the last time my colleagues and I reviewed our institution's mission?
- What values does the mission represent?
- What implications do those values have for our program and courses?

Intended learning outcomes are in alignment at the course, academic program, and institutional levels

The intended learning outcomes of a program or course should be compatible with the institution's intended outcomes—if they exist. The faculty and administration at all institutions expect that students will know more and be more skilled when they leave the institution than when they entered. However, not all institutions have formulated institution-wide learner-centered outcomes that describe what graduates should know and be able to do. As reflected in the previous section, the process of formulating institution-wide outcomes has taken place intentionally and with broad faculty input at some institutions. Typically, these intended outcomes address the outcomes of the general education portion of the institutional program because this is the component of the curriculum that all students experience in common.

Not all institutions have formulated learner-centered outcomes or have even considered doing so. But as discussed in Chapter 1, external forces such as legislatures and accrediting associations have prompted this approach by requiring institutions to conduct assessments of student learning. All institutions have missions, a developing sense of uniqueness, and some form of a general education program. These factors should be taken into account when formulating program and course outcomes.

Just as institutional faculty should consider the appropriateness of developing common learner-centered outcomes for all students, so academic program faculty should consider developing discipline-related goals or intended learning outcomes for the students in their program. Intended learning outcomes at the program level should reflect the type of knowledge and skills expected in members of the program's discipline, but they should be compatible with and support institutional outcomes. The intended outcomes of courses should be compatible with academic program and institutional outcomes.

This relationship is displayed in Figure 8.7 which is an offshoot of the early work of Spady (W. Spady, personal communication, October 28, 1998). In designing course outcomes, we start first with the broad outcomes expected of all students in the institution. We then work backward to design academic program outcomes that are in harmony with them. Finally, we design course outcomes that will lead to the achievement of both program and institutional outcomes.

On the other hand, when the program is delivered, students experience the system in reverse. They first participate in experiences that address lesson outcomes. The learning that results from these experiences accumulates as students proceed through the courses and other experiences in the program. When the curriculum is designed so that it provides a coherent set of experiences leading

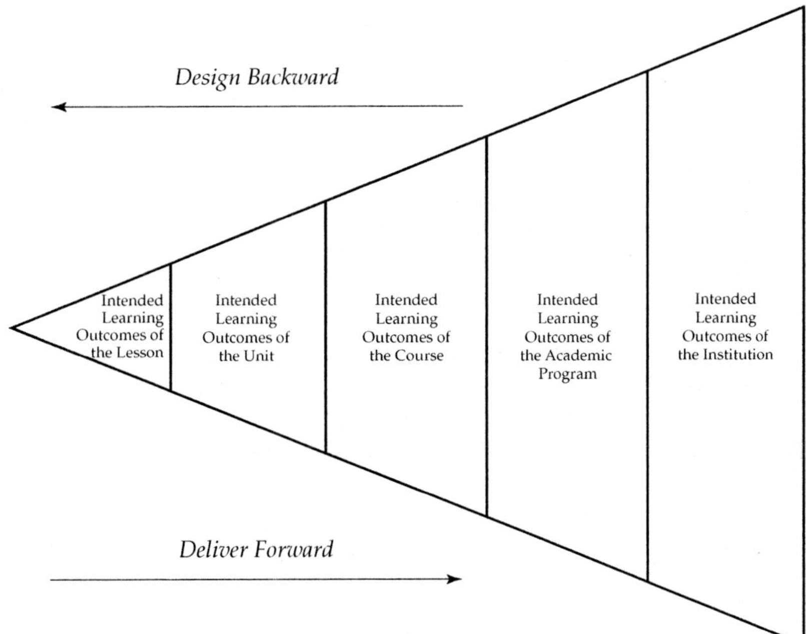

Figure 8.7
Plan for Designing and Delivering Learning Outcomes

to the development of desired knowledge and skills, students show increasing levels of sophistication and integration of skills as they progress through the program. By the end of their college years, they should have achieved both academic program learning outcomes and institutional outcomes.

Figure 8.8 shows examples of institution-wide, program area, and course outcomes that address the topic of environmental awareness. The institutional outcome is a broadly stated learning outcome addressing students' understanding of physical and biological properties of the environment. This outcome could be achieved in general education science courses by students in many different major disciplines.

In some cases, achievement in a major discipline will reinforce and deepen students' understanding in an area addressed in an institutional outcome. For example, the academic program outcome shown in Figure 8.8 represents the type of achievement expected of graduates who major in Horticulture. It is compatible with the institution-wide outcome that addresses understanding of the physical and biological properties of the environment, but it is much more specific in its focus on the discipline of Horticulture. It addresses student learning in the area of biotic and abiotic stresses and their relationship to plant development, and it also focuses on sensitivity to environmental concerns when reducing stresses. This is a culminating learning outcome of a major program, and more than one course in the curriculum would contribute to the achievement of this learning outcome.

The final outcome in Figure 8.8 addresses one aspect of the learning that might take place in a Horticulture course on Environmental Issues, that of the responsibility of the individual in the sustainable management of energy, soil, water, and plants. The learning outcome is narrowly focused, but it is compatible with both the academic program outcome and the institution-wide outcome. For Horticulture students, achieving this course outcome contributes to the achievement of program and institution-wide outcomes as well.

A program's outcomes should also address the general abilities and skills which are used in all academic disciplines, and they should reflect the unique ways in which they are applied in the program. For example, communication skills are desired in all students, but the way in which physicists communicate in their discipline is somewhat different from the way in which teacher education students communicate in theirs. Students in the arts will learn to communicate somewhat differently from students in engineering. This is illustrated in Figure 8.9.

Figure 8.9 presents an institution-wide outcome in the area of oral and written communication skills, followed by program outcomes in the area of communication for the majors of Political Science and Psychology. Notice that one focuses on using communication skills to express the ideas of the discipline, whereas the other focuses on communicating in the manner of the discipline.

Figure 8.8
Relationship Among Institutional, Program, and Course Outcomes: Example 1

Institutional Outcome

Students will understand the physical and biological properties of the environment and how these properties are interlinked within ecological systems.

Academic Program Outcome (Horticulture)

Students will recognize common biotic and abiotic stresses, their potential effects on plants at various stages of plant development, and options for reduction of stresses with minimal disturbance to the environment and human beings (Department of Horticulture, 1996).

Course Outcome (Environmental Issues)

Students will be able to articulate the responsibility of the individual in the sustainable management of energy, soil, water, and plants.

Figure 8.9
Relationship Among Institutional, Program, and Course Outcomes: Example 2

Institutional Outcome

Students will be able to speak and write effectively.

Academic Program Outcome	Academic Program Outcome
(Political Science) Students can articulate principles and concepts of the discipline of political science (Department of Political Science, 1996).	*(Psychology)* Students can speak and write effectively in the discourse of psychology (Department of Psychology, 1996).
Course Outcome	**Course Outcome**
(Current Issues in U.S. Foreign Policy) Students can make an accurate and engaging oral presentation analyzing one current issue in American foreign policy.	*(Psychological Measurement)* Students can prepare a written summary and interpretation of standardized test results.

The course outcomes in Figure 8.9 list the type of communication that might be typical for professionals in each field. The course outcome for Political Science addresses the ability to make an accurate and engaging oral presentation on a current issue, whereas the course outcome for Psychology addresses the development of an understandable and useful written report of standardized test results. It is clear that members of both disciplines need excellent communication skills, but the content and sometimes the format of their communication will differ.

When the intended course outcomes in an academic program are compatible with institutional and program outcomes, those of us who teach the courses—individually and collectively—are at the heart of a system that intentionally and effectively helps students develop desired characteristics. This system becomes more effective when, at the program level, we examine program and course outcomes to decide how to best deliver the curriculum, including who will teach which courses and how.

For example, we may wish to structure experiences in the curriculum in order to intentionally help students integrate general skills with discipline-related knowledge in the program. We should sequence courses and establish appropriate prerequisites in such a way that student learning develops in a planned fashion.

In accomplishing this, it would be helpful for all of us to reflect on our individual strengths and weaknesses and determine the ways in which we are best able to contribute to the development of student learning. Those of us who are good communicators may take (or be given) the responsibility for emphasizing communication skills in the courses we teach in the discipline. Others may emphasize critical thinking and problem solving. This may be done informally, or it could be formalized by designating certain courses as "communication intensive" or "problem-solving intensive" (Green & Mullen, 1993).

Attending to the development of general skills and abilities may also cause us to design new organizational structures. At Alverno College, a faculty member is not only a member of an academic department, but he/she is also a member of an interdisciplinary group focused on one of the eight abilities the institution seeks to have students develop (Alverno College Faculty, 1992; Hakel, 1997). In a system with dearly formulated learning outcomes, each course and each faculty member can be envisioned in terms of their role in a curricular system of experiences that are interrelated and outcome-oriented.

It is possible for us to pursue learner-centered instruction without consideration of program and institutional outcomes, and we might be quite effective in helping students develop certain skills

Reflections

As you create your own meaning from the ideas in this section, begin to think about . . .

- Have faculty at my institution formulated intended learning outcomes for all students?
- If so, what implications do they have for the outcomes in my program or courses?
- How would the intended learning outcomes of our program and courses differ if my faculty colleagues and I designed them backward, starting with institutional outcomes?
- As we deliver the curriculum forward, how are our courses helping students reach important institutional or program learning goals?

and abilities. However, as Chapters 1 and 3 point out, the ability of higher education institutions to serve society implies that faculty work in concert, developing a common vision of the desired qualities that our graduates should possess and a coherent curriculum to help students achieve them.

Intended learning outcomes focus on important, non-trivial aspects of learning that are credible to the public

One pitfall to avoid in formulating intended outcomes is focusing on easy-to-measure, but relatively unimportant outcomes like, "Students will recall the stages of mitosis." This can happen when we develop learning outcomes by carving up the content of the discipline into ever smaller pieces. Recalling the stages of mitosis may be important for some students, but it is probably more appropriate as an intended outcome of a class period than it is as a course or program outcome.

Statements of intended outcomes that "decompose" the content of the discipline into smaller parts are referred to by Erwin (1991) as "subject matter objectives" (p. 37). They tend to result from traditional, behavioral approaches to formulating learning goals and objectives that were advocated in the 1950s and 1960s. At that time, Bloom (1956) and others (Krathwohl, Bloom, & Masia, 1964; Mager, 1962) developed taxonomies of educational objectives and guidelines for developing them that encouraged teachers to think about student learning in terms of its cognitive, affective, and psychomotor components. The cognitive component focuses on the development of the intellect and related intellectual skills. The affective component focuses on the development of values and attitudes. The psychomotor area refers to the development of muscular skills and neuromuscular coordination.

Although it is helpful to think about these aspects of learning separately, it is important to remember that when students are engaged in learning, the cognitive, affective, and psychomotor aspects of their learning are inseparable (King & Baxter Magolda, 1996). All learning—even the acquisition of a new fact—requires the integration of new material with existing knowledge and is achieved through complex mental processes (Resnick & Resnick, 1992). Learning is influenced by feelings and attitudes, and in some cases, it involves feedback from muscular coordination. Thus, statements of intended outcomes at the course, program, and institutional levels should focus on desired outcomes with all of their complexities. They should address the integrated skills and abilities that are valued by educated people (Sizer, 1992; Wiggins, 1989).

This means that statements of desired outcomes should focus on the way the outcomes of the general education component of a student's program intersect with those in the major discipline. In general education, faculty help students to develop their skills and abilities in areas like communication and critical thinking. However, such abilities cannot develop in isolation from disciplinary content. One can learn effective communication and critical thinking skills only if one has something to communicate and think critically about. Furthermore, faculty should be helping students to communicate and think critically as members of their discipline. Process outcomes and content outcomes must be developed together, and the focus should be on *using* content effectively, not memorizing it. [See Chapter 7 for a discussion of Kurfiss's (1988) distinction between declarative knowledge and procedural knowledge.]

Marzano, Pickering, and McTighe (1993) have identified five types of learning outcomes that comprise the processes they believe will promote lifelong learning. The first category is that of complex thinking standards and includes students' ability to use various reasoning strategies and to translate "issues and situations into manageable tasks that have a clear purpose" (p. 19). The second is the area of information processing. Outcomes to be addressed in this area include using information-gathering techniques and resources, interpreting and synthesizing information, assessing the value of information, and knowing how and where additional information is needed. The third category is that of effective communication and includes communicating with diverse audiences in a variety of ways for different purposes. The fourth category addresses collaboration/cooperation outcomes, including effective performance in group situations, using interpersonal skills.

The final category, habits of mind, is concerned with students' ability to control their own thought processes and behavior. Marzano et al. (1993) include three types of outcomes in this category.

Self-Regulation

a. Is aware of own thinking.
b. Makes effective plans.
c. Is aware of and uses necessary resources.
d. Is sensitive to feedback.
e. Evaluates the effectiveness of own actions.

Critical Thinking

f. Is accurate and seeks accuracy.
g. Is clear and seeks clarity.
h. Is open-minded.
i. Restrains impulsivity.
j. Takes a position when the situation warrants it.
k. Is sensitive to the feelings and level of knowledge of others.

Creative Thinking

l. Engages intensely in tasks even when answers or solutions are not immediately apparent.
m. Pushes the limits of own knowledge and abilities.
n. Generates, trusts, and maintains own standards of evaluation.
o. Generates new ways of viewing a situation outside the boundaries of standard conventions (pp. 23–24).

King and Baxter Magolda (1996) support the importance of developing habits of mind in the college curriculum.

> Developing thinking skills is only one aspect of achieving educational success in college. . . . For example, effective problem solving requires such attributes as awareness of the problem, the ability to gather and interpret relevant information, a willingness to try overcoming obstacles by making the best decision, and the personal "wherewithall" to implement the desired solution (p. 167).
>
> Do students have the self-discipline to exert the appropriate amount of "time on task," the perseverance to see a problem or project through to completion, and the personal maturity to take responsibility for completing projects in a timely fashion. . . . The affective or personal development dimensions that affect student learning are painfully clear when the answer to questions like these is "no" (p. 168).

Some people react negatively to the suggestion that learning outcomes should focus on general abilities, "habits of mind," or attitudinal aspects of learning. They fear that a "process" focus will minimize the amount of content that students learn. However, these individuals may be confusing the amount of content that students *are exposed to* with the amount that they *actually internalize.* In traditional teaching, students are exposed to a great deal of content by professors, but the typical lament of professors is that students don't seem to understand or retain it. In courses in which students are expected to *use* content in meaningful ways, the amount of content internalized and recalled should actually increase.

Furthermore, students with little knowledge of the discipline will not be effective when they attempt to employ general abilities like communication, reasoning, and so forth. As Resnick and Resnick (1992) point out, the ability of individuals to think, reason, and make judgments like experts in the discipline depends on the amount of content they possess. Students who have mastered more content will be better able to think like members of their discipline. Thus, the focus is not on less content but rather is on what students can do with the content they have learned. Recall the problem of "inert knowledge" (Whitehead, 1929), stemming from the difficulty individuals have in knowing when, how, and where to use the information they acquire, When formulating intended learning outcomes, we should integrate the knowledge of essential facts and concepts with the development of habits of mind that will require their use.

This approach is compatible with a holistic model of college student development, one that blurs distinctions between cognitive and noncognitive achievements (Ewell, 1994). Outcomes that integrate content and thinking processes, as well as cognitive and affective components of learning, are referred to by Erwin (1991) as "developmental objectives" (p. 39). As Ewell points out, the conceptual foundations for an integrated developmental approach have been well established in the student development theories of Perry (1970), Chickering (1969), and Kohlberg (1981). The integrated developmental approach is becoming increasingly characteristic of curricular objectives on college campuses (Erwin, 1991).

The following intended outcomes are examples of learning outcomes that integrate intellectual skills and the use of disciplinary content.

- Students will reason using simplified economic models such as supply and demand, marginal analysis, benefit–cost analysis, and comparative advantage (Department of Economics, 1996).
- The student will be able to design and conduct original and independent biological research (Department of Biology, 1998).
- The student will be able to identify and present the implications of the various ethical and legal decisions facing Human Resources professionals and substantiate points of view with credible reasoning (Department of Human Resources Management, 1998).

Reflections

As you create your own meaning from the ideas in this section, begin to think about . . .

- If a panel of educated people were to review the intended learning outcomes that my faculty colleagues and I have developed for our program and courses, which ones would they agree are important?
- How do my colleagues and I focus on using knowledge rather than simply acquiring it?
- Which of our intended learning outcomes reflect an understanding that students are whole persons and not just minds?

These outcomes integrate intellectual and affective elements.

- Students will have greater respect for different races and cultures as their knowledge about them increases.
- As team members, students will reveal their commitment to the team through the effective use of group problem-solving techniques.

Intended learning outcomes focus on skills and abilities central to the discipline and based on professional standards of excellence

Intended learning outcomes should be credible to members of the profession in which they are formulated. Many professors in disciplines like the arts perceive that an outcomes approach to assessment is a reductionistic attempt to "quantify" the elusive and important qualities they seek to develop in students. They feel that the "special quality" that makes a painting, a sculpture, or a landscape artistic is difficult to describe in observable terms, let alone quantify.

It is true that there is no need to quantify the unquantifiable in assessment. On the other hand, if faculty in the arts are going to participate in assessment that promotes learning, they must attempt to describe and measure the quality or qualities that make a work artistic, and their description should be convincing to members of their disciplines. Even though it is difficult to articulate and assess what is really central in the arts, it is critically important to do so. It doesn't make sense to simply "count" superficial aspects of artistic endeavor just to fulfill a requirement to assess.

Intended learning outcomes should be compatible with the best thinking in the discipline in terms of what is important to know and how information in the discipline should be taught. Most disciplines have developed standards for student learning. The National Council of Teachers of Mathematics is a notable example. In recent years, this organization has developed standards that focus on conceptual understanding, problem solving, and the use of mathematics in the context of application rather than simply on the acquisition of procedural information leading to right answers. We should all consider turning to our professional associations for guidance in developing learner outcomes.

Intended learning outcomes are general enough to capture important learning but clear and specific enough to be measurable

Attaining an appropriate level of generality or specificity is often a difficult challenge when we begin formulating intended outcomes. As a basic principle, institution-wide outcomes will be more general than academic program outcomes. Academic program outcomes will be more general than individual course outcomes, and within a course, we may formulate day-to-day intended outcomes that are more specific than the course outcomes they support. If a professor's course outcome is that teacher education students will learn to use instructional media effectively, the specific outcome for today or this week may be that students will learn to make and use transparencies that enhance the effectiveness of instruction.

Even though program and institutional outcomes will be stated more generally than course or lesson outcomes, they should still be framed in measurable terms. For example, the outcome, "Students will be able to solve problems," gives little guidance for assessment. On the other hand, considerable direction for assessment is provided when the outcome is phrased in the following manner:

> Students will work effectively with others on complex, issue-laden problems requiring holistic problem solving approaches (College of Agriculture Curriculum Committee, 1994).

This outcome can be assessed by developing assessments that require teams of students to develop solutions to complex, issue-laden problems, as defined by the discipline. They can be judged on the effectiveness of their team skills, the quality of their solution, and their ability to use holistic problem-solving approaches. Rubrics are tools that can be used to describe and judge student work in important areas like team skills, areas that many have considered too subjective to be measured validly.

Intended learning outcomes focus on aspects of learning that will develop and endure but that can be assessed in some form now

Another issue that can arise has to do with the point at which learners are expected to achieve intended outcomes. Many faculty claim that the goals of an education are not really achieved until many years after graduation when individuals have the opportunity to use their knowledge and apply their skills in the context of their adult life and professional development.

This is probably true; however, it does not justify postponing the assessment of student learning until after graduation. We have a responsibility to gauge the extent of learning that can reasonably be expected to occur before students leave the institution. We also have the responsibility to assess whether or not it has occurred and how programs can be changed to make learning more effective.

Looking Ahead

Once we have written learning outcomes that form the basis for assessment at all levels in the institution, provide direction for all instructional activity, and inform students about our intentions, it is important that we collect data about whether or not we are helping students achieve them. Classroom assessment techniques and continuous improvement activities provide us with numerous ways to gather feedback for the purpose of improving learning and teaching.

Chapter 5 explains several techniques commonly used by professors who are committed to assessing learning and continually improving. These techniques help teachers collect feedback to understand how students are progressing and to help them make adjustments to remove barriers to learning. Equally important is the need to communicate back to students about progress in learning and changes that will be made in order to create a feedback loop. This loop or system of continuous feedback helps create a learner-centered environment in which teaching and learning are inseparable activities that reinforce one another.

Try Something New

1. Write five intended learning outcomes, and evaluate them according to the criteria discussed in this chapter and listed in Figure 8.2.
2. Write a set of intended learning outcomes for one of your courses and discuss them with students.
3. With a group of colleagues, formulate intended learning outcomes for your program and discuss how your courses help students reach them.

Reflections

As you create your own meaning from the ideas in the previous sections, begin to think about . . .

- How do our intended learning outcomes reflect current thinking in our discipline?
- How would leaders in our discipline react to our intended learning outcomes?
- Do my colleagues and I have a clear idea of how we would measure the learning represented in our intended learning outcomes?
- How could we rephrase our learning outcomes to represent the type of learning that we have in mind?
- What aspects of our intended learning outcomes could be measured while students are still at the institution?
- What aspects can only be assessed later in students' lives?

References

Alverno College Faculty. (1992). *Liberal learning at Alverno College.* Milwaukee, WI: Alverno College Productions.

Astin, A. W. (1993). *Assessment for excellence.* Phoenix, AZ: Oryx Press.

Babson College. (1998). *Undergraduate program guide.* Wellesley, MA: Babson College.

Baxter Magolda, M. B. (1996). Epistemological development in graduate and professional education. *The Review of Higher Education, 19* (3), 283–304.

Bloom, B. (Ed.) (1956). *Taxonomy of educational objectives. Handbook 1: Cognitive domain.* New York: Longman.

Chickering, A. W. (1969). *Education and identity.* San Francisco: Jossey-Bass.

College of Agriculture Curriculum Committee. (1994). *Unpublished general education outcomes for the College of Agriculture.* Ames, IA: Iowa State University.

Department of Biology. (1998). *Competency growth plan in critical thinking for students majoring in Biology.* Unpublished document. Wilkes-Barre, PA: King's College.

Department of Economics. (1996). *Annual student outcomes assessment report.* Unpublished document. Ames, IA: Iowa State University.

Department of Horticulture. (1996). *Annual student outcomes assessment report.* Unpublished document. Ames, IA: Iowa State University.

Department of Human Resources Management. (1998). *Competency growth plan in critical thinking for students majoring in Human Resources Management.* Unpublished document. Wilkes-Barre, PA: King's College.

Department of Political Science. (1996). *Annual student outcomes assessment report.* Unpublished document. Ames, IA: Iowa State University.

Department of Psychology. (1996). *Annual student outcomes assessment report.* Unpublished document. Ames, IA: Iowa State University.

Erwin, T. D. (1991). *Assessing student learning and development.* San Francisco: Jossey-Bass.

Ewell, P. T. (1991). To capture the ineffable: New forms of assessment in higher education. In G. Grant (Ed.), *Review of Research in Education, 17,* 75–125. Washington, DC: American Educational Research Association.

Ewell, P. T. (1994, November/December). A matter of integrity: Accountability and the future of self-regulation. *Change, 26* (6), 25–29.

Green, D. E., & Mullen, R. E. (1993). Doing it our way—revising a College of Agriculture curriculum. *Agronomy Abstracts,* 2.

Hakel, M. D. (1997, July–August). What we must learn from Alverno. *About Campus,* 16–21.

Julian, F. (1996). The capstone course as an outcomes test for majors. In T. W. Banta, J. P. Lund, K. E. Black & F. W. Oblander (Eds.), *Assessment in practice: Putting principles to work on college campuses* (pp. 79–82). San Francisco: Jossey-Bass.

King, P. M. (1999, March-April). Putting together the puzzle of student learning. *About Campus,* 2–4.

King, P. M., & Baxter Magolda, M. B. (1996). A developmental perspective on learning. *Journal of College Student Development, 37* (2), 163–173.

King, P. M., & Kitchener, K. S. (1994). *Developing reflective judgment: Understanding and promoting intellectual growth and critical thinking in adolescents and adults.* San Francisco: Jossey-Bass.

Kohlberg, L. (1981). *The meaning and measure of moral development.* Worcester, MA: Clark University Press.

Krathwohl, D. R., Bloom, B. S., & Masia, B. B. (1964). *Taxonomy of educational objectives. Handbook 2: Affective domain.* New York: Longman.

Kurfiss, J. G. (1988). *Critical thinking: Theory, research, practice, and possibilities.* (ASHE-ERIC Higher Education Report No. 2). College Station, TX: Association for the Study of Higher Education.

Mager, R. F. (1962). *Preparing instructional objectives.* Palo Alto, CA: Fearon Publishers.

Marzano, R. J., Pickering, D., & McTighe, J, (1993). *Assessing student outcomes: Performance assessment using the dimensions of learning model.* Alexandria, VA: Association for Supervision and Curriculum Development.

Perry, W. G. (1970). *Forms of intellectual and ethical development in the college years.* New York: Holt, Rinehart and Winston.

Resnick, L., & Resnick, D. (1992). Assessing the thinking curriculum: New tools for educational reform. In B. R. Gifford & M. C. O'Connor (Eds.), *Changing assessments: Alternative views of aptitude, achievement and instruction* (pp. 37–75). Boston: Kluwer Academic Publishers.

Rogers, B. (1991). Setting and evaluating intended educational (instructional) outcomes. In J. O. Nichols (Ed.), *A practitioner's handbook for institutional effectiveness and student outcomes assessment implementation* (pp. 168–187). New York: Agathon Press.

Rutgers University. (1998). *Middle States Association self-study: Assessing our vision for excellence.* New Brunswick, NJ: Rutgers, The State University of New Jersey.

Schechter, E. (1999). *Internet resources for higher education outcomes assessment.* http://www2.acs.ncsu.edu/UPA/survey/resource.htm

Sizer, T. R. (1992). *Horace's school: Redesigning the American high school.* Boston: Houghton Mifflin Company.

Southern West Virginia Community and Technical College. (1998a). *Mission statement.* Mount Gay, WV: Southern West Virginia Community and Technical College.

Southern West Virginia Community and Technical College. (1998b). *Plan for assessment of student academic achievement.* Mount Gay, WV: Southern West Virginia Community and Technical College.

The College of St. Scholastica. (1999). *Undergraduate and graduate catalog 1999–2000.* Duluth, MN: The College of St. Scholastica, Office of the Registrar.

Whitehead, A. N. (1929). *The aims of education.* New York: MacMillan.

Wiggins, G. (1989). A true test: Toward more authentic and equitable assessment. *Phi Delta Kappan, 70,* 703–713.

ALIGNING TEACHING FOR CONSTRUCTING LEARNING

JOHN BIGGS

Summary

'Constructive alignment' starts with the notion that the learner constructs his or her own learning through relevant learning activities. The teacher's job is to create a learning environment that supports the learning activities appropriate to achieving the desired learning outcomes. The key is that all components in the teaching system—the curriculum and its intended outcomes, the teaching methods used, the assessment tasks—are aligned to each other. All are tuned to learning activities addressed in the desired learning outcomes. The learner finds it difficult to escape without learning appropriately.

Biography

John Biggs obtained his Ph.D. from the University of London in 1963, and has held Chairs in Education in Canada, Australia, and Hong Kong. He retired in 1995 to act as a consultant in Higher Education, and has been employed in this capacity in many institutions in Australia, Hong Kong, and the United Kingdom.

Keywords

intended learning outcomes, constructive alignment, criterion-referenced assessment, teaching for active learning, systems approach to teaching

Introduction

Teaching and learning take place in a whole *system,* which embraces classroom, departmental and institutional levels. A poor system is one in which the components are not integrated, and are not tuned to support high-level learning. In such a system, only the 'academic' students use higher-order learning processes. In a good system, all aspects of teaching and assessment are tuned to support high level learning, so that all students are encouraged to use higher-order learning processes. 'Constructive alignment' (CA) is such a system. It is an approach to curriculum design that optimises the conditions for quality learning.

For an example of a poor system, here is what a psychology undergraduate said about his teaching:

> *'I hate to say it, but what you have got to do is to have a list of 'facts'; you write down ten important points and memorize those, then you'll do all right in the test . . . If you can give a bit of factual information—so and so did that, and concluded that—for two sides of writing, then you'll get a good mark.'* Quoted in Ramsden (1984: 144)

The problem here was not the student. In fact, this student liked writing extended essays, and finally graduated with First Class Honours, but he was contemptuous of these quick and snappy

Reprinted from *The Higher Education Academy* (2003).

assessments. So in psychology, he made a strategic decision to memorise, knowing that it was enough to get him through, saving his big guns for his major subject. The problem here was the assessment: it was not aligned with the aims of teaching.

So often the rhetoric in courses and programmes is all that it should be, stating for example that students will graduate with a deep understanding of the discipline and the ability to solve problems creatively. Then they are told about creative problem solving in packed lecture halls and tested with multiple-choice tests. It's all out of kilter, but such a situation is not, I strongly suspect, all that uncommon.

What is constructive alignment?

'Constructive alignment' has two aspects. The 'constructive' aspect refers to the idea that students *construct meaning* through relevant learning activities. That is, meaning is not something imparted or transmitted from teacher to learner, but is something learners have to create for themselves. Teaching is simply a catalyst for learning:

'If students are to learn desired outcomes in a reasonably effective manner, then the teacher's fundamental task is to get students to engage in learning activities that are likely to result in their achieving those outcomes . . . It is helpful to remember that what the student does is actually more important in determining what is learned than what the teacher does.' (Shuell, 1986: 429)

The 'alignment' aspect refers to what the teacher does, which is to set up a learning environment that supports the learning activities appropriate to achieving the desired learning outcomes. The key is that the components in the teaching system, especially the teaching methods used and the assessment tasks, are *aligned* with the learning activities assumed in the intended outcomes. The learner is in a sense 'trapped', and finds it difficult to escape without learning what he or she is intended to learn.

In setting up an aligned system, we specify the desired outcomes of our teaching in terms not only of topic content, but in the *level of understanding* we want students to achieve. We then set up an environment that maximises the likelihood that students will engage in the activities designed to achieve the intended outcomes. Finally, we choose assessment tasks that will tell us how well individual students have attained these outcomes, in terms of graded levels of acceptability. These levels are the grades we award.

There are thus four major steps:

1. Defining the intended learning outcomes (ILOs);
2. Choosing teaching/learning activities likely to lead to the ILOs;
3. Assessing students' actual learning outcomes to see how well they match what was intended;
4. Arriving at a final grade.

Defining the ILOs

When we teach we should have a clear idea of what we want our students to learn. More specifically, on a topic by topic basis, we should be able to stipulate how well each topic needs to be understood. First, we need to distinguish between *declarative* knowledge and *functioning* knowledge.

Declarative knowledge is knowledge that can be 'declared': we tell people about it, orally or in writing. Declarative knowledge is usually second-hand knowledge; it is about what has been discovered. Knowledge of academic disciplines is declarative, and our students need to understand it selectively. Declarative knowledge is, however, only the first part of the story.

We don't acquire knowledge only so that we can tell other people about it; more specifically, so that our students can tell us—in their own words of course—what we have recently been telling them. Our students need to put that knowledge to work, to make it function. Understanding makes you see the world differently, and behave differently towards that part of the world. We want lawyers to make good legal decisions, doctors to make accurate diagnoses, physicists to think and behave like physicists. After graduation, all our students, whatever their degree programmes, should see a section of their world differently, and to behave differently towards it, expertly and wisely. Thus, simply telling our students about that part of the world, and getting them to read about it, is not likely to achieve our ILOs with the majority of students. Good students will turn declarative into functioning knowledge in time, but most will not if they are not required to.

Accordingly, we have to state our objectives in terms that require students to demonstrate their understanding, not just simply tell us about it in invigilated exams. The first step in designing the curriculum objectives, then, is to make clear what levels of understanding we want from our students in what topics, and what performances of understanding would give us this knowledge.

It is helpful to think in terms of appropriate verbs. Generic high level verbs include: Reflect, hypothesise, solve unseen complex problems, generate new alternatives

Low level verbs include: Describe, identify, memorise, and so on. Each discipline and topic will of course have its own appropriate verbs that reflect different levels of understanding, the topic content being the objects the verbs take.

Incorporating verbs in our intended learning outcomes gives us markers throughout the system. The same verbs need to be embedded in the teaching/learning activities, and in the assessment tasks. They keep us on track.

Choosing teaching/learning activities (TLAs)

Teaching and learning activities in many courses are restricted to lecture and tutorial: lecture to expound and package, and tutorial to clarify and extend. However, these contexts do not necessarily elicit high level verbs. Students can get away with passive listening and selectively memorising.

There are many other ways of encouraging appropriate learning activities (Chapter 5, Biggs 2003), even in large classes (Chapter 6, op. cit.), while a range of activities can be scheduled outside the classroom, especially but not only using educational technology (Chapter 10, op cit.). In fact, problems of resourcing conventional on-campus teaching, and the changing nature of HE, are coming to be blessings in disguise, forcing learning to take place outside the class, with interactive group work, peer teaching, independent learning and work-based learning, all of which are a rich source of relevant learning activities.

Assessing students' learning outcomes

Faulty assumptions about and practices of assessment do more damage by misaligning teaching than any other single factor. As Ramsden (1992) puts it, the assessment is the curriculum, as far as the students are concerned. They will learn what they think they will be assessed on, not what is in the curriculum, or even on what has been 'covered' in class. The trick is, then, to make sure the assessment tasks mirror the ILOs.

Teacher perspective → objectives → ILOs → teaching activities → assessment
↓
Student perspective → assessment → learning activities → outcomes

To the teacher, assessment is at the end of the teaching-learning sequence of events, but to the student it is at the beginning. If the curriculum is reflected in the assessment, as indicated by the downward arrow, the teaching activities of the teacher and the learning activities of the learner are both directed towards the same goal. In preparing for the assessments, students will be learning the curriculum. The cynical game-playing we saw in our psychology undergraduate above, with his 'two pages of writing', is pre-empted.

Matching individual performances against the criteria is not a matter of counting marks but of making holistic judgments. This is a controversial issue, and is dealt with in more detail in Biggs (2003, Chapters 8 and 9). Just let me say here that the ILOs cannot sensibly be stated in terms of marks obtained. Intended outcomes refer to sought-for *qualities of performance,* and it is these that need to be stated clearly, so that the students' actual learning outcomes can be judged against those qualities. If this is not done, we are not aligning our objectives and our assessments.

Conclusion

Constructive alignment is more than criterion-reference assessment, which aligns assessment to the objectives. CA includes that, but it differs (a) in talking not so much about the assessment matching the objectives, but of first expressing the objectives in terms of intended learning outcomes (ILOs), which *then* in effect define the assessment task; and (b) in aligning the teaching methods, with the intended outcomes as well as aligning just the assessment tasks.

References

Biggs, J.B. (2003). *Teaching for quality learning at university.* Buckingham: Open University Press/Society for Research into Higher Education. (Second edition)

Ramsden, P. (1984). The context of learning. In F. Marton, D. Hounsell, and N. Entwistle, N. (eds), *The Experience of Learning.* Edinburgh: Scottish Academic Press.

Ramsden, P. (1992). *Learning to teach in higher education.* London: Routledge.

Shuell, T.J. (1986). Cognitive conceptions of learning. *Review of Educational Research,* 56, 411–436.

Chapter 9

Considerations of Design for Different Learning Contexts and Learners

Learning Styles and Culturally Diverse Students: A Literature Review

Jacqueline Jordan Irvine
Emory University

Darlene Eleanor York
Emory University

The research on the learning styles of culturally diverse students is neither a panacea nor a Pandora's box. The complexity of the construct, the psychometric problems related to its measurement, and the enigmatic relationship between culture and the teaching and learning process suggest that this body of research must be interpreted and applied carefully in classrooms of culturally diverse students. The analyses presented in this chapter suggest that the widespread conclusions in the literature that African American, Hispanic, and Indian students are field-dependent learners who prosper academically when taught with comparable field-dependent teaching strategies are premature and conjectural. However, the learning-styles research has significant possibilities for enhancing the achievement of culturally diverse students. This body of research reminds teachers to be attentive not only to individual students' learning styles but to their own actions, instructional goals, methods, and materials in reference to their students' cultural experiences and preferred learning environments.

Consequently, the purpose of this chapter on the learning styles of culturally diverse students is to review critically: (a) the definitions of the construct and the instruments used to measure it; (b) assumptions regarding the cultural influences on teaching and learning; (c) conclusions about the field-dependent learning styles of African American, Hispanic, and Indian students; (d) suggested field-dependent teaching strategies: (e) problems of the learning-styles research; and (f) potential promises of the learning-styles research.

Definitions and Instrumentation

The concept of learning styles is based on the theory that an individual responds to educational experiences with consistent behavior and performance patterns. These patterns are composed of a constellation of cognitive, affective, and physiological behaviors that are created and maintained by the interaction of culture, personality, and brain chemistry (American Association of School Administrators, 1991, Bennett, 1990). Technically, *learning styles* is an umbrella term encompassing three distinct styles or substyles: cognitive, affective, and physiological.

The division of learning styles into cognitive styles, affective styles, and physiological styles serves both to differentiate and to specify related research. Cognitive-styles research, for example, focuses on how learners prefer to receive and process information and experiences, how they create

Reprinted from *Handbook of Multicultural Education,* edited by J. Banks and C.M. Banks, Jossey-Bass Publishers, Inc.

concepts, and how they retain and retrieve information. Affective-styles research, in contrast, emphasizes differences in interpersonal skills and self-perception, curiosity, attention, motivation, arousal, and persistence. Finally, physiological-styles research measures how gender, circadian rhythms, nutrition, and general health impact learning processes. In education, the central focus of research is on cognitive styles, defined by Messick (1984) as "characteristic self-consistencies in information processing that develop in congenial ways around underlying personality trends" (p. 61). Thus, although cognitive styles can be distinguished theoretically from affective and physiological styles, in research and in practice the terms *learning style* and *cognitive style* are often used interchangeably.

When learning-styles measures began to appear, the diagnosis of a specific student-learning preference seemed so simple and accessible, its applicability so apparent, and its potential so vast that learning-style identification was believed to be a fundamental key in reconceptualizing what educators meant by thinking and learning. Contributing theorists such as Benjamin Bloom (1976) proposed that learning occurred as a result of the interactions of an individual's prior knowledge, attitudes toward learning, self-perception, and his or her immediate environment. Others suggested that "thinking" could be subdivided into several distinct, measurable processes (McKenney & Keen, 1974). Kolb's (1984) theory that learning is a cycle based on the learner's preferences for some combination of concrete-abstract and reflective-active experiential learning dimensions further enhanced the idea that learning is a negotiated activity, not the display of an ascriptive ability. These theories have called into question both the appropriateness and efficacy of the traditional search for "pure" intelligence.

Maintaining a theoretical distinction between learning style and ability has proven difficult. For example, Anthony Gregore (1979) explored "mindstyles," suggesting that learners filter, order, process, and evaluate information congruent with their perceptions of reality. These filtering, ordering, processing, and evaluative functions seem related both to ability and style. Gregore suggests that learning ability is mediated by deep psychological constructs, sociocultural variables, and socialization patterns—a consortium influencing learning style. More recently, Howard Gardner (1983) suggested that the interaction of culture, affect, and cognition allows the learner to develop "multiple intelligences," including spatial sensitivity, musical ability, kinesthetic/body intelligence, interpersonal intuition, and deep knowledge of oneself. Hence the theoretical distinction between style and ability is unclear.

In a recent review of cognitive styles research, Tiedemann (1989) used Messick's (1984) contrasting properties of cognitive styles and intellectual abilities as a means of differentiating style from ability. First, intellective abilities concern the learner's scope of information, the level of complexity of the information, and the quality and speed of information processing. Cognitive styles concern how the information is processed, the modes or patterns of information processing.

Second, ability implies a "measurement of competencies in terms of maximal performance, with the emphasis on accuracy and correctness of response" (Tiedemann, 1989, p. 263). In contrast, style is a measure of preference or habit. It measures not potentials, but propensities.

Third, ability is unidimensional. That is, it is a higher measure of some ability, such as abstract reasoning, and implies that more of that particular competency is present in the learner with a higher score than in the learner with a lower score. Cognitive style, however, is presumed to be multidimensional. Ranges of style indicate a variety of cognitive responses; each direction is a type of zero-sum equation. For example, a learner whose style is less concrete is therefore more abstract.

Fourth, the multidimensionality of styles implies that all styles are appropriate within given learning contexts, and when the context is congruent with style, learners with that style may enjoy an advantage. The measure of ability is presumed to be more universal. Higher-ability learners are believed to have an advantage over those with lower abilities in every learning context.

Fifth, ability indicates the presence of domain-specific competencies such as verbal or mathematical ability. Cognitive styles, however, represent learning preferences across domains and thus may signal the pattern of underlying personality constructs.

Finally, ability is viewed as a variable that helps or enables the learner to achieve a given competency. Style, in contrast, is presumed to be a variable that "contribute[s] to the selection, combination, and sequence of both substance and process" as well as regulating "the direction, duration, intensity, range, and speed of functioning" (Tiedemann, 1989, p. 263). In other words, ability aids behavioral competency; style organizes and controls the processing of information.

Since the development of learning-style theory, a search has been underway to capture and observe distinct cognitive, affective, and physiological behaviors. Testing instruments have been developed in recent years in an attempt to measure different styles and to categorize them along a meaningful and reliable continuum. More than 30 learning-styles instruments have been constructed, and the tests have been administered to a broad cross-section of populations. Table 27–1 is a representative, though not exhaustive, list of some of the major learning-styles instruments presently in use.

Despite the continuing popularity of the instruments, the surrounding research has not fully supported the underlying theory of learning styles. As early as 1963, Zigler suggested that cognitive-style instruments were confounded with measures of cognitive ability, a distinction that continues to be problematic. Other researchers have addressed other problems. Paulsen (1978), for example, suggests that cognitive style may be partially a function of physiological maturity. O'Leary, Calsyn, and Fauria (1980), in a comparison test of brain-impaired and non-impaired subjects, found that learning-styles instruments may measure cognitive impairment more accurately than they do underlying personality constructs. Many have suggested that learning-styles measures are gender related (Zeitoun & Fowler, 1981) or age related (Gjerde, Block, & Block, 1985). Furthermore, several learning-style tests, such as the Rod-and-Frame Test (RFT) and the Group Embedded Figures Test (GEFT), which are designed to measure the same construct, have produced low correlations when administered to the same subjects (Witkin, Dyk, Faterson, Goodenough, & Karp, 1962). Hence, the theory and measurement of learning styles are the focus of ongoing debate. In broad terms, the concept of learning style continues to face three central challenges: (a) the persistence of weak links between instruments and theory; (b) the persistence of internal weaknesses in the learning-style instruments themselves, particularly the difficulties with validity and reliability; and (c) the importance of these weaknesses in light of the growing popularity of the instruments and calls for the creation of style-sensitive educational environments based on the results of learning-style measures.

Recent reviews of learning style have been critical of both the theory and instrumentation used to explain and identify style. For example, in a longitudinal study of children at ages 3, 4, 5, and 11, Gjerde et al. (1985) found that the consistency of error scores over time using the Matching Familiar Figures Test (MFFT) was related to IQ measures. They conclude that this learning-style instrument may measure cognitive competence rather than the underlying theoretical construct of conceptual tempo it is designed to measure. Similarly, in a thorough review of the research on the 1976 Learning Style Inventory (LSI), Atkinson (1991) found that the design strategy, reliability, and validity of the inventory were largely unsupported by the research evidence. Furthermore, Atkinson suggests that the revised LSI, the LSI 1985, may be vulnerable to similar weaknesses. The "feeling," "watching," "thinking," and "doing" differences in preferred learning modalities remain unsubstantiated Tiedemann (1989), in a review of the research on five theoretical characteristics believed to qualify as style indicators, concludes that the research fails to support the theory or to legitimize the continued use of style measures: "The gap between the conceptual and empirical level is enormous. It cannot be reduced by revising the theory" (p. 272). Tiedemann's criticisms rest in what he views as an irreconcilable conflict. If the theory were modified to "fit" research results, Tiedemann argues that the current concept of learning style would have to be abandoned. If, however, current definitions of the concept are retained, some new method of measuring the concept is needed. Researchers have as yet had little success in devising an instrument that operationally distinguishes "behavior correlates of different performance dimensions," or competence, from style (p. 273).

There has been rapid growth, not only in the use of learning-style measures within education, but also in the research surrounding learning styles. Even a cursory examination of the educational and psychological research literature reveals several thousand studies conducted within the last decade. One area of interest has been the link between measures of learning style and academic achievement. This is an important field of examination, particularly since learning-style theory sug-

TABLE 9.1.

Selected Learning-Styles Identification Instruments

Title and Reference	Assessment Type	Categories of Learners	Format Style and Length
ELSIE (Edmonds Learning Style Identification Exercise) (Reinert, 1976)	Cognitive style	Visualisation Reading Listening Kinesthetic	50 common English words are analyzed according to learner's patterns of response.
GEFT [Group Embedded Figures Test] (Witkin, 1971)	Cognitive style	Analytical Global	Subjects are asked to identify simple shapes hidden in complex figures. The test takes 15 minutes.
Transaction Ability Inventory (Gregore, 1982)	Cognitive style	Concrete Abstract Random Sequential	Subjects rank their responses to learning using 40 words in 10 sets of 4 words each.
Cognitive Profiles (Letteri, 1980)	Cognitive style	Field independence/ dependence Scan/focus Breadth of categorization Cognitive complexity/ simplicity Reflectiveness/ Impulsiveness Leveling/sharpening Tolerant/Intolerant	7 separate tests used in combination to predict standardized achievement-test scores.
Group Embedded Figures Test (Witkin, 1971)	Cognitive style	Field-dependence Field-independence	15-minute test in which subjects must find geometric figures within larger patterns, differentiated by task.
MFFT (Matching Familiar Figures Test) (Kagan, 1965)	Cognitive style	Impulsivity-reflectivity	12 pictures are shown with, in each case, 6 alternatives, only one of which is correct. Impulsives tend to choose more quickly and inaccurately than reflectives.
Student Motivation Information Form (Wlodkowski, 1978)	Affective style	Intrinsic motivation Extrinsic motivation	35 incomplete sentences are used to elicit information about motivation.
UE Scale (Rotter, 1959)	Affective style	Internal/external locus of control	29 paired alternatives that describe beliefs about life events. Subjects choose one alternative they believe to be true.
LSI (Learning Style Inventory) (Myers & Briggs, 1976)	Learning style	Environmental Emotional Sociological Physical	Comprehensive style indicator containing 36 computer-scored subscales.
MBTI (Myers-Briggs Type Indicator) (Dunn, Dunn, & Price, 1978)	Learning style	Judgment Perception Introversion Extraversion Feeling Thinking Sensing Intuition	550 questions assessing multilevel personality indicators. Requires training to administer and score.
CSII (Cognitive Style Interest Inventory) (Hill, 1971)	Learning style	Abstract Visual Tactile Auditory Coordination Social interaction	Self-reported ranking of learning preferences and beliefs. Test takes 50 minutes.
Swassing-Barbe Modality Index (Barbe & Swassing, 1979)	Learning style	Visual Auditory Tactile/kinesthetic	Subject must process the order of geometric shapes in each of the three modalities. Scores from each tell the preferred modality.

Note No measures exist to isolate physiological style preferences. The learning-styles measures include both cognitive and affective; those listed also contain items that address physiological aspects of learning.

gests that educational experiences designed to be more congruent with student learning style may enhance academic achievement.

The prediction (not simply the correlation) of academic achievement plays a critical role in both research and application. In research, the presence of predictive validity enables one to forecast individual performance or estimate current performance on variables that are different from a learning-styles inventory (American Psychological Association, 1966). This form of validity is an important tool in educational test design and construction. In practice, the prediction of performance based on the results of a test can exert a powerful influence over thousands of transactions between teacher and student. When children's scores on a learning-style measure are used as a predictor of future achievement, and when teaching and learning environments are correspondingly mediated to enhance future achievement, the strength of the predictive validity of learning-styles measures becomes apparent.

Since 1966, only 29 studies have been conducted measuring the predictive validity of learning-styles instruments. Of those published since 1978, several address predictive validity in areas other than academic achievement, such as studies that try to predict emotional or psychological maturity, levels of skill, or coordination in sports. Other studies examine whether learning-styles instruments can be used to predict career choices. Several others draw from a preschool or postsecondary population. However, there are limited studies published since 1978 that test the predictive validity of learning-styles instruments relative to academic achievement among K–12 populations; this research can be analyzed using the categories of field dependence/independence, locus of control, impulsivity-reflectivity, and other learning-styles measures.

Field Dependence/Independence

Field dependence/independence refers to psychological constructs that define the ways individuals respond cognitively to confusing information or unfamiliar situations. These responses produce observable behaviors. Field-dependent behaviors include high levels of impulsivity, low reflectivity, and reliance on the social environment and on authority figures. Field-dependent persons prefer to work with people rather than in isolation and tend to conform to the prevailing social context. Field-independent behaviors are more conceptual and analytical in nature. Field-independent persons tend to be autonomous, detached, goal oriented, and self-aware. Neither of these styles is mutually exclusive. All individuals may exhibit, at different times, elements of both field-dependent and field-independent behaviors (Ramirez & Castaneda, 1974; Saracho & Spodek, 1984).

In a 1978 study, Buriel tested a mixture of Mexican American and Anglo American first and second graders and compared them with a mixture of Mexican American and Anglo American third and fourth graders to see if three separate measures of field dependence/field independence could predict achievement on reading and math sections of the Metropolitan Achievement Test. Only one instrument, the Children's Embedded Figures Test (CEFT), revealed a relationship strong enough to predict mathematics scores, and only for Mexican American children. Given achievement domains, culture, gender, and age, Buriel found that none of the instruments used to measure field dependence/independence could predict academic achievement.

In a later study of the predictive strength of field dependence/independence, Swanson (1980) tested learning-disabled third-grade females. The CEFT, the Nowicki-Strickland Locus of Control test for children, and an intelligence test were given, and the results compared with scores on the Peabody Achievement Test in reading and mathematics. Swanson, like Buriel (1978), found that the CEFT contained some predictive power, but related more to intelligence than to style. Swanson concludes that learning style measures are no better than IQ tests for predicting academic achievement.

Blaha (1982) measured fifth-grade African American and White children in three domains: attitude toward reading, locus of control measure, and field dependency/independency. The measures were used to predict scores on the Iowa Test of Basic Skills (ITBS) in reading, mathematical concepts, and mathematical computation. Blaha found that attitude toward reading was strongly related to reading achievement. Field independence related more strongly to reading achievement than to achievement in mathematics. The locus of control measure proved to be an important predictor for reading and mathematical computation but not for mathematical concepts. These results call into question the generalizability of learning styles and the validity of learning-styles measures. Interestingly, Blaha found no predictions that could be made based on gender or race.

Taken together, these three studies challenge the ability of current field-dependence/independence measures to predict academic achievement. Three problems exist. First, there seems to be no configuration of school-aged subjects that has yet established a predictive relationship. For example, although testing has involved different-aged male and female children from different cultures, from different backgrounds, and with different abilities, no "group style" has been found that can predict academic achievement. Second, although there are some indications that some tests seem related to the achievement of some children, the relationship does not establish one of the fundamental tenets of learning-style theory: that "style" supersedes content-based knowledge. For example, tests of field independence that show the presence of a dominant learning style in reading should show evidence of the same preferred style in mathematics as well. They do not. Finally, these learning-styles measures fail to produce as strong a predictive relationship as intelligence tests. In theory, learning style may be distinct from learning ability, but the instruments used to measure style have made little distinction between them.

Locus of Control

The distinction between internal and external locus of control was first measured by Julian Rotter (1959). His I/E Scale measures the degree to which respondents feel some sense of control over their lives. For example, a student who believes that high test scores occur because of a "lucky pencil" is more externally controlled than one who believes that high test scores are attributable to drive and effort.

As pointed out earlier, Blaha (1982) found that locus of control was a predictor of reading and mathematical computation but not of mathematical concepts. Other researchers have examined the strength of locus of control measures as predictors of academic achievement. For example, in a study of third, fourth, and fifth graders, Creek, McDonald, and Ganley (1991) divided the children into gifted (average IQ of 140) and nongifted (average IQ of 120). They then subdivided the groups, using the Nowicki-Strickland Locus of Control Scale, into those internally motivated and externally motivated. All the children were given the California Achievement Test. The test results showed that the nongifted internals scored as high as the gifted externals. As noted earlier, the relationships among intelligence, style, and achievement are unclear. If learning styles supersede intelligence in the determination of school achievement, then Creek, McDonald, and Ganley's work should have produced different results. Instead, their results suggest that the construct of learning styles and the instruments used to measure it are receiving more attention than they deserve.

Impulsivity-Reflectivity

Impulsivity and reflectivity refer to the speed and accuracy of a student's response to questions. An impulsive learner is one who is likely to answer quickly and inaccurately; a reflective learner is likely to take more time pondering a question (Becker, Bender, & Morrison, 1978).

In a longitudinal study of kindergarten children, Wood (1979) investigated the predictive power of four measures of cognitive style. She tested the kindergarten children using the MFFT, an instrument designed to measure potential learning problems, the Metropolitan Readiness Test (MRT), and the teacher's assessment of student self-concept. At the end of their first-grade year, these measures were compared with their scores on the ITBS. Wood found that none of the measures predicted achievement scores. The single exception was the MFFT, which predicted achievement for boys only, and only when the MRT was removed from the equation.

In another study of impulsivity-reflectivity, Margolis and Brannigan (1978) found that impulsivity predicts achievement in reading. They also used a kindergarten sample of average-ability children, administering the MRT, the MFFT, and several other cognitive-style measures. These results were compared with scores on a reading inventory. Although Margolis and Brannigan found that impulsivity is related to achievement, it is perhaps significant that separate equations for achievement were calculated based on outcomes from the MFFT. This reliance on a single measure of impulsivity-reflectivity, coupled with their small sample size (n = 22 for each group), suggests the need for replication of the study.

Butter, Kennedy, and Shoemaker-Kelly (1982) used a similar design to measure third-grade children whose IQ scores were unknown. The MFFT was administered, as was the Auditory Impuisivity Test (AIT)—a test of how well students can select a series of sounds that mimics a previously heard series of beeps and pauses. These results were compared with the California Achievement Test of reading comprehension and vocabulary. Butter et al. found that both cognitive-styles measures predicted reading achievement; however, the combined scores accounted for only 22% of the variance in achievement. In this study, both reflectives and impulsives were considered in a single regression equation. Furthermore, because no IQ scores were taken, it is unclear how well ihe instruments predict compared to intelligence tests.

Other Learning-Styles Measures

Raile (1980) compared outcomes on the Structure of Intellect–Learning Abilities Test (SOILAT) with a test that predicts foreign-language achievement. The tests were administered to secondary students enrolled in Spanish classes and in French classes, and to students not enrolled in foreign-language classes. Raile found that, although there was a significant relationship between the measures, the relationship was not consistent across the two foreign languages. Furthermore, the correlations between bilingual Mexican American students and English-speaking students studying a foreign language were insignificant. Although some of the six SOILAT subtests showed a greater predictive ability than others, the test was an inconclusive predictor of achievement.

Asbury, Stokes, Adderley-Kelly, and Knuckle (1989) tested 100 right-handed African American sixth graders. In all, 16 predictor variables were tested, including intelligence, dexterity, ethnic identity, and brain function. These were used to categorize the students into a modified scoring scheme of the Wechsler Intelligence Scale for Children-Revised (WISC-R) and to compare with students' grades in academic subjects. Asbury et al. found no predictive ability from ethnic identity, but they did find that the Symbol Digit Modalities Test (SDMT)—a test that asks respondents to substitute numbers for geometric designs in written and oral responses—was significant and was also related to IQ scores. Along with the SDMT, gender was also a significant predictor, leading the authors to conclude that "sex, an organismic variable, and SDMT-O, a neuropsychological measure . . . may suggest an intimate connection between physiological function . . . and test performance" (p. 188).

In another interesting study of the relationship of learning styles to achievement, Kampwirth and MacKenzie (1989) tested first graders using the Swassing-Barbe Modalities Index (SBMI) and the visual and auditory subtests of the Illinois Test of Psycholinguistic Abilities (ITPA). These were compared with the children's scores on a lesson in which they were to learn nonsense words. The children were assigned to two groups based on their learning style preferences. In one group a lesson in the words was presented using primarily auditory teaching methods; in the other group primarily visual teaching methods were presented. Kampwirth and MacKenzie found that the strongest correlations were between the scores of the children taught by auditory means and those taught by visual means. No significant difference between groups or methods was noted. Children whose learning-style tests indicated a preferred modality were taught in accordance wirh that modality, but even under those circumstances the learning-style measures could not predict the achievement of the children.

Although all learning-style measures have produced equivocal findings on many different scales of reliability and prediction, these results across the field-dependence/independence, locus of control, reflectivity-impulsivity, and other dimensions suggest that learning-style instruments perform more of a dialogic than a diagnostic function. Results from learning-styles measures may alert both teachers and students to individual learning preferences, but to use the results as an indicator of potential achievement is clearly unwarranted from research findings. Furthermore, while teachers who utilize a variety of teaching styles undoubtedly encourage learning in their students, a repertoire of teaching styles tailored to the learning styles of students will not assure student achievement because there is evidence that matching teaching styles with learning style will not predict achievement (Kampwirth & Mackenzie, 1989). This research suggests that a wider, more inclusive understanding of children is necessary in order to encourage achievement.

The Relationship Between Learning Styles and Culture

Culture is the sum total of ways of living (Hoopes & Pusch, 1979), a way of life that is shared by members of a population (Ogbu, 1988) and includes rites and rituals, legends and myths, artifacts and symbols, and language and history, as well as "sense-making devices that guide and shape behavior" (Davis, 1984, p. 10). Culture is what one thinks is important (values); what one thinks is true (beliefs), and how one perceives things are done (norms) (Owens, 1987).

The cultures of students of color or their "way of life" (Ogbu, 1988) are often incongruous with expected middle-class cultural values, beliefs, and norms of schools. These cultural differences often result in cultural discontinuity or lack of cultural synchronization between the student and the school (Irvine, 1990), and has led researchers to conclude that cultural differences, particularly differences among mainstream and diverse students' approaches to learning, are major contributors to the school failure of students of color.

Bennett (1990) identifies five cultural factors that appear to influence learning: (a) childhood socialisation, (b) sociocultural tightness, (c) ecological adaptation, (d) biological effects, and (e) language. *Childhood socialization* refers specifically to the child-rearing practices of a particular culture. For example, authoritative socialization practices are associated with field dependence, laissez-faire practices with field independence. Serpell (1976) claims that mothers of field dependents hamper independence in their children because they tend to be overly protective, restrictive of their children's exploration and originality, impulsive and arbitrary disciplinarians, and overly indulgent. Chimezie (1988) attributes African American children's more developed motor proficiency skills to the observed fact that African American mothers have more physical contact with their babies than do Euro-American mothers. Since African American homes generally have more people in them, African American children receive more frequent and intense verbal and physical stimulation than white children. Bermudez's (1986) research on Hispanics concludes that Hispanic parenting styles are significantly different from the parenting styles of Anglos. She found that Hispanic parents were less likely than Anglo parents to encourage self-dependent and analytic skills.

The concept of *sociocultural tightness* (Hall, 1989) distinguishes between high-and low-context cultures. High-and low-context cultures differ along several dimensions: time orientation, social roles, interpersonal relations, reasoning, verbal messages, and social organization. Field-dependent learning styles are typical for individuals in high-context cultures. For example, high-context cultures operate on polychronic time, with loose schedules and multiple and simultaneous activities. Knowledge is gained through intuition and spiral logic. Low-context, cultures are thought to operate on tight schedules with linear events, with knowledge gained through analytical reasoning.

Ecological adaptation affects learning styles. For example, some cultures depend on highly developed perceptual skills for survival in their environment. Navajo children are taught to recognize their families' herd at great distances and are cognizant of danger signs of changing weather and approaching predators (Swisher & Deyhle, 1989).

The *biological effects* refer to such factors as nutrition, physical development, and brain development McShane and Plas (1982) conclude that the psychoneurological literature suggests that Indians may have a neurologically based cognitive style that "may interfere in some cases with left hemisphere processing of its own specialized function, resulting in deficit linguistic processing and overuse of the spatial mode" (p. 14). They also suggest that otitis media, or middle-ear infection, a condition that plagues half of the Indian population, may be related to Indian students' preference for certain learning styles. Pasteur and Toldson (1982) hypothesize that African Americans and Whites are governed by different hemispheres of the brain. These authors note that African Americans are thought to be right-brain dominated—intuitive, nonverbal, creative, spontaneous, and expressive—while Whites are likely to be left-brain dominated—logical, mathematical, and sequential. Perhaps the most extreme example of the biological basis of learning style is the assertion by Dunn, Gemake, and Jalali (1990) that boys are less able to sit for long periods of time because they are "less well padded exactly where they need to be" (p. 71). These authors conclude that there appears to be a biological basis for learning style.

Finally, *language* is an important variable in learning style. For African American students, there are obvious differences from mainstream language usages not only in students' pronunciation, vocabulary, rhythm, pacing, and inflection, but also in assumptions regarding what is spoken and left unspoken, whether one interrupts, defers to others, or asks direct or indirect questions (Erickson, 1986). Many Asian and Hispanic students who are not native speakers encounter barriers in school because their language is not valued and is perceived as a cultural deficit rather than an asset. Some researchers believe that the Navajo language has influenced Indian students' mastery of mathematics; the absence from the language of agreed-upon meanings for concepts such as multiply, divide, if, cosine, and sine is thought to be a contributory factor to some Indian students' difficulty with certain mathematical functions and syllogistic reasoning (Bradley, 1984; Moore, 1982).

The Learning Styles of African American, Hispanic, and Indian Students

In spite of methodological, conceptual, and pedagogical problems in the learning-styles research (discussed later in this chapter), researchers persist in identifying certain learning-styles characteristics of various ethnic groups. The following represents a summary of some of these works.

African American Learning Styles

A summary of the research (Baruth & Manning, 1992; Boykin & Toms, 1985; Cushner, McClelland, & Safford, 1992; Hale-Benson, 1986; Shade, 1982, 1989a, 1989b) suggests that African Americans are field-dependent learners as contrasted to field-independent (some writers prefer to use the terms *relational, field sensitive,* or *global* learners) and tend to:

- respond to things in terms of the whole instead of isolated parts;
- prefer inferential reasoning as opposed to deductive or inductive;
- approximate space and numbers rather than adhere to exactness or accuracy;
- focus on people rather than things;
- be more proficient in nonverbal than verbal communications;
- prefer learning characterized by variation and freedom of movement;
- prefer kinesthetic/active instructional activities;
- prefer evening rather than morning learning;
- choose social over nonsocial cues;
- proceed from a top-down processing approach rather than a bottom-up approach;
- prefer "vervistic" (Boykin & Toms, 1985) learning experiences.

Hispanic Learning Styles

The research (Baruth & Manning, 1992; Casteñeda & Gray, 1974; Grossman, 1984; Ramírez & Castañeda, 1974), like that on African American students, characterizes Hispanic students as field-dependent and relational learners, indicating that these students tend to:

- prefer group learning situations;
- be sensitive to the opinions of others;
- remember faces and social words;
- be extrinsically motivated;
- learn by doing;

- prefer concrete representations to abstract ones;
- prefer people to ideas.

Indian Learning Styles

Many researchers (Baruth & Manning, 1992; Bradley, 1984; McShane & Plas, 1982; Sawyer, 1991; Swisher & Deyhle, 1989; Tharp, 1989) have noted that Indian students also tend to be field dependent, although Shade (1989b) identifies most Indians, regardless of tribe, as field independent. However, a summary of the findings reveals that Indians tend to be field dependent, like their African American and Hispanic counterparts, and:

- prefer visual, spatial, and perceptual information rather than verbal;
- learn privately rather than in public;
- use mental images to remember and understand words and concepts rather than word associations;
- watch and then do rather than employ trial and error;
- have well-formed spatial ability;
- learn best from nonverbal mechanisms rather than verbal;
- learn experientially and in natural settings;
- have a generalist orientation, interested in people and things;
- value conciseness of speech, slightly varied intonation, and limited vocal range;
- prefer small-group work;
- favor wholistic presentations and visual representations.

Suggested Field-Dependent Teaching Strategies

Advocates believe that the closer the match between a student's learning style and the teacher's instructional methods, the more likely the student will experience academic success (Cushner et al., 1992; Gregorc, 1979; Dunn & Dunn, 1979; cited in Bennett, 1990). Shade (1982) speculates that the differences in performance between African American students and mainstream students can be related to "Afro-American cognitive or perceptual style preference which emphasizes a person rather than an object orientation" (p. 236).

Several researchers have translated these findings into recommendations for teaching and organizing instruction. Clarkson (1983) describes field-dependent instructional techniques for an "urban" learning style, although he notes that minorities and women also are likely to be field-dependent learners. He recommends that teachers develop a strong personal relationship with their students, deliver clear and direct verbal instructions, and use advance organizers in a highly structured presentation of instructional materials. He advises teachers to arrange classroom seating so that field-dependent learners are physically close to the teacher and physically distant from other students in order to minimize distractions and discourage interaction. He recommends "that nondirect teaching strategies, such as independent project work, independent seatwork, and 'do-your-own thing-times,' in the classroom *not* [emphasis in original] be used with this type of student" (p. 124).

Clarkson's work is contradictory to recommendations by Gilbert and Gay (1989), who state that field-dependent African American students function better in loosely structured, cooperative environments in which teachers and students work together. These researchers state that "multimodal, multidimensional" (p. 278) classrooms are not distracting to African American students, and "the orderly environment that the teacher considers most desirable for learning seems dull, stagnant, and unstimulating to black students" (p. 279). Hale-Benson's (1986) observations are similar, indicating that physical and motoric activities like dancing and hand dapping contribute to the achievement of African American students.

In reference to Hispanics, Ramirez and Casteñeda (1974) advise instructional methods such as cooperative learning, a curriculum humanized through use of humor, fantasy, or drama, personalized rewards, modeling, informal class discussions, global emphasis on concepts rather than attention to details, and explicit rules regarding classroom behavior. Grossman (1984) extends these researchers' work and advocates that teachers who work with Hispanic students include community group projects, use personal rewards such as hugs and pats, avoid debating as an instructional technique, avoid long-term projects in favor of daily assignments, include religion, saints, and the supernatural in the curriculum, de-emphasize the question-answer format, and stand close to the students when teaching.

A list of teaching behaviors for Indian students is presented by Sawyer (1991). She suggests that teachers avoid highlighting individual students' success, accept silence, reduce lecturing, de-emphasize competition, use personal teaching styles, allow longer pauses after questions, use whole-language approaches to language instruction, and use minimal teacher directions. Bradley (1984) cautions teachers to avoid discovery learning when planning instruction for Indian students; peer learning and learning stations with visual, motor, tactile, or auditory games or tasks are advised.

Cooperative teaching is one of the techniques most often recommended for all culturally diverse students, Slavin (1987) found that African American students' achievement is enhanced when cooperative learning groups incorporate group rewards based on group members' individual learning. He speculates that African American students excel in cooperative learning because it captures "the social and motivational dynamics of team sports" (p. 66).

Problems of the Learning-Styles Research

The research on learning styles and culturally diverse populations should be interpreted cautiously. Several aspects of this emerging body of knowledge warrant careful consideration and further deliberation. The critical questions for consideration are:

1. Is culture the primary variable that influences learning styles of students of color? Are there other significant variables?
2. Do characteristics of the cultural group apply uniformly to individual members of the group?
3. What is the relationship between teachers' instructional methods and students' learning style?
4. Should students of color always be taught using their preferred learning style?

Critical Variables that Influence Learning Styles

The research on learning styles of culturally diverse students is based preponderantly on the cultural anthropological literature. Relevant examples can be found in the works on African Americans' African cultural retentions and are summarized by Boykin (1986), who proposes that African American culture contains at least nine interrelated dimensions: (a) spirituality—an approach in which life is viewed as vitalistic rather than mechanistic; (b) harmony—the idea that humans and nature live interdependently; (c) movement—an emphasis on rhythm, music, and dance; (d) verve—a propensity for high levels of stimulation; (e) affect—an emphasis on emotions and feelings; (f) communalism—a commitment to social connectedness; (g) expressive individualism—a value on genuine personal expression; (h) oral tradition—a preference for oral/aural communication; and (i) social time perspective—an orientation to time as social rather than material space, These observations are directly related to consequent instructional recommendations, summarized in this chapter, that suggest that African American students learn best through physical movements, personal teacher-student relationships, cooperative groups, and oral/aural communication.

Similarly, Slonim (1991) posits that Hispanic culture is founded on core values of (a) mutualism that stresses sharing and cooperation; (b) interpersonal relationships based on trust and respect; (c) modesty in regard to personal or sexual matters; (d) a relaxed perception of time; (e) a fatalistic attitude toward life; (f) a preference for physical proximity; and (g) a value on machismo in which men embrace traditional sex-role behavior. The recommended instructional strategies for Hispanic students are synchronous with the values of cooperation and a focus on interpersonal relationships.

Although it is clear that culture, particularly ethnicity, is a powerful force that influences students' predispositions toward learning, it must be emphasized that cultural practices are learned behavior that can be unlearned and modified. Culture is neither static nor deterministic; people of color are not solely products of their culture. Consequently, culture affects individuals in different ways. Hanson (1992) states that culture is not a strict set of prescribed behaviors, but is a "framework through which actions are filtered or checked as individuals go about daily life" (p. 3). She adds that culture is constantly evolving and that although some students may share the same cultural background and predispositions, not all members of the same cultural group behave in identical ways.

Individuals who belong to a particular cultural group vary in the degree to which they identify with their culture. Banks (1987) identifies a six-stage typology of ethnic identity that traces development from ethnic psychological captivity, through ethnic encapsulation, ethnic identity clarification, biethnicity, and multiethnicity, to global competency. Banks emphasizes that his schema is not a hierarchy in the sense that individuals begin at stage one and move progressively to stage six; rather, individuals can move among the stages depending on their experiences.

The cultural influence on learning styles is mediated by such additional factors as social class and gender. Banks (1988) writes that although people in the same social class do exhibit some similar learning-styles characteristics, there is evidence that the effects of ethnicity persist across social-class segments within an ethnic group (p. 462). Women tend to be more field dependent than men (Cushner et al., 1992). Although Shade's (1989a) review of studies does not identify social class or gender differences in African American cognition, she speculates that her findings are probably related to previous researchers' omission of these variables in their work. Child-rearing practices and the home environment are also significant factors, although Nieto (1992) notes that children raised in the same home can have different learning styles. Using the LSI, Jacobs (1990) found differences between the learning approaches of high- and low-achieving African American students. African American high achievers were teacher motivated and preferred less structure than low achievers. Bell and McGraw-Burrell (1988) found that African American high achievers shared similar learning styles with White students, a finding consistent with Kreuze and Payne's (1969) conclusion that Hispanic and White students' learning styles did not differ significantly from each other.

Not to be underestimated is the growing number of various ethnic subcultures. Valentine (1971) observes that there are at least 14 African American subcultures "with more or less distinct cultures" (p. 140). Hispanics also are represented by many subcultures. They do not all share a common language, religion, or racial identification. Hispanics in the United States come from 19 different countries and have disparate socioeconomic and migrational characteristics (Marin & Marin, 1991). These subcultural differences have surfaced in learning-styles differences. Ramírez and Castañeda (1974) found that the variability of learning styles within Hispanic populations is related to degree of assimilation, distance from the Mexican border, length of residence in the United States, degree of urbanization, and degree of prejudice experienced.

In summary, it appears that culture and ethnicity are frameworks for the development of learning-styles preferences. However, other factors can play a significant role in changing and modifying initial cultural predilections.

The Dangers of Generalizations

Stereotyping exists when exaggerated and inaccurate characteristics of a group are ascribed to an individual. This phenomenon is different from sociotyping, which involves accurate generalizations about groups (Bennett, 1990). For example, we know that the majority of students of color score lower on standardized tests than their White counterparts. This is an accurate generalization or sociotype, but it is a stereotype when extrapolated to a particular individual Indian or Hispanic student. The learning-styles research, if not carefully interpreted and implemented, poses some danger in this regard, particularly when style assumptions limit students' experiences or infer negative characteristics about ability. For example, students thought to be field dependent may be discouraged from participating in solo performances or from taking leadership roles. Negative teacher expectations can be fueled if teachers incorporate generalized and decontextualized observations about children of color without knowledge of the limitations of learning-styles labels. Research in which conclusions are unsupported or insufficiently supported by the data may be not only misleading but harmful. For example, Cureton (1978), in describing African American students' auditory skills, states: "They are not accustomed to listening for long periods" (p. 752). Dunn et al. (1990) revealed that Whites, in comparison to African Americans, prefer bright lights while learning, a trait correlated with a successive-analytic-left processing style. On the other hand, they add, low-light preference is associated with a simultaneous-global-right processing style. Based on such limited evidence, the authors conclude. "Thus Euro-Americans may be more analytical than Afro-Americans" (p. 73).

Teachers' Instructional Methods and Students' Learning Style

As indicated earlier in this chapter, numerous writers (Clarkson, 1983; Cureton, 1978; Gilbert & Gay, 1989; Ramírex & Castañeda, 1974; Sawyer, 1991) have presented recommendations that associated learning-styles research with specific instructional strategies for culturally diverse students. Other researchers (Boykin, 1986; Foster, 1989) have extended this application from teaching methods to teaching style, and inferred that there are teacher personality types that are more effective with particular groups. Boykin (1986; Boykin & Toms, 1985) describes African American students' preference for verve or high stimulation and their low tolerance for routine and monotonous tasks, and implies (Chimezie, 1988) that teachers of African American students must also be vervistic, a personality style characterized by high energy and performance. Other researchers suggest that effective teachers of African American students use a "style filled with rhythmic language, rapid intonation, and many encouraging gestures" (Foster, 1989. p. 5), with many instances of repetition, call and response, variation in pace, high emotional involvement, creative analogies, figurative language, vowel elongation, catchy phrases, gestures, body movements, symbolism, aphorisms, and lively discussions with frequent and spontaneous student participation. Foster, quoting Piestrup (1972), calls this the Black Artful Style reminiscent of the admired Black preaching style.

Irvine (1990) suggests that all children, regardless of race, would benefit from more active and stimulating teaching approaches. In his seminal work, *A Place Called School,* Goodlad (1984) observed over 1,000 classes and found that 60% of class time in elementary school was spent doing the following: preparing for and cleaning up after assignments, listening to teachers explain or lecture, and carrying out written assignments. What Goodlad discovered was a lack of variability for most children. Seldom (except in art, music, and physical education) were children being taught with methods involving physical movement, varied techniques, or high affect. There was minimal student movement, minimal student-to-student interaction, minimal teacher-to-student interaction, and minimal intimate affect. Irvine notes, "Given these conditions, all children, particularly black children, would welcome 'verve inducement' in these classrooms" (p. 91).

Kleinfeld (1992) and Shade (1989a) agree that, given the limitations of the learning-styles research, it is premature to conclude that any one method of teaching is effective with a particular cultural group. Shade, who appears to have modified her earlier position (Shade, 1982), refers to the learning-styles research as propositions that have strong intuitive elements, yet are "insufficient to produce the types of changes necessary in the teaching-learning process and in the assessment of skills" (1989a, p, 110). Hilliard (1989/90) makes a more definitive statement by warning educators that "it is premature to draw conclusions for classroom strategy based on style; or to prescribe pedagogical practice in a general way" (p. 3).

Teaching to Preferred Learning Style

Inherent in the learning-styles literature is the assumption that diverse students can learn only if they use their preferred style. One avenue for examining this assumption critically is to pose a historical question: Prior to the emergence of a defined learning style for African American students, is there any evidence that African American teachers in segregated schools employed teaching techniques that attended to learning style? In an impressive ethnographic study of a pre-*Brown* (*Brown v. Board of Education of Topeka,* 1954) segregated school in North Carolina, Siddle Walker (1993) documents that African American teachers' success was related to their interpersonal caring rather than to a particular method or teaching style. She states: "Students spoke much more vehemently about the degree to which they felt cared about than they did about the particular teaching methods used by the teachers" (p. 75). The works of Sowell (1976), Jones (1981), and Baker (1982) support Siddle Walker's observations.

The assumption that diverse students can learn only if they use their preferred style also ignores what developmental psychologists call the malleability (Gallagher & Barney, 1987) and plasticity (Lerner, 1987) of children. These researchers note that people do not develop in a standardized or normative fashion; researchers have too often ignored the active role that individuals play in shaping their own development. Culturally diverse students have demonstrated their resilience and adaptability and can, if provided the psychological and instructional support, master various learning styles, Hilliard (1992) adds: "All students have an incredible capacity for developing the ability to use multiple learning styles, in much the same way that multiple language competency can be accomplished" (p. 373). Gilbert and Gay (1989) and Chimezie (1988) recommend, in fact, that African American students shift their preferred verbal and kinesthetic style to more school-compatible written and sedentary performance.

Saracho and Spodek (1984) acknowledge the work of several learning-styles theorists who advocate this kind of bicognitive flexibility for culturally diverse students. Although the authors support the theoretical concept, they raise concerns about the teachability of cognitive flexibility. Some research (Kogan, 1971) indicates that field-independent learners are better able to switch learning strategies than field-dependent learners, and that field dependents may resist style modification. Furthermore, a culturally diverse student who is achieving with his or her preferred style has no obvious or compelling reason to switch learning styles. Teaching cognitive flexibility to certain students is not only an unwise use of valuable instructional time, but may also be frustrating to students and lead to less, not more, learning. More important, there is no empirical evidence that these strategies enhance student achievement.

Promising Aspects of the Learning-Styles Research

Although the research on learning styles is plagued by methodological, conceptual, and pedagogical problems, and is "thin and fragmented" (Banks, 1988, p. 465), there are many aspects of the literature that have significant potential for enhancing the achievement of culturally diverse students.

First, learning-styles research emphasizes the cultural context of teaching and learning (Irvine, 1992). Cultural variables are powerful, yet often overlooked, explanatory factors in the school failure of children of color. African American, Hispanic, and Indian students bring to the school setting a distinctive set of cultural forms and behaviors, including their group's history, language, values, norms, rituals, and symbols.

It must be emphasized that effective teachers of these students must contextualize the teaching act, giving attention to their students' cultural forms, behaviors, and experiences. Teachers also must negotiate and construct their understanding of teaching by examining the intersection of contexts and culture as well as their own behaviors, talents, and preferences. The cultural context of teaching and learning reminds teachers to be attentive not only to individual students' learning styles but to their own actions, instructional goals, methods, and materials as they relate to their students' cultural experiences and preferred learning environment. The teacher should probe the school, community, and home environments in a search for insights into diverse students' abilities, preferences, motivations, and learning approaches. Villegas (1991) calls this process "mutual accommodation in which both teachers and students adapt their actions to the common goal of academic success with cultural respect" (p. 12).

The learning-styles research reminds teachers to (a) understand and appreciate students' personal cultural knowledge, and (b) use their students' prior knowledge and culture in teaching. This process calls for the construction and design of relevant cultural metaphors and images in an effort to bridge the gap between what the students know and appreciate and the new knowledge or concepts to be taught. This process requires finding pertinent cultural examples, applying, comparing, and contrasting them, and creating authentic discourse and authentic teacher questions that relate what is being taught to what the student knows. Giroux (1992) adds:

> This is not meant to suggest that the experiences that students bring to school be merely affirmed. On the contrary, one begins with such experiences but does not treat them as undisputed nor allow them to limit what is taught. Knowledge needs to be made meaningful in order to be made critical and transformative. (p. 9)

Second, the learning-styles research documents the importance of affect in teaching culturally diverse students. Teaching is an act of social interaction, and the resultant classroom climate is related directly to the interpersonal relationship between student and teacher. Learning-styles theories accentuate the significance of teacher-student interactions that include eye contact, facial expressions, body posture, physical space, use of silence, and interpersonal touching (Longstreet, 1978). The foundation for success for students of color appears not to be teacher knowledge of specific learning styles, but committed, caring, dedicated teachers who are not afraid, resentful, or hostile, and who genuinely want to teach at schools with culturally diverse populations.

Third, learning-styles research is extremely helpful in that it rightly places the responsibility for student learning with teachers, instead of ascribing blame to students and their parents. It holds teachers responsible and accountable for designing instruction to meet students' individual learning needs by making them aware that all students are capable of learning, provided the learning environment attends to a variety of learning styles. In addition, learning-styles research alerts teachers to ways in which their unique teaching styles and pedagogical preferences may contribute to lack of achievement by certain students. It stresses the importance of increasing the number of instructional methods and amount of materials in the classroom and abandoning more traditional teacher-dominated methods of teaching. Kleinfeld (1992) states that learning styles "reminds teachers to create rich and interesting classrooms where children learn in different ways" (p. 2).

Conclusion

Learning-styles research is based on the theory that individuals respond to learning situations with consistent patterns of behavior. When applied to culturally diverse students, learning-styles research proposes to explain why children of the same culture and ethnicity often employ similar strategies for learning.

Learning-styles instruments, which attempt to operationalize the theoretical variables, have been moderately successful in distinguishing many of these styles. However, the applicability of the learning-styles research is limited. Understanding this limitation is particularly important in the education of children of color. One core assumption inherent in the learning-styles research is that children outside of mainstream culture learn better when teaching matches their preferred style. However, research on learning styles using culturally diverse students fails to support the premise that members of a given cultural group exhibit a distinctive style. Hence, the issue is not the identification of a style for a particular ethnic or gender group, but rather how instruction should be arranged to meet the instructional needs of culturally diverse students. Teachers who understand the preferred style of a student can use that knowledge to design and plan instruction and to encourage students to experiment with a wider repertoire of learning approaches. Clearly, learning-styles research is a useful beginning point in designing appropriate instruction for culturally diverse students, and not an end in itself.

References

American Association of School Administrators. (1991). *Learning styles: Putting research and common sense into practice.* Arlington, VA: Author.

American Psychological Association, (1966). *Standards for educational and psychological tests and manuals.* Washington, DC: Author.

Asbury, C. A., Stokes, A., Adderly-Kelly, B., & Knuckle, E. P. (1989). Effectiveness of selected neuropsychological, academic, and sociocultural measures for predicting Bannatyne pattern categories in black adolescents. *Journal of Negro Education, 58(2),* 177–188.

Atkinson, G. (1991). Kolb's Learning Style Inventory: A practitioner's perspective. *Measurement and Evaluation In Counseling and Development, 23*(4), 149–161.

Baker, S. (1982, December). *Characteristics of effective urban language arts teachers: An ethnographic study of retired educators.* Paper presented at the meeting of the American Reading Forum, Sarasota, FL.

Banks, J. A. (1987) *Teaching strategies for ethnic studies* (4th ed.). Boston: Allyn and Bacon.

Banks, J. A. (1987). Ethnicity, class, cognitive, and motivational styles: Research and teaching implications. *Journal of Negro Education, 57*(4), 452–466.

Barbe, W., & Swassing, R. (1979). *Swassing-Barbe modality index.* Columbus, OH: Zaner-Bloser.

Baruth, L. G., & Manning, M. L. (1992). *Multicultural education of children and adolescents.* Boston: Allyn and Bacon.

Becker, L. O., Bender, N. N., & Morrison, G. (1978). Measuring impulsivity-reflection: A critical review. *Journal of Learning Disabilities, 11*(10), 626–632.

Bell, Y. R., & McGraw-Burrell, R. (1988). Culturally-sensitive and traditional methods of task presentation and learning performance in black children. *The Western Journal of Black Studies, 21*(4), 187–193.

Bennett, C. J. (1990). *Comprehensive multicultural education* (2nd ed.). Boston: Allyn and Bacon.

Bermudez, A. (1986, March). *Examining the effects of home training on problem-solving styles.* Paper presented at the meeting of the Teachers of English to Speakers of Other Languages, Anaheim, CA.

Blaha, J. (1982). Predicting reading and arithmetic achievement with measures of reading attitudes and cognitive styles. *Perceptual and Motor Skills, 55,* 107–114.

Bloom, B. S. (1976), *Human characteristics and school learning.* New York: McGraw-Hill.

Boykin, A. W. (1986). The triple quandary and the schooling of Afro-American children. In U. Neisser (Ed.), *The school achievement of minority children* (pp. 57–92). Hillsdale, NJ: Lawrence Erlbaum Associates.

Boykin, A, W., & Toms, F. D. (1985). Black child socialization. In H. P. McAdoo & J. L. McAdoo (Eds.), *Black children: Social, educational, and parental environments* (pp. 33–51). Beverly Hills, CA: Sage Publications.

Bradley, C. (1984), Issues in mathematics education for Native Americans and directions for research. *Journal for Research in Mathematics Education, 15* (2), 96–106.

Brown v. Board of Education of Topeka, 347 *U.S. 483 (1954).*

Buriel, R. (1978). Relationship of three field-dependence measures to the reading and math achievement of Anglo American and Mexican American children. *Journal of Educational Psychology, 70*(2), 167–174.

Butter, E. J., Kenned, C. B, & Shoemaker-Kelly, K. E. (1982). Prediction of third grade reading ability as a function of performance on visual, auditory and visual-auditory cognitive style tasks. *The Alberta Journal of Educational Research, 28*(4), 347–359.

Casteñeda, A., & Gray, T. (1974). Bicognitive processes in multicultural education, *Educational Leadership, 32,* 203–207.

Chimezie, A. (1988), Black children's characteristics and the schools: A selective adaptation approach. *The Western Journal of Black Studies, 12*(2), 77–85.

Clarkson, J. (1983). Urban learning styles. In J. M. Lakebrink (Ed.), *Children's success in school* (pp. 115–139). Springfield, IL; Charles C. Thomas.

Creek, R. J., McDonald, W. C, & Ganley, M. A. (1991). *Internality and achievement in the intermediate grades* (Report No. SP-032-968). Office of Educational Research and Improvement. (ERIC Document Reproduction Service ED No. 330656)

Cureton, G. O. (1978). Using a black learning style. *The Reading Teacher, 31*(7), 751–756.

Cushner, K, McClelland, A., & Safford, P. (1992), *Human diversity in education.* New York: McGraw-Hill.

Davis, S. M. (1984). *Managing corporate culture.* Cambridge, MA: Ballinger Press.

Dunn, R. S., & Dunn, K.J. (1979). Learning styles/teaching styles: Should they . . . Can they be matched? *Educational Leadership, 36,* 238–244.

Dunn, R., Dunn, K, & Price, G. E. (1978). *Learning style inventory.* Lawrence, KS: Price Systems.

Dunn, R, Gemake, J. G., Jalali, F. (1990). Cross-cultural differences in learning styles of elementary-age students from four ethnic backgrounds. *Journal of Multicultural Counseling and Development, 18*(2), 68–93.

Erickson, F. (1986). Culture difference and science education. *The Urban Review, 18*(2), 117–124.

Foster, M. (1989). "It's cooking now": A performance analysis of the speech event of a Black teacher in an urban community college. *Language in Society, 18,* 1–29.

Gallagher, J, J., & Barney, C. T. (1987). *The malleability of children.* Baltimore, MD: Paul H. Brookes Publishing Co.

Gardner, H. (1983). *Frames of mind: The theory of multiple intelligences.* New York: Basic Books.

Gilbert, S, E., & Gay, G. (1989). Improving the success in school of poor black children. In B. J. R. Shade (Ed.), *Culture, style, and the educative process* (pp. 275–283). Springfield, IL: Charles C. Thompson.

Giroux, H. A. (1992). Educational leadership and the crisis of democratic government. *Educational Researcher, 21*(4), 4–11.

Gjerde, P. F., Block, J., & Block, J. H. (1985). Longitudinal consistency of Matching Familiar Figures Test performance from early childhood to preadolescence. *Developmental Psychology, 21*(2), 262–271.

Goodlad, J. (1984). *A place called school.* New York: McGraw-Hill.

Gregore, A. F. (1979). Learning/teaching styles: Potent forces behind them. *Educational Leadership, 36,* 234–236.

Gregore, A. F. (1982). *Transaction ability inventory.* Department of Secondary Education. University of Connecticut, Storrs.

Grossman, H. (1984), *Educating Hispanic students.* Springfield, IL: Charles C. Thomas.

Hale-Benson, J. E. (1986). *Black children: Their roots, culture, and learning styles.* Baltimore, MD. Johns Hopkins University Press.

Hall, E. T. (1989). Unstated features of the cultural context of learning. *The Educational forum, 54,* 21–34.

Hanson, M. J. (1992). Ethnic, cultural, and language diversity in intervention settings. In E. W. Lynch & M. J. Hanson (Eds.), *Developing cross-cultural competence* (pp. 3–18). Baltimore, MD; Paul H. Brookes Publishing Co.

Hill, J. (1971). *Personalized education programs utilizing cognitive style mapping.* Bloomfield Hills, MI: Oakland Community College Press.

Hilliard, A. G, (1989/90). Teachers and cultural styles in a pluralistic society. *Rethinking Schools, 14*(2), 3.

Hilliard, A. G. (1992). Behavioral style, culture, and teaching and learning. *Journal of Negro Education, 61*(3), 370–377.

Hoopes, D. S., & Pusch, M. D. (1979). Definitions of terms. In M. D. Pusch (Ed,), *Multicultural education: A cross-cultural training approach* (pp. 2–8). Yarmouth, ME: Intercultural Press.

Irvine, J, J. (1990). *Black students and school feature: Policies, practices, and prescriptions.* Weapon, CT: Greenwood Publishing Group

Irvine, J. J. (1992). Making teacher education culturally responsive. In M. E. Dilworth (Ed), *Diversity in teacher education* (pp. 79–92). San Francisco: Jossey-Bass.

Jacobs, R. L. (1990). Learning styles or black high, average, and low achievers. *The Clearing House, 63,* 253–254.

Jones, F. C. (1981). *A traditional model of educational excellence.* Washington, DC: Howard University Press.

Kagan, J. (1965). *Learning and the educational process.* Chicago: Rand McNally.

Kampwirth, T.J., & MacKenzie, K. (1989). Modality preference and word learning: The predictive ability of the Swassing-Barbe Modality Index and the Illinois Test of Psycholinguistic Abilities. *Educational Research Quarterly, 13*(2), 18–25.

Kleinfeld, J. (1992), *Learning styles and culture.* Fairbanks: University of Alaska Press.

Kogan, N. (1971). Educational implications of cognitive styles. In G. S. Lesser (Ed.), *Psychology and educational practice* (pp. 242–292). Glenview, IL: Scott, Foresman.

Kolb, D. A. (1984). *Experiential learning: Experience as the source of learning and development.* Englewood Cliffs, NJ: Prentice-Hall

Kreuze, J, G., & Payne, D. D. (1989). The learning styles preference of Hispanic and Anglo college students. A comparison. *Reading Improvement, 26*(2), 166–169.

Lerner, R. M. (1987). The concept of plasticity in development. In J. J. Gallagher & C. T, Ramey (Eds.), *The malleability of children* (pp. 3–14). Baltimore, MD: Paul H. Brookes Publishing Co.

Letteri, C. A. (1980). *Cognitive profile: Basic determinant of academic achievement.* Burlington, VT: Center for Cognitive Studies.

Longstreet, W. C. (1978). *Aspects of ethnicity.* New York: Teachers College Press.

Margolis, H., & Brannigan, G. G. (1978) Conceptual tempo as a parameter for predicting reading achievement. *Journal of Educational Research, 71*(6), 342–345.

Marin, G., & Marin, B. V. (1991). *Research with Hispanic population.* Newbury Park, CA: Sage Publishers.

McKenney, J. L., & Keen, P. G. W. (1974). How managers' minds work. *Harvard Business Review, 53,* 79–90.

McShane, D. A., & Plas, J. M. (1982) Wechsler scale performance patterns of American Indian children. *Psychology in the Schools, 19*(1), 8–17.

Messick, S. (1984). The nature of cognitive styles: Problems and promise in educational practice. *Educational Psychologist, 19,* 59–74.

Moore, C. G. 0932). *The Navajo culture and the learning of mathematics.* Washington, DC: The National Institute of Education. (ERIC Document Reproduction Service No. ED 214 708)

Myers, L B., & Briggs, K. C. (1976). *Myers-Briggs type indicator.* Palo Alto, CA: Consulting Psychologists Press.

Nieto, S. (1992). *Affirming diversity: The sociopolitical context of multicultural education.* New York: Longman.

Ogbu, J. (1988). Cultural diversity and human development. In D. T. Slaughter (Ed.), *Black children and poverty: A developmental perspective* (pp. 11–28). San Francisco: Jossey-Bass.

O'Leary, M., Calsyn, D. A., & Fauria, T. (1980). The Group Embedded Figures Test: A measure of cognitive style or cognitive impairment *Journal of Personality Assessment, 44*(5), 532–557.

Owens, R. G. (1987). *Organizational behavior in education.* Engle-wood Cliffs, NJ: Prentice-Hall.

Pasteur, A. B., & Toldson, I. L. (1982). *The roots of soul: The psychology of black expressiveness.* New York: Anchor Press.

Paulsen, K. (1978). Reflection-impulsivity and level of maturity. *Journal of Psychology, 99*(1), 109–112.

Piestrup, A. M. (1972). *Black dialed interference and accommodation of reading instruction in first grade* (Monograph of the language Behavior Research Laboratory). Berkeley: University of California.

Raile, F. N. (1980). *Structure of intellect factors and foreign language learning* (Structure of intellect studies Report No. FL-016-807). (ERIC Document Reproduction Service No. ED 288346)

Ramírez, M., & Casteñeda, A. (1974). *Cultural democracy, bicognitive development, and education.* New York: Academic Press.

Reinert, H. (1976). One picture is worth a thousand words? Not necessarily! *The Modern Language Journal, 60,* 160–168.

Rotter, J. B. (1959). Generalized expectations for internal versus external control of reinforcements. *Psychological Issues, 1* (4), 11–12.

Saracho, O. N., & Spodek, B. (1984). *Cognitive style and children's learning: Individual variation in cognitive processes.* Urbana, IL: ERIC Clearinghouse on Elementary and Early Childhood Education. (ERIC Document Reproduction Service No. 247 034)

Sawyer, D, (1991). Native learning styles: Shorthand for instructional adaptations? *Canadian Journal of Native Education, 18*(1), 99–104.

Serpell, R. (1976). *Culture's influence on behaviour.* London: Methuen & Co.

Shade, B. J. (1982). Afro-American cognitive styles: A variable in school success? *Review of Educational Research, 52*(2), 219–244.

Shade, B.J. (1989a). Afro-American cognitive patterns: A review of the research. In B. J. Shade (Ed.), *Culture, style, and the educative process* (pp. 94–115). Springfield, IL: Charles C. Thomas.

Shade, B. J. (1989b). The influence of perceptual development on cognitive style: Cross ethnic comparisons. *Early Child Development and Care, 51,* 137–155.

Siddle Walker, E. V. (1993). Interpersonal caring in the "good" segregated schooling of African American children: Evidence from the case of Caswell County Training School. *Urban Review, 25,* 63–77.

Slavin, R E. (1987). Cooperative learning and the education of black students. In D. S. Strickland & E. J. Cooper (Eds.). *Educating black children: America's challenge* (pp. 63–68). Washington, DC: Howard University Press.

Slonim, M, B. (1991). *Children, culture, and ethnicity.* New York: Garland.

Sowell, T. (1976) Patterns of black experience. *The Public Interest, 43,* 26–58.

Swanson, L. (1980) Cognitive style, locus of control, and school achievement in learning disabled females. *Journal of Clinical Psychology, 36*(4), 964–967.

Swisher, K., & Deyhle, D. (1989). The styles of learning are different, but the teaching is just the same. *Journal of American Indian Education* [Special Issue], 1–13.

Tharp, R, G. (1989). Psychocultural variables and constants: Efects on teaching and learning in schools. *American Psychologist, 44*(2), 349–359.

Tiedemann, J. (1989). Measures of cognitive style: A critical review. *Educational Psychologist, 24*(3), 261–275.

Valentine, C. A. (1971. Deficit, difference, and bicultural models of Afro-American behavior. *Harvard Educational Review, 41*(2), 137–157.

Villegas, A. M. (1991). *Culturally responsive pedagogy for the 1990s and beyond.* Washington, DC: American Association of Colleges of Teacher Education.

Witkin, H. A. (1971). *Group embedded figures test.* Palo Alto, CA: Consulting Psychologists Press.

Witkin, H. A., Dyk, R. B., Paterson, H. F., Goodenough, D. R., & Karp, S. A. (1962). *Psychological differentiation.* New York: Wiley.

Wlodkowski, R. J. (1978). *Student motivation information form.* Washington, DC: National Education Association.

Wood, C. M. (1979, April). *Cognitive style, school readiness and behavior as predictors of first-grade achievement.* (Report No. PS-011-098). Paper presented at the annual meeting of the American Educational Research Association, San Francisco. (ERIC Document Reproduction Service ED No. 182 014)

Zeìtoun, H. H., & Fowler, H. S. (1981, April). *Predicting Piagetian cognitive levels of teacher education students at the Pennsylvania State University.* (Report No. SP-O16-376). Paper presented at the annual meeting of the National Association for Research in Science Teaching, Ellenville, NY. (ERIC Document Reproduction Service No. ED 204 136)

Zigler, E. A. (1963). A measure in search of a theory. *Contemporary Psychology, 8,* 133–135.

CHAPTER 10

ASSESSING STUDENT LEARNING

Classroom Assessment: Guidelines for Success

Thomas A. Angelo,
The School for New Learning, DePaul University

If you've ever wondered, as a class ended, how well your students really understood that day's material, then you'll understand the impetus behind Classroom Assessment. If you've ever been unhappily surprised by students' performance on a midterm, final, or major assignment, then you'll understand the need for Classroom Assessment. And if you'd like to benefit from lessons learned since 1986, by practitioners and researchers, on how to use Classroom Assessment to improve teaching and learning, then you may find this essay useful.

What is Classroom Assessment?

Researchers have long known that both students and teachers need clear, timely, and focused feedback to improve performance. Classroom Assessment is a simple method—and a toolbox full of techniques—which faculty use to collect such feedback, early and often, on how well students are learning. Its purpose is to provide faculty and students with information and insights needed to improve teaching effectiveness and learning quality. Faculty use feedback gleaned through Classroom Assessment Techniques (CATs) to inform changes in their teaching. Faculty also share feedback from CATs with students to help them improve their learning and study strategies. Since 1986, when K. Patricia Cross and I first introduced Classroom Assessment, this practical feedback method has been employed by tens of thousands of college teachers in the United States and abroad.

The "Minute Paper" is one of the simplest, most widely used CATs, and a good example of the method. Attributed to Dr. Charles Schwartz, a physics professor at UC Berkeley, the Minute Paper has, been adapted and used since the mid-1980s in virtually every discipline. The Minute Paper asks students to respond anonymously to some variant of these two questions: (1) What are the 2–3 most important things you learned in class today? And (2) What questions remain uppermost in your mind? The "Muddiest Point," a variation on the Minute Paper developed by Professor Frederick Mosteller of Harvard, elicits useful feedback with just one question: "What was the muddiest point in today's lecture?"—or in today's discussion, lab, reading, quiz, or other learning activity.

By quickly scanning and summarizing responses to the CAT, the teacher can make well-targeted adjustments to the next class, recognize and capitalize on what students have learned well (or not learned)), and clear up questions that might impede further learning. We've learned that Classroom Assessment is most effective when teachers: (1) explain why they are asking these questions, (2) share a summary of responses with students, and (3) discuss how they and the students can make best use of the feedback. Letting students in on the process helps promote active engagement, participation, and more reflective learning.

Reprinted from *Essays on Teaching Excellence: Toward the Best in the Academy,* edited by K.H. Gillespie (2000), The POD Network.

At first glance, faculty sometimes confuse Classroom Assessment Techniques (CATs) with the questions we ask in class, with tests and quizzes, or with familiar teaching techniques. Most teachers ask questions to check understanding. And most of us have noticed that typically only a small, not very representative percentage of students volunteers to answer. CATs, by contrast, elicit anonymous responses, usually in writing, from all or nearly all of the students. Unlike quizzes and tests, CATs are for quickly assessing the whole group's learning, not for evaluating the work of individual students to assign grades. And while all faculty use teaching techniques, whether they know it or not, some faculty go a step further, using CATs to find out how well those techniques are promoting learning.

Since the late 1980s, several researchers have studied the effects and effectiveness of using Classroom Assessment Techniques in college and university classrooms. From these studies, which involved observations, interviews, focus groups, survey questionnaires, and/or document analysis, several clear trends have emerged. Below, I'll summarize key lessons and guidelines from that research and, in particular, from an extensive study of faculty and student attitudes about the use of CATs carried out by Mimi Harris Steadman (1998).

What's in it for students?

Across many different studies, the great majority of students whose teachers employed CATs describe the process as advantageous. These students see CATs as evidence that instructors are interested in and responsive to their concerns and suggestions. They report feeling more involved, engaged, and interested in class. They tend to rate teachers who use CATs as more effective than those who don't. And some students feel that CATs help them learn how to learn—as well as to learn course content.

Surprisingly, students rarely identify any disadvantages in using CATs. The few negative comments tend to focus on faculty who either do not respond or respond defensively to feedback, or on the fact that CATs "force" passive students to participate actively. On the whole, it appears that students both value and benefit from the effective use of Classroom Assessment.

What's in it for teachers?

Since most faculty who use Classroom Assessment do so voluntarily, it is perhaps less surprising that they tend to see its benefits as far outweighing its costs. The advantage teachers most often note is that CATs provide a quick and easy way to monitor what and how their students are learning. They also mention the importance of gaining tools and data to reflect on and improve their teaching. Teachers believe that this simple assessment and feedback method raises student involvement and learning quality. Those who share their Classroom Assessment experiences and data with other teachers are the most enthusiastic. Faculty, like students, report few disadvantages. However, some note the amount of time CATs require and the challenges posed by negative feedback. Overall, like their students, most faculty who use Classroom Assessment are convinced it benefits teachers and learners. Both teachers and learners recognize intrinsic (more satisfaction and learning) and extrinsic (higher grades and student evaluations) motivators for using CATs.

This suggests that both groups see this as a way of "doing well by doing good."

Getting Started Successfully

One way to get started is to borrow and skim through a copy of *Classroom Assessment Techniques: A Handbook for College Teachers,* a how-to resource for faculty. It contains 50 different CATs, examples and case studies from many disciplines, guidelines for success, as well as information on the theory and research behind the method.

In the last decade, several other books, articles, and dissertations have been published on Classroom Assessment, and a growing number of websites, particularly those of teaching and learning centers, offer useful information on CATs. After fifteen years of working with faculty, we've learned that it's wise to start small, to limit risk-taking and time invested initially, and to share ideas and outcomes with colleagues. The most satisfied and successful Classroom Assessors are those who belong to face-to-face (or virtual) "learning communities" of teachers interested in improving their practice and their students' learning.

Seven Guidelines for Success

The list that follows is based on recommendations from hundreds of experienced Classroom Assessors.

- Don't ask if you don't want to know. Don't ask for feedback on things you can't or won't change.
- Don't collect more feedback than you can analyze and respond to by the next class meeting.
- Don't simply adopt assessment techniques from others; adapt them to your own subject and students.
- Before you use a CAT, ask yourself: How might responses to this question(s) help me and my students improve? If you can't answer that question, don't do the assessment.
- Take advantage of the "Hawthorne Effect." If students know that you're using CATs to promote involvement, they're likely to be more involved. Alternately, if you explain that you are using it to promote more reflection and metacognition, you're likely to get just that.
- Teach students how to give useful feedback. If a CAT is worth doing, it's worth showing students how.
- Make sure to "close the feedback loop" by letting students know what you've gleaned from their responses and how you and they can use that information to improve learning.

From Classroom Assessment to Classroom Research

Classroom Assessment is one method of inquiry within the larger framework of Classroom Research—systematic, ongoing, scholarly inquiry into student learning by faculty. As such, Classroom Assessment serves many teachers as a natural introduction to the scholarship of teaching and learning.

References and Resources

Angelo, T.A. (Ed.) (1998). *Classroom Assessment and Research: Uses, approaches, and research findings.* New Directions for Teaching and Learning, no. 75. San Francisco: Jossey-Bass, 1998.

Angelo, T.A. and Cross, K.P. (1993). *Classroom assessment techniques: A handbook for college teachers,* (2nd ed.). San Francisco: Jossey-Bass.

Angelo, T.A. (Ed.). (1991). *Classroom research: Early lessons from success.* New Directions for Teaching and Learning, no. 46. San Francisco: Jossey-Bass.

Cross, K.P., & Steadman, M. H. (1996). *Classroom research: Implementing the scholarship of teaching.* San Francisco: Jossey-Bass.

Steadman, M.H. (1998). Using classroom assessment to change both teaching and learning. In T.A. Angelo (Ed.), *Classroom assessment and research: Uses, approaches, and research findings.* New Directions for Teaching and Learning, no. 75. San Francisco: Jossey-Bass.

Rethinking formative assessment in HE: A theoretical model and seven principles of good feedback practice

Dr David Nicol, University of Strathclyde
Debra Macfarlane-Dick, University of Glasgow

This section explores how higher education institutions might use assessment more effectively to promote student learning. Assessment provides a framework for sharing educational objectives with students and for charting their progress. However, it can generate feedback information that can be used by students to enhance learning and achievement. This feedback information can also help teachers realign their teaching in response to learners' needs. When assessment serves these purposes it is called 'formative assessment'. It is argued that formative assessment should be an integral part of teaching and learning in HE and that 'feedback' and 'feed-forward' should be systematically embedded in curriculum practices.

Formative assessment aids learning by generating feedback information that is of benefit to students and to teachers. Feedback on performance, in class or on assignments, enables students to restructure their understanding/skills and build more powerful ideas and capabilities. However, the provision of feedback information is not the sole province of the teacher. Peers often provide feedback—for example in group-work contexts—and students generate their own feedback while engaging in and producing academic work (see below). Formative assessment also provides information to teachers about where students are experiencing difficulties and where to focus their teaching efforts.

This section summarises the research on formative assessment and feedback. It includes the following:

- A conceptual model of the formative assessment/ feedback cycle
- Seven principles of good feedback practice: these are drawn from the model and a review of the research literature
- Some examples of good practice strategies related to each principle.

There are two central arguments within this section (i) that formative assessment and feedback should be used to empower students as self-regulated learners and (ii) that more recognition should be given to the role of feedback on learners' motivational beliefs and self-esteem. A number of writers have argued that feedback is under-conceptualised in the theoretical literature in HE and elsewhere, and that this makes it difficult to design effective feedback practices or to evaluate their effectiveness (Yorke, 2003; Sadler, 1998). While there has been a move over the last decade to conceptualise 'learning' from a constructivist perspective (Laurillard, 2002, for example), approaches to feedback have, until recently, remained obstinately focused on simple 'transmission' perspectives. Teachers 'transmit' feedback messages to students about strengths and weaknesses in their work assuming that these messages are easily decoded and turned into action. In contrast, in this paper,

Reprinted from *The Higher Education Academy* (2004).

students are assumed to construct actively their own understanding of feedback messages from tutors. Moreover, these messages are assumed to be complex and difficult to decipher (Higgins, Hartley and Skelton, 2001; Ivanic, Clark and Rimmershaw, 2000).

The conceptual model and the seven principles presented in this paper are intended as tools that teachers might use to analyse and improve their own formative assessment and feedback practices.

A conceptual model

In a review article, Black and Wiliam (1998) drew together over 250 studies of formative assessment with feedback carried out since 1988 spanning all educational sectors. The studies that formed part of their meta-analysis were ecologically valid in that they were drawn from real teaching situations. Black and Wiliam's analysis of these studies showed that feedback resulted in positive benefits on learning and achievement across all content areas, knowledge and skill types and levels of education. One of the most influential papers underpinning the Black and Wiliam review, and the writings of other researchers, is that by Sadler (1989). Sadler identified three conditions necessary for students to benefit from feedback. The student must:

- Possess a concept of the goal/standard or reference level being aimed for
- Compare the actual (or current) level of performance with that goal or standard
- Engage in appropriate action which leads to some closure of the gap.

Sadler argued that in many educational settings teachers give students feedback information on (b)—that is, how their performance compares to the standard—but that this feedback often falls short of what is actually necessary to help students close the gap. For example, such information might be difficult to understand (such as a comment that 'this essay is not sufficiently analytical') and especially if the learning goal (a) has not been fully assimilated in the first place. Black and Wiliam (1998) further elaborate on this communication issue when they discuss the links between the way a feedback message is received and what students do with that message.

> *... those factors which influence the reception of a [feedback] message and the personal decision about how to respond ... [include]. ... beliefs about the goals of learning, about one's capacity to respond, about the risks involved in responding in various ways and about what learning should be like (p21).*

Any model of feedback must take account of the way students make sense of, and use, feedback information. More importantly, however, is Sadler's argument that for students to be able to compare actual performance with a standard, and take action to close the gap, they *must already possess some of the same evaluative skills as their teacher.* For many writers, this observation has led to the conclusion that as well as focusing on the quality of the feedback messages, teachers should focus their efforts on strengthening the skills of self-assessment in their students (Yorke, 2003; Boud, 2000).

Figure 10.1 presents a conceptual model of formative assessment and feedback that synthesises current thinking by key researchers into this topic (Sadler, 1983, 1989; Black and Wiliam, 1998; Yorke, 2003; Torrance and Pryor, 1998). The figure is based on a model of feedback and self-regulated learning originally published by Butler and Winne (1995). A key feature in the model that differentiates it from commonplace understandings of feedback is that the student is assumed to occupy a central and active role in all feedback processes. They are always actively involved in monitoring and regulating their own performance both in terms of their goals and in terms of the strategies being used to reach those goals.

In the model, an academic task set by the teacher (in class or set as an assignment) is the starting point for the feedback cycle.

Engagement with the task requires that students draw on prior knowledge and motivational beliefs and construct a personal interpretation of the requirements and properties of the task. Based on this internal conception, they formulate their own task goals (which may be different from those of the teacher) and engage in actions to achieve these goals by applying tactics and strategies that generate outcomes. Monitoring these interactions with the task and the outcomes that are being cumulatively produced, generates *internal feedback.*

Figure 10.1
A Model of the Formative Assessment and Feedback.

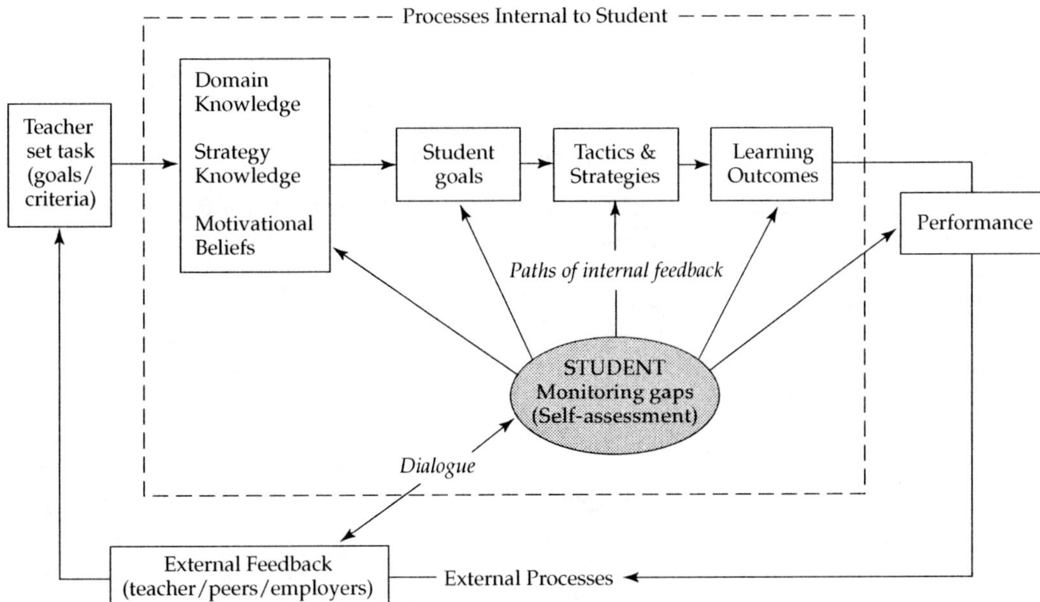

This feedback is derived from a comparison of current progress against internal goals or standards—gaps are identified (between progress and goals) and further actions are taken to close these gaps (Sadler, 1989). This self-generated feedback information might lead to a re-interpretation of the task or to the adjustment of internal goals or of tactics and strategies. Students might even revise their domain knowledge or beliefs which, in turn, would influence subsequent processes of self-regulation. If *external feedback* is provided, this additional information might augment, concur or conflict with the student's interpretation of the task and the path of learning (Butler and Winne, 1995).

In the model, external feedback to the student might be provided by teachers, peers or others (placement supervisor, for example). However, students are always actively engaged in feedback processes. First, they generate aspects of their own feedback as they monitor performance and identify and make sense of gaps while carrying out tasks. Second, they interpret and filter feedback information from external sources. The teacher's feedback response (based on their monitoring and assessment of student performance) must be interpreted and internalised by the student before it can influence subsequent action (Ivanic, Clark and Rimmershaw, 2000). This has important implications for feedback processes in HE. If students are always involved in monitoring and assessing their own work, then rather than just thinking of ways of enhancing the teacher's ability to deliver high quality feedback we should be devising ways of building upon this capacity for self-regulation (Yorke, 2003).

Seven principles of good feedback practice

From the conceptual model and the research literature on formative assessment it is possible to identify some broad principles of good feedback practice. A provisional list might include the following seven.

1. Facilitates the development of self-assessment (reflection) in learning.
2. Encourages teacher and peer dialogue around learning.
3. Helps clarify what good performance is (goals, criteria, standards expected).
4. Provides opportunities to close the gap between current and desired performance.
5. Delivers high quality information to students about their learning.

6. Encourages positive motivational beliefs and self-esteem.
7. Provides information to teachers that can be used to help shape the teaching.

The following sections provide the rationale for each principle in terms of the conceptual model and the associated research literature. Brief examples of how these principles might be applied are also suggested.

1. Facilitates the development of self-assessment in learning

Over the last decade there has been an increasing interest in strategies that encourage students to take a more active role in the management of their own learning (see Nicol, 1997). Black and Wiliam (1998) make the argument that 'a student who automatically follows the diagnostic prescription of a teacher without understanding of its purpose will not learn' (p54) while Sadler (1989) argues that the purpose of formative assessment should be to equip students gradually with the evaluative skills that their teachers' possess. These writers are concerned that an over-emphasis on teacher assessment might increase students' dependency on others rather than develop their ability to self-assess and self-correct.

In the conceptual model, the student or learner is always engaged in *monitoring gaps* between internally *set task and personal goals* and the *outcomes* that are being progressively produced. This monitoring is a by-product of purposeful engagement in a task. However, in order to build on this process, and the student's capacity for self-regulation, teachers should create more formal and structured opportunities for self-monitoring and the judging of progression to goals. Self-assessment tasks are a good way of doing this, as are activities that encourage reflection on both the processes and the products of learning.

Research shows that direct involvement by students in assessing their own work, and frequent opportunities to reflect on goals, strategies and outcomes are highly effective in enhancing learning and achievement (McDonald and Boud, 2003). Moreover, if the skills of self-assessment are developed progressively over the course of an undergraduate degree this would support a model of higher education where students are prepared for lifelong learning (Boud, 2000).

An important aspect of self-assessment involves helping students both to identify standards/criteria that apply to their work and to make judgements about how their work relates to these standards (Boud, 1986).

Examples of structured reflection and/or self-assessment are varied and might include students:

(1) requesting the kinds of feedback they would like when they hand in work;
(2) identifying the strengths and weaknesses in their own work in relation to criteria or standards before handing it in for teacher feedback;
(3) reflecting on their achievements and selecting work in order to compile a portfolio;
(4) setting achievement milestones for a task and reflecting back on progress and forward to the next stage of action;
(5) having students give feedback on each other's work (peer feedback) also helps support the development of self-assessment skills (for example, Gibbs, 1999).

2. Encourages teacher and peer dialogue around learning

While research shows that teachers have a central role in helping a develop student's own capacity for self-assessment in learning, external feedback from other sources (such as tutors or peers) is also crucial. Feedback from tutors and peers provides additional information that helps challenge students to reassess their knowledge and beliefs. Teacher feedback also serves as an authoritative external reference point against which students can evaluate, and self-correct their progress and their own internal goals.

In the conceptual model (figure 1), for external feedback to be effective it must be understood and internalised by the student before it can be used productively. Yet in the research literature (Chanock, 2000; Hyland, 2000) there is a great deal of evidence that students do not understand the feedback given by tutors (for instance, 'this report is not logically structured') and are therefore not able to take action to close the gap (that is, he or she may not know what to do to make the report more 'logical in structure'). External feedback as a transmission process involving 'telling' ignores the active role the student must play in constructing meaning from feedback messages.

One way of increasing the effectiveness of external feedback and the likelihood that the information provided is understood is to conceptualise feedback more as a *dialogue* rather than as information transmission. Feedback as dialogue means that the student not only receives initial feedback information but also has the opportunity to engage the teacher in discussion about that feedback. This is shown in the conceptual model by the two-way arrows that link external processes to those internal to the student. The idea that feedback encourages dialogue is considered good practice by many writers on assessment. For example, Freeman and Lewis (1998) argue that the teacher 'should try to stimulate a response and a continuing dialogue—whether this be on the topics that formed the basis of the assignment or aspects of students' performance or the feedback itself' (p51). Discussions with the teacher help students to develop their understanding of expectations and standards, to check out and correct misunderstandings and to get an immediate response to difficulties.

Unfortunately, with large class sizes it can be difficult for the teacher to engage in dialogue with students. Nonetheless, there are ways that teachers might increase feedback dialogue even in these situations. For example, by reporting feedback in class and structuring break out discussions of feedback or by using classroom technologies that collate student responses in class and then feed the results back visually as a histogram. This feedback can act as a trigger for teacher-managed discussion (for example, Nicol and Boyle, 2003).

Another source of external feedback are the students themselves. Peer dialogue is beneficial to student learning in a variety of ways. First, students who have just learned something are often better able than teachers to explain it to their classmates in a language and in a way that is accessible. Second, peer discussion exposes students to alternative perspectives on problems and to alternative tactics and strategies. Alternative perspectives enable students to revise or reject their initial hypothesis and construct new knowledge and meaning through negotiation. Thirdly, by commenting on the work of peers, students develop objectivity of judgement (about work in relation to standards) which can be transferred to the assessment of their own work ('I didn't do that either', for example). Fourthly, peer discussion can be motivational in that it encourages students to persist and gives a yardstick to measure their own performance against (see Nicol and Boyle, 2003). Finally, it is sometimes easier for students to accept critiques of their work from peers rather than tutors.

Good examples of feedback dialogue in class include:

(1) providing feedback using one-minute papers (Angelo and Cross, 1990);
(2) reviewing feedback in tutorials where students are asked to read the feedback comments they have been given and discuss these with peers—they might also be asked to suggest strategies to improve performance next time;
(3) asking students to find one or two examples of feedback comments that they found useful and to explain how they helped.

Other ways of using feedback dialogue in a planned way, for assignments, might involve:

(1) having students give each other descriptive feedback on their work in relation to published criteria before submission;
(2) group projects.

3. Helps clarify what good performance is

Students can only achieve a learning goal if they understand that goal, assume some ownership of it, and can assess progress (Sadler, 1989; Black and Wiliam, 1998). In the model (figure 10.1), understanding the goal means that there must be a reasonable degree of overlap between the task goal set by the student and the goal originally set by the teacher. However, there is considerable research evidence to suggest that there are often mismatches between tutors' and students' conceptions of goals and of assessment standards and criteria.

Hounsell (1997) has shown that tutors and students often have quite different conceptions about the goals and criteria for essays in undergraduate courses in history and psychology and that poor essay performance is correlated with the degree of mismatch. In a similar vein, Norton (1990) has shown that when students were asked to rank specific assessment criteria for an essay task they produced quite different rankings from those of their teachers. Weak and incorrect conceptions of goals not only influence what students do but also the value of feedback information. If students do not share (at least in part) their tutor's conceptions of assessment goals (criteria/standards) then the feedback information they receive is unlikely to 'connect' (Hounsell, 1997). In this case, it will be difficult for students to evaluate gaps between required and actual performance.

One way of clarifying task requirements (goals/ criteria/standards) is to provide students with written documents embodying descriptive statements that externalise assessment goals and the standards that define different levels of achievement. However, many studies have shown that it is difficult to make explicit assessment criteria and standards through written documentation or through verbal descriptions in class (Rust, Price and O'Donovan, 2003). Most criteria for complex tasks are difficult to articulate; they are often 'tacit' and unarticulated in the mind of the teacher. As Yorke notes:

> *Statements of expected standards, curriculum objectives or learning outcomes are generally insufficient to convey the richness of meaning that is wrapped up in them (Yorke, 2003, p480).*

Hence there is a need for strategies that complement written materials and simple verbal explanations. An approach that has proved particularly powerful in clarifying goals and standards has been to provide students with 'exemplars' of performance (Orsmond, Merry and Reiling, 2002) alongside other resources. Exemplars are effective because they define an objective and valid standard against which students can compare their work.

Strategies that have proved effective in clarifying criteria, standards and goals therefore include:

(1) providing better definitions of requirements using carefully constructed criteria sheets and performance level definitions;
(2) providing students with exemplar assignments with attached feedback;
(3) increasing discussion and reflection about criteria and standards in class;
(4) involving students in assessment exercises where they mark or comment on other students' work in relation to defined criteria and standards;
(5) workshops where students in collaboration with their teacher devise their own assessment criteria for a piece of work;
(6) combinations of the above five have proved particularly effective.

4. Provides opportunities to close the gap

According to Yorke (2003) two questions might be asked regarding external feedback. First, is the feedback of the best quality and second, does it lead to changes in student behaviour? Many researchers have focused on the first question but the second is equally important. External feedback provides an opportunity to close the gap in the learning process between the current learning achievements of the student and the goals set by the teacher. If feedback information is not turned into action soon after it is produced then this is a missed opportunity. As Boud notes:

> *The only way to tell if learning results from feedback is for students to make some kind of response to complete the feedback loop (Sadler, 1989). This is one of the most often forgotten aspects of formative assessment. Unless students are able to use the feedback to produce improved work, through for example, re-doing the same assignment, neither they nor those giving the feedback will know that it has been effective (Boud, 2000, p158).*

In the conceptual model (figure 1), Boud's arguments about closing the gap can be viewed in two ways. First, closing the gap is about supporting students while engaged in the act of production of a piece of work. Second, it is about providing opportunities to repeat the same 'task-performance-feedback cycle' by, for example, allowing resubmission. External feedback should support both processes: it should help students to recognise the next steps in learning and how to take them both during production and for the next assignment.

Supporting the act of production requires the generation of concurrent or intrinsic feedback that students can interact with while engaged in an assessment task. This feedback would normally be built into the task (a group task with peer interaction is an example here) or the task might be broken down into components each associated with its own feedback. Many forms of electronic feedback can be automatically generated to support task engagement (multiple choice, FAQs). Providing feedback at sub-task level is not significantly different from other forms of feedback described in this paper.

In HE, most students have little opportunity to use directly the feedback they receive to close the gap, especially in the case of planned assignments. Invariably they move on to the next assessment task soon after feedback is received. While not all work can be resubmitted, many writers argue that resubmissions should play a more prominent role in learning (Boud, 2000). In addition, the external feedback provided to students often focuses on identifying specific errors rather than providing constructive advice about how performance relates to standards and about how to make improvements in subsequent tasks; and even when corrective guidance about how to improve is given, students often do not fully understand it or know how to turn it into action.

Specific strategies to help students use external feedback to close the gap are:

(1) to increase the number of opportunities for resubmission;

(2) for teachers to model the strategies that might be used to close a performance gap in class (for example, model how to structure an essay when given a new question);

(3) teachers might also write down some 'action points' alongside the normal feedback they provide. This would identify for students what they should do next time to improve their performance;

(4) a more effective strategy might be to involve students in identifying their own action points in class based on the feedback they have just received. This would integrate the process into the teaching and learning situation and involve the students more actively in the generation and planned use of feedback.

5. Delivers high quality information to students about their learning

Another finding from the research is that a great deal of external feedback given to students is not of good quality: it may be delayed, not relevant or informative, or overwhelming in quantity, and so on. Good quality external feedback is defined as information that helps students trouble-shoot their own performance and take action to close the gap between intent and effect. In the model (figure 10.1) processes internal to the student (shown by the dotted line) are strongly influenced by contextual factors in the environment over which the teacher has considerable control. The teacher sets the task, assesses performance and provides feedback. Research shows that in each of these areas there is considerable scope for improvement.

Feedback needs to be relevant to the task in hand and to student needs. Despite this, research shows that feedback information is often about strengths and weaknesses in handed-in work or about aspects of performance that are easy to identify (such as spelling mistakes) rather than about aspects that are of greater importance to academic learning but that are more abstract and difficult to define (strength of argument, for example).

Students might also receive too much feedback, making it difficult to decide what to act on. In the literature on essay assessment, researchers have tried to formulate guidelines regarding the quantity and tone of feedback comments. For example, Lunsford (1997) has advocated providing only three well thought out feedback comments per essay. Moreover, these comments should indicate to the student how the reader experienced the essay as it was read—'playing back' to the students how the essay worked—rather than offering judgemental comments. Such comments help the student to understand the difference between his or her intentions and the effects. Comments should always be written in a non-authoritative tone and where possible, they should offer corrective advice (both about the writing process as well as about content) instead of just information about strengths and weaknesses.

Other researchers have argued against following positive comments with lists of criticisms (such as 'this essay was well-structured . . . However . . .') arguing instead that descriptive information about performance in relation to defined assessment criteria is better received by students and is more likely to be acted upon.

It has become common practice in recent years to provide feedback sheets with assessment criteria as a way of informing students about task requirements and of providing consistent feedback in relation to expected goals. However, the construction of such feedback sheets does not always encourage students to engage with a task in a way desired by teachers. Sadler (1983) has argued that the use of such criteria sheets often has unwanted effects. For example, if there are a large number of criteria (12–20) they may convey a conception of an assessment task (an essay, for instance) as a list of things to be done ('ticked off') rather than a holistic process—something involving the production of a coherent argument supported by evidence. So as well as being responsive to student needs, teachers should also consider whether the instruments they use to deliver feedback are commensurate with the expected goals and task requirements.

Strategies that increase the quality of feedback drawn from research include:

(1) making sure that feedback is provided in relation to pre-defined criteria but paying particular attention to the number of criteria;
(2) providing feedback soon after a submission;
(3) providing corrective advice, not just information on strengths/ weaknesses;
(4) limiting the amount of feedback so that it is used;
(5) prioritising areas for improvement;
(6) providing online tests so that feedback can be accessed anytime, any place and as many times as students wish;
(7) focusing on students with greatest difficulties.

6. Encourages positive motivational beliefs and self-esteem

How can we make assessment a positive learning experience for students? A key feature of the model of feedback (figure 10.1) presented in this paper is the importance attached to motivational beliefs and self-esteem. In the model, students construct their own motivation based on their appraisal of the teaching, learning and assessment context. This influences the goals that students set (personal and academic) as well as their commitment to these goals. However, research has shown that external feedback can have a positive or negative effect on motivational beliefs and on self-esteem. It influences how students feel about themselves which, in turn, affects what and how they learn.

Many studies have shown that, contrary to expectation, frequent high stakes assessment (where marks or grades are given) can lower the motivation to learn (Harlen and Crick, 2003). Such assessments encourage students to focus on performance goals (passing the test) rather than learning goals (Elliott and Dweck, 1988). In one study, Butler (1988) demonstrated that feedback comments alone improved students' subsequent interest in learning and performance when compared with controlled situations where marks alone or feedback and marks were given. Butler argued that students paid less attention to the comments when given marks and consequently did not try to use the comments to make improvements.

Butler (1987) has also argued that grading student performance has less effect than feedback comments because it leads students to compare themselves against others (egoinvolvement) rather than to focus on the difficulties in the task and on making efforts to improve (task-involvement). Feedback given as grades has also been shown to have especially negative effects on the self-esteem of low ability students (Craven, et al., 1991).

Dweck (2000) has interpreted some of these findings in terms of a developmental model that differentiates students into those who believe that ability is fixed and that there is a limit to what they can achieve (the 'entity view') and those that believe that their ability is malleable and depends on the effort that is input into a task (the 'incremental view'). These views affect how students respond to learning difficulties. Those with an entity view (fixed) interpret failure as a reflection of their low ability and are likely to give up whereas those with an incremental view (malleable) interpret this as a challenge or an obstacle to be overcome.

These motivational beliefs, however, are not immutable. In part, they depend on how teachers provide feedback. Praising effort and strategic behaviours and focusing students on learning goals leads to higher achievement than praising ability or intelligence which can result in a learned-helplessness orientation. In summary, 'feedback which draws attention away from the task and towards self-esteem can have a negative effect on attitudes and performance' (Black and Wiliam, 1998, p23).

The implication of these studies for teaching practice is that motivation and self-esteem are more likely to be enhanced when a course has many low-stakes tasks with feedback geared to providing information about progress and achievement rather than high stakes summative assessment tasks where information is only about success or failure or about how students compare with peers.

Other strategies that would help encourage high levels of motivation to succeed include:

(1) providing marks on written work only after students have responded to feedback comments;
(2) allocating time for students to re-write selected pieces of work—this would help change students' expectations about purpose;
(3) automated testing with feedback;
(4) drafts and resubmissions.

7. Provides information to teachers that can be used to help shape the teaching

Good feedback practice is not only about providing good information to the students about learning—it is also about providing good information to teachers. As Yorke notes:

> The act of assessing has an effect on the assessor as well as the student. Assessors learn about the extent to which they [students] have developed expertise and can tailor their teaching accordingly (Yorke, 2003, p482).

In order to produce feedback that is relevant and informative teachers themselves need good data about how students are progressing. They also need to be involved in reviewing and reflecting on this data and in taking action to help close the learning gap.

In the conceptual model (figure 101) information about students is provided when the learning outcomes are translated into public performances. Teachers generate this public information about students through a variety of methods—by setting assessment tasks and in class, through questioning of students and through observation. Such information helps teachers uncover student difficulties with subject matter (conceptual misunderstandings, for example) and difficulties with study methods while carrying out assessment tasks.

Frequent assessment tasks, especially diagnostic tests, can help teachers generate cumulative information about students' levels of understanding and skill so that they can adapt their teaching accordingly. This is one of the key ideas behind the work of Angelo and Cross (1990) in the United States. They have shown how teachers can gain regular feedback information about student learning within large classes by using short test-feedback cycles. These strategies benefit both the student and the teacher (Steadman, 1998) and they can be adapted to any classroom situation or discipline. Moreover, implementation allows teachers and students to share, on a regular basis their conceptions about both the goals and processes of learning (Stefani and Nicol, 1997).

A variety of strategies are available to teachers to help generate and collate quality information about student learning and help them decide how to use it. For example:

(1) one-minute papers where students carry out a small assessment task and hand this in anonymously at the end of a class, such as . . .
What was the main point of this lecture? What question remains outstanding for you at the end of this teaching session?;

(2) having students request the feedback they would like when they make an assignment submission;

(3) having students identify where they are having difficulties when they hand in assessed work;

(4) asking students in groups to identify 'a question worth asking', based on prior study, that they would like to explore for a short time at the beginning of the next tutorial;

(5) quick evaluation strategies at key points in teaching.

THE ART AND SCIENCE OF CLASSROOM ASSESSMENT

S. M. BROOKHART

Options For Classroom Assessment

A Framework for Understanding Assessment Options

Student assessment should be multidimensional and the focus of ongoing communication with students about their achievement of objectives for the course. The methodology for classroom assessment can be thought of as a toolkit that faculty members use for accomplishing their purposes. Students' involvement in assessment, at all stages of the process from design through scoring, is also recommended as a strategy for teaching and learning and for enhancing motivation.

Several versions of a framework for understanding types of classroom assessment have been offered (see Stiggins, 1992, 1997, particularly 1992). Assessment methods can be grouped into three general categories: paper-and-pencil tests, performance assessments of processes or products, and oral communication. For each category, objective (right/wrong or present/absent) and subjective (judgment of degree of quality) scoring can be developed. Objective scoring is easier to do than subjective rating, but objectively scored questions are more difficult to write well than are subjectively scored questions and exercises. Depending on the author one consults, portfolios can be considered a fourth category of assessment or a different sort of beast that falls between the cracks: part assessment method and part collection and communication of assessment results.

Different assessments are necessary to cover the full range of achievement targeted: knowledge, thinking, processes, products, and dispositions. Table 10.1 describes and gives some examples of the various kinds of assessments that can be used to evaluate achievement of learning goals.

Paper-and-Pencil Tests

College instructors are generally familiar with both objectively and subjectively scored tests. Test development should be keyed to the learning objectives for the course. It should be obvious to the student that what has been stressed in the course and what is valued knowledge are the focus of the exercises the students are asked to do. If, for example, a course had stressed interpreting poetry but a large portion of the final examination includes identifying poets, dates, and titles of poems, then scores on the final would not reflect what the instructor intended the students to learn, nor would they reflect what students thought they were supposed to learn.

To design a test, the learning targets must first be identified and then assessed to decide whether they represent knowledge, thinking, skills, products, or dispositions. Knowledge and thinking are usually captured well by well-written tests, but if the target includes skills or products, a test will be only a proxy for complete assessment. Two steps are necessary to make sure the test really taps into students' knowledge or thinking and not something else. The first is to design the general form of the exam, giving space and weight to various topics as appropriate to the instructional intent. A test

Reprinted from *ASHE-ERIC Higher Education Report* (1999), George Washington University.

TABLE 10.1

Classroom Assessment Options

	Objective scoring	Subjective scoring	Most appropriate uses	Major advantages	Potential pitfalls
Paper-and-pencil tests	Multiple choice, true/false, matching, fill in the blanks	Essays or show-the-work problems judged with rubrics or rating scales	To assess knowledge and thinking over a range of content *or* to assess dispositions and interests (ungraded)	Most reliable way to assess knowledge and thinking in a content area domain; best way to cover a large number of facts and concepts	Require clearly written items that appropriately sample a range of content material; easiest to write recall-level questions
Performance assessments	Judgments of performance on a task using a checklist	Judgments of performance on a task using rubrics or rating scales	To assess in-depth thinking in one area *or* to assess skills attained or products created	Allow measurement of in-depth thinking, skills, or products not readily assessable by tests	Require clear expectations for tasks and scoring to provide meaningful assessment information
Oral questions	In-class questions with right/wrong answers	Discussions or interviews evaluated with rubrics or rating scales	To assess knowledge and thinking during instruction *or* to assess dispositions and interests (ungraded)	Provide feedback for instruction; identify students' concepts and misconceptions; tap students' interests and opinions	Students may prefer not to speak up or give their honest responses in class.
Portfolios	Could use a checklist for portfolio entries but not recommended except for special purposes	Collection of a student's work and reflections over time, entries can be rated separately or as a whole	To document progress or development *or* to showcase complex achievement of a range of skills	Allow for assessment of student's development and some ownership and control by student	Require clear purpose, focused construction, and long-term attention to give any more useful information than stand-alone assessments

Source: Adapted from Stiggins, 1987, 1992, 1997.

blueprint can help accomplish this aim. The second step is to write clear, unambiguous test questions. Students can help with this step, but instructors who ask students to write questions should make sure that final, edited items are well written, according to the guidelines in this subsection, and that the final set of items used for a test matches its blueprint.

Objective test items

Table 10.2 presents some general guidelines for writing objective test items. The purpose of these dos and don'ts is an important one that contributes to the validity of the information instructors will get from students' performance on the test. If a test item is written in such a way as to tap into general logic or cleverness, then a student's score will reflect general ability as well as the particular knowledge or application that the instructor meant to teach. General cleverness is not a bad quality, but it is not the basis on which a student's work in a course should be judged. A poorly written test item also increases the risk that students who know how to answer the question will get it wrong, which will cause the test score to reflect less achievement of whatever the course was designed to teach than is actually the case.

Each "do" and "don't" has a reason behind it. For example, the suggestion to put matching and multiple-choice answers in logical order, if there is one, is to save students who know the answer some reading and processing time they should be spending on the substance of the test material. If the question is "In what year was the Battle of Hastings fought?" some students may need to look over a list of choices and decide among them. But for some students, answering this question is really a matter of saying to themselves, "Where did she put 1066?" If the dates are listed in order, it is easier to answer such a question, and the student can answer the question quickly and move on, saving his or her serious thinking for more important parts of the test. Alphabetical order works well for lists of names or places. If no logical order is apparent, or if putting the answers in order would give clues to the answers of other items on the test, then the choices should be scrambled for the same reason—to have students' scores be as accurate a representation as possible of what they really know.

Writing good test items is a skill that requires practice, drafting, editing, and all the other elements of good writing in any format. Writing unambiguous test items is a more understandable task after an instructor has studied the reasons behind each suggestion. (See the resources described in "Conclusions and Further Resources for Faculty.")

Essays and partial-credit problems

Assessing thinking and problem solving is a good use of the time and effort it takes to read and score essay tests or show-the-work and partial-credit problems in math or science. To really assess thinking, and not merely recall, the question must present a new problem to the student, one that he or she has not seen before. The question does not have to be truly *new*, just new to the student. As described earlier, even the most complex reasoning question becomes a matter of recall if the textbook or class discussion has already laid out the reasoning for students.

This approach will sound harsh to instructors who are used to hearing complaints about exams: "We never went over that in class." The way around this complaint is to make sure that class time includes work on new problems, students' analysis of issues, and the like, so that students understand why new thinking is important and called for, and learn how to do it. The solution is *not* to preview everything on a test; otherwise, no higher order thinking can be demonstrated. Table 10.3 presents some suggestions for writing essay questions.

Only the instructor of the class can determine what is new and what is not. Consider the example of a freshman English class that is reading the Declaration of Independence. An essay question about the structure and persuasiveness of Jefferson's argument could require thorough, original thought—or not! Suppose a whole class period had been devoted to discussing "the structure and persuasiveness of Jefferson's argument." Then this question would tap students' recall of the day's discussion.

TABLE 10.2

Dos and Don'ts for Writing Objective Test Items

General

1. Use clear and concise language.
2. Prepare a draft and edit it.
3. Proofread the draft from a student's point of view.
4. Test important ideas, not trivial points.
5. Write short, clear directions for *all* sections of the test.
6. Don't copy statements from the textbook.

True/false items

1. Make statements definitely true or definitely false.

   NOT: The advent of the computer is the strongest force for social change in the 20th century.

   BETTER: Some authors have compared the social impact of the advent of the computer with that of the printing press.
2. Keep statements short.
3. Have only one idea per statement.

   NOT: Captain Ahab was not afraid of death, whereas Ishmael wanted very much to live.

   BETTER: Captain Ahab was not afraid of death.
4. Use positive statements; if the statement contains a "not," highlight it.

   NOT: The issue of the Emancipation Proclamation in 1863 did not result in immediate freedom for any slaves.

   BETTER: The issue of the Emancipation Proclamation in 1863 did NOT result in immediate freedom for any slaves.
5. Make "trues" and "falses" about the same length.
6. Avoid patterns of answers (e.g., TTFF or TFTF).

This point about novelty of problem and level of thought required from the student shows clearly that assessment and instruction are related enterprises. Many authors have polemicized that assessment and instruction *should* be related and have demonstrated ways to do it well. But whether an instructor realizes or intends it or not, assessment and instruction *will* be related, because both are experiences the student has with material he or she is supposed to learn. Therefore, it is important for instructors to understand the nature of this relationship. Writing better essay questions and problems will be only one of many good results from this understanding. Consider the following scenario:

> This is a true story. A colleague of ours teaches an introductory calculus section. Early one term, he and his class were working through some standard motion problems: "A boy drops a water balloon from a window. If it takes 0.8 seconds to strike his erstwhile friend, who is 5 feet tall, how high is the window?" On the exam, the problem took this form: "Someone walking along the edge of a pit accidentally kicks into it a small stone, which falls to the bottom in 2.3 seconds. How deep is the pit?" One student was visibly upset. The question was not fair, she protested. The instructor had promised that there would not be any material on the exam that they had not gone over in class. "But we did a dozen of those problems in class," our colleague said. "Oh no," shot back the student, "we never did a single pit problem." (McClymer & Knoles, 1992, p. 33)

TABLE 10.2 *(Continued)*

Matching items

1. Number the items in the first column; letter the response choices in the second column.
2. Make items and response choices homogeneous.

NOT: Match the word with its definition.

1. Solid bodies bounded by planar surfaces	a. Absolute zero
2. At a constant temperature, the volume of a given amount of gas varies inversely with pressure.	b. Boyle's law
3. Temperature at which the kinetic energy of molecules is zero	c. Crystal
4. Process of passing from solid to gas without going through the liquid state, or vice versa	d. Enthalpy of fusion
5. Heat required to melt 1 mole of a substance	e. Ionic radii
	f. Sublimation

BETTER: Match each gas law with the name of the scientist associated with it.

1. The volume of a certain mass of gas is inversely proportional to the pressure, at constant temperature.	a. Avogadro
2. The total pressure in a mixture of gases is the sum of the individual partial pressures.	b. Boyle
3. The rates of diffusion of two gases are inversely proportional to the square roots of their densities.	c. Charles
4. Equal numbers of molecules are contained in equal volumes of different gases if the temperature and pressure are the same.	d. Dalton
5. The volume of a given mass of gas is directly proportional to the absolute temperature, at constant pressure.	e. Graham
	f. Kelvin

3. Each response choice should look like a plausible answer for any item in the set. If not, the list is not similar enough to be a set of matching items.
4. Keep the lists short (5 to 10 items).
5. Separate longer lists into two or more shorter ones, using the principle of homogeneity.
6. Avoid having the same number of items and response choices so that the last answer is not really a choice.
7. Put the longer phrases in the left column and the shorter phrases in the right column.
8. Arrange response choices in a logical order, if there is one.
9. Avoid using incomplete sentences as items.
10. Keep all items and response choices in a set on the same page of the test.

Completion/fill-in-the blank items

1. Don't put too many blanks together.
   NOT: The_______left_______over issues of________
   BETTER: The Puritans left England over issues of_______
2. Make the answer a single word if possible.
3. Make sure there is only one way to interpret the blank.
   NOT: Abraham Lincoln was born in_______ (A log cabin? Poverty? Kentucky? 1809? A bed?)
   BETTER: Abraham Lincoln was born in the year_______
   OR: In what year was Abraham Lincoln born?_______
4. A word bank (a set of choices in a box or list) is often helpful, depending on whether total recall is important or not and whether spelling counts.

TABLE 10.2 *(Continued)*

Multiple-choice items

1. The stem (the numbered section) should ask or imply a question.
2. If the stem is an incomplete sentence, the alternatives should be at the end and should be the answer to an implied question.
3. If "not" is used, underline it.
4. Avoid statements of opinion.
5. Don't link two items together so that getting the second one correct depends on getting the first one correct.

   NOT: 1. What is the next number in the series 1, 5, 13, 29, . . . ?
   a. 43 b. 57 c. 61 d. 64
   2. What is the following number in the series in question #1?
   a. 122 b. 125 c. 127 d. 129

   BETTER: 1. What is the next number in the series 1, 5, 13, 29, . . . ?
   a. 43 b. 57 c. 61 d. 64
   2. What is the next number in the series 1, 4, 16, 64, . . . ?
   a. 128 b. 256 c. 372 d. 448
6. Don't give away the answer to one item with information or clues in another item.
7. Use three to five functional alternatives (response choices). Silly alternatives (e.g., "Mickey Mouse") do not draw serious consideration and should not be used. To inject humor into a test, use a whole silly item, not part of a serious one.
8. All alternatives should be plausible answers for those who are truly guessing.
9. Repeated words go in the stem, not the alternatives.

   NOT: Computer-based tutorials are called "adaptive" if they change based on information
   a. about the student.
   b. about the content material.
   c. about the computer.

   BETTER: Computer-based tutorials are called "adaptive" if they change based on information about the
   a. student.
   b. content material.
   c. computer.
10. Punctuate all alternatives correctly, given the stem.
11. Put the alternatives in logical order, if there is one.
12. Avoid overlapping alternatives.

   NOT: Which of the following possibilities enabling communication over the Internet is the best choice for a class discussion in a distance learning course?
   a. E-mail
   b. Usenet news
   c. Chat systems
   d. Conferencing software

   BETTER: Which of the following possibilities enabling communication over the Internet is the best choice for a class discussion in a distance learning course?
   a. E-mail
   b. Usenet news
   c. Chat systems
13. Avoid "all of the above" as an alternative.
14. Use "none of the above" sparingly.
15. Adjust the difficulty of an item by making the alternatives more or less alike. The more similar the alternatives, the more difficult the item.

Note: For more detail, see Linn & Gronlund, 1995; Nitko, 1996; Ory & Ryan, 1993.

TABLE 10.3

Dos and Don'ts for Writing Essay Test Items

Restricted range essay items (usually one to three paragraphs per answer)

1. For most purposes, use several restricted essays rather than one extended essay.
2. Ask for a focused response to one point; state the question so the student can tell what kind of response is required.
3. Do not ask a question that requires merely extended recall. Questions should require some critical thinking; for example:
   - explain causes and effects
   - identify assumptions
   - draw valid conclusions
   - present relevant arguments
   - state and defend a position
   - explain a procedure
   - describe limitations
   - apply a principle
   - compare and contrast ideas.
4. Use clear scoring criteria.
5. Don't use optional questions.

Extended range essay items (answer will be a true "essay" form)

1. Use to test in-depth understanding of a small range of content.
2. Call for students to express ideas in an organized fashion. Specify both what should be discussed and how it should be discussed.
3. Allow enough time for students to think and write.
4. Assign the essay as a paper or theme if out-of-class time is needed or if students' choice and resources are required.

Note: For more detail, see Linn & Gronlund, 1995, Nitko, 1996.

This illustration is used to introduce a discussion about how "inauthentic" assessment leads students to develop problem-solving strategies that help them pass exams but do not help them reach the intended learning goals. The discussion goes on to describe two categories of these maladaptive student responses, "shapes" and "clumps," which are discussed later.

The student who had trouble with the "pit problem" had not availed herself of a problem-solving strategy that the instructor had recommended, namely, drawing the problem (McClymer & Knoles, 1992, p. 34). Thus, her inability to solve this problem, and the low score that would result, would be an accurate and meaningful (reliable and valid) reflection of her learning about motion problems. The "inauthenticity" or contrived nature of the problem was not the only reason for her failure.

Viewed from the perspective of developing concepts, the "pit problem" shows how true concept development and application skills require variation in instruction, not just in novel problems on exams, and how the two are related. When students learn concepts, they are learning a set of defining characteristics. The characteristics that are important in a concept's definition are called "essential attributes." Characteristics that just happen to be there, but are not relevant to the concept's definition, are called "nonessential attributes." The best way to teach a concept to learners who are not familiar with it is to present the best examples, plus some counterexamples, and include variation on all attributes that might plausibly be confused with the definition.

For example, an essential characteristic of a simile is that a comparison of two like things is explicitly stated, commonly with "like" or "as," and an essential characteristic of a metaphor is that the comparison is implied. Metaphor and simile are often taught together, so that the similarity (both are comparisons of two things that are alike in some way) and difference (one comparison is explicit, the other implicit) are easy to point out. This approach helps with development of the concept. A variety of examples are needed, too, so that students can learn which attributes are essential. All the examples should not be about flowers, or even always about concrete things, lest students get the mistaken idea or misconception that metaphors and similes have to compare things to concrete objects. Similarly, all the examples should not be from poems, lest students get the misconception that comparisons have to be in poetry to be called metaphors and similes.

During instruction, then, the series of motion problems should not all have been dropping-from-window problems. The collection of "dropping problems" could have included various settings, buildings, cliffs, holes, scaffolds, and so on, and the students could have been asked what they all had in common, forcing students to articulate what their working understanding of the concept was in time for further explanation if misconceptions were apparent. Then students' task would have been to recognize the novel "pit problem" on the test as one of the "dropping problems" they had learned how to solve. One suspects, however, from the authors' account and the instructor's suggestion that students draw the problems, that attention had already been paid to essential and nonessential attributes in that particular calculus class. The student who protested may have been demonstrating that she did not, in fact, understand the concept. If that is the case, then a low score on that problem would correctly indicate her lack of understanding.

When instructors do not attend well to concept development and make sure that examples and counterexamples are clear for students, students will sometimes, understandably, attune to aspects of the format of problems or arguments. After all, in their essays or solutions, students will be trying to convince the instructor who is grading their work that they deserve high scores. A well-constructed test will not compensate for a lack of concept development in instruction. If instruction has been appropriate, however, a well-constructed test and a carefully prepared scoring scheme can minimize cases when students score well because they were skilled at *appearing* to understand.

Two different ways that students present responses demonstrate a less than deep and critical understanding of concepts, problems, or arguments—"clumps" and "shapes" (McClymer & Knoles, 1992, pp. 38-39). Clumps are parts of arguments, solutions to problems, or critical analyses that pile up analytical elements without the logic and explanations that should hold them together. Three kinds of clumps include "data packing," in which students write many facts but do not make clear what the facts are intended to show; "jargon packing," in which students use much terminology to make it sound as though they understand but do not, in fact, explain anything with the terms: and "assertion packing," in which students report *that* something is the case (for example, that the poet John Donne used imagery) without identifying, explaining, or citing any actual evidence. Sometimes several of these clumps are used in the same essay or analysis.

Shapes are approximations of the logic of criticism, the form without the substance (or the words without the music). Students might copy the form of someone else's analysis, perhaps from a textbook, or uncritically apply an algorithm that looks as though it should fit without understanding why it is appropriate. Students may stick to a surface recitation of a piece of literature or textbook, demonstrating that they have read the material but not that they have used it to think critically. A third shape students sometimes use is a one-note analysis, describing part but not all of the meaning required to answer the question fully.

McClymer and Knoles (1992) interpreted students' tendencies to answer higher level questions with clumps and shapes in light of some survey data collected at their institution. Entering freshmen reported that their main responsibilities as students were to master informational content and acquire critical skills. They did not express much support for the purposes of becoming scholars in their own right. Freshmen are known to have this expert-oriented, content-based understanding of learning; eventually more personal ownership of knowledge and thinking abilities becomes important for those who make progress through the stages of adult intellectual development (Perry, 1970). There is some truth to the claim, however, that students in higher education will be interested in passing courses as well as in learning, as students have invested time and money in enrolling in courses. Good instruction, coupled with high quality assessment, can help them do both. Clear scoring plans can help instructors judge the quality of the range of students' responses, from incorrect, to clumps, shapes, and other approximations, to appropriate, clear, well-reasoned answers.

Scoring essays and partial-credit problems may be done by a point method or a rubric method. If the problem or essay is one that requires a discrete amount of information and one solution or organizational strategy, it is easy to set up a system assigning points for each aspect, with a total number of points for a complete, correct answer. The instructor must make sure that the points reflect the relative importance of each aspect's contribution to the whole. Some aspects that are more important than others may be worth more points. Moreover, total points for the essay must reflect that essay question's contribution to the whole test. If it does not, the question should be weighted accordingly. For example, if an essay should be worth 20 points on a test but it has only 10 logical points, the score for the essay should be doubled and then added to the rest of the score for the test.

Rubrics are descriptive rating scales that are particularly useful for scoring when judgment about the quality of an answer is required—when, for example, it is not so much that the student remembered all the right concepts and organized them correctly, but more that the essay was well conceived, strongly argued, included original perspectives, or the like. Rubrics are good at indicating a range of poor quality through excellent quality work, making them ideal for scoring many college-level essay questions, show-the-work problems, and performance assessments.

To write rubrics, begin with a description of the criteria for good work. Envision a well-constructed, complete, and clear answer to the question or problem. What would its important characteristics be? They should be directly related to the knowledge, critical thinking, or skills that the instructor intended the students to acquire, and therefore they ought to be related to activities and instruction for the course, what students read and studied, and therefore what students will expect the test to require.

List the criteria for good work, then describe levels of performance. Be careful to use descriptions (e.g., "grammar and usage errors are rare and do not interfere with meaning") rather than judgments (e.g., "good"). Use as many levels as there are meaningful distinctions. Meaning is more important than having some particular number of levels. The term "analytic rubrics" is used when each criterion has a separate scale and the essay is rated on each separately, with the several ratings summed or averaged for a total score. Table 10.4 presents an example of analytic rubrics. The term "holistic rubrics" is used when all criteria are considered together on one descriptive rating scale and the answer is scored at the level that best describes it. Table 10.5 presents an example of holistic rubrics using the same criteria. Rubrics can be shared with students ahead of time so they better understand what they are being asked to do and what counts as good work.

Two good ways to share rubrics also enable students' involvement in assessment, which in turn enhances motivation and learning. When instructors share the rubrics, they can also give students some examples of work done at various levels. Ask students to rate the examples and tell why they scored them as they did. If descriptions of levels are well written, students will have to articulate the qualities of the work to justify their ratings. A variation on this strategy is to share the examples of work with students and have the students reason inductively from the examples to write the rubrics themselves. This approach works well and helps students develop a sense of ownership of the criteria for good work. Students are also likely to internalize and remember these criteria for good work if they develop them themselves. The cost for this instructional benefit is time; therefore, it is wiser to use this strategy on very important and authentic work than on simpler, more contrived classroom assignments.

TABLE 10.4

Analytic Rubrics for a Question on an Essay Test

Thesis and organization

4—Thesis is defensible and stated explicitly; appropriate facts and concepts are used in a logical manner to support the argument.

3—Thesis is defensible and stated explicitly; appropriate facts and concepts are used in a logical manner to support the argument, although support may be thin in places and/or logic may not be made clear.

2—Thesis is not clearly stated; some attempt at support is made.

1—No thesis or indefensible thesis; support is missing or illogical.

Content knowledge

4—All relevant facts and concepts included; all accurate.

3—All or most relevant facts and concepts included; inaccuracies are minor.

2—Some relevant facts and concepts included; some inaccuracies.

1—No facts or concepts included, or irrelevant facts and concepts included.

Writing style and mechanics

4—Writing is clear and smooth. Word choice and style are appropriate for the topic. No errors in grammar or usage.

3—Writing is generally clear. Word choice and style are appropriate for the topic. Few errors in grammar or usage, and they do not interfere with meaning.

2—Writing is not clear. Style is poor. Some errors in grammar and usage interfere with meaning.

1—Writing is not clear. Style is poor. Many errors in grammar and usage.

TABLE 10.5

Holistic Rubrics for a Question on an Essay Test

4—Thesis is defensible and stated explicitly; appropriate facts and concepts are used in a logical manner to support the argument. All relevant facts and concepts included; all accurate. Writing is clear and smooth. Word choice and style are appropriate for the topic. No errors in grammar or usage.

3—Thesis is defensible and stated explicitly; appropriate facts and concepts are used in a logical manner to support the argument, although support may be thin in places and/or logic may not be made clear. All or most relevant facts and concepts included; inaccuracies are minor. Writing is generally clear. Word choice and style are appropriate for the topic. Few errors in grammar or usage, and they do not interfere with meaning.

2—Thesis is not clearly stated; some attempt at support is made. All or most relevant facts and concepts included; inaccuracies are minor. Writing is not clear. Style is poor. Some errors in grammar and usage interfere with meaning.

1—No thesis or indefensible thesis: support is missing or illogical. No facts or concepts included or irrelevant facts and concepts included. Writing is not clear. Style is poor. Many errors in grammar and usage.

Performance Assessment

Performance assessment refers to assessment in which a student's product or participation in a process is observed and judged. Performance assessments have two parts: a task and a scoring scheme. One without the other constitutes an incomplete performance assessment.

Performance tasks differ from essay tests in that they usually require sustained performance, often allow the use of resources, and often encourage revision and refinement before a final product is submitted. (Suggested frameworks for categorizing assessments range from multiple choice at one end of the continuum to presentations [Bennett, 1993] or collections of work over time [Snow, 1993] at the other.) A performance task in which a student is asked to solve a problem and explain the solution in one or two class periods is closer in kind to an essay question than a performance in which a student is asked to write a paper about a research question, using library and Internet resources, over the course of a semester.

One benefit of some performance assessment tasks is the requirement that students write reflections or explanations. Writing explanations makes students' reasoning explicit. It is a no-lose situation: Either a student gives evidence of clear, logical, appropriate reasoning in a discipline or demonstrates where his or her reasoning is flawed, thus identifying specifically what area needs more work. Writing reflections affords students the opportunity to think about what they have learned and what it means. "Knowing what they know" is a metacognitive achievement for students, an awareness of comprehension that is required for students to become self-sustaining, self-directed learners in a discipline.

Performance assessment tasks should not be simply interesting, novel, or appealing activities chosen for their novelty or appeal. Performance tasks should be constructed to elicit evidence of learning outcomes achieved—which requires thought and care. The following example shows how thought must be given to performance tasks to ensure that they give evidence of students' achievement of specific learning targets. In the example, a novice teacher thinks it would be a good idea to make an assessment out of the instructional activity of putting the Socrates of Plato's *Apology* on trial (Wiggins, 1998). But what is wrong with that idea, and what should be done about it?

- *Although the desired achievement involves the text and its implications, the activity can be done engagingly and effectively by each student with only limited insight into the entire text and its context. If a student merely has to play an aggrieved aristocrat or playwright, he or she can study for that role with only a limited grasp of the text. Also, the student's trial performance need not have much to do with Greek life and philosophy. The question of assessment validity (Does it measure what we want it to measure?) works differently, requiring us to consider whether success or failure at the proposed task depends on the targeted knowledge (as opposed to fortunate personal talents): [The] performance of the student playing, say, one of the lawyers may be better or worse relative to his or her debating and lawyering skills rather than relative to his or her knowledge of the text.*
- *It is highly unlikely that we will derive apt and sufficient evidence of understanding of the text from each individual student through this activity, even if we can hear an understanding of the text in some comments by some students. In fact, in the heat of a debate or mock trial, students might forget or not be able to use what they understand about the text, depriving themselves and us of needed assessment evidence. This is a crucial problem, common to many proposed assessment tasks: [When] we employ a particular performance genre, such as a trial, essay, or report, as a means to some other assessment end, we may fail to consider that the performance genre itself is a variable in the task and will affect the results.*
- *Although the trial may provide some evidence, it is far more likely that in this case a thorough and thoughtful piece of writing, combined with an extensive Socratic seminar on the text, would tell us more of what we need to know about students' knowledge and understanding. Such writing and discussion can certainly supplement the trial, but in considering such an idea we should be alert to the fact that no single complex performance task is sufficient for sound assessment.* (pp. 31–32)

Assessment should be both "authentic" and "educative" (Wiggins, 1998). "Authentic assessment" means that assessment tasks, whether test questions or performance assessment tasks, are grounded in the kind of work people actually do in a discipline. That is, tests are not inappropriate, but they should be used the same way that drills in athletic practice are, for mastery and review of component skills, while keeping in mind the end or goal of real work or performance in the discipline (Wiggins, 1998). And at least some of the time, the "game must be played," or real-world performance must be attempted, to help students see what is required for real practice and how they measure up. "Educative assessment" means that a primary purpose of students' participation in assessment is to teach, to help students improve on dimensions of performance that are required for genuine or authentic work, to help them conceptualize what that work looks like (Wiggins, 1998).

Scoring criteria for evaluating performance tasks are constructed in a similar manner to the scoring schemes used for essay test questions. Their content should reflect the nature of the process or product that is to be scored.

Criteria for evaluation can be used holistically, considering all criteria simultaneously and assigning a single score, or analytically, considering each criterion separately and assigning a separate score for each. Analytical scoring is more helpful as feedback to students than holistic scoring, because students can see where their strengths and weaknesses are and work on their skills accordingly. Holistic scoring takes less time, because one judgment is required of the scorer instead of many. Analytic and holistic rubrics for performance assessments are similar in form to rubrics for essays and partial-credit test problems.

Table 10.6 presents a set of rubrics for scoring a Web page design project, a performance assessment. It is an analytic rubric, chosen as an example here because two of its scales, HTML Creation Skills and Navigation, illustrate rather concrete descriptions of work at each level (e.g., "at least two lists"), while the Web Page Layout scale illustrates more abstract quality descriptions (e.g., "hierarchy closely follows meaning") that require substantive judgment. Both kinds of descriptions are appropriate for rubrics; the important point is that the descriptions match what genuinely reflects levels of quality. Depending on the purpose of the assignment, this set of rubrics could include a fourth scale to evaluate the accuracy, importance, or impact of the content included on the student's Web page.

TABLE 10.6

Performance Assessment Rubrics for a Web Page Design

Level 1	Level 2	Level 3	Level 4	Level 5
		Web page (HTML) creation skills		
No HTML formatting tags; text is not broken into paragraphs.	Text is broken into paragraphs; headings are used; no other HTML tags.	Headings, title, tags such as preformatted text, styles, centering, horizontal lines, lists, etc.	Same as Level 3 plus images and hyperlinks to related material.	Same as Level 4 plus at least 2 lists, images as hyperlinks; color or background image, frames, tables, or imagemap.
		Web page layout		
Layout has no structure or organization.	Text broken into paragraphs and sections.	Headings label sections and create hierarchy; some consistency.	Hierarchy closely follows meaning; headings and styles consistent within pages; text, images, and links flow together.	Consistent format; extends the information from page to page; easy to read; attention to different browsers and their quirks.
		Navigation		
One page	One page with title bar added, heading, etc.	Two pages (or one page with links within page or to other resources); navigation between pages; links work.	Three or more pages with clear order, labeling, and navigation between pages; all links work.	Title page with other pages branching off and atleast four pages total; navigation path clear and logical; all links work.

Source: San Diego County, 1998. Used with permission.

Another way scoring scales can vary is with regard to whether they are generalized or task specific. Generalized rubrics can be used in assessment, but they also can be used instructionally, shared with students to help them understand the nature of the achievement target. Generalized rubrics are one way to communicate the characteristics of good quality work. Students can use them in their work and in evaluation of others' work. Task-specific scoring rubrics are easier to apply reliably the first time, but they cannot be shared with students ahead of time, when the assignment is made, because they contain answers (e.g., "uses Newton's Law of Cooling" instead of "selects relevant principles and procedures").

Instructors who regularly involve students in their own assessment can use this distinction to advantage. Share generalized rubrics with students or have them develop their own rubrics, then present a specific task for students to work and then score together. In describing why a performance deserves a certain score, students will articulate the specifics. In the example above, students would defend a score by saying, "They selected Newton's Law of Cooling, which in this case was a relevant principle for solving the problem."

Grading cooperative assignments presents an unusual challenge. Performance assessment highlights this difficulty, because most cooperative assignments are some type of performance assessment. Group reports, skits, or other projects can result in performance by a group in cases where an individual paper or other assessment is not really feasible. Yet college grades are given to individuals. Table 10.7 presents an example of a peer evaluation that group members can use. If students are aware ahead of time of the expectations and the fact that they will be monitored, many problems will take care of themselves. If the peer evaluations indicate that one group member was not contributing at the same level as others, and if the instructor's observations agree, then the instructor can intervene in several different ways, from speaking to the student or group to adjusting the grade.

Oral Questions

Oral questions during class time help both instructors and students to clarify what they know and where misconceptions have occurred. They work best in small classes. The instructor must know students' names to call on them, and students must know their classmates well enough so that they do not perceive the questions as public grilling. Oral questions can be factual in nature and check for simple recall or for whether or not assigned reading was done. "Why did your author say that Thomas Jefferson became interested in education?" "What is the chemical reaction that happens during nuclear fission?"

For oral questions to indicate accurately what the class as a whole understands, it is important to sample a range of students. The range should include various abilities as well as various interests. Always calling on students who have their hands raised will bias the information gained about class members' understanding. Most of the time, a disproportionate number of students who do understand the material in a lesson will be represented among those who volunteer to participate.

Handled well, oral questions provide good assessment information for instructors about students' understanding and interest. This information is best interpreted for the group (class). The use of assessment information about individual's participation in class discussions for grading is more problematic, as personal and group dynamics as well as availability of "air time" mean such information gives an incomplete picture of an individual's understandings.

Ask students questions that require knowledge at all cognitive levels. As for test questions, it is easier to pose recall questions in class than to ask questions that require application of principles, analysis of issues, or other complex thinking. Similarly, it is easier to judge the adequacy of responses to recall questions than to questions requiring more thought. The kind of questions the instructor asks should match the kind of information the instructor needs to know. Preparing some higher order questions ahead of time is a good strategy, as questions made up on the spot in a class are likely to be recall questions. Asking "why" as a follow-up to concept questions is also a good way to elicit thinking from students.

TABLE 10.7

Sample Peer Evaluation for Cooperative Learning Assignments

Group members	Worked cooperatively to complete assignments	Attended and participated in scheduled meetings	Supported and respected other members' efforts and opinions	Prepared adequately for sessions	Made substantial contributions to group's under standings—shared ideas, resources, information

Write the names of each member of the group, including yourself, in the boxes in the first column. Put a check in each cell in the grid to indicate "fine job, as expected" for each group member for each criterion. For any box in which you have reservations about making a check because a group member did not meet your expectations for a criterion, write a brief comment. For any box in which you would like to comment on truly exceptional performance, please do so.

Source: Adapted from Munson, 1995.

Portfolios

A portfolio is a purposeful collection of a student's work, often with samples of work collected over time and with reflections about what was learned or what a piece is supposed to demonstrate (Arter, Spandel, & Culham, 1995; Nitko, 1996). Some authors consider portfolios an option for assessing work in their own right. Others consider portfolios a collection of various assessments.

Portfolios constructed for a single course are usually designed to reflect achievement of the particular goals for that course. This purpose contrasts with the traditional artist's portfolio, which is designed to show best work in a field and may represent work done in several courses and outside courses. Some students, most notably in the fine arts, will develop such portfolios during their college careers, but they are not the focus of this discussion. The following review is limited to portfolios used to demonstrate achievement of learning goals for a course.

The most important point to decide when a portfolio is selected as an assessment tool is its purpose. What learning or accomplishments is it intended to show? And is it intended to illustrate progress, the process on the journey toward achievement, or just final products? A portfolio for a writing class, for instance, may include a series of drafts of various works with reflections on how revisions were made and what improvement was shown to demonstrate how a student understands the writing process, or it may be a collection of finished works to demonstrate the quality of final products.

Another consideration for portfolios is the extent to which a portfolio itself, as a collection, would be more valuable than the uncollected assessments individually. What would be gained by holding a collection of work over time, in one location and with periodic review, over simply assigning, discussing, and evaluating each assignment separately? For some purposes, such as demonstrating students' development into "writers" by showing how they have progressed, and for leaving the evidence where they will look over it repeatedly to reflect upon it (which in itself will contribute to development as a writer), the collection of work is the answer. But portfolios consume time and space, and if they are simply a storage box for a series of reports, they are not worth the extra time and space they take to construct and review.

For portfolios to be effective methods of assessment, it is essential to define clear and complete performance criteria against which the work will be compared (Arter, Spandel, & Culham, 1995). Although the criteria are used to score or grade students, it is not their most important function in a portfolio. The importance of criteria is to ensure that students use them as guides for selecting what goes into their portfolios and as guides for reflecting on their work. Thus, how the criteria are written is very important, because the language used in the criteria becomes the language in which descriptions of quality work are phrased. The contribution a portfolio can make that other forms of assessment commonly do not is this aspect of reflection by students, of living with and revisiting past work, of setting goals for future work and then evaluating whether and to what degree the goals were met.

A survey of academic vice presidents and deans at all Carnegie classification Baccalaureate College II institutions found that of 395 respondents, 202 used portfolios for institutional outcomes assessment, classroom assessment, and/or other purposes such as admissions or placement (Larson, 1995). Those 202 administrators were sent a second survey, asking for more details, to which 101 responded. Among respondents using portfolios, 47% used them for classroom assessment. Administrators reported up to 29 years of classroom use of portfolios, with a mean of 6.4 years. The most common portfolio contents reported included final drafts of papers (50%), student projects (47%), journals/logs (41%), self-evaluations (35%), faculty evaluations (26%), videos (26%), and drafts of final work (23%). Selecting contents of portfolios used in the classroom included selection by faculty and student together (37%), selection by student using faculty guidelines (34%), selection by faculty alone (9%), and selection by student alone (4%). Rubrics or scoring schemes for evaluating classroom portfolios were reported as not used (44%), developed by faculty for institutional outcomes assessment (31%), developed by faculty to serve their own purposes (29%), developed by an accrediting agency (4%), and "other" (5%). Classroom portfolios were typically returned to the student (Larson, 1995).

On the positive side, administrators reported that portfolios were useful, powerful assessment tools whose chief strengths involved participation by students, the collection of multiple assessments, and the ability to demonstrate progress over time. On the negative side, administrators reported concerns about the logistics, accuracy, and grading of portfolios.

Summary

Options for classroom assessment include paper-and-pencil tests, performance assessment, oral questions, and portfolios. Each has its strengths and weaknesses and is particularly appropriate for different learning goals. Students' involvement in any of these methods increases their motivation, learning, and sense of ownership of the material. Once an instructor has decided what methods are most appropriate for assessing learning goals for students, it is important to communicate the decision to students. The syllabus is an appropriate place to do so. If a syllabus makes clear to students what their goals for learning are, how they will be assessed, and how those assessments will be combined for their course grade, students can monitor their own learning, itself a worthwhile goal for higher education.

CHAPTER 11

EVALUATING TEACHING

The Paradigm Shifts: Examining Quality of Teaching Through Assessment of Student Learning

Barbara L. Cambridge

Abstract Student learning is the strongest criterion for evaluating effective teaching. This article looks at three practices which partner students, teachers, and faculty peers in understanding the quality of teaching and learning through student course portfolios and teacher course portfolios, majors portfolios and teaching portfolios, and collaborative classroom assessment. Two outcomes of using a learning paradigm are building community and representing successes in higher education through documentation of effective teaching and learning.

Introduction

We have long known that teaching which results in learning is effective teaching: this is the fundamental criterion. Yet many colleges and universities in the past have relied primarily on student evaluations to determine the link between learning and teaching. In his study of over 500 liberal arts colleges from 1983–1993, Peter Seldin (1993) learned, over that period of time, that "Student ratings have become the most widely used source of information to assess teaching" (p. 8). Student evaluations administered regularly by individual faculty, departments, and schools have indeed resulted in changes of pedagogy and decisions about promotion and tenure.

Yet faculty have reservations about the validity of certain kinds of student evaluations. What does a faculty member learn from a high rating in response to the question "Is this faculty member current in her field?" On what basis can a student answer such a question? As learners entering a discipline, students understandably do not have sufficient background to respond knowledgeably to such a question. Even a question which seems more suitable to student input may be problematic. What does a faculty member learn from a high or a low rating on a question such as "Would you recommend that your friends take a course from this professor?" Students may be rating the faculty member according to pedagogical method, faculty attitude, course content, or any one or more of a multitude of factors which influence what students say to their friends. Although student evalua-

Barbara L. Cambridge, Professor of English and Associate Dean of the Faculties at Indiana University-Purdue University Indianapolis, serves on the IUPUI Program Review and Assessment Committee and recently chaired the Task Force on Accountability and Assessment for Indiana University's Strategic Directions Long-range Planning. She has made presentations and written on portfolio assessment, assessment and evaluation of faculty work, and issues in undergraduate education. Editor of the *Journal of Teaching Writing*, she is past President of the National Council of Writing Program Administrators.

Reprinted from *Innovative Higher Education* (1996), Springer.

tions carefully constructed and administered offer some information for assessing teaching, faculty need additional ways of describing the relationship of learning and teaching.

Indeed, faculty need first to reconsider the relationship of learning and teaching. A significant article in *Change* describes in clearcut terms a paradigm shift that is taking place in American higher education. In "From Teaching to Learning—A New Paradigm for Undergraduate Education," Robert Barr and John Tagg (1995) make a persuasive case for the shift from the Instruction Paradigm, in which a college or university exists to provide instruction, to the Learning Paradigm, in which the institution exists to produce learning. In the Learning Paradigm, faculty and students are both responsible for the amount and quality of student learning. "The aim in the Learning Paradigm is not so much to improve the quality of instruction—although that is not irrelevant—as it is to improve continuously the quality of learning for students individually and in the aggregate" (p. 15). Barr and Tagg's chart of features of the Teaching Paradigm and the Learning Paradigm (p. 16) reveals contrasts in Criteria for Success:

The Instruction Paradigm	The Learning Paradigm
Inputs, resources	Learning and student success
Quality of entering students	Quality of exiting students
Curriculum development, expansion	Learning technologies development, expansion
Quantity and quality of resources	Quantity and quality of outcomes
Enrollment, revenue growth	Aggregate learning growth, efficiency
Quality of faculty, instruction	Quality of students, learning

The implication for peer review of teaching is clear: a focus on student learning and assessing student learning must be central to the assessment of teaching. The Peer Review Project of the American Association for Higher Education places groups of faculty peers in the foreground of assessing teaching. Practices developed and implemented on campuses across the country enable faculty to work together to describe and assess the effectiveness of teaching. Collaborative teams are best constituted, however, when each member of the team contributes that which other team members are unable to do as well. If student learning is the chief goal of teaching, students are important members of the collaborative effort to determine the extent and quality of learning. Focusing on ways in which students demonstrate and assess their learning reveals ways in which faculty can learn about their teaching. This article looks at three practices in which students, teachers, and faculty colleagues work as partners to understand the quality of teaching and learning. Student and teacher course portfolios, majors and teaching portfolios, and classroom assessment combine to yield a rich picture of student learning.

Student Course Portfolios and Teacher Course Portfolios

From the assessment of student learning, we can learn some useful lessons about faculty learning as reflected in teaching. Research in composition, for example, has concluded that multiple pieces of writing are necessary for evaluating a writer's competencies. Ascertaining the ability of a writer based on one piece of writing is invalid because the writer may perform better or worse depending on the occasion, purpose, and audience for the writing. Based on this knowledge, writing faculty in many colleges and universities have adopted portfolio assessment, in which students present at points during and/or at the end of a term a portfolio of writings which have different purposes and audiences. Sometimes required pieces must be submitted, such as a narrative, a critical analysis, and a position paper; other times students select their best work based on criteria determined by their department, professor, or themselves. Usually students can revise their work in order to represent in the portfolio evidence of their learning throughout the term. Multiple pieces of writing represent the range of abilities of the writers, who can, therefore, be evaluated more accurately by themselves and by their professors. Some writing programs, in fact, have more than one faculty reader so that students have the benefit of self assessment, teacher assessment, and departmental assessment, the same tripartite perspective that is useful in validly assessing excellence in teaching.

We as teachers can learn about assessing teacher learning from examining how we assess student learning. Just as students deserve evaluation of their full range of work, so, too, do faculty also deserve evaluation of all elements of their teaching. In the scholarship of research, or, in Ernest Boyer's terms (1990), the scholarship of discovery, a case for excellence in research is not based on a single article or book but on the corpus of published research. The corpus of work important in a course must also be considered in order to understand the effectiveness of a faculty member's teaching in that course.

Just as students produce portfolios for writing courses and for other courses as well, teachers can produce course portfolios. At the June 1995 meeting of the AAHE Peer Review Project teams, the course portfolio evoked a great amount of interest as a potentially valid demonstration of the scholarship of teaching. Richard Turner, an Indiana University-Purdue University Indianapolis (IUPUI) Professor of English, asked for response to a set of materials which he had assembled concerning an introductory English course. He included the mission and goals statements of the University, the department, and the course; the syllabus; student assignment sheets; and his own explanation of the rationale and practices of the course.

Peer responders, however, were stymied in fully assessing Turner's teaching materials because they did not include evidence from student portfolios. Although faculty understood well the ways in which assignments were directed at course goals and the way in which pedagogical methods emerged from assignment objectives, they found themselves unable to assess teaching without evidence of the learning that had taken place from students' completion of the assignments. Upon request of faculty readers of his materials, Turner subsequently added students' work from their own portfolios to demonstrate how the course generated student learning and how students assessed their own learning. Faculty from his own and other disciplines have since become more and more excited about the possibilities of understanding the context for learning and the learning outcomes of courses through analysis of such a comprehensive body of materials. Different responses to the materials by faculty peers in different disciplines have raised important questions about the strengths and weaknesses of cross-disciplinary evaluations of teaching. Faculty want to consider further what combination of materials provides the best opportunity for evaluating the scholarship of teaching. The combination of student learning outcomes, self analysis, and peer response, however, is clearly a powerful move toward valid assessment of teaching.

Moreover, student learning may be enhanced if faculty share course portfolios with students. One method is to make the evolving course portfolio available to students as they prepare their own portfolios. Students may then understand more clearly reasons for pedagogical choices or sequences of assignments, thus enabling them to draw more valid conclusions about their own learning. Another method is sharing portfolios at the end of a course. Both students and faculty can learn from completed portfolios by comparing students' assessments of their individual work and of the class's accomplishment contained in student portfolios with the instructor's assessments of students' individual learning and of the class's accomplishment contained in the course portfolio. Although faculty have had access in the past to student portfolios, an addition to student learning can occur through student access to faculty learning evidenced in the course portfolio. The symbiotic assessments of students and faculty can result in more effective teaching and learning.

Majors Portfolios and Teaching Portfolios

In *Assessment in Higher Education: Politics, Pedagogy, and Portfolios,* Patrick Courts and Kathleen McInerney (1993) analyze a portfolio program for English Education majors at SUNY-Fredonia. Students include materials generated in courses and their reflections on their learning experiences in portfolios which are used by students, teachers, and academic advisors to plan and understand progress in the students' degree programs. The authors conclude that "one of the most revealing facts in Fredonia's assessment project is the finding that we often seriously overestimate how much and what our students are learning" (p. 91).

On the other hand, I find that students sometimes underestimate how much and what they have learned. In an IUPUI English Department Senior Seminar in Writing in which students create capstone portfolios from materials in previous course portfolios, they often are amazed at the improvement between critical analyses written in their elementary composition course and their upper-division literature course, at the variety of genres in which they have written during their undergraduate career, and at the judgements about sufficiency of evidence and audience adaptation which they are capable of making by the time they are seniors. English majors who develop portfolios for the audience of a future employer, a graduate school admissions officer, or themselves as lifelong learners discover what the students and faculty at Fredonia also have found: "Portfolios have the potential to work powerfully as part of the teaching-learning process as they reveal confusions and encourage explorations of experience that students have across courses and disciplines" (Courts & McInerny, 1993, p. 93). Students are encouraged through their capstone portfolio statements to integrate their learning and to identify areas of progress and areas in which more progress is desired.

Consider the following summary of four attributes of portfolios. First, portfolios can capture the intellectual substance and learning situation in ways that other methods of evaluation cannot. Second, because of this capacity, portfolios encourage students to take important, new roles in the documentation, observation, and review of learning. Third, because they prompt students to take these new roles, portfolios are a particularly powerful tool for improvement. Fourth, as more students come to use them, portfolios can help forge a new campus culture of professionalism about learning. Students see their learning as an object of study and reflection, influenced by all the circumstances of that learning. Students become involved in assessment of their own learning instead of only receiving the judgement of others. They, therefore, can take responsibility for change because they have self knowledge about their areas of strength and areas for improvement, and they can gain more control and sophistication in their approaches to learning.

Changing each reference in the four attributes above from "student" to "teacher" and "learning" to "teaching" would yield a direct quote from Russell Edgerton, Patricia Hutchings, and Kathleen Quinlan's book *The Teaching Portfolio: Capturing the Scholarship in Teaching* (1991, p. 4). The conscientious and comprehensive compilation of evidence of effective teaching in a teaching portfolio serves a parallel purpose to the students' majors portfolio. Over time faculty are able to demonstrate their increasing ability as effective teachers, both in the classroom and in the other activities involved in the scholarship of teaching. Faculty can reflect on the evolution of their teaching practices and the effect of those practices on students. Once again, teachers can learn about teaching from the ways in which students document and assess their learning.

For example, Jay Howard, who teaches sociology at Indiana University-Purdue University Columbus, believes that effective teaching takes place outside as well as inside the classroom. From 1993–1995 Howard has taken ten students to the Midwest Student Sociology Conference, where they present refereed papers. In his teaching portfolio Howard not only identifies the students who have participated each year at three different locations in the Midwest but also details the benefits to the learning of students and to his own learning. Howard (1995) draws conclusions based on his students' assessment of their learning. Using student comments, he demonstrates that the conference sparks their interest in sociology; helps them learn to think critically; gives them experience in professional presentations; provides opportunities for students and instructor to discuss sociological issues during the trip to and from the conference; and affirms the value of their work, enabling students to compare themselves to students from other colleges and universities. Howard, too, has assessed the relative quality of his students' work which has led him to reconsider his pedagogical strategies, including the importance of teaching that goes on outside the classroom.

Peer reviewers of Howard's written description and self analysis of his out-of-classroom teaching warranted student testimony about the worth of conference participation, but they wanted more informarion from Howard about the relationship of that learning to the goals of the course and to other learning activities in the course. When Howard placed this description with other student assignments and with an annotated syllabus in his teaching portfolio, peer reviewers recognized a teacher who was dedicated to students' application of theoretical knowledge, their research skills, and their professional development. The combination of student evaluation of the experience, which could also appear in the students' portfolios, and Howard's own evaluation of the experience over time in terms of student and teacher was a powerful addition to Howard's teaching portfolio, enabling valid peer review based on substantive evidence.

Classroom Assessment

Classroom assessment calls on students and faculty to look periodically at progress in a learning situation. For example, the minute paper promoted by Tom Angelo and Patricia Cross in their book *Classroom Assessment Techniques* (1988) asks students at the end of a class meeting to answer quick questions about the class like "What remains the most confusing point for you from the class today?" The teacher then reads all the student responses, classifying the kinds of confusing points or determining the most confusing point to clarify the next class hour. Sharing the results of the minute papers with students, the teacher shows the importance of honest student response by altering the subsequent class to address difficulties in student learning. The teacher herself could not know the most confusing points: only the students are able to identify what baffles them, even if only to say "I didn't get it." The teacher's responsibility is then to take another approach to help the students understand the problematic material.

Faculty peers can contribute to this process of evaluating teaching by responding to a teacher's analysis of her use of classroom assessment. For example, if a teacher were to write about changes in her teaching based on her use of the minute paper five times in one class and six times in another during a semester, a faculty peer might conclude that the teacher cares about student perception, is flexible enough to change plans to respond to student need, and is capable of varying pedagogical approaches. If other evidence such as student test scores and student satisfaction ratings are positive, a faculty peer might rate the teacher highly in teaching effectiveness. The student provides what only he can: honest responses to the classroom assessment measure. The teacher provides what only she can: a detailed description of reasons for use of the classroom assessment measure, the outcomes in terms of her pedagogical choices, and her analysis of the effect on student learning. The faculty peer provides what only he can: the perspective and analysis of another knowledgeable teacher about the description of this assessment practice, the compatibility of this evidence with other evidence of student learning, and the conclusions that might be drawn about teaching effectiveness.

An example illustrates the power of multiple perspectives on teaching effectiveness. At IUPUI, Carol Brown teaches a Master's course in management information systems for the School of Business. This Master's program accepts students in sixty-member cohort groups who take their program together. Because working effectively in cross-functional teams is a highly valued management skill, the course is structured into twelve-member student teams with team assignments for class presentations. Class presentations are assessed by the faculty member and student peers. Both the faculty and student evaluation forms focus on content and delivery separately.

Brown (1995) writes that "this is because many times very good content eludes the student audience due to a less effective delivery. Similarly, a really slick delivery can mask mediocre content" (p. 6). When students submit their rating and comments to the faculty member, she prepares a one-page summary with an average score on each rating and an aggregation of the comments. Her own faculty assessment form identifies strengths and weaknesses and offers descriptive comments on approach, organization, and content.

As a result of analysis of this double mode of feedback for students, Brown has not only revised the evaluation forms, but also revised the instructions to the students; she now asks for constructive suggestions for improvement as well as weaknesses. She has also revised the wording of the assessments so that the students improve their comments on content, rather than focusing only on delivery. Brown also finds that by having students participate in peer evaluations for team presentations throughout the semester, they learn both analytical and communication skills, along with teamwork skills and the course content itself.

When Brown shared her self analysis with faculty peers in a workshop on documenting teaching, she asked her colleagues what conclusions they might make based on her students' work, examples of which she included, and on her own analysis. Faculty peers who read her description were able through their fresh perspectives to conclude that Brown had many attributes of an excellent teacher. She valued students as able partners for one another in presenting and evaluating presentations, and she adjusted her contributions accordingly, i.e. focusing on content more than delivery. Moreover, her pedagogy and assessment processes were consonant with the goals of the course; and she structured the course for the benefit of presenters and listeners.

In this case, if we examined all Brown's documents from her class, we would be able to look at student work and evaluations, teacher self analysis, and faculty peer analysis as a rich description of Carol Brown's teaching in this course. This description already shows the formative value of examining teaching: Brown changed her response practices based on what she learned from student response forms, and she reported that she continued this type of dual response to student presentations based on her faculty peer responses. This description might also provide some data for summative purposes: a faculty peer could affirm the attributes mentioned above in a high stakes outcome situation like promotion or merit consideration.

More data, however, is useful and even necessary, especially for summative purposes. One instance of student learning and teacher response to that learning, while illustrative, may be anomalous and not provide the substantive description that we need to understand a faculty member's quality of teaching. Faculty benefit from having multiple ways of documenting student learning.

Consequential Validity of the New Paradigm

A central consideration in any assessment of teaching is consequential validity. In other words, what are the consequences of our choices about ways to describe, document, assess, and evaluate teaching? With good choices we have better opportunities to improve teaching and learning and to affirm effective teachers and learners. Two other benefits, however, are significant: building community and representing higher education to multiple publics.

Parker Palmer writes and speaks often about ways to foster the kind of community within the academy that enables faculty and students to do their work better. In "Good Talk about Good Teaching: Improving Teaching through Conversation and Community," Palmer (1993) laments the privatization that results from faculty reluctance to engage regularly in concentrated talk about teaching. He suggests that three elements are essential to generating discussion about teaching and learning: leaders who expect and invite conversation, topics of conversation that go beyond teaching methods, and ground rules for the discussion. I would add to Palmer's list another essential element: collaborative practices of students and faculty. If we believe that the strongest criterion for assessing effective teaching is effective learning, we must go to the learners. When students examine, document, and assess their own learning; when faculty examine, document and assess their own teaching; and when faculty peers examine and assess the relationship of the learning and teaching, a powerful model emerges for creating a discourse about teaching and learning and a means of improving and evaluating both.

Omnipresent calls for improvement of undergraduate teaching can then be met with two responses. First, students are learning and learning well: we have evidence of effective teaching through documented learning analyzed by students, teachers, and faculty colleagues. Secondly, faculty are continually improving their teaching: we have evidence of change based on student work, teacher self-analysis, and faculty peer evaluation. Uniting the student, faculty member, and faculty peer in the process of representing teaching and learning forges a powerful coalition for the affirmation of higher education.

References

Angelo, T. & Cross, K. R (1988). *Classroom assessment techniques: A handbook for faculty.* Ann Arbor: University of Michigan.

Barr, R. B., & Tagg, J. (1995). From teaching to learning: A new paradigm for undergraduate education. *Change,* (November/December), 12–25.

Boyer, E. L. (1990). *Scholarship reconsidered: Priorities of the professoriate.* Princeton, NJ: The Carnegie Foundation for the Advancement of Teaching.

Brown, C. B. (1995). "Documenting teaching workshop: Toward the development of a teaching portfolio." Unpublished paper.

Courts, P. L., & McInerney, K. H. (1993). *Assessment in higher education: Politics, pedagogy, and portfolios.* Westport, CT: Praeger.

Edgerton, R. E., Hutchings, P., & Quinlan, K. (1991). *The teaching portfolio: Capturing the scholarship in teaching.* Washington, DC: American Association for Higher Education.

Howard, J. (1995). *Teaching outside the classroom: The Midwest Student Sociology Conference.* Unpublished paper.

Palmer, R J. (1993). Good talk about good teaching: Improving teaching through conversation and community. *Change,* (November/December), 8–13.

Seldin, R (1993). How colleges evaluate professors: 1983 v. 1993. *AAHE Bulletin,* 46(2), 6–8.

Evaluating College Teaching: Myth and Reality

Peter Seldin

No group is more full of myths about teaching and its evaluation, more reluctant to admit that there are good and bad teachers, and more resistant to the idea that teaching skills can be acquired than teachers themselves.

This mythology is often grounded in dubious assumptions about the nature of teaching and learning and about the characteristics of teachers and students. Rarely are these myths confronted by practical experience, thoughtful observation, or careful reasoning. For that reason, this chapter examines five common assumptions—touched on in one way or another by the *Change* articles in this section—that help create or dispel a mythology of teaching and its evaluation.

1. **There is no way to identify good teaching.** Meech (1976) took this position in his *Change* article, suggesting that since we do not know what effective teaching is, we are unable to evaluate it properly. Cross (1989, p. 12) saw it differently. She said, "We cannot continue to hide behind the excuse that we . . . can't tell a good teacher from a poor one. The sentiment defies our common sense and is contrary to most research on the question." Carson (1996) identified effective teachers as those remembered by their students decades later for their special ability to: (1) link students to their discipline; (2) use stories, examples, anecdotes to explain tough concepts; and (3) truly care about their students and their learning.

   Eble (1986) agreed, pointing out that faculty singled out for making a difference are also heavily involved in assisting student learning by providing extra help, working closely with teaching assistants, and setting up mentoring programs.

   The critical characteristics of effective teaching have been identified in the more than 10,000 studies on teaching effectiveness published in the last 20 years. Those studies are in general agreement. In addition to the characteristics mentioned above, the important teacher qualities include professional competence, the ability to motivate students and effectively communicate at their level, fairness, and positive attitude. These points of important teaching traits are not far removed from those employed by Socrates.

2. **Good teachers are born not made.** The marginal truth in this belief applies no more to teachers than it does to those in any other profession. Hence, there are born dentists, born accountants, born physical therapists. In truth, though, born anythings spend an enormous amount of time conditioning their minds, acquiring skills, and endlessly practicing. Potentially great teachers become great teachers by the same route: through conditioning mind and spirit, acquiring skills, and through endlessly practicing in the classroom.

   It is true, of course, that some teachers have certain natural advantages—charm, verbal fluency, an ability to communicate well with students, a warm smile, patience—but the skills are as likely to be acquired as inborn. Perhaps that is why Kunz (1978) said that teacher evaluation must be linked to specific strategies for improvement, and why Carson (1996) argued

Reprinted from *Learning from Change,* edited by D. DeZure (2000), Stylus Publishing.

that teachers can increase their effectiveness by learning how to communicate their love for their academic field, to be attentive to their words and action so their respect and concern for students is apparent, and to find strategies for signaling their availability.

Tobias (1986) described an innovative teaching improvement approach: non-science professors are taught science by their colleagues for the express purpose of providing feedback to the instructor. As part of the process, the non-science professors respond to two questions: what is making this subject difficult for me? What could be done differently to make it more clear?

Too often, professors look upon evaluation of teaching and professional development as unrelated processes. The fact is that they are a single process and make most sense as such. While administrative evaluation can be helpful in making tenure, promotion, or retention decisions, its core purpose is to identify areas of needed or desired improvement and to point the way to professional development.

The movement to improve teaching has been adopted, in various forms, by a rapidly increasing number of institutions. Although reliable numbers are hard to come by, it is estimated that today as many as 1,000 colleges and universities have centers devoted to improving teaching—a stunning jump from the 80 centers cited by Meeth (1976) some 24 years ago in *Change.*

3. **There are no differences in effectiveness of different methods of instruction.** This may be the case if the criterion used is student performance on final examinations, certainly an important outcome of higher education. However, there are others. As McKeachie (1969) correctly pointed out, other important goals include problem-solving and critical thinking skills, interest in the field, motivation, and attitudinal or value changes. It is in these areas, rather than student performance on final examinations, that differences in teaching methods appear.

   In truth, there is no one best way of teaching. What is best for one teacher may be quite different from what is best for another (McKeachie, 1999), and no one method is best for all goals, students, or teachers. Perhaps that is why Whitfield (1982), in his *Change* review of a book by Epstein on preeminent professors, reported that some were fluent lecturers and delivered histrionic performances while others used the Socratic method. Some took a personal interest in their students; others did not. While most were mentors, some had a coherent set of doctrines, while others did not.

4. **Student ratings are the only source of information needed to determine teaching effectiveness.** It has become as common for students to grade teachers as for teachers to grade students. In fact, student ratings have become the most widely used—and, in many cases, the only—source of information on teaching effectiveness (Seldin, 1993). Tapping just one source of information is a dangerous approach, however. In her article, Carson worried that many will confuse such simplistic assessment outcomes with quality of teaching. Frey said that even properly developed student ratings that provide reliable and valid data about teaching should be considered with other evidence.

   Cashin (1989) argued that students are unqualified to provide valid reports on a number of important matters of teaching effectiveness. These include an array of factors related to subject matter mastery, course design, and curriculum development. Seldin (1999) agreed, saying that no single source of evaluative information can capture the individuality and complexity of teaching.

5. **The evaluation of teaching has not changed much over the years.** In truth, both the conversation and the process have changed significantly.

How has the conversation changed? Perhaps the best way to see it is to compare the table of contents of two well-received books by the same author on the topic of evaluating teaching, one published in 1980, the other in 1999.

The table of contents in the 1980 book listed only the following chapters:

- Student ratings
- Colleague evaluation

- Self-evaluation
- Other ways to evaluate teaching.

By comparison, the table of contents in the 1999 book contained the following chapters:

- Student ratings
- Using student feedback to improve teaching
- Peer observation
- Self-evaluation
- Post-tenure review: evaluating teaching
- Evaluating teaching through classroom assessment
- Using the World Wide Web to improve teaching
- Teaching portfolios
- Administrative courage to evaluate the complexities of teaching
- Building a climate conducive to effective evaluation
- Building successful teaching evaluation programs

Without doubt, the conversation about evaluating teaching has changed, becoming broader and deeper. New approaches, such as the teaching portfolio, have been developed. The technology movement is in full swing. There is greater concern for creating an environment conducive to meaningful evaluation. Beyond that, however, there is now a keen awareness that evaluation data can and should be used to improve teaching performance, not just for personnel decisions.

Clearly, the conversation has changed. More significantly, so has the process used to evaluate teaching performance. In his *Change* article, Seldin (1984) documented those changes over the five-year period from 1978 to 1983. Since then, Seldin (1999) has extended his study and now has documented the changes over the 20-year period between 1978 and 1998. (See below.)

Information Sources Cited as "Always Used" in Evaluating Teaching, 1978, 1988, and 1998

Information Source*	1978	1988	1998
Systematic student ratings	54.8%	80.3%	88.1%
Evaluation by department chair	80.3%	80.9%	70.4%
Evaluation by dean	76.9%	72.6%	64.9%
Self-evaluation	36.6%	49.8%	58.7%
Committee evaluation	46.6%	49.3%	46.0%
Colleagues' opinions	42.7%	44.3%	44.0%
Classroom visits	14.3%	27.4%	40.3%
Course syllabi and examinations	13.9%	29.0%	38.6%
Scholarly research/publication	19.9%	29.0%	26.9%
Alumni opinions	3.4%	3.0%	9.0%
Grade distribution	2.1%	4.2%	6.7%

*In descending order by 1998 scares
Source. Seldin (1999)

Seldin (p. 21) cites the following key changes in the evaluation of teaching in this period:

- Systematic student ratings have become the most widely used source of information.
- The department chair and dean are still important sources of information but with sharply diluted power.

- Self-evaluation, classroom visits, and course syllabi and exams are far more widely used.
- Committee evaluation and colleagues' opinions continue to play major roles.
- In altering their evaluation practices, colleges are gathering more information from more sources and doing so more systematically.

Why has the evaluation of teaching been so dramatically transformed? Some of the answer is found in administrative displeasure with the inadequacies of systems used in the past. Another part is a response to competition from Internet-based providers like the University of Phoenix and University Access that offer academic modules, courses, and entire degree programs. The movements to promote peer review and more recently the scholarship of teaching also contribute to these changes.

More of the answer likely lies in the burgeoning teaching portfolio movement. Portfolios are factual descriptions of a professor's teaching strengths and accomplishments. They often include student ratings, classroom observation reports, syllabi and other teaching materials, and a reflective statement addressing teaching philosophy, objectives, and strategies (Seldin, 1997).

It is clear that teaching evaluation methods are changing. Some factors are getting more weight and others less. What is unresolved is which of the shifts will turn out to be improvements and which will be short-lived fads. More certain is the likelihood that a direct outgrowth of improved teaching evaluation practices will be improvements in teaching performance.

References

Cashin, W. E. (1989). Defining and evaluating college teaching. *IDEA Paper* no. 32, IDEA Center, Kansas State University.

Carson, B. H. (1996, November/December). Thirty years of stories: The professor's place in student memories. *Change, 28,* 11–17.

Cross, K. P. (1989). A proposal to improve teaching or what "taking teaching seriously" should mean. *AAHE Bulletin, 39,* 9–15.

Eble, K. E. (1986, July/August). A group portrait. *Change, 18,* 21–47.

Kunz, D. (1978, February). Viewpoint 2: Learning to live with evaluation. *Change, 10,* 10–11.

McKeachie, W. J. (1969, November/December). Letters: Effects of teaching. *Change, 1,* 4.

McKeachie, W. J. (1999). *Teaching tips* (10th ed.). Boston, MA: Houghton Mifflin.

Meeth, L. R. (1976, June). An overview: The stateless art of teaching evaluation. *Change, 8,* 3–5.

Seldin, P. (1984, April). Faculty evaluation: Surveying policy and practices. *Change, 16,* 28–33.

Seldin, P. (1993, July 21). The use and abuse of student ratings of professors. *The Chronicle of Higher Education,* p. A-40.

Seldin, P. (1997). *The teaching portfolio* (2nd ed.). Bolton, MA: Anker.

Seldin, P. (1999). *Changing practices in evaluating teaching.* Bolton, MA: Anker.

Tobias, S. (1986, March/April). Peer perspectives on the teaching of science. *Change, 18,* 36–51.

Whitfield, S. J. (1982, March). Review: Masters: Portraits of great teachers. *Change, 14,* 53–54.

PART III—COURSE/CURRICULUM: DESIGNING FOR LEARNING

Recommended Readings

Achacoso, M. V. (Ed.). (2005). *Alternative strategies for evaluating student learning.* San Francisco, CA: Jossey-Bass.

Alfred, M. (2002). *Learning and sociocultural contexts: Implications for adults, community, and workplace education.* San Francisco, CA: Jossey-Bass.

Allen, M. J. (2006). *Assessing general education programs.* Bolton, MA: Anker.

Anderson, L. W., & Krathwohl, D. R. (Eds.). (2001). *A taxonomy for learning, teaching, and assessing: A revision of Bloom's taxonomy of educational objectives.* New York, NY: Addison Wesley Longman.

Angelo, T. A. (1995). Classroom assessment for critical thinking. *Teaching of Psychology, 22*(1), 6–7.

Angelo, T. A. (Ed.). (1998). *New Directions for Teaching and Learning: No. 75, Classroom assessment and research: Uses, approaches, and research findings.* San Francisco, CA: Jossey-Bass.

Angelo, T.A., & Cross, K. P. (1993). *Classroom assessment techniques: A handbook for college teachers.* San Francisco, CA: Jossey-Bass.

Arter, J., & McTighe, J. (2001). *Scoring rubrics in the classroom: Using performance criteria for assessing and improving student performance.* Thousand Oaks, CA: Corwin.

Astin, A. W. (1993). *Assessment for excellence: The philosophy and practice of assessment and evaluation in higher education.* American Council on Education Series on Higher Education. Phoenix, AZ: Oryx Press.

Banta, T. W. (2002). *Building a scholarship of assessment.* San Francisco, CA: Jossey-Bass.

Banta, T. W. (Ed.). (2007). *Assessing student achievement in general education: Assessment update collection.* San Francisco, CA: Jossey-Bass.

Banta, T. W., Jones, E. A., & Black, K. E. (2009). *Designing effective assessment: Principles and profiles of good practice.* San Francisco, CA: Jossey-Bass.

Baxter Magolda, M.B., & King, P.M. (2004). *Learning partnerships: Theory and models of practice to educate for self-authorship.* Sterling, VA: Stylus.

Berk, R. A. (2005). Survey of 12 strategies to measure teaching effectiveness. *International Journal of Teaching and Learning in Higher Education, 17*(1), 48–62.

Bloom, B. S., & Krathwohl, D. R. (1956). *Taxonomy of educational objectives: The classification of educational goals by a committee of college and university examiners. Handbook I: Cognitive domain.* New York, NY: Longman, Green.

Bothel, R. T. (2002). Epilogue: A cautionary note about on-line assessment. In R. Anderson and B. Speck (Eds.), *New Directions for Teaching and Learning: No. 91, Assessment Strategies for the on-line class from theory to practice* (pp. 99–104). San Francisco, CA: Jossey-Bass.

Boud, D., & Falchikov, N. (2007). *Rethinking assessment in higher education.* New York, NY: Routledge.

Borden, V. M. H. (2005, March/April). Accommodating student swirl: When traditional students are no longer the tradition. *Change, 36,* 10–17.

Braxton, J. M. (Ed.). (2006). *New Directions for Institutional Research: No. 129, Analyzing faculty work and rewards: Using Boyer's four domains of scholarship.* San Francisco, CA: Jossey-Bass.

Bresciani, M. J. (Ed). (2007). *Assessing student learning in general education.* Boston, MA: Anker.

Brinko, K. (1991, February). Visioning your course: Questions to ask as you design your course. *The Teaching Professor,* 3–4.

Brown, S., & Glasner, A. (Eds.). (1999). *Assessment matters in higher education: Choosing and using diverse approaches (Society for Research into Higher Education).* London, UK: Open University Press.

Bryan, C., & Clegg, K. (2006). *Innovative assessment in higher education.* New York, NY: Routledge.

Campbell, A., & Norton, L. (Eds.). (2007). *Learning, teaching and assessing in higher education: Developing reflective practice.* Exeter, UK: Learning Matters.

Chatterji, M. (2003). *Designing and using tools for educational assessment.* Boston, MA: Allyn and Bacon.

Chetro-Szivos, J., & Gray, P. (2004). Creating conversational spaces on campus: Connecting students and faculty through appreciative inquiry and circular questioning. *The Journal of Student Centered Learning, 2*(1) 35–42.

Comeaux, P. (Ed.). (2005). *Assessing online learning.* Bolton, MA: Anker.

Davis, B. G. (1993). *Tools for teaching.* San Francisco, CA: Jossey-Bass.

Diamond, R. M. (2008). *Designing and assessing courses and curricula: A practical guide* (3rd ed.). San Francisco, CA: Jossey-Bass.

Durning, B., & Jenkins, A. (2005). Teaching/research relations in departments: the perspectives of built environment academics. *Studies in Higher Education, 30*(4), 407–426.

Espey, M. (2008). Does space matter? Classroom design and team-based learning. *Review of Agricultural Economics, 30*(4), 764–775.

Evans, N. J. (2000). Creating a positive learning environment for gay, lesbian, and bisexual students. In T. C. Guy (Ed.), *New Directions for Teaching and Learning: No. 82, Identity, learning, and the liberal arts* (pp. 81–87). San Francisco, CA: Jossey-Bass.

Fox, R., & Rowntree, K. (2004). Linking the doing to the thinking: using criterion-based assessment in role-playing simulations. *Planet, 13,* 9–15.

Gates, S., Augustine, C., Benjamin, R., Bikson, T., Kaganoff, T., Levy, D., Moini, J. S., & Zimmer, R. W. (2002). *Ensuring quality and productivity in higher education: An analysis of assessment practices.* San Francisco, CA: Jossey-Bass.

Grunert, J. (1997). *The course syllabus: A learning-centered approach.* Bolton, MA: Anker Publishing.

Gurin, P., Dey, E., Hurtado, S., & Gurin, G. (2002). Diversity and higher education: Theory and impact on educational outcomes. *Harvard Educational Review, 72*(3), 330–366.

Howard-Hamilton, M. F. (2000). Creating a culturally responsive learning environment for African American students. In T.C. Guy (Ed.), *New Directions for Teaching and Learning: No. 82, Identity, learning, and the liberal arts* (pp. 45–53). San Francisco, CA: Jossey-Bass.

Hutchings, P. (Ed.). (1998). *The course portfolio: How faculty can examine their teaching to advance practice and improve student learning.* Washington, DC: American Association for Higher Education.

Irons, A. (2008). *Enhancing learning through formative assessment and feedback.* London, UK: Routledge.

Jamieson, P. (2003). Designing more effective on campus teaching and learning spaces: A role for academic developers. *International Journal for Academic Development, 8*(1/2), 119–133.

Jamieson, P., Fisher, K., Gilding, T., Taylor, P., & Trevitt, A. C. F., (2000). Place and space in the design of new learning environments. *Higher Education Research and Development, 19*(2), 221–236.

Klenowski, V., Askew, S. & Carnell, E. (2006). Portfolios for learning, assessment and professional development in higher education. *Assessment and Evaluation in Higher Education, 31*(3), 267–286.

Kreber, C. (2001). Learning experientially through case studies? A conceptual analysis, *Teaching in Higher Education, 6*(2), 217–228.

Kurz, L., & Banta, T. W. (2004). Decoding the assessment of student learning. In A. J. Petrosino, T. Martin and V. Svihla (Eds.), *New Directions for Teaching and Learning, 98, Decoding the disciplines: Helping students learn disciplinary ways of thinking* (pp. 85–94). San Francisco, CA: Jossey-Bass.

Lawrence, R. L. (Ed.). (October 2005). Artistic ways of knowing: Expanded opportunities for teaching and learning. In C. Kreber (Ed.), *New Directions for Teaching and Learning: No. 107, Exploring research-based teaching.* San Francisco, CA: Jossey-Bass.

Leskes, A., & Wright, B. (2005). *The art and science of assessing general education outcomes: A practical guide.* Washington DC: Association of American Colleges and Universities.

Linn, R. L., & Gronlund, N. E. (2008). *Measurement and assessment in teaching* (8th ed.). New Jersey: Prentice Hall.

Livingston, K. (2000). When architecture disables: Teaching undergraduates to perceive ableism in the built environment. *Teaching Sociology, 28*(3), 182–91.

Louie, B. Y., Drevdahl, D. J., Purdy, J. M., & Stackman, R. W. (2003). Advancing the scholarship of teaching and learning through collaborative self-study. *The Journal of Higher Education, 74,* 150–171.

Lyons, R. E., McIntosh, M., & Kysilka, M. L. (2003). *Teaching college in an age of accountability.* Boston, MA: Allyn and Bacon.

Macdonald, R. (2006). The use of evaluation to improve practice in learning and teaching. *Innovations in Education and Teaching International, 43*(1), 3–13. http://dx.doi.org/DOI10.1080/14703290500472087

Maki, P. L. (2004). *Assessing for learning: Building a sustainable commitment across the institution.* Sterling, VA: Stylus

Mansilla, V. B. (2005). Assessing student work at disciplinary crossroads. *Change, 37*(1), 14–21.

Messick, S. J. (Ed.). (1999). *Assessment in higher education: Issues of access, quality, student development, and public policy.* Mahweh, NJ: Lawrence Erlbaum Associates.

Meyer, J. H. F., & Land, R. (2003). Threshold concepts and troublesome knowledge (1): Linkages to thinking and practising within the disciplines. In C. Rust (Ed.), *Improving student learning theory and practice - ten years on* (pp. 412–424). Oxford, UK: OCSLD.

Meyer, J. H. F., & Land, R. (2005). Threshold concepts and troublesome knowledge (2): Epistemological considerations and a conceptual framework for teaching and learning. *Higher Education, 49*(3), 373–388.

Middendorf, J., & Pace, D. (2007). Easing entry into the scholarship of teaching and learning through focused assessments: The 'decoding the disciplines' approach. In D. Robertson and L. Nilson (Eds.), *To Improve the Academy: Vol. 26, Resources for Faculty, Instructional and Organizational Development* (pp. 53–67). San Francisco, CA: Jossey-Bass.

Miller, A., Imrie, B., & Cox, K. (1998). *Student assessment in higher education: A handbook for assessing performance.* London, UK: Kogan Page.

Mundhenk, R. T. (2004). Communities of assessment. *Change, 36*(6), 36–41.

Nilson, L. B. (2007). *The graphic syllabus and the outcomes map: Communicating your course.* San Francisco, CA: Jossey-Bass.

Oliver, R. (2007). Exploring an inquiry-based learning approach with first year students in a large undergraduate class. *Innovations in Education and Teaching International, 44*(1), 3–15.

Palomba, C., & Banta, T. (1999). *Assessment essentials: Planning, implementing, and improving assessment in higher education.* San Francisco, CA: Jossey-Bass

Palomba, C. A., & Banta, T. W. (Eds.). (2001). *Assessing student competence in accredited disciplines: Pioneering approaches to assessment in higher education.* Sterling, VA: Stylus.

Pellegrino, J., Chudowsky, N., & Glaser, P. (2001). *Knowing what students know: The science and design of educational assessment.* Washington, DC: National Academy of Sciences.

Pickford, R., & Brown, S. (2006). *Assessing skills and practice.* New York, NY: Routledge.

Ryan, K. E. (Ed.). (2000). *Evaluating teaching in higher education: A vision for the future.* San Francisco, CA: Jossey-Bass.

Schwartz, P., & Webb, G. (Eds.). (2002). *Assessment: Case studies, experience and practice from higher education.* London, UK: Kogan Page.

Scott, S. S., & Gregg, N. (2000). Meeting the evolving education needs of faculty in providing access for college students with LD. *Journal of Learning Disabilities, 33*(2), 158–167.

Scott-Webber, L. (2004). *In sync: Environmental behaviour research and the design of learning spaces.* MI: The Society for College and University Planning.

Simm, D. and McGuiness, M. (2004). Crisis resolution of student-led research projects at distant locations, *Planet, 13,* 8–11. http://www.gees.ac.uk/pubs/planet/index.htm#P13

Simonson, M., Smaldino, S., Albright, M., & Zvacek, S. (2003). *Teaching and learning at a distance: Foundations of distance education* (2nd ed.). Upper Saddle River, NJ: Pearson Education.

Strange, C. C., & Banning, J. H. (2001). *Educating by design: Creating campus learning communities that work.* San Francisco, CA: Jossey-Bass.

Suskie, L. (Ed.). (2000). *Assessment to promote deep learning.* Washington, DC: American Association for Higher Education.

Suskie, L. (2004). *Assessing student learning: A common sense guide.* Bolton, MA: Anker.

Theall, M., & Franklin, J. L. (1990). Student ratings in the context of complex evaluation systems. In M. Theall and J. Franklin (Eds.), *New Directions for Teaching and Learning, No. 43, Student ratings of instruction: Issues for improving practice.* San Francisco, CA: Jossey-Bass.

Theall, M., Abrami, P. A., & Mets, L. (Eds.). (2001). The student ratings debate. Are they valid? How can we best use them? *New Directions for Institutional Research,* No. 109. San Francisco: Jossey-Bass

Walvoord, B. E. (2003). Assessment in Accelerated Learning Programs. In R. J. Wlodkowski and C. E. Kasworm (Eds.), *New Directions for Adult and Continuing Education, No. 9, Accelerated learning for adults: The promise and practice of intensive educational formats.* San Francisco, CA: Jossey-Bass.

Walvoord, B. C. (2004). *Assessment clear and simple.* San Francisco, CA: Jossey-Bass.

Walvoord, B. C., & Anderson, V. J. (1998). *Effective grading: A tool for teaching and learning.* San Francisco, CA: Jossey-Bass.

Wehlburg, C. (2006). *Meaningful course revision: Enhancing academic engagement using student learning data.* Bolton, MA: Anker.

Williams, D. D., Hricko, M., & Howell, S. L. (2006). *Online assessment, measurement, and evaluation: Emerging practices.* Hershey, PA: Information Science Publishers.

Willis, D., & Millis, B. J. (2004). An international perspective on assessing group projects. In C. Wehlburg and S. Chadwick-Blossey (Eds.), *To Improve The Academy: Vol. 22, Resources for Faculty, Instructional, and Organizational Development* (pp. 268–286). Bolton, MA: Anker.

Wolf, P. & Christensen Hughes, J. (Eds.). (2008). *New Directions for Teaching and Learning: No. 112, Curriculum development in higher education: Faculty-driven processes and practices.* San Francisco, CA: Jossey-Bass.

Wulff, D. H., Jacobson, W. H., Freisem, K., Hatch, D. H., Lawrence, M., & Lenz, L. R. (Eds.). (2005). *Aligning for learning: Strategies for teaching effectiveness.* Bolton, MA: Anker.

Zubizarreta, H. (2004). *The learning portfolio: Reflective practice of improving student learning.* Bolton, MA: Anker.

Web Resources

The American Distance Education Consortium
http://www.adec.edu/online-resources.html

Google Distance Learning Directory
http://directory.google.com/Top/Reference/Education/Distance_Learning

Part IV

Methods: Choosing the Best Strategies and Techniques

Part IV—Methods: Choosing the Best Strategies and Techniques

Part IV of this reader is intended to provide information on methods that can be strategically matched with learning outcomes. Gone are the days when lecture can be allowed to function as the default means of knowledge transmission and acquisition, as contemporary theories of learning move us toward appreciating the promise of students' active involvement in knowledge creation.

General—Active Learning

We begin this section with some concepts about active learning, the baseline of most pedagogical assumptions in higher education today. Dee Fink, known for his work in promoting the design of "significant learning" experiences, provides us with a holistic model of active learning that includes activities related to knowledge acquisition as well as reflection and action.

Problem-Based Learning

Problem-based learning (PBL) is an approach that requires a commitment to student group processing and flexible, responsive teaching. However, it first requires careful planning on the part of the instructor. To assist faculty interested in promoting a problem-based activity, course, or curriculum, the second reading in this section, "Getting started in problem-based learning" by Harold White, is packed with helpful advice and considerations to guide someone using PBL for the first time.

Integrative Learning

As the complex problems of contemporary society demand complex solutions, educators preparing tomorrow's leaders feel more compelled than ever to promote "thinking outside of the box," or integrative learning. Huber and Hutchings highlight the irony of this need given our current higher education structures and practices. Tradition can often get in the way of, rather than facilitate, collaboration across disciplinary boundaries. The authors challenge modern teaching and learning views by citing examples where the terrain of higher education is beginning to change. Huber and Hutchings maintain that there must be intentional effort on the part of administrators, faculty, and students to actively seek opportunities for integration.

Team-Based/Cooperative/Collaborative Learning

There is much more to collaborative learning than placing students in groups. Like an orchestra, each member must have a role combined with goals and ongoing guidance to be successful. We selected two readings for this section. The first, by Michaelsen, Fink, and Knight, examines the group process and how we can best design tasks for group experiences. They offer helpful advice to tackle the most common problems associated with group work. Barbara Millis, in the second reading titled "Enhancing learning—and more!—through cooperative learning," emphasizes the importance of providing adequate structure for group activities. She instructs us about theory, research, and principles that can be used to create a cooperative classroom.

Discussion

The two names that come to mind most when raising the issue of classroom discussion are Brookfield and Preskill. Their collaboration on this topic has added value to the literature on teaching and learning. While comprehensively covering the subject of discussion is not possible given the breadth of this reader, we have chosen a piece by these authors that supplies some practical ideas for how to facilitate group discussions and structure student engagement.

Citizenship/Service Learning

Community service and service learning can be viewed on a continuum, with service reflecting a one-time event or even long-term commitment of an individual providing assistance to those in need. It is often used as a form of active learning in that it has the potential to inform student understanding of various communities, cultures, races, and social classes. Service learning, while sharing the above attributes of service, adds a layer of learning by including an academic component characterized by intentionally structured, reflective activities and discussions. Service learning, a deliberate pedagogy as well as philosophy, has the potential to fundamentally transform students' views of the world and can make course content come to life. In the selection by Vogelgesang and Astin, the authors present research that directly compares service-learning and co-curricular community service (p. 25). Their findings conclude that pairing service with academic work enhances eleven outcomes related to student growth, intellectual development, and leadership ability.

Technology

No collection of readings on teaching and learning today would be complete without addressing the online environment. Palloff and Pratt, two authorities emerging in this arena, impart "best practices in delivering online courses" (p. 1) in their presentation "Lessons from the cyberspace classroom." Their insights include shifts in relationships and expectations this environment creates—between students and faculty, faculty and the institution, and students and the institution. In addition, they provide valuable suggestions for making institutions, faculty, and students more successful in the transition from face-to-face to online teaching and learning.

Scholarship of Teaching and Learning as Method

Faculty members at community colleges have different expectations placed on them than those at four-year institutions. Often their teaching load and service expectations are great while their requirements for publishing are of secondary concern. However, at an institution where teaching is of primary value, the scholarship of teaching and learning (SoTL) can simultaneously be a teaching method and contribution to the research base of higher education. Tinberg, Duffy, and Mino share the "promise and peril" of SoTL within the two-year college environment. They charge administrators and faculty "to create a far more complex and productive vision of the two-year college teacher/scholar than exists today . . . includ[ing] time for inquiry, discovery, and collegial exchange—all the critical components of the scholarship of teaching and learning" (p. 33).

CHAPTER 12

GENERAL—ACTIVE LEARNING

A SELF-DIRECTED GUIDE TO DESIGNING COURSES FOR SIGNIFICANT LEARNING (EXCERPTS)

D. FINK

Active Learning. One of the more powerful ideas to emerge in the literature on college teaching in the last decade or so is the concept of active learning. In essence, the concept of active learning supports research that shows: students learn more and retain their learning longer if they acquire it in an active rather than a passive manner.

What do we mean by "active learning"? Active-learning advocates Bonwell and Eison (1991) describe active learning as "[involving] students in doing things and thinking about the things they are doing." By "doing things," they are referring to activities such as debates, simulations, guided design, small group problem solving, case studies, etc. My way of illustrating that definition is shown in Figure 12.1. When students listen to a lecture or read a texbook, they are receiving "Information and Ideas"—an important part of the learning process but also one that is relatively passive. To make the learning more active, we need to learn how to enhance the overall learning experience by adding some kind of experiential learning and opportunities for reflective dialogue.

An Enlarged View of "Active Learning." In order to create a complete set of learning activities capable of achieving significant learning, we need an enlarged and more holistic view of active learning—one that includes "getting information and ideas" as well as "experience" and "reflection." Figure 12.2 illustrates a new conceptualization of active learning, one that makes all three modes of learning an integral part of a more complete set of learning activities.

Figure 12.1
Initial View of Passive and Active Learning

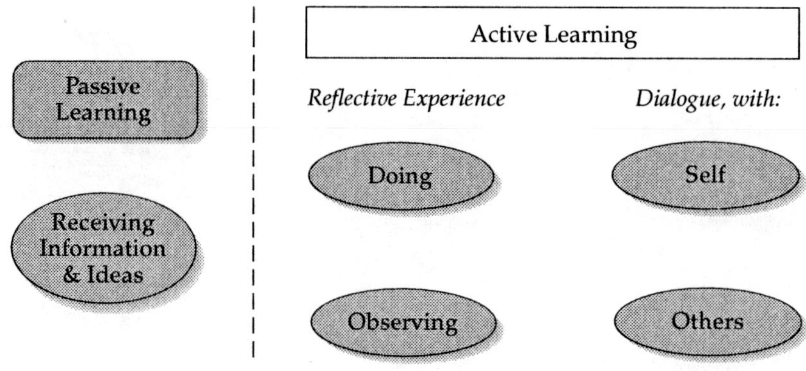

Reprinted from *A Self-Directed Guide to Designing Courses for Significant Learning*, by permission of the author.

Figure 12.2
A Holistic View of Active Learning

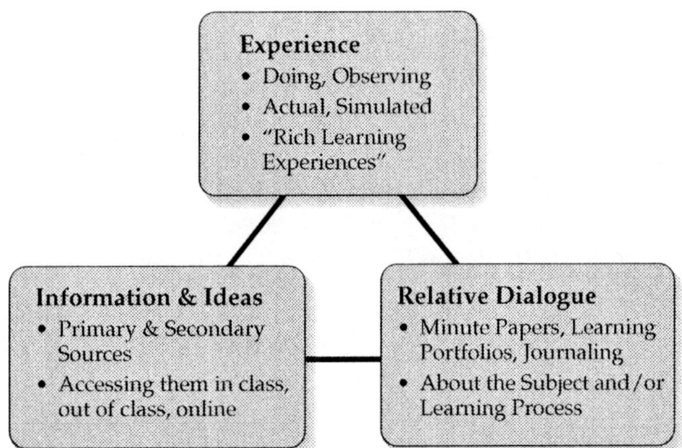

Two principles should guide our choice of learning activities. First, an effective set of learning activities is one that includes activities from each of the following three components of active learning: information and ideas, experience, and reflective dialogue. Second, we should try to find *direct* kinds of learning activities, whenever possible. *Indirect,* or vicarious, forms may be necessary in some cases. But when we can find *direct* ways of providing active learning, the quality of student learning expands.

From my own experience and from reading the literature on what effective teachers actually do in terms of this holistic view of active learning, I have found that good teachers incorporate all three components of active learning in a variety of ways. As shown in Table 12.1, sometimes teachers pro-

TABLE 12.1

Learning Activities for Holistic, Active Learning

	GETTING INFORMATION & IDEAS	**EXPERIENCE**		**REFLECTIVE DIALOGUE, with:**	
		"Doing"	**"Observing"**	**Self**	**Others**
DIRECT	• Primary data • Primary sources	• "Real Doing," in authentic settings	• Direct observation of phenomena	• Reflective thinking • Journaling	• Dialogue (in or out of class)
INDIRECT, VICARIOUS	• Secondary data and sources • Lectures, textbooks	• Case Studies • Gaming, Simulations • Role Play	• Stories (can be accessed *via:* film, oral history, literature)		
ONLINE	• Course website • Internet	• Teacher can assign students to "directly experience _____." • Students can engage in "indirect" kinds of experience online.		• Students can reflect and then engage in various kinds of dialogue online.	

vide information and ideas, experience, and reflective dialogue directly; at other times it is done indirectly or even online.

To help you explore ways of developing more powerful learning experiences for your students, I suggest some ideas for each of three components of active learning: Rich Learning Experience, In-Depth Reflective Dialogue, and Information and Ideas.

Rich Learning Experiences. As you try to add an experiential component to the learning experience, look for "Rich Learning Experiences." Certain learning experiences are "rich" because they allow students to acquire several kinds of significant learning simultaneously. What are some ways this can be done? The list below identifies in-class and out-of-class activities that promote multiple kinds of significant learning—all at the same time.

In Class:	**Outside of Class:**
• Debates	• Service learning
• Role playing	• Situational observations
• Simulations	• Authentic projects
• Dramatizations	

Action: Identify some learning activities to add to your course that will give students a "Doing" or "Observing" Experience. What "Rich Learning Experiences" are appropriate for your course?

In-Depth Reflective Dialogue. Another important ingredient of active learning is giving students time and encouragement to reflect on the meaning of their learning experience. There are various forms of reflective dialogue (See Table 12.2). One can reflect with oneself (as in writing in a journal or diary) or with others (as in engaging in discussions with a teacher or others). Another key distinction is between substantive writing, in which one writes about a subject (e.g., a typical term paper), and reflective writing, in which one writes about one's

TABLE 12.2

In-Depth Reflective Dialogue

With Whom?

- **Oneself** (journaling, learning portfolios)
- **Others** (teacher, other students, people outside class)

About What?

- **Subject of the Course:** (*Substantive* writing)

What is an <u>appropriate and full understanding</u> of this concept or topic?

- **Learning Process:** (*Reflective* writing)
- <u>What</u> am I learning?
- Of what <u>value</u> is this?
- <u>How</u> did I learn: best, most comfortably, with difficulty, etc.?
- <u>What else</u> do I need to learn?

Written Forms?

- **One-minute papers**
- **Weekly journal writing**
- **Learning portfolios** (end-of-course, end-of-program)

own learning. In reflective writing, students address a different set of questions, such as: *What* am I learning? What is the *value* of what I am learning? *How* am I learning? *What else* do I need to learn?

The literature on college teaching identifies numerous procedures to promote reflection. In the *one-minute paper,* the teacher poses a short, but well-focused, question for students to answer once a week or at the end of each class. Sample questions include: "What is the most important thing you learned today? What is the "muddiest point" of this class?" Slightly more ambitious is the practice of having students write weekly *learning journals.* Ask students to periodically reflect on their learning experience. You may need to guide this effort by providing some questions like the four listed above (or more specific versions of them).

Another excellent practice is for students to put together a *learning portfolio* at the end of the course. This is an 8–12 page narrative with an appendix of materials to support and illustrate the content of the narrative. In the narrative, students write reflectively about their learning experiences, again addressing questions like the those listed above.

Action: What kinds of *Reflective Dialogue* can you incorporate into your course?

Information and Ideas. In order to free up some class time for the experiential and reflective activities identified above, you will probably need to explore alternative ways of introducing students to the key information and ideas of the course, i.e., the content. This might involve having them do more reading before they come to class. Or it may mean creating a course-specific website where you put content-related material. Or you can direct students to go to selected websites that have good content related to the course.

Action: Other than lectures, what ways can you identify to cause students to get their initial exposure to subject matter and ideas (preferably outside of class)?

CHAPTER 13

PROBLEM-BASED LEARNING

Getting Started in Problem-Based Learning

Harold B. White, III

Chapter Summary

The transition from traditional instruction to a problem-based approach to learning requires many changes and, without proper preparation, can frustrate the best intentions. Among the issues one needs to address are preparing a syllabus that reflects revised learning objectives, finding appropriate problems to address content, introducing students to group process and learning skills, and dealing with the uncertainty of a different classroom strategy.

Introduction

It takes a certain amount of independence and determination to change the way one teaches. It also takes time and involves risks. Where do instructors acquire the commitment to get started with problem-based learning (PBL)? Frequently, commitment grows out of the recurring frustration most instructors experience when they realize how little their students understand or remember from a semester of charismatic lectures. If not ignored, that frustration leads to reflection on what it means "to teach" and "to learn." Problem-based learning addresses these issues and offers an attractive alternative to traditional education by shifting the focus of education from *what faculty teach* to *what students learn.* Content remains important, but emphasis shifts more to the process. For those used to lecturing, the trade-offs can intimidate, but the promise of greater student understanding sustains the effort. Fundamentally, adopting PBL requires a transformation of the classroom role of the instructor from a "sage on the stage to a guide on the side" (King, 1993). With that change in perspective comes the commitment to accept the risks and take the time. However, commitment alone is insufficient. Advanced planning is necessary to anticipate pitfalls encountered by blind enthusiasm (McKeachie, 1986; White, 1996a).

Getting Started Ahead of Time

Mentoring

Getting started begins well before the semester begins. Sometimes the idea of transforming a course to one with a PBL format incubates for several years. The change in perspective requires getting used to. Finding others who have experience helps this transition, because few instructors have themselves been taught in a PBL classroom, and it is sometimes difficult to envision how a PBL class operates or to anticipate all the situations one might encounter. Instructors who use PBL have traveled the same path and appreciate the problem. In most cases, they welcome visitors to their classes. Those getting started should take advantage of such opportunities and find a mentor. An occasional coffee break or lunch with others using PBL can help deal with new situations. Most concerns relate to process; thus, colleagues from diverse disciplines can contribute constructively to each other's

Reprinted from *The Power of Problem-Based Learning,* edited by B.J. Duch and S.E. Groh (2001), Stylus Publishing.

effective teaching. The University of Delaware PBL website (see electronic resources for PBL at the end of the list of references for this chapter), and related PBL listserver also provide information and a forum for discussion.

Decisions

While circumstances may limit choices, some ways of getting started are easier than others. Occasionally, one might start by creating an entirely new course with a PBL format, but more often, instructors will transform one of their existing lecture-based courses into one that uses PBL. Because existing courses are already built into the curriculum, they have an established content and clientele, and they constitute part of the regular workload. These factors legitimatize the effort. Most faculty choose to make the transition gradually by introducing a problem-based exercise every week or two at first. They also tend to start with smaller classes and courses within a major. Once comfortable with PBL, instructors often transform other courses they teach.

Course Goals and Learning Objectives

Once the decision to transform a course has been made, formulating a list of instructional goals focused on student learning helps subsequent decisions. Examples of such goals can be found elsewhere in this volume. Because PBL addresses behavioral issues in addition to content issues, the course goals probably will change the way a course is structured and conducted. For example, oral and written communication skills or the ability to find and use new resources often become explicit goals that may have been subordinated to content goals without a PBL format. The new priorities lead to new assignments and restructured schedules.

Finding Problems

With the exception of a few disciplines, notably medicine and business, good PBL problems usually do not appear in textbooks. As a consequence, an instructor needs to find problems, modify textbook problems, or write new problems that address the course content goals and learning objectives. The "learning issue matrix" (White, 1996b; White, Chapter 12 of this book) provides a strategy for selecting a set of problems that covers the course content. While having to write problems may be necessary and seem to be a significant barrier, most instructors find writing problems an enjoyable scholarly activity (White, 1995; Duch, Chapter 5 of this book). Furthermore, because of the need, there are outlets for publishing good problems. The *PBL Clearinghouse* and *Case Studies in Science* are two web-based opportunities, while educational journals, such as *Biochemistry and Molecular Biology Education* (see electronic resources for PBL at the end of the list of references for the URLs to these three sites) or the *Journal of College Science Teaching* will accept manuscripts describing PBL problems.

Using the Syllabus to Get Started

Because the syllabus defines a course, it needs to be completed before the first class and should distinguish the new PBL format from the format of previous offerings of the course. Its contents provide a framework for discussing the issues in introducing PBL, while the course goals, noted previously, provide the basis for making decisions relating to these issues. Altman and Cashin (1992) identify the following seven major topics that should be in a syllabus: course information; instructor information; text, readings, and materials; course description and objectives; course calendar and schedule; course policies; and available support services. These will be discussed in turn with respect to decisions associated with getting started with PBL.

Course Information

This includes basic syllabus material, such as course title, course number, prerequisites, credit hours, meeting time, and meeting place. Some of these items will be influenced by a change to a PBL format. For instance, when and where will the class meet? To provide longer time for discussion, it may be useful to have two 75-minute classes per week rather than three 50-minute classes. It may be worth considering nonstandard meeting times, such as 75 minutes on Monday and Friday to distribute time for out-of-class research if this is possible at your institution. The classroom itself is quite important. A room with tables where students can work comfortably in groups is preferable to a room with fixed seating in a tiered auditorium. A room with lots of blackboard space provides opportunities for effective communications within groups.

Instructor Information

As for every course, the syllabus should contain information about who the instructor is and where, how, and when he or she may be contacted. Not only is student communication with the instructor important in a PBL course, but other lines of communication are important and can be established ahead of time. E-mail newsgroups, chat rooms, and electronic class-mailing lists can be used to facilitate student-student and intergroup communication, which can be more important than in a typical class and may need to be structured ahead of time.

Instructor information in a syllabus might include a statement of teaching philosophy that relates to PBL. That information might also accompany a friendly e-mail message to the class during the week before the semester starts. Such a gesture can set a positive tone for the course and let the students know something about the course as well. If the syllabus is on a course website, the message can provide its URL. This also is a good time to get feedback from students that might be helpful in assigning them to groups. If the course involves teaching assistants or tutor-facilitators (Allen & White, 2000, and Chapter 8 of this book), that information can be included with information about the instructor.

Text, Readings, and Materials

Frequently, a PBL format changes the way instructors and students see and use textbooks. A decision that an instructor needs to make is whether to have a text, and if so, does a different text fit the PBL format better than texts used previously. For an advanced course built around problems in which students need to access multiple primary resources, a text may be unnecessary. For a course that uses a PBL format only part of the time to emphasize certain concepts during class time, a textbook is an important reference and may be selected for its encyclopedic character rather than its readability in independent study. Decisions on a textbook may be driven on whether the significant learning issues are (or are not) covered and whether this fits with the course goals.

Depending on the course goals, an instructor may provide supplementary readings in the library or eliminate them in courses where students need to find resources for themselves. With increased use of the Internet and the enormous variability in the quality of websites, some instructors choose to provide a list of Internet sites that provide reliable information. In another approach, instructors direct students to websites that provide guidance in evaluating other websites because students frequently equate an attractive layout with "good" informational quality. If one plans to make greater use of library and Internet resources, the availability to students also must be considered. Not all students have computers, and commuting students can be put at a disadvantage.

Course Description and Objectives

What is the purpose of the course? Where does it fit into the curriculum? How will students change as a result of taking the course? While many of the decisions identified so far appear in a syllabus as statements with little elaboration, the course description is the meat of a syllabus and requires a narrative, particularly if one plans to use PBL. For example, the course goals and learning objectives belong here. Students need to know what they are expected to do and why groups are important. Most certainly, a PBL format will lead to unfamiliar types of assignments, such as generating a concept map as a group. These may be introduced in a syllabus.

If the students entering the course have little or no experience with PBL, the syllabus is the place for the instructor to explain what PBL is. It also is a good place to explain why PBL fits in with the instructor's teaching philosophy and why it is important for student learning. Much of the resistance to PBL by students, particularly in the early weeks of a course, comes from the surprise of doing something unfamiliar and not knowing why the instructor is "doing this to them." As noted earlier, PBL relies on good communication, and it is the instructor's responsibility to discuss teaching philosophy in the syllabus and at the beginning and throughout a course.

Course Calendar and Schedule

The use of a PBL format implies that the instructor values group process and problem-solving abilities. Typical course examinations given during class time often do not incorporate such values. Consequently, a significant decision is whether or not to schedule out-of-class examinations with relaxed time constraints and incorporate group elements. For example, a three-hour evening examination permits successive individual and group parts (White, 1997). Such an arrangement extracts a cost because in most courses there will be a few students who have conflicting schedules. Furthermore, a room, perhaps the normal classroom, needs to be available and reserved. Many schools require that the dates and times of out-of-class examinations be printed in the registration booklet so that students can arrange their schedules accordingly when they register. This means that the decision for an out-of-class examination needs to be made and approved quite early.

One must decide how often to use a PBL format and incorporate that into the course schedule. Good PBL problems are open-ended and may take more time than anticipated. Students need sufficient time to research, discuss, and come to closure on a problem. Consequently, the schedule and instructor need to be flexible. One way to allow for changes during the semester is to title the schedule as "tentative."

Course Policies

PBL affects many course policies and thus requires decisions. Group progress and group dynamics depend strongly on full participation. Thus, absences and tardiness disrupt a PBL class in ways that would be unimportant in a lecture class. An instructor should have a firm attendance policy, which also is affirmed by group guidelines. In a lecture class, individual students can do quite well and not have to say one word in class during an entire semester. Such silence would undermine the PBL process. There are ways for introverted students to contribute significantly to group process. Ideally, the instructor's policies should be discussed and agreed to by all groups and appropriate consequences specified for noncompliance, for example, some groups may agree to exclude repeat offenders from group portions of examinations.

PBL also affects grading policies. What is the proper balance between individual and group work? How much will peer evaluation contribute to individual grades? How much are process skills valued, and how is that factored into a grade? What constitute criteria that distinguish one level of achievement from another?

Academic honesty creates a dilemma for some students in PBL classes. Throughout their academic career, teachers have discouraged collaboration with other students. Now the rules seem reversed. What constitutes academic dishonesty? What can be shared for credit? These issues need to be discussed and clearly defined in the course policies. Students need to know that they learn on their own and that there is individual accountability. Working in groups facilitates learning, but it is not a license to use the work of others as one's own.

Available Support Services

Students have access to a wide variety of academic support services. Some of these resources are especially useful for courses using a PBL format, and instructors may decide to set aside time to ensure that their students know about them and can use them. For example, a PBL course often requires students to identify and locate resources that they need. However, many students have only rudimentary skills in exploiting library resources and may need guidance. While they may be familiar with surfing the Internet, they may have little ability to distinguish authoritative information from the biased information available on a myriad of advocacy sites. In most disciplines, there are particular search strategies that are preferred to others. These may be laid out in a syllabus or on a course website. Given these needs, an instructor may arrange for a library tour or a presentation on web resources.

Getting Students Started with PBL

The First Week of Class

Despite all of the advanced preparation, a certain amount of apprehension and self-doubt accompanies the beginning of a first-time PBL class. What if something goes wrong? What if the students don't like it? Imagine a classroom full of students who have spent their entire education in lectures and are seated nicely in rows facing the front of the room. This course will be unfamiliar to them or, if not unfamiliar, something they may have found unpleasant. Will they buy into PBL?

There are many approaches and, as noted earlier, sending an e-mail message to the whole class a week before the semester starts can ease both student and instructor apprehensions about PBL. It is important, however, not to call PBL an *"experiment."* The students need to know what will be different and why, but they do not wish to be guinea pigs. The introduction could take the form of a lecture—but that may send the wrong message in a PBL course. A successful approach is to initiate group discussions that evolve into a whole-class discussion about the students' prior experiences with groups and why they liked or disliked those experiences. This demonstrates that discussion is expected and that student concerns are heard. In addition, an "ice breaker" exercise often shows in an experiential way what a lecture or discussion cannot. I have developed the following activity, *Stand and Deliver,* that provides a visceral appreciation of the importance of teacher-to-student, student-to-teacher, and student-to-student communication in learning.

Stand and Deliver

Much of what we do when we lecture is to describe things and create mental images with words. These words have discipline-specific meaning that students sometimes misinterpret or don't understand. The following group activity deals with verbal communication of images. The rules of this "game" are simple.

1. Teacher Selection. Within each group of four or five students, determine who has the birth date closest to today. That person will be the *teacher* for this activity.
2. Lesson Plan. Assemble all of the teachers in the hall outside the classroom and show them a simple geometric figure that they will have to describe orally to their group of "students." The figure should have about three simple components; for example, a square, a triangle, and a circle and of different sizes, in different positions, and overlapping in different ways so that the sizes, relationships, and orientations become important details to communicate.
3. The Lecture. The teachers return to their groups for two minutes while they describe, as accurately as they can, what they saw. The teachers *cannot use hand gestures,* and the students *cannot ask questions* of the teacher or talk among themselves during the "lecture." The students may take notes, but cannot draw pictures yet.
4. Teacher Conference. After the lecture, the teachers leave the room and can discuss the experience among themselves until step 7.

5. Individual Work. Without talking to each other, each student must draw, as closely as he or she can, a copy of the figure described by the teacher. The objective is to be as close to a carbon copy of the original drawing as possible. They have two minutes to do this.
6. Group Work. The members within each group compare their drawings and discuss the differences in an attempt to come to consensus. In five minutes, each group should have a revised consensus drawing to show to their teacher.
7. Teacher Assessment. The teachers return and see what their students have drawn. Groups then can discuss the exercise. At this time, each group receives a photocopy of the original drawing to compare with their drawing.
8. Reflection. Among the questions groups might consider in discussing the implications are: Did everyone in your group draw the same picture? Did subsequent discussion improve the representation? Was the teacher happy with the results? What were your frustrations, if any? Can you make any conclusions?

This activity generates a lot of discussion and raises important questions about how we communicate and the importance of feedback. It also addresses what it means to teach and to learn. Given additional time, groups can discuss how such an assignment might be graded. Clearly, there will be many things going on during the first week of classes, and this is just one idea for getting started.

Keeping Going with PBL

For anyone getting started with PBL, the learning curve is steep. It may seem a bit overwhelming to have to deal with issues of group dynamics, educational psychology, and student learning skills in addition to the subject matter. However, practitioners need not be experts and one need not implement everything at once. The change in perspective that accompanies the adoption of a few PBL exercises in one course usually leads to more and to the transformation of other courses. It also leads to a revitalized interest in education. Once started, it is easy to keep going.

Author Biography

Harold B. White, III is Professor of Biochemistry in the Department of Chemistry and Biochemistry and Director of the Howard Hughes Medical Institute's Undergraduate Biological Sciences Education Program at the University of Delaware.

References

Allen, D. E., & White, H. B., III. (2000). Peer facilitators of in-class groups: Adapting problem-based learning to the undergraduate setting. In J. E. Miller, J. E. Groccia, & M. S. Miller (Eds.), *Student-assisted teaching: A guide to faculty-student teamwork.* Bolton, MA: Anker Publications.

Altman, H. B., & Cashin, W. E. (1992). *Writing a syllabus.* Idea Paper No. 27, Lawrence, KS: Kansas State University, Center for Faculty Evaluation and Development.

King, A. (1993). From sage on the stage to guide on the side. *College Teaching, 4* (1), 30–35.

McKeachie, W. J. (1986). *Teaching tips—A guidebook for the beginning college teacher.* Lexington, MA: D. C. Heath and Company.

White, H. B., III. (1995). Creating problems for PBL. *About Teaching 47.* (Distributed by the University of Delaware Center for Teaching Effectiveness, Newark, DE. Also posted at http://www.udel.edu/pbl/cte/jan95-chem.html)

White, H. B., III. (1996a). Dan tries problem-based learning: A case study. *To Improve the Academy, 15,* 75–91. (also posted at http://www.udel.edu/pbl/dancase3.html)

White, H. B., III. (1996b), Addressing content in problem-based courses: The learning issue matrix. *Biochemical Education, 24* (1): 41–45.

White, H. B., III. (1997). Untimed individual/group exams, problem-based learning. In S. Tobias and J. Raphael (Eds). *The hidden curriculum: Faculty-made tests in science. Part 2. Upper-division courses,* pp. 102–103. New York: Plenum Press.

Electronic Resources for Problem-based Learning

Biochemistry and Molecular Biology Education.
http://www.elsevier.nl/inca/publications/store/6/2/1/2/4/5/

Cases Studies in Science. http://ublib.buffalo.edu/libraries/projects/cases/new.htm
PBL Clearinghouse. https://www.mis3.udel.edu/Pbl
UD PBL: Problem-Based Learning. http://www.udel.edu/pbl/

CHAPTER 14

INTEGRATIVE LEARNING

Integrative Learning: Mapping the Terrain

Mary Taylor Huber and Pat Hutchings

A background paper for Integrative Learning: Opportunities to Connect, An Initiative of The Carnegie Foundation for the Advancement of Teaching and Association of American Colleges and Universities (AAC&U)

One of the great challenges in higher education is to foster students' abilities to integrate their learning over time. Learning that helps develop integrative capacities is important because it develops habits of mind that prepare students to make informed judgments in the conduct of personal, professional, and civic life. On the other hand, even when higher education has identified such learning as a goal, it has been difficult to incorporate into the undergraduate experience because the normal structures of academic life encourage students to see their courses simply as isolated requirements to complete. How can campuses help students pursue their learning in more intentionally connected ways?

As documented in AAC&U's report, *Greater Expectations: A New Vision for Learning as a Nation Goes to College* (2002), many colleges and universities are creating opportunities for more integrative, connected learning through practices like first-year seminars, learning communities, interdisciplinary studies, capstone experiences, portfolios, and student self-assessment. Often, however, such innovative educational programs involve small numbers of students or exist in isolation, disconnected from other parts of the curriculum and from other reform efforts. What would it look like to design or link such programs so that all students have multiple and varied opportunities to develop and display the capacity for integrative learning throughout their college experience?

As The Carnegie Foundation for the Advancement of Teaching and AAC&U embark upon a new initiative with campus partners to explore these questions, we offer the following thoughts to help locate integrative learning in the larger territory of liberal education today.

Learning that Is Greater than the Sum of its Parts

At the heart of liberal education lies the idea that learning should be greater than the sum of its parts. Resonant with the classical tradition of educating the "whole" person, liberal education has historically encouraged "breadth of outlook, a capacity to see connections and hence an ability to make fundamental decisions and judgements" (Rothblatt 1993:28). Historically, this work of integration has been credited with countering the forces that narrow perspective, liberating students from the darker sides of human nature and social constraint, and preparing them for responsible participation in civic life. The promise that "integrative learning" leads to personal liberation and social empowerment inspires and challenges higher education to this day (See AAC&U 1998).

Integrative learning inspires in part because of its intellectual appeal. The capacity to connect is central to scholarship broadly conceived—whether focused on discovery and creativity, integrating

Presented as paper at *Making Connections: A CUNY General Education Conference on Integrative Learning at LaGuardia Community College on May 6, 2005* (2004).

and interpreting knowledge from different disciplines, applying knowledge through real-world engagements, or teaching students and communicating with the public (Boyer 1990). Done well, these activities all require taking account of different dimensions of a problem, seeing it from different perspectives, and making conceptual links among those dimensions and perspectives (Suedfeld et al. 1992: 393). Integrative learning also has emotional appeal. Indeed, emotion can be a catalyst for integrative learning. When students become passionate about their learning, when a topic ignites their enthusiasm, integration is more likely to happen. As E.M. Forster famously said in his novel, *Howard's End*, "Only connect the prose and the passion, and both will be exalted. . . ."

Educators have long endorsed the value of integrative learning. Today, however, there is new appreciation of its importance to contemporary thought and life. For one thing, disciplines are now less bounded, with new areas of scientific knowledge emerging on the borders of old ones, and the humanities and social sciences engaged in lively trade of concepts, methods, and even subject matter (Geertz 1983; Bender and Schorske 1997; Gallison 1997). Technology and globalization are transforming knowledge practices in all the disciplines, professions, and arts (Gibbons et al. 1994). Indeed, we are awash in information in all areas of life, challenging the integrative abilities of experts and students alike.

The workplace, too, has been transformed. The "knowledge society" places a premium on higher education, making college a virtual necessity for American students aspiring to a middle-class style of life. With flexibility and mobility the keywords of the new economy, people can no longer count on a career with the same employer or even in the same line of work. Students are now advised that the knowledge they gain in their majors will not be useful for long unless coupled with skills and dispositions that enhance their ability to find and take advantage of new opportunities when the need arises. To be sure, many educators remain wary about linking liberal education to vocational ends, but others are more sympathetic to the concerns of students and their families about preparation for work, and see in students' search for vocation a humane activity that liberal education should inform. As Ellen Lagemann argues: "One might even venture that vocation, broadly defined. . . . tends usually to be the theme that links the different experiences that define an individual's education" (2003: 8; see also Shulman 1997).

If students today would benefit from taking a more intentional, deliberative, and reflexive stance towards vocation, which requires integrative learning during and beyond their college years, the same is true for other parts of life. Scientific and technological development and globalization have made everything more complex, bringing many advantages to the fortunate, but also exacerbating inequalities and elevating risk for all (Beck 1992). We no longer live in a world where it is easy to feel in control or empowered to affect what is happening in our neighborhoods, much less in the nation or the world, but by the same token our own actions—even the food, clothing, and cars we buy—have immediate consequences for those far away (Giddens 1994). These conditions make high demands on our capacities for moral judgment and practical reason (Sullivan 2002). To participate responsibly as citizens, students must be able to synthesize learning from a wide array of sources, learn from experience, and make productive connections between theory and practice.

Our colleges and universities can play an important role in helping students develop this integrative cast of mind, and many campuses espouse such a goal. College catalogs make powerful promises about students' personal and intellectual development as thinkers and citizens—and certainly there are inspiring models and "existence proofs" to show what may be possible (Colby et al. 2003). To meet these commitments to integrative learning more fully, and to meet them for *all* students, is the difficult challenge ahead.

Against the Grain: Challenges to Achieving Integrative Learning

Integrative learning does not just happen—though it may come easier for some of us than for others. Whether one is talking about making connections within a major, between fields, between curriculum and co-curriculum, or between academic knowledge and practice, integrative learning requires work. Of course students must play a role in making this happen (a theme we will return to shortly), but it is unlikely to occur without commitment and creativity from our educational institutions.

Today, many colleges and universities are developing new kinds of institutional "scaffolding" to support integrative learning—courses that invite students to take different perspectives on an issue, capstone projects that ask students to draw on learning from earlier courses to explore a new topic or solve a problem, experiences that combine academic and community-based work, or systems of journaling and reflection like those known as "learning portfolios."

Such developments meet obstacles at every turn. As Carol Schneider and Robert Schoenberg (1999) suggest, organizing for integrative learning goes against the grain of many structural features of campus life. They cite academic departments and schools which often see their responsibility as socializing students into a particular discipline or profession; the split between general education and the major which exacerbates the problem; the bachelor's degree that is defined more in terms of courses and credits than by a vision of what the degree should mean; systems of faculty roles and rewards that have been slow to recognize interdisciplinary and applied scholarship, not to mention the extra efforts entailed in designing, teaching, and assessing courses aimed at integrative learning (See Huber 2001). Other familiar disconnects include the gaps between programs in the professions and the liberal arts and sciences, the curriculum and the co-curriculum, and campus and community life.

Among the many organizational structures cited by Schneider and Shoenberg that create barriers to integrative learning, one of the more difficult to address is the course and credit system (1999:32–33; also see Wellman and Ehrlich 2003). Since the replacement of the required curriculum with "free electives" in the late 19th and early 20th century, the provision of content through courses counted in standard credit units has long encouraged faculty and students alike to think of learning in course-like modules or chunks. Recalling his doctoral studies in English Literature in the early 1960s, Gerald Graff writes:

> I experienced graduate school not as an intellectual community that sharpened my thinking about important issues, but as a set of disconnected courses and mixed messages. I coped by giving each professor what he or she seemed to want, even when it contradicted what the professor the previous hour had wanted. . . . In the end I internalized the compartmentalizations of the curriculum rather than wrestled with its conflicts, either resolving the conflicts too easily on one side . . . or ignoring them (2003:2–3).

Graff has made "teaching the conflicts" (and along with them, something about the nature of academic knowledge) a keystone in his ideas for pedagogical reform. Indeed, his work underlines the value of pedagogy as a key to integrative learning, even in contexts where curriculum and other structures work against it. Whatever the mechanism, helping *undergraduates* develop strategies for going beyond the tacit message of curricular fragmentation in order to connect their learning is becoming a priority at many colleges and universities today.

The need to find ways to help students connect their learning is underlined by the fact that a growing proportion are now taking advantage of the portability provided by the course-credit accounting system to attend more than one institution over their college career. The exact numbers of students who do so nationwide is not known, but one study indicates that fully half of the bachelor's degree recipients in 1992–93 took courses at more than one college or university (sometimes concurrently), including a fifth who attended at least three (McCormick 2003:17). Some are students who transfer from two- to four-year institutions; others experiment with their first college to see if they like it and then transfer to another; some accelerate their programs by taking one or two terms elsewhere; others just take a supplementary course or two. Some educators see this trend as a reflection of more consumerist attitudes on the part of today's students (Levine and Cureton 1998; Fallon 2002). Certainly, these "swirling" patterns of enrollment make integrative learning across courses and contexts harder to achieve. They suggest, too, that curriculum cannot be the only solution. What's needed are approaches that develop students' capacity to make connections for *themselves* (See AAC&U 2002; Schneider and Shoenberg 1999:33).

Intentional Learning

The idea that integrative learning depends on *students* to make connections is hardly a new one. Indeed, the burden of integration has traditionally fallen primarily on the learner, with campuses assuming that bright students would have the wit and grit to pull the pieces together as they moved through their studies. What's new, perhaps, is a conviction that "intentional learning," as it is called in *Greater Expectations,* is a capacity that we can and should help all students develop as a key to integrative learning.

Several core insights lie at the heart of this idea. Intentional learners have a sense of purpose that serves as a kind of "through line" (as the playwrights call it), connecting the sometimes far-flung and fragmentary learning experiences they encounter. They approach learning with high levels of self-awareness, understanding their own processes and goals as learners, and making choices that promote connections and depth of understanding. They know how to regulate and focus their efforts as learners—how to make the most of their study time, to practice new skills, to ask probing questions. They are, if you will, on the road to life-long learning. In a nutshell, intentional learning entails "cognitive processes that have learning as a goal rather than an incidental outcome" (Bereiter and Scardamalia 1989: 363).

The good news for educators committed to integrative learning is that the concept of intentional learning—though the phrase may be new for many—offers a powerful set of ideas and tools. Several established lines of work offer lessons for students and teachers seeking to connect learning in meaningful ways.

One relevant line of research and practice can be traced to adult learning and professional education, for instance in medicine and social work, where we find several decades of attention to "self-directed learning," a fairly scripted process in which the student reflects on and formulates her own learning goals (Brookfield 1986; Sabral 1997; Taylor and Burgess 1995). Advocates of this approach point to the power of explicit goals in which students are personally invested to propel meaningful learning.

A related line of work goes by the label of "learning how to learn." A recent volume on new classroom approaches describes three abilities associated with this term: how to be a better student, how to conduct inquiry and construct knowledge in certain disciplines or fields, and how to be a self-directing learner (Fink 2003). Or, consider Claire Ellen Weinstein's framework of the "strategic learner," characterized by student knowledge in five broad categories: 1) knowledge about themselves as learners, 2) knowledge about different types of academic tasks, 3) knowledge about strategies and methods for acquiring, integrating, thinking about, and using new knowledge, 4) knowledge about how prior content knowledge can be applied, and 5) knowledge of present and future contexts in which new information could be useful (1996: 49–50).

Work from cognitive science, which is increasingly invoked in discussions of teaching and learning (Bransford, Brown, and Cocking 1999; Halpern and Hakel 2003) also reinforces emergent notions of intentional learning. Most notable perhaps is the emphasis on "metacognition," a term that speaks to a very robust area of research—and to common sense about how learning happens. As summarized by Glaser, for instance, metacognition entails knowing what one knows and does not know, predicting outcomes, planning ahead, efficiently apportioning time and cognitive resources, and monitoring one's efforts to solve a problem or learn (1984).

Finally, intentional learning can be viewed through the lens of extensive work on reflection. Echoing Dewey in many ways, Donald Schon's work on reflective practice highlights the connection between thought and action as a key foundation of learning in which "doing and thinking are complementary" (1983: 280). Through reflection, Schon argues, we "surface and criticize the tacit understandings that have grown up around the repetitive experiences of a specialized practice, and can make new sense of . . . situations of uncertainty or uniqueness . . ." (1983: 61). Schon's work focuses primarily on professional education and practice but the role of reflection in undergraduate education has also garnered attention. For instance, a current project of the Carnegie Foundation has identified "structured reflection" as one of six pedagogies in preparing students for political engagement. In composition studies, reflection is seen as a key component in the writing process and a necessary ingredient, therefore, in the teaching of writing, one in which "we call upon the cognitive, the affective, the intuitive, putting these into play with each other," says Kathleen Yancey (1998: 6).

Indeed, in her recent volume on the role of reflection in the teaching and learning of writing, Yancey's description of the process pulls together elegantly many of the themes of intentional learning:

> In method, reflection is dialectical, putting multiple perspectives into play with each other in order to produce insight. Procedurally, reflection entails a looking forward to goals we might attain, as well as a casting backward to see where we have been. When we reflect, we thus project and review, often putting the projections and the reviews in dialogue with each other, working dialectically as we seek to discover what we know, what we have learned, and what we might understand (1998: 6).

Reflection. Metacognition. Learning how to learn. Whatever the language or lineage, the idea of making students more intentional, self-aware, and purposeful about their studies is a powerful one. What's also clear is that assisting students to develop such capacities poses important challenges for campus reforms around teaching and learning.

Intentional Teaching

Efforts to promote intentional, integrative learning are clearly on the rise. General education curricular reform around explicit cross-cutting outcomes such as critical thinking or problem solving offers opportunities for students to see connections as well as differences among disciplines. Learning communities, which link courses with each other in various configurations, often around interdisciplinary themes, are opportunities to help (and indeed require) students to connect concepts from one course with those of another. When experiences like these occur in the first year, students may begin to develop habits of connection-making that can be cultivated and refined in subsequent years.

At the other end of the trajectory, some campuses are now creating or recreating capstone courses and experiences. Typically the capstone course has been situated in the major, and often it has been framed as a transition or rite of passage for students going on to graduate school. But capstones *can* serve more broadly integrative purposes. Several faculty working with the Carnegie Academy for the Scholarship of Teaching and Learning are focusing their efforts on culminating experiences, with a goal, as one of them says, of creating "a set of experiences that captivate, encapsulate, synthesize, and demonstrate learning" (Hamilton, 2002).

Whether as part of a culminating experience or earlier in the curriculum, experiences that connect course content with more applied contexts also represent steps toward intentional, integrative learning. The service-learning movement, for instance, requires students to test out and refine academic concepts in community-based settings. While such experiences are typically elective, some campuses—including several featured in Carnegie's recent volume, *Educating Citizens*—require all students to engage in some form of community-based learning, and to do so at several points in the curriculum.

Intentional learning may also require scaffolding that extends beyond individual courses. In this spirit, we find a growing use of portfolios as vehicles for students to document, connect, and reflect upon their learning *across* courses. More explicit rubrics for self-assessment, sometimes connected with portfolio development, may also serve powerful integrative purposes by making students more self-aware, self-directed learners (Loacker 2002). Strategies such as these are particularly relevant to the challenge of shifting enrollment patterns since (in theory at least) they can be carried with the student as she moves from setting to setting.

Behind these developments is a move toward asking students to "go meta" with their learning, in order to identify, assess and strategize about next directions. But many educators would argue that students are unlikely to develop such habits of reflection and intentionality if *faculty* do not do the same. In part, this involves designing better opportunities for students to connect their learning within and between courses and contexts. It means getting smarter about the look and feel of integrative learning so that students' efforts can be recognized and fostered. And it also means faculty modeling, through their teaching, the thoughtful approach to learning that they want their students to develop.

In fact, teaching and learning are *both* complex processes—situations of "uncertainty and uniqueness" (to use Schon's phrase), in which particular circumstances trump general rules and theories. What is needed in teaching for integration, then, is similar to what is needed in learning—an intentional approach. For faculty, this means systematic reflection and inquiry into the specific challenges and dilemmas faculty face in the classroom—bringing the habits, skills and values of scholarship to their work as teachers. "Intentional teaching" thus entails what many today are calling "the scholarship of teaching and learning."

> A scholarship of teaching . . . requires a kind of "going meta," in which faculty frame and systematically investigate questions related to student learning—the conditions under which it occurs, what it looks like, how to deepen it, and so forth—and do so with an eye not only to improving their own classroom but to advancing practice beyond it" (Hutchings and Shulman 1999:13).

Here, too, there is great progress to report. Over the past decade, the scholarship of teaching and learning has come to represent a set of practices and commitments around which new communities of faculty are forming, both within disciplines and across them. Understood broadly, such work draws on a variety of approaches from a range of disciplines that support a more scholarly, intentional approach to the work of the classroom (See Hutchings 2000; Huber and Morreale 2002; Huber, Hutchings, and Shulman n.d; McKinney n.d.) Faculty working with the Carnegie Academy for the Scholarship of Teaching and Learning, for example, have used focus groups, design experiments, close readings of student work, and course portfolios to explore questions about their students' learning (see www.carnegiefoundation.org), including, in many cases, questions about whether and how their students are able to integrate learning across various settings and contexts. Indeed, evidence about learning, and thus assessment, is an essential ingredient in the kind of intentional teaching and learning that is needed for the work of integration.

Integrative Assessment

Like learning and teaching, assessment is a complex process, and its challenges are magnified when complex forms of learning are its focus. Indeed, assessment that captures significant forms of integration is the exception rather than the rule. Whether at the institutional, program, or classroom level, it is far easier to document simpler forms of learning.

What then would be entailed in focusing assessment more sharply on integrative outcomes? For one thing, integrative assessment would seem to imply more collaboration among faculty to identify key points and elements of integration. That is, to develop assessment instruments and approaches one would need to know not simply that connections are a goal but to specify what *kinds* of connections (between theory and practice? across disciplines?), in what contexts (a service learning requirement? a capstone experience?) and in what ways they would be demonstrated. Assessment aimed at such learning needs to go beyond the individual classroom but may also stop short of the full program, focusing instead on clusters of related courses and experiences. This "middle ground" has thus far been fairly underdeveloped assessment territory.

Integrative assessment may also raise conceptual questions about how, exactly, students develop such abilities. Surely we would expect graduating students to engage in different kinds and levels of connection-making than we would expect of first-year students. How does integration correlate with, say, the developmental stages mapped out in the work of William Perry (1970)? How can assessment tap into the kinds of integration that adult learners with extensive life experience bring to their academic work? Progress with integrative assessment will require that we think through questions like these.

Integrative assessment almost certainly implies more focus on student self-assessment, as well—an approach that carries intentional learning to its logical conclusion. As suggested by work at Alverno College, a pioneer in this regard, self-assessment, taken seriously, implies not just a general injunction for students to reflect on their work but more structured frameworks for that reflection (Loacker 2002). Such frameworks have yet to be developed on most campuses.

Again, however, there are signs of progress. Student portfolios, mentioned earlier as a vehicle for fostering integrative abilities, can also be a vehicle for assessment. A typical focus of portfolio assessment is writing ability (highly relevant to integrative learning) but some campuses are employing the approach around a broader set of outcomes, as well (Cambridge 2001). Capstone experiences, similarly, can serve both a learning and an assessment function.

More indirect measures may also be an important part of the mix. The National Survey of Student Engagement, used by 437 four-year colleges and universities in spring 2003, provides evidence of experiences that might contribute to integration—for instance, participation in community-based learning, writing across the curriculum, and opportunities to test out academic learning in co-curricular settings. (There is also a newer community college version.) Although it is too early to tell if data from these instruments get "down" to a level that faculty can use to improve their courses and advising, early findings are already suggesting to administrators and policymakers that colleges and universities can do better at providing opportunities to develop their students' capacities to connect.

Still, the challenges of assessing integrative learning run deep and will not be easily met. They are both technical and political, both theoretical and practical. They underline how important it is for educators to work together to build knowledge about the varieties of integrative learning, how they are best fostered, and how they can be most helpfully assessed.

Building Knowledge about Integrative Learning

For many college-educated adults of a certain age—the parents and grandparents of today's college students—the image of undergraduate education set forth here is unfamiliar in a number of ways. To be sure, most undergraduate programs are still comprised of general education requirements, a major concentration, and free electives, as they have been for much of the last century. Periodic reforms have brought renewed attention to general education (that part of the program that is more or less shared by all students), and to the major, in the attempt to keep the curriculum coherent and in tune with educational goals of the time (see Boyer and Levine 1981; AAC&U 1991). More recently, as we discuss in this paper, educators have begun to focus on creating opportunities for students to develop capacities for integrative learning that will prepare them for living productively, responsibly, and meaningfully amidst the uncertainties of the world today.

To this end, the Carnegie Foundation and AAC&U are seeking eight to ten campuses to participate in a joint project, *Integrative Learning: Opportunities to Connect.* Selected both on the basis of work already accomplished and on a desire to extend that work, participants will develop new models to provide students with more purposeful, progressively challenging, integrative educational experiences. Campuses could choose, for example, to scale up student participation, expand the number of opportunities, better link opportunities to explicit learning goals and to other parts of the curriculum, and assess students' ability to integrate knowledge across fields and experiences. Campuses could also propose to implement new practices to complement and supplement existing programs.

Whatever the specific student experience or curricular structure selected as the focus of work, we are seeking institutions that will be deliberate about promoting integrative learning throughout a student's undergraduate career, serious about assessment, and committed to knowledge-building.

Indeed, we believe that efforts to strengthen programs that foster integration cannot be effectively pursued alone. Too often good work in teaching and learning remains with its creators, unavailable for others to consult, review, and build on. Campuses need to work together to share what they are finding out about integrative learning, to develop new ideas about assessment, and to learn from each other's designs. Local efforts can be reinvigorated by participation in a community of educators working towards similar goals, and that community in turn can contribute to building knowledge that can inform efforts to foster integrative learning at colleges and universities around the country and around the world.

References

AAC&U (Association of American Colleges and Universities). 1991. *The Challenge of Connecting Learning*

AAC&U (Association of American Colleges and Universities). 1998. Statement on Liberal Learning. http://www.aacu.org/about/liberal_learning.cfm

AAC&U. (Association of American Colleges and Universities). 2002. *Greater Expectations: A New Vision for Learning as a Nation Goes to College.* http://www.greaterexpectations.org/

Beck, Ulrich. 1992. *Risk Society: Towards a New Modernity.* London: Sage.

Bender, Thomas, and Carl E. Schorske, eds. 1997. *American Academic Culture in Transformation: Fifty Years, Four Disciplines.* Princeton: American Academy of Arts and Sciences.

Bereiter, C. and M. Scardamalia. 1989. Intentional Learning as a Goal of Instruction. In L. Resnick (ed), *Knowing, Learning and Instruction: Essays in Honor of Robert Glaser.* Hillsdale, NJ: Lawrence Erlbaum, 361–392.

Boyer, Ernest L. 1990. *Scholarship Reconsidered: Priorities of the Professoriate.* San Francisco: Jossey-Bass.

Boyer, Ernest L. and Arthur Levine. 1981. *A Quest for Common Learning: The Aims of General Education.* Princeton, NJ: The Carnegie Foundation for the Advancement of Teaching.

Bransford, John D., Anne L. Brown, and Rodney R. Cocking, eds. 1999. *How People Learn: Brain, Mind, Experience, and School.* Committee on Developments in the Science of Learning, Commission on Behavioral and Social Sciences, and Education, National Research Council. Washington, DC: National Academy Press.

Brookfield, Stephen. 1986. *Understanding and Facilitating Adult Learning.* Milton Keynes: Open University Press.

Cambridge, Barbara, ed. 2001. Electronic Portfolios: emerging Practices in Student, Faculty and Institutional Learning. Washington, DC: American Association for Higher Education.

Colby, Anne, Thomas Ehrlich, Elizabeth Beaumont, and Jason Stephens. 2003. *Educating Citizens: Preparing America's Undergraduates for Lives of Moral and Civic Responsibility.* San Francisco: Jossey-Bass.

Fallon, Daniel. 2002. On the Past, Present, and Future of the Liberal Arts. Paper presented at the Cornell Conference on The Idea of a University. Ithaca, NY, October 18, 2002.

Fink, L. Dee. 2003. *Creating Significant Learning Experiences: an Integrated Approach to Designing College Courses.* San Francisco: Jossey-Bass.

Forster, E. M. [1910] 1985. *Howard's End.* New York: Bantam Books.

Gallison, Peter. 1997. *Image and Logic: A Material Culture of Microphysics.* Chicago: University of Chicago Press.

Geertz, Clifford. 1983. *Local Knowledge: Further Essays in Interpretive Anthropology.* New York: Basic Books.

Gibbons, Michael, Camille Limoges, Helga Nowotny, Simon Schartzman, Peter Scott, Martin Trow. 1994. *The New Production of Knowledge: The Dynamics of Science and Research in Contemporary Societies.* London: Sage Publications.

Giddens, Anthony. 1994. Living in a Post-Traditional Society. In *Reflexive Modernization: Politics, Tradition and Aesthetics in the Modern Social Order,* by Ulrich Beck, Anthony Giddens, and Scott Lash, pp. 56–109. Stanford, CA: Stanford University Press.

Glaser, Robert. 1984. Education and Thinking: The Role of Knowledge. *American Psychologist* 39: 93–104.

Graff, Gerald. 2003. The PhD in English: Towards a New Consensus. Menlo Park, CA: Carnegie Essays on the Doctorate.

Hamilton, Sharon. 2002. Campus Action Plan for Indiana University – Pursue University Indianapolis, unpublished document developed at the 2002 AAC&U Institute for Sustaining Innovation.

Halpern, Diane F and Milton K. Hakel. 2003. Applying the Science of the Learning to the University and Beyond: Teaching for Long-Term Retention and Transfer. *Change* 35 (4): 36–41.

Huber, Mary Taylor. 2001. Balancing Acts: Designing Careers Around the Scholarship of Teaching. *Change* 33 (4): 21–29.

Huber, Mary Taylor, and Sherwyn P. Morreale, eds. 2002. *Disciplinary Styles in the Scholarship of Teaching and Learning: Exploring Common Ground.* Washington, DC: The American Association for Higher Education and The Carnegie Foundation for the Advancement of Teaching.

Huber, Mary Taylor, Pat Hutchings, and Lee S. Shulman. n.d. The Scholarship of Teaching and Learning Today. In *Encouraging Multiple Forms of Scholarship: Voices from the Field,* ed. Kerry Ann O'Meara and R. Eugene Rice. Washington, DC: American Association for Higher Education. In press.

Hutchings, Pat. ed. 2000. *Opening Lines: Approaches to the Scholarship of Teaching and Learning.* Menlo Park, CA: The Carnegie Foundation for the Advancement of Teaching.

Hutchings, Pat, and Lee S. Shulman. 1999. The Scholarship of Teaching: New Elaborations, New Developments. *Change* 31 (5):10–15.

Lagemann, Ellen Condliffe. 2003. The Challenge of Liberal Education. *Liberal Education* 89 (2): 6–13.

Levine, Arthur and Jeanette S. Cureton. 1998. College Life: An Obituary. *Change* 30 (3): 12–17.

Loacker, Georgine, ed. 2002. Self Assessment at Alverno College. Milwaukee, WI: Alverno College Press.

McCormick, Alexander C. 2003. Swirling and Double-Dipping: New Patterns of Student Attendance and Their Implications for Higher Education. *New Directions for Higher Education* 121: 13–24.

McKinney, Kathleen. n.d. The Scholarship of Teaching and Learning: Past Lessons, Current Challenges, and Future Visions. *To Improve the Academy,* 22. In press.

National Survey of Student Engagement. 2003. NSSE 2004 Registration Begins. http://www.indiana.edu/~nsse/

Perry, William G, Jr. 1970. *Forms of Intellectual Development in the College Years.* New York: Henry Holt.

Rothblatt, Sheldon. 1993. The Limbs of Osiris: Liberal Education in the English-Speaking World. In *The European and American University Since 1800: Historical and Sociological Essays,* ed. Sheldon Rothblatt and Bjorn Wittrock, pp. 19–73. Cambridge: Cambridge University Press.

Sabral, Dejano T. 1997. Improving Learning Skills: A Self-Help Group Approach. *Higher Education* 33 (1): 39–50.

Schneider, Carol Geary, and Robert Shoenberg. 1999. Habits Hard to Break: How Persistent Features of Campus Life Frustrate Curricular Reform. *Change* 31 (2): 30–35.

Schon, Donald A. 1983. *The Reflective Practitioner: How Professionals Think in Action.* New York: Basic Books.

Shulman, Lee S. 1997. Professing the Liberal Arts. In *Education and Democracy: Re-imagining Liberal Learning in America,* ed. Robert Orrill, pp. 151–173.

Suedfeld, Peter, Philip E. Tetlock, and Siegried Streufert. 1992. Conceptual/Integrative Complexity. In *Motivation and Personality: Handbook of Thematic Content Analysis,* ed. Charles P. Smith, pp. 393–400. Cambridge: Cambridge University Press.

Sullivan, William M. 2002. A Life of the Mind for Practice: Professional Education and the Liberal Arts. Manuscript. Menlo Park: The Carnegie Foundation for the Advancement of Teaching.

Taylor, Imogen and Hilary Burgess. 1995. Orientation to Self-Directed Learning: Paradox nor Paradigm. *Studies in Higher Education* 20 (1) 87–99.

Weinstein, Claire Ellen. 1996. Learning How to Learn: An Essential Skill for the 21st Century. *Educational Record* 77 (4): 48–52.

Wellman, Jane and Thomas Ehrlich, ed. 2003. *How the Student Credit Hour Shapes Higher Education: The Tie That Binds.* Jossey-Bass, 2003.

Yancey, Kathleen Blake. 1998. *Reflection in the Writing Classroom.* Logan, Utah: Utah State University Press.

CHAPTER 15

TEAM-BASED/COOPERATIVE/ COLLABORATIVE LEARNING

Designing Effective Group Activities: Lessons for Classroom Teaching and Faculty Development

Larry K. Michaelsen
L. Dee Fink
Arletta Knight
The University of Oklahoma

Abstract The primary objective of this article is to provide readers with guidance for designing effective group assignments and activities for classes and workshops. In doing so, we examine the forces that foster social loafing (uneven participation) in learning groups and identify four key variables that must be managed in order to create a group environment that is conducive for broad-based member participation and learning. We then discuss the impact of various types of activities and assignments on learning and group cohesiveness. Finally, we present a checklist that has been designed to evaluate the effectiveness of group assignments in a wide variety of instructional settings and subject areas.

Over the last few years group activities have become increasingly popular. However, instructors and workshop leaders frequently report three common problems that greatly reduce the effectiveness of small-group based learning activities. Two of the three problems typically occur while students or workshop participants are actually engaged in the group work. Probably the most common problem is that one or two vocal individuals often dominate the discussions to the point that quieter members' ideas are either unexpressed or largely ignored. Alternatively, groups frequently have difficulty staying focused on the assigned task because they get side-tracked on inconsequential or irrelevant details. The third problem occurs when groups are reporting the results of their work to the total class. Even when there has been a high level of engagement in the small groups subsequent whole-class discussions sometimes "fall flat."

Based on our experience, these "problems" are actually symptoms that are almost always the result of poorly conceived group tasks. Further, we believe that all three of these problems can be avoided if classroom teachers and faculty developers use activities that are designed to take into account: 1) the developmental level of the groups in which they will be used and, 2) the impact of the activity on the cohesiveness of the groups.

With this in mind, our primary objective in writing this article is to provide a set of conceptual tools to provide guidance for designing effective group assignments and activities for classes and workshops. Overall, the most important idea in the paper is that the most reliable way to gauge the learning value of group assignments is to examine their impact on group cohesiveness.

Reprinted from *To Improve the Academy: Resources for Faculty, Instructional and Organizational Development*, edited by D. DeZure (1997), by permission of John Wiley & Sons, Inc.

Accordingly, a second objective in writing the article is to help readers understand how different types of learning tasks contribute to or detract from group cohesion.

In the pages that follow, we:

1. discuss the psychological processes that result in uneven participation by group members;
2. identify four key variables that must be managed in order to create a group environment that is conducive for broad-based member participation and learning;
3. describe the cognitive processes through which learning occurs and discuss the implications for designing effective learning activities;
4. outline the impact of assignment wording on learning and group development;
5. present a checklist for evaluating and/or designing effective group activities in a variety of subject areas and educational settings;
6. Use a "before-after" example of a group assignment from one of our colleague's classes to illustrate why the effectiveness of group activities is so closely tied to their impact on group cohesiveness.

The Nature of Group Interaction

Under certain conditions, a high percentage of group members would prefer to sit back and let "someone else" work on their behalf. This phenomenon, which has come to be known as "social loafing" (Latane, Williams & Harkins, 1979) can be a serious problem in classrooms and workshops because it heavily constrains the interaction necessary for a productive learning environment. Further, if left unchecked, the conditions that produce social loafing can prevent the development of the social fabric that is necessary for effectively functioning learning groups. More assertive members will inevitably "take charge" and, by doing so, will both reduce the need for additional input and create a sort of a "caste" system in which quieter members often feel that their ideas might not be welcomed.

We have identified six forces which, unless recognized and dealt with by the instructor or workshop leader, will produce a level of social loafing that will be a serious problem in most learning groups. Three of these have to do with the characteristics of group members. First, some people are naturally resistant to participation (e.g., shy). Second, others prefer to dominate a discussion. Third, members who feel they lack content knowledge of the task at hand are usually reluctant to speak because they are concerned about being seen as incompetent. Two others are especially problematic in newly formed and/or temporary groups. These are that members of new and/or temporary groups are typically more concerned about their own personal image than that of the group and also see themselves as having little to lose if the group fails to perform effectively. Finally, the group task promotes social loafing when it can be completed by one member working alone and/or doesn't require members to reach an agreement (see Figure 15.1).

The forces that promote social loafing in learning groups, however, can largely be offset by assignments and practices that foster the development of cohesive learning groups. There are two reasons for this. First, as groups become more cohesive, trust and understanding typically build to the point that even naturally quiet members are willing and able to engage in intense give-and-take interactions without having to worry about being offensive or misunderstood (Michaelsen, Watson & Black, 1989; Watson, Michaelsen & Sharp, 1991; Watson, Kumar & Michaelsen, 1993; Michaelsen, Black & Fink, 1996). Second, a primary characteristic of cohesive groups is that members see their own well-being as being integrally tied to the success of their group. As a result, members of cohesive groups are often highly motivated to invest personal energy doing group work (Shaw, 1981; Michaelsen, Jones & Watson, 1993).

Figure 15.1
Forces that Promote Social Loafing

Forces that Promote Social Loafing
(Uneven Contributions in Group Discussions)

- Some individuals naturally resist participation (shyness).
- Some individuals prefer to dominate discussions.
- Members may believe they lack the content knowledge required for making a meaningful contribution.
- Members may be concerned about appearing to be disagreeable or overly aggressive.*
- Members may not be committed to the success of the group.*
- The task may be inappropriate for groups because it:
  - can be completed by one or two members working alone.
  - does not require members to reach an agreement.

**These are especially important problems with new groups.*

Characteristics of Learning Tasks that Promote Group Cohesiveness

The single most effective strategy for eliminating social loafing is to ensure that four key dimensions of the learning tasks cause members to interact in ways that promote the development of cohesive groups. Specifically, the tasks should be explicitly designed to: 1) require a high level of individual accountability for group members and/or workshop participants, 2) motivate a great deal of discussion among group members, 3) ensure that members receive immediate, clear and meaningful feedback (preferably involving direct comparisons with the performance outputs from other groups), and 4) provide explicit rewards for high levels of group performance (see Figure 15.2).

Figure 15.2
Impact of Task Characteristics on Team Development and Social Loafing

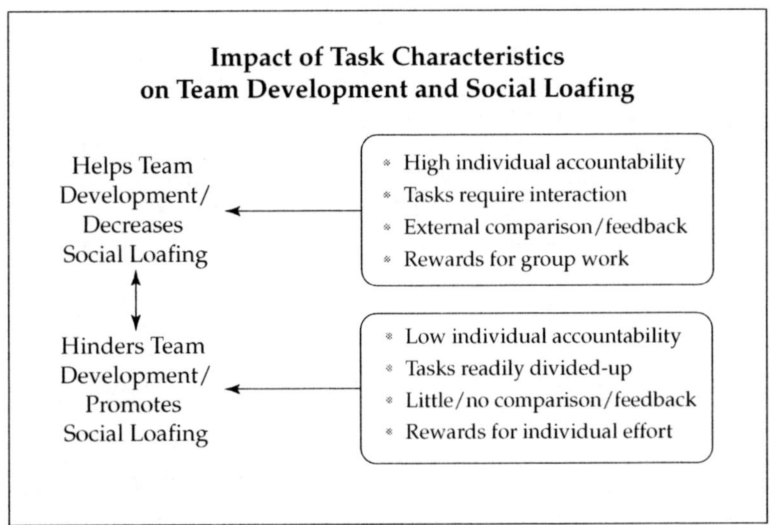

Ensuring individual accountability

Instructors or workshop leaders often inadvertently foster social loafing by failing to ensure that their group assignments (especially the first one) require input from every group member. The initial assignment is key for two reasons. First, the innate forces against broad-based participation in new groups (see Figure 15.1) are so powerful that they must be offset early on. Second, if the group is even modestly successful with input from only one or two members, then it is highly likely that the group will develop a norm supporting at least partial *non*-participation of members (Feldman, 1984).

On the other hand, if the task explicitly requires input from group members, then the question of whether their input is needed becomes a moot point. As a result, at least two of the negatives are turned into positives. One is that members are faced with the possibility of being seen in a negative light if they *don't* contribute. The other is that, because of the additional input, the groups are both more likely to succeed, which reinforces a norm that everyone is expected to provide input to the group (Feldman, 1984). These dynamics are two of the main reasons that giving an individual test followed immediately by a group test is such a powerful learning and group-building tool (Michaelsen & Black, 1994; Michaelsen, Black & Fink, 1996). Another way to ensure broad-based input in small group discussions is to hand out an individual worksheet and ask participants to take a few minutes to think through the issues and write down their ideas prior to the start of the group discussions (see the discussion of "Think, Pair Share" in Cottell, Millis & Engrave, 1996).

Motivating intensive group interaction

The most common cause of social loafing is the use of assignments that can be completed by independent individual work. When the rational way to complete a task is to "delegate" the work to individual members, that is exactly what will happen. Delegating commonly occurs in two situations. One situation is when the assignments are too easy (i.e., group interaction isn't needed). In this case, one member will simply act on behalf of the group. The other situation occurs when the task requires a great deal of writing. Since writing is *inherently* an individual activity, the only real group activity will be deciding how to divide up the work. When group members work independently, cohesiveness is reduced for at least two reasons. The first reason is that some members always feel like they are having to do more than their fair share (and in most cases, they probably are correct). The other reason is that, depending on the group's performance, the top students are likely to resent having to choose between carrying their less able or less motivated peers or risk getting a low grade.

Although a number of different types of tasks will reliably produce high levels of group interaction, a highly reliable "rule-of-thumb" is that assignments increase group cohesiveness (and, over time, eliminate social loafing) when they require members to make a concrete decision based on the analysis of a complex issue. In other words, when we ask students or workshop participants to apply a rule or solve a problem. This type of task typically requires students to use a broad range of intellectual skills including: recognizing and defining concepts, making discriminations, and applying principles or procedural rules (Gagne, 1970). Further, everyone typically has both opportunities and incentives to participate actively in completing the task because of the genuine need for broad-based member input. The net result is that problem-based tasks almost universally immerse students and/or workshop participants in a information-rich, give-and-take discussions through which their content learning increases. Further, if the assignment is thoughtfully crafted, they are also likely to learn two important lessons about their group. They are: 1) other members' input is a valuable resource, and 2) *we* can accomplish something by working together that none of us could have accomplished on our own.

Facilitating external [meaningful] performance feedback

The single most powerful force for the development of group cohesiveness is the presence of an outside influence that is perceived to be threatening to member goals and/or the well-being of the group (Shaw, 1981). Differences among members become less important as they pull together to protect themselves and/or their public image. As a result, providing performance data that allow comparisons with other groups is a very powerful tool for increasing group cohesiveness.

Some assignments are clearly better than others at providing such comparisons. In general, the more assignments provide unambiguous performance feedback (especially if it is in a form that enables direct comparisons with similar groups) the better they are at promoting team development. Further, the more immediate the feedback, the greater its value to both learning and group cohesiveness. By contrast, assignments are likely to limit the development of group cohesiveness (and encourage social loafing) if they force groups to do the majority of their work in the absence of feedback. When groups have no way of knowing how they are doing (e.g. when groups are asked to produce some sort of a complex "product" such as a group paper), members are likely to experience a great deal of stress in working with each other. For example, differences in members' work styles often produce a great deal of tension in the group. Members who have a strong preference for a systematic and orderly approach and have time to work on the project often become so anxious that they alienate their peers who either have different time pressures or who feel they do better work when they are faced with a performance deadline.

Rewarding group success

Although it would be wonderful if students or workshop participants would complete group assignments because of a love of learning, if we fail to create a situation in which doing good work as a group "pays off" in some meaningful way, we are, in effect, asking them to behave irrationally. One obvious way to use group rewards as a means of building group cohesiveness is to include group performance in our grading system. Failing to do so will greatly increase the probability that group cohesiveness will be blocked by the fact that students will correctly see themselves competing with other members of their own group.

Including group performance in the grading system is not, however, the most effective way to use rewards for building groups (and minimize social loafing) for three reasons. First, unless the grading system also promotes individual accountability (e.g., grading individual work that prepares students for group work, using a peer evaluation system, etc.), social loafing can still become a serious problem. Second, groups often contain members with very different needs—what may be an acceptable grade for one student might be a disaster for another. Third, giving grades isn't even a possibility in workshops and many other educational settings in which we should use group work.

In our judgment, the reward that offers the greatest potential for both classrooms and workshops is the basic human need for social validation. *Everyone* wants to feel they can offer something of value to others. Thus, by creating a situation where the output from group work will be scrutinized and challenged by peers from other groups, we are creating an environment that promotes both group cohesiveness and learning.

The best and the worst

Based on our experience, the best activity available for building group cohesiveness and minimizing social loafing is the Readiness Assurance Process which constitutes the first four steps in the learning activity sequence in team-based learning (Michaelsen, Watson & Schraeder, 1985; Michaelsen, 1992; Michaelsen & Black, 1994) and the worst activity is group term papers. The Readiness Assurance Process is used at the very beginning of each major instructional unit (i.e., prior to any lectures) to ensure that students master basic course content. It involves four steps: 1) individual students complete a test over a set of pre-assigned readings and turn in their answers, 2) groups then re-take the same test and turn in their consensus answers for immediate scoring (group scores are posted on the board to provide immediate cross-group comparisons), 3) groups are given time re-study their assigned readings to prepare written appeals for any questions they have missed, and 4) the instructor provides input that is specifically focused on correcting student misunderstandings that have come to light in the previous three steps of the process. The power of the Readiness Assurance Process comes from the fact that its activities, in combination, clearly meet all four of the criteria for building groups (see Figure 15.2 and Figure 15.3).

Figure 15.3
Impact of the Readiness Assurance Process

Impact of the Readiness Assurance Process:

Individual Accountability from:

* Completing individual exam over assigned readings prior to group exam (*counts toward the course grade*).
* Revealing/defending individual answers during the group exam.
* Preparing written appeals to justify their point of view on questions on which they influenced the group to select an incorrect answer.

Intense Give-and-take Group Discussion from:

* Having to agree on a group answer on each test question.
* Agreeing on a rationale for written appeals justifying their point of view on questions incorrectly answered during the group test.

External (Meaningful) Performance Feedback from:

* Immediate scoring of individual and group exams.
* Posting group test scores to provide external comparisons.
* Feedback and corrective input from instructor.

Rewards for Group Success from:

* Group exam scores count toward course grade.
* Public awareness of group exam scores.

By contrast, group term papers seldom provide any support for building group cohesiveness and almost universally result in at least the perception of social loafing. Because writing is inherently an individual activity, the rational way to accomplish the overall task is to divide up the work so that each member independently completes part of the assignment (usually the part that he or she already knows the most about). As a result, there is seldom any significant discussion after the initial division of labor, and feedback is generally unavailable until it is too late to create either individual accountability or meaningful comparisons with other groups. Further, under these conditions, having part of the grade based on group performance is as much of a negative as a positive. Members are well aware that the failure of any member of the group could force the rest to accept a low grade or engage in a last-minute attempt to salvage a disaster. In fact, high-achieving students often express the feeling that getting an acceptable grade on a group term paper feels like having crossed a freeway during rush hour without being run over.

Differences in group process that result from the specific requirements of learning tasks not only affect group cohesiveness; they also have a profound impact on learning. Before we try to link group processes and learning, however, we will briefly set the stage by reviewing some of what is known about the way we learn, i.e., process information. As a result, the following paragraphs focus on cognitive processes that occur as we take-in, store, and use ideas and information.

Learning Processes: Implications for Assignment Design

On the surface, what we know would seem to be the sum total of the information to which we have been exposed. Taking in information is, however, only part of the learning process (Bruning, Schraw & Ronning, 1994). Information that is taken in and stored in short-term memory decays very rapidly. Thus, from a practical standpoint, what we "know" is more a function of our ability to retrieve and use the information than the sum total of the information that we have taken in.

Impact of what we know

Our ability to learn is profoundly affected by both information to which we have previously been exposed and the way this information is stored in our long-term memory. Most importantly, our capability to learn depends on the extent to which the related components of our memory are clustered into well organized structures (i.e., sometimes referred to as schemata—see Anderson, 1993; Mandler, 1984; Bruning et al., 1994). These information structures are important because they provide "hooks" that help establish links between new information that is related to what we already "know" and between the individual components of our existing structures. In addition, the structures provide a backdrop that helps us to recognize what we don't know (i.e., information that doesn't "fit").

Information structures and learning

What we "know," then, is largely a function of the number, complexity and inter-connectedness of the information structures in our long-term memory and, for practical purposes, consists of the information that we are able to retrieve and use. Significant learning takes place when our set of useful information increases. This usually occurs when new information motivates us to: 1) add to existing structures, 2) establish new structures, or 3) establish new links within or between existing structures.

Elaborative Rehearsal

If a learning activity exposes us to new information that neatly connects to a "hook" in one of our information structures, then it is simply "attached" to the appropriate link. If new information appears to conflict with existing grouping, the learning process takes a very different, but even more beneficial, course. Initially, we will "search through" our long-term memory to review the linkages upon which the apparent conflict is based. If this review confirms the existence of a conflict, we will be in a state of discomfort until we find a harmonious accommodation. If none is found and the information's credibility is sustained, we are motivated to eliminate the conflict by modifying and/or adding to existing information grouping. This memory retrieval and examination process, called *elaborative rehearsal* (Craik & Lockhart, 1986), facilitates learning because each stage has a positive impact on our long-term memory. As a result, the greater the extent to which an assignment exposes students or workshop participants to credible information that conflicts with their existing information structures, the greater its impact on their long-term memory.

Promoting the development of higher-level cognitive skills

The importance of providing opportunities for elaborative rehearsal is dramatically illustrated by a series of studies involving learning groups that are summarized in Slavin (1995). In all of the studies, students were divided into four member "Jigsaw" groups. Each member was assigned to become a subject-matter expert with respect to one of four areas and then given the opportunity to teach the material to the other members of his or her Jigsaw team. In most instances, students in Jigsaw groups scored higher on an overall summative test than students from a control group who had been taught with a more traditional method. The positive benefits of the Jigsaw activity, however, were primarily due to students' mastery of the material that they had "taught" to their peers. Hearing someone else explain a set of concepts (i.e., listening to a lecture) had a minimal positive effect as compared to the impact of having to synthesize the information, organize a presentation and present the information to a group of peers.

In two other studies, Lazarowitz (1991) and Lazarowitz and Karsenty (1990) added an additional learning task for the Jigsaw groups. After the Jigsaw peer instruction, each of the groups was given a discovery-oriented problem to solve that required actively using information presented by each of the four subject-matter experts. The most significant finding from these studies was that requiring students to engage in a higher level thinking (Gagne, 1970) increased students' ability to recall and use the information that was originally presented by the other subject-matter experts.

Based on the overall results of the Jigsaw studies, it appears that listening to another peer in a learning group, even when combined with the opportunity to ask clarifying questions, produces only modest gains in long-term memory. On the other hand, learning activities that require higher-level thinking skills (Gagne, 1970) such as acting in a teaching role (see also Bargh & Schul, 1980) or using concepts to solve a discovery-oriented problem, produce substantially greater long-term gains in students' ability to recall and use course concepts. Other types of learning activities that focus on using higher level thinking skills have also been shown to produce similar gains compared to simple cognitive tasks such as listening to lectures or going over one's notes. These include taking tests (see Nungester & Duchastel, 1982), writing "minute papers" (Wilson, 1986), and being exposed to opposing views on a subject then having to resolve the conflicts in the process of making a decision (Smith, Johnson & Johnson, 1981). In combination, these findings convincingly argue that the long-term impact of group work will be much greater if group assignments go beyond simply exposing learners to new information by requiring them to actively engage in the use of higher-level cognitive skills.

Phrasing Assignments to Promote the Use of Higher-level Cognitive Skills

The degree to which assignments stimulate higher-level cognitive skills (i.e., elaborative rehearsal) is largely a function of what we ask students to "produce." For example, suppose an English composition instructor wanted to ensure that his or her students were able to recognize the effective use of active vs. passive voice in written communication. Three alternative versions of the assignment are shown in Figure 15.4 (see also Michaelsen, Black & Fink, 1996).

In the examples shown in Figure 15.4, the order of the tasks reflects the degree to which they would require the use of higher-level cognitive skills. It is unlikely that alternative #1 would stimulate higher-level thinking because students could "make-a-list" by simply extracting items from one or more reference sources and recording them in another location. Assignment #2 is considerably better. Having to "make-a-choice" would require students to examine critically the sentences in the sample passage and use the criteria that define active vs. passive voice to identify examples of active and passive voice. Alternative #3 would provide the most practice using higher-level cognitive skills for two reasons. First, students could not complete task #3 unless they could also complete tasks #1 and #2. Second, as is typical of "make-a-specific-choice" assignments, picking a single best example of correct use of passive voice would require students to use/develop a number of higher-level cognitive skills. At a minimum, these would include making multiple comparisons and discriminations, analysis of content information and, verification of rule application (see Gagne, 1970).

Figure 15.4
Wording Assignments to PromoteHigher-level Cognitive Skills

Wording Assignments to Promote Higher-level Cognitive Skills

"Make-a-list"

1. "List the 'mistakes' that writers frequently make that detract from their efforts to write in active 'voice.'"

"Make-a-choice"

2. "Read the following passage and identify a sentence that is a clear example of: a) active, and b) passive 'voice.'"

"Make-a-specific-choice"

3. "Read the following passage and identify the sentence in which passive 'voice' is used most appropriately."

Implications for Effective Group Assignments

Although "make-a-specific-choice" assignments (e.g. Figure 15.4) are beneficial for individual students working alone, they produce the greatest gains in conjunction with learning groups. In part, this occurs because students/workshop participants have an additional source of motivation to take the assignment seriously. In addition, group interaction provides two additional opportunities to stimulate active learning. One is during discussions within the groups. The other occurs during subsequent class discussions (i.e., between groups). Further, when used in a group context, "Make-a-specific-choice" assignments increase learning in each step of the process and set the stage for greater learning in the next (see Figure 15.5).

Individual preparation for group work

As long as group members are given the assignment as preparation for group work (e.g. in the example from Figure 15.4, having everyone read the same passage and select the sentence in which passive voice is used most appropriately), having students make a specific choice ensures that members will be individually far more accountable (see above) for having engaged in higher-level thinking than is the case with "make-a-list" assignments for three reasons. First, learners have to use higher-level thinking skills in order to make choices (e.g. see Gagne, 1970). Second, members expect to be asked to share their choice with their group. Third, they are also aware that, unless the group is in complete agreement, the differences will be so evident that proponents of each of the alternatives will almost certainly be asked to explain the reasons behind their choices. As a result, "make-a-specific-choice" assignments motivate most students/workshop participants to enter the group discussion with a clearly defined position and the ability to defend it (see Figure 15.5).

Figure 15.5
Impact of Assignment Phrasing

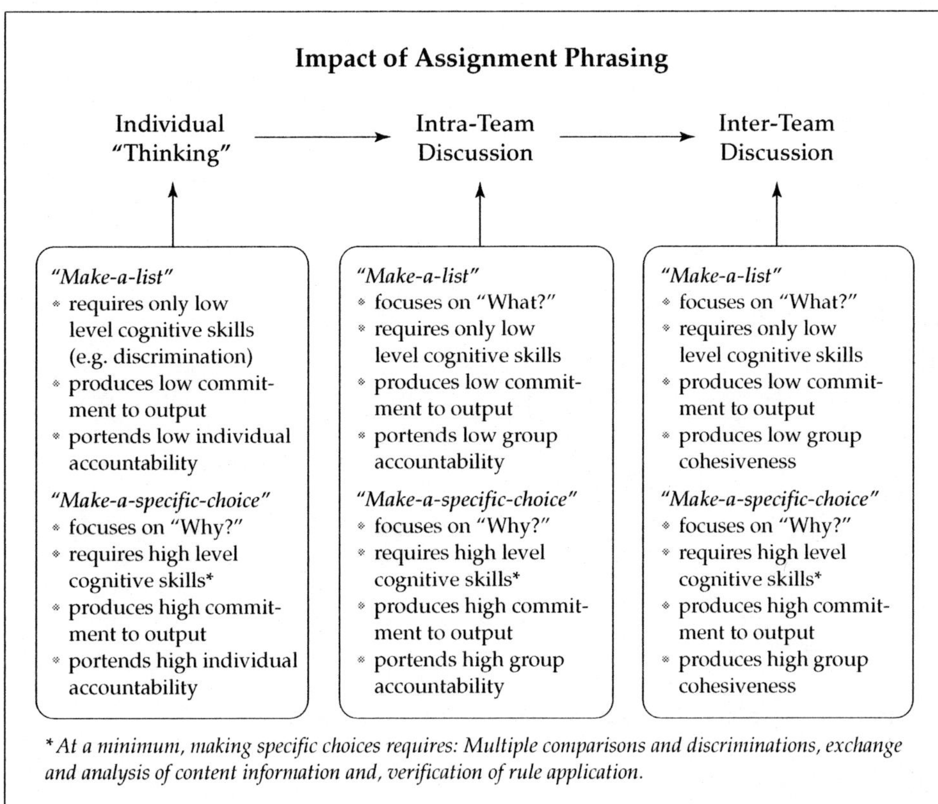

Discussions within groups

The difference between "make-a-list" and "make-a-specific-choice" assignments is even more evident in intra-team discussion. Listing possibilities tends to be a low energy team task for several reasons. One is that a search for what should be on a list focuses on quantity rather than quality. Another is that once several items go on the list, it is easy for quieter and/or less self-assured participants to get "off the hook" by saying that their ideas are already listed. Finally, making a list seldom leads to a feeling of pride in the group output because the majority of the items are likely to be in common with other groups.

By contrast, when groups are asked to select a single best choice based on specific criteria and know that other groups have been given the same assignment, members are likely to engage in an intense give-and-take discussion of why any given choice is better than another. No one wants to be the only group to have made a particular choice (e.g. which sentence is the best example of the correct use of passive voice—see Figure 15.4) and not be able to present a clear and cogent rationale for their position. As a result, most groups will engage in "make-a-specific-choice" tasks with a great deal of energy and are also likely to be willing and able to defend their choices.

Discussions between groups

Group assignments phrased in "make-a-specific-choice" terms produce their greatest gains in subsequent class discussions (i.e., between-groups). Two of the benefits come from the simplicity of the output. One is that they invariably promote *group* accountability because any differences between groups are absolutely clear. For example, an assignment that asked groups to select the single best example of an appropriate use of passive voice (see Figure 15.4) would produce a much more productive class discussion than an assignment that asked groups to identify examples of appropriate use of active and passive voice (see Figure 15.4). Comparing "best examples" is likely to produce a more intense and informative discussion than either listing examples or the choice of a clear example. When comparing "best examples," groups have a vested interest in defending their position and the discussion will focus on the reasons that one choice is better than another.

By contrast, group assignments that result in either lists or non-specific choices often result in low-energy class discussion and allow relatively poor group analyses to go unchallenged. The lack of energy results from the fact that groups tend to be far more interested in their own work than that of other groups. Poor analysis often goes unchallenged because: 1) having students/workshop participants either make a list or a non-specific choice is likely to produce so much data that the task of finding something to challenge can be quite difficult and, 2) the absence of clear comparisons allows groups to overlook inconsistencies in both their own and other groups' analyses.

Group cohesiveness

Another important benefit of properly designed "make-a-specific-choice" group assignments is their positive impact on cohesiveness. Because reaching consensus on a difficult choice requires a great deal of thought and effort, students/workshop participants intuitively realize that differences between teams represent an important source of feedback. Thus, because differences between team choices are so clear, they represent a significant external threat. By contrast, "make-a-list" assignments seldom promote group cohesiveness because the output is poorly suited for inter-group comparisons. This becomes most apparent when groups share the results of their discussions. Even though groups generally do a pretty good job of making lists, there is almost always a "nose-dive" in the energy level when the groups "report" to the class. In fact, simply getting students/workshop participants to pay attention to each other as representatives go over each item in their list can be a serious problem. Differences that groups might otherwise take pride in and be motivated to defend, are both obscured and diminished in significance by the sheer volume of data.

Assignments that Facilitate Inter-group Comparisons

There are two keys to ensuring that "make-a-specific-choice" assignments facilitate intergroup comparisons. One is keeping the "output" as simple as possible. The other is organizing the inter-group sharing process to minimize the amount of time used in a lecture-like mode (i.e., a series of representatives giving a report of what happened in their group).

For example, suppose a marketing instructor wanted to create a "make-a-specific-choice" assignment that would ensure him or her that students understood the key variables that should be considered in selecting a site upon which to locate a new business. One way to word the assignment would be, "Select what you think would be the ideal site to locate a new dry cleaning establishment in _______ (i.e., filling in the name of a specific city about which students could gain access to relevant data), identify, and be prepared to explain the rationale for the single most important site selection factor that led to your decision (Michaelsen, Black & Fink, 1996)."

Although the assignment involves making a specific choice, the degree to which it would support inter-group comparisons depends on both the specific "product" that was used to represent their choice and the nature of the group reporting process. One common approach would be to assign each of four groups to make a 10-minute presentation revealing their chosen location and the rationale for selecting it followed by a few minutes for questions and class discussion.

Alternatively, the instructor could require students to come to class having made their choice and, instead of using class time for presentations, he or she could:

1) Give each group a post-it-note with their group number on it, a felt-tipped marker and a legal-sized sheet of paper.
2) Allow 5-minutes to decide on and record their single most important reason for their decision.
3) Require groups (after 5 minutes), to place their post-it on their selected location on a city map attached to the classroom wall.
4) Allow groups 10 minutes to formulate questions they would like to ask the other groups.
5) Use the remainder of the class for questions and discussion.

In this example, the "post-it-note" version of the assignment would provide far more explicit inter-group comparisons. With presentations, the differences are obscured by three factors. First, the sheer volume of data in three other 10-minute presentations makes it difficult for students to keep track. Second, the relevant facts are presented over a 40-minute span. As a result, the key points will be temporally separated by far less significant information. Third, since the groups are likely to use a variety of presentation modes, establishing links between key ideas is likely to seem like comparing apples and oranges. By contrast, using the "post-it-note" approach ensures that, instead of being overwhelmed with data, students are exposed to a simultaneous, common, permanent, and highly visual representation of only the essential data: 1) the proposed locations and 2) the foundation of each group's rationale for their choice. Further, they have a designated time to carefully process and digest the information in an integrated way.

A Checklist for Effective Group Activities

Probably the most important key in designing effective group assignments is viewing the entire context within which they will be used. This includes taking into account the developmental level of the groups, individual preparation for group work, discussions within groups, post-group class discussions, and the extent to which the group will work together again. The following checklist (see Figure 15.6) provides prompts for taking these factors into account as you evaluate and or design group assignments.

Figure 15.6
Criteria for Effective Group Assignments

Criteria for Effective Group Assignments

Prior to Group Discussions:

* Are group members required to use newly acquired concepts to make a specific choice, individually and in writing? (*Note: This individual accountability is especially important in newly formed groups.*)

During Discussions within Groups:

* Are groups required to share members' individual choices and agree (i.e., reach a group consensus) on a specific choice?
* Will the discussion focus on "Why?" (and/or "How?")
* Will the groups' choice(s) be represented in a form that enables immediate and direct comparisons with other groups*?

During Discussions between Groups:

* Are group decisions reported simultaneously*?
* Do group "reports" focus attention on the absolutely key issues*?
* Are groups given the opportunity to digest and reflect on the entire set of "reports*" before total class discussion begins?
* Will the discussion focus on "Why?" (and/or "How?")

The more "Yes" answers, the better. If the answer to all eight questions is "Yes", the assignment will effectively promote both learning and group development.

**The form in which individual and group choices are represented largely determines the dynamics of the discussions that follow. Both individual reports to groups and group reports to the class should be as absolutely succinct as possible. One-word reports are the very best (e.g. yes/no, best/worst, up/down/no change, etc.) because they invariably stimulate a discussion of why one choice is better than another.*

Making Good Group Assignments into Great Ones

Regardless of its primary intent, every learning activity affects learning in two very different ways. First, the specific characteristics of the activity determine how much active learning can be achieved by its use. Second, each activity inherently fosters (or inhibits) the peer interactions that have a major impact on team development. Further, modifying an activity in an attempt to change the impact on either dimension is likely to affect the other.

For example, we have an agronomist colleague who wants his students to develop the ability to recognize the weeds that commonly infest turf grass lawns in our region. Initially, he used an assignment that required groups to "identify and appropriately tag an example of each weed variety growing in plot #1 [which he had laid out] on the lawn on the east side of this building." The assignment worked quite well but, he decided to modify the group portion of the activity in an attempt to increase its value for building cohesiveness. The revised assignment uses 5 plots (one for each group in the class) and requires an additional 20 minutes to complete. During the first 10 minutes the group members, working individually within their team's plot, find and temporarily tag an example of each weed variety. During the next 20 minutes, the groups: agree on (and permanently tag) a sample of each weed variety in their plot (and receive 10 points for each correctly tagged weed variety) and, 2) prepare for a "weed finders challenge" (WFC). During the WFC, groups have 5 minutes to examine each others' plots and "challenge" incorrectly tagged weeds. If their challenge is valid, they receive 10 bonus points but, if the challenge is bogus, they lose 10 points to the group who elicited the challenge.

Although the changes were modest in nature, they produced positive changes in all four of the factors that affect group cohesiveness (see Figure 15.2). The assignment now provides rewards for group work (the opportunity to earn points for correctly tagging weeds and extra points by successfully challenging other groups). The assignment provides external comparison/feedback (by giving other groups the opportunity to challenge each other). The assignment produces high levels of group interaction (reaching consensus on your own samples and preparing members to scout other plots). Finally, the assignment promotes individual accountability on both ends (individual tagging prior to group work and individuals serving as scouts during the WFC). As a result, the assignment is much more effective in building group cohesiveness. Groups typically use the first half of their time to make sure they have a correctly tagged sample of each weed variety. Then they turn their attention to preparing for the WFC by: 1) preparing members to scout for a potential challenge because they don't have time to go to each of the other plots as a group and 2) shifting their tags to atypical examples of the weed varieties in an attempt to "set-up" other groups for a bogus challenge.

Even though the impact on cohesiveness has been highly positive, the impact on learning has been even greater. The knowledge that they will have to work on their own causes group members to be more serious about advance preparation. Thus, members start out with a reasonably high level of understanding that is further enhanced during the group discussions in preparation for the weed finders' challenge. Nor does the learning end there. Many of the students who have participated in the weed finders challenge report that they can't have a picnic any more without thinking about what kind of weeds are going to be covered by their picnic blanket.

Energy—the Acid Test for Effective Group Activities

Our colleague's experience with modifying the group assignment for his agronomy class illustrates two key concepts about effective group assignments. First, the best way to increase the effectiveness of group assignments is to focus on increasing the extent to which they build group cohesiveness. Assignments simply will not increase group cohesiveness unless they produce a great deal of task-focused energy. Thus, if you ask yourself the question, "How can I change this assignment so that it will increase group cohesiveness?" you are also asking, "How can I change this assignment so that students/workshop participants will commit a higher level of energy to this learning task?" Second, the single best indicator of the effectiveness of a group assignment is what happens when groups share the results of their discussions with the class as a whole. The higher the energy (i.e., the extent to which groups are interested in and willing to spontaneously challenge each others thinking and defend their own), the more confident you can be that: 1) they have taken their group work seriously and 2) their ability to tackle even more difficult learning tasks has been significantly enhanced.

Conclusion

Overall, we hope that four messages have come through in this paper. First, group activities and assignments can be a highly effective tool for developing both students' mastery of basic conceptual material and their higher-level thinking and problem solving skills. Second, the vast majority of student or workshop participants' dysfunctional behaviors (e.g., social loafing, one or two members dominating the discussion, etc.) and complaints (e.g., having to carry the dead wood, the instructor isn't teaching, etc.) are the result of bad assignments *not* bad learners. Third, the key to designing effective group assignments is to maximize the extent to which the learning tasks promote the development of cohesive learning groups. Finally, the single best way to gauge the effectiveness of group assignments is the observe the level of energy that is present when the results of the small group discussions are reported to the class as a whole.

References

Anderson, J. R. (1993). Problem solving and learning. *American Psychologist, 48,* 35–44.

Bargh J. A., & Schul, Y. (1980). On the cognitive benefits of teaching. *Journal of Educational Psychology, 74*(5), 593–604.

Bruning, R. H., Schraw, G. J., & Ronning, R. R. (1994). *Cognitive Psychology and instruction* (2nd ed.). Englewood Cliffs, NJ: Prentice Hall.

Cottell, P., Millis, B. J. & Engrave, R. W. (1996). *Cooperative learning techniques and teaching notes: Financial accounting.* Cincinnati, OH: Southwestern College Publishing.

Craik, F. L. M. & Lockhart, R. S. (1986) CHARM is not enough: Comments on Eich's model of cued recall. *Psychological review, 93,* 360–364.

Feldman, D. (1984). The development and enforcement of group norms. *Academy of Management Review, 9,* 47–53.

Gagne, R. M. (1970). *The conditions for learning* (2nd Ed.). New York: Holt, Rinehart & Winston.

Latane, B., Williams, K. and Harkins, S. (1979). Many hands make light the work: The causes and consequences of social loafing. *Journal of Personality and Social Psychology, 37,* 822–832.

Lazarowitz, R. (1991). Learning biology cooperatively: An Israeli junior high school study. *Cooperative Learning, 11*(3), 19–21.

Lazarowitz, R. and Karsenty, G. (1990). Cooperative learning and student's self-esteem in tenth grade biology classrooms. In Sharon, S. (ed.) *Cooperative learning theory and research* (pp. 143–149). New York: Praeger Publishers.

Mandler, J. M. (1984). *Stories, scripts, and scenes: Aspects of schema theory.* Hillsdale, NJ: Lawrence Erlbaum.

Michaelsen, L. K. (1992). Team learning: A comprehensive approach for harnessing the poser of small groups in higher education. In *To Improve the Academy: Resources for Faculty, Instructional and Organizational Development, 1992.* Wulff, D. H. & Nyquist, J. D. (Eds.). Stillwater, OK: New Forums Press Co.

Michaelsen, L. K. & Black, R. H. (1994). Building learning teams: The key to harnessing the power of small groups in higher education. In *Collaborative Learning: A Sourcebook for Higher Education Vol. 2.* State College, PA: National Center for Teaching, Learning and Assessment.

Michaelsen, L. K., Black, R. H. & Fink, L. D. (1996). What every faculty developer needs to know about learning groups. In *To Improve the Academy: Resources for Faculty, Instructional and Organizational Development, 1996.* Richlin, L. (Ed.). Stillwater, OK: New Forums Press Co.

Michaelsen, L. K., Jones, C. F. & Watson, W. E. (1993). Beyond Groups and Cooperation: Building High Performance Learning Teams. In *To Improve the Academy: Resources for Faculty, Instructional and Organizational Development, 1993.* Wright, D. L. & Lunde, J. P. (Eds.). Stillwater, OK: New Forums Press Co.

Michaelsen, L. K., Watson, W. E. & Black, R. H. (1989). A realistic test of individual versus group consensus decision making. *Journal of Applied Psychology, 74*(5), 834–839.

Michaelsen, L. K., Watson, W. E. & Schraeder, C. B. (1985). Informative testing: A practical approach for tutoring with groups. *Organizational Behavior Teaching Review, 9*(4), 18–33.

Nungester, R. J. & Duchastel, P. C. (1982). Testing versus review: Effects on retention. *Journal of Applied Psychology, 74*(1), 18–22.

Shaw, M. E. (1981). *Group dynamics: The psychology of small group behavior* (3rd Ed.) New York: McGraw-Hill.

Slavin, R. E. (1995). *Cooperative Learning* (2nd Ed.). Boston, MA: Allyn & Bacon.

Smith, K., Johnson, D. W. & Johnson R. T. (1981). Can conflict be constructive? Controversy versus concurrence seeking in learning groups. *Journal of Educational Psychology, 73*(5), 651–663.

Watson, W. E., Kumar, K. & Michaelsen, L. K. (1993). Cultural diversity's impact on group process and performance: Comparing culturally homogeneous and culturally diverse task groups. *The Academy of Management Journal, 36*(3), 590–602.

Watson, W. E., Michaelsen, L. K. & Sharp, W. (1991). Member competence, group interaction and group decision-making: A longitudinal study. *Journal of Applied Psychology, 76,* 801–809.

Enhancing Learning—and More!—Through Cooperative Learning

Barbara J. Millis, U.S. Air Force Academy

Some of higher education's most challenging goals include enhancing critical thinking, promoting "deep" (as opposed to superficial) learning, encouraging both self-esteem and the acceptance of others, and improving interpersonal effectiveness (with an emphasis on team skills). This paper describes cooperative learning, an instructional approach designed especially with these objectives in mind.

What is Cooperative Learning?

Cooperative learning, like collaborative learning, entails small groups working on specific tasks. It seeks to overcome some of the weaknesses of traditional small group approaches by structuring activities carefully. Cooper (1990, p. 1), in fact, regards the key to successful cooperative learning as "Structure! Structure! Structure!" Macaulay and Gonzalez (1996, p. 2) characterize it as:

> The instructional use of small groups so that learners are able to work together in a manner that enhances both group and individual learning. The key to cooperative learning is the careful structuring of learning groups. There are many ways to structure such groups, but some of the key elements are the building of interdependence, the designing of interactive processes, and accountability. The building of social skills around such areas as decision-making, communication, and conflict management is also fundamental to cooperative learning.

Tang (1998, p. 116) offers an international perspective on cooperative learning, emphasizing some of its practices and effects:

> Co-operative learning provides a non-threatening learning context for interaction between students. During co-operative learning, students are exposed to other perspectives and alternatives, they share and exchange ideas, criticise and provide feedback. Peer feedback can help students increase their awareness of their learning aims, and of the strategies to employ to achieve those aims. Collaboration provides "scaffolding" for mutual support and enables students to learn from each other. The function is a teaching function, although the major interaction is student-student, rather than teacher-student, as teaching is normally understood.

Barbara Millis is Director of Faculty Development, US Air Force Academy, Colorado Springs, Colorado. She has presented workshops at academic conferences (including American Association for Higher Education and Lilly Teaching Conferences), as well as at various colleges and universities. She has published numerous articles on such topics as cooperative learning, classroom observations, peer review, academic games, and microteaching, and has co-authored Cooperative Learning for Higher Education Faculty (Oryx Press, 1998). She was awarded the US Air Force Academy's prestigious McDermott Award for Research Excellence in the Humanities and Social Sciences and Outstanding Educator Award.

Reprinted from *Idea Paper # 38* (2002), The IDEA Center, Inc.

Regardless of the definition of cooperative learning, most experts agree that its foundation rests on several significant premises.

The Premises Underlying Cooperative Learning

The first premise underlying cooperative learning is respect for students—regardless of their ethnic, intellectual, educational, or social backgrounds—and a belief in their potential for academic success. Sapon-Shevin, Ayres, and Duncan (1994, p. 46) suggest: "Cooperative learning . . . builds upon heterogeneity and formalizes and encourages peer support and connection. . . . ***All*** students need to learn and work in environments where their individual strengths are recognized and individual needs are addressed. ***All*** students need to learn within a supportive community in order to feel safe enough to take risks."

Second, cooperative learning promotes a shared sense of community. Learning, like living, is inherently social. This approach offers students support and encouragement through systematic classroom interactions. An intellectual synergy develops, and positive relationships typically develop.

Third, cooperative learning is predicated on the premise that learning is an active, constructive process. Myers and Jones (1993, xi) find that such learning "provides opportunities for students to ***talk and listen, read, write,*** and ***reflect*** as they approach course content through problem-solving exercises, informal small groups, simulations, case studies, role playing, and other activities—of all which require students to ***apply*** what they are learning." As a result, learning is not passively absorbed nor are facts simply added systematically to existing knowledge. Students often take new material—including conflicting viewpoints—and integrate, reinterpret, and transform it until new knowledge is forged. Thus, learning is produced, not reproduced.

The role of the instructor changes from a deliverer-of-information to a facilitator of learning. This does not mean that faculty members, who will always remain authorities in the definitive sense, abdicate their responsibility to students; rather, it means that they assume the role of "midwife professors" who "assist . . . students in giving birth to their own ideas, in making tacit knowledge explicit and elaborating on it" (Belenky, Clinchy, Goldberger, & Torule, 1986, p. 217).

Theory and Research

Establishing a cooperative classroom entails understanding the underlying theory in order to select effective teaching approaches. Leamnson (1999, p. 8) emphasizes that "a good pedagogy *selects* what is appropriate and is not wedded to a method, no matter how innovative or popular." Similarly, Palmer (1996, p. 12) reminds us that, "Our challenge is not to reduce good teaching to a particular form, model, methodology, or technique, but to understand its dynamics at the deeper levels, the underpinnings, to understand the dynamics that make connectedness a powerful force for learning in whatever forms it takes."

Using a connected, cooperative approach also reinforces the concepts of "deep learning." Four key components—totally consistent with cooperative learning practices—characterize a deep, rather than a surface approach to learning. Rhem (1995, p. 4) summarizes them as follows:

> **Motivational context:** We learn best what we feel a need to know. Intrinsic motivation remains inextricably bound to some level of choice and control. Courses that remove these take away the sense of ownership and kill one of the strongest elements in lasting learning.
>
> Learner activity: Deep learning and "doing" travel together. Doing in itself isn't enough. Faculty must connect activity to the abstract conceptions that make sense of it, but passive mental postures lead to superficial learning.
>
> **Interaction with others:** As Noel Entwistle put it in a recent email message, "The teacher is not the only source of instruction or inspiration." Peers working as groups enjoin dimensions of learning that lectures and readings by themselves cannot touch.
>
> A well-structured knowledge base: This doesn't just mean presenting new material in an organized way. It also means engaging and reshaping the concepts students bring with them when they register.

> Deep approaches and learning for understanding are integrative processes. The more fully new concepts can be connected with students' prior experience and existing knowledge, the more it is they will be impatient with inert facts and eager to achieve their own synthesis.

Deep learning and cooperative learning mesh perfectly when teachers capitalize on the underlying theories by—among other things—assigning motivating homework assignments that get students involved with the knowledge base. Students often become motivated when the material is relevant to their own lives and learning. When students can place content knowledge in a personal context, they are more likely to retain the information and be able to retrieve it (the "self-referral" effect), This research is the basis for Jensen's (2000, p. 282) advice to help students "discover their own connections rather than imposing your own" and encouraging "learners to use their own words with regard to new learning."

What becomes of the out-of-class homework assignment is critically important. Too often, teachers merely collect and grade homework, suggesting to students that their work is merely an artificial exercise intended for evaluation by a bored expert (the teacher). To avoid this perception and to build in the active learning and interaction with peers in the deep learning/cooperative learning models, teachers should consider peer reviews or other meaningful uses of the out-of-class assignment. Because students have already prepared individually, group activities based on that preparation should result in deeper learning.

The cooperative use of homework assignments also builds on what we know about cognitive development. Leamnson (1999, p. 5), for example, defines learning as "stabilizing, through repeated use, certain appropriate and desirable synapses in the brain." Teachers preparing lectures strengthen their own synapses, but the real test of learning is how students' synapses are affected. When a teacher deliberately couples well-thought-out homework assignments with cooperative in-class activities and targeted feedback, the repetition needed for student learning occurs through various approaches to the same content material, not through rote memorization.

Bransford, Brown, and Cocking (2000, p. 59) emphasize that "students need feedback about the degree to which they know when, where, and how to use the knowledge they are learning." The value of repetition is apparent when cooperative learning is added to a "learning to write" out-of-class activity such as the Double Entry Journal (DEJ).

With a DEJ, students identify on the left side of a grid (a Word table template e-mailed or distributed to students) the key points of an article, chapter, or guest lecture. Just opposite the key point they respond, linking the point to other academic material, current events, or their personal experiences and opinions (see Exhibit A). To avoid overloading students, faculty members can limit either the length of the DEJ or the number of key points.

Instead of jamming the DEJs into a briefcase for later evaluation, cooperative teachers can pair students, encouraging them to engage in discussions of their key points and responses. This paired discussion builds on the premises of critical thinking. Brookfield (1987) and others have emphasized that critical thinking depends on identifying and challenging assumptions and subsequently exploring and conceptualizing alternatives.

This linking of out-of-class work with in-class "processing" also results in meaningful on-target repetition with students more likely to complete an assignment they know will be shared with peers. The reading is exposure one. Then, crafting the DEJ draws the student back into the material—with personally relevant responses—for repetition two. The paired discussion in class provides a third repetition. (Students coming unprepared do not pair: they sit in the back of the class and work on their DEJ.) As a fourth repetition, students are likely to review their DEJ when the teacher returns them with marginal comments. (Although marked, DEJs need not receive a labor-intensive letter grade: a pass-fail grade—with a "pass," for example, counting 10 points counting toward a criterion referenced point-based final grode-motivates students without adding significantly to the grading load.) A fifth repetition occurs when teachers "coach" students on preparing an ideal DEJ by presenting exemplary examples as an in-class follow-up.

Faculty reluctant to consider cooperative learning can be reassured by the fact that the research base supporting it is long-standing and solid. Both the learning outcomes and the social dynamics of

EXHIBIT A

Sample Double Entry Journal (Two Points Cited Only)

Name: Barbara J. Millis

Article: "Investing in Creativity: Many Happy Returns" by Robert J. Sternberg

Key Points	**Responses**
Creative thinking is every bit as malleable as critical thinking.	Judging from the academic literature and discussions with faculty, critical thinking is not easy to define, let alone to each. I believe that critical thinking is taught by "doing" and by doing things specifically within the discipline. Activities such as The Double Entry Journal encourage critical thinking. Creativity is even more elusive. For me, creativity emerges from thinking—you can't separate the creative from the critical. I'm not certain I understand Sternberg's point about "malleability."
The investment theory of creativity holds that creativity gifted people share common characteristics.	Do we find gifted people and look for these characteristics or do we find the people who have these characteristics in common and then look for their creativity?

cooperative learning have been studied under a number of conditions. Slavin (1989–1990, p. 52) regards it as "one of the most thoroughly researched of all instructional methods." Johnson, Johnson and Smith (1991, p. 43) describe the amount of research conducted over the past 90 years as "staggering." In addition to cooperative learning's positive effect on student achievement, they also find that it significantly affects interpersonal relations:

> As relationships within the class or college become more positive, absenteeism decreases and students' commitment to learning, feeling of personal responsibility to complete the assigned work, willingness to take on difficult tasks, motivation and persistence in working on tasks, satisfaction and morale, willingness to endure pain and frustration to succeed, willingness to defend the college against external criticism or attack, willingness to listen to and be influenced by peers, commitment to peer's success and growth, and productivity and achievement can be expected to increase.

Cooper and Mueck (1990, p. 71) note: "The most consistent positive findings for cooperative learning . . . have centered on affective or attitudinal change. Outcome measures such as racial/ethnic relations, sex difference relations, self-esteem, and other prosocial outcomes have all been documented in the Cooperative Learning research."

Knowing only the underlying theory and the research base, however, will not result in a smoothly functioning cooperative classroom: teachers need to know how to establish and maintain a cooperative classroom.

Effective Cooperative Learning Experiences

Conducting the Cooperative Classroom

Much of the well-intentioned literature on higher education reform tends to be theoretical and exhortative: "Use active learning techniques;" "Be responsive in the classroom;" "Promote respect for diversity;" "Foster critical thinking." Too often such challenges leave faculty with a sense of schizophrenic overload, feeling almost like an early Picasso with eyes, ears, and mouth—to say nothing of brain!—permanently askew. How can they respond simultaneously and responsibly to these multiple demands? Inserting new elements into existing courses without a clear sense of purpose, commitment, or competence can result in a half-hearted "Band-Aid" approach. A strength of cooperative learning is that it provides a practical means to operationalize these new challenges in pedagogically sound, systematic ways.

When structuring a cooperative classroom, the following key principles should guide all decisions:

1. Positive interdependence fosters cooperative behaviors

Johnson, Johnson, and Smith (1991, p. 3) describe positive interdependence in these words:

> Cooperation results in participants' striving for mutual benefit so that all members of the group benefit from each other's efforts (your success benefits me and my success benefits you), their recognizing that all group members share a common fate (we sink or swim together) and that one's performance depends mutually on oneself and one's colleagues (we cannot do it without you), and their feeling proud and jointly celebrating when a group member is recognized for achievement (You got an A! That's terrific!).

In a traditional educational setting, students tend to work either on their own or in competition with one another. In a cooperative, group-oriented setting, all class members, particularly those grouped in instructor-selected teams, contribute to each other's learning. Through careful planning, positive interdependence can be established by having students achieve: (a) mutual goals, such as reaching a consensus on specific solutions to problems or arriving at team-generated solutions; (b) mutual rewards, such as individually assigned points counting toward a criterion-referenced final grade, points which only help, but never handicap; (c) structured tasks, such as a report or complex problem with sections contributed by each team member; and (d) interdependent roles, such as having group members serve as discussion leaders, organizers, recorders, and spokespersons.

2. Individual accountability promotes fair evaluation

No matter how much mutual support, coaching, and encouragement they receive, students must be individually responsible for their own academic achievements. Because students have been acclimated to academic settings where they compete against fellow classmates, this aspect of cooperative group work is reassuring: final course grades will be based on personal efforts, uncompromised and uncomplicated by the achievements of others. Teachers can grade quizzes, projects, and final exams just as they would in a class where group work is not the norm.

Positive interdependence and individual accountability can be fostered through carefully structured in-class activities. For example, when students receive a specific task such as worksheet or case study to complete cooperatively, teachers can tell students that one group member—unidentified ahead of time—will be responsible for reporting the group's work. This is a cooperative structure called "Numbered Heads Together" (Kagan, 1989), "Problem Solving Lesson" (Johnson, Johnson, and Smith, 1991), or "Structured Problem-Solving" (Millis and Cottell, 1998). Such an approach has several positive outcomes: (a) It encourages all students to learn the material because they don't know who will be called upon; (b) It encourages weaker students to request—and typically receive—peer coaching; (c) It encourages shyer or less-able students to accept leadership roles because their selection as the spokesperson is random and the report they give is not their personal report, but the team's.

3. A clear, non-competitive, criterion-referenced grading scheme encourages cooperation

Both positive interdependence and individual accountability can also be affected by the grading system adopted. Nothing undercuts a cooperative classroom more than a grading system that pits students against one another in competition for a set number of A's or B's. In contrast, a criterion-referenced grading scheme allows all students to receive appropriate grades. Standards should be high, but they should theoretically be within the grasp of all students who work cooperatively toward the established benchmark.

Another grading concern relates to grades for team projects. Undifferentiated group grades for a single project, particularly if the majority of the work is expected out-of-class, invite inequity problems—or even ethical or legal issues—and undermine individual accountability. Too often one student ends up doing the majority of the work. That student often relishes the power associated with this role but resents the lack of input from students who will benefit from the same grade. The students who contribute little receive signals that their efforts are unappreciated or unwanted, and they learn a negative lesson: they can receive a grade they did not earn. Thus, it is important to build in accountability through responsible peer and self-assessment so that all students receive grades reflecting their contributions. Some instructors, especially those in preprofessional disciplines, may argue that "real world" preparation should put students in situations where one team member's performance—or lack of performance—drags down the achievement of the team as a whole. In reality, no savvy corporate leader allows teams to dissolve in bickering or exclusive behavior when a contract or a job deadline is looming. Nor do responsible supervisors write the same performance appraisals for all their personnel.

4. Students and teachers should monitor group behaviors

Group processing of behaviors and of social skills, such as listening and providing constructive feedback, often distinguish cooperative learning from less structured forms of group work. These proactive practices allow students to reflect on their learning process and outcomes. Group processing involves evaluating skills such as leadership, decision-making, communication, and conflict resolution. "Process" focuses not on the content, but on how the group is functioning. After an assignment or activity, for instance, students could respond to questions such as: "Did all members of the group contribute?" "What could be done next time to make the group function better?" or "What were the most important things I learned today?"

Social skills are important, although students may not initially see their connection with academic learning. Interpersonal skills go well beyond mere politeness. Students should understand the value of cooperative interaction and mutual respect in adult living. Teachers should model appropriate social skills, including ways of providing constructive feedback or eliciting more in-depth responses through probing questions. They can also reinforce these social skills by publicly commenting on ways students use them effectively.

In a cooperative classroom, the teacher monitors group behavior and learning by moving group to group as teams complete cooperative tasks. Teachers benefit by: (a) discovering what students actually know or when and why they are struggling; (b) encouraging, through their proximity, students to remain on task; (c) building rapport by showing obvious interest in students' progress; (d) being perceived as "approachable," a special advantage for students afraid to ask "dumb" questions in front of the entire class; (e) learning new ways to approach material by hearing students translate "professorese" into concepts their peers can understand; and (f) acquiring opportunities to integrate ideas overheard into a follow-up mini-lecture, building self-esteem in the designated students and their teams and signaling to the class as a whole that student insights are valued.

5. Classroom Assessment Techniques (CATs) can shed light on student progress

Monitoring can also include written exercises designed to find out if students are learning what teachers think they are teaching. Angelo and Cross (1993) offer fifty techniques for assessing student learning. Many of these, such as the One-Minute Paper or the Muddiest Point, can be conducted, analyzed, and "debriefed" rapidly. Classroom assessment practices not only help teachers understand the extent of student learning, but they also get students involved in monitoring their own academic progress. Most cooperative activities, when properly monitored, have assessment value.

A Visible Quiz (Staley, 2003, 104–110), for example, when conducted cooperatively, can help both students and teachers determine how well students are grasping content and concepts. In a

Visible Quiz, students in pairs or small groups discuss the appropriate response to quiz questions typically displayed on an overhead screen. The answers can be multiple choice (A, B, C, or D) or True (T) and False (F). Each team has a set of color-coded cards (all A's could be orange, for example, and all T's, blue). At a given signal, one person from each team displays the team's choice. A quick survey of the room shows how well students understood the question. If most students gave inappropriate responses, then an impromptu mini-lecture can capitalize on the "teachable moment." Groups can also explain the rationale for their inappropriate selection, a process that may uncover misconceptions or poorly constructed, ambiguous questions. Besides proving immediate feedback for both students and teachers, this technique also promotes peer coaching when the teams discuss each question. Johnston and Cooper (1997, p. 4) label a variation of the Visible Quiz, "Select the Best Response."

Even in-class activities as relatively straightforward as a Visible Quiz need to be appropriately introduced.

Establishing a Cooperative Activity

Four important guidelines can help teachers and students establish—and value—cooperative activities.

1. Teachers should think through the proposed group activity by answering key questions

A pundit once quipped: "If you don't know where you're going, you'll probably end up somewhere else." This saying is certainly true for group activities. As a general rule, teachers will want to ask themselves the following questions: What will I do? Why am I doing it? How will this activity further my course objectives? How will I introduce this activity to students? How will I form groups? How will I monitor students' interactions and learning? How will I foster positive interdependence (goal, resource materials, evaluation methods, roles, etc.)? How will I maintain individual accountability? How will I access student learning, student interactions/contributions, and the overall success of the activity? What problems/challenges do I expect? Careful planning tied to course objectives is essential.

2. Students need to understand the nature and value of the proposed activity

Many students will come to classes with learning styles that predispose them to work independently. Furthermore, they may have been "burned" in the past by ineptly managed group work. Thus, they must understand why group interactions will further immediate course goals and lead to other desirable outcomes such as acquiring the teamwork skills needed in the modern work place.

3. Clear instructions are essential

Group work can be frustrating for both students and faculty if instructions are unclear. Students may question a teacher's organizational skills, and they may waste precious class time puzzling over directions. For complex tasks, teachers can provide instructions as handouts given either to individuals or to teams. Projecting tasks and expectations on a screen or writing them on a chalkboard can prove helpful. For simpler activities, asking a single student or the class to repeat the instructions will reinforce them.

Clear instructions not only explain the task, but they also specify the time involved. Students cannot manage their time wisely, even during short in-class activities, if they cannot plan ahead. As a general rule, it is better to allow too little time and then expand it as needed rather than to give students a twenty-minute in-class activity that many groups will complete in ten.

Studies, such as *The Seven Principles for Good Practice in Undergraduate Education* (Chickering and Gamson, 1987), have identified "time on task" as a factor critical to student achievement. To maximize time on task, teachers can include in the instructions a "sponge" or extension activity that teams turn to if they complete the initial assignment early. This "sponge" typically involves more challenging problems to solve or more complex issues to discuss.

4. Students appreciate a sense of closure

As indicated earlier, students may be unwilling group members unless they see the value of cooperative learning. The instructor must avoid the appearance of "toying" with students by withholding information while a group struggles with a difficult problem. Generally, it is appropriate to offer help when all group members admit that they need it. A better tactic might be to send a student "adviser" from a different learning team.

Sometimes the instructor, as the authority, will need to summarize a lesson, validating the learning that has occurred in groups. Report-outs—particularly those that do not take too much time—can provide a sense of closure. When time is short, reporters can e-mail the group report for later circulation or for posting on a course web page.

E-mail reports work well, for example, for class summaries of an activity called Roundtable. Roundtable, a cooperative learning structure useful for brainstorming, reviewing, predicting, or practicing a skill, uses a single sheet of paper and pen for each cooperative learning group. In response to a question or problem, students in turn state their ideas aloud as they write them on the paper. Team members ideally should not skip turns, but if their thoughts are at a standstill, then they are allowed to say "Pass" rather than turn the brainstorm into a brain drizzle.

Roundtable is most effective when used in a carefully sequenced series of activities. The brainstorming can reinforce ideas from the readings or can be used to set the stage for upcoming discussions. Students, for example, could identify the characteristics of an effective leader or the attributes of terrorism before these topics are formally introduced. Comparing a student-generated list with those of "experts" creates interest. The multiple answers encourage creativity and deeper thinking. This activity builds positive interdependence among team members because of the shared writing surface. More importantly, it builds team cohesion and reinforces the power of teamwork because students see in action the value of multiple viewpoints and ideas.

Organizing Groups/Teams Effectively

Three guidelines can optimize team cohesion and eliminate many of the dysfunctional aspects of groups.

1. Group size should remain small

Most teachers experienced with group work advocate groups composed of three to four students. Four, or a quad, is generally considered the ideal because the group is large enough to contain students who will bring diverse opinions, experiences, and learning styles to aid in problem solving. If a group member is absent, the group can continue to function smoothly. A group of four is not so large, however, that students can hide. All must carry their fair share of the workload. A quad has the additional advantage of offering easy pair formation within the group.

2. Teacher-selected heterogeneous groups usually function better than randomly selected or student-selected groups

Stein and Hurd (2000, p. 12) state: "Teams should be heterogeneous: diverse in gender, ethnic background, and academic ability." Felder and Brent (1994, p. 7) give a reasoned case for heterogeneity in ability:

> The drawbacks of a group with only weak students are obvious, but having only strong students in a group is equally undesirable. First, the strong groups have an unfair advantage over other groups in the class. Second, the team members tend to divide up the homework and communicate only cursorily with one another, omitting the dynamic interactions that lead to most of the proven benefits of cooperative learning. In mixed ability groups, on the other hand, the weaker students gain from see-

ing how better students study and approach problems, and the strong students gain a deeper understanding of the subject by teaching it to others.

Besides enhancing the likelihood of success with academic tasks, heterogeneous grouping will typically permit students to work constructively with varied individuals who bring different strengths and approaches to academic tasks. Positive interactions with diverse individuals prepare students for the modern work place and for society as a whole.

It is wise to explain to students the rationale for grouping them rather than allowing them to select their own teammates. Self-selected groups tend to be homogenous, reducing the likelihood of divergent thinking. Roles and expectations tend be more fixed, eliminating the "dating dance" where students unknown to one another are on their best behaviors.

3. Groups should remain together long enough to establish positive working relationships and to develop team-building

It is dangerous to assume that students will bring with them the skills needed to function effectively in cooperative groups. Permanent learning teams should remain together long enough to pass through the "forming," "storming," "norming," "performing," and "adjourning" phases cited in the group dynamics literature (Tuckman, 1965; Tuckman & Jensen, 1977). Students need time to become acquainted, to identify one another's strengths, and to learn to support and coach one another. Most practitioners recommend that groups remain together for the duration of an extended project or for a series of ongoing activities, usually for about half a semester. It is important to clearly explain to students when and why they will be re-grouped to forestall the inevitable laments that come from closely bonded teams "rent asunder."

Managing Group Activities

Instructors concerned about wasted time want to move quickly in and out of group work. Thus, students noisily engaged in group activities must understand that when they receive a given signal, they must give the teacher their immediate attention. In small classes, merely calling "time" may suffice. In larger classes, it may be necessary to use a visual signal such as a raised hand (called a quiet signal, students raise their hand also as they cease talking to create a ripple effect). Combining the quiet signal with an auditory signal such as a timer beep helps to conclude the activity as well as to keep track of time.

With effective classroom management, many cooperative activities can be completed within a few minutes. A Think-Pair-Share, for example, gives students thirty-seconds of "wait time" to ***think*** independently on the answer to a content-related question or a critical question such as, "I've been lecturing for the past fifteen minutes. Please summarize the three most important points I've made." (To contribute to classroom assessment, many instructors allow two minutes for students to write their responses on index cards for later collection and review.) Then students ***pair*** to compare their responses, rehearse their answers, and receive feedback on their ideas. During the third phase, students are called on to respond ***(share).*** Those with raised hands will now typically include introverts who have had time for reflection; shy students who have received reinforcement; and thoughtful students who have "processed" the question in depth. A quiet signal helps teachers move through these phases expeditiously.

Time is also saved by using team folders—even in a small class—when students are assigned to permanent (course-long) or semi-permanent groups (typically half-a-term). At the beginning of each class session, a designated group member picks up the team folder, which contains all relevant class materials and papers to be returned. During class, students put in the folder their homework and any in-class written activities, including classroom assessment responses such as the Think-Pair-Share index cards or a Roundtable sheet. The designated student returns the folder to the instructor at the conclusion of class. Students can use sheets stapled in the folder to keep track of attendance or homework completion.

To delineate tasks and assign roles rapidly, it is important to identify quickly both teams and team members. Students can number off within their teams (one, two, three, four), or teams and team members can be identified through the use of playing cards. The playing cards allow teachers to communicate readily to the students their group assignments (by the rank of the card) and the roles they are to play within that group (by the suit of the card). They also enable the instructor to keep track of students already called upon—an equity concern—by checking off from an ongoing list, for example, the "Jack of Hearts" or the "Two of Clubs." When extra members are added, bringing some team totals to five, jokers (called "wild cards") can be used for the fifth member, who fills in for anyone absent. For ready identification in larger classes, two or more decks of cards can be used—red and blue-backed, for example—with different colored folders corresponding to each different deck of cards.

The roles assigned within the groups—typically leader, recorder, reporter, and folder monitor—should be rotated frequently to form positive interdependence. This practice discourages domination by one person, a problem common in less structured group work, and gives all students an opportunity to practice various social, communication, and leadership skills.

Team-building activities can build team cohesion, but they should never be frivolous, off-task exercises. Content-based activities, such as a Three-Step Interview, encourage students to focus on the course material, while interacting positively with one another. In a Three-Step Interview, one student interviews another within specified time limits (step one). An extra question can be added for pairs working more rapidly than others, the "extension" or "sponge" recommended for many cooperative learning activities. The two then reverse roles and conduct the interview again (step two). The students then form a quad where students share not their own viewpoints, but the information or insights gleaned from their partners (step three). This structure reinforces listening and probing skills, helps students process and rehearse information, and results in shared insights. Teachers can encourage preparation by announcing, "Chapter Eight is so important that I will be asking you to interview one another to be certain that you understand the critical concepts." Used at the beginning of a class period, the content-based questions give students immediate feedback on their understanding of the assigned material. As teachers monitor the interviews, they can determine how well the students have responded to the readings and incorporate some of their ideas in a follow-on lecture/discussion.

No matter how carefully teachers plan, some things will invariably go wrong. Risk-taking, however, is essential for professional growth. The point is not to give up ("Oh, I tried cooperative learning, and it didn't work at all"). A myriad of helpful books, articles, and websites, such as those found in the references or at http://www.tltgroup.org/resources/millis.html, offer constructive advice. Faculty members can ask knowledgeable colleagues or faculty development consultants to observe their classes, or they can sit in on theirs. Faculty can also attend cooperative learning workshops that model classroom management techniques and activities such as the Double Entry Journal, Structured Problem Solving, Think-Pair-Share, Visible Quiz, Roundtable, and Three-Step Interview discussed here.

Conclusion

Faculty understanding the research and theory behind cooperative learning—and the classroom management techniques that insure smooth implementation—can adapt it to virtually any curriculum. As a result, learning can be deepened, students will enjoy attending classes, and they will come to respect and value the contributions of their fellow classmates. Millis (2000–2001, p. 4) explains why cooperative learning is far from a "trendy" fad:

> It allows us to be student-centered without abrogating the responsibility of shaping a class based on our experience and expertise. It provides us with the tools to structure activities that maximize learning. It helps us foster not only learning, but also a host of other positive outcomes such as increased self-esteem, respect for others, and civility. It can transform our large, diverse lecture classes into a community of supportive teams. Cooperative learning satisfies, for students, a human desire for connection and cooperation. In addition to keeping them energized and awake, it gives them the social

support to tackle complex tasks impossible to complete alone. It gives them essential social and communication skills needed for success in the workplace. Finally, for both teachers and students, cooperation makes learning fun.

References

Angelo, T. A. & Cross, K. P. (1993). *Classroom assessment techniques: A handbook for college teachers.* 2nd Ed. San Francisco: Jossey-Bass.

Belenky, M. F., Clinchy, B. M., Goldberger, N. R., & Tacule, J. M. (1986). *Women's ways of knowing: The development of self, voice, and mind.* New York: Basic Books, Inc.

Bransford, J. D., Brown, A. L., & Cocking, R. R. (Eds.). (2000). *How people learn: Brain, mind, experience, and school.* Commission on Behavioral and Social Sciences and Education National Research Council. Washington, DC: National Academy Press.

Brookfield, S. D. (1987). *Developing critical thinkers: Challenging adults to explore alternative ways of thinking and acting.* San Francisco: Jossey-Bass.

Chickering, A. W. & Gamson, A. F. (1987). Seven principles for good practice in undergraduate education. Racine, WI: The Johnson Foundation, Inc./Wingspread. http://www.aahe.org/bulletin/sevenprinciples1987.htm

Cooper, J. (1990, May). Cooperative learning and college teaching: Tips from the trenches. *The Teaching Professor,* pp. 1–2.

Cooper, J. & Mueck, R. (1990). Student involvement in learning: Cooperative learning and college instruction. *Journal on Excellence in College Teaching,* 1, 68–76. [Article is reprinted in Goodsell, A., Mayer, M., Tinto, V., Smith, B. L., & Macgregor, J. (Eds.). (1992). *Collaborative learning: A sourcebook for higher education* (pp. 68–74). University Pork, PA: National Center on Postsecondary Teaching, Learning, & Assessment.]

Felder, R. M. & Brent, R. (1994). Cooperative learning in technical courses: Procedures, pitfalls, and payoffs. Eric Document Reproduction Service Report ED 377038. 22 September 2002. http://www2.ncsu.edu/unity/lockers/users/f/felder/public/papers/Coopreport.html

Jenson, E. (2000). *Brain-based learning.* Revised Ed. San Diego: The Brain Store.

Johnson, D. W., Johnson, R. T., & Smith, K. A (1991). *Cooperative learning: Increasing college faculty instructional productivity.* (ASHE-ERIC Higher Education Report No. 4). Washington, DC: The George Washington University School of Education and Human Development.

Johnston, S. & Cooper, J. (Fall, 1997). Quick thinks: Active-thinking tasks in lecture classes and televised instruction. *Cooperative Learning and College Teaching.* Stillwater, OK: New Forums Press.

Kagan, S. (1989). *Cooperative learning resources for teachers.* San Capistrano, CA: Resources for Teachers, Inc.

Leamnson, R. (1999). *Thinking about teaching and learning: Developing habits of learning with first year college and university students.* Sterling, VA: Stylus Press.

Macaulay, B. A & Gonzales, V. G. (1996, March). Enhancing the collaborative/cooperative learning experience: A guide for faculty development. Workshop presented at the AAHE National Conference on Higher Education.

Millis, B. (2000–2001). Cooperative learning: It's here to stay. *Teaching Excellence: Toward the Best in the Academy,* 12(8). The Professional and Organizational Development Network in Higher Education.

Millis, B. & Cottell, P. (1998). *Cooperative learning for higher education faculty.* American Council on Education, Oryx Press [Now available through Greenwood Press].

Myers, C. & Jones, T. B. (1993). *Promoting active learning: Strategies for the college classroom.* San Francisco: Jossey-Bass.

Palmer, P. J. (1996). The renewal of community in higher education. In W. E. Campbell & K. A. Smith (Eds.), *New Paradigms for College Teaching* (pp. 1–18). Edina, MN: Interaction Book Company.

Rhem, J. (1995). Close-Up: Going deep. *The National Teaching & Learning Forum,* 5(1), 4.

Sapon-Shevin, M., Ayres, B. J., & Duncan, J. (1994). Cooperative learning and inclusion. In J.S. Thousand, R. A. Villa, & A. I. Nevin (Eds.), *Creativity and collaborative learning: A practical guide to empowering students and teachers* (pp. 45–58). Baltimore: Paul H. Brookes Publishing Co.

Slavin, R. E. (1989–1990). Research in cooperative learning: Consensus and controversy. *Educational leadership,* 47(4), 52–55.

Staley, C. (2003). *Fifty Ways to Leave your Lectern.* Wadsworth/Thompson.

Stein, R. F. & Hurd, S. (2000). *Using Student Teams in the Classroom: A Faculty Guide.* Bolton, MA: Anker Publishing Company.

Tang, C. (1998). Effects of collaborative learning on the quality of assignments. In B. Dart & G. Boulton-Lewis (Eds.), *Teaching and Learning in Higher Education* (pp. 102–123). Melbourne, Australia: The Australian Council for Education Research Ltd.

Tuckman, B. (1965). Developmental sequence in small groups. *Psychological Bulletin,* 63(6), 384–399.

Tuckman, B. & Jensen, M. A. C. (1977). Stages of small-group development revisited. *Group and Organizational Studies,* 2(4), 419–427.

Chapter 16

Discussion

Strategies for Reporting Small-Group Discussions to the Class

Stephen D. Brookfield and Stephen Preskill

It is common practice to divide students into small groups to discuss a topic or to answer a few questions, and then to invite them to report the substance of their conversations to the group as a whole. How we teachers do that can make the difference between students' feeling that they are just going through their paces and the sense that they are engaged in a powerful exchange of ideas.

Typically, we approach the task of reporting to the whole group in a number of ways. We might invite each group to summarize the themes explored in response to the question or issue. Although admirably thorough, that can also be repetitive. Or we call on each small group to share the one or two insights group members found most surprising or illuminating. It also is useful to direct each group to ask the whole class a particularly challenging question that emerged from group discussion. On other occasions, small groups can offer the key themes or concepts that seemed to recur throughout their conversation. These can spark strong reactions from others, stimulating new lines of inquiry.

Newsprint Dialogue

We have found that one way to avoid the more ponderous aspects of reporting is to suggest that small groups summarize their conversations on large sheets of newsprint or the chalkboard. Individual members of the class are then free to wander about the room reading all the responses and comparing them to those of their own groups.

Here are the instructions we give to students:

> In this activity, you will be working in small groups most of the time. We have prepared some questions for you to consider in these groups, but don't follow them too slavishly. Use them as a jumping-off point for ideas you find worth exploring.
>
> You will have thirty minutes to discuss these questions in your groups and to write your answers on the newsprint provided. You should appoint someone to be recorder, but don't start writing immediately. Take some time to let your responses emerge from the discussion. Covering all the questions is not important, but you should begin to jot down some ideas on the newsprint within fifteen or twenty minutes of starting.
>
> When the thirty minutes are up, post your newsprint sheets around the classroom and tour the answers recorded by other groups. Look especially for common themes that stand out on the sheets and for possible contradictions that arise within and between groups' responses. If possible, write your comments on the same sheet of newsprint containing the point you're addressing.
>
> Finally, note any questions that were raised for you during the discussion on the separate sheets of newsprint specially provided for this. We will bring the activity to a close with a short debriefing in the large group.

Reprinted from *College Teaching* (1999), Heldref Publications.

Attractions of this activity are that it provides a different approach to reporting by taking students out of groups for a while and letting them act as relatively autonomous free agents. It also reminds people that dialogue can be a written, as well as a spoken, exchange. On the downside, written exchanges often lack the spontaneity and excitement of group talk. And in the limited space and time allotted, it is frequently difficult for students to provide full explanations of the words and phrases on the newsprint. Still, it is an interesting way to keep the conversation going.

Rotating Small-Group Stations

Another way to avoid the usual format is to place each small group at a station where members have ten minutes to discuss a provocative issue and record their ideas on newsprint or a chalkboard. When time is up, the groups move to new positions in the classroom, where they continue their discussions, treating the comments written on the newsprint or chalkboard by the preceding group as a new voice in the mix. Rotations continue every ten minutes until each group has been at all of the positions and has had a chance to consider all of the other groups' comments.

Here are the instructions we give to students for this exercise:

> We're going to do another small group activity, but this time you won't be staying in one place for long. Each of you should join a group of about five participants at one of the stations that has been established around the classroom. Together you will have the responsibility to answer some questions by making comments on the newsprint directly in front of your group. You will have ten minutes to do this. When the time is up, move with your group to the next station, where you will continue your conversation by responding to the comments left behind by the group that has just vacated that station. You have ten minutes to record the main points of your discussion at this station. When that time is up, move on to the next station, where you will now have the comments of two other groups to consider.
>
> Again take ten minutes to respond, and move on when the time is up. When every group has occupied each station, leaving remarks behind at all of them, break out of your groups and read all of the newsprint comments. Add questions, comments, criticisms to these sheets whenever you are inspired to do so. Remember that each station will include comments from all groups, making orderliness a challenge. Write as small and as legibly as you can, please!

In addition to fostering healthy confusion, rotating stations encourages students to examine critically ideas that originate outside their group. The safety and intimacy of small groups is retained while incorporating the diversity of viewpoints in whole-class discussion. Momentum and excitement tend to grow as groups rotate from one station to another, and students enjoy a sense of exhilaration and connectedness unusual in small-group activities. People feel they have heard and responded to many voices in the classroom in a way that is less threatening than in large-group exchanges.

On the debit side, the ten-minute period for each rotation does not allow much deep discussion. But longer periods of thirty to forty minutes, we have found, are impractical. Using fewer groups with a greater number of members is one option for getting around the problem, but the larger group size makes it harder for shy or introverted members to contribute.

Snowballing

One way to make a discussion developmental and increasingly inclusive is to use a process called "snowballing" or "pyramiding" (Jacques 1992). Students begin this activity by responding to questions or issues as individuals. They then create progressively larger conversation groups by doubling the size of these groups every few minutes until the large group has been re-formed. Here are the instructions students follow:

> We are going to try something a little different today. It is called "snowballing," and it gives you a chance to think and talk about issues in a variety of configurations. Notice that there are some questions at the bottom of this sheet.

> Begin this activity by gathering your thoughts on these questions in private reflection. Jot down some of these reflections as you wish. After five minutes of solitary thought, you will begin a dialogue on the questions with one other person. After another five minutes, you and your partner should join another pair to form a group of four.
>
> You will continue the discussion for ten minutes and then merge with another foursome to create a group of eight. The discussion proceeds for twenty minutes this time, after which two groups merge again, and the process continues in twenty-minute intervals until the whole class has been brought together at the end of the session. The discussion can end when the class is reunited, or continue for a final twenty minutes (or however much time is available).

On the one hand, this exercise gets a lot of people talking to each other while retaining much of the value of small groups. It also contributes a festive quality to the class. People mill about excitedly and greet each other warmly as they meet in new configurations. On the other hand, snowballing can have a frenetic feeling. But sometimes the regular changing of group membership is just the thing needed to shake students up a little.

Cocktail Party

A variation on snowballing is the cocktail party. In this exercise, the teacher brings in and serves hors d'oeuvres and nonalcoholic drinks. The ground rules couldn't be simpler. To create the right mood, the teacher serves students from a tray carried around the room, frequently replenishing it with more food and drink. Just as at a party, students munch and drink as they mingle with as many of their peers as they can. The only expectation is that in chatting with different people, students find interesting and engaging ways to explore an issue. Like snowballing, this exercise encourages a festive atmosphere while offering a relaxed setting for conversation. Strange and sometimes wonderful things happen in unique settings such as these. Although we don't promise miracles, we do recommend an occasional activity/surprise/treat such as this to cultivate the unexpected and the spontaneous.

Jigsaw

Still another way to retain the advantages of small groups but infuse them with more diverse perspectives is to use the cooperative teachnique called "jigsaw" (Aronson 1978; Slavin 1990). Teachers and students begin by generating a short list of topics they would like to study. Each student becomes an "expert" on one of these topics, first individually and then in discussion with other students who are experts on the same topics. Later these student experts become responsible again, through dialogue, for helping nonexperts to become as informed as they are.

The following is an example of the jigsaw technique as applied to a graduate course that one of us taught called Leadership and Biography.

> For today's class I am going to hand out six biographies for you to read. Each person will read one biography and since there are 36 people in the class each person will read the same biography as five other class members. You should read your chosen biography carefully so that you are knowledgeable enough about this person's life to be designated an "expert" for the purposes of our discussion. When we return to class, you will meet in a small group with the other people who have chosen the same biography—thus everyone reading about Susan B. Anthony will meet together, everyone reading about Frederick Douglass will form a group, and so on. In these groups you will touch on as many different aspects of the person's life as possible, focusing on key accomplishments, missed opportunities, character flaws, personal history, and unanswered questions.
>
> Once all the members of each group have mastered their chosen subject, we will form a second set of small groups, containing one representative from each of the expert groups. Thus each group will include one person who read about Anthony, one who read about Douglass, and so on. These second discussions allow each expert to share perspectives from the expert group and to lead the rest of the group in a discussion of the chosen person's life. These discussions should not come to a conclusion until each expert has had a chance to lead the group in discussion and everyone is reasonably familiar with each life discussed. The activity will end with debriefing as a class.

In this activity, students benefit from having more discussion with twice the usual number of students. The jigsaw gives even the most reticent students reason to speak up, thereby bolstering their confidence. Both sets of discussions are rich, but in different ways. In the initial expert conversations, everyone is on roughly equal ground. They have a common focus and a lot to share with one another. In the second round of discussions, everyone has a basis for contributing substantively, and everyone is obligated to participate. Each person has a chance to be in the spotlight for part of the discussion. The chief drawback to the jigsaw is that the amount of information to absorb in the second round of discussion can be overwhelming.

Many creative ways exist to make good use of small groups, and groups' deliberations can be communicated to the class as a whole using a variety of imaginative strategies. Teachers who often use small-group discussion should avoid relying too heavily on traditional reporting procedures, which tend to induce boredom and bring diminishing returns. The alternative suggestions we have put forward are all flawed in various ways, and none should be overused. Still, these strategies may rejuvenate classrooms that have become dull. We believe that they will introduce a spontaneous, improvisational spirit that is highly motivating for many of today's jaded students.

Added Material

Stephen D. Brookfield is Distinguished Professor at the University of St. Thomas in St. Paul, Minnesota. Stephen Preskill is an associate professor of education and director of the Division of Educational Leadership and Organizational Learning, at the University of New Mexico in Albuquerque. This article is derived from their new book, *Discussion as a Way of Teaching* (1999).

References

Aronson, E. 1978. *The jigsaw classroom*. Thousand Oaks, Calif: Sage.

Jacques, D. 1992. *Learning in groups*. 2nd ed. Houston: Gulf Publishing.

Slavin, R. 1990. *Cooperative grouping: Theory, research, and practice*. Upper Saddle River, N.J.: Prentice-Hall.

CHAPTER 17

CITIZENSHIP/SERVICE LEARNING

Comparing the Effects of Community Service and Service-Learning

Lori J. Vogelgesang and Alexander W. Astin
University of California, Los Angeles

This paper presents results from a study that compares course-based service-learning and generic community service. The study was a quantitative, longitudinal look at over 22,000 students at diverse colleges and universities. Student outcome comparisons are made related to values and beliefs, academic skills, leadership, and future plans. Of particular interest is the finding that connecting service with academic course material does indeed enhance the development of cognitive skills. Limitations and directions for future research are identified.

Service-learning represents a potentially powerful form of pedagogy because it provides a means of linking the academic with the practical. The more abstract and theoretical material of the traditional classroom takes on new meaning as the student "tries it out," so to speak, in the "real" world. At the same time, the student benefits from the opportunity to connect the service experience to the intellectual content of the classroom. By emphasizing cooperation, democratic citizenship and moral responsibility through service-learning, higher education connects to the wider community and enables students to contribute to the alleviation of society's urgent needs.

There is a mounting body of evidence documenting the efficacy of participating in service during the undergraduate years (Astin, Sax & Avalos, 1999; Batchelder & Root, 1994; Eyler, Giles & Braxton, 1997; Eyler & Giles, 1999; Hesser, 1995; Rhoads, 1997; Sax, Astin & Astin, 1996). Yet, though there is broad support for engaging students in community service, there has been some resistance to incorporating service into academic courses. The thinking has been that the place for service is outside the classroom—done on a student's "own time." Those who doubt that service-learning belongs in undergraduate curricula ask, What is the "value-added" for course-based service? For proponents of service-learning, it is important to be able to know whether engaging in service *as part of an academic course* has benefits over and above those of co-curricular community service.

This study directly compares service-learning and co-curricular community service, in order to identify the unique contributions, if any, of course-based service beyond those of community service.[1] We address these issues through a quantitative longitudinal study of a national sample of students at diverse colleges and universities.

LORI J. VOGELGESANG is director of the Center for Service Learning Research and Dissemination at the Higher Education Research Institute (HERI), University of California, Los Angeles. She has conducted research and evaluation of service learning programs for HERI and for RAND.

ALEXANDER W. ASTIN is Allan M. Cartter Professor of Higher Education and Director of the Higher Education Research Institute at the University of California, Los Angeles.

Reprinted from *Michigan Journal of Community Service Learning* (2000).

Research that contributes to understanding the educational value of course-based service is important for several reasons. First, it contributes to our understanding of how student learning takes place. Second, such understanding directly addresses faculty concerns about the value of participating in service as part of a course. As a recent study of federally funded service-learning programs points out, "at the institutional level, the most serious obstacle [to expanding and sustaining service programs] is faculty resistance to service-learning. Faculty are reluctant to invest the extra time that teaching service-learning courses entails, and many are skeptical of the educational value of service-learning" (Gray et. al., 1999, p. 103). As a result of research on service-learning, faculty may not only gain a broader understanding of how learning takes place, but also be more likely to support service-learning if they see evidence documenting its educational value.

Method

In this article, we report the results of quantitative analyses which directly compare service-learning and community service. For this purpose we do a longitudinal comparison of three student groups: service-learning participants, "generic" community service participants, and non-service participants.

Participants

The data from this study were collected as part of the Cooperative Institutional Research Program (CIRP), with sponsorship from the American Council on Education. Conducted by the Higher Education Research Institute (HERI) at the University of California, Los Angeles, the CIRP annually collects data on entering first-year students using the Student Information Form (SIF), a questionnaire which is designed as a pre-test for longitudinal assessments of the impact of college on students. The College Student Survey (CSS), which provides longitudinal follow-up data, is typically administered four years after college entry.

This study uses 1998 CSS data, and draws on SIF data from 1991 through 1997. Most students who participated in the 1998 CSS completed their SIF in 1994 (69%). The remaining cases either entered college before 1994 (8%), or were at institutions that administer the CSS to students less than four years after college entry (22%). For instance, some schools administer the CSS to students at the end of their sophomore year. The total number of students in this study is 22,236. Detailed information on the data collection process for the 1998 CSS is available from HERI.

The sample represents most institutional types and selectivity levels, but two-year institutions are only marginally represented, and among four-year institutions, private four-year colleges are over-represented. Table 17.1 shows the number of institutions and students from each institutional type that participated in the study.

Measures

Principal Independent Variables

The main independent variables used in this study come from the 1998 CSS instrument: "generic" community service and "course-based"service (or service-learning). To measure the frequency of "generic"community service, students were asked: "Please indicate how often you performed volunteer work during the past year,"and students could mark *frequently, occasionally,* or *not at all.*

To determine participation in service-learning, students were asked, "Since entering college, have you performed any community/ volunteer service? If yes, how was the service performed?"Students were instructed to mark all that applied: as part of a course or class; as part of a collegiate-sponsored activity (sorority, campus org., etc.); or independently through a non-collegiate group (church, family, etc.). Students who indicated they had performed community/ volunteer service as part of a course (regardless of whether they also marked another choice) were considered to have participated in service-learning.

TABLE 17.1

Description of Study Sample by Institutional Type

Type of Institution	Number of Institutions	Number of Students	% of Sample
Public university	9	2,435	9.7
Private university	12	4,364	17.5
Public College	11	1,317	5.6
Non-sectarian private college	35	4,445	21.2
Catholic college	33	4,338	21.2
Protestant college	71	5,064	23.5
Predominantly Black College	1	111	.5
Public two-year college	3	64	.3
Private two-year college	2	98	.4
Total	177	22,236	100

These two service variables were coded into two partially overlapping variables:

- "Generic"service participation: participated in service (including service-learning) frequently (score 3), occasionally (score 2) or not at all (score 1).
- Service-learning: a dichotomous variable in which those who took one or more service-learning courses (score 2) were contrasted with non-service-learning participants (score 1) (i.e., non-service participants plus community service participants who were not in a service-learning course).

Note that these two variables differ only in the placement of the community service participants who did not take a service-learning course (see below for how these two variables were used in the analysis).

Dependent Variables

Existing research on community service influenced our choice of dependent variables. Since the study seeks to compare the effect of course-based service with the effect of "generic"community service, we chose outcomes that have been shown to be impacted by participation in any type of service.

Given the existing research, we chose eleven dependent measures, reflecting behavioral and cognitive outcomes as well as values and beliefs. Many of these items were pretested when students entered college. Dependent variables include:

Three measures of values and beliefs:

- degree of commitment to the goal of promoting racial understanding (4 = *essential*, 3 = *very important*, 2 = *somewhat important*, 1 = *not important*)
- degree of commitment to activism (see below)
- agreement with the statement "realistically, an individual can do little to bring about changes in our society" (4 = *agree strongly*, 3 = *agree somewhat*, 2 = *disagree somewhat*, 1 = *disagree strongly*);

Three measures of academic skills:

- GPA (grade-point-average)
- growth in writing skills ("compared with when you entered college as a freshman, how would you now describe your writing skills?" 5 = *much stronger*, 4 = *stronger*, 3 = *no change*, 2 = *weaker*, 1 = *much weaker*)

- critical thinking skills ("compared with when you entered college as a freshman, how would you now describe your ability to think critically?" 5 = *much stronger*, 4 = *stronger*, 3 = *no change*, 2 = *weaker*, 1 = *much weaker*);

Three measures of leadership:

- growth in interpersonal skills ("compared with when you entered college as a freshman, how would you now describe your interpersonal skills?" 5 = *much stronger*, 4 = *stronger*, 3 = *no change*, 2 = *weaker*, 1 = *much weaker*)
- leadership activities (see below)
- leadership ability ("compared with when you entered college as a freshman, how would you now describe your leadership abilities?" 5 = *much stronger*, 4 = *stronger*, 3 = *no change*, 2 = *weaker*, 1 = *much weaker*);

And two measures of future plans:

- career choice (see below)
- plans to engage in community service during the forthcoming year (see below).

Several of the dependent variables reflect responses to more than one survey item. Commitment to activism is a composite measure of the eight items listed below. The first seven items are responses (4 = *essential*, 3 = *very important*, 2 = *somewhat important*, 1 = *not important*) to the item "indicate the importance to you personally of each of the following:" The last item (about politics) is a response to, "for the activities listed below, please indicate how often you engaged in each during the past year" (3 = *frequently*, 2 = *occasionally*, 1 = *not at all*)

- influencing the political structure
- influencing social values
- helping others who are in difficulty
- becoming involved in programs to clean up the environment
- participating in a community action program
- keeping up to date with political affairs
- becoming a community leader
- frequency of discussing politics

The activism composite measure was factorially derived (alpha =.8021). The composite measure "leadership activities" was derived in an *a priori* manner, and includes the following dichotomous items:

- participating in student government,
- being elected to student office, and
- participating in leadership training

The composite measure of "plans to engage in community service the following year," also derived in an *a priori* manner, includes:

- plans to do volunteer work, and
- plans to participate in a community service organization.

Other Independent Variables

In addition to the two principal independent variables—"generic" community service participation and taking a service-learning course—several freshman "input" or "control" variables were included in the analysis to minimize the potentially biasing effect of characteristics such as previously held beliefs and high school activities (Astin, 1993). These input variables from the SIF also include pretests for most of the dependent measures on the CSS. In examining writing, critical thinking and leadership ability, we chose to use self-perceived change during college as the dependent measure. Although there is no pretest that would allow us to assess actual change in writing, critical thinking, or leadership ability, we were able to control for self-rated writing ability and leadership ability at the time of college entry. Similarly, since "plan to engage in community service next year" does not have a pre-test on the SIF, we used the freshman response to "plan to engage in volunteer work" (in college) as a proxy.

Since we were interested in isolating the effect of service during college as distinct from antecedent factors that might predispose the student to engage in service, we also controlled for freshman self-selection factors that are known to predict subsequent participation in service (Astin & Sax, 1998; Sax, Astin & Astin, 1996). These eight variables include: sex (women are more likely than men to participate), doing volunteer work in high school, tutoring another student, attending religious services, being a guest in teacher's home, commitment to participating in a community action program, endorsing "to make more money" as a reason for attending college (which is a *negative* predictor), and self-rated leadership ability. We also controlled for freshman student characteristics such as religious preference (4 dichotomous variables), parental education and income, and race (8 dichotomous variables), because some of the outcome measures may be affected by these characteristics (Astin, 1993).

In addition to entering student characteristics, activities and attitudes, we controlled for a set of college environmental variables, reflecting differences in college size, type and control. This was done in order to make sure that any observed effects of community service and service-learning are not confused with the environmental effect of attending a given kind of college. The nine institutional variables used in the regression are measures of institutional selectivity, size, and seven dichotomous variables reflecting type/control combinations (private university, public university, public college, non-sectarian college, Catholic college, Protestant college, and Historically Black College/University).

Data Analyses

The purpose of the study was to see if participating in service as part of an academic course has any effects on each of the 11 outcome measures beyond those of "generic" community service. A secondary objective of the study is to replicate previously reported effects of service participation using a new sample of students and several new outcome measures.

For these purposes we utilized a method of causal modeling which uses blocked, stepwise linear regression analysis to study the changes in partial regression coefficients for all variables at each step in the analysis (Astin, 1991). The advantage of this form of analysis is that it allows us to observe and understand the effects of multicollinearity—especially involving the variables representing community service and service-learning—in a complex longitudinal data set.

The approach we used enables us to view each step or block in a stepwise regression as a new model, different from the previous steps or blocks because of the newly added variable in the model. We can see how the new variable or block of variables affects the relationship of the dependent variable to every other variable, both in and out of the model. All such changes in relationships can be seen because SPSS has a feature that computes the "Beta in" for each such variable. "Beta in" shows what the standardized regression coefficient for a nonentered variable would be if it were the variable entered on the next step. By tracking step-by-step changes in Betas (for variables already in the model) and in "Beta-ins" (for variables not yet in the model), we can understand how multicollinearity is affecting the entire data set. Because community service and service-learning are treated as independent measures in this study, we are able to examine closely how their relationship with the dependent variable is affected by the entry of every other variable (including each other).

For each of the eleven stepwise regressions in this study, there are thus three blocks of variables in the regression equation: (1) entering freshman (input) variables; (2) variables for college size and type; and (3) variables representing participation in generic community service and in service-learning. By placing all the entering freshman variables in the first block, we controlled for pre-test differences on each outcome measure as well as for each individual's predisposition to engage in service—the self-selection bias.

We entered our primary independent variables in the third block: "generic" community service and service-learning. As already noted, the service-learning variable is a dichotomous measure of whether the student participated in service as part of a course, and the "generic" community service reflects any kind of community service experience, including service-learning.

A separate analysis was conducted for each dependent measure. All subjects who were missing data on either the dependent measure, the pre-test of the dependent measure, or the primary independent variables (community service and service-learning) were excluded from the analysis. The final sample sizes thus ranged from 19,268 to 20,254. Analyses used a very stringent confidence level ($p < .001$) to select input variables in each regression, except for the career choice regressions, for which we used subsamples. The confidence levels for all regressions are noted in the results tables.

Results and Discussion

Of the 22,236 students in our study, 29.9% indicated that they had participated in course-based community service (service-learning), an additional 46.5% reported participation in some other form of community service (the sum of these two define "generic" community service participation), and 23.6% said they did not participate in any community service during college. Service-learning participants were more likely to say they performed volunteer work *frequently* (28.5%) compared to those who participated in non-course-based community service (22.7%).

Confirming earlier research (Astin & Sax, 1998), we found that there were certain characteristics that pre-dispose students to participation in community service. Among the strongest predictors of participation in community service are volunteering in high school, being a woman, tutoring other students in high school, expressing a commitment to participate in community action programs, attending religious services, and not placing a high priority on making money.

In addition to confirming earlier research on the predictors of service, this study affirms some earlier findings about the *effects* of service participation. All eleven student outcomes are positively affected both by community service and by taking service-learning courses, even after "inputs" and "environments" (entering characteristics and institutional type) are controlled. We will briefly discuss these overall findings, and then address affective, academic, leadership and future plans outcomes in more detail.

In some cases—most notably with certain affective outcomes—community service appears to have a stronger effect than does service-learning.[2] Moreover, while both of these participation measures show significant partial correlations with the affective outcomes after inputs and college-type variables are controlled, for the self-efficacy and leadership outcomes the partial regression coefficient for service-learning shrinks to nonsignificance when generic service is entered into the equation. In other words, for these outcomes, the effect of service-learning is accounted for by the fact that students who engage in service-learning are also participating in generic community service.

In such comparisons between the effects of community service and service-learning, it is important to keep in mind a couple of considerations. First, service-learning is still an emerging form of pedagogy for faculty. Some faculty may not conduct service-learning well, or service placements might not work out for some students; we have not attempted to assess the quality of the service experience in these analyses. Given the range of such experiences that students might have, the possible effect of participating in a service-learning course may not be as strong as it might be if only "excellent" service-learning courses were analyzed.

Second, elements that make course-based service a potentially powerful pedagogy can also be found in some "generic" community service. For instance, co-curricular leadership development programs that require service might also have a strong reflection component (such as structured discussions with a student affairs professional). In such cases, one might expect the outcomes of such an experience to resemble outcomes that would be expected in service-learning courses, especially for the affective outcomes. These kinds of issues are important when comparing the effects of service-learning with those of community service.

Despite these considerations, there are a few outcomes for which service-learning is a stronger predictor than is community service. Further, for all academic outcomes as well as for some affective ones, participating in service as part of a course has a positive effect over and above the effect of generic community service. Service-learning participation is also a clearly superior predictor of choosing a service-related career, exhibiting a stronger effect than generic community service in almost all career-choice analyses. We now discuss each group of outcomes in more detail.

Values and Beliefs

We have intentionally chosen affective measures that reflect social concern and interest in civic engagement. In this way, our research directly addresses the extent to which community service and service-learning are tools that higher education can use to strengthen democracy by fostering a sense of civic responsibility and community participation in students.

Two of the three measures of values—"commitment to promoting racial understanding" and "commitment to activism"—are significantly affected by participation in course-based service over generic community service. A third outcome—the belief that an individual can effect change in our society—is impacted by service, but service-learning shows a significant effect only until generic service is controlled. In other words, service-learning does strengthen a student's sense of social self-efficacy, but only because it provides an opportunity to do community service. In this connection, it is important to realize that service-learning *would* have shown a significant direct effect on this belief if generic community service had not been included in the analysis.[3] Table 17.2 shows the Beta values at the end of each regression block for the outcome measures.

That service-learning has an independent effect both on a student's commitment to promoting racial understanding and activism is noteworthy. This suggests that service-learning provides a concrete means by which institutions of higher education can educate students to become concerned and involved citizens. (Recall that our measure of activism includes such things as helping others who are in difficulty, influencing the political structure, influencing social values and participating in community action programs.) In short, while participating in community service positively affects these values, participating in course-based service can strengthen them even more.

TABLE 17.2

Affective Outcomes: Community Service (c/s) and Service-Learning (s/l) Beta Values

	Simple r		Beta after Controlling for: Inputs		Institutional Environment		Service (Final step)	
Outcome	c/s	s/l	c/s	s/l	c/s	s/l	c/s	s/l
Commitment to Activism N=19,789	.28	.11	19	07	19	07	18	03
Promoting Racial Understanding N=19,439	.19	.10	12	06	12	06	11	04
Self-efficacy N=19,268	.15	.07	09	03	09	03	09	01*

Note: Unless indicated, all coefficients are significant at the $p < .001$ level of confidence. Decimals omitted from Beta coefficients. *$p < .05$

Academic Outcomes

One of the most interesting findings of our study is the positive effect that participating in service has on all the academic outcomes: growth in critical thinking and in writing skills and college GPA (grade-point average). Table 17.3 shows the Beta values for community service and service-learning at the end of each of the three blocks of these regression analyses.

For all three academic outcomes, both community service and service-learning have a significant effect after controlling for "inputs" (including entering characteristics such as high school GPA) and institutional type. In other words, both kinds of service are associated with greater self-reported gains both in critical thinking and in writing skills, and higher college GPAs.

Of particular significance is the finding that service-learning has an effect on all these cognitive outcomes that is independent of the effect of community service. This is different from what we found with the affective outcomes just discussed, where the impact of service-learning is largely due to the fact that it provides an opportunity to engage in community service. In fact, for both writing skills and college GPA, the effect of service-learning is *stronger* than that of generic community service. Since these outcomes are academic in nature, one might expect that course-based service would provide benefits beyond those of generic community service. Though the differences are modest, it is important to keep in mind that we have not limited our analysis to what might be considered "ideal" service-learning courses (where academic learning and the service are both meaningful and connected in clear ways).

The reason that students who participate in service-learning courses exhibit higher GPAs is not entirely clear. Could it be that service-learning courses tend to be "easy" courses, that is, graded on a more lenient basis than other courses? While it may seem far-fetched to argue that a course or two will significantly improve a student's overall GPA, could it be that students who take service-learning courses tend to enroll in other courses that are "easy" as well?[4] Another explanation, of course, is that participating in service-learning helps to get students more engaged in the overall academic experience, thereby enhancing their overall academic performance. Clearly, these alternative interpretations need to be tested in further research.

Taken together, these findings present powerful evidence to suggest that *connecting service with academic course material does indeed enhance the development of cognitive skills.* In other words, even if the only goal of coursework is to strengthen students' cognitive development, this study suggests that service-learning has a place in the curriculum, and should not be relegated solely to co-curricular efforts.

TABLE 17.3

Academic Outcomes: Community Service (c/s) and Service-Learning (s/l) Beta Values

			Beta after Controlling for					
	Simple r		Inputs		Institutional Environment		Service (Final step)	
Outcome	c/s	s/l	c/s	s/l	c/s	s/l	c/s	s/l
Critical Thinking Skills N=20,129	.09	.07	07	06	06	04	06	03
Writing Skills N=19,974	.06	.07	04	06	03	04	02*	04
College GPA N=19,972	.08	.10	04	07	03	04	02	04

Note: Unless indicated, all coefficients are significant at the $p < .001$ level of confidence. Decimals omitted from Beta coefficients. $^{*}p < .01$

Leadership Outcomes

The leadership measures we examined—growth in leadership *ability*, involvement in leadership *activities* (being elected to student government office, participating in student office or participating in leadership training) and self-perceived growth in interpersonal skills—do not appear to benefit more from a service-learning experience than from involvement in generic community service. Service-learning does not retain its significance once generic service enters the regression, primarily because the effect of generic service is so strong. (The final coefficients for service-learning reach the .01 level of confidence for leadership ability and leadership activities, but not the .001 level.) See Table 17.4 for the Beta values of the leadership measures at key points in the regression analysis.

One possible explanation of these results is that academic courses incorporating service-learning focus more on cognitive skill development (critical thinking, writing, etc.) than on the development of leadership and interpersonal skills. Another possible explanation is that co-curricular leadership development programs (in contrast to service-learning courses) may in many cases be designed and operated by the students themselves, thereby affording them an opportunity to develop leadership skills not present in most service-learning courses. Or, co-curricular service programs designed to enhance leadership development may be designed more like service-learning courses, thereby producing the same effects in students.

Career Outcomes and Plans for Future Service

Choosing a service-related career is more strongly affected by participating in community service and by service-learning than most other student outcomes. For the preliminary descriptive analyses, freshman career choices were grouped into two kinds of service-related careers:

- medical careers (clinical psychologist, dentist, nurse, optometrist, physician and therapist),
- non-medical service careers (elementary, secondary or college teacher, clergy, forester/ conservationist, foreign service, law enforcement, school counselor, and principal).

Table 17.5 shows that students who participate in community service—regardless of freshman year career choice—are more likely than their nonparticipant classmates to say they plan to pursue a service-related career on the post-test. Moreover, those students who complete their service as part

TABLE 17.4

Leadership Measures: Community Service (c/s) and Service-Learning (s/l) Beta Values

	Simple r		Beta after Controlling for: Inputs		Institutional Environment		Service (Final step)	
Outcome	c/s	s/l	c/s	s/l	c/s	s/l	c/s	s/l
Leadership Ability N=20,254	.21	.09	18	07	17	05	17	02[a]
Leadership Activities N=20,046	.25	.10	18	06	17	05	17	02[b]
Interpersonal Skills N=20,124	.14	.07	11	05	10	03	10	01[c]

Note: Unless otherwise indicated, all coefficients are statistically significant at the $p < .001$ level of confidence. Decimals omitted from Beta coefficients. [a] .01 $p < .05$ [b] .001 $p < .01$ [c] $p > .05$

TABLE 17.5

Effects of Service Participation on Choosing a Service Career

Freshman Career Choice	Percent Choosing Service Career Four Years Later Among: Service-Learning Participants	Other Volunteers	Students
Medical n=3942	71.3 (n=987)	64.4 (n=1226)	54.7 (n=357)
Non-Medical Service N=3177	78.7 (n=1022)	68.2 (n=901)	60.6 (n=337)
Non-service N=7604	19.1 (n=380)	13.1 (n=488)	10.3 (n=223)
"other" N=1374	43.5 (n=176)	28.6 (n=178)	24.4 (n=85)
undecided N=2635	41.3 (n=318)	27.8 (n=345)	18.5 (n=116)
All Freshmen N=18,732	29.8 N=5,585	47.0 N=8,806	23.2 N=4,341

Note: N's in parentheses do not sum to row or column totals because of missing data. Decimals omitted from Beta coefficients.

of a course exhibit the most dramatic shifts in career choice. For example, among those 3,942 students who indicated on the Freshman Survey that they were interested in pursuing a medical career, 71.3% of those who participated in service-learning confirmed their commitment to a service related career on the follow-up survey; of those who were engaged in generic community service, 64.4% maintained their initial commitment, while among other students only 54.7% maintained their freshman commitment to a service-related career. The differences among the 2,635 freshman "undecided" students are particularly remarkable: 41.3% of those who engaged in service-learning during college planned to pursue a service-related career on the follow-up, compared to only 18.5 of undecided students who didn't participate in service.

The regression results for "plans to participate in community service" mirror those for the values and beliefs we examined, in that generic community service is the stronger predictor. However, in this case, service-learning maintains a unique (though slight) direct affect on the outcome measure. Not surprisingly, participation in (any kind of) service during college is a powerful predictor of plans to do so in the future.

Career choice regression analyses are limited to the sub-group of students for whom we had post-test career choice information. Since the dependent measure is necessarily dichotomous (chose a service career or a non-service career), we made a decision to eliminate the cases who marked "other" or "undecided" on the follow-up survey.

Because the various career-choice groups looked so different in our preliminary descriptive analyses, we chose to run four separate regressions, one each for:

1. the entering group that planned to pursue service-related careers (medical and non-medical were combined),
2. the group planning non-service-related careers as freshmen,
3. the group who chose "other" on the freshman survey and
4. those who marked "undecided" on the freshman survey.

Table 17.6 shows the regression results for these four career-choice groups.

TABLE 17.6

Service & Career Plans: Community Service (c/s) and Service-Learning (s/l) Beta Values

	Simple r		**Beta after Controlling for**					
			Inputs		**Institutional Environment**		**Service (Final step)**	
Outcome	c/s	s/l	c/s	s/l	c/s	s/l	c/s	s/l
Service plans next yr. N=20,254; $p < .001$	.31	.09	28	06	26	07	16	02
service career SIF* service N=5,671; $p < .005$	.12	.13	12	09	12	09	11	07
service career SIF* non-service N=6,068; $p < .005$	.12	.14	12	09	11	08	09	05
service career SIF* "other" N=814; $p < .01$	.19	.18	13	15	13	15	10	15
service career SIF* "undecided" N=1,662; $p < .01$	.23	.20	19	17	19	17	16	13

* SIF = freshman survey. *Note:* Decimals omitted from Beta coefficients.

Service-learning appears to impact these career outcomes in two different ways. First, it affects students' career choices indirectly by providing an opportunity to participate in generic community service. This indirect effect is evidenced by the decrease in the Beta value for service-learning that occurs when community service enters the regression. For example, in the regression for undecided students, the coefficient for service-learning after controlling for inputs and institutional characteristics is .17, but drops to .13 when community service enters the regression. So service-learning has a unique ("direct") effect on initially undecided students, but also a weaker ("indirect") effect that is shared with community service. This same shared effect is evidenced in the case of generic community service, where the Betas show a decrease from .19 to .16 when service-learning enters the equation. However, the fact that the Betas for service-learning in all four groups retain most of their size even after community service is controlled suggests that service-learning's primary effect on career choice is a direct one.

Given that one's career choice often represents a lifelong commitment that consumes a large part of one's waking hours, there is perhaps no stronger expression of commitment to service than to choose a career that is service-based. Thus, the positive effects of service-learning on the student's career choice may well represent the most significant finding to emerge from this inquiry.

Limitations and Future Research

Perhaps the greatest limitation of this study is that the quality of the community service and classroom experiences are not measured, and as Eyler and Giles' (1999) research suggests, "the quality of the service-learning makes a difference" (p. 187). Echoing other researchers and practitioners (Mabry, 1998; Zlotkowski, 1996), we suggest that future research focus on the specifics of the service experience.[5] For instance, how do factors such as training, type of experience, and length of experience affect student development?

Second, this study examines outcomes from the perspective of the student (self-reported measures). Research that provides different perspectives—faculty assessment of learning or standardized assessments—will also benefit our understanding of how learning takes place. The self-efficacy measures in this study are not intended to substitute for independently assessed skills, though one would expect the two to be related (e.g., one who believes he/she has good leadership skills is likely to become more effective than one who doesn't). Research examining the validity of self-reported growth in cognitive learning in general suggests that self-reported growth is related to cognitive constructs (Anaya, 1999). A more detailed study of critical thinking in particular offers support for the use of self-reports to measure this construct (Tsui, 1999).

The analyses conducted on the academic outcomes in this study only begin to enhance our understanding of how students participating in service learning can benefit from the experience. There is still a need to understand how the learning of various disciplines might be enhanced by service-learning. This concern is being addressed directly by the American Association for Higher Education (AAHE) Series on Service-Learning in the Disciplines. There is also a need to better understand how different kinds of students might benefit (e.g. does race or gender matter?), and the benefits of placing a service-learning experience at different points in a student's college experience (e.g. first-year experience, in the major, or throughout the college years).

Conclusion

The results of this study add weight to the belief that course-based service has benefits over and above those of "generic" community service. Because it is a longitudinal study, we have been able to control for many student and institutional characteristics which predispose students to participate in service, and which may shape the service-learning experience. Even when such student and institutional characteristics were controlled, service-learning has a significant effect on all eleven outcomes examined.

Notes

This research was funded in part by an anonymous donor.

The authors gratefully acknowledge the work of Elaine K. Ikeda and Jennifer A. Yee, who were part of a larger research project on the effects of service-learning, and who gave valuable feedback on earlier drafts of these findings.

1. For this study, we define service-learning as service done as part of a course or class.
2. In most cases this difference may be attributed simply to the greater variance in generic community service.
3. Here we have a clear demonstration of the "multicollinearity problem:" Our conclusion about whether a particular variable (i.e., course-based service-learning) "affects" any given outcome may depend on what *other* variables (i.e., generic service) are included in the analysis of that outcome.
4. Further analyses of these data suggest that college major does not play a significant mediating role between service-learning and college GPA (Astin, Vogelgesang, Ikeda, and Yee., 2000).
5. For a discussion of the effects of reflection on this particular set of students, see Astin, Vogelgesang, Ikeda & Yee (2000).

References

Anaya, G. (1999). College impact on student learning: Comparing the use of self-reported gains, standardized test scores, and college grades. *Research in Higher Education, 40* (5), 499–524.

Astin, A. W. (1991). *Assessment for excellence: The philosophy and practice of assessment and evaluation in higher education.* New York: Macmillan/Onyx.

Astin, A. W. (1993). *What matters in college? Four critical years revisited.* San Francisco, CA: Jossey-Bass.

Astin, A. W. & Sax, L. J. (1998). How undergraduates are affected by service participation. *Journal of College Student Development, 39* (3), 251–263.

Astin, A.W., Sax, L.J., & Avalos, J. (1999). Long-term effects of volunteerism during the undergraduate years. *The Review of Higher Education, 22* (2), 187–202.

Astin, A.W., Vogelgesang, L.J., Ikeda, E.K. & Yee, J.A. (2000). *How Service Learning Affects Students.* Los Angeles: University of California Los Angeles, Higher Education Research Institute.

Batchelder, T. H. & Root, S. (1994). Effects of an undergraduate program to integrate academic learning and service: Cognitive, prosocial cognitive, and identity outcomes. *Journal of Adolescence, 17*(4), 341–355.

Eyler, J. & Giles Jr., D. E. (1999). *Where's the learning in service-learning?* San Francisco: Jossey-Bass.

Eyler, J., Giles Jr., D. E., & Braxton, J. (1997). The impact of service-learning on college students. *Michigan Journal of Community Service Learning, 4*, 5–15.

Gray, M. J., Ondaatje, E., Fricker, R., Geschwind, S., Goldman, C. A., Kaganoff, T. Robyn, A., Sundt, M., Vogelgesang, L., & Klein, S. P. (1999). *Combining Service and Learning in Higher Education: Evaluation of the Learn and Serve America, Higher Education Program.* Santa Monica, CA: RAND.

Hesser, G. (1995). Faculty assessment of student learning: Outcomes attributed to service-learning and evidence of changes in faculty attitudes about experiential education. *Michigan Journal of Community Service Learning, 2*, 33–42.

Mabry, J. B. (1998). Pedagogical variations in service-learning and student outcomes: How time, contact and reflection matter. *Michigan Journal of Community Service Learning, 5*, 32–47.

Rhoads, R. A. (1997). *Community service and higher learning: Explorations of the caring self.* Albany: State University of New York Press.

Sax, L.J., Astin, A.W., & Astin, H.S. (1996). What were LSAHE impacts on student volunteers? Chapter in *Evaluation of Learn and Serve America, Higher Education: First Year Report.* Santa Monica, CA: RAND Corporation.

Tsui, L. (1999). Courses and instruction affecting critical thinking. *Research in Higher Education, 40* (2), 185–200.

Zlotkowski, E. (1996). Linking service-learning and the academy: A new voice at the table? *Change, 28* (1), 20–27.

CHAPTER 18

TECHNOLOGY

Lessons from the Cyberspace Classroom

Rena M. Palloff, Ph.D.
Crossroads Consulting Group and
The Fielding Institute
Alameda, CA

and

Keith Pratt, Ph.D.
Datatel, Inc. and Crossroads Consulting Group
Oklahoma City, OK

Abstract: Teaching in cyberspace involves more than taking traditional teaching models and transferring them to a different medium. The use of online distance learning is creating changes in the delivery of education in general. Changes in online distance learning are also occurring rapidly, predominantly in the way courses are developed and delivered. This paper and session, based on the presenters' experience of over 7 years of online teaching and their two books, *Building Learning Communities in Cyberspace* and *Lessons from the Cyberspace Classroom,* explores best practices in delivering online courses.

Online Distance Learning: More of the Same?

Institutions are rushing to get in on the distance learning craze, many for the wrong reasons. Administrators see it as a way to increase flagging enrollments and extend the reach of the institution or, in simple terms, an easy way to maximize profits. They believe that they will attract students from far beyond their current geographic reach. They also believe that they will save money by not needing as many classrooms and even as many faculty. All faculty need to do is to post their lectures online, right? How difficult can that be?

Many students see online courses as a more convenient way to go to school and even sometimes as a softer, easier way to earn credit. Faculty, however, given the responsibility to develop and teach online courses may not see online education in such a positive light. As they struggle to move materials and pedagogy to the web, faculty complain in ever increasing numbers about the time it takes to effectively teach an online course—a complaint that often goes unheeded.

Regardless of the motivation to engage in online teaching and learning, the use of instructional technology in higher education is having a significant impact in a number of ways. The impacts fall into four broad categories:

- Faculty/Institutional (or administrative) Relationships
- Faculty/Student Relationships

Reprinted from *Proceedings of the 17th Annual Conference on Distance Teaching and Learning* (2001), University of Wisconsin System Board of Regents.

- Student/Institutional Relationships
- How Education is Delivered and Learning Happens

We will now review each of these categories in brief and conclude with the lessons learned from the problems and successes encountered in online learning.

Faculty/Institutional Relationships

One of the major issues facing faculty and their institutions as they prepare to teach online is compensation. Because we know that it takes approximately three times as long to prepare for and teach an online course (Palloff and Pratt, 1999), the question regarding equitable compensation surfaces. At many institutions, faculty are offered incentives for the development of online courses, in the form of stipends, reduced course loads, reimbursement for attending conferences on the topic of online teaching and learning, sabbaticals, etc. However, there are still many institutions where online teaching is considered simply a part of the overall course load or, worse yet, is considered an overload and treated as such. Related to the issue of compensation is that of promotion and tenure. Online teaching is still not treated as scholarly work, although preparing an online course is often likened to writing a textbook on a given topic. Course ownership is another issue that is being hotly debated—who owns a course that has been prepared by a member of the faculty of an institution and taught online, especially if that faculty member has received a stipend for its preparation? There are no easy answers to the questions that surface regarding these issues. However, with good planning and policymaking at the institutional level, problems in these areas can be avoided.

Faculty/Student Relationships

It has been noted in research regarding the students who enroll in online courses, that the online student tends to be a mid-career adult returning to school (Hammonds, Jackson, DeGeorge, and Morris, 1997). The increasingly non-traditional student with life and career experience is not satisfied with a traditional approach to them as students (Carr, 2000). They tend to return to school with career goals in mind and a directed course of study to get them there. Thus, the more typical online student is seeking an active approach to learning and more involvement in the learning process itself. Not content with being *taught to,* the online student seeks to engage with faculty in a more collaborative learning partnership resulting in the achievement of their learning objectives (Palloff and Pratt, 2001). Consequently, the faculty-centered approach found at many institutions of higher education must give way to a more learner-center approach.

Student/Institution Relationships

The demand from online students for increased involvement and responsiveness goes beyond their relationships with faculty to relationships with the institutions in which they enroll. Because they are not on campus and generally have little interest in campus life per se, the needs of the online student are different, but equally in need of attention. Issues such as ease of registration, integration of admission functions, access to library services, and access to advising all must be addressed by the institution in order to effectively retain online students in courses and programs. When their needs are not addressed, online students can become disgruntled and withdraw. Although no comprehensive research exists to date that describes retention issues with online students, it can be assumed that if a solid connection is forged with the institution through the provision of services at a distance, students will be more likely to stay in their online courses and programs.

How Education is Delivered and Learning Happens

The major impact of online education, and the area in which we are seeing the greatest amount of change, is in the area of teaching and learning. The online environment is conducive to an interactive, collaborative, facilitated approach wherein the instructor acts as a guide to the process rather than its director. By paying attention to the development of a learning community, the instructor creates the vehicle through which the learning happens (Palloff and Pratt, 1999; Palloff and Pratt, 2001). Through the development of a learning community, students learn that their greatest and most profound learning comes through reflection and interaction with one another. Dependence on the instructor is reduced and students are empowered to take responsibility for their own learning.

Lessons Learned

As more institutions and their instructors enter the cyberspace classroom and encounter both successes and difficulties in the process, they are coming face-to-face with the realities of online teaching and asking more, not fewer, questions about how to make the transition to this environment successfully. What, then, are the lessons learned from the experiences and noted changes that are occurring as the result of the implementation of online distance learning? How can institutions and instructors more effectively deliver instruction online? And lastly, but probably most important, how can students become effective online learners? The following are suggestions that address these questions:

- **Course development should focus on facilitation and interactivity rather than content.** Often, we are asked how instructors can "teach" the content that is the core of the class. Our response is to reframe the way in which content is delivered. When students are encouraged to embark on a process of discovery with one another, rather than being told what they need to memorize or know, the outcome is a deepening of the learning experience and satisfactory achievement of learning objectives. In general, when students evaluate a class, it is the interactions that they have had with the instructor and with other students that they often cite as the most important aspect of the class (Phipps and Merisotis, 1999). For the online student, this is where the learning occurs.
- **Faculty and student roles need to change.** In order for a high degree of interactivity to occur in a course, faculty need to let go of the control of the course and empower students to take responsibility for the learning process. For this to happen successfully, students need to be oriented to the differences in learning online. A good student orientation to the online environment would include not only training in the courseware used, but also the difference in the role of the instructor and the expectations of the student as a learner. We cannot expect that students will simply know how to learn online or that faculty will know how to teach in this environment. Training for both is essential.
- **Adequate support for faculty and students must be provided.** Many institutions are engaging in creative ways to meet this important need, such as using students to staff a help desk 24/7 or by outsourcing technical support. Regardless of how it is offered, support for both students and faculty is critical to the success of an online course or program. There is nothing more frustrating to a student who is working late at night than to be unable to access the course site. If and when this occurs, help needs to be available.
- **Good institutional planning is critical to the success of online courses and programs.** Rather than simply jumping on the bandwagon with little to no infrastructure, institutions need to engage in an inclusive planning process to address: Policy issues such as faculty compensation and course ownership; infrastructure issues such as the purchase of servers and courseware; the provision of training and support; and the future of online courses and programs in that institution, including a budget that allows for growth and development.

The Challenges

By slowing the process and paying attention to issues of quality, involvement, and empowerment, institutions and their faculties can develop effective online courses and programs that help to develop a culture of lifelong learning for all involved. As James Duderstadt (1999) notes, "Today's technology is rapidly breaking the constraints of space and time. It has become clear that most people, in most areas, can learn—and learn well—using asynchronous learning (that is 'anytime, anyplace, anywhere' education) . . . Lifetime education is becoming a reality, making learning available for anyone who wants to learn, at the time and place of their choice, without great personal effort or cost . . . Rather than an 'age of knowledge,' could we instead aspire to a 'culture of learning,' in which people are continually surrounded by, immersed in, and absorbed in learning experiences? . . This may become not only the great challenge but the compelling vision facing higher education as it enters the next millennium" (pp. 24–25).

References

Carr, S., "As distance education comes of age, the challenge is keeping the students." *Chronicle of higher education.* April 26, 2001.

Duderstadt, J., "Can colleges and universities survive in the information age?" In R. Katz and Associates (eds) (1999), *Dancing with the devil.* San Francisco: Jossey-Bass.

Hammonds, K., Jackson, S., DeGeorge, G. and Morris, K., "The new university: A tough market is reshaping colleges." *Business week,* Dec. 11, 1997. [http://www.businessweek.com/1997/51/b3558139.htm].

Palloff, R. and Pratt, K. (2001), *Lessons from the cyberspace classroom.* San Francisco: Jossey-Bass.

Palloff, R. and Pratt, K. (1999), *Building learning communities in cyberspace.* San Francisco: Jossey-Bass.

Phipps, R. and Merisotis, J. (1999). *What's the difference?* Washington, DC: Institute for Higher Education Policy.

Biographical Sketches

Rena Palloff, Ph.D. is a member of the faculty of the Fielding Institute, teaching in their completely online masters degree program in Organizational Management and Capella University, teaching in the School of Education. She is also an Assistant Professor at John F. Kennedy University, teaching in the Graduate School for Holistic Studies, an adjunct Associate Professor in the Chemical Dependency Studies Department at California State University-Hayward, and an adjunct professor in Samuel Merritt College's program in Health and Human Sciences. **Keith Pratt, Ph.D.** is a Project Manager for Datatel. Keith also teaches at the Fielding Institute, Capella University, California State University-Hayward, John F. Kennedy University, and Samuel Merritt College. In addition, Rena and Keith are the managing partners of Crossroads Consulting Group and the authors of the Frandson Award winning book ***Building Learning Communities in Cyberspace: Effective Strategies for the Online Classroom*** *(Jossey-Bass, 1999)* and ***Lessons from the Cyberspace Classroom: The Realities of Online Teaching*** *(Jossey-Bass, 2001).* The books are based on their many years of teaching experience in the online environment and contain vignettes and case examples from a variety of successful online courses. Drs. Palloff and Pratt have been presenting this work across the United States and internationally since 1994.

Chapter 19

Scholarship of Teaching and Learning as Method

THE SCHOLARSHIP OF TEACHING AND LEARNING AT THE TWO-YEAR COLLEGE: PROMISE AND PERIL

HOWARD TINBERG, DONNA KILLIAN DUFFY, AND JACK MINO

The emergence of the scholarship of teaching and learning (commonly shortened to SoTL) as a viable alternative to traditional scholarship should come as no surprise to readers of *Change.* In recent years the magazine has featured the work of Lee Shulman, Pat Hutchings, Mary Huber, Eileen Bender, and others who have traced the trajectory of this movement. Hutchings and Huber also have begun to map out what an intellectual "commons" generated by this scholarship might look like—including case studies of strong work done in and across a wide variety of disciplines.

None of these scholars, however, has any illusions as to the obstacles facing those who wish to pursue such scholarship—obstacles erected most conspicuously by committees on tenure and promotion, which may be loath to credit anything other than the scholarship of discovery, to use Ernest Boyer's term for basic research.

Such obstacles have persisted despite the very strong case that has been made for teaching as a legitimate object of scholarly inquiry. Like conventional scholarship, as Lee Shulman has pointed out, the scholarship of teaching and learning, while differing from the scholarship of discovery in its focus on the classroom, calls for a systematic investigation of a research question, a survey of the best scholarship on the subject, going public with one's findings in the form of conference presentations and scholarly publication, a "critical review and evaluation" by peers, and the use of such research as a foundation for further work in the field.

But while candid about the various "balancing acts" necessitated by a dual allegiance to the scholarly disciplines and to SoTL, the latter's advocates spend less time on obstacles to change created by the nature of institutions themselves. What distinctive challenges await those of us who teach in public two-year colleges and who wish to engage in SoTL, for example?

Obstacle One: Attitudes Toward Scholarship and Research at the Two-Year College

While logic would suggest that teaching-centered institutions such as two-year colleges would welcome any national movement that paid serious attention to classroom instruction, the reality is otherwise. Where the fight at research-centered universities and college is to valorize teaching as a legitimate subject of scholarship and research, the struggle at two-year colleges is to convince faculty and administrators that intellectual inquiry and scholarly exchange are activities appropriate to the mission of the institutions.

In a sharply utilitarian culture, shaped most recently by calls for accountability and shrinking state support, reflecting on one's teaching and sharing that reflective work with a community of scholars are activities that often are perceived as, at best, luxuries and, at worst, distractions from

Reprinted from *Change* (2007), by permission of Taylor and Francis Group.

the teaching mission of the college. When teachers become researchers, they assume the role of knowledge-makers, adding to what is already known about a subject. But two-year college faculty rarely see themselves in this role. Instead, they are likely to view themselves as transmitters of knowledge or translators of specialized material to novice learners.

Since tenure and promotion at two-year college are typically linked to teaching excellence and college service (required committee work and advising duties), scholarship and research fail to carry the urgency that they do at research-intensive institutions. In the five years during which I (Tinberg) edited a peer-reviewed journal, *Teaching English at the Two-Year College,* I cannot recall one inquiry from a two-year college author on the brink of tenure regarding the readership and editorial policy of the journal—a routine question from authors who are preparing for tenure review at four-year institutions.

Obstacle Two: "Pedagogical Solitude"

If scholars of teaching and learning wish to become true knowledge-builders, they need to "go public" by sharing their findings and methods with colleagues beyond their own institutions. It is only through such an exchange that this scholarship can begin to assemble its own central "texts" and construct foundational thinking about teaching and learning that transcends local circumstances.

But a two-year college teacher/scholar typically works in what Lee Shulman has called "pedagogical solitude." With work routines driven by a relentless teaching schedule that leaves little time to meet with colleagues (two-year faculty usually teach five sections per term), and with conference travel money modest at best, two-year college faculty struggle to break through that solitude, despite the opportunities for exchange afforded by electronic forums such as listservs and blogs.

What Two-Year College Faculty Bring to the Scholarship of Teaching and Learning

So I do not minimize all the challenges facing two-year college faculty who wish to engage in the scholarship of teaching and learning. But I propose a sea-change in the way they view their work. Inquiry, reflection, and critical exchange ought not to be "add-ons" to that work; rather, these need to be at its center (with all the recognition for such work that institutions can provide). I'd even add that without such introspection and collaboration, teaching becomes more labor intensive, not to mention less rewarding, because it is less informed.

But such an argument does not touch upon two critical reasons that two-year college faculty need to engage in SoTL. The first is to represent in a capable and authentic way the range of student accomplishment, from the mediocre to the truly sterling, that we see at the two-year college. With the bulk of these students fully capable to holding their own at four-year colleges, they can achieve great things if faculty keep the bar high and construct the scaffolding that makes student success possible.

The second reason is to raise the intellectual profile of two-year college faculty and teaching within higher education and among the public at large. With the opportunities afforded by small classes and close attention to individual students learning needs—both hallmarks of two-year-college instruction—faculty at these colleges have extraordinary advantages as teacher/scholars. And then students—most of whom have working lives outside the college—bring with them richly textured experience that could provide equally rich contexts for study and research.

A Potential Area for Research: Integrative Learning

Two-year college faculty have another advantage over their four-year colleagues when embarking on the scholarship of teaching and learning: the mission of the two-year college. With its focus on general education as well as the promotion of workplace and civic literacy, the faculty who teach there have few disciplinary axes to grind. They are not generally expected to publish papers on conventional scholarship rooted in specific disciplines, relying on discipline-sanctioned methods of research. They are instead defined as teachers first and specialists second.

While that fact may at times contribute to the crisis of professionalism to which I alluded above, it may also make it easier for faculty to engage in new forms of scholarship that require crossing disciplinary boundaries, as SoTL does. If, as Mary Huber and Pat Hutchings of the Carnegie Foundation for the Advancement of Teaching observe, "one of the great challenges in higher education is to foster students' abilities to integrate their learning across contexts and over time," then two-year colleges have a significant role to play in "mapping the terrain" of a new educational landscape.

I'm not saying that this task will be easy, not by a long shot—especially in light of the various pressures placed on two-year colleges to conform to the curricular norms of transfer institutions and to prepare students for the exigencies of the workplace. But it makes perfectly good sense to expect a two-year college faculty member in biology to ask—as Crima Pogge at the City College of San Francisco has in her Carnegie-supported research project, "Is There A Need for 'Culturing' Ecology Education?"—whether there is a way to determine the impact of students diverse backgrounds on their views of ecological conservation. It makes just as much sense for Mike Burke, a mathematics faculty member at the College of San Matco, to ask his students to apply scientific thinking—in the form of mathematical models—to such pressing social problems as global warming and population growth. Both Pogge and Burke have taken to heart the gold of creating opportunities for students to, in E.M. Forster's famous phrase, "Only connect."

The same integrative model of teaching and learning that can be the two-year college's contribution to the scholarship of teaching and learning might also serve as a powerful means of promoting improved articulation between two- and four-year institutions. If students emerge from integrative learning experiences at the two-year college with an enhanced ability to solve problems by drawing upon perspectives and methods from a variety of disciplines, they are primed to succeed at four-year institutions that have a commitment to interdisciplinary general education. Moreover, faculty at two- and four-year institutions who practice and study integrative teaching and learning have a fruitful basis for dialogue and an exchange of ideas.

Three Carnegie Scholars Report on Their Research

To demonstrate what the scholarship of teaching and learning looks like within the context of the two-year college, I offer descriptions of three projects done under the auspices of the Carnegie Academy for the Support of Teaching and Learning (CASTL) with additional support from our institutions.

The View Ahead

Given the challenges of the two-year college setting, particularly the burdensome workloads of community-college faculty, a creative approach to scholarship is required. A common thread that runs through all the projects highlighted in this essay is the embedded nature of their research strategies. From Duffy's "resiliency" model of mental illness to my table of reading to Mino's mechanisms of integration, the research methods function as instructional methods, not just data-gathering strategies. Teaching and research go hand in hand.

The scholarship of teaching and learning promises two-year college faculty recognition as bona fide teacher/scholars. The importance of such recognition cannot be overstated as two-year college faculty continue their struggle to construct an identity as higher-education professionals. If these faculty play to their strengths—their intense engagement with students, their passion for teaching and learning—the research possibilities afforded by SoTL are rich indeed. Moreover, their enhanced identity as both teachers and scholars may assist two-year college faculty in forming collegial partnerships with their counterparts at four-year institutions who are similarly committed to scholarly exchanges.

But challenges remain to complicate matters for two-year college teachers, most fundamentally the threat of becoming production workers with little time for reflection, instead of teaching professionals whose work is continually reviewed, shared, and revised. Administrators and faculty alike need to create a far more complex and productive vision of the two-year college teacher/scholar than exists today. That vision ought to include time for inquiry, discovery, and collegial exchange—all the critical components of the scholarship of teaching and learning.

Resources

Bender, E. "CASTLs in the Air: The SoTL Movement in Mid-Flight." *Change.* (Sept. 2005) 37.5: 40–49.

Boyer, E. L. *Scholarship Reconsidered: Priorities of the Professoriate.* Princeton, NJ: The Carnegie Foundation for the Advancement of Teaching, 1990.

Burke, M. "Integrative Learning in the Mathematics Classroom: June 2006 Snapshot." Carnegie Foundation, 12 July 2006, 5 June 2006. http://sakai.cfkeep.org/html/snapshot.php?id=83270972392774

Duffy, D. K. "Service-Learning, Resilience, and Community: The Challenges of Authentic Assessment." In D. S. Dunn. C. M. Mehrotra, and J. S. Halonen, Eds. *Measuring Up: Educational Assessment Challenges and Practices for Psychology.* Washington, DC: American Psychological Association, 2004: 243–256.

(Forthcoming). "Service-Learning as a Pathway to The Scholarship of Teaching And Learning." In *Course Design Guidebook.* Providence, RI: Campus Compact.

Grubb, W. N. *Honored But Invisible: An Inside Look at Community Colleges.* New York: Routledge, 1999.

Huber, M. T. and P. Hutchings. *The Advancement of Learning: Building the Teaching Commons.* San Francisco: Jossey-Bass, 2006.

Levin, J. S., S. Kater, and R. L. Wagoner. *Community College Faculty: At Work in the New Economy.* New York: Palgrave Macmillan, 2006.

Pogge, C. "Is There A Need For 'Culturing' Ecology Education? February 2006 Snapshot." Carnegie Foundation. 12 July 2006. 2 March 2006. http://sakai.cfkeep.org/html/snapshot.php?id=17752376308434

Shulman, L. S. *Teaching As Community Property: Essays on Higher Education.* San Francisco, CA: Jossey-Bass, 2004.

Tinberg, H. *Border Talk: Writing and Knowing in the Two-Year College.* Urbana, IL. National Council of Teachers of English, 1997.

Vess, D. and S. Linkon. "Navigating the Interdisciplinary Archipelago: The Scholarship of Interdisciplinary Teaching and Learning." In Huber, M. T. & S. P. Morreale, Eds. *Disciplinary Styles in the Scholarship of Teaching and Learning: Exploring Common Ground.* Washington, DC: American Association of Higher Education and The Carnegie Foundation for the Advancement of Teaching, 2002: 87–106.

Part IV—Methods: Choosing the Best Strategies and Techniques

Recommended Readings

Albers, C. (2003). Using the syllabus to document the scholarship of teaching and learning. *Teaching Sociology, 31*, 60–72.

Altany, A. (2001). Teaching: Emptiness, compassion, failures, & the art of disappearing. *The National Teaching and Learning Forum, 10*(5), 4–5.

Backx, C. (2008). The use of a case study approach to teaching and group work to promote autonomous learning, transferable skills and attendance. *Practice and Evidence of Scholarship of Teaching and Learning in Higher Education, 3*(1), 68–83.

Bain, K. (2004). *What the best college teachers do.* Cambridge, MA: Harvard University Press.

Baiocco, S. A. & DeWaters, J. N. (1998). *Successful college teaching: Problem-solving strategies of distinguished professors.* Old Tappan, NJ: Allyn & Bacon, Prentice Hall.

Barkley, E., Cross, K. P., & Major, C. H. (2004). *Collaborative learning techniques: A handbook for college faculty.* San Francisco, CA: Jossey-Bass.

Bash, L. (Ed.). (2005). *Best practices in adult learning.* Bolton, MA: Anker.

Bates, A. W., & Poole, G. (2003). *Effective teaching with technology in higher education: Foundations for success.* San Francisco, CA: Jossey-Bass.

Baume, D., & Beaty, L. (2006). Developing pedagogic research. *Educational Developments, 7*(2), 1–6.

Baxter Magolda, M. B. (1999). *Creating contexts for learning and self-authorship.* Nashville, TN: Vanderbilt University Press.

Bean, J. (2001). *Engaging ideas: The professor's guide to integrating writing, critical thinking, and active learning in the classroom.* San Francisco, CA: Jossey-Bass.

Benjamin, J. (2000). The scholarship of teaching in teams: What does it look like in practice? *Higher Education Research and Development, 19*, 191–204.

Berge, Z. L. (Ed.). (2001). *Sustaining distance education: Integrating learning technology into the fabric of the enterprise.* San Francisco, CA: Jossey-Bass.

Bernstein, D. J., Nelson, A., Goodburn, A., & Savory, P. (2006). *Making teaching and learning visible: Course portfolios and the peer review of teaching.* San Francisco, CA: Jossey-Bass/Anker.

Bligh, D. (2000). *What's the use of lectures?* San Francisco, CA: Jossey-Bass.

Blumberg P. (2009). *Developing learner-centered teaching: A practical guide for faculty.* San Francisco, CA: Jossey-Bass.

Boice, R. (1996). *First-order principles for college teachers.* Bolton, MA: Anker.

Bonwell C., & Sutherland, T. (Eds.). (1996). *Using active learning in college classes: A range of options for faculty.* San Francisco, CA: Jossey-Bass.

Boud, D., & Feletti, G. (1997). *The challenge of problem-based learning* (2nd ed.). London, UK: Kogan Page.

Boyle, E., & Rothstein, H. (2003). *Essentials of college and university teaching: A practical guide.* Stillwater, OK: New Forums Press.

Breivek, P. S. (2005). 21st century learning and information literacy. *Change, 37*(2) 20–27.

Brew, A., & Ginns, P. (2007). The relationship between engagement in the scholarship of teaching and learning and students' course experiences. *Assessment & Evaluation in Higher Education, 33*(5), 535–545.

Brookfield, S. D. & Preskill, S. (1999). *Discussion as a way of teaching.* San Francisco: Jossey-Bass.

Brookfield, S. D. (2005). *The power of critical theory: Liberating adult learning and teaching.* San Francisco, CA: Jossey-Bass.

Brown, D. G. (2000). *Interactive learning.* Bolton, MA: Anker Publishing Company, Inc.

Bush, L., Maid, B., & Roen, D. (2003). A matrix for reconsidering, reassessing, and shaping e-learning pedagogy and curriculum. In C. M. Wehlburg & S. Chadwick-Blossey (Eds.), *To Improve the Academy: Vol. 21, Resources for Faculty, Instructional, and Organizational Development* (pp. 302–318). Bolton, MA: Anker.

Campbell, W. E., & Smith, K. A. (1997). *New paradigms for college teaching.* Edina, MN: Interaction Book Company.

Cannon, R., & Newble, D. (2000). *A handbook for teachers in universities and colleges: a guide to improving teaching methods* (4th ed.). London: Kogan Page.

Cantor, J. A. (1995). *Experiential learning in higher education: Linking classroom and community.* ASHE-ERIC Higher Education Report No. 7. Washington, DC: The George Washington University, Graduate School of Education and Human Development.

Carrell, L. (2007). A scholarly teaching adventure. . . . *International Journal for the Scholarship of Teaching and Learning, 1*(2). http://www.georgiasouthern.edu/ijsotl

Colby, A., Ehrlich, T., Beaumont, E., & Stephens, J. (2003). *Educating citizens: Preparing America's undergraduates for lives of moral and civic responsibility.* San Francisco, CA: Jossey-Bass.

Collison, G., Elbaum, B., Haavind, S., & Tinker, R. (2000). *Facilitating online learning: Effective strategies for moderators.* Madison, WI: Atwood.

Conrad, R.M. (2004). *Engaging the online learner.* San Francisco, CA: Jossey-Bass.

Cooper, W. (2003). Cyberphilosophy, learning cells, and distance education. In M. M. Watts (Ed.), *New Directions for Teaching and Learning: No 94, Technology: Taking the Distance out of Learning* (pp. 83–87). San Fransciso, CA: Jossey-Bass.

Cooper, J. L., MacGregor, J., & Smith, K. A. (Eds.). (2000). *New Directions for Teaching and Learning: No. 81, Implementing small group instruction: Insights from successful practitioners* (pp. 63–76). San Francisco, CA: Jossey-Bass.

Cross, K. P. (2006). Teaching for the sake of learning. *Change, 38*(3), 5.

Davis, J. R. (1993). *Better teaching, more learning: Strategies for success in postsecondary settings.* Phoenix, AZ: America Council on Education and The Oryx Press.

Delisle, R. (1997). *How to use problem-based learning in the classroom.* Alexandria, VA: Association for Supervision and Curriculum Development.

Dennick, R., & Exley, K. (2004). *Small group teaching: Tutorials, seminars and beyond (Effective teaching in higher education series).* London, UK: Routledge Falmer.

Dewey, J. (1938). *Experience and education.* New York, NY: Collier Books.

Dille, B. (2005). The impact of community-based research on student learning. In S. K. Miller & J. Moore (Eds.), *Transforming practice through reflective scholarship* (pp. 127–133). Tempe, AZ: Maricopa Center for Learning and Instruction.

Dinan, F. J. (2006). Opening day: Getting started in the cooperative classroom. *Journal of College Science Teaching, 35*(4), 12–14.

Dolmans, D. H. F. H., Wolfhagen, I. H. A. P., van der Vleuten, C. P. M., & Wijnen, W. H. F. W. (2001). Solving problems with group work in problem-based learning. *Medical Education, 35,* 884–889.

Dorman, W. (2004). Scholarship of teaching and learning: Affecting students' points of view in a survey of methods class. *Communication Education, 53,* 274–280.

Driscoll, A., Glemon, S. B., Holland, B. A., Kerrigan, S., & Spring, A. (2001). *Assessing service-learning and civic engagement: Principles and techniques.* Providence, RI: Campus Compact.

Duffy, T. M., & Kirkley, J. R. (Eds.). (2004). *Learner centered theory and practice in distance education cases from higher education.* Mahwah, NJ: Lawrence Erlbaum and Associates.

Dwyer, C. (2001). Linking research and teaching: A staff-student interview project. *Journal of Geography in Higher Education, 25*(3), 357–366.

Ehrlich, T. (Ed.). (2000). *Civic responsibility and higher education.* Phoenix, AZ: Oryx Press.

Elmendorf, H. (2006). Learning through teaching: A new perspective on entering a discipline. *Change, 38*(6), 37–41.

Ernst, H., & Colthorpe, K. (2007). The efficacy of interactive lecturing for students with diverse science backgrounds, *Advances in Physiology Education 31*, 41–44.

Evensen, D. H., & Hmelo, C. E. (2000). *Problem-based learning: A research perspective on learning interactions.* Mahwah, NJ: Lawrence Erlbaum Associates, Publishers.

Eyler, J., & Giles D. E. (1999). *Where's the learning in service learning?* San Francisco, CA: Jossey-Bass.

Falbo, M. C. (2002). *Serving to learn: A faculty guide to service learning* (2nd ed.). Granville, OH: Campus Compact.

Fink, L. D. (2003). *Creating significant learning experiences: An integrated approach to designing college courses.* San Francisco, CA: Jossey-Bass.

France, K. (2004). Problem-based service learning: Rewards and challenges with undergraduates. In C. Wahlburg and S. Chadwick-Blossey (Eds.), *To Improve the Academy: Vol. 22, Resources for Faculty, Instructional, and Organizational Development* (pp. 239–250). San Francisco, CA: Jossey-Bass.

Fry, H., Ketteridge, S., & Marshall, S. (Eds.). (2003). *A handbook for teaching and learning in higher education: Enhancing academic practice* (2nd ed.). London, UK: Kogan Page.

Gahr, A. A. (2003). Cooperative chemistry. *Journal of College Science Teaching, 32*(5), 311–315.

Garrison, D. R., & Vaughan, N. D. (2008). *Blended learning in higher education: Framework, principles, and guidelines.* San Francisco, CA: Jossey-Bass.

Gijselaers, W. H. (1996). Connecting problem-based practices with educational theory. In L. Wilerson and W. H. Gijselaers (Eds.), *New Directions for Teaching and Learning: No. 68, Bringing problem-based learning to higher education: Theory and practice* (pp. 13–21). San Francisco, CA: Jossey-Bass.

Goodsell, A., Maher, M., & Tinto, V. with Smith, B. L., & MacGregor, J. (1992). *Collaborative learning: A sourcebook for higher education.* University Park, PA: National Center on Postsecondary Teaching, Learning, and Assessment, Pennsylvania State University.

Grasha, A. F. (1996). *Teaching with style.* Pittsburgh, PA: Alliance Publishers.

Gurung, R. A. R., & Schwartz, B. M. (2009). *Optimizing teaching and learning: Practicing pedagogical research.* Malden, MA: Wiley-Blackwell.

Haidet, P., Richards, B., Morgan, R. O., Wristers, K., & Moran B. J. (2004). A controlled trial of active versus passive learning strategies in a large group setting. *Advanced Health Science Education, 9*(1), 15–27.

Hake, R. R. (1998). Interactive-engagement vs. traditional methods: A six-thousand-student survey of mechanics test data for introductory physics courses. *American Journal of Physics, 66*, 64–74.

Halpern, D. F., & Hakel, M. D. (2003, July/August). Applying the science of learning to the university and beyond: Teaching for long-term retention and transfer. *Change, 35*(4), 36–41.

Harwood, W. S. (2003). Course enhancement: a road map for devising active-learning and inquiry based science courses, *International Journal of Developmental Biology 47*, 213–221.

Healey, M. (2000, February 4). How to put scholarship into teaching. *The Times Higher Education Supplement, 1421*, 40–1.

Hecke, G. R. V., Karukstis, K. K., Haskell, R. C., McFadden, C. S., & Wettack, F. S. (2002). An integration of chemistry, biology, and physics: The interdisciplinary laboratory. *Journal of Chemical Education, 79*(7), 837–844.

Hertel, J. P. & Millis, B. J. (2002). *Using simulations to promote learning in higher education: An introduction.* Sterling, VA: Stylus.

Hoffman, E. A. (2001). Successful application of active learning techniques to introductory microbiology. *Microbiology Education, 2*(1), 5–11.

Hofmeyer, A., Newton, M., & Scott, C. (2007). Valuing the scholarship of integration and the scholarship of application in the academy for health science scholars: Recommended methods. *Health Research Policy and Systems, 5*(5). http://www.biomedcentral.com/content/pdf/1478-4505-5-5.pdf

Hostetter, C., & Busch, M. (2006). Measuring up online: the relationship between social presence and student learning satisfaction. *Journal of Scholarship of Teaching and Learning, 6*(2), 1–12.

Hudspith, B., & Jenkins, H. (2001). *Teaching the art of inquiry, Green Guide 3.* Halifax, Nova Scotia: Society for Teaching and Learning in Higher Education.

Hussain, R. M. R., Mamat, W. H. W., Salleh, N., Saat, R. M., & Harland, T. (2007). Problem-based learning in Asian universities. *Studies in Higher Education, 32*(6), 761–772.

Jennings, T. E. (1997). *Restructuring for integrative education: multiple perspectives, multiple contexts.* Westport, CT: Bergin & Garvey.

Johnson, D. W., Johnson, R. T., & Smith, K. A. (1996). *Academic controversy: Enriching college instruction through intellectual conflict.* ASHE-ERIC Higher Education Report Volume 25, No. 3. Washington, DC: The George Washington University, Graduate School of Education and Human Development.

Johnson, D. W., Johnson, R. T., & Smith, K. A. (1998). *Active learning: Cooperation in the college classroom.* Edina, MN: Interaction.

Johnson, K., & Magusin, E. (2005). *Exploring the digital library: A guide for online teaching and learning.* San Francisco, CA: Jossey-Bass.

Jonassen D. (2000). Toward a design theory of problem solving. *Educational Technology, Research, Development, 48,* 63–85.

Jonassen, D. H., Peck, K. L., & Wilson, B. G. (1999). *Learning with technology: A constructivist perspective.* Upper Saddle River, NJ: Merrill, Prentice Hall.

Jones, M. G., & Harmon, S. W. (2002). What professors need to know about technology to assess on-line student learning. In R. Anderson and B. Speck (Eds.), *New Directions for Teaching and Learning: No. 91, Assessment strategies for the on-line class from theory to practice* (pp. 19–30). San Francisco, CA: Jossey-Bass.

Jones, S. R., & Hill, K. (2001). Crossing high street: Understanding diversity through community service learning. *Journal of College Student Development, 42*(3), 204–216.

Justice, C., Rice, J., Warry, W., Inglis, S., Miller, S. and Sammon, S. (2007). Inquiry in higher education: reflections and directions on course design and teaching methods, *Innovative Higher Education, 31*(4), 201–214.

Justice, C., Rice, J., and Warry, W. (2009). Academic skill development—inquiry seminars can make a difference: evidence from a quasi-experimental study, *International Journal for the Scholarship of Teaching and Learning, 3*(1). http://www.georgiasouthern.edu/ijsotl

Kanuka, H. (2006). Inquiry-based learning with the net: Opportunities and challenges. In C. Kreber (Ed.), *New Directions in Teaching and Learning: No. 107, Exploring research-based teaching* (pp. 57–65). San Francisco, CA: Jossey-Bass/Wiley.

Kember, D. (2000). *Action learning and action research: Improving the quality of teaching and learning.* London, UK: Kogan Page.

Kember, D. & Gow, L. (1994). Orientations to teaching and their effect on the quality of student learning. *Journal of Higher Education, 65*(1), 58–74.

Keyser, M. W. (2000). Active learning and cooperative learning: understanding the difference and using both styles effectively. *Research Strategies, 17,* 35–44.

Klein, J. T. (2005). *Humanities, culture, and interdisciplinarity: The changing American academy.* Albany, NY: State University of New York Press.

Knight, P. (2002). *Being a teacher in higher education.* Buckingham, UK: Society for Research into Higher Education & Open University Press.

Knowlton, D. S., & Sharp, D. C. (Eds.). (2003). *New Directions for Teaching and Learning: No. 95, Problem-based learning in the information age.* San Francisco, CA: Jossey-Bass.

Kobrin, M., Smith, M., & Mareth, J. (2000). *Introduction to service-learning toolkit: Readings and resources for faculty.* Providence, RI: Campus Compact.

Kramer, T., & Korn, J. (1999). Class discussions: Promoting participation and preventing problems. In B. Perlman, L. McCann, and S. McFadden (Eds.), *Lessons learned: Practical advice for the teaching of psychology.* Washington, DC: The American Psychological Society.

Lang, J. M. (2008). *On Course: A week-by-week guide to your first semester of college teaching.* Cambridge, MA: Harvard University Press.

Laurillard, D. (1993). *Rethinking university teaching: A framework for the effective use of educational technology.* London, UK: Routledge.

Lomicka, L., & Cooke-Plagwitz, J. (2004). *Teaching with technology.* Boston, MA: Thomson/Heinle.

Lorents, A., Morgan, J., & Tallman, G. (2003). The impact of course integration on student grades. *Journal of Education for Business, 78*(3), 135–138.

Lowman, J. (1990). *Mastering the techniques of teaching.* San Francisco, CA: Jossey-Bass.

Lyons, R. E. (Ed.). (2007). *Best practices for supporting adjunct faculty.* Bolton, MA: Anker Publishing Company.

Magnan, R. (Ed.). (1990). *147 practical tips for teaching professors.* Madison, WI: Atwood Publishing.

Margetson, D. (1994). Current educational reform and the significance of problem-based learning. *Studies in Higher Education, 19*(1), 5–19.

Marsh, P. (2007). What is known about student learning outcomes and how does it relate to the scholarship of teaching and learning? *International Journal for the Scholarship of Teaching and Learning, 1*(2). http://www.georgiasouthern.edu/ijsotl

Maudsley, G. (1999). Do we all mean the same thing by problem-based learning? A review of the concepts and a formulation of the ground rules. *Academic Medicine, 74,* 178–85.

McKeachie, W. J., & Svinicki, M. (2006). Problem-based learning: Teaching with cases, simulations, and games. In W. J. McKeachie and M. Svinicki (Eds.), *Teaching tips: Strategies, research, and theory for college and university teachers* (12th ed.). (pp. 221–228). Boston, MA: Houghton Mifflin.

Mendel-Reyes, M. (1998). A pedagogy for citizenship: Service learning and democratic education. In B. A. Quigley and G. W. Kuhne (Eds.), *New Directions for Teaching and Learning: No. 73, Creating practical knowledge through action research* (pp. 31–38). San Francisco, CA: Jossey-Bass.

Meyers, C., & Jones, T. B. (1993). *Promoting active learning: Strategies for the college classroom.* San Francisco, CA: Jossey-Bass.

Meyer, K. A. (Ed.). (2002). *Quality in distance learning: Focus on on-line learning.* ASHE-ERIC Higher Education Report, 29(4).

Michaelsen, L. K. (2004). *Team-based learning.* Sterling, VA: Stylus.

Michaelsen, L. K., Parmelee, D. X., McMahon, K. K., & Levine, R. E. (Eds.). (2008). *Team-based learning for health professions education: A guide to using small groups for improving learning.* Sterling, VA: Stylus.

Michaelsen, L. K., Peterson, T., & Sweet, M.S. (2009). Building learning teams: The key to harnessing the power of small groups in management education. In S. Armstrong and C. Fukami (Eds.), *Handbook of managerial learning, education, and development.* Thousand Oaks, CA: Sage Publications.

Miller, J. S. (2004). Problem-based learning in organizational behavior class: Solving students' real problems. *Journal of Management Education, 28*(5), 578–589.

Miller, W. R., & Miller, M. F. (1997). *Handbook for college teaching.* Sautee-Nacoochee, GA: PineCrest Publications.

Millis, B. J. (2003). How cooperative learning can fulfill the promises of the "seven principles." In J. L. Cooper & D. Ball (Eds.), *Small group instruction in higher education: Lessons from the past, visions of the future* (pp. 39–43). Stillwater, OK: New Forums Press, Inc.

Millis, B. J., & Cottell, P. G. (1998). *Cooperative learning for higher education faculty.* Phoenix, AZ: Oryx Press.

Monolescu, D., Schifter, C., & Greenwood, L. (2004). *The distance education evolution: Issues and case studies.* Hershey, PA: Information Science Publications.

Moon, J. (2004). *A handbook of reflective and experiential learning: Theory and Practice.* London, UK: Routledge Falmer.

Naidu, S. (2003). *Learning & teaching with technology: Principles and practices.* London, UK: Sterling, VA: Kogan Page.

Nash, R. N., & Murray, M. C. (2010). *Helping college students find purpose: The campus guide to meaning-making.* San Francisco, CA: Jossey-Bass.

Neville, A. J. (2009). Problem-based learning and medical education forty years on: A review of its effects on knowledge and clinical performance. *Medical Principles and Practice, 18,* 1–9.

Nicholls, G. (2002). *Developing teaching and learning in higher education.* London, UK: Routledge.

Orlich, D. (2006). *Teaching strategies* (8th ed.). Boston, MA: Houghton Mifflin.

Palmer, P. (1993). Good talk about good teaching: Improving teaching through conversation. *Change, 25*(6), 8–13.

Paswan, A. K., & Gollakota, K. (2004). Dimensions of peer evaluation, overall satisfaction, and overall evaluation: An investigation in a group task environment. *Journal of Education for Business, 79*(4), 275–231.

Prince, M. J. (2004). Does active learning work? A review of the research. *Journal of Engineering Education, 93,* 223–231.

Prince, M. J., & Felder, R. M. (2006). Inductive teaching and learning methods: Definitions, comparisons, and research bases. *Journal of Engineering Education, 95*(2), 123–138.

Qualters, D. (2001). Do students want to be active? *Journal of Scholarship of Teaching and Learning, 2*(1), 52–59.

Race, P. (2001). *The lecturer's toolkit: A resource for developing learning, teaching and assessment.* London, UK: Kogan Page.

Ramsden, P. (2003). *Learning to teach in higher education.* London, UK: Routledge Falmer.

Redlawski, D. P., Rice, T., & Barnes, K. W. (2009). *Civic service: Service-learning with state and local government partners.* San Francisco, CA: Jossey-Bass.

Rockman, I. F. (2004). *Integrating information literacy into higher education curriculum: Practical models for transformation.* San Francisco, CA: Jossey-Bass.

Ryan, G. (1993). Student perceptions about self-directed learning in a professional course implementing problem-based learning. *Studies in Higher Education, 18*(1), 53–63.

Sadlo, G., & Richardson, J. T. E. (2003). Approaches to studying and perceptions of the academic environment in students following problem-based and subject-based curricula. *Higher Education Research and Development, 22*(3), 253–296.

Savin-Baden, M. (2000). *Problem-based learning in higher education: Untold stories.* Buckingham, UK: Open University Press/SRHE.

Savin-Baden, M. (2003). *Facilitating problem-based learning: Illuminating perspectives.* Philadelphia, PA: The Society for Research into Higher Education & Open University Press.

Savin-Baden, M. (2004). *Challenging research in problem-based learning.* Maidenhead, UK: McGraw-Hill.

Savin-Baden, M., & Major, C. H. (2004). *Foundations of problem-based learning.* Berkshire, England: Society for Research into Higher Education & Open University Press.

Savin-Baden, M., & Wilkie, K. (Eds.). (2006). *Problem-based learning online.* Maidenhead, UK: McGraw-Hill.

Schön, D. A. (1988). *Educating the reflective practitioner: Toward a new design for teaching and learning in the professions.* San Francisco, CA: Jossey-Bass.

Schwartz, P. (2001). Problem-based learning: Case studies, experience and practice. London, UK: Kogan Page.

Scott, D. K. (2002). General education for an integrative age. *Higher Education Policy, 15*(1), 7–18.

Shapiro, D. F. (2003). Facilitating holistic curriculum development. *Assessment & Evaluation in Higher Education, 28*(4), 423–434.

Shore, M. A., & Shore, J. B. (2003). An integrative curriculum approach to developmental mathematics and the health professions using problem based learning. *Mathematics and Computer Education, 37*(1), 29–38.

Shulman, L. S. (2005). Signature pedagogies in the professions. *Daedalus, 134*(3), 52–59.

Shulman, L. S. (2005). *The wisdom of practice: Essays on teaching, learning, and learning to teach.* San Francisco, CA: Jossey-Bass.

Silberman, M. (1996). *Active learning: 101 strategies to teach any subject.* Needham Heights, MA: Allyn & Bacon.

Smith, G. A. (2008). First day questions for the learner-centered classroom. *National Teaching and Learning Forum, 17*(5), 1–4.

Smith, S. (2004). Designing collaborative learning experiences for library computer classrooms. *College & Undergraduate Libraries, 11*(2), 65–83.

Smith, B. L., & McCann, J. (2001). *Reinventing ourselves: Interdisciplinary education, collaborative learning, and experimentation in higher education.* Bolton, MA: Anker.

Smith, M. K., Wood, W. B., Adams, W. K., Wieman, C., Knight, J. K., Guild, N., & Su, T. T. (2009). Why peer discussion improves student performance on in-class concept questions. *Science, 323,* 122–124.

Spronken-Smith, R., & Harland, T. (2009). Learning to teach with problem-based learning, *Active Learning in Higher Education, 10*(2), 138–153.

Staley, C. C. (2003). *50 ways to leave your lectern: Active learning strategies to engage first-year students.* Belmont, CA: Wadsworth/Thomson Learning.

Stanley, C. A. (2000–2001). Teaching in action: Multicultural education as the highest form of understanding. *Teaching Excellence, 12*(2).

Stanley, C. A. & Porter, M. E. (Eds.). (2002). *Engaging large classes: Strategies and techniques for college faculty.* Bolton, MA: Anker.

Stein, R. F., & Hurd, S. (2000). *Using student teams in the classroom: A faculty guide.* Bolton, MA: Anker Publishing Company.

Stephenson, F. J. (2001). *Extraordinary teachers: The essence of excellent teaching.* Kansas City, MO: Andrews McMeel.

Su, A. Y. (2007). The impact of individual ability, favorable team member scores, and student perception of course importance on student preference of team-based learning and grading methods. *Adolescence, 42*(168), 805–26.

Sutherland, T., & Bonwell, C. (Eds.). (1996, Fall). Using active learning in college classes: A range of options for faculty. *New Directions for Teaching and Learning: No. 67, Facilitating distance education.* San Francisco, CA: Jossey-Bass.

Sweet, M. S., & Michaelsen, L. K. (2007). How group dynamics research can inform the theory and practice of postsecondary small group learning. *Educational Psychology Review, 19*(1), 31–47.

Timpson, W. M., Yang, R., Borrayo, E., & Canetto, S. S. (2005). *147 practical tips for teaching diversity.* Madison, WI: Atwood Publishing.

Tomei, L. A. (2003). *Challenges of teaching with technology across the curriculum: Issues and solutions.* Hershey, PA: Information Science Publishers.

Ward, K., & Wolf-Wendel, L. (2000). Community-centered service learning: Moving from doing *for* to doing *with. American Behavioral Scientist, 43*(5), 767–780.

Watts, M. M. (Ed.). (2003). *New directions for teaching and learning: No. 94, Technology: Taking the distance out of learning* [Special issue]. San Francisco, CA: Jossey-Bass.

Weiss, R. E. (2003). Designing problems to promote higher-order thinking. *New Directions for Teaching and Learning, 95,* 25–31.

Weiss, R. E., Knowlton, D. S. & Speck, B. W. (Eds.). (2000). *New Directions for Teaching and Learning: No. 84, Principles of effective teaching in the online classroom.* San Francisco, CA: Jossey-Bass.

Westheimer, J., & Kahne, J. (2004). Educating the 'good' citizen: Political choices and pedagogical goals. *Political Science & Politics, 37,* 1–7.

Wildman, T., Hable, M., Preston, M., & Magliaro, S. (2000). Faculty student groups: Solving "good problems" through study, reflection, and collaboration. *Innovative Higher Education, 24*(4), 247–263.

Wilkerson, L. & Gijselaers, W. H. (Eds.). (1996). *New Directions for Teaching and Learning: No. 68, Bringing problem-based learning to higher education: Theory and practice.* San Francisco, CA: Jossey-Bass.

Wright, W. A. & Associates. (1995). *Teaching improvement practices: Successful strategies for higher education.* Boston, MA: Anker.

Wulff, D. H. (Ed.). (2005). *Aligning for learning: Strategies for teaching effectiveness.* Bolton, MA: Anker Publishing.

Yelon, S. (1996). *Powerful principles of instruction.* White Plains, NY: Longman Publishers.

Young, S. (2006). Student views of effective online teaching in higher education. *American Journal of Distance Education, 20*(2), 65–77.

Web Resources

AAC&U Center for Liberal Education and Civic Engagement
http://www.aacu.org/civic_engagement/index.cfm

Association for Integrative Studies (AIS)
http://www.units.muohio.edu/aisorg/

Campus Compact
http://www.compact.org/

The Carnegie Foundation's Integrative Learning Project: Opportunities to Connect
http://www.carnegiefoundation.org/general/index.asp?key=24

Distance Education Clearinghouse: University of Wisconsin-Extension
http://www.uwex.edu/disted/

EduCause: Transforming Education through Information Technology
http://www.educause.edu/

The Higher Education Academy: Sociology, Anthropology and Politics (C-SAP)
Sharing ideas and research in social sciences learning and teaching
http://www.c-sap.bham.ac.uk/resources/project_reports/ShowOverview.asp?id=4

Journal of Online Teaching and Learning
http://jolt.merlot.org/

Learn and Serve: America's National Service-Learning Clearinghouse
http://www.servicelearning.org/

National Center for Learning and Citizenship (NCLC)
www.ecs.org/ecsmain.asp?page=/html/projectsPartners/nclc/nclc_main.htm

Ohio Learning Network
http://oln.org

Teaching Style Inventory (Grasha-Riechmann)
http://longleaf.net/teachingstyle.html

Teaching Perspectives Inventory.
http://teachingperspectives.com/

UD-PBL-UNDERGRAD (owned by the University of Delaware)
http://www.udel.edu/pbl/ud-pbl-undergrad.html

Part V

Shared Expectations: Creating Supportive Learning Environments

Part V—Shared Expectations: Creating Supportive Learning Environments

Part V is dedicated to perspectives and practices that help educators to develop productive contexts for learning. Contemporary thinking about creating an environment for learning often translates to building a community built on trust, respect, and participation. The following readings aid us in understanding how we might construct a supportive classroom atmosphere in which learning is valued and shared.

Ethics/Establishing Trust

According to the studies shared by Kuther in "College Student Views," students turn to faculty to model the ethical behaviors and high standards of professionals. Her findings indicate that students agree on some behaviors or actions of faculty that they consider unethical. This information can suggest a "profile of the ethical professor" from a student standpoint, informing faculty of the expectations students may hold.

Learning Communities

There are many types of student learning communities being developed on college campuses; examples range from linked courses in a curriculum to cohorts of students living in the same residence hall and experiencing classes and co-curricular events situated around a theme together. At their most basic level, learning communities promote the sharing of knowledge among students and working toward common goals. In the reading titled "Student ownership of learning in an interdisciplinary community: expectations make a difference," Wiersema and Licklider share an example of a learning community and notable outcomes that resulted from the program based on their research. They state that "by focusing on effective interpersonal skills and by valuing the contributions of diverse individuals, each team member was able to work increasingly interdependently while genuinely caring for and supporting others—the very essence of community" (pp. 114–115). The authors conclude with recommendations to encourage students to assume leadership roles within any given community.

It is difficult to consider the notion of community in higher education without mention of the influence that Parker Palmer has had on this topic. *Change* magazine featured the article "Community, conflict, and ways of knowing" in 1987, and yet it has applicability for our work in colleges and universities today. He challenges those within the academy to "think about community in ways that deepen the *educational* agenda" (pp. 20–22) and calls for a change from the purely objectivist approach to knowledge that dominates much of higher education, to an approach that balances the objective with the relational.

Classroom Management

As cultural expectations and norms shift, so do behaviors in the classroom. It is difficult to imagine how a class might function as a community if members do not hold some shared values and norms. However, the "gap" between faculty member and current student experience in college widens with each year, and so can perceptions about appropriate behavior. Large classes have a tendency to create an additional challenge if students remain anonymous. Mary Deane Sorcinelli provides essential advice for faculty who teach large sections in her chapter "Promoting civility in large classes." While we should always strive to believe the best about our students, her "solutions for dealing with misbehavior" can help educators deal with issues if/when they arise. After all, the instructor, no matter the teaching philosophy employed, is the one ultimately responsible for making sure the learning environment is protected from disruption.

Student Engagement

The work that is being done by George Kuh and colleagues from the Center for Postsecondary Research at Indiana University is revolutionizing assessment efforts on many college campuses by focusing on student engagement. Findings from their widely used survey "show that the time and energy that students devote to their studies and other educationally purposeful activities positively influence their grades and persistence" (p. 2). In this brief but informative article, Kuh provides insights from research that can help institutions engage students more effectively.

Teaching Through Tragedy

Faculty in higher education, with the exception of those in colleges or schools of education, are not usually formally trained as teachers. We are experts in our field who often teach as our mentors taught or who seek out support for teaching on our own. When the terrorist attacks of September 11 occurred, many faculty members were struggling to make their own sense of what was happening, much less thinking about how to invite students into reflective conversations. How can we better prepare instructors to take helpful actions in the midst of tragedy? Huston and DiPietro conducted a research project that helps us understand what some students may expect of faculty in times of crisis, and further, what faculty developers and administrators can do to provide support through such tragic events.

Recognizing Student Diversity

In order to create an inclusive learning environment, faculty need to recognize and demonstrate appreciation for the diversity among their community of learners. We cannot assume, for instance, that international students have the same needs and reactions in the classroom as American students. In a chapter titled "Improving teaching and learning practices for international students," Janette Ryan identifies the "gaps in understanding" or misconceptions that often exist between faculty and international students. She provides some constructive suggestions to lessen the gaps and improve the learning experience for all students.

In the next reading, Gloria Ladson-Billings, a leader deeply committed to improving the public education experience of African-American (as well as all underserved) students describes her notion of "culturally relevant teaching." In this article, she shares her definition of this pedagogy and three criteria: "(a) Students must experience academic success; (b) students must develop and/or maintain cultural competence; and (c) students must develop a critical consciousness through which they challenge the status quo of the current social order" (p. 160). While this research is specific to African-American students in a public, K-12 context, there is much to be learned from the teachers she observed for making improvements in higher education practice for all students.

The language we use in higher education is supposed to be selective, intentional, and articulate of the ideas we hope to share, but as Ben-Moshe points out, many commonly used phrases can hurt and exclude others. The lexicon related to disability has been, essentially, disabling; operating from a deficit model. The authors share some examples of how the language related to ability is shifting and encourage faculty to be cognizant of these shifts in order to educate others and create more inclusive learning environments.

Another way of taking diversity into account is through "connected teaching," advanced by

Blythe Clinchy. In connected knowing, an approach believed to be used more often by women, a student would "prefer 'thinking with' to 'thinking against' others" (p. 103). Thus a connected teacher acts as "midwife" to facilitate the emergence of students' ideas. Using a course she teaches on developmental psychology, Clinchy demonstrates the ways that she privileges the active construction of collective thinking over passive adherence to existing knowledge. The author posits that men benefit from a connected approach to teaching as well, as it is one way to challenge all students to ask questions and seek new answers within a context of mutual trust.

Student Motivation

How can we motivate others? This question has driven inquiry in various disciplines for years. In her chapter on motivating students to learn, Svinicki applies this question to the postsecondary classroom environment. She surveys the landscape of motivation theory and proposes an "amalgamated" model that captures the latest thinking about motivation and learning. This model assumes that "the strength of the motivation is . . . a function of the type of goal selected, the value of the goal being pursued in relationship to other goals, and the learners' beliefs in their own ability to achieve the goal" (p. 145). The author examines the three major tenets of this model, weaving in examples and vignettes from college teaching and learning.

CHAPTER 20

ETHICS/ESTABLISHING TRUST

A Profile of the Ethical Professor: Student Views

Tara L. Kuther

Abstract Two studies examined college students' perceptions of professors' ethical responsibilities. Students agreed that professors must demonstrate respect for students, teach objectively, and grade honestly, and they should not tolerate cheating or plagiarism. Results indicate that students expect professors to act with professionalism, to employ a vast base of content knowledge, and to show concern for student welfare. Many view professors as exemplars of scholarship and professional behavior. Professors must be cognizant of student expectations and should reflect on their behavior both in and out of the classroom.

Ethics education has been recognized as an essential component of the liberal arts curriculum because it encourages the development of critical thinking and fosters the values and standards that guide responsible behavior (APA 1992, 2002; AAC&U 1985; Baum et al. 1993; Fisher and Kuther 1997; Hobbs 1948; McGovern 1993). Proponents of the ethics across the curriculum movement recommend that ethics permeate all undergraduate courses to illustrate that it pervades all aspects of life (Ashmore and Starr 1991; Navarre 1994). Despite the increasing attention to integrating ethics across the undergraduate curriculum, recent reports of the prevalence of cheating and plagiarism have led faculty to question the integrity of their students (Kleiner and Lord 1999; Sohn 2001). For example, it has been estimated that more than 80 percent of college students have cheated or plagiarized material at least once (Pullen et al. 2000). Why is academic dishonesty rampant?

Some scholars point to faculty's failure to "serve as exemplars of decent moral behavior" (Callahan 1982, 336), yet the scant data on this topic indicate that faculty rarely engage in unethical actions (Tabachnick, Keith-Spiegel, and Pope 1991). What are the ethical responsibilities of faculty? The American Association of University Professors (1987) has outlined a statement of professional ethics, but the statement is not binding and often is not acknowledged (Birch, Elliott, and Trankel 1999). Ethics in academia rarely is broached in the literature. The few discussions of academic ethics to date tend to focus on sexual harassment, the rights of participants, teaching values to students, and scientific misconduct (Keith-Spiegel, Tabachnick, and Allen 1993). The ethical obligations and ambiguities in teaching largely have been ignored (Kuther 2002; in press). Understanding how college students view their professors' actions may help delineate the professional role of teaching professors.

In a landmark study, Keith-Spiegel, Tabachnick, and Allen (1993) surveyed nearly five hundred Midwest and West Coast college students about the ethical nature of more than one hundred behaviors in which faculty might engage. Eighty percent or more of the students agreed that unethical behaviors on the part of faculty include dishonest grading practices (e.g., using a grading procedure

TARA L. KUTHER is an assistant professor in the Department of Psychology at Western Connecticut State University, in Danbury.

Reprinted from *College Teaching* (2003), Heldref Publications.

that does not measure what students have learned, allowing how much a student is liked to influence grading, or giving every student an "A" regardless of the quality of work). Unprofessional interactions with students (e.g., insulting or ridiculing a student or flirting with students), unprofessional classroom practices (e.g., teaching while under the influence of drugs or alcohol, requiring students to disclose sensitive information in class discussions, or ridiculing a student in class), and professional dishonesty (e.g., ignoring strong evidence of cheating or including misleading information in a student's letter of recommendation) also were seen as unethical behaviors on the part of faculty. A decade has passed since the publication of their initial study; therefore, the present study provides an updated account of college student views of the ethics of faculty behavior. The present article specifically describes two research studies designed to provide information about how college students perceive the ethical responsibilities of professors. Part 1 examines students' ratings of the ethical nature of twenty-five behaviors in which faculty might engage. Part 2 gathers qualitative data to examine students' perspectives on eight behaviors in which faculty might engage.

Part 1

Given current findings that cheating and plagiarism are commonplace among college students, as well as recent criticisms of the ethical integrity of professors (Callahan 1982; Pullen et al. 2000), this study provides an updated portrait of students' views of the ethical professor. Specifically, students rated the ethical dimension of twenty-five actions in which professors might engage.

Method

Participants were 249 undergraduate students (72 percent female and 38 percent freshmen) enrolled in introductory and advanced courses in psychology at a public university in the Northeast. Participants completed a survey adapted from Keith-Spiegel, Tabachnick, and Allen (1993) that asked them to rate the ethical appropriateness of twenty-five behaviors. Participants responded on a five-item scale: (1) not ethical under any circumstance; (2) ethical under rare circumstances; (3) ethical under some circumstances; (4) ethical under most circumstances; and (5) ethical under all circumstances. The behaviors included academic honesty (e.g., ignoring cheating or plagiarism), student-professor relationships (e.g., hugging, asking for favors, accepting gifts), teaching (e.g., teaching material that has not been mastered, teaching unprepared, using films to reduce work), drug and alcohol use (e.g., while teaching, in one's personal life), and respect for students (e.g., revealing confidential disclosures, ridiculing a student).

Results

Table 20.1 presents the mean, standard deviation, and skew for each item. The means indicate that students viewed most behaviors as not ethical under any circumstance or as ethical under rare circumstances. Several items were highly positively skewed, indicating high levels of student agreement on the unethical nature of each.

Table 20.2 presents student responses for each item. Ten behaviors emerged as particularly unethical (75 percent or more of students rated them as never ethical or ethical under rare circumstances): substance use while teaching (97 percent for teaching while under the influence of alcohol and teaching while under the influence of cocaine or other illegal drugs); lack of respect for students (97 percent for insulting or ridiculing a student in his or her absence, 96 percent for telling colleagues confidential disclosures made by a student, 92 percent for insulting or ridiculing a student in his or her presence, and 78 percent for telling the class confidential disclosures made by a student without revealing the student's identity); dishonest grading practices (91 percent for ignoring strong evidence of cheating, 86 percent for allowing a student's likability to influence grading, and 88 percent for ignoring strong evidence of plagiarism in a written assignment); and nonobjective teaching (89 percent for criticizing all theoretical orientations except those personally preferred, and 88 percent for teaching content in a nonobjective or incomplete manner).

TABLE 20.1

Mean, Standard Deviation, and Skew

Behavior	Mean	*SD*	Skew
1. Ignoring strong evidence of cheating	1.43	.83	2.21
2. Dating a student	2.13	.99	.68
3. Asking small favors from students	2.84	.91	−.05
4. Hugging a student	2.90	.97	−.10
5. Accepting a student's expensive gift	2.23	.98	.47
6. Teaching when too distressed to be effective	2.10	.91	.50
7. Ignoring strong evidence of plagiarism in a written assignment	1.47	.78	1.72
8. Accepting a student's invitation to a party	2.53	1.01	.20
9. Teaching material that has not been mastered	2.16	.98	.61
10. Accepting a student's inexpensive gift	3.18	1.14	−.34
11. Teaching a class without adequate preparation that day	2.40	.92	.09
12. Teaching while under the influence of alcohol	1.13	1.00	.51
13. Teaching content in a nonobjective or incomplete manner	1.63	.77	1.34
14. Teaching while under the influence of cocaine or other illegal drugs	1.10	.49	5.67
15. Allowing a student's likability to influence grading	1.49	.81	1.68
16. Using profanity in lectures	2.64	1.00	−.05
17. Using films to fill class time and reduce teaching work	2.38	.94	.37
18. Telling colleagues confidential disclosures made by a student	1.29	.63	2.76
19. Failing to update lecture notes when reteaching a course	2.03	.94	.84
20. Criticizing all theoretical orientations except those personally preferred	1.50	.74	1.46
21. Using cocaine or other illegal drugs in his or her personal (nonteaching) life	1.90	1.19	1.10
22. Insulting or ridiculing a student in the student's presence	1.31	.72	2.70
23. Insulting or ridiculing a student in his or her absence	1.21	.55	3.77
24. Becoming sexually active with a student only after he or she has completed the course and the grade has been filed	2.66	1.31	.30
25. Telling the class confidential disclosures made by a student without revealing the student's identity	1.85	.99	1.09

Students demonstrated more ambiguous perspectives (60 percent to 75 percent agreement as never or rarely ethical) with regard to several behaviors: excellence in teaching (73 percent for failing to update lecture notes when reteaching a course, 68 percent for teaching when too distressed to be effective, and 66 percent for teaching material that has not been mastered); student-professor relationships (64 percent for dating a student and 61 percent for accepting a student's expensive gift); and drug use in a professor's personal (nonteaching) life (72 percent).

Chi square analyses compared ratings by freshmen students and upperclass students for all items (% = .002 to correct for multiple analyses). Only two comparisons emerged as significant. Seventy-six percent of upperclass students viewed ignoring strong evidence of plagiarism as unethical, as compared with 54 percent of freshmen, $P^2(3, N = 246) = 16.79, p = .002$. Ninety-five percent of upperclassmen and 81 percent of freshmen viewed criticizing all theoretical orientations except those personally preferred as unethical or as ethical only in rare circumstances, $P^2(3, N = 245) = 14.72, p = .002$.

TABLE 20.2

Student Ratings of the Ethical Nature of Twenty-five Professorial Behaviors (Percentages Shown)

Behaviour	1 Not ethical under any circumstance	2 Ethical under rare circumstances	3 Ethical under some circumstances
1. Ignoring strong evidence of cheating	72	19	4
2. Dating a student	31	33	3
3. Asking small favors from students	8	25	40
4. Hugging a student	9	23	43
5. Accepting a student's expensive gift	26	35	30
6. Teaching when too distressed to be effective	29	39	20
7. Ignoring strong evidence of plagiarism in a written assignment	68	20	9
8. Accepting a student's invitation to a party	17	34	32
9. Teaching material that has not been mastered	29	37	20
10. Accepting a student's inexpensive gift	11	15	33
11. Teaching a class without adequate preparation that day	19	33	38
12. Teaching while under the influence of alcohol	92	5	20
13. Teaching content in a nonobjective or incomplete manner	52	36	10
14. Teaching while under the influence of cocaine or other illegal drugs	95	2	2
15. Allowing a student's likability to influence grading	67	19	12
16. Using profanity in lectures	16	26	40
17. Using films to fill class time and reduce teaching work	18	39	33
18. Telling colleagues confidential disclosures made by a student	78	18	2
19. Failing to update lecture notes when reteaching a course	32	41	21
20. Criticizing all theoretical orientations except those personally preferred	62	27	10
21. Using cocaine or other illegal drugs in his or her personal (nonteaching) life	55	17	15
22. Insulting or ridiculing a student in the student's presence	80	12	6
23. Insulting or ridiculing a student in his or her absence	84	13	2
24. Becoming sexually active with a student only after he or she has completed the course and the grade has been filed	24	24	25
25. Telling the class confidential disclosures made by a student without revealing the student's identity	47	31	15

Discussion

Students generally agreed that professors must not use alcohol or substances while teaching. They also are morally obligated to demonstrate respect for students by not ridiculing them or revealing confidential disclosures. In students' eyes, ethical professors teach objectively, grade honestly, and do not tolerate cheating or plagiarism. These findings are remarkably similar to those from a survey of faculty ratings of professorial ethics (Birch, Elliott, and Trankel 1999), suggesting that faculty and students share similar perspectives on the ethical professor.

Most interesting in light of recent accounts of the prevalence of plagiarism and cheating is that 72 percent and 68 percent of students reported that it was never or rarely ethical, respectively, for professors to ignore cheating and plagiarism. Freshmen students tended to view ignoring plagiarism as less problematic for professors than did upperclass students, suggesting that freshmen may require additional socialization into a culture of academic honesty and integrity.

Part 2

Given that students agreed to a surprising extent on the scope of unethical behavior on the part of professors, the second research study examines issues about which students were more ambiguous: relationships with students, excellence in teaching, and using illegal drugs in one's personal life. The following items in particular were assessed: dating a student, accepting an expensive gift from a student, becoming sexually active with a student only after the student has completed the course and the grade has been filed, teaching when too distressed to be effective, teaching material that has not been mastered, failing to update lecture notes when reteaching a course, and using cocaine or other illegal drugs in his or her personal (nonteaching) life. Because of recent concerns about the rise in plagiarism among college students (Kleiner and Lord 1999; Sohn 2001), an item on plagiarism ("ignoring strong evidence of plagiarism in a written assignment") was added.

Method

Participants were fifty-eight undergraduate students (66 percent female and 21 percent freshmen) enrolled in introductory and advanced courses in psychology at a public university in the Northeast. Similar to part 1, participants completed a survey that asked them to rate the ethical appropriateness of eight behaviors. Participants responded on a five-item scale: (1) not ethical under any circumstance; (2) ethical under rare circumstances; (3) ethical under some circumstances; (4) ethical under most circumstances; and (5) ethical under all circumstances. After rating the ethical appropriateness, students were instructed to write a short answer response explaining why the behavior was ethical or unethical.

Results

Table 20.3 presents student responses for each item. Chi square analyses comparing the ratings generated by participants in part 1 with those of part 2 (% = .006 to correct for multiple analyses) revealed no differences among the ratings provided by participants across the two samples. Participant short answer responses were analyzed for themes and were categorized accordingly.

Relationships with Students

Three items examined participant views of the ethics of professor-student relationships:

Accepting a student's expensive gift. Sixty-two percent of participants indicated that accepting an expensive gift is rarely or never ethical on the part of a professor. Most argued that an expensive gift could be interpreted as a bribe or persuasive device and may be permissible only after the semester ends or after graduation:

> "Why would a student give an expensive gift unless he or she wants a better grade?"
>
> "This is appropriate only if the teacher-student relationship has been terminated prior to the gift. During the relationship a teacher's acceptance of such a gift sends mixed messages to the student and his or her peers."

TABLE 20.3

Student Ratings of the Ethical Nature of Eight Professorial Behaviors (Percentages Shown)

Behaviour	1 Not ethical under any circumstance	2 Ethical under rare circumstances	3 Ethical under some circumstances	4 Ethical under most circumstances	5 Ethical under all circumstances
1. Dating a student	35	34	19	5	7
2. Accepting a student's expensive gift	29	33	29	4	5
3. Teaching when too distressed to be effective	26	25	35	12	2
4. Teaching material that has not been mastered	27	36	31	4	2
5. Failing to update lecture notes when reteaching a course	29	15	35	17	4
6. Using cocaine or other illegal drugs in his or her personal (nonteaching) life	53	19	7	8	13
7. Ignoring strong evidence of plagiarism in a written assignment	75	19	2	2	2
8. Becoming sexually active with a student only after he or she has completed the course and the grade has been filed	24	22	13	23	18

Three participants suggested that accepting an expensive gift would interfere with the normal professor-student relationship:

> "This is not appropriate because the teacher is getting paid for the job and gifts would interfere with the normal student-teacher relationship."

Twenty-nine percent of participants reported that it is sometimes permissible for a professor to accept an expensive gift from a student, and 9 percent reported that it is often or always ethical. Many students explained that accepting an expensive gift is ethical if the professor has a preexisting relationship with the student.

> "Perhaps if the professor was a friend of the family or had a profound effect on the student, it might be appropriate."
>
> "It depends on the relationship between the student and the professor. If the relationship is a friendship and both parties are mutual in this friendship then it seems fine to me, but if it seems as though the student is using bribery then I don't think it should be accepted."

Others argued that accepting an expensive gift from a student is appropriate if the gift is a token of the student's appreciation:

> "Sometimes students just want to show their appreciation for what their teacher has done for them without expecting anything in return."

Dating a student. Sixty-nine percent of participants rated dating a student as rarely or never ethical. Most argued that it leads to favoritism and provides some students with an unfair advantage:

"Dating a student is a complete failure to uphold a professional relationship which could influence factors such as grading and classroom distractions."

"A professor's job is to teach students and to grade students solely on their performance in class and the work they do. If a professor was to date a student, the student wouldn't be graded fairly, etc."

A minority of students argued that a relationship with a student disrupts the power differential between professor and student:

"The power dynamic is not egalitarian and the power imbalance inherent to the student-teacher relationship precludes personal autonomy in both relationships. As both lovers and participants in a student-teacher relationship, both stand to lose. This is a time when it is essential to know one is valued and judged based on the merits of one's ideas and work, not on other criteria. It all becomes confused when boundaries are burned."

Nineteen percent judged dating a student as sometimes ethical, and 12 percent reported that it was often or always ethical, especially if it occurs after the course has ended. The majority of these respondents argued that dating a student is permissible if it does not interfere with the classroom and if the professor and student are in love:

"Regardless of context, teacher and student are two people with feelings and they can fall in love with one another. Why not? If they feel uncomfortable with gossip, the student may take another class."

"If the fact that the professor is dating their student does not interfere with school and grading etc, then I don't see a problem with it, but if it does, then it should not be allowed."

Interestingly, several participants mentioned that the professor's age plays a role in how acceptable it is to date a student:

"Usually professors are much older than students; however, if the professor and student are close in age and don't have a relationship until the course is over, it might be ok."

"If the professor and the student are around the same age and they can carry out a relationship that won't affect anything in the classroom then the professor can do it."

Becoming sexually active with a student only after he or she has completed the course and the grade has been filed. Forty-six percent of participants indicated that becoming sexually active with a student after the grade has been filed is rarely or never ethical. Most of these students explained that there was at least the appearance of impropriety and that the professor's reputation would suffer:

"I think they would encounter disbelief, the tendency would be to think that an exchange of sorts had taken place."

"Down the road, the teacher may be accused of having sexual relations with this person while in class. How can the teacher prove that it wasn't going on until the student was no longer in the class?"

Others explained that sexual relations between professor and student are unethical because they violate the special professor-student relationship:

"Since the grade has already been filed, you won't have to worry about the relationship being about a better grade. But there should be a professional relationship with all teachers and students. The students are here to learn and the teachers are here to teach, not find a love interest. Plus it would probably look bad from other students' perspectives."

Thirteen percent of participants judged becoming sexually involved with a student as sometimes ethical on the part of a professor, especially if the student has graduated:

"If the student has graduated from the college and the relationship begins after graduation then I think it will be ok but if the student is still going to the college but just not taking any more classes with that professor it's wrong."

Forty-two percent judged sexual involvement with a student after a course ends as usually or always ethical. Most of the respondents reasoned that such involvement is ethical because the grade has already been filed:

"If they are past where they have to be professional, and emotions won't hinder their judgment or behavior in class, then that is their business."

> "This is their own choice—both student and teacher and should not be questioned at all. Personal life is personal and should not be related to the profession at all. I don't think this would interfere with the teacher's job at all."
>
> "The student should be allowed to be sexually active with a professor after he or she has completed the course because it has nothing to do with the course or the grade. Sex is on a personal level not a professional level like school is."

One student warned that sexual involvement with students, even former students, is perilous because it jeopardizes the professor-student bond:

> "Depends on the pre-existing relationship. Yes it's ethical and legal but if you have been a Svengali to this person, they may be overly influenced by your past relationship."

Excellence in Teaching

Three items examined student perspectives on professors' roles in the classroom and on ethical issues that may arise in teaching.

Teaching when too distressed to be effective. Fifty-one percent of participants judged teaching when too distressed to be effective as rarely or never ethical. Most argued that in such situations class time would be wasted, which hurts students:

> "If they're not going to be effective, it's a waste of time for everyone."
>
> "Stressed professors are not effective and the stress then spread to the students."
>
> "When the teacher isn't into what he's doing, why should we be?"
>
> "When a professor teaches they need to be able to teach effectively and when that is not happening then it negatively effects the students and their grades."

Others added that professors must separate their private lives from the classroom:

> "In cases of tragedy (national or personal) one would be expected to be distressed. However, as a professional, one is expected to separate their private lives from the classroom."

Thirty-five percent explained that teaching when distressed is sometimes ethical, especially if the professor takes the time to review the material at a later date, while 14 percent responded that teaching while distressed is usually or always ethical:

> "It depends on how distressed. If a teacher does this then I believe it is necessary for them to go over the material a second time and when they are less distressed to be fair and sure that everyone understands it."
>
> "Some people have bad days. Some more than others. Once in a while it's ok. In my opinion, canceling class isn't the worst if one feels that they are wasting time anyway."

Teaching material that has not been mastered. Sixty-three percent of participants rated a professor's teaching material that has not been mastered as rarely or never ethical:

> "The professor is just going to confuse the students if he has not mastered the material."
>
> "If the teacher doesn't totally understand the material how is the student supposed to master it? It's impossible."
>
> "This is not fair! A teacher should in all circumstances know about what they are teaching otherwise they can not teach the students. Students need guidance and are here to learn. What good does a teacher who doesn't know what he or she is talking about to anyone?"
>
> "You should know what you're teaching otherwise you're cheating the student."

Thirty-one percent responded that teaching material that has not been mastered is sometimes ethical, and 6 percent responded that it is usually or always ethical. Many mentioned that it is not possible for a professor to master all of his or her field, but intellectual integrity is essential; professors must know their limitations and be honest:

> "Teaching material for the first time is always difficult and not usually 100 percent mastered. If the teacher still presents his teaching in an organized manner creating a learning environment, I think this way is acceptable."

"People are always learning and can't expect their professor to know everything. If the professor admits to lacking information, it's fine."

Failing to update lecture notes when reteaching a course. Forty-four percent of participants judged failing to update lecture notes as rarely or never ethical. Many explained that the pace of change and information gathering places an ethical responsibility on professors to maintain and expand their lecture notes and pedagogy accordingly:

"The material constantly changes or the way to teach that material changes from year to year. Students change with time."

"That's teaching old things which can allow students to believe false statements that were once true. You would be misleading them or basically lying to them."

Others noted that professors are responsible for providing students with a quality education and that students may perceive the failure to update lecture notes as indicative of laziness on the part of the professor:

"A teacher is supposed to be in charge and ahead of the game. If they fall behind, they won't get the respect they need to have from their students. Students will see that their teacher is a slacker."

"Every teacher should be on top of everything especially since the students pay them."

Thirty-five percent judged failing to update lecture notes as sometimes ethical, and 20 percent judged it as usually or always ethical:

"Most of the information is constant, so there really isn't a need unless the professor finds something interesting to add to his or her teaching."

"If a professor feels that it is unnecessary to update notes in order to keep teaching at the same level, then its fine. If the students are learning information, then why change it?"

Professional and Personal Dishonesty

Ignoring strong evidence of plagiarism in a written assignment. Ninety-five percent of participants judged ignoring evidence of plagiarism in a written assignment as rarely or never ethical on the part of a professor. Many explained that plagiarism is illegal and that ignoring it is not helpful to students:

"Due to the fact that plagiarism is illegal, ignoring the strong evidence is clearly unethical. If no administrative action is taken, the student should at least be informed of the implications of plagiarism."

"This isn't teaching the student how to do independent work."

"If the teacher knows that a student plagiarized then he should speak up. Because the student is not learning anything by just copying and the student should learn that plagiarism is wrong and that you can't get away with it."

Four percent of participants judged ignoring plagiarism in a written assignment as usually or always ethical on the part of a professor. Each of these students qualified their responses by explaining that the professor should not ignore plagiarism but should use it as a teaching opportunity and should not penalize the student:

"If a student genuinely doesn't know what plagiarism is and it is their first offense, let them write it over and don't count it against them."

"In most colleges, plagiarism is addressed with expulsion. Do you really want to ruin a kid's whole career because of one paper? Use discretion and talk to him or her about it."

Using cocaine or other illegal drugs in his or her personal (nonteaching) life. Seventy-two percent of participants judged that a professor's use of illegal drugs in his or her personal life is rarely or never ethical. Many students explained that professors are role models and that drug use tarnishes their credibility and harms students:

"Its not ethical for a teacher to do something illegal. Teachers are supposed to be role models."

"It is not ethical because it is illegal to begin with and if caught it will make the school look bad and lose some credibility in the eyes of the students and public."

> "Regardless of whether the teacher uses the drugs at school or not they still effect how the teacher is as a person and as a teacher. This may endanger the students and cannot possibly be considered safe."
>
> "Teachers are supposed to be role models and help students to the best of their ability. I don't see how one could do this while using drugs."

Eight percent judged a professor's use of illegal drugs in his or her personal life as sometimes ethical, and 21 percent judged it as usually or always ethical. Most of these respondents explained that professional life is separate from private life:

> "Do what you do in your own life. Just as long as you are professional when you come to class and around campus. Everybody has a vice just control it and don't bring it to the workplace."

Discussion

Part 2 examined student views about the ethical nature of a variety of behaviors in which professors might engage. Qualitative analyses of participant responses revealed that college students expect excellence on the part of their professors. Specifically, students expect professors to act with professionalism, to employ a vast base of content knowledge, and to show concern for student welfare.

Professionalism and the Professor

The present sample of college students viewed the ethical professor as one who can separate his or her personal life and institutional life. Ethical professors do not allow their personal problems to affect their teaching or to adversely affect students. They do not teach when they are too distressed to be effective, and they learn to compartmentalize their personal and professional lives.

Professionalism also entails refraining from inappropriate behaviors. More than two-thirds of the students surveyed argued that ethical professors do not date their current students and do not use illegal drugs in then personal lives. Despite this, some respondents acknowledged that professors are people as well and that what happens in professors' personal lives is their business as long as their professional duties are not affected. A number of respondents explained that drug use and relationships with former students are personal choices on the part of professors and are not subject to judgment unless they adversely affect a professor's institutional life. Students' emphasis on personal choice is consistent with a body of research suggesting that adolescents tend to view many behaviors and dilemmas as personal choices, rather than moral or ethical decisions (Killen, Leviton, and Cahill 1991; Kuther and Higgins-D'Alessandro 2000; Nucci, Guerra, and Lee 1991). The importance ascribed to personal choice is consistent with the developmental tasks of adolescence and young adulthood, individuation, autonomy, and identity formation (Erikson 1950; Hill and Holmbeck 1986).

Content Knowledge and the Professor

The present findings suggest that college students expect professors to have a vast amount of content knowledge. Ethical professors remain competent in then content area, are cognizant of new developments, and generally understand their field. Students varied in the extent to which they expected their professors to master the content of their field and remain up-to-date. Some participants argued that knowledge is absolute and static (e.g., "If they haven't mastered the material, who are they to tell you what is right or wrong?" or "Someone who has not mastered a subject completely should not be allowed to teach") and that professors, therefore, cannot excuse themselves from thoroughly grasping their field. Others noted that knowledge is constantly changing and that despite all efforts it may not be possible for a professor to completely master his or her field. These variations in student responses are likely influenced by their level of cognitive development and epistemological views. During adulthood, cognitive development tends to shift from viewing knowledge as absolute to understanding knowledge as relative and uncertain (King and Kitchener

1994; Perry 1968). Further research might examine how intellectual development influences college students' perceptions of the responsibilities and duties of professors.

Student Welfare and the Professor

Finally, the data suggest that college students expect professors to promote their welfare and not to engage in activities that may harm them. Specifically, students in the present sample expected professors to act on cases of plagiarism, using such cases as teaching opportunities. Although professors must not ignore plagiarism, many participants reported that professors should exercise judgment in how such cases are handled. Some argued that professors are obligated to act with compassion and should allow students a second chance—the opportunity to rewrite plagiarized work.

Conclusion

The present findings suggest that college students hold high expectations of their professors that may vary with development. Many view professors as role models who act as exemplars of scholarship and professional behavior. The American Association of University Professors' (1987) ethical guidelines explain that professors must act with beneficence, and the present findings suggest that students expect faculty to act on their behalf and to promote their welfare. Professors must be cognizant of student expectations and should begin to reflect on their behavior both in and out of the classroom. It appears that professors hold not merely a professional obligation to their students, but a moral one as well.

Key words: ethics, ethics education, role models

Note

An early draft of this paper was presented at the 2002 annual meeting of the American Educational Research Association in New Orleans, La. Address correspondence to Dr. T. Kuther, Department of Psychology, Western Connecticut State University, 181 White Street, Danbury, CT 06810, or e-mail at kuther@wcsa.edu

References

American Association of University Professors, 1987. Statement on professional ethics, *Academe* 73 (4): 49.

American Psychological Association. 1992. Ethical principles of psychologists and code of conduct. *American Psychologist* 47:1597–611.

———. 2001. National guidelines and suggested learning outcomes for the undergraduate psychology major (draft #10). http://www.apa.org/ed/draft10.html (accessed 28 January 2002).

Ashmore, R. B., and W. C. Starr. 1991. *Ethics across the curriculum: The Marquette experience.* Milwaukee, Wis.; Marquette University Press.

Association of American Colleges and Universities. 1985. *Integrity in the college curriculum: A report to the academic community.* Washington, D.C.: AAC&U.

Baum, C., L. T. Benjamin, D. Bernstein, A. Crider, J. Halonen, R. Hopkins, T. McGovern, W. McKeachie, B. Nodine, P. Reid, R. Suinn, and C. Wade. 1993. Principles for quality undergraduate psychology programs. In *Handbook for enhancing undergraduate education in psychology,* edited by T. V. McGovern. Washington, D.C.: American Psychological Association.

Birch, M., D. Elliott, and M. A. Trankel. 1999. Black and white and shades of gray: A portrait of the ethical professor. *Ethics and Behavior* 9:243–61.

Callahan, D. 1982. Should there be an academic code of ethics? *Journal of Higher Education* 53:335–44.

Erikson, E. H. 1950. *Childhood and society.* New York: W. W. Norton and Company.

Fisher, C. B., and T. L. Kuther. 1997. Integrating research ethics into the introductory psychology curriculum. *Teaching of Psychology* 24 (3): 172–75.

Hill, J. P., and G. N. Holmbeck. 1986. Attachment and autonomy during adolescence. *Annals of Child Development* 3:145–89.

Hobbs, N. 1948. The development of a code of ethical standards for psychology. *American Psychologist* 3:80–84.

Keith-Spiegel, P. C., B. G. Tabachnick, and M. Allen. 1993. Ethics in academia: Students' views of professors' actions. *Ethics and Behavior* 3:149–62.

Killen, M., M. Leviton, and J. Cahill. 1991. Adolescent reasoning about drug use. *Journal of Adolescent Research* 6:336–56.

King, P. M., and K. S. Kitchener. 1994. *Developing reflective judgment: Understanding and promoting intellectual growth and critical thinking in adolescents and adults.* San Francisco: Jossey-Bass.

Kleiner, C., and M. Lord. 1999. The cheating game. *U.S. News and World Report* 127 (20): 54–65.

Kuther, T. L. 2002. Ethical conflicts in the teaching assignments of graduate students. *Ethics and Behavior* 12 (2): 197–204.

———. In press. Ethical issues in teaching. In *What every graduate student should know or ask themselves about ethics in graduate school,* edited by B. Schrag. Bloomington, Ind.: Association for Practical and Professional Ethics.

Kuther, T. L., and A. Higgins-D'Alessandro. 2000. Bridging the gap between moral reasoning and adolescent engagement in risky behavior. *Journal of Adolescence* 23:409–22.

McCabe, D. L., and P. Drinan. 1999. Toward a culture of academic integrity. *Chronicle of Higher Education.* http://chronicle.com/weekly/v46/i08/08b00701.htm (accessed 31 July 2001).

McGovern, T. V. 1988. Teaching the ethical principles of psychology. *Teaching of Psychology* 15:22–26.

———, ed. 1993. *Handbook for enhancing undergraduate education in psychology.* Washington, D.C.: American Psychological Association.

Navarre, M. 1994. Implementing ethics across the curriculum. In *Teaching ethics: An interdisciplinary approach,* edited by R. B. Ashmore and W. C. Starr. Milwaukee, Wis.: Marquette University Press.

Nucci, L., N. Guerra, and J. Lee. 1991. Adolescent judgment of the personal, prudential, and normative aspects of drug usage. *Developmental Psychology* 27:841–48.

Perry, W. G. 1968. *Forms of intellectual and ethical development in the college years: A scheme.* San Francisco: Jossey-Bass.

Pullen, R., V. Ortloff, S. Casey, and J. B. Payne, 2000. Analysis of academic misconduct using unobtrusive research: A study of discarded cheat sheets. *College Student Journal* 34:616–25.

Sohn, E. 2001. The young and the virtueless. *U.S. News and World Report* 130 (20): 51.

Tabachnick, B. G., R. Keith-Spiegel, and K. S. Pope. 1991. Ethics of teaching: Beliefs and behaviors of psychologists as educators. *American Psychologist* 46:506–15.

CHAPTER 21

LEARNING COMMUNITIES

Student Ownership of Learning in an Interdisciplinary Community: Expectations Make a Difference

Janice Wiersema
Barbara Licklider
Iowa State University

In many college courses students can succeed by memorizing facts and principles. But solving ill-defined problems of the future requires critical thinking and continuous learning. The authors examine findings from a phenomenological study of an interdisciplinary student learning community focused on developing lifelong learners. Although not surprising that students said the high expectations set for them impacted their learning, it is significant that every student, independently, identified being held accountable for meeting those expectations was critical to becoming a responsible learner. The implications for educators are that students must be challenged with ambiguous, complex tasks that are relevant to them as professionals and be held accountable for meeting high expectations.

A primary goal of higher education should be to help students become professionals and citizens who use their minds effectively to solve challenging problems and seek new insights. A series of studies reviewed by Gardiner (1998), however, "consistently show that the college experience for most students comprises a loosely organized, unfocused curriculum, with undefined outcomes, classes that emphasize passive listening, [and] lectures that frequently demand only the recall of memorized material or low-level comprehension of concepts" (p. 72). But the good grades students typically receive from passive practices, such as memorizing and recall, are not necessarily accurate indicators of their ability to solve the ill-defined, real-world problems they will face for the rest of their lives (Huba & Freed, 2000). Developing citizens who can meet the challenges of the future requires not only technical knowledge and skills, but also the ability to communicate effectively, think critically, and form meaningful relationships. The challenge for post-secondary educators, therefore, is to engage students in learning opportunities that will allow them to develop a mix of both cognitive and interpersonal abilities while mastering the content of the discipline. The key for students' success in these endeavors, as uncovered in this study, is to challenge them with ambiguous, complex tasks relevant to them as professionals and to hold them accountable for meeting the challenge.

Background for the Study

We (the authors) recently had the opportunity to combine our knowledge of human learning and the principles of learning organizations in a leadership development program for National Science

Reprinted by permission from *Learning Communities Journal* (2009).

Foundation (NSF) Scholarship for Service (SFS) students at a Land Grant, Research I university in the Midwest. As part of the NSF SFS program, students are awarded full scholarships in exchange for two years of federal government work in cyber security following graduation. The NSF SFS program is an interdisciplinary effort involving students and faculty in computer engineering, computer science, mathematics, political science, management information systems, and education. Fellowship recipients participate in a two-year leadership development program in addition to the requirements of their majors. The leadership program is designed with six emphases: (a) learning about learning, (b) learning about self, (c) purposefully developing community, (d) deliberately practicing and refining skills to support and encourage the growth of self and others, (e) practicing metacognition, and (f) engaging in intentional mental processing (Wiersema, 2006). During the first year of the program, we observed juniors, seniors, and graduate students take responsibility for their own learning when they were deliberately engaged in activities designed to create a learning community. They learned to help all members understand more about their brains and how learning happens, about themselves as learners, about the power of metacognition, and about the need for continuous intentional mental processing to achieve transfer of learning for future use (see the Appendix for our general philosophy of learning and a list of our expectations). Eventually, these students were able to enhance their learning regardless of the teaching/learning style of the professor. In addition, by focusing on effective interpersonal skills and by valuing the contributions of diverse individuals, each team member was able to work increasingly interdependently while genuinely caring for and supporting others—the very essence of community.

According to the students, the knowledge, skills, and dispositions determined as outcomes of this program are certainly outside the experiences and comfort zones of their previous educational encounters. For example, students had been able to attend many classes without getting involved in discussions. We expected them not only to express and defend their thinking publicly, but also to challenge the thinking of their peers. Students had not previously been expected to use rubrics to critique their own performances or to set their own goals for growth and development. One of the greatest challenges for most of the students was to engage regularly in reflection and to record those thoughts and feelings in a journal.

By the end of the first year, it was clear both from their behaviors prior to and during class and in personal reflections captured in their journals that the students were not only taking responsibility for their own learning, but also developing into a productive community of learners. For example, not only did the students come to class having done the reading, they also met with each other outside of class to discuss the assignments and to challenge each other to think more deeply. Without being prompted, students developed questions to engage each other in perspective taking or problem solving. They began analyzing current events and applying theories studied in class to real-world situations.

It seemed appropriate to try to discern some of the reasons for these changes in the students' behaviors. This study, therefore, sought to determine the important factors affecting students' self-responsibility for their own learning and for the growth and development of their peers.

Theoretical Framework

Our study was based in qualitative research. According to Merriam (2002), during the past 20 years qualitative research has gained respect in the social science and helping professions. Procedures used in qualitative studies, however, differ distinctly from the more traditional methods of quantitative research. In this section we provide a rationale for the selection of phenomenology to guide the study, briefly explain our roles as researchers and our efforts to set our own beliefs and biases aside, and describe the processes we used for data collection and analysis.

Epistemology

The constructionist view of the source of knowledge informed this study. Constructionism rejects the view of objectivism—that truth exists in the world and is just waiting to be discovered. Instead, the constructionist stance is that "truth, or meaning, comes into existence in and out of our engagement with the realities in our world. There is no meaning without a mind. Meaning is not discovered, but constructed" (Crotty, 2004, p. 9). According to this understanding of knowledge, individuals are likely to construct different meanings from similar experiences. This epistemology gives rise to a number of theoretical perspectives for conducting qualitative research.

Theoretical Perspective

The theoretical perspective provided a context for the process involved in as well as a basis for the logic of the study. According to the theoretical perspective, "Different ways of viewing the world shape different ways of researching the world" (Crotty, 2004, p. 66). Interpretivism was the way of viewing the world that informed this study. Interpretivism "looks for culturally derived and historically situated interpretations of the social life-world" (Crotty, p. 67). The purpose of the study was to discover, from the student respondents' voices, their culturally derived interpretation of learning in community. An interpretive theoretical perspective informed several of our methodologies (Crotty, 2004).

Methodology

Phenomenology derives from the interpretivist theoretical perspective. This study was a descriptive phenomenological study that allowed the essence of the experience of learning in community to emerge from the eight students (Creswell, 2003). As developers and co-facilitators of the leadership program, we witnessed the phenomenon of learning in community and observed the students develop into responsible learners and worthy team members. The growth we witnessed in these students far surpassed any similar successes we had observed in all of our nearly 60 combined years of experience in public education. It was our desire, therefore, to uncover the factors that contributed to this growth.

Research Methods

Epoche Process

We realized while conducting this study that our own biases and beliefs are the result of many years of experience in education and are very strong. It was necessary for us as researchers, therefore, to bracket our own viewpoints in order to uncover the essence of the students' experiences. We did so by following the phenomenological epoche process. According to Moustakas (1994), the epoche is

> . . . a preparation for deriving new knowledge but also an experience in itself, a process of setting aside predilections, prejudices, predispositions, and allowing things, events, and people to enter anew into consciousness, and to look and see them again, as if for the first time. (p. 85)

The best way for us to engage in the epoche process was through reflection—identifying, first, our own beliefs based on our experiences of helping others learn, and second, our biases as a result of our interpretation of the students' experiences in the leadership program. Before we could experience the phenomenon of learning in community through the perceptions of the student participants, then, it was necessary to make explicit our beliefs, biases, and assumptions about learning and the development of community. Drawing on our years of experience in education, each of us individually identified our own notions of learning and community. Then, through much discussion, we compiled and agreed on the list below:

- Learning occurs in the mind of the individual.
- Each individual is responsible for his/her own learning.
- Much learning occurs through social interaction.
- Each individual has a responsibility to contribute to the learning of others.
- Interdependence is a more complex and higher state of being than independence.

- Intentional mental processing and metacognition are critical for constructing meaning.
- A safe environment enhances learning.
- Interpersonal skills must be deliberately taught and practiced.
- Development of community requires learners to engage in team learning opportunities.

Although we never formally presented the list to the students, it became evident that their paradigms of learning and community had been changed through their experiences in the leadership development program. Reviewing this list frequently before engaging in the interviews with students and while working with the data allowed us to focus on the lived experiences of the students.

The Participants

The study participants were the cohort of students who experienced the leadership development phenomenon. The cohort was small enough that we had the luxury of not having to select a subset of participants. Of the nine students, eight consented to be a part of the study: four undergraduate men, one undergraduate woman, and three graduate men. (The NSF SFS program is open to juniors, seniors, and graduate students. Very few women are involved in the program at our institution.) Two male undergraduates were majoring in computer engineering, one in management information systems, and one in computer science. The female undergraduate student also was a computer science major. Two of the graduate students were computer science majors, and the other was a math major. Although the eight participants, who had always received high academic grades, were in the fourth semester of the NSF SFS program, the retrospective study was designed to focus on their learning experiences during the first two semesters of the leadership development program.

Data Collection

The goal in data collection for a phenomenological study is to collect rich, meaningful data that accurately depict the participants' interpretation of the phenomenon. The primary method we used to achieve the data was the interview (Merriam, 2002). Phenomenologists usually use in-depth, semi-structured interviews guided by open-ended questions to increase the probability of gathering comparable data across subjects. In addition, this type of interview allows the researcher to gather descriptive data in the subjects' own words to provide insights into the interpretation of the experience (Bogdan & Biklen, 2003).

The first interview we conducted was a focus group with all eight participants. The open-ended questions were e-mailed to students one week prior to the interview. Students were encouraged to engage in reflection before the meeting and bring written thoughts with them. The focus group lasted approximately 90 minutes and was audiotaped and transcribed.

The same researcher interviewed each of the eight participants individually. Even though we were interested in identifying everything related to the phenomenon that was important to each participant, we chose to use semi-structured interviews because of our desire to uncover each individual's own personal interpretation of the experience that lead to his or her development as a responsible learner. Additional interviews with individual participants were not deemed necessary due to the abundance of data available in the students' journals and self-assessments.

Frequent reflection and periodic written self-assessments were required of the students throughout the leadership development program. They recorded their reflections in journals, which were copied and used as sources of data for the study. At the end of each semester, students also were required to complete self-assessments describing their growth and development as leaders. Those written self-assessments were also used as data in this study.

Data Analysis and Interpretation

The data were analyzed and interpreted by both researchers independently following steps suggested by Colaizzi (1978): Read all data, extract significant statements, formulate meanings, organize into clusters of themes, integrate into an exhaustive description, and formulate the exhaustive description in as unequivocal a statement of identification of the phenomenon's fundamental structure as possible. We began the analysis by reading through all data to become familiar with them and to begin listening to the words of the participants as they described their experiences. We then read through the data a second time and began coding by highlighting significant statements using various colors. Any coding discrepancies that arose were resolved by discussing our individual interpretations and by returning to the data for additional evidence to support claims. It was also through our discussions that themes began to emerge. We validated the findings by taking these themes back to the participants and asking for feedback. When this member checking provided no new data or insights about our interpretations, we proceeded to the final step in the analysis: to formulate as unequivocal a statement of identification of the phenomenon's fundamental structure as possible.

Findings

The eight general themes that emerged from the coding were as follows: (a) self-identified growth and development, (b) continuous reflection, (c) metacognition, (d) high expectations for addressing challenging tasks, (e) interdependence, (f) accountability, (g) a supportive environment, and (h) working together over time. The fundamental structure of learning in community as perceived by these eight participants, then, was a self-recognized transformative development that resulted from being engaged in intentional mental processing before, during, and after being challenged with and held accountable for addressing complex, meaningful tasks in an interdependent and supportive environment over time. This complex statement embodies a great many possibilities with implications for educators and students alike—far too many to explore in one study. This article, therefore, addresses the nature and role of the high expectations set and the importance of being held accountable for working to meet those expectations that made a difference in this transformative experience for students.

Initially, it may not seem like a significant finding that high expectations are key to transformative learning. Faculty are fully aware of the importance of setting high expectations for their students (Schilling & Schilling, 1999; Weimer, 2002). Much time is invested in carefully constructing student learning outcomes for a course, planning the learning opportunities to achieve those outcomes, and developing assessment tools to evaluate student growth and development (Huba & Freed, 2000; Wiggins & McTighe, 1998). Most would certainly agree that students will live up—or down—to our expectations.

Professors do want and expect their students to be diligent and to engage in every learning opportunity planned for them. Unfortunately, educators may unwittingly send messages that less is expected. For example, class interaction may require students to read and think before coming to class, but how do instructors respond when students have not prepared? Are students held accountable, or does the instructor change the plan for the day to "take care of" those students who didn't prepare? For example, does he or she spend the class time conveying to students the content they were to have studied on their own instead of engaging them in thinking related to the content? Our findings support a claim by Weimer (2002), "Expectations for more responsible student behavior are conveyed not by what we say but by what we do. And we compromise what we say when what we do contradicts it" (p. 106). According to Weimer (2002): "[S]tudents will start assuming more responsibility for their learning once we start making them accountable for their actions" (pp. 105–106). If, in fact, we expect students to take responsibility for their own learning, our behaviors must consistently hold them accountable for doing the thinking required for learning. In addition, our findings reveal that students can identify, as contributing to their growth, the importance of their instructors holding them accountable for meeting expectations. The challenge is for faculty to maintain high expectations by holding students accountable for meeting them. In addition, our findings indicate that high expectations *must not* be mundane activities that students can merely check off a list, but instead need to be upheld by challenging tasks that are relevant to students as professionals and that have enough ambiguity to allow them to guide and direct their own learning.

Becoming Responsible Learners

Our ultimate expectation in the leadership development program is that students learn to take responsibility for their own growth and development—that they do their own thinking and take ownership of their choices of action. Every learning opportunity we plan has this outcome in mind, and we continually communicate to students that the assignments are for them, not us. It was no surprise to us that students realize the importance of high expectations. It was, however, a revelation when students identified the differences in our expectations and the kinds of expectations they were accustomed to meeting in order to get a desired grade. An entry from Kim's[1] journal toward the end of the first year, for example, revealed that she had discovered a new personal meaning for learning:

> My beliefs about learning at the start of the semester were the norm for someone institutionalized by the public school system. I believed that the key to success in learning was to do whatever professors asked. Learning in my mind was to show up, do the required assignments, and study for the tests. Granted, I knew on some level that learning in that fashion is superficial learning only. In fact, my learning philosophy back then could even be said to be more of a general belief in doing exactly what I was told rather than a real learning belief system.

Even early in the semester, students' journal reflections described the difference in expectations between the leadership class and many other classes:

> . . . you have to like the type of learning we were doing. I used to just like memorization, memorizing computer knowledge and spitting it back out on a test or something. I don't think I've had any non-test classes.
>
> I went ahead and did the second assignment and created the chart based on the relational leadership model; that took a lot of thought. I don't think it is complete; I'm sure I'll be adding to it every once in a while. By assigning us to go back and look at things we've done or somewhat completed, reflect upon them and then apply new things to them, we are learning more and getting more out of topics and materials. We don't just read a chapter and then never go back, we are required to apply those things learned to new assignments later on.

It became clear to us that students were accustomed to following strict guidelines and checking items off a list to meet the requirements for many courses. There was security for students in knowing exactly what they had to do to get the desired grade in many courses. They were more than a little uncomfortable being expected to take responsibility for their own learning. For example, several participants admitted the leadership class was not only different from most other classes, it was even a bit scary:

> When I first heard we were going to be doing a journal, I was apprehensive and a little disconcerted. . . . I was reluctant to do it, fearing I wouldn't be able to put my thoughts on paper.
>
> It [journaling] was painful to start out with, but it got less so.
>
> When you required us to talk, I was scared to say anything. I would always pass—well, not always, but a lot of the times.

We did expect some cognitive dissonance as students were given more control of their own growth and development, but what we didn't realize was how deceptively simple our expectation was. Our desire was, simply, for students to take responsibility for their learning—to do their own thinking and own their choices of actions. We expected each student to engage fully in every learning opportunity and to develop skills and abilities accordingly. We were pleasantly surprised that students interpreted this as much more of a challenge than they were accustomed to facing:

> This is, in some ways my most challenging class, because I can always do more. I see people around me doing more than I am, and I think, 'I should be doing what they are doing.' However, I realize that I have not reached that point yet. That is the goal (i.e., to work as hard as I can in order to learn as much as possible).

As revealed by Kenna's words above, students not only recognized a very different kind of expectation, they also began to understand their own role in making choices and setting their own expectations. It was our challenge to plan activities that would move them along on the journey to becoming lifelong learners.

Kinds of Expectations

As stated earlier, every learning opportunity was designed to support and encourage students to take responsibility for their own growth and development. The analysis of our data, in the words of the participants, revealed that the expectations and assignments that had the greatest impact on their learning were interacting with others, recording their thoughts in a journal, doing special projects like interviewing leaders or preparing for an academic controversy, and engaging in self-assessment. We offer the following examples, in the voices of the participants, to illustrate each type of assignment or expectation.

Interacting With Others

We believe students have an obligation not only to take responsibility for their own learning, but also to contribute to the learning of everyone else in the class. As previously identified in our list of biases, we expect students to come to class prepared to engage in discussion and interaction. For many students, this is one of the first big challenges to their learning paradigms, as revealed by Sam in a journal entry early in the year:

> In the vast majority of my other classes, I show up for class, jot down a few notes, do the homework, and take the tests. I am not forced to share thoughts of my own or involve myself with others. Indeed, most college classes allow students to work in isolation, which is a grievous error. Leadership class is dramatically different. I am required to voice my own values and perform teamwork. I am not allowed to just sit back and listen. I must synthesize my own thoughts and express them.

Meeting this expectation is a bigger challenge for some students than for others. We work hard to establish a safe environment early in the semester where all students will be willing to contribute. To encourage contributions early, we start and end every class meeting with one of our favorite interaction strategies: a "go 'round." The facilitator poses a question or a notion to elicit a response, and after some individual think time, each person is expected to speak. Discussion is discouraged during the actual go 'round, but those individuals who speak early will be more likely to engage in interaction later in the meeting when discussion is desired. During the focus group interview, participants reflected on those first classes and the early go 'rounds. Alex, for instance, recognized how much his willingness to speak up in other groups had changed. When questioned about the reason, he replied that it was due to "Having go 'rounds every week, you know, always having to say something once or twice every class."

Recording Thoughts in a Journal

In addition to being expected to reveal their thinking publicly, all students are required to monitor their progress in a reflection journal—another big challenge. The following honest reflection from Pat's journal is typical of many students who have not previously engaged in deeper thinking and learning through reflection:

> Journaling is still not easy for me and still takes a lot of time, but I am working at it. . . . When I was told at the beginning of the year that journaling was required, I laughed to myself; I knew I was not going to like doing it and I thought it was sort of weird. While I still do not take pleasure in writing journal entries, I do enjoy having them. I understand how vital they are for me to learn about myself. They serve as great evidence of my development at certain points along the way.

Most students undergo similar attitude changes from when we first introduce them to the notion of learning more deeply through reflection to after they have struggled through learning to record their thoughts in their journals and publicly reveal their thinking to colleagues. Early on, we provide questions to guide students' journaling, but eventually we expect them to monitor their own thinking and writing with the aid of rubrics. We often need to "persist longer than they resist"—our mantra when students work hard to have us "tell them what to do and how to do it."

Writing in a journal is not easy; neither is thinking on your feet and explaining your thoughts publicly. But both are critical for development into a responsible learner. While many students realize this by the end of the first semester, for others it takes nearly the entire academic year. Regardless, students' newly developed skills of engaging in critical thinking and meaningful reflection are usually revealed to them after they have done the hard work necessary to complete an assigned task.

Engaging in Special Projects

One major project during first semester required students to interview three individuals whom they considered leaders and write a paper describing their insights. Bert's candid reflection reveals the frustration of facing a challenging task, the discipline required to complete it, and the awareness of his growth and development as a result:

> When we were given the assignment I dreaded it. I knew it was going to be hard and that it was not something I could just do and get over with. Choosing three people to interview was difficult, writing three sets of questions was not easy, setting up times to do the interviews was complicated, giving the interviews was a new and challenging experience, and writing the paper that went along with the project was time consuming and, again, difficult. I am so glad I did it.

Alex admitted in his journal to being frustrated with the ambiguity of this same assignment:

> I have been having quite a bit of trouble with the interview assignment. I sort of wish there were clearly defined guidelines on what we are supposed to learn, because I'm used to that. This is sort of stepping outside my comfort zone, having to decide what I want to learn and all.

These words confirm the importance of designing learning activities that are relevant to students as they prepare to be become professionals in their chosen discipline but that contain enough ambiguity to allow students to guide and direct their own learning.

Another challenging and ambiguous task was an academic controversy designed to challenge students to do the kind of thinking necessary for those preparing to protect our nation's information infrastructure. An academic controversy (Johnson, Johnson, & Smith, 1991) is a specific learning strategy we like to use to engage students in critically examining both sides of an issue before making an important decision. Typically, we describe a controversial matter, and students then research it to learn as much about both sides of the topic as possible. Then, with a partner, they are assigned to defend one side (whether they believe in it or not) as forcefully as possible. They must, in turn, also listen to an opposing pair defend the contrary viewpoint. Next, both student pairs reverse their stance and present their best case for the opposing side. The final challenge is to engage in a discussion to make the best decision possible.

Students were given the task of preparing to engage in an academic controversy about an issue pertinent to them not only as citizens, but also as professionals: the Patriot Act. Kim's journal reflection about this experience is evidence that students enjoy being challenged with meaningful tasks and recognize the rewards from their investments of time, energy, and engagement:

> I have even poured my heart into little things. We were asked to read up on the Patriot Act so that we would be able to do a quick debate during one of our class periods. I spent so much time looking up different materials and sources and reading over all of it, probably too much considering how quickly it was over and done with. I worked extremely hard in preparation for that 20-minute activity, and I do not regret it—and that is how I have done almost everything else in this class as well.

These words confirmed for us that we were on the right track in planning learning opportunities to challenge our students. They recognized that growth and development is not an easy process; in fact, it is hard work—but it is worth the effort. More of the students came to this realization as they engaged in the final assignment of the first semester: engaging in self-assessment.

The final project for each semester requires students to summarize their growth and development. Words taken from Kelly's final project revealed an appreciation for the hard work necessary for deep, meaningful learning:

> Something that I have to bring up in a summary of this semester is the effort I have put into this class and all that has been asked of me. For me, this class is not easy; it is trying and different from all the other classes I have taken in college. The thinking, analyzing, and reflecting we do is not common practice here. . . . It is challenging and out of the ordinary for me, and I have put forth a great deal of effort and time to produce my best work. There is a reason I take pride in my journaling as a whole and my interview project, and that is because I gave them all that I could. Through hard work and effort I was/am able to learn more from these activities than if I could do them with ease.

The Nature of Expectations

The learning opportunities we developed to help our students meet our expectation of taking responsibility for their own learning, thinking, and behaviors had a greater impact than we anticipated. Further analysis of the data revealed to us that the learning opportunities most likely to promote student growth and development were those that were challenging enough to require deep thinking and new learning, relevant to students as professionals, and ambiguous enough to allow students to guide and direct their own thinking and learning. In addition, we found that even when students didn't like the task given them, they usually enjoyed meeting our challenge.

None of our findings about the nature of expectations that promote student growth and development should be much of a surprise. All are well supported in the literature. Students really do like to learn (Leamnson, 2000; Sprenger, 2005); learning is innate (Caine & Caine, 1997). In spite of what faculty may think, there is nothing wrong with the way the brains of their students work. For example, students who are fans of professional sports have no trouble remembering specific details and statistics related to their favorite player or team. Because of their emotional involvement in the game, they are capable of "one-trial learning." That is, "They readily learn what captures their imagination" or that with which they become emotionally involved (Leamnson, 2000, p. 38). Once students understand that their brains seek challenge (Caine & Caine, 1997), which results in strong positive emotions, they find their own emotional hooks to enhance memory formation. The lesson is that students can become more involved with the content of their courses if they intentionally seek out these emotional hooks.

We believe the emotional hooks for our students emerged as they engaged in activities that allowed them to develop the skills required of a professional in their chosen field of information assurance—securing information in application areas ranging from software to networks to electronic democracy. Students' emotional involvement allowed them to set goals and challenge themselves to take risks inherent in deep and meaningful growth and development—to become responsible learners—as evidenced in the following excerpt from Alex's journal:

> The thing I want to continue to work on is applying leadership in the real world. Doing so this semester was a real eye opener for me, and a lot of what I've learned about leadership started to make a lot more sense. This shouldn't have come as a huge shock since I learn the most about engineering in the labs, but for some reason it did. Be that as it may, I now know that the more I apply leadership in the real world, the more I will learn and the easier it will become. It still is somewhat difficult to do, so I have to keep in the front of my mind that I can't just give in or give up. I have to keep pushing through because the benefits are certainly worth it.

Once students accept the challenge to take greater ownership of their learning, the ambiguity of assigned tasks became even more important. Students began to seek opportunities to do their own thinking and choose their own actions. Again, this is no surprise. Self-directedness is an important aspect of adult learning (Cranton, 1994). Two of the four aspects of self-directedness described by Candy (in Cranton, 1994) are particularly salient to our work with the students: self-management and learner control. Self-management is the willingness and capacity to conduct one's own education. Learner control is the learner's decision making about objectives, sequence, strategies, and evaluation in an education setting. Ambiguous tasks allowed the students to make choices about their own growth and development.

Pat's words from the final assessment reiterate our earlier point—that even though students might not like the task(s), they usually liked meeting the challenge:

In reality, the second semester this year was a long, intense, difficult, rewarding and growing trial. However, it felt more like a racing blur, where you cannot separate one lesson learned from the next because there were so many insights and realizations to take in and absorb. I firmly stand by this statement. If there is *one* thing that could be said about [these courses], it would be that it is the biggest challenge one will face at [Midwestern university]; it is also the most rewarding.

In addition, we were delighted by the honesty in the students' reflections throughout the experience. A section from Brent's journal suggests the possibility of having too much of a good thing:

Having the rubric there was the key to accomplishing the object of the assignment (I know we were supposed to use it, but it was an essential tool). It allowed me to look for specific things (objectively), whereas I would've been lost without it. I do agree that you have to be challenged, and put outside of your comfort zone sometimes in order to grow. So these assignments are good for us, but they should be used sparingly and in moderation.

The Importance of Accountability

Even though our notions about high expectations were not explicit in our original list of beliefs, biases, and assumptions, they certainly were implicit. Missing from the list, however, was another important finding from the study—student recognition of the importance of being held accountable for meeting the high expectations that have been set. In retrospect, our years of experience with learners of all ages developed within us an assumption about accountability and learning. Intuitively, we *know* accountability is always critical. It was, however, surprising to us that *every* student participant, independently, identified that being held accountable for meeting the high expectations was critical to his or her development.

The students' words revealed their progress along the journey to becoming responsible learners. The first stage seemed to be one of resistance. The expectations and the type of learning we were asking of them were unfamiliar. It was not uncommon to read journal entries where students were working through their frustrations:

{I'm feeling] pressured to share my own thoughts and ideas in more of a public setting than I am used to. I've always felt the most comfortable speaking about topics of any substance with only one or two people at a time.

. . . at first I did it simply because it was a requirement. . . .

It was really hard at first. The standard was to try and do five [journal entries] a week, and for me that was impossible. I knew that changing my own standard to four [entries] made it a little more accomplishable.

I guess if I didn't have to [journal], I probably wouldn't.

In the case of the leadership journal, at first I did it simply because it was a requirement of being in the class. Over time it developed into a valuable tool for me, but the problem is that I wouldn't have done it in the first place if I wasn't "forced" to.

Knowing that it would be more or less a weekly requirement to share my personal feelings with a larger group, I realized that it was not something I just had to get through; it was something I had to become better at.

I think the discussion we do in a large group gives everyone the opportunity to place ideas on a stage, including pushing those of use who are less prone to do so on our own. . . .

Holding students accountable through this resistant stage was our responsibility. Because that was usually not easy, or pleasant, we often drew on our own mantra—persist longer than they resist. Eventually, students recognized the rewards as a result of engaging in the hard work of growth and development, and we met with less resistance. For example:

I think one of the biggest areas I have grown in is my willingness to share my ideas without having to be directly asked. I worked on this in class by offering to go first in a go 'round and participating more actively in the group activity discussions. However, this is still an area I need to improve upon a lot.

Our job became easier once students realized the importance of accountability and asked for help in developing ways to hold themselves accountable. One extremely shy student found it very difficult to express ideas publicly. Even though he accepted the notion that each student had a responsibility to contribute to the learning of others, it was a constant challenge. Together we devised a strategy to encourage him to contribute:

> One plan to contribute more visibly is to offer input without being called on, such as raising my hand to start a go 'round. I kind of asked [my instructor] to keep me accountable for visible contributions to the team, and that if she feels I have not shown enough, she should let me know. She would like to see more effort. I think this plan will help others see me as more of a contributor, as well as allowing me to get more out of the course.

It was the realization that being held accountable was critical to their development as professionals that eventually prodded the students to take the final step of holding themselves accountable for working at learning, as revealed by Taylor: "Knowing I have the inclination to allow myself to become disempowered, I have to force myself out of my comfort zone regularly. When I need to speak up, I will just have to bite the bullet and force myself." Alex took this responsibility for his own learning to his other classes:

> I figured out how I was going to try and [get more out of lectures]. Instead of just sitting there like some wilting plant trying to just soak up the information like sunlight in the hopes that it would help me, I needed to make myself a lot more active in the class. A lot of professors are very bad at involving the class and making us active participants in our learning, but if they weren't going to do it, I was. So I resolved to take notes in more of my own words, try my own little examples of concepts they were explaining, and generally try to become a more active participant in the lecture process.

Finally, as students resisted returning to old habits, we acknowledged in their journal reflections their transformation into the responsible learners they needed to be:

> To help with this new way of thinking, I had to become motivated to learn for myself, and not just to please others. For example, I could complete half of the activities or not do much reading if I really wanted to, but since I know it's for my personal development and I would only be disabling myself, it becomes worthwhile to put a true effort into the activities.
>
> . . . I have learned that I need to take leadership by asking questions and taking responsibility for learning the material. On the other hand, I have also thought much about how I can take leadership in my less challenging classes and take it upon myself to go beyond the required class work. In both cases, I have to take a leadership role to learn.
>
> . . . I had to become motivated to learn for myself, and not just to please others.
>
> I believed what I was told: "This learning is for you." This has allowed me to have a different kind of expectation (maybe even a higher expectation) than I have for my other classes. I do not set out to learn a certain set of material; I set out to learn as much as I can.

The entire journey of becoming a responsible learner is probably best summed up by one of the participants, who succinctly said, "At first we tried to refuse to do what you asked. Then we did it because you made us. Now we do it because it works!"

Limitations

Because the purpose of this phenomenological study was to uncover the essence of the participants' experiences of learning in community, the findings are limited to a specific small group of students at a Midwestern university during the first year of a two-year program. No attempt has been made to generalize the results to other student populations; however, early observations from our work with three other groups of students learning in community indicate that similar results may be occurring. Therefore, the findings from this study about the importance of having high expectations and of holding students accountable for meeting them offer implications for educators as they plan for the learning of their students.

Implications

Most students—and many faculty—are deeply entrenched in the paradigm of learning where students come to class expecting to be told exactly what to do and how to think, check assignments off a list, take tests that measure how much information has been stored in (short-term?) memory, and then dump the information before moving on to the next class. Faculty have a responsibility to help students break through that paradigm and become responsible learners. Faculty owe it to students to

- make them do the preparation and thinking required for deeper learning;
- challenge them with addressing complex, meaningful real-world tasks;
- help them develop emotional connections by planning assignments that are relevant to their future professional lives;
- create enough ambiguity to require students to guide and direct their own thinking and learning; and
- hold them accountable for meeting the expectation of becoming responsible learners.

Students may not initially like these new kinds of expectations, but they do realize that being held accountable for meeting them makes a difference in their learning. And they come to appreciate the freedom and power associated with becoming responsible learners.

Footnotes

[1]Kim and all other student names used in the article are pseudonyms.

References

Bogdan, R. C., & Biklen, S. K. (2003). *Qualitative research for education—An introduction to theories and methods* (4th ed.). Boston: Allyn & Bacon.

Caine, R. N., & Caine, G. (1997). *Education on the edge of possibility*. Alexandria, VA: Association for Supervision and Curriculum Development.

Colaizzi, P. F. (1978). Psychological research as the phenomenologist views it. In R. Valle & M. King (Eds.), *Existential-phenomenological alternatives for psychology* (pp. 48–70). New York: Oxford University Press.

Cranton, P. (1994). Self-directed and transformative instructional development. *Journal of Higher Education, 65* (6), 726–744.

Creswell, J. W. (2003). *Research design: Qualitative, quantitative, and mixed methods approaches* (2nd ed.). Thousand Oaks, CA: Sage.

Crotty, M. (2004). *Foundations of social research: Meaning and perspective in the research process*. Thousand Oaks, CA: Sage.

Gardiner, L. (1998). Why we must change: The research evidence. *Thought and Action, 14*, 71–87.

Huba, M., & Freed, J. (2000). *Learner-centered assessment on college campuses: Shifting the focus from teaching to learning*. Needham Heights, MA: Allyn & Bacon.

Johnson, D., Johnson, R., & Smith, K. (1991). *Cooperative learning: Increasing college faculty instructional productivity* (ASHE-ERIC Higher Education Report No. 4). Washington, DC: The George Washington University, School of Education and Human Development.

Leamnson, R. (2000). Learning as biological brain change. *Change, 32* (6), 34–40.

Licklider, B., Thompson, J., Hendrich, S., Boylston, T., Zachary, L., Jungst, S., Nonnecke, G., Hayes, C., & Freeman, S. (2004). *Leading the learning revolution*. Retrieved April 12, 2005, from http://www.iastate.edu/~newplan/2010/process/docs/learnrev.shtml

Merriam, S. B., and associates. (2002). *Qualitative research in practice: Examples for discussion and analysis*. San Francisco: Jossey-Bass.

Moustakas, C. (1994). *Phenomenological research methods*. Thousands Oaks, CA: Sage.

Robertson, D. R. (2001). Beyond learner-centeredness: Close encounters of the systemocentric kind. *Journal of Faculty Development, 18* (1), 7–13.

Schilling, K. M., & Schilling, K. L. (1999). Increasing expectations for student effort. *About campus, 4* (2), 4–10.

Sprenger, M. (2005). *How to teach so students remember*. Alexandria, VA: Association for Supervision and Curriculum Development.

Weimer, M. (2002). *Learner-centered teaching*. San Francisco: Jossey-Bass.

Wiersema, J. (2006). *Learning in community: Student perceptions and experiences.* Unpublished dissertation, Iowa State University, Ames, IA.

Wiggins, G., & McTighe, J. (1998). *Understanding by design.* Alexandria, VA: Association for Supervision and Curriculum Development.

Appendix

General Philosophy and Expectations

We view the four leadership courses as developmental in nature. They are listed as courses to fit the university structure, but we do not see the outcomes as simply items to be checked off of a list. Development is a process of adding something, such as thoughts, feelings, or behaviors, to what was there already and, as that something is integrated, causing the whole that it is joining, such as a perspective or frame of reference, to be transformed (Robertson, 2001). Therefore, we think the assignments listed below are the most appropriate ones, but they may change, and others might be added as needed.

Assessment/Evaluation

Letter grades earned in the course will be based on the quality of student performance on the assignments described below. It is expected that all completed assignments will be high quality. If an assignment appears to be a "work in progress," the student will receive feedback with suggestions about what needs to be done to reach completion.

1. **Work with a learning partner.**
   a. Hold each other accountable for completing work.
   b. Help with make-up if late or absent from any meeting.
   c. Ask questions to cause intentional mental processing and deeper learning.
   d. Challenge and encourage each other to develop in all areas.

   Accountability:
   (1) Critical self-assessment of the action plan
   (2) Identification of learning as a result of the action plan
   (3) Evidence of peer-editing on written assignments
2. **Connect with leaders in the field (but within geographic area) by interviewing three leaders outside the university.**

   Accountability: Complete a paper after the interviews that includes a:
   (1) Summary of each interview
   (2) Analysis of leadership skills
   (3) Summary of learning
3. **Engage in personal conversation with facilitator.**

   Accountability: Write a summary of the conversation in which you:
   (1) Identify and provide evidence of team contributions.
   (2) Set goals for self-development.
   (3) Outline a plan to meet those goals.
4. **Implement selected applications of learning theories.**

   Accountability: Complete relevant assignments as given.

5. **Actively practice interactive skills.**
   a. Complete "Practices Inventories."
   b. Reflect and record progress in your journal.
   c. Make connections with your learning of skills.
   d. Implement a plan for improvement.

   Accountability:
   (1) Observations of actions during meetings
   (2) Critical self-assessment and analysis of growth to be included with final project
6. **Complete self-inventories as given (with reflection and analysis).**
   Accountability: Reflection and analysis to be included with final project
7. **Read & study assigned portions of texts.**
   a. Engage in discussion and activities.
   b. Apply information for self-improvement.

   Accountability:
   (1) Completion of written assignments related to readings
   (2) Critical self-assessment and analysis of growth to be included with final project
8. **Journal.** Reflect on:
   a. Current issues and policies in information assurance
   b. Ethical dilemmas in the news
   c. Evidence of your development of specific interactive skills
   d. Analysis of team your team's development
   e. Evidence of **[your?]** development as a lifelong learner
   f. Consequences of **[your?]** choices and decisions

   Accountability: See rubric.
9. **Participate in class go 'rounds, discussions, and activities:** Experiential learning and modeling of effective strategies are important parts of this course. Your comments during discussions and go 'rounds will provide evidence that you are making the transfer to your own leadership situation.
10. **Prepare and interact between sessions.**
    Accountability: Team, learning partners, reflection, and written work as assigned
11. **Complete final project:** Reflection on your development as a leader: The final project will be an organization and analysis of your work and thinking for this semester. Please include:
    - your reflection journal;
    - your assessment of your efforts at completing a reflection journal based on the rubric;
    - evidence of your work on each enduring understanding;
    - all assignments;
    - a brief (no more than one page) written analysis of each artifact,* considering:
      - what you did,
      - what was effective,
      - what you might change another time, and
      - what you learned;

*Artifacts include all assignments as listed above as well as any additional given during the semester.

- your beliefs about learning and leadership both at the beginning of the course and at the time you are writing the analysis.

From the above analyses, prepare a **summary** of your understandings, learnings, practices, and future plans to continue your growth as a leader. Describe what growth you think you have made. Be sure to include your assessment of your progress on each of the enduring understandings. Provide evidence for your assessments.

Community, Conflict, and Ways of Knowing

Parker J. Palmer

Ways to Deepen Our Educational Agenda

Twelve years ago, my own yearning for community in education led me out of the mainstream of higher education to a small place called Pendle Hill, a 55-year-old Quaker living/learning community near Philadelphia. It is a place where everyone—from teachers to cooks to administrators—receives the same base salary as a witness to community. At Pendle Hill, rigorous study of philosophy, nonviolent social change, and other subjects, goes right alongside washing the dishes each day, making decisions by consensus, and taking care of each other, as well as reaching out to the world.

Out of that long, intense experience, what might I share that would somehow be hopeful and encouraging? I learned, of course, that community is vital and important, but it is also terribly difficult work for which we are not well prepared; at least I was not. I learned that the degree to which a person yearns for community is directly related to the dimming of memory of his or her last experience of it.

I came up with my own definition of community after a year at Pendle Hill: Community is that place where the person you least want to live with always lives. At the end of my second year, I came up with a corollary: When that person moves away, someone else arises immediately to take his or her place.

But the question I want to address is this: How should we be thinking about the nature of community in the modern college and university? I think that question puts the issue where it belongs. We need a way of thinking about community in higher education that relates it to the central mission of the academy—the generation and transmission of knowledge. The way we think about community in settings of higher learning, in other words, must be different from the way we think about community in other settings, like the civil society, the neighborhood, the church, or the workplace. Within the academy, we need to think about community in ways that deepen the *educational* agenda.

As I listen to the current conversation about the place of community in the academy, it seems to go something like this. First, there has been a collapse of civic virtue in the society around us, a collapse into expressive and competitive individualism, and a loss of integrated vision. This view was articulated for us most recently by the work of Robert Bellah and his colleagues in *Habits of the Heart*.

Second, the argument runs, higher education can and should respond to this collapse by becoming a model of community in at least two ways. One is to develop new, cooperative social forms for campus life (i.e., in dormitory and classroom life, where cooperative habits can be formed). Second,

PARKER J. PALMER is director of the Resident Program at St. Benedict Center, Box 5070, Madison, Wisconsin, 53705. He is the author of *To Know As We Are Known: A Spirituality of Education* (published by Harper and Row). The above article was taken from a speech given at the AAHE annual meeting in Chicago earlier this year.

higher education should reorganize curricula toward a more integrated vision of the world, offer more interdisciplinary studies, and do more ethical- and value-oriented work.

There is value in this line of argument, but I think much of it parallels the way we think about renewing the civil society itself, where we argue that we must build structures and teach the content of civic virtue to bind the community together. The argument is valuable, but it does not respond to the unique heart-and-core mission of higher education.

So I would like to press the question of community in education a step further. I want to go beyond altering the social forms of education, as valuable as that may be, go beyond altering the topical content of courses, as valuable as that may be, and try to reach into the underlying nature of our knowledge itself. I want to reach for the relation of community to the very mode of knowing dominant in the academy.

To put it in philosophical terms, I want to try to connect concepts of community to questions of epistemology, which I believe are the central questions for any institution engaged in a mission of knowing, teaching, and learning. How do we know? How do we learn? Under what conditions and with what validity?

***

I believe that it is here—at the epistemological core of our knowledge and our processes of knowing that our powers for forming or deforming human consciousness are to be found. I believe that it is here, in our modes of knowing, that we shape souls by the shape of our knowledge: It is here that the idea of community must ultimately take root and have impact if it is to reshape the doing of higher education.

My thesis is a very simple one: I do not believe that epistemology is a bloodless abstraction; the *way* we know has powerful implications for the *way* we live. I argue that every epistemology tends to become an ethic, and that every way of knowing tends to become a way of living. I argue that the relation established between the knower and the known, between the student and the subject, tends to become the relation of the living person to the world itself. I argue that every mode of knowing contains its own moral trajectory, its own ethical direction and outcomes.

Let me try to demonstrate this thesis, this link between epistemology and life. The mode of knowing that dominates higher education I call objectivism. It has three traits with which we are all familiar.

The first of these traits is that the academy will be objective. This means that it holds everything it knows at arm's length. It distances the knower from the world for a very specific purpose; that is, to keep its knowledge from contamination by subjective prejudice and bias. But even as it does this distancing, it divorces that knowledge—a part of the world—from our personal life. It creates a world "out there" of which we are only spectators and in which we do not live. That is the first outcome of the objectivist way of knowing.

Secondly, objectivism is analytic. Once you have made something into an object (in my own discipline, that something can be a person), you can then chop that object up into pieces to see what makes it tick. You can dissect it, you can cut it apart, you can analyze it, even unto death. And that is the second habit formed by the objectivist mode of knowing.

Third, this mode of knowing is experimental. And I mean this in a broad and metaphoric sense, not laboratory operations *per se*. I mean by experimental that we are now free with these dissected objects to move the pieces around, to reshape the world in an image more pleasing to us, to see what would happen if we did. It is this "power over the world" motif that I am reaching for when I say "experimentalism" in the epistemology called objectivism.

Objective, analytic, experimental. Very quickly this seemingly abstract way of knowing, this seemingly bloodless epistemology, becomes an ethic. It is an ethic of competitive individualism, in the midst of a world fragmented and made exploitable by that very mode of knowing. The mode of knowing itself breeds intellectual habits, indeed spiritual instincts, that destroy community. We make objects of each other and the world to be manipulated for our own private ends.

Remember if you will those students in an earlier Carnegie study, Arthur Levine's *When Dreams and Heroes Died*. These were the students who thought, 80 to 90 percent of them, that the world was going to hell in a handbasket, that its future was dim and grim. But when asked about their own personal futures, 80 and 90 percent of them said, "Oh, no problem. It's rosy. I'm getting a good education, good grades, I'm going to a good school, I'm going to get a good job." A psychoanalyst looking at this data would say, "schizophrenia."

I want to argue that it's a *trained* schizophrenia: It is the way these students have been taught to look at reality through objectivist lenses. They have always been taught about a world out there somewhere apart from them, divorced from their personal lives; they never have been invited to intersect their autobiographies with the life story of the world. And so they can report on a world that is not the one in which they live, one they've been taught about from some objectivist 's fantasy.

They have also been formed in the habit of experimental manipulation. These students believe they can take pieces of the world and carve out for themselves a niche of private sanity in the midst of public calamity. That is nothing more than the ethical outcome of the objectivism in which they have been formed, or deformed. It is a failure to recognize their own implication with society's fate.

Objectivism is essentially anticommunal. As long as it remains the dominant epistemology in higher education, I think we will make little progress on communal agendas. I do not believe that any interdisciplinary combining of objectivist courses can overcome this kind of ethical impact: You can't put all the objectivisms together and come up with something new. I don't believe that courses on ethics placed around the perimeters of this objectivism can in any way deflect its moral trajectory, because objectivism is not about neutral facts that can somehow be reshaped by add-on values—it is a kind of knowledge that has its own ethical and moral course.

My definition of community is simple, if partial: I understand community as a capacity for relatedness within individuals—relatedness not only to people but to events in history, to nature, to the world of ideas, and yes, to things of the spirit. We talk a lot in higher education about the formation of inward capacities—the capacity to tolerate ambiguity, the capacity for critical thought. I want us to talk more about those ways of knowing that form an inward capacity for relatedness. Objectivism, which destroys this capacity, must be countered if the academy is to make a contribution to the reweaving of community.

***

On a hopeful note, I believe there are promising movements towards community in the world of intellect today. They are found in the emergence of new epistemologies, which emerge most often in fringe areas of the academy's work. The underlying theme in all of these "fringe" areas is the theme of the relatedness. Let me give examples.

First and most prominent is feminist thought. Feminist thought is not primarily about equal pay for equal work. It is not primarily about equal power and status for women. It *is* about those things, but it is primarily about another way of seeing and therefore another way of being in the world. It is about an alternative epistemology. It is vital for that reason.

I see an alternative epistemology evolving in black scholarship. If you read a book called *There is a River,* by Vincent Harding, you are reading another kind of history, history that refuses to allow you to divorce your own story from the story being told. It is history told with a passion that draws you in; it will not let you escape. It is factual, it is objective, *and* it is passionate. It refuses to let you off the hook.

Native American studies have much the same quality. Ecological studies are also giving rise to new epistemologies, as are the philosophies of the new physics, the work of people like David Bohm, and the work of someone like geneticist Barbara McClintock. These latter have a "feeling for the organism." In all of these places we are learning that the act of knowing itself, if we understand it rightly, is a bond of community between us and that which we know. The act of knowing itself is a way of building and rebuilding community, and it is this we must reach for in our education.

Throughout the literature in the fields I have mentioned, certain words keep popping up—words like organic, bodily, intuitive, reciprocal, passionate, interactive, and communal. These are words of epistemology, long before they are words of ethics. They are words about a way of knowing that then becomes a way of living.

What happens when higher education and its dominant epistemology are challenged by studies such as these, or by virtually any other problem? If the problem will not go away, the strategy is add-a-course. And so we add a course in black studies, or feminist thought, or Native American literature, or in ethics or ecology to try somehow to bleed off the pressure that these new epistemologies put on objectivism.

The strategy misses the point. These studies are a challenge to an outmoded way of knowing, and to an ethic that is essentially destructive to community.

I want to make it clear that these new epistemologies do not aim at the overthrow of objectivity, analysis, and experimentation. Indeed, the feminist thinkers that I know use those very tools in their writing. But they want to put those tools within a context of affirming the communal nature of reality itself, the *relational* nature of reality. So in these studies, objectivist modes are used in creative tension with their relational counterparts. For example, the mode of objectivity is held in creative tension with another way of knowing, the way of intimacy, the way of personally implicating yourself with the subject. Virtually every great scholar finds this way of appropriating knowledge, of living it and breathing it and bringing it so close to your heart that you and it are almost one. Objectivity and intimacy can go hand in hand; that's what the new epistemologies are calling for.

Alongside analysis, the same principle holds. These new epistemologies juxtapose analysis with synthesis, integration, and the creative act. Alongside experimentation—that need we have to manipulate the pieces to see how things might go if it were otherwise—these scholars cultivate the capacity appreciatively to receive the world as it is given as a gift, not as an exploitable playground for our minds.

These paired and paradoxical modes of knowing need to find a more secure and prominent place in higher education if we are to make our unique contribution to community. They help us uncover what Thomas Merton once called the "hidden wholeness" of things. They enhance community by enlarging our capacity for relatedness.

***

Let me push my argument further by saying that the job cannot be completed on the epistemological level alone. These insights must be carried over into our pedagogies as well. Community must become a central concept in ways we teach and learn.

Many communal experiments in pedagogy have been tried in the history of American higher education, and many have fallen by the wayside. And the reason, I think, is simple: The underlying mode of knowing remained the same. You cannot derive communal ways of teaching and learning from an essentially anticommunal mode of knowing. The pedagogy falls apart if the epistemology isn't there to support and sustain it.

The root fallacy in the pedagogy of most of our institutions is that the individual is the agent of knowing and therefore the focus for teaching and learning. We all know that if we draw the lines of instruction in most classrooms, they run singularly from teacher to each individual student. These lines are there for the convenience of the instructor, not for their corporate reality. They do not reveal a complex web of relationships between teacher and students and subject that would look like true community.

Given this focus on the individual in the classroom, competition between individuals for knowlege becomes inevitable. The competitive individualism of the classroom is not simply the function of a social ethic; it reflects a pedagogy that stresses the individual as the prime agent of knowing. But to say the obvious, knowing and learning are *communal* acts. They require many eyes and ears, many observations and experiences. They require a continual cycle of discussion, disagreement, and consensus over what has been seen and what it all means. This is the essence of the "community of scholars," and it should be the essence of the classroom as well.

At the core of this communal way of knowing is a primary virtue, one too seldom named when we discuss community or set community against competition. This primary virtue is capacity for creative conflict. It troubles me when we frame the issue as community vs competition, because too often we link competition with conflict, as if conflict were what needed to be eliminated. But there is no knowing without conflict.

Community in the classroom is often advocated as an affective or emotional supplement to cognitive education; the debate often poses the "hard" virtues of cognition against the "soft" virtues of community. My point is that there is very little conflict in American classrooms, and the reason is that the soft virtues of community are lacking there. Without the soft virtues of community, the hard virtues of cognitive teaching and learning will be absent as well. Our ability to confront each other critically and honestly over alleged facts, imputed meanings, or personal biases and prejudices—*that* is the ability impaired by the absence of community. The ethos of competitive individualism breeds silent, *sub rosa,* private combat for personal reward—it's all under the table, it never comes out in the open—that's what competitive individualism is all about. Competitive individualism squelches the kind of conflict I am trying to name. Conflict is open, public, and often very noisy. Competition is a secret, zero-sum game played by individuals for private gain. *Communal conflict* is a public encounter in which the whole group can win by growing. Those of you who have participated in consensus decision making know something of what I mean.

A healthy community, while it may exclude this one-up, one-down thing called competition, includes conflict at its very heart, checking and correcting and enlarging the knowledge of individuals by drawing on the knowledge of the group. Healthy conflict is possible only in the context of supportive community. What prevents conflicts in our classrooms is a simple emotion called fear. It is fear that is in the hearts of teachers as well as students. It is fear of exposure, of appearing ignorant, of being ridiculed. And the only antidote to that fear is a hospitable environment created, for example, by a teacher who knows how to use every remark, no matter how mistaken or seemingly stupid, to upbuild both the individual and the group. When people in a classroom begin to learn that every attempt at truth, no matter how off the mark, is a contribution to the larger search for corporate and consensual truth, they are soon emboldened and empowered to say what they need to say, to expose their ignorance, to do, in short, those things without which learning can't happen.

Community is not opposed to conflict. On the contrary, community is precisely that place where an arena for creative conflict is protected by the compassionate fabric of human caring itself.

***

If you ask what holds community together, what makes this capacity for relatedness possible, the only honest answer I can give brings me to that dangerous realm called the spiritual. The only answer I can give is that what makes community possible is love.

I would like to think that love is not an entirely alien word in the academy today, because I know that in the great tradition of intellectual life it is not. It is a word very much at home in the academy. The kind of community I am calling for is a community that exists at the heart of knowing, of epistemology, of teaching and learning, of pedagogy; that kind of community depends centrally on two ancient and honorable kinds of love.

The first is love of learning itself. The simple ability to take sheer joy in having a new idea, reaffirming or discarding an old one, connecting two or more notions that had hitherto seemed alien to each other, sheer joy in building images of reality with mere words that now suddenly seem more like mirrors of truth—this is love of learning.

And the second kind of love on which this community depends is love of learners, of those we see every day, who stumble and crumble, who wax hot and cold, who sometimes want truth and sometimes evade it at all costs, but who are in our care, and who—for their sake, ours, and the world's—deserve all the love that the community of teaching and learning has to offer.

CHAPTER 22

CLASSROOM MANAGEMENT

Promoting Civility in Large Classes

Mary Deane Sorcinelli
University of Massachusetts, Amherst

I have been meeting in a bimonthly, cross-disciplinary seminar with ten tenured professors who teach large, lower-division lectures in which class sizes range from 100 to 500 students. Our goal, supported by a grant from the Hewlett Foundation, is to consider how we might improve general education at the university. A key focus is to examine how inquiry-based, active and engaged learning can be infused into large lecture courses in ways that deepen students' abilities in learning. Discussions have been stimulating, exploring such teaching practices as cooperative learning, writing to learn, and classroom-based assessment. Early on in our meetings, however, a desire to share strategies for managing student behavior in the large lecture class surfaced. Promoting classroom civility became the topic of a full seminar meeting and the discussion proved so helpful that the "teaching fellows" are now planning to share their experiences with their colleagues in a campus-wide forum.

Unfortunately, the erosion of classroom decorum appears to be a shared concern among college teachers on many campuses. The last decade has seen an increasing stream of commentary and advice in higher education publications on troublesome behaviors, indecorum, incivility, and misconduct among college students, both in and outside of the classroom (Amada, 1999; Baldwin, 1997; Boice, 1996; Dannells, 1997; Downs, 1992; Kilmer, 1998; Richardson, 1999; Schneider, 1998; Trout, 1998). This chapter looks specifically at issues of civility in the large lecture classroom, where management and discipline problems seem to plague teachers the most (Carbone, 1998, 1999; Carbone & Greenberg, 1998; Sorcinelli, 1994; Weimer, 1987). It first suggests specific ways in which college teachers can promote a classroom community in which mutual respect is expected from day one. No matter how careful teachers are, however, they will still run into some disruptive behaviors in the large classroom. A few recurrent misbehaviors—and ways to work with them—will be discussed as well.

What Constitutes Incivil Behaviors in Large Classes?

Richardson (1999) suggests that classroom incivility is a "slippery concept" because teachers' and students' expectations for classroom decorum are often quite different. For example, what bothers a faculty member with an authoritarian teaching style might not bother a teacher who takes a more laissez-faire approach. In turn, some students might not be fazed by side-bar chatting while other students' learning is impeded by such distractions.

We culled and categorized the kinds of student behaviors in large classes that faculty members in our seminar perceived as most negatively affecting the teaching and learning process. While faculty tolerance stretched across a continuum, we found considerable consensus about student behaviors that faculty regarded as irritating, and the results mirrored other formal and informal surveys

Reprinted from *Engaging Large Classes: Strategies and Techniques for College Faculty,* edited by C. A. Stanley and M. E. Porter (2002), by permission of John Wiley & Sons, Inc.

(Appleby, 1990; Boice, 1996; Carbone & Greenberg, 1998; Sorcinelli, 1994). Most common were behaviors such as arriving late and leaving early, coming unprepared, acting bored (loud yawns, reading the newspaper, sleeping), side-talking, using cell phones, working on assignments for other classes, causing disruption by packing books and materials before class is over, skipping classes, especially as the semester progressed, and missing deadlines. More serious problems such as cheating, notably plagiarism using the Internet, or challenging authority were much less frequently mentioned but raised considerable angst when they occurred.

Why Do Incivilities Occur?

In an online colloquy in *The Chronicle of Higher Education* (1998) on the issue of civility in the classroom, the finger of blame pointed in a myriad of directions—at students, teachers, administrators, and the larger society. Some argued that in large classes, students may be more willing to engage in rude behavior because class size renders them anonymous and detached from the teacher. Others suggested that students might see little value in large classes, especially required, general education courses. Also, students are separated from each other and teachers by many gaps (age, race, gender, sexual orientation, social class, academic preparation, learning styles, etc.) and bridging those gaps in a large setting is difficult. Some reasoned that because the current generation of students was raised on television, MTV, and video games, it no longer is able to attend to the unidirectional, largely verbal transmission of information often found in large lectures. Finally, faculty members reminded each other that issues outside of class (e.g., a roommate conflict, not getting into a preferred course) might anger and frustrate students, affecting their behavior during class.

Teachers and administrators did not escape fault. Some discussants wondered why more attention is not paid to pedagogical issues in training for an academic career, leaving PhDs without the knowledge and skills to deal with disruptive students. Others asked why teachers themselves devote little attention to learning about instructional practices and pedagogy. Still others called for teachers to examine their own behavior (e.g., over- or under-using authority, expertise, and power) when faced with inappropriate deportment. Some blamed campus administrators for catering to students rather than punishing unacceptable behavior. Even society took a hit for encouraging cultures of consumerism, entitlement, youth orientation, and confrontational oratory, all of which discourage good manners, respect, and civil behavior in the home, school, and community.

Creating a Constructive Large-Class Environment

As instructors, while we may not agree on definition, standards, and reasons for classroom incivility, we can be sure of two things. First, when confronted with behaviors that do not match our basic expectations for classroom behavior, we need to do something. The longer inappropriate behavior continues, the more acceptable it becomes and the more difficult it is to stop it. Second, it is easier to prevent disruptive behaviors than it is to deal with them after the fact. Establishing a positive climate and expectations for large-class learning, for example, can avert many problems.

This section discusses four groups of specific strategies that college teachers can use to guide their efforts in creating a constructive large-class environment: 1) define expectations for student behavior at the outset, 2) decrease anonymity by forming personal relationships with students, 3) encourage active learning, and 4) self-assess your behavior and seek feedback from students and colleagues (Sorcinelli, 1994).

Define Expectations at the Outset

The importance of defining a class at the outset cannot be overstated. The first class meeting offers an ideal opportunity both for welcoming students and for communicating expectations for classroom conventions, such as arriving, leaving, and talking in class. The challenge lies in establishing both a pleasant atmosphere and a code of conduct. One professor on my campus, a microbiologist who routinely teaches a lecture course with 500 students, starts each first class by acknowledging the worries that go with beginning a course in the sciences, by discussing the constraints and the benefits of a large class, and by encouraging students to get to know him (e.g., bringing in topical articles from the local and campus paper, stopping by his desk before or after class). At the same time, he conveys to students the notion that they have certain responsibilities. He explicitly states expectations for behavior, asserting that, especially because the class is large, inattendance, tardiness, and idle chatter can only serve to break down the respect between teacher and students. Another colleague in business law videotapes her first class meeting so that students who are still completing their schedules or waiting in line for a parking sticker will not miss the setting of both tone and conduct.

A clear, informative syllabus can reduce student confusion about appropriate behavior. Teachers should describe, in a positive manner, what they anticipate and would like to see in terms of classroom behavior. Equally important, they should outline, with candor, what they dislike. Put simply, the syllabus should indicate whatever rules are deemed necessary for the course to run smoothly. For example, a professor who teaches introductory sociology adds a classroom behavior contract to his syllabus so that everyone starts out with the same assumptions. It describes rules of classroom conduct for the student (e.g., to cease talking at the bell, to refrain from speaking to seatmates during class, to enter by the front door and sit in the designated front rows when unavoidably arriving late, or having to leave early). It also outlines responsibilities of the instructor (e.g., to be on time for class, to spend at least five minutes after class for individual questions, to put a lecture outline on the overhead daily, to never hold the class for more than 30 seconds after class ends). He explains that the rules have one goal—to make the experience of the course more rewarding and enjoyable for all—fellow students as well as the teacher.

The large-class atmosphere also can be enhanced significantly when the instructor is willing to entertain reasonable suggestions and objections. Giving students some choices for shaping classroom policies within prescribed limits is likely to be appreciated. For example, an instructor might tell students he cannot tolerate side-talking during his lectures, but can live with students drinking a Coke or munching on a candy bar. Other possibilities for choice might include whether to drop the lowest quiz score, how much work to assign over a vacation break, or how many chapters in the text to cover for a given test.

Decrease Anonymity

When a student creates a personal relationship with the teacher as well as peers, civility comes more easily. Large classes present many more challenges than do smaller, more personal classes, however, in reducing anonymity. Lowman (1995) has asserted "the easiest way to begin forming personal relationships with students is to learn their names," (p. 67). A rare teacher can memorize hundreds of names, but there are other ways to make personal contact with students. One way is to administer a background questionnaire on the first day of class. A professor in Germanic languages and literature asks students to share their hometown, what dorm they live in, why they are taking the course, whether they work and how much, and their extracurricular interests or experiences. She tabulates the data and shares it in the next class, announcing that "a fifth of our class is from the Boston area" (the Bostonians cheer), or "will the 12 students in the marching band raise their hands," etc. She uses the questionnaire throughout the term to draw on students' common and unique interests and experiences. A professor in organic chemistry asks her 100 students to fill out background information on an index card and to tape a picture to it. She goes through the cards, repeating each student's name and scanning the face that goes with it. She can identify nearly every student's name within a week. Yet another professor, in information systems, chooses both to lead a computer lab section and spot visit other sections as a way to get to know students outside of lecture and to keep a pulse on how the lectures and labs work together to integrate student learning.

While announced office hours may signal an instructor's accessibility to students, many students are reluctant to use them. A journalism professor encourages personal contact with students by coming to class early. This allows her to work the aisles, chatting informally with students and eliciting their concerns. Similarly, she stays awhile after class to allow students to follow-up with a question or idea that they might have been reticent to bring up in class. Other faculty members find it helpful to schedule their office hours right after class. In that way, students who approach them after class have a chance to accompany the teachers to their offices to continue discussion.

A teacher in classics found that her 475 mostly first-year students were so reluctant to take advantage of office hours that she set up a coffee hour in the student center, reminding students that she would be at a corner table on most mornings at 10:00 a.m. and inviting them to come for coffee and conversation. She discovered students were more likely to arrive in groups of two or three and now encourages small-group visits.

Encourage Active Learning

Studies on active learning suggest that such methods engage students with content in ways that develop positive relationships among students as well as competencies and critical thinking skills—rather than solely the acquisition of knowledge. In large classes, however, students may resist non-lecturing approaches because they are in sharp contrast to the familiar passive listening role to which they have become accustomed. Faculty may fear that the use of active learning strategies will reduce the amount of available lecture time that can be devoted to content coverage (Bonwell, 1996).

Carbone (1998) offers three useful guidelines for getting started. First, be prepared. Decide on the goal of the activity, using an overhead to spell out the assignment (oral directions can lead to confusion). Make sure the task is clear and specific. For example, "Summarize the most important points you heard in today's lecture," or "List as many (fill-in-blank) as you can in the next four minutes." Second, ensure participation by requiring that individual or group assignments are handed in. These may or may not be graded but should require students' names to encourage attendance and participation. Finally, maintain order by limiting time and group size. Most large-lecture teachers that I work with use periods of two to ten minutes for group activities, interspersed with segments of lecture. This format stimulates student thinking, discussion, and learning without requiring large blocks of time. Also, in large lecture halls, even groups of four or five students can prove unwieldy. Having students simply turn to the person next to them and pair up, or twist around to form triads helps keep noise levels down and encourages task completion.

There are a number of active learning strategies that are particularly suited to large classes (Bonwell, 1996; Carbone, 1998; Sorcinelli, 1994). Four effective and low-risk activities include:

Pause procedure. Stop the lecture every 13-18 minutes to allow students to work in pairs to compare and rework their notes for three to five minutes. Ask what questions arose from their review.

Short writes. Punctuating a lecture with short writing assignments is a powerful way to assess the degree to which students understand presented material. Twenty minutes into the lecture, questions might include, "What was the main concept presented in this portion of the lecture?" "Give an example of this principle or concept." "Explain this concept in your own words." "How does his idea relate to your own experience?" Five or ten minutes before the end of lecture, use the "one-minute paper," advocated by Angelo and Cross (1993), and simply ask, "What was the most important thing you learned in this lecture?" or "What questions remain unanswered?" Short writes can be submitted or form the basis for questions or class discussion.

Think-pair-share. About 15-20 minutes into the lecture, put a question or problem up on the overhead. Ask students to think, write, and then talk about the answer with the person next to them. (Writing and then talking about their answers can take five to ten minutes depending on the question's complexity). You may ask several pairs to share their answers with the whole class. You can also collect the writing and grade it simply: check for "okay," check-plus for "great." This technique can reveal how much students are learning from the lecture and lead to a major improvement in student understanding of fundamental concepts.

Formative quizzes. Formative—that is ungraded—quizzes can be used to efficiently determine how students comprehend material. Using the kinds of questions that might be used on your exams, place questions on the overhead, giving students appropriate time to respond. If the question entails multiple choices, students can raise their hands in agreement, as each prompt is featured. (An essay question might be broken into component parts.) This preview can help you determine student understanding and show students problem areas that warrant further study.

Examine Your Behavior and Seek Feedback from Students and Colleagues

Examine your own behavior when faced with inappropriate deportment in the large classroom. Surveys of students' pet peeves about teaching reveal that many are concerned about lecturing behaviors—including poor organization of the lectures; blocking the blackboard; talking too fast, softly, or slowly; poor use of class time (e.g., coming in late and stopping early). Other top complaints include intellectual arrogance—talking down to or showing a lack of respect for students, being unhelpful or not approachable, and employing confusing testing and grading practices (Appleby, 1990; Perlman & McCann, 1998).

Asking students for help in determining what is working and what merits some attention can be incredibly valuable in encouraging communication, establishing a responsive tone, and providing self-correcting feedback. One effective technique is to administer an informal course evaluation early in the semester (many teaching and learning centers will facilitate a midsemester feedback session with your students). Our center's staff ask students either in small groups or individually what they most like about the course and teaching of it, what they would like to see changed or improved, and what would make the course a better learning experience for them. When asked at midterm, we find that most students' responses are substantive and constructive—the technique demonstrates respect for and interest in students' voices and promises to improve their learning experience while the course is in process.

Colleagues can prove a sounding board and offer suggestions on how they approach civility issues in the classroom. For example, we facilitate a process by which early career faculty can visit large lecture classes that are taught by some of our outstanding teachers. After the observations, these senior colleagues join our junior faculty for an informal session in which we talk about what worked, raise questions about large-class problems, and brainstorm solutions. And over the last decade, our teaching and learning center has offered periodic campus-wide workshops on teaching large classes well. Again, we call on seasoned large-lecture teachers to help workshop participants to identify civility problems in large classes and to share best practices.

Some Solutions for Dealing with Misbehavior in the Large Class

Ideally, creating an atmosphere that is conducive to positive, respectful behavior should allow instructors to work smoothly with all students. However, instructors may still run into some students or classes that present problems. Beyond notes in syllabi, instructors need to take a sensible stance on student misbehavior in terms of identifying it, responding to it, and doing so reasonably and consistently. The suggestions offered below address the behaviors that faculty report as most irritating and troublesome. There are several excellent resources to consult when confronted with more serious breaches of classroom conduct; for example, cheating, physical intimidation, harassment, drug or alcohol abuse (Amada, 1999; Dannells, 1997; McKeachie, 1999; Richardson, 1999).

Talking and Inattention

- If students are chatting, make direct eye contact with them so that they know you see them. Sometimes stopping the lecture, looking directly at the students, and resuming the lecture when you have full attention is enough to resolve the problem.
- Physically move to that part of the room, again making eye contact with the students. Often stepping into student space gets the message across.
- Direct a question to the area in which the chatting students are sitting. This focuses attention to that area of the class but avoids confrontations or putting anybody on the spot.
- Call the offending student or students up after class. Students usually appreciate a private reminder rather than public embarrassment. Tell students who talk in class (or read the newspaper, etc.) that their behavior distracts you and the other students, and ask them please to refrain.

- There is peer pressure among students not to confront each other about rude behavior; it is difficult to directly enlist students to reinforce your expectations. An accounting professor uses a subtler tactic. On the first day, she reads excerpts from past student evaluations that make it clear that rude behavior, especially noise during the lecture, irritates students as much as it does the instructor and that students appreciate it when she discourages such behavior.

Arriving Late and Leaving Early

- Establish an understanding with students. You expect them to come to class on time; in return, you will start and finish as scheduled.
- Institute a starting ritual: moving to the podium, dimming the lights, playing music, raising your hand, reading a notable quotation or passage—whatever suits your teaching style.
- Require students to inform you if they need to arrive late or leave early, either verbally or in writing. Some instructors reserve a section in the front or back, near an exit, where such students can sit so that their arrival or departure causes as little disruption as possible.
- Station your TAs along the back of the classroom, and if students arrive or leave early, have them ask students if they are okay, why they are leaving, etc.
- Use the last five minutes of class in ways that circumvent the temptation for students to pack up early. A biology teacher put a multiple choice or short answer question on the overhead projector during the last few minutes of each class. The question gets at the heart of the concluding lecture or previews the next lecture and the students know that they will see some variation of this question on the exam.
- Let students know that there are costs for arriving late or missing class. Don't teach a class twice—make students responsible for getting missed assignments and material.

Inattendance

- Many Instructors of large classes leave the question of attendance up to individual students. If you require attendance, be sure to have a system for reliably recording it, such as collecting homework, an in-class assignment, or a quiz at the end of class.
- A psychology professor divides the lecture hall and assigns TAs and their student discussion sections to specific areas. He asks TAs to note empty seats and to follow up on those who are excessively absent.
- A professor in accounting builds into class ten unannounced, short, extra credit writing assignments that essentially reward students for attending class. Roughly once a week, he shows a segment of video, poses an open-ended question on the overhead, etc., and asks students to respond from what they've learned in lecture and through personal experience. To ease the burden of grading, he scans the assignments, evaluates them with a check (or a zero for an absent student), and figures them toward the total grade.
- If a large percentage of students don't come to class, consider the possibility that they do not find sessions useful or that notes on the Internet or sold by companies inadvertently signal that attending class is not important. Make sure not only that the material covered in class is vital to students' mastery of the subject and their performance on tests and papers, but also that students understand the connection.
- On the day you give a test (attendance should be high), ask students to write on a piece of paper the reasons why they are not attending classes regularly.

Deadlines

- Clearly state your policy on missed exams, make-up exams, late homework, writing assignments, written university-sanctioned excuses, etc., in writing and orally at the beginning of the semester. Periodically remind students of such policies in advance of deadlines.
- Make it clear to students that there are logical consequences if they turn in assignments late. If the policy is not to accept late papers, then don't accept them except under the most extraordinary circumstances—and then in private. Always document the rationale for a change in policy should your decision be challenged by a third party.
- Regularly meet deadlines. If you say tests will be graded and returned Friday, then get them back on Friday.

Challenges to Authority

At some point in the large class, most teachers will have to face a student who is resentful, hostile, or challenging. The following are a few suggestions for gaining the cooperation of an oppositional student.

- As a rule of thumb, avoid arguments with students during class. If a student continues to press, table the discussion until later and then continue it with the student privately, in a more neutral setting. Listen carefully, openly, and calmly to the grievance. Sometimes the opportunity to ventilate and express a felt grievance may be more important to a student than is a resolution.
- When talking to a disruptive student, tell the student that you value his or her good contributions, but point out how the behavior that he or she is engaging in negatively affects you when you are teaching. Try to enlist the student's cooperation in setting ground rules for acceptable behavior.
- Don't become defensive and take a confrontation personally. Respond honestly to challenges, explaining—not defending—your instructional objectives and how assignments and exercises contribute to them. Although the purpose of class activities and lectures may be obvious to you, students often need to have these objectives made explicit.
- If the behavior is reoccurring, you may want to write a letter to the student. Describe the behavior, indicate how it disrupts you and other students, restate your expectations for behavior, and outline specific changes you would like to see. Copy the letter to the student's academic advisor or to the dean of students.
- On the rare occasion that a student is alarmingly hostile or threatening, contact the ombudsman's or the dean of student's office. Most campuses have disciplinary procedures that protect faculty as well as students.

Conclusion

For most instructors, teaching the large lecture is one of the most challenging of classroom assignments. Although we have expertise in our content areas, we often have little training for developing positive interpersonal relationships with and managing such large numbers of students. Yet we all want to create a classroom environment of mutual respect, not one rife with adversarial relationships. Paramount to establishing a positive environment in the large class and deterring disruptive behavior is to let students know from the outset what you expect of them and then to hold them to those expectations—intervening directly (e.g., talking privately, setting limits) to deal with inappropriate conduct. Perhaps most importantly, as instructors we need to consider our own behavior as well as that of our students. An honest attempt to understand how our classroom deportment might contribute to a difficult situation may help to reduce incivilities in our classrooms.

References

Amada, G. (1999). *Coping with misconduct in the college classroom: A practical model.* Asheville, NC: College Administration Publications.

Angelo, T.A., & Cross, K.P. (1993). *Classroom assessment techniques* (2nd ed.). San Francisco, CA: Jossey-Bass.

Appleby, D. C. (1990). Faculty and student perceptions of irritating behaviors in the college classroom. *Journal of Staff, Program and Organizational Development,* 8(2), 41–46.

Baldwin, R. G. (1997-98), Academic civility begins in the classroom. *Essays on teaching excellence: Toward the best in the academy,* 9 (8), Athena, GA: The Professional and Organizational Development Network in Higher Education.

Boice, B. (1996). Classroom incivilities. *Research in Higher Education, 37* (4), 453–487.

Bonwell, C. C. (1996). Enhancing the lecture: Revitalizing a traditional format In T. E. Sutherland & C. C. Bonwell (Eds.), *Using action learning in large classes: A range of options for faculty.* New Directions for Teaching and Learning, No. 67. San Francisco, CA: Jossey-Bass.

Carbone, E. (1998). *Teaching large classes: Tools and strategies.* Thousand Oaks, CA: Sage.

Carbone, E. (1999). Students behaving badly in large classes. In Richardson, S. (Ed,), *Promoting civility: A teaching challenge.* New Directions for Teaching and Learning, No. 77. San Francisco, CA: Jossey-Bass.

Carbone E., & Greenberg, J. (1998). Teaching large classes: Unpacking the problem and responding creatively. In M. Kaplan & D. Lieberman (Eds.), *To Improve the Academy: Vol. 17. Resources for faculty, instructional, and organizational development* (pp. 311-326), Stillwater, OK: New Forums Press.

Chronicle of Higher Education. (1998). *Is rudeness on the rise?* Online discussion, 3/23/98. www.chronicle.com/colloquy/98/rude/01.html

Dannells, M. (1997). *From discipline to development: Rethinking student conduct in higher education.* Washington DC: Office of Educational Research and Improvement. (ASHE-ERIC Higher Education Report, Vol. 25, No. 2).

Downs, J. R. (1992). Dealing with hostile and oppositional students. *College Teaching, 40* (3), 106–08.

Kilmer, P. (1998). When a few disruptive students challenge an instructor's plan. *Journalism & Mass Communication Educator,* 53 (2), 81–84.

Lowman, J. (1995). *Mastering the techniques of teaching* (2nd ed.). San Francisco, CA: Jossey-Bass.

McKeachie, W. J. (1999). *Teaching tips: A guide for the beginning college teacher* (10th ed.), Lexington, MA: D.C. Heath.

Perlman, B., & McCann, L. I. (1998). Students' pet peeves about teaching. *Teaching of Psychology,* 25, 201–02.

Richardson, S. (Ed.). (1999). *Promoting civility: A teaching challenge.* New Directions for Teaching and Learning, No. 77. San Francisco, CA: Jossey-Bass.

Schneider, A. (1998, March 27). Insubordination and intimidation signal the end of decorum in many classrooms. *Chronicle of Higher Education,* pp. A12-A14.

Sorcinelli, M. D. (1994). Dealing with troublesome behaviors in the classroom. In Prichard, K. W. and R. M. Sawyer (Eds.), *Handbook of college teaching: Theory and applications.* Westport, CT: Greenwood Press.

Trout, P. (1998, July 24). Incivility in the classroom breeds 'education lite'. *Chronicle of Higher Education,* p. A40.

Weimer, M. J. (Ed.), (1987). *Teaching large classes well.* New Directions for Teaching and Learning, No. 32. San Francisco, CA: Jossey-Bass.

CHAPTER 23

STUDENT ENGAGEMENT

How to Help Students Achieve

By George D. Kuh

As many as four-fifths of high-school graduates will need some form of postsecondary education if they are to become self-sufficient and the nation is to remain economically competitive. At the same time, policy makers, business leaders, and national study groups say the quality of student learning is subpar and want measures of institutional and student performance made public. Yet surprisingly little attention focuses on what higher-education institutions can do to help students survive and thrive in college.

The situation is complicated as tens of thousands of undergraduates today must deal with one or more circumstances that seriously challenge their ability to succeed. Socioeconomic background, financial means, college readiness, and support from home substantially influence whether a person will earn a credential or degree.

Javier, for instance, is the first in his family to go to college. His residence hall houses 600 other first-year students, but no one on his floor is in any of his classes, so he is on his own and adrift when it comes to studying.

Nicole left college after her first year to get married. Now divorced with a child, she works 30 hours a week and is taking two courses this term. Her life at college is limited mostly to finding a place to park near the campus and going to class.

Unsure of her major, Sarah struggles with her writing, which was a problem in high school as well. After three semesters of college, only her composition course has required a few short papers, while all her tests have been multiple choice or true-false. She is worried because two of her finals this term will be essay exams.

Yet whatever their situations, once students like Javier, Nicole, and Sarah start college, whether they persevere and how much they get out of their studies are largely the result of their individual effort and involvement. That is one of the key findings of the annual National Survey of Student Engagement that I direct at the Center for Postsecondary Research at Indiana University at Bloomington. The results of the survey, which records actual student experiences at more than 600 institutions across the country, show that the time and energy that students devote to their studies and other educationally purposeful activities positively influence their grades and persistence. In other words, a key to academic success for students is their engagement.

Ernest T. Pascarella of the University of Iowa and Patrick T. Terenzini of Pennsylvania State University came to a similar conclusion in their book, *How College Affects Students* (2nd edition, Jossey-Bass, 2005), after summarizing thousands of studies. As Lee S. Shulman, president of the Carnegie Foundation for the Advancement of Teaching, says, because student engagement is a precursor for knowledge and understanding, it is both a proxy for learning as well as a desired outcome in itself. By being engaged—something not represented in outcomes measures—students develop habits that promise to stand them in good stead for a lifetime of continuous learning.

The results of our survey and my own extensive research into the topic suggests six concrete steps that institutions can take to engage students like Javier, Sarah, and Nicole:

Reprinted from *Chronicle of Higher Education* (2007).

Teach first-year students as early as possible how to use college resources effectively. Most institutions offer a blend of summer orientation or advising sessions and a fall welcome week. While helpful, those practices cannot teach most students all they need to know and do to make the most of college. Simply living on the campus increases the odds that a student like Javier will return for a second year of study, but it does not guarantee that he will take advantage of academic-support services, participate in co-curricular activities, or interact with faculty members or friends on a meaningful level. That is especially the case for first-generation students who don't know what to expect from college life.

Institutions that are serious about helping more-vulnerable students succeed employ other mechanisms like first-year seminars, supplemental instruction, and placement tests that ensure students are in courses for which they are prepared. They also provide "intrusive advising"—like George Mason University's academic-advising office, which contacts students with low grades who have not declared a major, and Ursinus College, where a residence-life staff member or faculty adviser meets with students who seem to be struggling academically or socially. Prompt feedback about academic performance is also essential, since midterm-exam time is often too late for a student to salvage a semester.

In addition, one increasingly common activity that has proved to be effective for students like Javier is participating in a learning community. For example, freshman students in residence-based learning communities at the University of Missouri at Columbia live in the same building and take the same three core courses and an additional class focused on the skills needed to succeed in college, giving them common ground both in and out the classroom.

According to our survey results, students who live in learning communities tend to interact more with their professors and diverse peers, study more, and excel at synthesizing material and analyzing problems. They also reported gaining more from their college experience. Moreover, the "engagement advantage" for students in learning communities lasts through senior year, suggesting that the experience—which most students have in their first college year—positively affects what they do later in college. Vincent Tinto, distinguished university professor and chair of the higher-education program at Syracuse University, and researchers at the Washington Center for Improving the Quality of Undergraduate Education at Evergreen State College have found that nonresidential learning communities generally have similar salutary effects for community-college students.

Make the classroom the locus of community. Decades ago, when most undergraduates lived near their classmates and teachers, proximity and serendipity established the social order and instilled shared values and understandings. Today the majority of students are like Nicole; they commute to classes and work many hours a week. As a result, they spend a limited amount of time on the campus and have less contact with faculty members, as the results of our 2006 survey show.

For them, the classroom is the only venue where they regularly have face-to-face contact with faculty or staff members and other students, learn how the institution works, and absorb the campus culture. That makes professors' jobs in the classroom much more demanding and complicated. They must cultivate an atmosphere in which a group of strangers will listen attentively to others with respect, and challenge and support one another to previously unimagined levels of academic performance.

Professors who are skilled at managing class discussion make use of cooperative learning activities that get students working together during and after class on meaningful tasks. Along with subject matter, they teach institutional values and academic norms; they inform students about campus events and such nontrivial matters as course-registration deadlines and when and how to apply for financial aid.

Faculty members should not have to do this alone, however. For example, at the University of Texas at El Paso, an instructional team for the required first-year seminar in critical inquiry consists of a faculty member, an undergraduate peer leader, and a librarian. They emphasize active-learning approaches that engage students who prefer concrete, hands-on learning activities—like group projects that sometimes take students off the campus and into their home communities.

Develop networks and early-warning systems to support students when they need help. Three-fifths of students in public two-year colleges and one-quarter of students in four-year institutions must complete at least one remedial course. No wonder nine out of every 10 students starting college say they intend to use an academic-assistance or learning-skills center. But by the end of the first year, only about half as many have done so, according to our surveys. To make sure that students who need help get it, some colleges create first-year-student "tag teams" composed of some combination of faculty members, peer mentors, advisers, student-affairs officials, librarians, and other staff members. Academic-support staff members monitor class-attendance patterns, drop/add information, early-semester and midterm grades, and preregistration information to identify and intervene with students who are experiencing academic difficulties.

For example, instructors in Fayetteville State University's Early Alert program contact a student's adviser if the student seems to be struggling. At Wheaton College, in Massachusetts, a first-year student's advising team is made up of a faculty member, a student preceptor, and an administrative adviser—usually a student-life staff member or a librarian. Other programs that have proved successful include supplemental instruction, using peers as mentors, theme-based campus housing, on-campus work, internships, and service learning.

Connect every student in a meaningful way with some activity or positive role model. When students are responsible for tasks that require daily decisions over an extended period, they become invested in the activity that deepens their commitment to the college and their studies. Our survey shows that members of athletics teams, choirs and bands, and fraternities and sororities tend to graduate at higher rates, in part because the momentum of the group carries them forward, buoying them during difficult times. They also derive personal satisfaction by being a part of something larger than themselves. Working on the campus, writing for the student newspaper, or conducting research with a faculty member have numerous benefits, not the least of which is having another source of support and encouragement for persevering when times get tough.

Connecting students to somebody or something worthwhile is everyone's business. At the University of Kansas and other institutions, faculty members occasionally take a moment of class time to encourage students to get involved with a campus-based organization or to volunteer in the local community. Advisers, counselors, student-life staff members, and faculty members can make a big difference in the life of more than a few students by encouraging them to get involved with one or more of these kinds of activities or people.

If a program or practice works, make it widely available. Most institutions have small, boutiquelike programs for honors students or student-government leaders, but they typically include only a small fraction of undergraduates. Granted, no single teaching approach, classroom structure, or out-of-class experience will be effective with every student. But we should not ignore evidence, for example, that students who encounter diverse perspectives in their classes benefit more in desirable ways than their counterparts with less exposure, or that students who apply what they are learning in classes to real-world problems—as often happens during well-designed internships, study abroad, or service learning—deepen their learning and sharpen their critical-thinking skills.

In fact, if a program is successful, some students should be required to take it. Left to their own devices, students (and faculty members) do not always choose wisely, as Carol A. Twigg, president and chief executive officer of the National Center for Academic Transformation, discovered in her successful experiments with technology-enriched course redesigns. She concluded that first-year students "don't do optional"—even when it is in their interest to do so.

Remove obstacles to student engagement and success. One roadblock found on scores of campuses is "the runaround." Variations abound, but the basic story line is that no matter where students turn, they cannot get the information or help they need, whether from residence-life administrators, the registrar, or others. That stands in stark contrast to colleges with cultures marked by a sense of positive restlessness, where people are constantly asking how they can improve what they do, and administrators regularly evaluate campus priorities, policies, and programs. Such examinations can be formal, such as program reviews or accreditation self-studies. Informal reviews stimulated by faculty curiosity or visionary leaders also can lead to positive change.

The University of Michigan, for instance, conducted six major studies of the quality of the undergraduate experience between the mid-1980s and 2000, resulting in new online counseling and information services, a systemic revision in science and mathematics instruction, and the placement of faculty fellows in residence halls, among other new programs.

Several years ago, the math faculty on my own campus retooled a math course in which more than a third of the students in any given term either received a D or F, or withdrew from the class. They created a reduced-pace, two-semester course using the same material and exams. The number of students who now complete the course with a C or better has jumped by about 30 percent.

Even when institutions establish programs like those that I've outlined and faculty members use effective teaching and learning approaches, such efforts will not in every case make up for students' inadequate academic preparation in elementary and secondary school. Still, we can do better by the likes of Javier, Sarah, and Nicole by engaging them in purposeful activities that enhance their learning and personal development. The real question is whether we have the will to increase the odds that more students will get ready, get in, and get through.

George D. Kuh is a professor of higher education and director of the Center for Postsecondary Research at Indiana University at Bloomington. His most recent book, with other authors, is *Piecing Together the Student Success Puzzle* (Jossey-Bass, 2007).

CHAPTER 24

TEACHING THROUGH TRAGEDY

In the Eye of the Storm: Students' Perceptions of Helpful Faculty Actions Following a Collective Tragedy

Therese A. Huston
Seattle University

Michele DiPietro
Carnegie Mellon University

Abstract On occasion, our campus communities are shaken by national tragedies such as hurricane Katrina and the terrorist attacks of September 11, 2001, or by local tragedies such as the murder of a faculty member or student. Because these are unusual circumstances, faculty are often initially confused about how to respond, and later have little or no sense of how effective their actions have been (DiPietro, 2003). This paper investigates the most common instructor responses following a tragedy and which of those responses students find most helpful. Implications for faculty and faculty developers are discussed.

Campus communities deal with tragedy on both the national and local level. In the past decade, students and faculty across the country have struggled with the implications of the destruction brought about by hurricane Katrina, the September 11th attacks, the Columbine shootings, and Matthew Shephard's brutal beating and death. Even though these events were geographically localized, their impact has been far reaching. In particular, following hurricane Katrina, students from the affected colleges and universities were relocated in institutions across all 50 states, generating unpredicted ripples in campus dynamics everywhere (Mangan 2005). There are also local tragedies that receive less national attention but still leave faculty, staff, and students feeling frightened, angry, and vulnerable. For example, in the fall of 2002, a student at the University of Arizona, Tuscon killed three professors in the nursing school with an automatic weapon before killing himself (Rooney, 2002). Another disturbing example occurred at Gallaudet University, where two students were murdered in the same dormitory within a period of a few months (Guterman, 2001). Sadly, these are only a few of the violent losses that campuses have faced in recent years.

Tragedies and disasters have a strong emotional and cognitive impact on students, even if the students are not directly affected by the catastrophe (Honos-Webb, Sunwolf, Hart, & Scalise, 2006; Silver, Holman, McIntosh, Poulin, Gil-Rivas, 2002). Many students in the Boston area, for example, who were not directly impacted by the September 11th terrorist attacks, were nonetheless severely psychologically affected for two months or more following the attacks (Liverant, Hofmann & Litz,

Reprinted from *To Improve the Academy: Resources for faculty, instructional, and organizational development*, edited by D. R. Robertson and L. B. Nilson (2007), by permission of John Wiley & Sons, Inc.

2004). Recognizing the distress caused by natural and man-made disasters, the American Psychiatric Association has provided mental health guidelines for helping college students deal with the loss and disruption caused by such tragedies (American Psychiatric Association, 2005).

Given the widespread impact of such tragedies, how do most campuses respond? Many college and university administrations have created "crisis response teams," either in anticipation of or in response to a collective tragedy (Asmussen & Creswell, 1995; Farrell, 2001). Campus officials also increase support for the members of their community; many schools issue campus-wide policies to give everyone time to grieve, and University officials often create venues for students, faculty, and staff to learn more about the threatening events or to cope with heightened stress levels (e.g. Hurst, 1999). Administrators also have access to published guidelines on how to prepare a crisis response team, itemized lists of things to say and do immediately following a security threat, and recommendations for ensuring prompt and effective communication (Larson, 1994; Paine & Sprague, 2000; Whiting, Tucker & Whaley, 2004).

Although administrators have benchmarks to follow before, during, and after a crisis, faculty members receive precious little guidance as to what to say or do in their classrooms. As a noteworthy exception, the Center for Research on Teaching and Learning at University of Michigan (n.d.) has consistently assumed a leadership role on this issue by providing timely guidelines for discussions of hurricane Katrina, the December 2004 tsunami, the war on Iraq, and September 11th on the "Publications and Links" page of their website. Other exceptions we uncovered include the Faculty Center for Excellence in Teaching at Western Kentucky University (2002), which produced a booklet of short papers and reports on "Teaching and Learning in Times of Crisis," and Michigan State University (2005), which compiled a list of resources for doing research on hurricanes as a way to address the Katrina crisis as a course project.

Given that faculty represent the arm of the campus community that has the most day-to-day student contact, it is crucial that they receive the tools to best support students in the context of their classes. This includes deciding whether to address the tragic events, and if so, knowing some different ways to do so and the comparative value of those options.

The crisis literature for administrators does not define which events constitute a crisis warranting a response from the administration. It only advices that the crisis management plans be as flexible as possible, because they might include emergencies as diverse as crimes, natural disasters, suicide, plant failures, riots, bomb threats, disease, and scandals, among others (Larson 1994; Siegel 1994).

In the same vein, we too resist an inevitably narrow treatment of tragic events. Instead, this chapter reports the results of a study designed to categorize instructor responses, or lack thereof, following one specific crisis, the terrorist attacks of September 11th, 2001. The survey asked students to identify how their instructors responded to the attacks and to evaluate the usefulness of those actions. Even though the survey refers to a specific event, all the strategies listed and collected generalize to other catastrophes, so that the insights from this research are widely applicable.

Literature Review

Clinical researchers have examined psychological interventions to help people cope with the events of September 11, but their reports have focused on recommendations for psychologists and mental health professionals. For example, one study found that college students who participated in a journal writing exercise or who listened to a story that addressed themes relevant to the terrorist attacks showed greater improvements and fewer signs of trauma than a control condition (Honos-Webb et al., 2006). Another study found that adults who took an active approach, such as getting involved in their community efforts to help others, felt less distressed by the attacks (Silver et al., 2002).

Few researchers, however, have directly examined faculty responses to a national crisis, and the only relevant research we were able to uncover was a faculty survey developed by DiPietro (2003). Faculty were asked to report what, if anything, they had done in class after the September 11th attacks, their rationale for the response, and their perceptions of effectiveness. Three main themes emerged from that investigation:

- Faculty responded in many different ways. Even in this high-end, self-selected sample, where most people were eager to share what they had done, quite a few instructors (11%) admitted that they did not address the attacks in class. When faculty did address the attacks directly, their responses ranged from quick, low-effort strategies (e.g., a minute of silence) to more lengthy, involved responses (e.g., incorporating the tragedy into the course topics or the final project).
- There was a general sense of confusion; some instructors were unsure about what their role should be. Other instructors, even though they felt a strong need to do something, were confused about what would be appropriate or advisable and, as a result, did nothing. Men and international instructors reported the most confusion.
- Some confusion persisted after the fact. Several instructors had no idea whether their actions had any impact. Likewise, some instructors who did nothing reported that even though it seemed like the best thing to do at the time (to foster a sense of normalcy), they later had no idea if that was indeed the best course of action.

These findings clearly reveal that faculty members need to be equipped with appropriate pedagogical tools, well in advance of tragic events.

Method

Sample

A sample of 2000 students from a private, medium-sized university was selected from the enrollment database by randomly generating the names of 400 students from each of the following five groups: first-year students, sophomores, juniors, seniors, and masters/PhD students. Students completed the online survey voluntarily and were offered a lottery incentive: two randomly drawn respondents from each group won a $50.00 gift certificate toward purchases on Amazon.com.

Instrument

The survey was an online adaptation of an instructor survey (DiPietro, 2003), and most questions were simply modified to address students' perspectives. For instance, the original question "How many academic classes were you *teaching* in September 2001?" was changed to "How many academic classes were you *taking* in September of 2001?"

We administered the online survey using SurveyMonkey, a survey administration and data collection service. The survey included nine questions about demographics and academics, the last of which asked how many courses the student was taking in September, 2001. For each course, the respondent answered six questions concerning the instructor-led activities following September 11th (see Appendix for the complete survey).

Procedure

Each student received a brief email message in March of 2002 inviting the student to participate. The initial invitation included a link that took respondents to the online consent form. The software monitored which students had completed the survey to ensure that they could only complete the survey once. Two names were randomly drawn from each class for the online gift certificates, and prizes were awarded via email.

The results were calculated in terms of the number of reports (e.g. the number of reports in which faculty teaching labs offered extensions, led discussions, etc.). Helpfulness was only coded for the first two courses that each student reported because incrementally fewer and fewer students ranked the helpfulness of their third, fourth, and fifth courses.

Results and Discussion

Respondents

A total of 484 respondents (24.2% of the original 2000 students in the sample) completed the survey. Table 24.1 provides a breakdown of respondents by gender, academic discipline, and year in school. An equal number of men and women completed the survey, but this was surprising because the student body at this institution for the 2001–02 academic year was 65% male/35% female. Either females were over-represented in the original sample of 2000 students, or a greater proportion of females were interested in the survey or the lottery prize. Table 24.1 also shows the proportion of respondents by academic discipline. Overall, the response rates were representative of the relative distribution of students across schools. For example, the school of engineering had the highest response rate (26.4%), but engineering is also the largest school at the institution with 23.6% of all students in 2001–02.

In summary, the survey data represent first-year students through graduate students, a variety of academic disciplines, and equal numbers of men and women.

Responses to the Attacks

Courses where the attacks were addressed. Students reported taking an average of 4.43 classes on September 11, 2001, ranging from one class to five classes, with a median of five classes. As shown in the first row of Table 24.2, the majority of the reports came from small lecture (<50 students), large lecture (>=50 students), and discussion classes.

TABLE 24.1

Demographic Characteristics of Participants (N=484)

Gender	***n***	**%**
Male	243	50%
Female	242	50%
Year in School		
First-year	123	25%
Sophomore	116	24%
Junior	82	17%
Senior	90	19%
Masters or Ph.D.	73	15%
Academic Discipline		
Fine Arts	85	18%
Engineering	128	26%
Sciences and Computer Science	106	22%
Humanities and Social Sciences	90	19%
Business and Public Policy	69	14%
Other*	6	1%

*"Other" includes enrolled students who had not yet declared their major or students who were taking classes but were not working towards a specified degree.

TABLE 24.2

Types of Instructor Responses Across Different Types of Courses

Instructor Response	Discussion N=342	Small Lecture N=338	Large Lecture N=674	Lab N=81	Studio N=157	Project N=87	Total N=1679
No Response	22%	38%	47%	37%	27%	54%	38%
Types of Responses							
A	38%	31%	26%	36%	46%	18%	31%
B	13%	13%	15%	15%	9%	9%	13%
C	5%	5%	5%	4%	8%	2%	5%
D	12%	12%	9%	12%	23%	5%	11%
E	20%	24%	22%	25%	32%	13%	23%
F	14%	14%	9%	12%	25%	8%	13%
G	24%	22%	14%	14%	49%	7%	20%
H	12%	11%	6%	5%	17%	8%	10%
I	10%	11%	8%	6%	11%	6%	9%
J	1%	1%	0%	1%	2%	1%	1%
K	2%	1%	1%	0%	1%	0%	2%
L	12%	7%	6%	5%	13%	5%	8%
M	35%	17%	8%	10%	36%	23%	19%
N	6%	4%	3%	5%	4%	3%	5%

Key to Instructor Responses

A) Acknowledged that the class needs to go on with the material but reassured the class that if students were too distressed to process the material that there will be other opportunities to review it down the road

B) Acknowledged that the attacks had occurred and said that the class needs to go on with no mention of opportunities for review or extra help

C) One minute of silence

D) Mentioned Counseling Services

E) Excused students / offered extensions if assignments were due

F) Offered to talk privately with anybody who might want to

G) Had a brief discussion in class

H) Devoted the whole first class after the attacks to discussion

I) Incorporated the event into the lesson plan / curriculum

J) Decided to do a project as a class (i.e. quilt, fence-painting, etc.)

K) Read a passage from an inspirational book

L) Mentioned ways that people can help (i.e. gave out phone numbers for the Red Cross or charities, talked about the benefits of donating blood, etc.)

M) Asked students if their families and friends were physically affected

N) Other ___(write-in)____

According to the students, only 62% of their instructors addressed the attacks, and the remaining 38% of their instructors failed to mention the attacks in class at all. Students indicated that faculty were more likely to mention the attacks in some types of courses than others: most frequently in discussion and studio courses (in 78% of discussion courses and 73% of studios) and least frequently in large lecture and project classes (53% and 46%, respectively).

It is not surprising that the terrorist attacks were addressed more frequently in discussion and studio courses, where enrollments are typically smaller and classes are usually structured with a relatively high degree of faculty-student interaction. Using the same reasoning, one might have predicted that faculty would be less likely to mention the attacks in lecture halls with 50 students or more because faculty are less likely to know their students (particularly in the second week of classes, which is when the tragedy occurred for this campus). Faculty in large lectures may also have experienced more confusion about their roles with respect to the attacks, and DiPietro (2003) found that faculty who felt confused often said nothing about the attacks.

The fact that the attacks were mentioned least frequently in project courses was surprising because students usually receive individualized faculty attention around a group or individual project in such courses. One would predict a relatively high level of faculty-student interaction, much like discussion or studio courses. The project courses reported in this survey, however, varied dramatically in size, ranging from very small courses (i.e. one student in a drama thesis course) to relatively large team-based courses (i.e. an information systems course with over 80 students). The size of the course could predict whether instructors addressed the attacks. It could also be that faculty (and perhaps students) in project courses were more focused on a specific product or outcome, so the tendency might have been to "get back to work" rather than linger on the terrorist attacks.

Fortunately, only eight students (1.7%) reported that none of their instructors addressed the terrorist attacks. Five of these students were freshmen or sophomores taking four to five classes each, predominantly in science, mathematics, and business.

Frequency of responses. When faculty addressed the terrorist attacks, what kinds of comments did they make, and what kinds of activities did they lead? The survey provided 14 possible responses based on DiPietro's (2003) faculty survey, as listed below in Tables 24.2 and 24.3. Table 24.2 presents the frequency of responses organized by different types of courses. Students reported that the most common response (Response A, 31% of the instructors) was to communicate a two-part message: that the class needed to go on with the material despite the attacks but there would be additional opportunities to review the material down the road. The second most common response (Response E, 23%) was to excuse students from class or offer an extension on an assignment. Faculty who addressed the attacks in class typically addressed them in multiple ways, so the total for each column on Table 24.2 exceeds 100%. For example, faculty who asked if family and friends were affected (Response M) were also likely to lead a brief discussion in class (Response G).

Table 24.2 shows that some responses were more common in certain types of courses. For example, students reported that instructors led brief discussions about the attacks (Response G) in studio classes more frequently than in other types of classes. In fact, brief discussions were reported in 49% of studio courses but in only 24% of traditional "discussion courses." One possible reason that discussions occurred with such high frequency in studio courses, most common in the fine arts (e.g. art, drama, architecture, etc.) is that the dean of the College of Fine Arts contacted all department chairs immediately following the attacks and encouraged faculty to be responsive with their students. To our knowledge, no other dean coordinated such efforts.

Likewise, certain responses were reported with less frequency for some classroom environments. For example, only 8% of the students in large lectures indicated that their instructors asked if friends or family had been affected by the attacks (Response M) whereas 10–36% of the students reported that instructors asked about their families in other types of classes. By definition, these large lecture classes have enrollments of 50 students or more, and the faculty may have felt unnatural or awkward posing such a personal question to large groups.

Helpfulness of responses. When an instructor did not mention the attacks at all, students did not rate the helpfulness of this non-response, so there is little quantitative data to report. Some students offered comments about their instructor's lack of response, and their comments conveyed frustration, disappointment, or apathy, but few conveyed that "doing nothing" was helpful or even appropriate. Table 24.3 provides sample comments from students whose instructors made no mention of the terrorist attacks.

When instructors did respond to the terrorist attacks, approximately two-thirds of the students evaluated the helpfulness of that response (66.4%). The 33.6% of students who did not rate the helpfulness of their instructor's actions may have lacked a clear sense of what did or did not help them cope with the events, or they may have been fatigued by the length of the survey. Table 24.4 lists students' helpfulness ratings for 14 instructor-led activities.

As revealed in Table 24.4, most students found most responses very helpful, with the exception of Response B, which we shall return to momentarily. For the other 13 possible responses, 69–100% of the respondents thought that the instructor's efforts to address the attacks were quite helpful, regardless of whether the instructor's response required relatively little effort, such as asking for one minute of silence (Response C), or a great deal of effort and preparation, such as incorporating the event into the lesson plan or topics for the course (Response I). When instructors developed a class project related to the attacks, 100% of their students found such projects helpful, but the N for this response was small with only two students (Response J). Some students indicated that their instructors' responses were not helpful, but at most, only 15% of the students found a response unhelpful or problematic (with the exception of Response B). The general conclusion, from the students' perspective, appears to be "do something, just about anything."

Several of the responses that students appreciated were consistent with the research on coping with highly stressful events. For example, 78% of the students found it very helpful when their instructor mentioned ways that people can support the rescue efforts: instructors provided phone numbers for the Red Cross and other charities, informed students where they could donate blood, etc. Taking action to address a problem is known as "problem-focused coping" and it is a relatively adaptive response to cataclysmic events, often more effective at reducing stress than simply venting or focusing on one's emotional reaction (Carver, Scheier, & Kumari Weintraub, 1989). Accordingly, one national study found that people who were indirectly affected by the attacks of September 11th had lower levels of long-term stress when they took active, problem-focused approaches, which may explain why students benefited when instructors offered something concrete that they could do (Silver et al., 2002). Other potential responses addressed the cognitive load of a disaster. Recall that 69% of the students who were offered extensions or who were excused from class found this

TABLE 24.3

Sample Student Comments When Instructors Made No Mention of the Attacks in Class

"The instructor's ignoring of the events was terrible. People were panicking and he was acting like nothing happened." (Female sophomore in a small lecture music class)

"My professor was a complete *** about the whole situation . . . not only did he fail to try to do anything positive related to the attack, he made us come in on a Saturday morning to make up the class period that we missed due to classes being cancelled on September 11." (Male graduate student in a small lecture business class)

"Very unhelpful. Showed little personal concern for the students." (Female senior in a psychology discussion class)

"The instructor appeared not to take the event seriously enough." (Male graduate student in a small lecture engineering class)

"The instructor didn't mention the tragedy at all and surprisingly didn't give a nice historical or informational perspective: something I was hoping a history teacher would explain." (Male first-year student, large lecture history class)

"None- no room for discussion at all." (Female sophomore, large lecture chemistry class)

". . . the lack of activity was not detrimental. It didn't matter to me whether the professor talked about it or not." (Male graduate student in a project computer science course)

TABLE 24.4

Students' Perceptions of the Helpfulness of Instructor Responses

Instructor Response	Number of reports which rated helpfulness	Helpfulness Rating			
		Uncertain or N/A	Not Helpful	Somewhat Helpful	Very Helpful
A	174	11%	7%	11%	71%
B	54	17%	41%	6%	36%
C	32	3%	10%	7%	80%
D	66	15%	9%	7%	69%
E	150	8%	7%	16%	69%
F	86	12%	9%	8%	71%
G	140	9%	13%	9%	69%
H	77	6%	6%	4%	84%
I	73	7%	15%	6%	72%
J	2	0	0	0	100%
K	9	11%	11%	0	78%
L	45	14%	4%	4%	78%
M	115	15%	8%	8%	69%
N	29	10%	15%	13%	62%

Key to Instructor Responses

A) Acknowledged that the class needs to go on with the material but reassured the class that if students were too distressed to process the material that there will be other opportunities to review it down the road

B) Acknowledged that the attacks had occurred and said that the class needs to go on with no mention of opportunities for review or extra help

C) One minute of silence

D) Mentioned Counseling Services

E) Excused students / offered extensions if assignments were due

F) Offered to talk privately with anybody who might want to

G) Had a brief discussion in class

H) Devoted the whole first class after the attacks to discussion

I) Incorporated the event into the lesson plan / curriculum

J) Decided to do a project as a class (i.e. quilt, fence-painting, etc.)

K) Read a passage from an inspirational book

L) Mentioned ways that people can help (i.e. gave out phone numbers for the Red Cross or charities, talked about the benefits of donating blood, etc.)

M) Asked students if their families and friends were physically affected

N) Other ___(write-in)____

short-term break from their academic responsibilities to be very helpful. Although one might cynically interpret these numbers as students' general eagerness to postpone work whenever possible, cognitive and neuroscience research demonstrates that working memory capacity is reduced immediately following an acutely stressful experience (e.g. Arnsten, 1998; Newcomer, Selke, Melson, Hershey, Craft, Richards, & Alderson, 1999). Since students would be less capable of learning new material in the initial wake of a collective tragedy, providing them with extensions or excusing them from class reduces their stress and allows them to produce work later that better reflects their normal abilities and study habits.

The one response that was clearly problematic, however, was Response B, which consisted of "acknowledging that the attacks had occurred and saying that the class needs to go on with no mention of opportunities for review or extra help." Relatively few students found this approach helpful (36%), and an almost equal number found this response unhelpful (41%). Some students explained that Response B was unhelpful because so little was done (e.g. "It wasn't really helpful because it was never really discussed"), and others found it unhelpful because students' needs were not addressed (e.g. "Very unhelpful – Showed little personal concern for the students"). In contrast, most students found Response A very helpful (71%), which, like Response B, emphasized moving on with the material, but unlike Response B, recognized students' needs by offering to review material later.

Implications

Previous research found that faculty generally felt uncertain about their responses to the events of September 11th (DiPietro, 2003). The current study offers some reassuring clarity at to how faculty and faculty developers can be most effective following a collective tragedy.

Implications for Faculty

The first issue for faculty is deciding which events qualify as a collective crisis that should be addressed in the classroom. This was not one of our research questions, but we believe that several converging factors can help identify such events. Some events are likely to affect students because of their *proximity* (local campus events) or the sheer *magnitude* and scale (national events with wide media coverage). Other factors include a significant likelihood that the event will have a *direct impact* on students' families or social networks. Faculty should also consider the degree to which students are likely to *identify* with the victim(s) of the tragedy and feel like "vicarious victims" (which occurred with the September 11 terrorist attacks and could also occur for members of a group targeted by a hate crime) (Wayment, 2004). Finally instructors can pay attention to a variety of situational cues. Are the students getting mobilized on campus (e.g., through vigils)? Do faculty themselves find it hard to go back to class after the event? In all these cases, our results indicate that from the students' perspective, it is best to do something. Students often complained when faculty did not mention the attacks at all, and they expressed gratitude when faculty acknowledged that something awful had occurred. Beyond acknowledging a tragic event, faculty would be well-advised to take the extra step of recognizing that students are distressed and to show some extra support, such as offering to grant extensions for students who request them.

It is perhaps a surprising relief to learn that an instructor's response need not be complicated, time-intensive, or even personalized. Students are likely to appreciate responses that require relatively little effort, such as taking a minute of silence or offering to review material later in the course, so faculty should not feel pressed into redesigning their course. Faculty responses that required high levels of effort were also viewed as helpful, so those who wish to use the lens of their discipline to examine the events surrounding a tragedy are encouraged to do so. A repeated issue that appeared in students' comments was that they appreciated an instructor who responded in a unique and humane way, so faculty should not feel pressured to homogenize their responses.

Implications for Faculty Developers

The results suggest that faculty developers can play several roles in the wake of a collective tragedy. First, faculty developers can provide resources and leadership to deans and department chairs. We know that one dean, the dean of the College of Fine Arts, contacted all of his department chairs to encourage faculty to address the attacks and support students. Professors teaching studio courses in the fine arts responded more strongly than most of their peers by leading more discussions, offering more extensions, offering to talk privately with more students, etc. Although these studio instructors might have been just as proactive and compassionate without their dean's leadership, faculty developers should note that deans and department chairs are the nexus of faculty action. Connecting these key personnel with the findings from this study, along with online resources such as those at University of Michigan, empowers administrators to help their faculty respond more effectively.

A second implication for faculty developers is that if time and resources are limited, as they are likely to be following a tragedy, it would be strategic to focus on schools or departments that offer a greater number of project courses or large lecture courses. Our results indicate that faculty in these two types of courses were the least likely to mention the attacks, which would suggest that they are the most likely to benefit from guidance on how to respond. Although a full class discussion may not suit these courses, some of the quick, low-effort activities might work well.

The third role for faculty developers is to reassure faculty after the fact that their actions were probably helpful to students, even if it was not clear in class. As DiPietro (2003) noted, many faculty were still unclear about whether their responses were helpful several weeks later. The good news is that most students found most instructor responses, with the one noted exception, to be very helpful.

Limitations

There are limitations to this research. First, the data were collected several months after the tragic event, so students' memories might have been prone to error. The survey was intentionally delayed for several reasons. First, students' high stress levels immediately following the attacks would have impaired their ability to judge the effectiveness of an activity (LeDoux, 1996; Lazarus & Lazarus, 1994; Liverant et al., 2004). Second, some instructors created final projects around the attacks, and students would not have completed such projects until the end of the course. Lastly, we were concerned that administering the survey too soon after the attacks might augment students' stress or emotional difficulty. Many students at this institution come from New York or New Jersey (22% of the undergraduate students for 2001–02), and students across campus experienced the events of September 11th quite personally.

A second limitation of this study is that the data were collected with respect to one tragic event that raised controversial issues of race, religion, cultural differences, and politics (to name a few), which could explain faculty hesitancy to mention the event in class. Faculty may be more likely to respond to other tragedies. However, as we observed with hurricane Katrina and Matthew Shepard's death, traumatic events are often controversial. In that respect, faculty responses to the events of September 11th are likely to shed some light on how faculty navigate their way through other highly charged collective tragedies.

Conclusion

A crisis raises anxiety and confusion throughout an institution, and faculty are likely to be unsure about what to do in the classroom. As faculty developers, we can provide suggestions and resources to administrators, and we can offer instructors a variety of approaches so they feel more empowered and less paralyzed. Faculty will be relieved to learn that most responses, even the simplest recognition that it will take time to adjust, are helpful to students.

References

American Psychiatric Association. (2005). *Disasters: Mental health recommendations for students and colleges.* Retrieved March 10, 2006 from American Psychiatric Association's Web Site: http://healthyminds.org/katrinatipsforcollege.cfm

Arnsten, A. F. (1998, June 12). The biology of being frazzled. *Science, 280,* 1711–1712.

Asmussen, K. J., & Creswell, J. W. (1995). Campus response to a student gunman. *Journal of Higher Education, 66* (5), 575–591.

Carver, C. S., Scheier, M. F., & Kumari Weintraub, J. (1989). Assessing coping strategies: A theoretically based approach. *Journal of Personality and Social Psychology, 56,* 267–283.

Center for Research on Learning and Teaching. (n.d.). *Publications and links.* Retrieved December 3, 2005 from University of Michigan, Center for Research on Learning and Teaching Web site: http://www.crlt.umich.edu/publinks/publinks.html

DiPietro, M. (2003). The day after: Faculty behavior in post–September 11, 2001, classes. In C. M. Wehlburg. & S. Chadwick-Blossey (Eds.), *To improve the academy: Vol 21. Resources for faculty, instructional, and organizational development* (pp. 21–39). Bolton, MA: Anker.

Faculty Center for Excellence in Teaching. (2002). *Teaching and learning in times of crisis.* Retrieved December 3, 2005, from Western Kentucky University, Faculty Center for Excellence in Teaching Web site: http://www.wku.edu/teaching/booklets/crisis.html

Farrell, E. F. (2001, December 21). Hedging against disaster. *The Chronicle of Higher Education,* p. A40.

Guterman, L. (2001, Feb. 16). Student murdered in dormitory at Gallaudet University. *The Chronicle of Higher Education,* p. A49.

Honos-Webb, L., Sunwolf, Hart, S., Scalise, J. T. (2006). How to help after national catastrophes: Findings following 9/11. *The Humanistic Psychologist, 34*(1), *75–97.*

Hurst, J. C. (1999). The Matthew Shepard tragedy: Management of a crisis. *About Campus, 4*(3), 5–11.

Larson, W. A. (Ed.). (1994). *When crisis strikes on campus.* Washington, DC: Council for Advancement and Support of Education.

Lazarus, R. S., & Lazarus, B. N. (1994). *Passion and reason: Making sense of our emotions.* Oxford: Oxford University Press.

LeDoux, J. (1996). *The emotional brain: The mysterious underpinnings of emotional life.* New York: Simon & Schuster.

Liverant, G. I., Hofmann, S. G., & Litz, B. T. (2004). Coping and anxiety in college students after the September 11th terrorist attacks. *Anxiety, Stress & Coping: An International Journal, 17*(2), 127–139.

Mangan, K. (2005, November 25). 'Katrina' students are in every state. *The Chronicle of Higher Education,* p. A45.

Michigan State University Libraries. (2005, October). *Hurricane Katrina: Research and resources.* Retrieved December 3, 2005 from Michigan State University, Libraries Web site: http://www.lib.msu.edu/libinstr/katrina.htm

Newcomer, J. W., Selke, G., Melson, A. K., Hershey, T., Craft, S., Richards, K., & Alderson, A. L. (1999). Decreased memory performance in healthy humans induced by stress-level cortisol treatment. *Archives of General Psychiatry, 56,* 527–533.

Paine, C., & Sprague, J. (2000). Crisis prevention and response: Is your school prepared? *Oregon School Study Council Bulletin, 43*(2), 1.

Rooney, M. (2002, Nov. 8). Student kills three University of Arizona professors. *The Chronicle of Higher Education,* p. A12.

Siegel, D. (1994). *Campuses respond to violent tragedy.* Phoenix, AZ: Oryx Press.

Silver, R. C., Holman, A., McIntosh, D. N., Poulin, M., & Gil-Rivas, V. (2002). Nationwide longitudinal study of psychological responses to September 11. *Journal of the American Medical Association, 288,* 1235–1244.

Wayment, H. A. (2004). It could have been me: Vicarious victims and disaster-focused distress. *Personality and Social Psychology Bulletin, 30*(4), 515–528.

Whiting, L. R., Tucker, M., & Whaley, S. R. (2004, June). *Level of preparedness for managing crisis communication on land grant campuses.* Paper presented at the meeting of the American Council of Education, Lake Tahoe, CA.

Appendix

Survey Questions for Activities Following Sept. 11th Terrorist Attacks

1. Do you give Drs. Huston and DiPietro and their associates permission to present this work in written and oral form without further permission? Yes No
2. Gender: (1) Male (2) Female
3. College: *Colleges listed*
4. Major(s) or department in which you'll be getting a degree: *Relevant departments for each college*
5. Indicate your status as a student: (1) U.S. Citizen (2) International student
6. Class: (1) First-year student, (2) Sophomore, (3) Junior, (4) Senior, (5) Masters / Graduate student
7. Please check the boxes of any *university-wide activities* you attended after 9/11: (1) Prayer / Candlelight Vigil (evening of the attacks), (2) A Time to Learn: Professors Explain the Crisis, (3) Peace Rally, (4) Other—please explain.
8. How effective do you think these university-wide activity(ies) was (were)?
9. How many academic classes were you taking in September of 2001?
10. Please think of one of the courses you were taking last September. What department offers this course?
11. What type of class was this? (You may select multiple answers): (1) Discussion, (2) Small lecture (< 50 students), (3) Large lecture (>= 50 students), (4) Lab, (5) Studio, (6) Recitation, (7) Project course
12. Did the professor or TA mention the 9/11 attacks in class or lead any activities related to them? Yes No
13. Please check the boxes next to the anything that your *professor* did in this class that was related to 9/11. This is easier if you read all of the options before you begin selecting them. You may check more than one. *See Key for Instructor Responses in Tables 2 and 3 for specific response items.*
14. If you had a TA for this course, did the TA do anything in class to help the students? If so, what did he or she do? *(Same list of activities A-N as above)*
15. How helpful or effective do you think the instructor's or the TA's activities were? If an activity was helpful, what made it helpful? If an activity was unhelpful, why didn't it help you?

Questions 10–15 were then repeated for each course that the student was taking in September 2001.

CHAPTER 25

RECOGNIZING STUDENT DIVERSITY

Improving Teaching and Learning Practices for International Students: Implications for Curriculum, Pedagogy and Assessment

Dr Janette Ryan, Monash University

If international students are the 'canaries' in the coalmine as we suggest in Chapter 1, then it is necessary to examine the issues at the 'coalface' for both international students and their lecturers. This chapter focuses on the 'operational' issues and dilemmas that may surface in multicultural classrooms. It provides a summary of the problematic areas cited by international students and lecturers and provides practical suggestions as to how lecturers can improve their teaching and learning for international students in ways that will benefit all students.

Meeting students' learning needs

There is often not time in lecturers' busy lives to step back and re-assess the assumptions underpinning their practice. Student feedback instruments give lecturers some measure of the areas of their teaching which they do well and the areas that are lacking. These instruments rarely give lecturers qualitative information, however, about how they can improve their practice, in ways that are systemic and sustainable. Exhortations to 'do it better' without saying how, generally result in lecturers trying to do more to satisfy increasing demands. Lecturers need to learn how to do things differently in ways that better suit their own needs as teachers as well as the needs of the range of their students. But first lecturers need to know what areas are problematic, both for lecturers themselves and for international students.

In my own research (Ryan, 2000), asking lecturers and international students what they believed to be 'good' teaching and learning practices, both groups gave remarkably similar responses. They cited a preparedness to tailor course content, teaching methods and assessment techniques to the needs and interest of students. In many cases, the students interviewed were in the classes of the lecturers interviewed, yet the reports of how well students' needs were being met fell short of what lecturers thought they were delivering. This gap between theory and practice happened despite lecturers' dedication to meeting the needs of their students as best they could. Lecturers were often aware of what was needed but putting this into practice, that is, operationalising these ideals, was much more difficult. The 'gap' in expectations between lecturers and international students is often the source of students' problems rather than a lack in students' own skills. Lecturers can do much to bridge this gap and so ensure that international students have better opportunities to successfully demonstrate their abilities.

Reprinted from *Teaching International Students: Enhancing Learning for All Students,* edited by Jude Carroll and Janette Ryan (2005), Routledge.

'Gaps' in understanding

Many lecturers interviewed held misconceptions about international students which have already been reviewed elsewhere in this book. My studies confirmed that teachers sometimes viewed international students as a homogeneous group with similar learning styles and expectations; as rote learners with a surface approach to learning; as unwilling to participate in class discussion; and as only wanting to interact with others from similar backgrounds. International students reported that they felt under-valued and misunderstood. They wanted to learn new skills, to demonstrate their experience and expertise, and to speak up and participate in class, but needed help to do so. My interviews showed that international students liked doing group work and using independent and critical approaches to learning. They needed lecturers to assist them by employing a range of strategies such us providing background knowledge; avoiding the use of slang and not speaking too fast; referring to international or multicultural as well as local examples; and by providing opportunities to work and mix with home students.

There were many examples where lecturers were making genuine attempts to improve their practice, generally through a trial-and-error process. Many found that one solution worked for one group of students in a given year but needed to be changed and adapted to the following cohort of students. That is, lecturers found that there are differences in the curriculum as 'intention' (as stated in course objectives and outcomes) and curriculum as 'outcome' (as evidenced by what the students had actually learnt and experienced). Lecturers who understood the nexus between these two were generally those who understood the need to be flexible and reflective practitioners. They understood that teaching and learning are dynamic parts of a whole and that they could learn as much from their students as students could from them. They appreciated that the interaction between teachers and learners determines and shapes educational outcomes. They were comfortable with the co-construction of knowledge and learning, with different approaches and strategies despite there often being variable success. The types of learning tasks and materials that they provided were designed to facilitate a broad range of learning styles and interests that could be negotiated and adapted to suit a diverse range of students. They provided for this diversity not just in classroom activities but in the whole range of teaching and learning activities—in the curriculum (materials), pedagogy (teaching methods) and assessment (judgements of outcomes). Students in these classes reported an increased sense of ownership of their learning and of respect for them as independent learners. This, of course, was of benefit to all students within the classroom but of particular importance for international students who may often have difficulty negotiating a sometimes very unfamiliar learning environment.

Although problematic areas for international students can vary according to discipline area, there are some key generic issues in curriculum content, pedagogy and assessment where lecturers can improve their teaching and learning practices in ways that will not only benefit international students, but all students.

Curriculum content and design

'Internationalisation' of curriculum content and design is dealt with in some detail in Chapters 12 and 13, which make clear that internationalisation goes beyond the mere addition of international examples. It needs to permeate the very nature of the discipline so that students gain a global understanding and perspective of the discipline. Both curriculum content and design need to foster both international and local perspectives of the discipline. It is not just a matter of adjusting, or 'adding' to curriculum content to ensure that it suits international students, but making sure that home students also gain global and international understandings. Two specific aspects of the curriculum, however, are highlighted here.

Reference/reading lists

Copious amounts of reading present problems for many international students (see Chapter 6) as it can take them huge amounts of time to translate the information, or to understand the background content of the materials. There are many ways that lecturers can assist international students to access relevant information more easily, such as:

- the selective use of references/readings
- providing annotated bibliographies
- marking key texts
- identifying relevant chapters or excerpts
- using electronic materials (for faster searching of relevant information)
- checking the accessibility of texts or websites used (for Plain English and straightforward and pertinent information)
- checking the relevance of the language used and making sure it is appropriate for the target audience
- including foundational or definitive texts
- providing reading lists early
- making unit or module descriptions available electronically
- providing a glossary of key terms and concepts.

Placements/field work

Field work and field placements provide opportunities for students to expand their perspectives, especially in areas where lecturers themselves may have little knowledge or experience. It can therefore be useful, especially in practice-based courses, to provide students with opportunities for:

- a placement outside the local region
- diverse placements/field trips within the local region
- opportunities for national or international placements or work.

Pedagogy

Teaching practices provide opportunities for the development of globally orientated knowledge and intercultural understandings and skills for all students, as well as for catering for the learning needs of international students. International students need to be given opportunities to be able to participate and demonstrate their skills, and equally home students need to learn how to listen to and learn from the experiences of others. In this way, international students become an important source of expertise for home students. In order to do this, lecturers also need to examine fundamental issues about their teaching and learning practices. These include questions such as:

- Do you provide a supportive learning environment where all students are able to participate successfully and demonstrate their abilities?
- Do you engage students in learning, drawing on their experiences and interests?
- Are you a critically reflective practitioner? Can you identify the assumptions underpinning your teaching and learning practices? Do you examine these to ensure that outcomes for students are equitable?

Creating supportive learning environments

Lecturers need to create the contexts where students feel that their contributions are valued and that they are given opportunities to participate and succeed. Lecturers need to:

- provide a range of opportunities for all students to demonstrate their abilities, such as through choice of assessment or group discussion topics or class activities;
- provide negotiable class discussions and assessment tasks and methods so that students can explore their own areas of interest and demonstrate their knowledge and expertise;
- examine whether learning objectives can be met in other, more inclusive, ways such as through different tasks, formats or methods, or in different time frames;
- facilitate contact between home students and students from other cultures through organising and facilitating multicultural group work and discussion (see Chapters 8 and 9).

Engaging students in learning

Lecturers need to ensure that international students can draw upon their background knowledge and experience in order to make the connections with and foundations for their new knowledge and understandings. Providing opportunities for students to express and discuss their views in tutorials or seminars is not easy but lecturers encourage this if they:

- experiment with a variety of approaches to encourage students' participation, such as giving them time to formulate responses or engineering small group composition differently;
- frequently check students' understandings as to unit content and assessment task requirements;
- draw on the diverse background experiences and knowledge of students to enrich the learning environment for all students.

Being a critically reflective teacher

Lecturers need to re-examine their own practices to ensure that they are relevant to the needs of international students and provide equitable outcomes. For lecturers, this means:

- being aware of the cultural underpinnings of their own teaching and learning practices;
- examining whether their teaching either advantages or disadvantages different groups of students;
- evaluating unit or module requirements, including unit content, materials, classroom practices, assessment tasks and student learning outcomes, to ensure that there are no barriers to students' participation and success;
- thinking about whether any class or assessment tasks may cause difficulties for any group of students (e.g. due to ethnic background, religious beliefs, gender).

Lecture design and delivery

The areas that international students find most problematic relate to lectures (i.e. understanding lecture content) and tutorials or seminars (i.e. being able to participate). The conventional lecture format can present many problems for international students, as described in Chapter 6. This is especially true when lectures include large amounts of information and assume certain background knowledge and language proficiency. Making minor changes to the style of presentation can assist many students to more effectively understand the content and concepts contained in the lecture. This can include:

- providing a framework for each lecture, stating its main objectives, and how it links to previous and future topics;
- summarising the main points of the lecture;
- 'flagging' important information through the use of phrases such as 'this is a key point';
- pausing after key information or repeating or re-phrasing the information to allow more time for note taking;

- speaking clearly, using Plain English, and clarifying any new or unfamiliar vocabulary or concepts, then spelling them out or writing them down;
- speaking a little more slowly, especially when key information is being covered;
- providing lecture notes in advance or via the web;
- providing a 'question box' where students can leave questions after the lecture which can be addressed in tutorials or in the following lecture.

Encouraging participation in tutorials and seminars

In tutorials, international students need to be given opportunities to participate and demonstrate their knowledge and abilities. This can mean encouraging students to talk about their own experiences and ensuring that these become part of the class discussion. Often international students want to contribute but might not yet have the language facility or be familiar with the appropriate cultural mores for participation. This may mean that the tutor needs to give international students adequate time to prepare their responses and be sensitive to different ways of responding. The tutor also needs to be sensitive to students' different approaches to knowledge and learning and ensure that these are given equal 'space' and respect in the classroom. The tutor can do much to model a 'tone' of acceptance and nurturing of diversity, even displaying their own learning from unfamiliar perspectives.

The most problematic area for international students is often group discussions as they may lack background information or language proficiency, and the tutor needs to engineer and monitor these discussions to ensure that all students learn to value others' contributions. The use of ground rules for participation can be very effective, especially if they explicitly cover both group processes as well as group product, and stipulate task allocation and roles, turn-taking in discussions, conflict management, identification of groups members' strengths and weaknesses, and how group diversity has been productively used.

Tutors can feel uncomfortable when their questions in tutorials are met with silence and they can rush to fill the gap, often gratefully letting more vocal local students dominate the discussion. Sometimes students perceive that tutors are playing a 'fishing' game where the tutor responds positively to the answer they are looking for and this can prevent students from taking risks. Most students (but not all) learn to play the 'game' and can display their knowledge more easily. It can be uncomfortable when students do not respond in class in the ways that tutors normally expect, and this can sometimes be communicated negatively to students. If tutors do not respond to the contributions made by international students, because they are difficult to understand or are unfamiliar, the tutor's body language or facial expression can sometimes betray a lack of understanding or acceptance. It is important that tutors take the time to try to understand what a student has said, even if this can take some effort at understanding and perhaps follow-up questions, and to try to 'translate' it for the class and ensure that it becomes part of the discussion. All students need to feel that they are accepted as full members of the class.

International students report that they do want to participate but they often don't know how, lack the language facility to express their opinion or any sophistication of thought, and that it takes much courage to make a verbal contribution when they know that their language is clumsy and that they may not have understood. Many international students report that it can take them at least six months to summon the courage to speak in class, and if they receive a negative response, it can take much longer to muster the confidence to make another attempt. Many lecturers underestimate the abilities of international students, especially in the early stages of their study when they may be struggling with mastering the language. International students are aware that they sound clumsy and even 'stupid'. This can make it difficult for them to work in groups and even to make friends. Sheer fear of embarrassment prevents them from participating.

Tutors may often ask international students if they understand and students will say 'yes' when it is clear that they do not. When placed in such a situation, international students may feel too embarrassed to repeatedly admit that they don't understand and may not want to hold the class back. They prefer to say 'yes' to avoid the uncomfortable attention. Many students (including home students) prefer to remain silent in class. The tutor cannot force participation but can act to ensure that there are ample opportunities for participation and that students feel safe and supported when they choose to participate. Some possible strategies for doing this include:

- jointly developing with students 'ground rules' for whole group and small group discussion and participation;
- modelling inclusive speaking and listening practices by taking time to understand international students' contributions and, if necessary, 'translating' them in a diplomatic way for the rest of the class;
- ensuring that international students' contributions become part of the class discussion, even if this takes the discussion in a different direction;
- giving students time to formulate their responses to questions (through early provision of questions or through small group or pair work);
- engineering the composition of groups (for example, through allowing students to choose one friend to work with and then pairing them into groups of four that are diverse);
- structuring group tasks so that diversity of skills and knowledge is required and rewarded;
- showing an interest in students' background knowledge and experiences (but don't expect them to talk on behalf of their culture);
- providing some time in class for one-on-one conversations and for checking of progress and understanding of the tasks.

Assessment

The evaluation and grading of student work is a contentious area for most students, but international students will often have the most difficulty in decoding lecturers' expectations. They may also have reduced opportunities for demonstrating their learning and knowledge. Lecturers need to recognise that what they consider to be academic ability can be culturally based. They may reward for facility with academic discourse rather than what students have actually learnt or the depth of their understanding. They need to ensure that their assessment techniques match the learning objectives. Lecturers need to ask themselves:

- Are they assessing students for their mastery of academic discourse rather than for their critical or original thinking?
- Do they recognise or encourage different styles and approaches to learning?
- Do they allow students to use their own words and ways of expressing themselves?
- Do they assess content rather than penalise for spelling or grammatical expression except in the cases where spelling and grammar are inherent in the assessment criteria?

Many assessment tasks, especially essays, contain hidden codes or 'prompts' only apparent to students familiar with the academic discourse. For example, an essay topic that comprises a controversial statement followed by the word 'Discuss' may not signal to an international student that they are expected to challenge the statement, and that the essay should contain the student's own evaluation and opinion. The ways that international students write might also reflect different views about the nature and ownership of knowledge. It is therefore imperative for all students that expected paradigms and conventions are clearly articulated and modelled so that accusations of plagiarism, for example, can be avoided. Many international students can find themselves being punished for behaviour that was previously rewarded. In such cases it is important to take an educative approach to plagiarism and syndication (shared work) rather than simply a punitive one. It is also important that international students receive early feedback and encouragement. Such comments need to be descriptive, indicating what has been done well and what needs to be done in order to improve. It can also be helpful to model appropriate responses in class or to provide exemplars of previous successful work.

Anyone reviewing their own assessment methods and tasks could include questions such as:

- Are requirements and expectations explicit?
- Are there hidden codes or 'prompts'?
- Do the assessment tasks match the learning objectives?
- Do assessment tasks allow for different ways of demonstrating achievement of the learning objectives?
- Are students being assessed on what they have learnt or what they already know?
- Are content and understanding, or style and facility with language being assessed?
- If facility with language is important, are you teaching this skill?
- Is there a choice of topics so that students can connect with their own background knowledge and experiences?
- Can students work on topics that are relevant to their backgrounds and futures?
- Are assessment tasks flexible and negotiable?
- Is there a range of modes of presentation e.g. written, oral, 'hands on'?
- Is there a mixture of individual and group tasks?
- Can students choose the weighting of the task within a range so that they can take advantage of their strengths?
- Are tasks self-directed?
- Can assessment topics be provided that are less parochial and more internationalised?
- Can opportunities for plagiarism be 'designed out' by the choice of assessment task and topic?

Conclusion

By re-examining their teaching and learning practices, lecturers can make changes that are more sustainable for them as teachers and more suitable for the diverse range of students, not just international students. The use of 'internationalised' pedagogy means that all students not only gain more globalised knowledge but also develop the skills and attitudes to work in global settings. This requires that the teacher also has some level of global knowledge, skills and attitudes and a willingness to create spaces for all students with full rights of participation and success. Such a broad worldview can underpin teaching and learning philosophies but may only require minor adjustments to teaching and learning practices as the teacher becomes a more active facilitator of learning rather than the bastion of conventional wisdom.

References

Ryan, J. (2000). *A Guide to Teaching International Students,* Oxford: Oxford Centre for Staff and Learning Development.

But That's Just Good Teaching! The Case for Culturally Relevant Pedagogy

Gloria Ladson-Billings

For the past 6 years I have been engaged in research with excellent teachers of African American students (see, for example, Ladson-Billings, 1990, 1992b, 1992c, 1994). Given the dismal academic performance of many African American students (The College Board, 1985), I am not surprised that various administrators, teachers, and teacher educators have asked me to share and discuss my findings so that they might incorporate them in their work. One usual response to what I share is the comment around which I have based this article, "But, that's just good teaching!" Instead of some "magic bullet" or intricate formula and steps for instruction, some members of my audience are shocked to hear what seems to them like some rather routine teaching strategies that are a part of good teaching. My response is to affirm that, indeed, I am describing good teaching, and to question why so little of it seems to be occurring in the classrooms populated by African American students.

The pedagogical excellence I have studied is good teaching, but it is much more than that. This article is an attempt to describe a pedagogy I have come to identify as "culturally relevant" (Ladson-Billings, 1992a) and to argue for its centrality in the academic success of African American and other children who have not been well served by our nation's public schools. First, I provide some background information about other attempts to look at linkages between school and culture. Next, I discuss the theoretical grounding of culturally relevant teaching in the context of a 3-year study of successful teachers of African American students. I conclude this discussion with further examples of this pedagogy in action.

Linking Schooling and Culture

Native American educator Cornel Pewewardy (1993) asserts that one of the reasons Indian children experience difficulty in schools is that educators traditionally have attempted to insert culture into the education, instead of inserting education into the culture. This notion is, in all probability, true for many students who are not a part of the White, middle-class mainstream. For almost 15 years, anthropologists have looked at ways to develop a closer fit between students' home culture and the school. This work has had a variety of labels including "culturally appropriate" (Au & Jordan, 1981), "culturally congruent" (Mohatt & Erickson, 1981), "culturally responsive" (Cazden & Leggett, 1981; Erickson & Mohatt, 1982), and "culturally compatible" (Jordan, 1985; Vogt, Jordan, & Tharp, 1987). It has attempted to locate the problem of discontinuity between what students experience at home and what they experience at school in the speech and language interactions of teachers and students. These sociolinguists have suggested that if students' home language is incorporated into the classroom, students are more likely to experience academic success.

Villegas (1988), however, has argued that these micro-ethnographic studies fail to deal adequately with the macro social context in which student failure takes place. A concern I have voiced

Reprinted from *Theory Into Practice* (1995), Ohio State University College of Education.

about studies situated in speech and language interactions is that, in general, few have considered the needs of African American students.[1]

Irvine (1990) dealt with the lack of what she termed "cultural synchronization" between teachers and African American students. Her analysis included the micro-level classroom interactions, the "midlevel" institutional context (i.e., school practices and policies such as tracking and disciplinary practices), and the macro-level societal context. More recently Perry's (1993) analysis has included the historical context of the African American's educational struggle. All of this work—micro through macro level—has contributed to my conception of culturally relevant pedagogy.

What is Culturally Relevant Pedagogy?

In the current attempts to improve pedagogy, several scholars have advanced well-conceived conceptions of pedagogy. Notable among these scholars are Shulman (1987), whose work conceptualizes pedagogy as consisting of subject matter knowledge, pedagogical knowledge, and pedagogical content knowledge, and Berliner (1988), who doubts the ability of expert pedagogues to relate their expertise to novice practitioners. More recently, Bartolome (1994) has decried the search for the "right" teaching strategies and argued for a "humanizing pedagogy that respects and uses the reality, history, and perspectives of students as an integral part of educational practice" (p. 173).

I have defined culturally relevant teaching as a pedagogy of opposition (1992c) not unlike critical pedagogy but specifically committed to collective, not merely individual, empowerment. Culturally relevant pedagogy rests on three criteria or propositions: (a) Students must experience academic success; (b) students must develop and/or maintain cultural competence; and (c) students must develop a critical consciousness through which they challenge the status quo of the current social order.

Academic success

Despite the current social inequities and hostile classroom environments, students must develop their academic skills. The way those skills are developed may vary, but all students need literacy, numeracy, technological, social, and political skills in order to be active participants in a democracy. During the 1960s when African Americans were fighting for civil rights, one of the primary battlefronts was the classroom (Morris, 1984). Despite the federal government's failed attempts at adult literacy in the South, civil rights workers such as Septima Clark and Esau Jenkins (Brown, 1990) were able to teach successfully those same adults by ensuring that the students learned that which was most meaningful to them. This approach is similar to that advocated by noted critical pedagogue Paulo Freire (1970).

While much has been written about the need to improve the self-esteem of African American students (see for example, Banks & Grambs, 1972; Branch & Newcombe, 1986; Crooks, 1970), at base students must demonstrate academic competence. This was a clear message given by the eight teachers who participated in my study.[2] All of the teachers demanded, reinforced, and produced academic excellence in their students. Thus, culturally relevant teaching requires that teachers attend to students' academic needs, not merely make them "feel good." The trick of culturally relevant teaching is to get students to "choose" academic excellence.

In one of the classrooms I studied, the teacher, Ann Lewis,[3] focused a great deal of positive attention on the African American boys (who were the numerical majority in her class). Lewis, a White woman, recognized that the African American boys possessed social power. Rather than allow that power to influence their peers in negative ways, Lewis challenged the boys to demonstrate academic power by drawing on issues and ideas they found meaningful. As the boys began to take on academic leadership, other students saw this as a positive trait and developed similar behaviors. Instead of entering into an antagonistic relationship with the boys, Lewis found ways to value their skills and abilities and channel them in academically important ways.

Cultural competence

Culturally relevant teaching requires that students maintain some cultural integrity as well as academic excellence. In their widely cited article, Fordham and Ogbu (1986) point to a phenomenon called "acting White," where African American students fear being ostracized by their peers for demonstrating interest in and succeeding in academic and other school related tasks. Other scholars (Hollins, 1994; King, 1994) have provided alternate explanations of this behavior.[4] They suggest that for too many African American students, the school remains an alien and hostile place. This hostility is manifest in the "styling" and "posturing" (Majors & Billson, 1992) that the school rejects. Thus, the African American student wearing a hat in class or baggy pants may be sanctioned for clothing choices rather than specific behaviors. School is perceived as a place where African American students cannot "be themselves."

Culturally relevant teachers utilize students' culture as a vehicle for learning. Patricia Hilliard's love of poetry was shared with her students through their own love of rap music. Hilliard is an African American woman who had taught in a variety of schools, both public and private for about 12 years. She came into teaching after having stayed at home for many years to care for her family. The mother of a teenaged son, Hilliard was familiar with the music that permeates African American youth culture. Instead of railing against the supposed evils of rap music, Hilliard allowed her second grade students to bring in samples of lyrics from what both she and the students determined to be non-offensive rap songs.[5] Students were encouraged to perform the songs and the teacher reproduced them on an overhead so that they could discuss literal and figurative meanings as well as technical aspects of poetry such as rhyme scheme, alliteration, and onomatopoeia.

Thus, while the students were comfortable using their music, the teacher used it as a bridge to school learning. Their understanding of poetry far exceeded what either the state department of education or the local school district required. Hilliard's work is an example of how academic achievement and cultural competence can be merged.

Another way teachers can support cultural competence was demonstrated by Gertrude Winston, a White woman who has taught school for 40 years.[6] Winston worked hard to involve parents in her classroom. She created an "artist or craftsperson-in-residence" program so that the students could both learn from each other's parents and affirm cultural knowledge. Winston developed a rapport with parents and invited them to come into the classroom for 1 or 2 hours at a time for a period of 2–4 days. The parents, in consultation with Winston, demonstrated skills upon which Winston later built.

For example, a parent who was known in the community for her delicious sweet potato pies did a 2-day residency in Winston's fifth grade classroom. On the first day, she taught a group of students[7] how to make the pie crust. Winston provided supplies for the pie baking and the students tried their hands at making the crusts. They placed them in the refrigerator overnight and made the filling the following day. The finished pies were served to the entire class.

The students who participated in the "seminar" were required to conduct additional research on various aspects of what they learned. Students from the pie baking seminar did reports on George Washington Carver and his sweet potato research, conducted taste tests, devised a marketing plan for selling pies, and researched the culinary arts to find out what kind of preparation they needed to become cooks and chefs. Everyone in Winston's class was required to write a detailed thank you note to the artist/craftsperson.

Other residencies were done by a carpenter, a former professional basketball player, a licensed practical nurse, and a church musician. All of Winston's guests were parents or relatives of her students. She did not "import" role models with whom the students did not have firsthand experience. She was deliberate in reinforcing that the parents were a knowledgeable and capable resource. Her students came to understand the constructed nature of things such as "art," "excellence," and "knowledge." They also learned that what they had and where they came from was of value.

A third example of maintaining cultural competence was demonstrated by Ann Lewis, a White woman whom I have described as "culturally Black" (Ladson-Billings, 1992b; 1992c). In her sixth grade classroom, Lewis encouraged the students to use their home language while they acquired the secondary discourse (Gee, 1989) of "standard" English. Thus, her students were permitted to express themselves in language (in speaking and writing) with which they were knowledgeable and comfortable. They were then required to "translate" to the standard form. By the end of the year, the students were not only facile at this "code-switching" (Smitherman, 1981) but could better use both languages.

Critical consciousness

Culturally relevant teaching does not imply that it is enough for students to chose academic excellence and remain culturally grounded if those skills and abilities represent only an individual achievement. Beyond those individual characteristics of academic achievement and cultural competence, students must develop a broader sociopolitical consciousness that allows them to critique the cultural norms, values, mores, and institutions that produce and maintain social inequities. If school is about preparing students for active citizenship, what better citizenship tool than the ability to critically analyze the society?

Freire brought forth the notion of "conscientization," which is "a process that invites learners to engage the world and others critically" (McLaren, 1989, p. 195). However, Freire's work in Brazil was not radically different from work that was being done in the southern United States (Chilcoat & Ligon, 1994) to educate and empower African Americans who were disenfranchised.

In the classrooms of culturally relevant teachers, students are expected to "engage the world and others critically." Rather than merely bemoan the fact that their textbooks were out of date, several of the teachers in the study, in conjunction with their students, critiqued the knowledge represented in the textbooks, and the system of inequitable funding that allowed middle-class students to have newer texts. They wrote letters to the editor of the local newspaper to inform the community of the situation, The teachers also brought in articles and papers that represented counter knowledge to help the students develop multiple perspectives on a variety of social and historical phenomena.

Another example of this kind of teaching was reported in a Dallas newspaper (Robinson, 1993). A group of African American middle school students were involved in what they termed "community problem solving" (see Tate, this issue). The kind of social action curriculum in which the students participated is similar to that advocated by scholars who argue that students need to be "centered" (Asante, 1991; Tate, 1994) or the *subjects* rather than the objects of study.

Culturally Relevant Teaching in Action

As previously mentioned, this article and its theoretical undergirding come from a 3-year study of successful teachers of African American students. The teachers who participated in the study were initially selected by African American parents who believed them to be exceptional. Some of the parents' reasons for selecting the teachers were the enthusiasm their children showed in school and learning while in their classrooms, the consistent level of respect they received from the teachers, and their perception that the teachers understood the need for the students to operate in the dual worlds of their home community and the White community.

In addition to the parents' recommendations, I solicited principals' recommendations. Principals' reasons for recommending teachers were the low number of discipline referrals, the high attendance rates, and standardized test scores.[8] Teachers whose names appeared as both parents' and principals' recommendations were asked to participate in the study. Of the nine teachers' names who appeared on both lists, eight were willing to participate. Their participation required an in-depth ethnographic interview (Spradley, 1979), unannounced classroom visitations, videotaping of their teaching, and participation in a research collective with the other teachers in the study. This study was funded for 2 years. In a third year I did a follow-up study of two of the teachers to investigate their literacy teaching (Ladson-Billings, 1992b; 1992c).

Initially, as I observed the teachers I could not see patterns or similarities in their teaching. Some seemed very structured and regimented, using daily routines and activities. Others seemed more open or unstructured. Learning seemed to emerge from student initiation and suggestions. Still others seemed eclectic—very structured for certain activities and unstructured for others. It seemed to be a researcher's nightmare—no common threads to pull their practice together in order to relate it to others. The thought of their pedagogy as merely idiosyncratic, a product of their personalities and individual perspectives, left me both frustrated and dismayed. However, when I was able to go back over their interviews and later when we met together as a group to discuss their practice, I could see that in order to understand their practice it was necessary to go beyond the surface features of teaching "strategies" (Bartolome, 1994). The philosophical and ideological underpinnings of their practice, i.e. how they thought about themselves as teachers and how they thought about others (their students, the students' parents, and other community members), how they structured social relations within and outside of the classroom, and how they conceived of knowledge, revealed their similarities and points of congruence.[9]

All of the teachers identified strongly with teaching. They were not ashamed or embarrassed about their professions. Each had chosen to teach and, more importantly, had chosen to teach in this low-income, largely African American school district. The teachers saw themselves as a part of the community and teaching as a way to give back to the community. They encouraged their students to do the same. They believed their work was artistry, not a technical task that could be accomplished in a recipe-like fashion. Fundamental to their beliefs about teaching was that all of the students could and must succeed. Consequently, they saw their responsibility as working to guarantee the success of each student. The students who seemed furthest behind received plenty of individual attention and encouragement.

The teachers kept the relations between themselves and their students fluid and equitable. They encouraged the students to act as teachers, and they, themselves, often functioned as learners in the classroom. These fluid relationships extended beyond the classroom and into the community. Thus, it was common for the teachers to be seen attending community functions (e.g., churches, students' sports events) and using community services (e.g., beauty parlors, stores). The teachers attempted to create a bond with all of the students, rather than an idiosyncratic, individualistic connection that might foster an unhealthy competitiveness. This bond was nurtured by the teachers' insistence on creating a community of learners as a priority. They encouraged the students to learn collaboratively, teach each other, and be responsible for each other's learning.

As teachers in the same district, the teachers in this study were responsible for meeting the same state and local curriculum guidelines.[10] However, the way they met and challenged those guidelines helped to define them as culturally relevant teachers. For these teachers, knowledge is continuously recreated, recycled, and shared by the teachers and the students. Thus, they were not dependent on state curriculum frameworks or textbooks to decide what and how to teach.

For example, if the state curriculum framework called for teaching about the "age of exploration," they used this as an opportunity to examine conventional interpretations and introduce alternate ones. The content of the curriculum was always open to critical analysis.

The teachers exhibited a passion about what they were teaching—showing enthusiasm and vitality about what was being taught and learned. When students came to them with skill deficiencies, the teachers worked to help the students build bridges or scaffolding so that they could be proficient in the more challenging work they experienced in these classrooms.

For example, in Margaret Rossi's sixth grade class, all of the students were expected to learn algebra. For those who did not know basic number facts, Rossi provided calculators. She believed that by using particular skills in context (e.g., multiplication and division in the context of solving equations), the students would become more proficient at those skills while acquiring new learning.

Implications for Further Study

I believe this work has implications for both the research and practice communities. For researchers, I suggest that this kind of study must be replicated again and again. We need to know much more about the practice of successful teachers for African American and other students who have been poorly served by our schools. We need to have an opportunity to explore alternate research paradigms that include the voices of parents and communities in non-exploitative ways.[11]

For practitioners, this research reinforces the fact that the place to find out about classroom practices is the naturalistic setting of the classroom and from the lived experiences of teachers. Teachers need not shy away from conducting their own research about their practice (Zeichner & Tabachnick, 1991). Their unique perspectives and personal investment in good practice must not be overlooked. For both groups—researchers and practitioners alike—this work is designed to challenge us to reconsider what we mean by "good" teaching, to look for it in some unlikely places, and to challenge those who suggest it cannot be made available to all children.

Notes

1. Some notable exceptions to this failure to consider achievement strategies for African American students are *Ways With Words* (Heath, 1983); "Fostering Early Literacy Through Parent Coaching" (Edwards, 1991); and "Achieving Equal Educational Outcomes for Black Children" (Hale-Benson, 1990).
2. I have written extensively about this study, its methodology, findings, and results elsewhere. For a full discussion of the study, see Ladson-Billings (1994).
3. All study participants' names are pseudonyms.
4. At the 1994 annual meeting of the American Educational Research Association, King and Hollins presented a symposium entitled, "The Burden of Acting White Revisited."
5. The teacher acknowledged the racism, misogyny, and explicit sexuality that is a part of the lyrics of some rap songs. Thus, the students were directed to use only those songs they felt they could "sing to their parents."
6. Winston retired after the first year of the study but continued to participate in the research collaborative throughout the study.
7. Because the residency is more than a demonstration and requires students to work intensely with the artist or craftsperson, students must sign up for a particular artist. The typical group size was 5–6 students.
8. Standardized test scores throughout this district were very low. However, the teachers in the study distinguished themselves because students in their classrooms consistently produced higher test scores than their grade level colleagues.
9. As I describe the teachers I do not mean to suggest that they had no individual personalities or practices. However, what I was looking for in this study were ways to describe the commonalties of their practice. Thus, while this discussion of culturally relevant teaching may appear to infer an essentialized notion of teaching practice, none is intended. Speaking in this categorical manner is a heuristic for research purposes.
10. The eight teachers were spread across four schools in the district and were subjected to the specific administrative styles of four different principals.
11. Two sessions at the 1994 annual meeting of the American Educational Research Association in New Orleans entitled, "Private Lives in Public Conversations: Ethics of Research Across Communities of Color," dealt with concerns for the ethical standards of research in non-White communities.

References:

Asante, M.K. (1991). The Afrocentric idea in education. *Journal of Negro Education, 60,* 170–180.

Au, K., & Jordan, C. (1981). Teaching reading to Hawaiian children: Finding a culturally appropriate solution. In H. Trueba, G. Guthrie, & K. Au (Eds.), *Culture and the bilingual classroom: Studies in classroom ethnography* (pp, 69–86). Rowley, MA: Newbury House.

Banks, J., & Grambs, J. (Eds.). (1972). *Black self-concept: Implications for educational and social sciences,* New York: McGraw-Hill.

Bartolome, L. (1994). Beyond the methods fetish: Toward a humanizing pedagogy. *Harvard Educational Review, 64,* 173–194.

Berliner, D. (1988, October). Implications of studies of expertise in pedagogy for teacher education and evaluation. In *New directions for teacher assessment* (Invitational conference proceedings). New York: Educational Testing Service.

Branch, C., & Newcombe, N. (1986). Racial attitudes among young Black children as a function of parental attitudes: A longitudinal and cross-sectional study. *Child Development, 57,* 712–721.

Brown, C.S. (Ed.). (1990). *Ready from within: A first person narrative,* Trenton, NJ: Africa World Press.

Cazden, C., & Leggett, E. (1981). Culturally responsive education: Recommendations for achieving Lau remedies II. In H. Trueba, G, Guthrie, & K. Au (Eds.), *Culture and the bilingual classroom: Studies in classroom ethnography* (pp. 69–86). Rowley, MA: Newbury House.

Chilcoat, G.W., & Ligon, J.A. (1994). Developing democratic citizens: The Mississippi Freedom Schools as a model for social studies instruction. *Theory and Research in Social Education, 22,* 128–175.

The College Board. (1985). *Equality and excellence: The educational status of Black Americans.* New York: Author.

Crooks, R. (1970). The effects of an interracial preschool program upon racial preference, knowledge of racial differences, and racial identification. *Journal of Social Issues, 26,* 137–148.

Edwards, P.A. (1991). Fostering early literacy through parent coaching. In E. Hiebert (Ed.), *Literacy for a diverse society: Perspectives, programs, and policies* (pp. 199–213). New York; Teachers College Press.

Erickson, F., & Mohan, C. (1982). Cultural organization and participation structures in two classrooms of Indian students. In G. Spindler, (Ed.), *Doing the ethnography of schooling* (pp. 131–174). New York: Holt, Rinehart & Winston.

Fordham, S., & Ogbu, J. (l986). Black students' success: Coping with the burden of "acting White." *Urban Review, 18,* 1–31.

Freire, P. (1970). *Pedagogy of the oppressed.* New York: Herder & Herder. Gee, J.P. (1989). Literacy, discourse, and linguistics: Introduction. *Journal of Education, 171,* 5–17.

Hale-Benson, J. (1990). Achieving equal educational outcomes for Black children. In A. Baron & E.E Garcia (Eds.), *Children at risk: Poverty, minority status, and other issues in educational equity* (pp. 201–215). Washington, DC: National Association of School Psychologists.

Heath, S.B. (1983). *Ways with words.* Cambridge, UK: Cambridge University Press.

Hollins, E.R. (1994, April). *The burden of acting White revisited: Planning school success rather than explaining school failure.* Paper presented at the annual Meeting of the American Education Research Association, New Orleans.

Irvine, J.J. (1990). *Black students and school failure.* Westport, CT: Greenwood Press.

Jordan, C. (1985). Translating culture: From ethnographic information to educational program. *Anthropology and Education Quarterly, 16,* 105–123.

King, J. (1994). *The burden of acting White re-examined: Towards a critical genealogy of acting Black.* Paper presented at the annual meeting of the American Educational Research Association, New Orleans.

Ladson-Billings, G. (1990). Like lightning in a bottle: Attempting to capture the pedagogical excellence of successful teachers of Black students. *International Journal of Qualitative Studies in Education, 3,* 335–344.

Ladson-Billings, G. (1992a). Culturally relevant teaching: The key to making multicultural education work. In C.A. Grant (Ed.), *Research and multicultural education* (pp. 106–121). London: Falmer Press.

Ladson-Billings, G. (1992b). Liberatory consequences of Literacy: A case of culturally relevant instruction for African-American students. *Journal of Negro Education, 61,* 378–391.

Ladson-Billings, G. (1992c). Reading between the lines and beyond the pages: A culturally relevant approach to literacy teaching. *Theory Intro Practice, 31,* 312–320.

Ladson-Billings, G. (1994). *The dreamkeepers: Successful teaching for African-American students.* San Francisco: Jossey-Bass.

McLaren, P. (1989). *Life in schools.* White Plains, NY: Longman.

Majors, R. & Billson, J. (1992). *Cool pose: The dilemmas of Black manhood in America.* New York: Lexington Books.

Mohatt, G., & Erickson, F. (1981). Cultural differences in teaching styles in an Odawa school: A sociolinguistic approach. In H. Trueba, G. Guthrie, & K. Au (Eds.), *Culture and the bilingual classroom: Studies in classroom ethnography* (pp. 105–119). Rowley, MA: Newbury House.

Morris, A. (1984). *The origins of the civil rights movement: Black communities organizing for change.* New York: The Free Press.

Perry, T. (1993). *Toward a theory of African-American student achievement.* Report No. 16. Boston, MA: Center on Families, Communities, Schools and Children's Learning, Wheelock College.

Pewewardy, C. (1993). Culturally responsible pedagogy in action: An American Indian magnet school. In E. Hollins, J. King, & W. Hayman (Eds.), *Teaching diverse populations: Formulating a knowledge base* (pp. 77–92). Albany: State University of New York Press.

Robinson, R. (1993, Feb. 25). P.C. Anderson students try hand at problem-solving. *The Dallas Examiner,* pp. 1, 8.

Shulman, L. (1987). Knowledge and teaching: Foundations of the new reform. *Harvard Educational Review,* 57, 1–22.

Smitherman, G. (1981). *Black English and the education of Black children and youth.* Detroit: Center for Black Studies, Wayne State University.

Spradley, J. (1979). *The ethnographic interview.* New York: Holt, Rinehart & Winston.

Tate, W.F. (1994). Race, retrenchment, and reform of school mathematics. *Phi Delta Kappan,* 75, 477–484.

Villegas, A. (1988). School failure and cultural mismatch: Another view. *The Urban Review, 20,* 253–265.

Vogt, L., Jordan, C., & Tharp, R. (1987). Explaining school failure, producing school success: Two cases. *Anthropology and Education Quarterly, 18,* 276–286.

Zeichner, K.M., & Tabachnick, B.R. (1991). Reflections on reflective teaching. In B.R Tabachnick & K.M. Zeichner (Eds.), *Inquiry-oriented practices in teacher education* (pp. 1–21). London: Falmer Press.

"Lame Idea": Disabling Language in the Classroom

Liat Ben-Moshe

As instructors, our job is to teach new material and prescribe new knowledge to our students. The way we choose to do this job is as significant as the educational content we are transmitting. As an instructor, a student and a person with a disability, I feel that it is up to all of us to convey our messages in ways that create the most comfortable and inclusive environment. Our classrooms should be safe places, not places that perpetuate oppression, exclusion and discrimination. The language that we use in the classroom is imperative for achieving these goals.

In the English language, using disability as a metaphor, an analogy and a derogatory term is common. Examples of such phrases and terms include: lame idea, blind justice, dumb luck, felt paralyzed, argument fell on deaf ears, crippling, crazy, insane, idiotic and retarded.

One might argue that using these words without relating them to particular individuals is not offensive. However, using disability as an analogy not only offends certain individuals, but it also impedes clear communication, perpetuates false beliefs about disability and creates an environment of unease and exclusion.

Disability Denotes Deficiency

Disability has negative connotations when used metaphorically, while the real experience of living with a disability can be quite enriching and empowering. In all the examples above disability is used in a value-laden way. "Lame idea" means bad idea or one that is not constructed in a sufficient and persuasive manner. When we call a notion or act "idiotic/moronic/retarded" we are trying to convey the message that the idea or notion is ill-conceived, lacking in thought or unintelligent. When we describe someone as "blind" to a fact (for example, men are blind to sexist practices), we mean that they are lacking knowledge or have no notion of what transpires around them. "Crazy" means excessive or without control. None of these signifying phrases carries positive and empowering interpretations.

As educators, we must bear in mind that disability labels have a history, and that those labels have been highly contested over the decades. These words were actually created to describe people with different abilities as inferior within particular value systems. For instance, the words "moron," "idiot" and "imbecile" were used throughout the 20th century as medical classifications to denote different levels of intellectual deficiency. Later on, all these terms were conflated under the umbrella of "mental retardation" (Clark & Marsh, 2002).

LIAT BEN-MOSHE is a Ph.D. student in Sociology, Disability Studies and Women Studies at Syracuse University.

Reprinted from *Building Pedagogical Curb Cuts: Incorporating Disability in the University,* edited by L. Ben-Moshe, R. C. Cory, M. Feldbaum and K. Sagendorf (2005), by permission of the author.

The category of mental retardation, by itself, is highly contested for its reification of all perceived differences in cognitive abilities into one unified category. The important fact here is that mental retardation is a social construction, not a real condition that is innate in people's minds. The only requirement for inclusion in this category is deviation from a norm (usually prescribed by the use of IQ test) and perceived incompetence. Mental retardation is by itself a linguistic metaphor that means "cognitively delayed." When used metaphorically in everyday speech, "retarded" stands for slow or underdeveloped thought processes.

When we use terms like "retarded," "lame" or "blind"—even if we are referring to acts or ideas and not to people at all—we perpetuate the stigma associated with disability. By using a label which is commonly associated with disabled people to denote a deficiency, a lack or an ill-conceived notion, we reproduce the oppression of people with disabilities. As educators, we must be aware of the oppressive power of "everyday" language and try to change it.

False Beliefs Contained in Disabling Phrases

We learn about disability through everyday use of language. In the same way that racist or sexist attitudes, whether implicit or explicit, are acquired through the "normal" learning process, so too are negative assumptions about disabilities and the people who are labeled as having them. Our notions of people who are blind, deaf or labeled as mentally retarded come into play when we use disabling phrases, and these notions are usually far from accurate. They do not convey the complexity of living in a society that regards people with disabilities as the Other on the basis of perceived mentally or bodily difference.

The use of disability as a metaphor perpetuates false beliefs about the nature of impairment and disability. People who are blind, for example, do not lack in knowledge; they simply have different ways of obtaining it. Paralysis does not necessarily imply lack of mobility, stagnancy or dependence since there are augmentative instruments, such as wheelchairs and personal aids, that secure independence and mobility. The continued use of disabling language in the classroom perpetuates ignorance and misconceptions in regards to the lived experience of people with disabilities.

Power Relations in the Classroom

As Marxists, feminists and anti-racist activists and scholars have claimed for decades, the world is viewed mostly from the perspective of the rulers, and language is created in their image as well. Therefore, we must not be surprised that the use of disabling language not only persists, but is neither contested nor acknowledged. Disabling language is language that accepts the assumption that disabilities *are* bad, unfortunate or denote lack/deficiency; that they *are* invisible and insignificant to society as a whole; and that disabilities belong to the Other and are distinct from what we would term as normal.

What this language hides is that there is a power struggle of definitions, that normalcy is culturally determined and ever-changing, and that there are more people who are defined as having disabilities than we acknowledge. The question that disability activists and scholars are asking is not who is disabled, but who gets to be defined as blind, mentally retarded or crippled and under what power relations? Using an oppressive abelist language to denote deficiency reproduces the same hierarchy and power relations in the classroom, and renders these phrases unproblematic.

Disability is not a metaphor. It is an identity.

Using disability as a metaphor to represent only negative aspects of a situation is problematic. It is made worse by the fact that blindness, deafness, paralysis, etc., are not floating signifiers, but have real referents behind them—people with disabilities. When using disabling language, we do not only de-value the lived experience of people with disabilities, but we also appropriate these lived experiences for our own use. This means that disabled people have been presented as socially flawed able-bodied people, not as people with our own identities. As responsible instructors, we must ask ourselves, when was the last time we discussed disability in our classrooms, not as metaphors, but as lived experiences?

The consequences of this exclusion are that most students know disability only metaphorically (unless they have disabilities themselves), and that we fail them as teachers by not providing descriptions of what disability actually means to the people who embody it. As critical teachers, we should counteract the use of disability as a metaphor in everyday language, in media and in literary representations. This pedagogical goal can be achieved by introducing more complex accounts of the disability experience through autobiographies, guest speakers or critical accounts by people with disabilities or by scholars of disability studies.

To make matters more complex, we must consider that some of our students might have disabilities themselves. These can be hidden and not visible. When we use disabling language, we alienate our students from our arguments and from feeling included in the classroom. As a wheelchair user, I find that when people use terms like "crippling" or "disabling" as rhetorical devices, I am distracted from the discussions. I cannot listen to arguments that make their point by using my identity as a rhetorical device. When a student tells me, "'I didn't know what do. I was paralyzed," I think to myself, "funny, I'm paralyzed, but I do know what to do." I stop listening to my student's complaint and feel offended by the conversation. When this happens, I feel "mugged by a metaphor" in the words of Wahneema Lubiano (1996).[1]

Talking About People with Disabilities Not as Metaphors

Disability is socially constructed and engulfs many labels under its umbrella. Although people with different impairments and disability labels are not similar in their thoughts, feelings or everyday lives, they are united under an oppressive label. The effects of being labeled as disabled have profound implications on disabled individuals in the areas of employment, education, built environment and product design, leisure activities, politics, family and sexual lives. "Disability," therefore, represents a complex system of social constraints imposed on people with impairments by a highly discriminatory society; to be disabled means being discriminated against. The problem is even more complex for disabled members of other marginalized locales such as the gay and lesbian communities, people of color and women.

How can we refer to disability as an identity and to the people who embody this identity and not be offensive? What follows is a list of terms currently in use by activists, academics and the media to refer to people with bodily or mental difference.

Disabled people

This is most commonly used in Great Britain. Traditionally, it was thought that innate medical conditions defined disability status and caused exclusion. As Laurence Clark and Stephen Marsh recall, "In the mid-seventies a new way of thinking about disability emerged from the disabled people's civil rights movement called the social model of disability. This stated that disabled people are those people with impairments who experience barriers within society. Therefore, the term 'disabled people' was redefined by the movement to mean "people with impairments who are disabled by socially constructed barriers" (2002, p. 2). "Disablement," therefore, refers to prejudice, stereotyping or "institutional discrimination" against disabled people.

People with disabilities

This is the most commonly used descriptor in the United States. It is used by disability rights activists and scholars. Like the term "disabled people," the phrase "people with disabilities" emerged from the disability movement in the United States where people-first phrasing was coined.

1. Lubiano is talking about the metaphor of multiculturalsm and the inequality produced by racial relations, and the way she experiences these effects on her indiviuality as a black woman. Although we do not share the same social location, I can empathize with her.

The tendency to place the noun "people" before "disability" is viewed positively because it emphasizes the fact that individuals with impairments are, first and foremost, people—something which historically has been denied.

deaf/Deaf

Most deaf people do not identify themselves as disabled, but consider deaf people a linguistic minority; they simply use sign instead of oral communications. Some Deaf people have also adopted a capital "D" in order to show their affiliation with Deaf culture and to politicize the word.

Handicapped or mentally handicapped

These terms alludes to a time when people with disabilities were viewed mostly as beggars who went "cap in hand" (Barnes, 1992). The use of "mentally handicapped," "feebleminded" or "retarded" has been replaced in the United States with the phrases "people with intellectual disabilities" or "people with developmental disabilities." These phrases are preferred terms by people who have been labeled in those ways, as well as by activists and scholars.

Challenged

Phrases based on "politically correct" language started to replace terms like "the handicapped" in the 1980s. Referring to impairment as "challenging" portrays them as obstacles to be overcome. However, these phrases ignore the disabling social barriers, placing the emphasis instead on impairments as the "challenging" factor (Clark & Marsh, 2002). In the US, this phrase is often used as a euphemism, such as the phrase 'vertically challenged' to refer to people who are short. The type of usage is generally considered patronizing. The phrase "physically challenged" also brings to mind the super-crip narrative of people with disabilities who climb mountains or are literary geniuses in spite of their "severe disabilities." Being physically challenged for able-bodied people and disabled people should be a matter of choice. We hope that *all* our students are intellectually challenged by the courses they take.

Special needs

"The phrase 'special needs' came about as an attempt to demedicalize the labeling of disabled children, changing it to what was hoped to be less negative labeling based on educational need" (Reiser & Mason, 1990, in Clark & Marsh, 2002, p. 12). "The 'needs' referred to here are typically determined by professional assessment, rather than by disabled people themselves" (Clark & Marsh, 2002, p. 12). Often these needs are commonplace: for example, disabled children "need" to receive a decent education, just like any other children. However, "the disabling culture transforms ordinary human needs into special needs and corrupts the identity of disabled children into special needs children" (Finklestein & Stuart, 1996).

Value-laden terms

"Emotive terms relating to disabled people, such as 'afflicted,' 'restricted,' 'stricken,' 'sufferer,' 'unfortunate' and 'victim,' tend to reflect a person's negative reaction's to a disabled person" (Clark & Marsh, 2002, p. 6). Describing a person as being "afflicted" by blindness or a "victim" of cerebral palsy takes away the agency from the individual and gives an active role to a constructed condition (Linton, 1998). Similarly, terms like "wheelchair bound" and "confined to a wheelchair" are value-laden and inaccurate, since wheelchairs are devices that empower rather than restrict the people who use them. Since paralysis or blindness do not have signifiers of their own, the augmentative devices attached to them (like canes or wheelchairs) carry the disabling stigma. In addition, many wheelchair users can walk short distances, and, therefore, are not "bound" to wheelchairs.

Conclusion

The language that we use in our classrooms has far-reaching implications on the education of students. Just as we would not tolerate sexist, misogynist or racist language, we must not tolerate disabling imagery and phrases. In particular, we should not contribute to reproducing it. Disability is not merely a metaphor or an analogy, but it is an identity for some of us as well as for some of our students. Disability is defined almost arbitrarily and the line between the disabled and the nondisabled is not a clear one. We must not assume disability, or the lack of it, by mere observation. Abelist language can be offensive and hurt some of our students while interfering with our original messages. We can either create barriers to communication or we can create classrooms in which we *all* feel equally challenged.

References

Barnes, C. (1992). *Disabling imagery and the media: An exploration of the principles for media representations of disabled people.* Derby: The British Council of Disabled People.

Clark, L. and Marsh, S. (2002); *Patriarchy in the UK: The language of disability.* Retrieved from the World Wide Web: http://www.leeds.ac.uk/disability-studies/archiveuk/titles.html

Finklestein, V. and Stuart, O. (1996). Developing new services. In Hales, G. (Ed.), *Beyond Disability: Towards an enabling society.* London: Sage Publications.

Linton, S. (1998). *Claiming Disability,* New York: New York University Press.

Lubiano, W. (1996). Like being mugged by a metaphor: Multiculturalism and state narratives. In Gordon and Newfield (Eds.), *Mapping Multiculturalism.* Minneapolis: University of Minnesota Press.

Reiser, R. (2001). Does language matter? *Disability Tribune,* October 2001.

Topical Articles: *A Connected Approach to the Teaching of Developmental Psychology*

Blythe McVicker Clinchy
Wellesley College

In this article, I describe ways in which a model of instruction called connected teaching can be applied to undergraduate courses in developmental psychology. The model contains features that women in interviews say they appreciated or wished had been present in their academic lives. The model emphasizes thinking over expertise; elicitation and exploration of students' narratives of personal experiences; respectful consideration of commonsense views of development derived from these experiences, especially among students whose backgrounds are poorly represented in the literature; and attention to the social context of the classroom, including facilitation of collaborative as well as adversarial forms of discourse. The overall goal is to convince students that they can actively construct, rather than just passively receive, knowledge about developmental psychology.

In *Women's Ways of Knowing* (Belenky, Clinchy, Goldberger, & Tarule, 1986), my co-authors and I proposed a model of instruction we call *connected teaching*, containing features that the women we interviewed had appreciated or wished had been present in their own college education. In this article, drawing on my experiences as a teacher in a small liberal arts college for women as well as on my research (Clinchy, 1987, 1989a, 1989b, 1990), I explore ways in which these features may be incorporated into the teaching of developmental psychology at the undergraduate level. Although my subjects and students have mainly been women, I suspect that men may benefit equally from connected teaching.

Sharing the Process

Most of the women we interviewed saw themselves as capable of taking in knowledge, but few saw themselves as capable of using their minds to create or construct knowledge. And they told stories of experiences in school that had served to convince them of their disabilities, not to enhance their thinking abilities.

Listening to these stories, I realized that I, as a teacher, was part of the problem. Like many of the teachers they described, I tended in my classroom to emphasize what Baron (1991) called knowledge over thinking. In lectures, I presented myself more as an expert than a thinker and, as Baron pointed out, "in many ways, experts appear to be the opposite of good thinkers. Because they *know* the answer to most questions, they do not have to think very often, compared to novices" (p. 177).

At most colleges and universities there are pressures on teachers and students to demonstrate and defend their knowledge rather than to exhibit their thinking. The Student Evaluation Questionnaires used at my college ask students to rate the degree to which the teacher appears to be "in com-

Reprinted from *Teaching of Psychology* (1995), Taylor and Francis Group

mand" of the subject matter. In turn, we ask the students to demonstrate in their written work that they too are in command of the material—not that they are puzzled, confused, or challenged by it, but that they have mastered it. Under such circumstances, teachers and students learn to conceal, rather than reveal, evidence of the puzzlement, confusion, ignorance, and uncertainty that usually accompany genuine thinking.

Yet, in interviews, students say that the teachers they appreciate most are not those who appear most knowledgeable but those who seem to be actively wrestling with the material. My own graduate school mentor, Jerome Bruner, was certainly capable of dazzling exhibitions of mastery, but it was not these performances that sealed my commitment to developmental psychology. Rather, it was occasions like the one on which, poring over the results of an experiment on infant perception, he smote his brow and exclaimed, "I can't stand how much I can't understand these results!" Both points made in that sentence were important to me: There was something this great man could not understand, and he could not stand not understanding it. This sort of statement offered promise of a relation to the material that was warmer and more intimate than a relation of control or command and infinitely more desirable. It looked like fun.

Real Questions

In trying as a teacher to behave less as a knower and more as a thinker and to encourage my students to do the same, I am bringing into the classroom more of myself as a researcher. I talk less and listen more than I used to. I try to design situations that will entice students to "show" me their thinking. For instance, I ask them the sorts of real questions I ask my interviewees. I ask them to tell me what they think. This may sound easy, but neither I nor the students find it easy, at least at first. Last semester, we were talking about Shirley Brice Heath's research showing the mismatch between the school culture and the home culture of Appalachian children. Heath noted that in the home community adults ask children questions to which they wish to know the answers; they count on the children to supply information about goings-on in the community. But school teachers do not ask children real questions. Teachers ask questions to which they already know the answers—ones such as "What color is that?" "What is 2 + 2?" The purpose of these questions is to see whether children know the answers that teachers already know. The Appalachian children have trouble adapting to that kind of question.

My students, contrarily, agreed that after more than 12 years of schooling they can handle these "teacher-type" questions with ease, but they have trouble adapting to real questions. They can answer a question such as "What is the concept of the permanent object?" When I go on to ask, "Do you think it's an important concept?" they treat it as a teacher-type question. They know the right answer is "yes" because important people like Piaget studied it, the topic occupies a half page of their 700-page textbook, and I gave them a handout on it. These are good objective measures of the importance of a topic (and the likelihood that it will appear on the exam). Students find it hard to believe that I really want to know whether they consider the concept important. In *Women's Ways of Knowing* (Belenky et al., 1986), we quote a woman who told us in tones of awe about a teacher—the only such teacher she could recall—who "was intensely, genuinely interested in everybody's feelings about things. She asked a question and wanted to know what your response was" (p. 225).

In my role as a teacher of developmental psychology, I am repeatedly struck by the degree to which I forget what I know as a developmental psychologist. Given my theoretical orientation, a son of Brunerized proto-post-Piagetian constructivist cognitive–developmentalism, I know that my student's minds do not come to me as blank slates or formless blobs of clay (however, sometimes I wish that they did), but I tend to forget it.

Students beginning the course in developmental psychology know or think they know quite a bit about human development. For the past five semesters, I have distributed a survey at the start of the course. Results of the survey show, for example, that between 98% and 100% of the students know or believe that events in the first 2 years of life have irreversible effects on development. Such beliefs are often implicit and usually unexamined; the survey is one strategy I use to try to make them explicit and open to examination.

I try to explore the basis for the students' beliefs. I ask, "Why?" "Why do you think that events in the first 2 years of life have irreversible effects on development?" Again, the students cannot "hear" the question as a real question. I want to enter the student's frame, to elicit the story of how she came to hold this belief, what experiences, in or out of school, led to it. But she hears the question as a challenge to the validity of her position and as a demand for rational justification, not as a quest for understanding.

This being so, I find it necessary to distinguish explicitly between occasions when we are in something akin to Bruner's (1985, p. 97) "paradigmatic mode," in which we do adopt a critical, even adversarial stance and make judgments of validity, and occasions when we are in the "narrative mode" (Bruner, 1985, p. 97) and are merely trying to understand. If we are in the narrative mode, I may assign a 10-min in-class "freeware" (Belanoff, Elbow, & Fontaine, 1991), an ungraded, uncensored, introspective, free-form account of the experiential basis for their beliefs about the effects of early events.

On other occasions, I take a more adversarial approach. Last year, I tried to disabuse my students of their views about early experience by presenting evidence for the psychological resilience of children. We discussed research by Rutter (1985), Werner and Smith (1992), and others, including dramatic case studies of hugely successful people raised under appalling circumstances. We talked about temperamental and environmental protective factors and how environmental interventions can undo negative effects. At the end of the semester, I distributed the survey again; between 98% and 100% of the students agreed that experience in the first 2 years of life had irreversible effects on behavior at a later age.

Other teachers in other fields reported similar findings. Driver and Easley (1978), for example, found that this sort of adversarial strategy did not produce a change in high school science students' thinking and "at times produced only confusion" (p. 78). According to Driver and Easley, "where an alternate theory was presented either by the teacher or by other pupils, which better accounted for the data it was not necessarily understood, but was accepted and learned at a verbal level" (pp. 78–79).

Writing about secondary science education, Hills (1989) argued that the students' theories may be inadequate from the standpoint of science but may be quite adequate in the commonsense realm of everyday life. If we treat these commonsense notions as "a naive or degenerate version of scientific theory" and offer scientific evidence to refute them, we are committing "the fallacy of the common ground" (Hills, 1989, p. 378). According to the philosopher–educator David Hawkins (1983), "teachers, in their own differently ordered minds, can often convict [students] of error, when in fact, the [students'] statements are right answers to questions different from those the teachers thought they had asked" (p. 74).

I believe that if I were to ask a question on the final exam concerning the effects of early experience, most students would answer correctly, citing Rutter (1985) and Werner and Smith (1992) among others. They would treat the exam question as a teacher-type question, whereas they treat the survey question as a real question—one that asks for their commonsense, nonacademic ungraded everyday opinions. Although I have forgotten the exact occasion, I recall Carol Gilligan quoting one of the women she interviewed as asking, "Do you want to know what I think? Or what I *really* think?" In their exams, students tell me what they think; in the anonymous and ungraded survey, they tell me what they really think.

In interviews, undergraduate women repeatedly tell us that, although they adopt for the duration of the course the truths that are foisted upon them, they discard them as soon as the grades are in, leaving their own prior convictions undisturbed. This seems to be true even of apparently abstract impersonal ideas. For instance, a first-year student reported that in her math course she was "having a hard time coming to grips with what these people think *infinity* is." She said,

> For the duration of the course, I'll go along with *their* right answer, and when it's over I'll go back to my idea of what infinity is, which I've done in every math course I've ever taken that has even involved anything that has to do with infinity, because I just can't picture it their way, and my way is right for me, but it's obviously not right for other people. You know, maybe some day I'll see the light, and their right will be right for me, but for now I have my own particular right, and I'll just stick to it.

If this is true of a concept as remote as infinity, surely it must also be true of presumably more hot-blooded convictions like "the best way to raise children is in a nuclear family with one consistent father and one consistent mother" (76% of the surveyed students agreed), or "no matter what changes occur in our society, women, on the whole, will remain more suited than men to the role of primary caretaker" (66% agreed).

At the end of this course, as at the beginning, approximately 95% of the students assert that common sense is a better guide to childrearing than is scientific knowledge, indicating that once the final exam is over, the scientific knowledge students have learned "at a verbal level" may be deleted from memory, whereas their commonsense views live on.

This being so, it seems to me critical that we elicit and explore these commonsense views, rather than ignore them or drive them underground. As Hills (1989) suggested, we teachers should view our students' notions not as wrong answers to our questions but as useful answers to other questions asked in other circumstances. We can try to distinguish between the different questions, and we can ask what purpose the students' commonsense concepts might serve in their daily lives. In Elbow's (1973) terms, we can play the Believing Game: We can look for what is right about the students' notions.

Narratives of Personal Experience

In order to do so, we will have to make room in the classroom for narratives of personal experience, because the students' naive conceptions about human development come from firsthand experience, not from textbooks. Although most of the women we have interviewed express considerable faith in this sort of knowledge, we in the academy tend to look down on it. We teach students either to keep quiet about personal experience or to preface their remarks with a modest disclaimer, "It's only my personal experience," "This is just my experience," or "I know it's just anecdotal evidence. . . ." (We professors often indulge in anecdote, of course, but we claim this is merely a device to liven up the lecture.) Students learn that narratives are not real evidence and that one's personal experience is limited and biased.

In the developmental psychology course, I have taught these lessons many times. For instance, a student interrupts my carefully crafted lecture on gender differences to say that the research results I am reporting are not at all true of her. "I'm much more competitive than my brother," she says, "and he's much more empathic than I am." I explain that this one case does not disconfirm the general finding, that of course there are many exceptions, but on the average . . . I drone on and on. My intention was to help this student see beyond the horizon of her personal experience, persuade her to think in general rather than specific terms, and think about data that had been collected using scientific procedures. This is the lesson I was trying to teach. But what lesson did she learn? Did she learn that her experiential knowledge was of limited value, or did she learn that it was of no value at all? Did she feel enlightened or alienated by my sermon?

When we (Belenky et al., 1986) asked women to tell us about good teachers they had known, they often described what we came to call *midwife teachers,* teachers who assumed that the student had something of value in her mind and took the time to draw it out and help her to reflect on it and carry it further. Had I practiced midwifery in this case, I would not have told the student that her experiences were beside the point; I might have asked her to think, talk, or even write about events that could have led to the differences between herself and her brother. And instead of telling her what was wrong with her position, I might have considered what was right about it. We might have used this occasion to discuss how the methods of our discipline lead to exaggeration of differences, including gender differences (e.g., Fine & Gordon. 1989; Riger, 1992), and we might look at different ways of representing gender comparisons—in terms of degree of overlap, for instance, as well us mean differences. We might talk about exploring exceptions to predicted results as a strategy for generating good questions for further research.

I might tell the students that the discovery that one's own experience is at odds with accepted developmental theory can occur, usually belatedly, even to teachers of developmental psychology, especially if they happen to be parents. One afternoon, as I was preaching to the students the Piagetian gospel concerning the concrete nature of the preoperational mind, an image floated into my mind from the morning I had just spent with my 4-year-old son and his 4-year-old friend. For nearly 1 hr, despite their presumably limited attention spans and incapacity for abstraction, the two had sat beneath a maple tree, with no props at all, discussing the question of what lay beyond the universe. A colleague remembers a similar occasion. While lecturing about toddlers' perceptual egocentrism, a phenomenon she had never doubted, she recalled her 18-month-old daughter at the breakfast table that morning carefully turning her open book around to enable her mother to see the picture.

Each student's perspective is biased by the limits of her experience, but psychology's sampling of persons and circumstances has hardly been unbiased, and one set of biases may serve as a corrective to the other. An African-American student taught me, before Baumrind (1972) did, that parental practices defined as *authoritarian* may have a different meaning and different consequences in African-American families than in White families. People who had little to do with designing the discipline of developmental psychology—for example, African Americans, Mexican Americans, Native Americans, and mothers without PhDs—often find that the data of their firsthand experience are at odds with the literature.

Last semester a Mexican-American student told me she felt excluded from the developmental psychology course because we paid so little attention to research by and about children of Color. Although I tried to appear tolerant and even receptive, I felt hurt, angry, and defensive. Driving home that night, I said to my dog, who was seated beside me and is always a good listener, "There just isn't much good research by and about children of Color, and much of what there is focuses on developmental deficits, and I just do not have time to look up all that stuff." The dog agreed, but, by the next day, I did not. I saw that the student was right and that I need not go searching out material to present from the podium. In the class were students of Korean, Mexican, Japanese, Indian, Pakistani, Portuguese, and African-American parentage. All could speak from positions of authority on their own experience to compensate for some of the omissions in the literature. And so we set up a multicultural panel in which, using Baumrind's (1971) model as a starting point, students described and analyzed their own parents' childrearing practices in terms of responsiveness and demandingness and speculated on the effects of these practices on their own competence. They also questioned the appropriateness of the definitions embedded in the model. For instance, how is *social competence* manifested in Mexican-American culture, and is *social assertiveness* one of its components? This panel presentation, I believe, did more than any lecture could do to extend the students' notions about childrearing beyond the bounds of their own individual experience while affirming that their own personal knowledge can be of value not only to themselves but to their classmates.

It may even be of value to the field of psychology. Students bring to our classrooms knowledge that has not merely been omitted but excluded from the disciplines (Minnich, 1990, p. 32), which Foucault (1980, p. 81) called "subjugated" knowledge, "the perspectives of those sufficiently low on the hierarchy that their interpretations do not reflect the predominant modes of thought" (Riger, 1992, p. 734). For instance, most of my students (women) have been engaged since childhood in the naturalistic study of the social world (Brown & Gilligan, 1992; Thorne & Luria, 1986); but, as Fine and Gordon (1989) pointed out, traditional experimental methods of studying personal relationships ignore the sort of knowledge they have accumulated.

> Removed from social relationships, interaction in the lab is typically limited to a "subject" and a white (often male) experimenter. There may be some strangers present, who are euphemistically called group members. Defining features of this context include a lack of trust, longevity, and connection. . . . The ostensible sterility and neutrality of the lab mean . . . that the social relationships and contexts in which women weave their lives are excluded as if irrelevant. (pp. 154–155)

The Social Context of the Classroom

Our classrooms, like our laboratories, are inhabited largely by strangers. Through written work and conferences, I get to know a little about each of my students, but the students rarely get to know each other. I believe that this lack of trust, longevity, and connection contributes to the purported passivity of female students. A first-year undergraduate complained that the peer-editing group in her writing course was not working: "We just talk about commas and junk like that." In contrast, she said,

> I had a peer editing group in high school, and it was terrific. But we all knew each other inside out, so you knew what each person was trying to do in her writing and you knew what kinds of criticisms helped her and what kind hurt her feelings. You can't really help if you don't know people. (Belenky et al., 1986, p. 222)

Most of the women I have encountered in teaching and in research are wary of argument. They do seem to prefer "thinking with" to "thinking against" others, and they do seem more skilled at collaborative than combative discussion (Mansfield & Clinchy, 1992). They cherish memories of "connected classes" (Belenky et al., 1986) in which each person served as midwife to each other person's thoughts, drawing out each other's ideas, entering into and elaborating on them, and building together a conception none of them could have constructed alone. I have to fight a tendency to think that the only good classes are those in which people argue with each other and that people are really thinking only when they are thinking against each other, even though I have learned through the practice of collaborative research that "thinking with" is really thinking.

I believe, too, that women find it easier to articulate and develop their ideas through argument in a context of trust, longevity, and connection, when they know and are known by their classmates and have less reason to fear hurting them or being hurt by them. In the absence of trust, my students tend to avoid initiating conflict and to forestall it whenever it threatens to emerge. Disagreements are politely tolerated but rarely explored. An Hispanic student once commented in the developmental psychology class that she found the children at our laboratory nursery school, where the students do internships and observations, rude, citing the example of a boy saying to his teacher, "It makes me angry when you touch me"—something no child from her culture would be allowed to say. A White student responded by saying, at least as the Hispanic student recalls, that we believe that, if children can verbalize their anger, they will not need to express it in physical aggression. The Hispanic student nodded, and we moved on to another topic. The subtext of this multicultural moment utterly escaped me until a few days later when the Hispanic student revealed, in conference, that she thought the White student was implying that Hispanics, being repressed, are prone to violence. I suspect that if the Hispanic student had known the White student better, she may have felt safe enough and may have cared enough to pursue the point in class.

In the developmental psychology course, I try in various ways to promote conversations among students and between students and the course material—to weave something like the nexus of I, Thou, and It that Hawkins (1967) described in his essay on children's education. Students keep journals in which they enter observations and reflections on current and past experiences relevant to the subject matter of the course. With the students' permission and with their names deleted if desired, I excerpt and distribute passages from the journals, and students sometimes write new journal entries reflecting on and responding to passages from other students' journals. Students also share their ideas and experiences by interviewing each other or discussing issues in small groups. For example, representatives of the 66% who believe that "no matter what changes occur in our society, women, on the whole, will remain more suited than men to the role of primary caretaker" are invited to join with representatives of the 34% who disagree to construct a position paper on the issue. Participants in these groups are provided with explicit instructions, and they practice careful listening and careful criticism (*careful* meaning concerned and interested as well as thorough and painstaking).

I have no special investment in the particular pedagogical techniques mentioned in this article, but I do believe passionately in the goal that they are designed to achieve. I am still haunted by a comment made by an undergraduate I interviewed several years ago. She said, "Science is not a creation of the human mind." (Scientists, in her view, merely gathered up facts strewn about the universe.) I will sleep well if I can be sure that students will emerge from my course convinced that developmental psychology is a creation of the human mind, rather than a gift of the gods, and that they, using their own good minds, can contribute to its continual construction and reconstruction.

References

Baron, J. (1991). *Beliefs about thinking.* In J. F. Voss, D. N. Perkins, & J. W. Segal (Eds.), *Informal reasoning and education* (pp. 169–186). Hillsdale, NJ: Lawrence Erlbaum Associates, Inc.

Baumrind, D. (1971). Current patterns of parental authority. *Developmental Psychology Monographs, 4,* 1–103.

Baumrind, D. (1972). An exploratory study of socialization effects on black children: Some black-white comparisons. *Child Development, 43,* 261–267.

Belanoff, P., Elbow, P., & Fontaine, C. I. (Eds.). (1991). *Nothing begins with N: New investigations of freewriting.* Carbondale: Southern Illinois University Press.

Belenky, M. F., Clinchy, B. M., Goldberger, N. R., & Tarule, J. M. (1986). *Women's ways of knowing.* New York: Basic Books.

Brown, L., & Gilligan, C. (1992). *Meeting at the crossroads: Women's psychology and girls' development.* Cambridge, MA: Harvard University Press.

Burner, J. S. (1985). Narrative and paradigmatic modes of thought. In E. Eisner (Ed.), *Learning and teaching the ways of knowing* (pp. 97–115). Chicago: University of Chicago Press.

Clinchy, B. M. (1987). Silencing women students. In L. D. Edmundson, J. P. Saunders, & E. S. Silber (Eds.), *Women's voices* (pp. 18–44). Littleton, MA: Copley.

Clinchy, B. M. (1989a). The development of thoughtfulness in college women: Integrating reason and care. *American Behavioral Scientist, 32,* 647–657.

Clinchy, B. M. (1989b). On critical thinking and connected knowing. *Liberal Education, 75*(5), 14–19.

Clinchy, B. M. (1990). Issues of gender in teaching and learning. *Journal on Excellence in College Teaching, 1,* 52–67.

Driver, R., & Easley, J. (1978). Pupils and paradigms: A review of the literature related to concept development in adolescent science students. *Studies in Science Education, 6,* 61–84.

Elbow, P. (1973). *Writing without teachers.* London: Oxford University Press.

Fine, M., & Gordon, S. M. (1989). Feminist transformations of/despite psychology. In M. Crawford & M. Gentry (Eds.), *Gender and thought* (pp. 146–174). New York: Springer-Verlag.

Foucault, M. (1980). *A history of sexuality: Vol. 1. An information.* New York: Random House.

Hawkins, D. (1967). *I, thou, it* (Reprint of a paper presented at the Primary Teachers' Residential Course, Loughborough, Leicestershire). Cambridge, MA: Elementary Science Study, Educational Services, Inc.

Hawkins, D. (1981). Nature closely observed. *Daedalus, 112,* 65–89.

Hills, G. L. C. (1989). Students' "untutored" beliefs about natural phenomena: Primitive science or common sense? *Science Education, 73,* 155–186.

Mansfield, A., & Clinchy, B. M. (1992, May). *The influence of different kinds of relationships on the development and expression of "separate" and "connected" knowing in undergraduate women.* Paper presented at the 22nd Annual Symposium of the Jean Piaget Society, Montreal, Québec.

Minnich, E. K. (1990). *Transforming knowledge.* Philadelphia: Temple University Press.

Riger, S. (1992). Epistemological debates, feminist voices: Science, social values, and the study of women. *American Psychologist, 47,* 710–740.

Rutter, M. (1985). Resilience in the face of adversity: Protective factors and resistance to psychiatric disorder. *British Journal of Psychiatry, 147,* 598–611.

Thorne, B., & Luria, Z. (1986). Sexuality and gender in children's daily worlds. *Social Problems, 33,* 176–190.

Werner, E. E., & Smith, R. S. (1992). *Overcoming the odds: High risk children from birth in adulthood.* Ithaca, NY: Cornell University Press.

Notes

1. An earlier version of this article was presented at the Biennial Meeting of the Society for Research in Child Development, March 1993, New Orleans, LA.
2. Requests for reprints should be sent to Blythe McVicker Clinchy, Department of Psychology, Wellesley College, Wellesley, MA 02181.

CHAPTER 26

STUDENT MOTIVATION

Motivating Students to Learn

M. D. Svinicki

Great teachers are often said to be those who can motivate their students to do their best work. Certainly that's what the students think, because when I ask groups of students to talk about their best teachers, motivation is almost always the number one quality listed. I find this a bit mystifying because I've certainly seen a lot of highly motivated students who didn't seem to learn very much, and I've been able to learn in the absence of any apparent motivation. Perhaps motivation is half the battle; if you've got that, learning at least becomes less onerous. But what is it about motivation that influences learning?

There is much of speculation in the literature about what motivation does for learning. Here are some of the ideas that have been offered:

1. Motivation directs the learners' attention to the task at hand and makes them less distractible. We know from the cognitive model that attention to the key variables is the first step to learning, so anything that focuses learner attention is bound to help learning.
2. Maybe motivation changes what learners pay attention to. As in item 1, attention is the focus here, but rather than dealing with the vigilance aspect of attention, here motivation influences what the learners focus on rather than that they simply pay more attention in general.
3. Motivation helps the learners persist when they encounter obstacles. This particular set of qualities is often referred to in the literature as volition rather than motivation, but they go together. Volition keeps the behavior going after motivation has gotten it started (Corno, 2000). Learning cannot occur unless learners are willing to engage the task.
4. Motivation in the form of goals may serve as benchmarks that the learners can use to monitor their own learning and recognize when they're making progress and when they've finished a task. So motivation may support the kind of metacognition controlling learning that was discussed in Chapter 5.

These different interpretations of what motivation is and does can help us think about what we do to support or frustrate those effects.

Alternative Theories of Motivation

There is no grand unifying theory of motivation in the psychological literature. Instead, bits and pieces of a theory have accumulated over the years. The recent ascendance of cognitive theory in the learning realm is being accompanied by a similar focus on thinking in the motivational realm.

Early Theories

Early theories of motivation depicted it as an inner force driving external behavior. Motivation was increased when some type of imbalance or deficit in needs was felt by the learners. Subsequent

Reprinted from *Learning and Motivation in the Post-secondary Classroom* (2004), by permission of John Wiley & Sons, Inc.

behaviors were then directed at rebalancing the system without much conscious action on the part of the learners. One early theory of motivation known as drive theory asserted that organisms were motivated to maintain a physiological balance. So for example, if something in their bodies was out of whack, such as a lack of water or food, the organisms would direct their behavior toward actions that would correct the imbalance. Initially, the deficits were focused on physical needs, but eventually the scope was expanded to include psychological needs, such as needs for approval, achievement, and affiliation. There was even a theory that held that humans had a need to keep their thinking and behavior in balance. When the two were at odds with one another, the condition was called "cognitive dissonance," and the behavior of the individual experiencing it was directed toward realigning thoughts and behaviors. Although the original theory is no longer around, the cognitive dissonance concept is a useful one and has remained in the repertoire of most psychologists and educators.

Behaviorally Based Theories

Most of us are more familiar with what passes for motivation in behavior theories. A strict behaviorist would not acknowledge the existence of motivation because the very idea implies some sort of cognitive planning or interpretation. Motivation comes before behavior. But a behaviorist would say that what influences behavior is what comes after it, not before it. A behaviorist would say that reinforcement and punishment cause behavior. We motivate an individual by reinforcing or punishing the target behaviors.

This strategy certainly is found in education at all levels. We praise students for their efforts, reward them with points and grades, scholarships and honors, and punish them with bad grades or points taken off when they don't learn fast enough or thoroughly enough. It would be foolish to think that these policies and practices would or should ever be abandoned, but things are never as simple and straightforward as these strategies would imply. What reinforces or punishes one student is not always reinforcing or punishing to another. We will continue to use these strategies because they work, but we will use them more effectively if we understand why they work or don't work and when, which brings us to cognitive theory.

Cognitive Theory

The advent of cognitive theory in the last part of the twentieth century spilled over into motivation theory. Psychologists began to shift the focus away from internal, pre-existing, semi-autonomous drives and needs, and started talking about motivation being a function of how learners interpret a situation. This was an important shift in focus because it placed motivation into the minds and hands of the learners. It was the learners' interpretation of a situation that determined whether they would be motivated by it. As an example, think about two children who receive new computers at Christmas. One of the children is happy with the gift. The other looks glum and depressed. What happened? It's the same computer; shouldn't the effects be the same? The difference here is in the perception of the computer by the child. The first child thinks of the computer as something to be used for fun, to play games, and surf the Internet. For the other child, the computer represents another tool for doing more schoolwork, thus not nearly as exciting. The perceptions of the two children make the computer a success or a failure at motivation. Paradoxically, this cognitive interpretation of motivation may make it seem like influencing motivation is beyond the reach of the instructor; it's the learner's interpretation that affects motivation. In a way that's true, but if we have a useful model about what influences learner perception, we also may be able to see how the environment influences those perceptions. In a sense, the source of motivation resides in both the learner and the environment; each influences the other. This is the basis of social cognitive theory, the latest and probably most complete theory about the sources and effects of motivation.

An Amalgamated Theory

For our purposes as instructors, the models of motivation that focus on learner perceptions are more interesting and more likely to suggest ways for us to intervene to enhance learner motivation than the old deficit models. To make your life a little easier, I have assembled into one diagram all the motivational theories currently being researched, based loosely on the model of motivation that I think is most useful (see Figure 26.1). The various components of this amalgamated model can suggest factors for instructors to consider in designing instructional methods to motivate students. The amalgamated model is based on three of the most prominent theories about motivation in use today. The first is the expectancy value model as refined by Wigfield and Eccles (2000), the second is Bandura's (1997) social cognitive model, and the third is the goal orientation model (Dweck & Leggett, 1988). A lot of the other models of motivation can be woven into this one amalgamated model.

As shown in the figure, the best way to think about motivation is to think about it as aiming at a specific goal, because much recent work approaches motivation through this avenue (Wentzel, 2000). The strength of the motivation is then a function of the type of goal selected, the value of the goal being pursued in relationship to other goals, and the learners' beliefs in their own ability to achieve the goal. These three aspects work together in a compounding fashion to create the motivational effectiveness and direction of a given goal.

To put that in everyday language, let's say that I am being asked to chair a departmental committee on academic integrity. How motivated would I be to accept this assignment? The theory says that part of the strength of my motivation would come from my orientation toward this goal. Am I thinking that this is a good way to develop myself and to make some change in the department? Or am I concerned about how competent I will appear to my colleagues and others in influential positions? Then I will factor in my perceptions of the value of chairing this committee. Is it something that I'm interested in? Will it be sufficiently challenging to be interesting? Or will it be too challenging and frustrating? Is it something that is needed by the department? Will the people on the committee be fun to work with? Will this add to my own value in the department, thus making tenure more secure? How much control will I have over the committee and its findings? Will my colleagues thank me for doing this and breathe a sigh of relief that the assignment wasn't given to them, or will they resent not being chosen? How would this goal compare with other goals I'm currently working on, either professional, personal or social? These are the kinds of questions that would assess the value of chairing this committee. Obviously the answers will influence my motivation.

But there is another set of considerations: How likely is it that I will be able to succeed with this committee? Are the people on the committee dedicated workers who will contribute to the task? Do I have enough time in my already crowded schedule to give it the attention it needs? If the committee issues recommendations, will they be accepted by the chair or the dean? And will they have any real impact on the students? No matter how valuable the committee's work might be, if there's no chance of getting it done or of it having any effect, I am less likely to be willing to spend my time on it. If I think that it is a good area to explore and that I can do it successfully such that the college benefits, my motivation to be the chair is increased.

Motivation involves a constant balancing of these two factors of value and expectations for success. Both must be present for motivation to occur, but their relative contributions will vary from situation to situation. Students perform this same balancing act as they approach the task of studying. They weigh the value of coming to class with estimates of whether they'll learn anything once they get there. They are constantly evaluating their chances for an A and making studying choices accordingly. Is there anything we as instructors can do to influence those choices? I believe so and now turn the discussion to each of the components of the amalgamated model shown in Figure 26.1 and how we as instructors might use this model to think of interventions to keep student motivation high.

The Value of the Goal

Let's begin on the side of value. We obviously think our course is the most valuable one that any student is taking, but we may have to convince the students. There are many factors that influence how valuable a course is perceived to be by the students.

Figure 26.1
An Amalgamated Model of Motivation

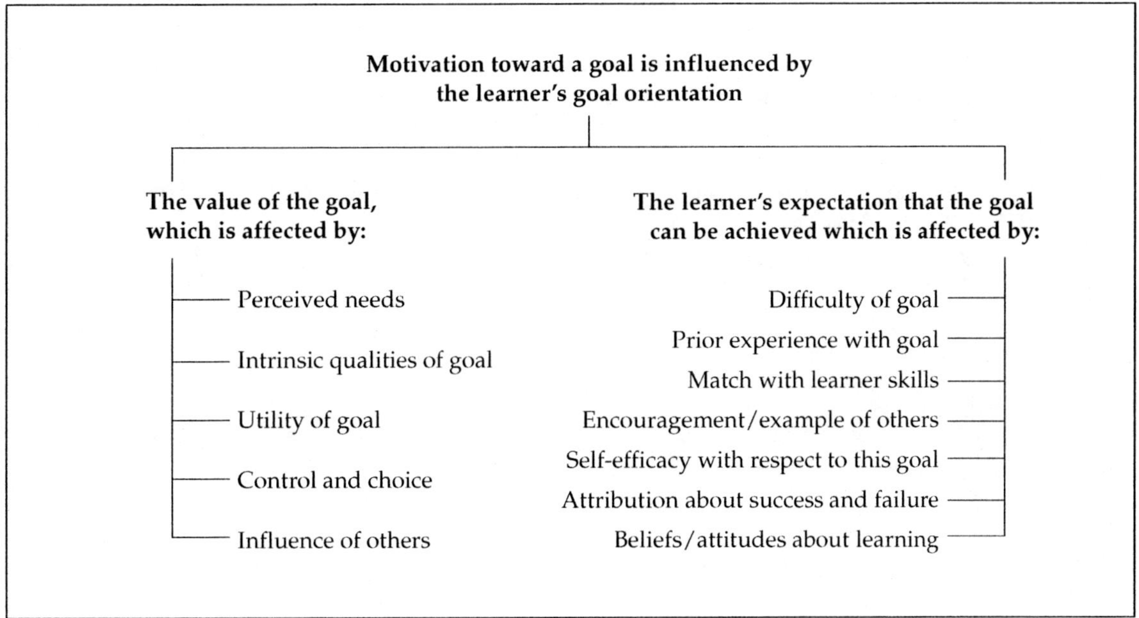

Value from expected outcome

The most obvious value of a goal comes from the outcomes of achieving it. What does the learner get if he or she is successful? The outcome might be a good grade, a higher salary, tenure, the satisfaction of a job well done. Actually this is what most people think of when we talk about motivation: the reward at the end of the line. Certainly this was how behaviorists interpreted motivation; it was the manipulation of rewards and punishments. And these are the easiest things for teachers to control. We give grades, we give praise, we give privileges, or we take them away. Most of the things that we can control, however, fall under the category of extrinsic motivators, things that exist outside the learner and the task. Extrinsic motivators are pretty good at getting a behavior going and keeping it going as long as they are in effect, but over the long haul, some intrinsic motivators are needed to keep learning strong and fresh. Intrinsic motivation also frees the instructor from having to constantly supervise and reinforce the learners. Students eventually need to be on their own.

There is an argument in the literature about the detrimental effects of extrinsic motivators on intrinsically motivated behavior (Pintrich & Schunk, 1996). The argument asserts that if you provide extrinsic motivation for a behavior that was initially already intrinsically motivating, you kill the intrinsic motivation and leave the learner dependent on the extrinsic motivator. Let me give an example. Let's imagine that you have a student who loves to study and enjoys working in the lab. Since his enthusiasm is so obvious, he would make a perfect lab assistant. So you hire him to work in the lab and help everyone else with their problems. Initially, this is a good thing for him, and he enjoys coming to work and helping others. Over time, however, the lab becomes a job rather than the fun activity that it used to be. He has to be there at specific times and he has to accomplish specific tasks whether he wants to or not. His enjoyment turns to annoyance and resentment. Theory says that what is happening has to do with perceptions of control. Once an extrinsic motivator (pay for the job) is in place, control over the behavior shifts from the learner to the person who is providing the extrinsic motivator, and that is a bad thing for motivation.

Extrinsic motivation has long been the staple of education, even though we say we want students to learn for the love of learning. Some students do love to learn; we professors were probably like that at least for courses in our majors. It's hard for us, then, when students aren't as fascinated by our subject as we are. However, reverting too strongly to a dependence on points, extra credit, or threats only compounds the problem. Those (minus the threats, please) can form a foundation of motivation to get learning started, but it is the intrinsic motivators that will keep it going over the long haul.

As instructors, we should find ways to enhance students' intrinsic motivation for the course by showing them the connection between the course and their own interests. Bringing things from their outside life into the course has many uses, only one of which is building on the intrinsic motivation of the students. Of course, we have to give grades, but the best way to lessen the influence of grades per se on student behavior is to have such clear expectations for grading that control over the grade is essentially in the hands of each individual student. They know what they have to do and if they do it, they get the grade. In the meantime, you make the rest of the course as intrinsically motivating as possible in hopes of successfully competing with their concerns about a grade.

Value from satisfying a need

Harkening back to the discussion of early models of motivation, we can glean from them some useful thoughts along these lines. Although it is unlikely that student physical needs (like food, water, and shelter) are being met by our courses, there is an association between a college degree and the eventual ability of students to purchase these necessities. Helping students understand how your course will give them an edge in the world of work increases the value of the course content in their eyes.

In terms of affiliative needs (the need to be accepted by a group), one thing that can influence motivation in a course is the degree to which the class becomes a community of learners. When students feel they are part of the social group of the class and are working with others in the class to achieve similar ends, their motivation to participate is enhanced. There is a lot of social psychological literature about the importance of others in shaping our behavior both on a daily basis and over time. Establishing rapport with the students and using that rapport to make them feel part of a bigger community can increase their willingness to come to class and participate in learning.

A related need that we might consider is the impact of approval (or lack of it) on behavior. Early theorists asserted that people had an inborn need for approval and would work to get it. I can give you a lot of other, simpler possible explanations for this phenomenon, but it can be useful to remember that approval is a powerful incentive. Extrinsic approval, such as praise from the instructor or other students, is something we can easily interject into our teaching. There is also a sense of something like internalized approval that most adults have developed. We have internalised the values of our social group, and we can assess our behavior in light of those values, even if no one else is around. This kind of self-approval based on internalized values is a powerful tool. To an instructor, it suggests that we should be overt in modeling and communicating the values of our classroom to the students: appropriate behavior, attitudes and behaviors we value in students or in thinking adults in general. Students who then adopt those values can provide self-reinforcement beyond the classroom.

Also dominant in the literature both in early theory and more recent cognitive theory is the need for achievement. Being successful at a task or in general appears to be something that motivates us. Actually, the basic value of need for achievement has been modified to say that, for some individuals, this is manifested as the need to succeed, while for others it is the need to avoid failing (Atkinson & Raynor, 1978). These two goals result in very different behaviors. I'll discuss this very interesting area later in the chapter when we talk about learning versus performance goals. As teachers, we can influence the possibilities for success by the way we set up and respond to the assignments we give students. Students will factor in our influence with that from other sources—their peers, their parents, and society—in determining what achievement means to them.

A broader need to feel competent or to have high self-worth can also influence motivation. We need to believe that what we do is valued by others and that our success at it reflects well on all aspects of our self, not just this particular instance. In this area, we are not simply trying to maintain an image of self-worth; we are also driven to enhance that self-image whenever possible. Instructors who help students see their strengths and how those fit into the larger picture of learning are making it easier for students to build a sense of self-worth based on important characteristics rather than shallow, immediately obvious qualities. For example, some students may be seduced by the idea that being able to do things quickly is the mark of worth in a field. While this might work for some situations (like game shows), in many cases a more valuable quality is an ability to do things accurately on the first try (like brain surgery). Instructors can help students focus on qualities that are valued in a particular setting or show how those qualities that a student already has have a place in the field. The most obvious instance of this misplaced source for self-worth in our society is appearance. Especially with girls and women, the equating of worth with standards of beauty does great harm. Turning their attention to other qualities as a source of worth is a wonderful way to counteract society's messages.

An interesting corollary to the work on students' need to protect or enhance their image of self-worth is research done on maladaptive strategies that some students use. Remember that the goal is to be considered competent. One inappropriate way that a lot of students do this is "self-handicapping" (Covington, 1992), in which learners sabotage their own chances for success by engaging in counterproductive behavior. For example, students who stay out all night before a big test can laugh off their poor showing as a result of their being such "party animals." If under these conditions they fail the test, they can protect their image by attributing that failure to their lack of preparation rather than their ability or understanding. And in the unlikely event that they do the same thing and pass the test, they can enhance their image as being so smart that they don't need to study. Either way their self-image is intact. Self-handicapping has been shown to take many forms. The one just described might be thought of as the reckless model of handicapping. Some students accomplish the same ends through procrastination. Putting things off and then rushing at the end provides an excuse for not doing your best work. Others take on too much responsibility and give themselves an excuse for failing by having too much to do. Whether this handicapping is deliberate or conscious is hard to say, but the effect is the same.

Another version of these attempts to protect self-worth is called "defensive pessimism." A defensive pessimist spends a lot of time worrying about and predicting failure, even when they have no history of failure to support their concerns. This can have two positive outcomes. For some students, the excess worry spurs them to study harder and therefore increases the probability of succeeding in the long run. For others, it protects them in case they do fail, for they have already prepared themselves for the pain of failure and can console themselves because their prediction was accurate.

A final motivational need is cognitive in nature but not in process. It is associated with some theories that have since given way to other more powerful explanations of behavior. Yet a kernel of this "need" remains in other forms in other theories and I think it has some useful implications for teaching. This is the need for cognitive balance mentioned earlier. The original notion was that individuals need their beliefs and behaviors to be consistent with one another. An imbalance leads to cognitive dissonance (in cognitive consistency theory). This is similar to the disequilibrium proposed as the mechanism for growth in Piagetian and other developmental theories. Individuals who run into situations they can't explain using their current world views or behavior systems engage in behaviors to bring perceptions and behavior back into balance. This is an important idea in explaining how students develop new world views, the conceptual change process.

The implications for instruction are obvious. When learners hold beliefs or misconceptions about a field, one of the best ways to get them to change is to confront them with the inconsistency between their views and reality. While this dissonance may not be totally capable of changing an individual's behavior or beliefs (there are some other factors operating as well), it can start the process of getting the individual to question his or her existing beliefs that the dissonance created.

As mentioned earlier, the concept of motivation as arising from the need to undo an imbalance or fill a need is a fairly old way of thinking about motivation. Yet, I believe it has some value in helping us think about ways to influence how students look at and react to the learning situation. We can make it physically pleasant and comfortable, a social group to which our students want to belong, a source of approval and achievement in a safe environment, a way to build their feelings of self-worth. And we can disrupt those feelings of safety and balance as a way of encouraging them to develop cognitively.

Value from intrinsic qualities of the task

This may sound simplistic, but some things are just more interesting than others. For example, I used to teach introductory psychology in the days when introductory psychology texts were completely text based—no pictures, no sidebars with interesting details, no biographies of the psychologists. They were, to put it mildly, capable of making a very interesting topic very boring. Then along came the textbook put out by *Psychology Today*. It was full of interesting details, pictures, graphs, stories, and so on. Students actually enjoyed reading it. Although students had learned from the old texts, the new models were much more likely to be read. Psychology textbooks haven't been the same since, thank heaven. So the presentation of material can be manipulated to enhance its motivational value by making it more interesting.

This particular source of value is one half of what we normally think of as intrinsic versus extrinsic sources of motivation. Richard Ryan and Edward Deci (2000) provide an updated look at this type of motivation. What is interesting about their discussion is that they propose that there is almost a continuum of motivation states, from totally intrinsic based on the type of enjoyment and inherent satisfaction that we usually associate with intrinsic motivation to what they call amotivation, or no motivation. In between are degrees of internality/externality of motivation. For example, external motivation in their system is what we normally think of as external, something imposed from the outside. Next is motivation that is internal to the learner but imposed from the outside. So when we do things to obtain the approval of others or to avoid censure, we are experiencing what they call introjected motivation. At the next level, the individual still is reacting to outside norms but has accepted those as important for him or her and so to some degree the individual identifies with the principle on which the motivation is based. Students who study content that might be relevant for their future are experiencing identification motivation. And one step beyond that is what Ryan and Deci call "integrated regulation," when the individual has fully accepted the principles that originated from the outside and no longer sees them as imposed on him or her. Most of our beginning students are still responding to outside pressure and are therefore extrinsically motivated to a degree. Majors and graduate students have probably integrated the motivation of learning the discipline into their value system and don't see it as imposed from the outside, so they'll work more autonomously. For a few, the activity of studying the discipline itself is motivating and we can experience that intense intrinsic motivation that comes from it.

Another source of intrinsic motivation derives from novelty and variety of the materials. Curiosity that arises from incongruity or change is an example of this type of motivational source. Posing questions and citing paradoxes are two ways for instructors to invoke the curiosity that is a natural characteristic of most learners. It is a mistake to hide the incongruities of our fields from students. The most interesting things are those that happen in the cracks between disciplines or those that turn out differently than predicted. That's where real learning occurs. Exposing students to the questions that still remain in the field is also a way to help them develop epistemologically. They move beyond what is safe and sure to what is still under development, and as a result they can vicariously participate in that development.

Another characteristic of the task that appeals to intrinsic sources of motivation is challenge. In fact, a whole area of research is devoted to the kind of motivation that arises from pitting the challenge of the task against the skill of the individual. When these two qualities are high and in balance, the individual will frequently experience "flow," the ultimate state of intrinsic motivation. This phenomenon was first studied in individuals who engaged willingly in very dangerous sports like sky diving and rock climbing. The researcher (Csikszentmihalyi, 1990) found that these individuals described their experiences in similar terms. They spoke of losing touch with their surroundings as they focused totally on their task. Time seemed to both shrink and expand because they lost track of it. They felt some danger, but a lot of control. The whole experience was a highly motivating one. Csikszentmihalyi went on to study other instances in which extremely intense focus was a characteristic of the condition and found the same sort of descriptions applied across situations and individuals. This area of intense intrinsic motivation is being studied for clues about how to produce it in more mundane circumstances. Although sometimes students almost seem to be in flow during a really stimulating class discussion, a fascinating experiment, or a difficult but doable assignment, I don't think we can produce it regularly. I'm not sure we'd even want that kind of intense experience on a regular basis, but it would be nice to be able to induce it when we want to.

What we can do to take advantage of this branch of the motivation model is to organize activities that challenge our students within their capacity to respond. We can use interesting examples and materials that relate to the interests that the students have or are experiencing outside the classroom. We can use a range of instructional methods and materials to keep the learning fresh. And we can help our students recognise and pursue their own interests as they relate to the course content.

Value derived from utility

A lament of many students is that they don't see any reason for learning important concepts. It's hard for novices to appreciate the value of foundational concepts unless they have a way of relating to them in a more concrete way. Two of the most useful ideas about influencing motivation revolve around this idea of giving students a reason to care about the concepts. They both deal with the functionality of the material, but one is immediate and the other is long range.

The immediate functionality arises when students learn things just in time, that is, right before they need the information or skill. In Chapter 4 I noted that this disconnect between what students are learning and when they are going to use the information is a possible source of failure to transfer ideas from the classroom to the real world. Lack of motivation is another reason why we should be better at timing when students are asked to learn things. In my experience as a psychology undergraduate and graduate student, I had to take a lot of statistics courses, something that is not my forte. I studied hard and learned what I needed to pass the tests but forgot most of it until I was working on my dissertation. Then, I had a functional need for statistics. I learned more statistics in the year I was working on my dissertation than I had in all the formal courses I had taken. My motivation to learn statistics was very high; I couldn't be distracted or discouraged. I had to do it. This is a cautionary tale for all of us who teach: Students who have an immediate need for something are more likely to learn it. As you think about when and how to introduce different skills and concepts, think about the natural flow of interdependence of topics and skills and design your curriculum accordingly. If you are going to have a guest speaker from the writing center talk about the process of writing, schedule that talk when students are about to start writing their papers. The same is true for presentations on library research or practical considerations in laboratories. There may be a similar interdependence of topics in your course. Juxtapose those that will best be learned in contrast to one another so that the immediate need to understand is underscored.

The second use issue has to do with longer range goals. It is difficult for novices in an area to understand how the minutiae of the immediate relate to their overall goals. They simply do not have the bigger picture to help them make the connections between what they are learning now and where they intend to be in five to ten years. You, on the other hand, may recognize this relationship. If so, you should make a point of drawing the connections for the students. In the undergraduate class I teach, I have education majors, nutrition majors, and speech therapist majors. Throughout the semester, whenever I get the chance I talk in terms of what they will be doing in later life and how it is supported by what we're doing in class. I try to give examples from all the fields often in class so the students can make the connection between now and the future. In fact, the final assignment is a "future uses" paper, in which students must select two or three ideas from the class and relate them to their future careers. I have had many papers begin with the statement, "when I started in this course, I didn't realize how many connections there would be for me as a . . ." Other colleagues have the students start the semester with a reflection on why they might be required to take this class. By example and content we instructors need to help students start thinking about the course content as a natural component of their future plans.

Value from choice and control

A strong source of motivation, negative or positive, comes from learner perceptions of self-determination and control (Deci & Ryan, 1987). The desire to be in control of our lives and fates is a strong source of motivation for most individuals. Students in classes in which there is little freedom of choice can easily abdicate responsibility for their own behavior; they're not in charge. When students have the opportunity to make decisions for themselves, they are most vested in the outcomes of those decisions and therefore more likely to invest the effort necessary to make the outcomes happen. Students who have made choices are also more likely to make the connection between their own behavior and the environmental consequences. This is an important developmental step toward adulthood. In fact, in some programs that work with juvenile offenders, the most common failure of these young people is an inability (not a reluctance) to make the connection between their choices and the outcomes. Some of the most successful programs for these individuals are those that force them to see that connection.

In a different part of the population, self-determination opportunities allow learners to develop more self-confidence and feelings of competence. If they are given a chance to determine either the process or product of their efforts, they take more ownership of the outcome, and when it's a success they experience it as affirmation of their self-worth. Research has shown that self-determination results in more creativity on the part of students and a willingness to take greater risk. This makes sense in terms of feeling in control; if you feel you are in control, you will be able to decide how much risk to take and when to get out. If you have that control, you are more willing to accept a challenge.

How do instructors allow students choice and control? There are almost always alternatives from which students can choose. They might not be able to choose the type of paper they need to write, but they can choose the topic and the schedule. Or if the topic is decided for them, perhaps they could choose the medium in which to express the learning. Instructors also can avoid excessive rules that seem to regiment or supervise student behaviors too closely. It is best to keep the rules to a few really important ones. It is even better to involve the students in determining the rules, which gives them much more control over what happens to them. If you as the instructor must make rules for safety or ethical reasons, explain the reasoning to the students. They'll usually understand and feel less like they are being controlled and more like they are being respected as thinking adults. And speaking of respect, respecting student opinions and questions is another way of giving them some control over their own fate. They know they can express those feelings without fear of ridicule or censure. Obviously, students can't control all that happens in a course, but to the degree that you can share control with them, you will have a more compliant audience.

Value that derives from the influence or opinion of others

When others appear to value a goal, learners will often adopt that value as their own, even in the absence of the qualities just listed. Something that everyone wants is something that we want, too. This probably works because of a combination of affiliation and approval, but it means simply that what society values will be valued by our students. Unfortunately, this sometimes leads to placing value on some fairly superficial things, like possessions or surface cleverness. This also can work against us as teachers when our students yield to social pressure and place value on counterproductive behaviors, such as binge drinking or slacker-type attitudes about work.

How do we overcome this? Fortunately, learners are also susceptible to influence by us as models and the things we value. When we show enthusiasm about a subject or a task, students will look at it in a different light. "If she thinks this is interesting, maybe it is," they might think to themselves. Certainly if it appears that we place no value on a particular behavior or outcome, students are likely to follow our lead. As noted in the chapter on modeling, teachers are models of much more than knowledge of the subject. Through our behavior we indicate what we value, and our students will take that into consideration as they are deciding on the value of various things we ask them to do. For example, I place a high premium on students coming to class prepared to work. That means that they will have read the assignment and thought about the questions in the textbook and possibly some of their own. I always come to class prepared to work with them, and what happens in class is always based on what they were to have read. This consistent behavior on my part speaks to them about what I value and what I think they should value. They can hardly be expected to put a premium on preparedness if I don't.

In summary on value

Helping to increase the value of a goal for students is the easier part of motivating them. As instructors we can intervene at just about every point as they decide how valuable a goal is and how much they're willing to do to obtain it. If you're having trouble with unmotivated students, trying to determine if and how they value what you're asking of them is the first step in motivating their best work.

The Expectancy That a Goal Can Be Achieved

Now that we've explored half of the motivation equation, increasing the value of the goal in the students' eyes, we can turn to the other half, increasing their belief that they will be successful at reaching the goal. This half is a little more difficult because we have less access to and ability to manipulate the bases for student expectations for success. These are internally generated by the learners rather than responses to qualities of the goal. Nevertheless, we can know something about why and how students think about their chances for success, and possibly help them develop healthy attitudes and strategies for building their self-efficacy with respect to our content.

Expectations based on learner self-efficacy

Self-efficacy refers to learners' beliefs that they have and can engage in the skills necessary to be successful at a task (Bandura, 1997). This doesn't necessarily mean they will be successful, but rather that they believe they have the capacity to be successful. In research on student achievement, self-efficacy is one of the strongest contributors to success (Zimmerman, 2000). In addition to influencing motivation, self-efficacy is itself influenced by most of the qualities below, but it would not be appropriate to equate self-efficacy with expectations of success. Research on self-efficacy and its influence on achievement has been growing lately as social cognitive theory has become more influential in psychology (Snow Corno & Jackson, 1996; Zimmerman, 2000). An implication of its importance is that, as instructors, we should adopt instructional strategies that help students make accurate estimates of their potential for success. A sample teaching strategy to enhance student self-efficacy would be to provide clear prerequisite statements that students could use to assess what they know and can do with regard to the content. This paired with information on ways to remediate one's skills or knowledge would help students plan their work and make them more confident about their ability to succeed at it.

Expectations based on difficulty of the goal

I said earlier that challenging goals are more motivating than easy goals. There is a balance here that has to be considered, however. Challenge is good, but too much challenge and you bump up against the learners' expectations for success. Let me give an example. I play tennis and because I am an average player, it is very motivating for me to be scheduled to play someone who is better than I am (high task value due to challenge). In that match I will have an opportunity to test myself, to try things that I haven't done before, and to evaluate my level of play. But suppose the person I'm scheduled to play is Venus Williams. In this case, my expectancy for success in the match is less than zero. I'd be lucky to get off the court without hurting myself. So, while playing Venus would be really exciting, I have no motivation to do so because I know I'd fail miserably. I'd be far more motivated to play someone who is slightly better than I am; that challenge would be doable. It would represent the best combination of challenge and expectations for success. (Think back to flow.) As instructors, we need to make our assignments challenging but doable if we want to motivate students to attempt them honestly.

Expectancy based on prior experience

One of the yardsticks learners use to decide on the probability of success at a task is their prior experience with it or related tasks. If students have been successful at math in the past, their estimates about success in a new math goal are likely to be high and therefore their motivation to pursue the goal is high as well.

Prior experience doesn't necessarily have to be with the exact task that is being considered at the moment. Expectations can be influenced by similar tasks. The problem is that a lot of students don't make the connection between what they have done before and their current task. It may fall to the instructor to point out those similar experiences to the students. Sometimes we even have to point out that they were successful in the past in addition to pointing out successful at what.

As instructors we can manipulate this aspect of expectancy for success by the way we structure the learning sequence. If goals early in the sequence are structured to produce student successes, later goals can be made more difficult without losing student enthusiasm. If we start the learning sequence with success, student motivation to continue will increase. Of course, it is important not to cultivate unreal expectations, so you want to quickly get the students to the right challenge level.

Expectancy based on skill matching

Sometimes the tasks we have for students are ones that they have not done before as a whole. But it is seldom that we ask our students to take on a totally new task. Most of the skills in education are built on previous skills, and there is the expectation that students will transfer what they have learned before to this new situation. Once again, however, students may not be able to recognize how a new skill derives from what they already know. It may be necessary for the instructor to help them analyze the requirements of the new task and find the component skills that they already have. Let me give an example. I frequently work with non-profit organizations in their training divisions. On one occasion I was charged with helping a group of mid-level managers develop teaching skills. The group members were very skeptical about their own abilities to take on this new set of skills, and they were quite nervous about it. I could see the link between their managerial skills and their teaching skills, but they didn't. So I first asked them to imagine that they had just been promoted and they had to hire their replacement. They had to analyze what skills they would look for in that applicant. There was a lot of consensus about what skills would be paramount. Then I had them think about a training session that they had attended that was really successful. I asked them to think about the person who led the session and what qualities that person had. When we compared the two sets of lists, we discovered that most of the skills that they already had as successful managers were closely related to the skills of a successful trainer. It was a definite "aha" experience for them. Their concerns about their abilities to succeed as trainers lessened considerably in light of the evidence that they already had many of the key skills.

The same might be true for your students. They might be approaching every class, every content area, as a brand new situation with nothing they can transfer in. You can help them see the connection between the skills and knowledge that they have and the kinds of goals that are going to be pursued in your course. This could dramatically increase their expectancy for success and therefore their motivation.

Expectancy based on the encouragement and modeling of others

A theme running through the previous discussion is that what you say to students influences their expectations for success. There is a wonderfully telling and famous piece of research that demonstrated that teacher expectations for students were more influential in the level of achievement reached than most other factors (Rosenthal & Jacobson, 1968). In this study teachers were led to believe that students were either about to bloom or not, even though students were chosen at random to be identified as bloomers. In subsequent classes, those students who had been randomly identified as bloomers did much better than the rest of the students. The researchers attributed the difference to the expectations of the teachers and how that influenced their treatment of the students. While this is a controversial study and replicating it has been a problem, it certainly makes sense that what you believe your students can do and how you communicate those beliefs to them will influence their motivation.

Usually the influence is a positive one. If you say, "This is a good class, and I know that you have the capacity to excel on this test," the students will respond positively. Of course, we have all heard and maybe even experienced a case where an instructor has motivated a group by telling them that there was no way they were going to succeed. The students then band together to show the instructor that he was wrong. I suppose this is the stuff of entertaining drama, but it is not the stuff of good teaching. You will get a far more motivated class when you set there a challenge and then tell them that you believe they have the ability to meet it.

There is another, less direct form of expectations based on the influence of others. It derives from the social learning theory discussed in Chapter 3 and deals with the influence of models. Learners' beliefs about success are strongly influenced when they see someone like themselves succeed. It's the case of, "if he can do it, then so can I." From an instructional perspective, this suggests that having other students demonstrate their own successes or their attempts at reaching the goal will influence all the students' beliefs about their own success probabilities. Alternatively, instructors can talk about their experiences of working toward similar goals, including the failures, false starts and attitudes they experienced. This is one strategy that may serve as a basis for the success of group learning methods. The opportunity to see other students in the group working with the same problems and succeeding serves as a source of motivation for everyone.

Expectancy as influenced by learner beliefs

One thing about expectancy beliefs is that they are strongly influenced by learners' other beliefs. This notion is less useful for teachers as designers of instruction, but more useful for teachers as interpreters of student behavior. Although there are ways to intervene with student beliefs, it's very difficult for any one instructor to have a large impact on a single student's deeply held beliefs. Nevertheless, understanding what some of them might be and how they might influence learner behavior is worthwhile.

A student's general self-confidence as a learner: Rightly or wrongly, some students are very confident about their own abilities to cope with anything we can throw at them. Students who have such high self-confidence are likely to believe that they can be successful at almost anything. Such students are also often fairly resilient and able to bounce back from failure. In the literature, a distinction is made between general self-esteem as a global trait and situation specific-confidence, which is the self-efficacy I described earlier (Ormrod, 1999). I can think that in general I am a good student, but have doubts about my ability to do well on high stakes tests, for example. The latter would be an indication of lower self-efficacy with regard to testing.

There isn't much you can do about most students' self-esteem, but you can help them make accurate appraisals of their abilities with regard to a specific task—that is, their self-efficacy. This won't hurt or help those with high general self-confidence, but it could help localize the confidence of those who have low general self-confidence. You can help them to see that, just because they haven't been successful overall, they have the possibility of being successful in this instance.

A student's beliefs about the nature of ability: There is a very interesting area of research that studies how student beliefs about the nature of intelligence and ability can influence their reactions to learning situations (Dweck & Leggett, 1988). The essence of the research revolves around whether an individual believes that ability is fixed or malleable. Students who hold the fixed perspective believe that one is born with a certain level of ability in an area and it cannot be changed. They are likely to say things like, "I'm just not good at math and never will be." These individuals will accept their failure at a goal or even their having to expend effort on a goal as evidence of the hopelessness of their situation. Why try if you are destined to fail? The flip side are the students who think they don't have to try because they've "always been an A student."

Students who hold the malleable perspective on ability believe that you may start out with a given level of some ability, but you're not stuck with that level for the rest of your life. Through hard work and effort, you can improve. You may not ever be the best at something, but you can always be better. These students interpret failure as a local phenomenon, something that indicates where they need to focus, and not as a condemnation of them personally.

Obviously, we would like our students to adopt the malleable attitude. Can we change student beliefs about ability? Yes, through modeling and through the way that we talk about student effort. If we focus on what can be done and on effort rather than focusing on some inborn ability, we are both modeling an appropriate belief and encouraging students to reframe their thinking.

A student's beliefs about the origins of success and failure is a very rich and growing area of theory and research. The theory associated with this area is called attribution theory, and it deals with how individuals explain what happens to them. Each individual has an "explanatory style," a way of thinking about why things happen. Of the several manifestations of this style, one primary manifestation is whether individuals believe that they are responsible for what happens to them (an "internal locus of control") or that forces outside their control are responsible (an "external locus of control"). Students who have an internal locus of control believe that it is something about them that determines the outcome of their effort. So, for example, a healthy internal locus of control statement is, "I can succeed if I am willing to put in a sufficient amount of effort." Students with an external locus of control place the responsibility for outcomes outside themselves. Someone with an external locus of control might say, "I got a good grade because I was lucky" or "I got a bad grade because the test was too tricky."

In most cases, it might seem that we would want students to develop an internal locus of control, to take responsibility for their own fate. But in reality, that is not always the case. What we really want is for students to make appropriate attributions about locus of control. Sometimes the test really is too hard, and no one is able to succeed at it. If that is the case, students shouldn't be blaming themselves and lowering their self-efficacy. However, when they do something or fail to do something and it results in their failure, they should be able and willing to accept that responsibility and make a change for the next time.

Can we as instructors influence student attributions for success and failure? Yes, at least within the context of our courses. The best strategy for attribution retraining (the technical name for it) is to put the learners in a situation in which they have to make choices and experience the consequences of those choices. If the instructor or some other force outside the students is always calling the shots and telling them what to do and how to do it, when things go wrong, students are very justified in pointing the finger at the instructor. "I was only following orders." If, however, the students make some of the choices about how to accomplish a goal and then monitor their progress (as in journaling), they are more likely to be able to recognize when their action leads to a particular outcome. This might help students make appropriate attributions, at least in that situation. For example, I have been very successful at getting students to think about the connection between their study behavior and the outcomes on their tests by having them write a learning analysis paper right after the first exam. In the paper, they describe how they studied for the exam and then analyze the exam performance itself. They look for commonly occurring errors, both in content and in the way they thought about and responded to the questions. For example, they sometimes discover on reflection that the questions they made the most mistakes on were those that called for application of concepts. Tying that back to their study strategies might show that they need to generate more of their own examples during studying. It doesn't work for everyone or for every kind of error, but for some of the students it's the first time they've ever analyzed what happened on an exam beyond just looking at the grade.

An interesting area of research related to attributions is the study of learned helplessness (Peterson, Maier, & Seligman, 1993). This phenomenon is characterized by a learner's belief that there is nothing he or she can do to affect the outcome of any situation, and as a result he or she simply stops trying. The literature in this area suggests that this is a learned response (as opposed to a personality trait) that came about by some past experiences in which the learner indeed had no control and could not predict the outcome of any behavior. They "learned" that they were helpless, and that situation then expanded to the rest of their functioning. Individuals who display learned helplessness are generally apathetic, indecisive, passive, and very susceptible to control by others. Some of these same characteristics are also common in people with depression, leading some researchers to speculate on the interrelatedness of the two phenomena. We may be seeing a learned helplessness syndrome in students who have a long history of failure in the school system. Because nothing they have done in the past has been successful, they simply stop trying and start believing that they never will be able to succeed. Working with students like this is particularly difficult, but some success can be achieved by starting with small goals that are achievable in a short span of time. If students see themselves as successful with these small goals, they might break out of the belief that they cannot do anything to help themselves. Certainly this is something we hope for any students caught in that downward spiral.

A Hybrid Source of Influence: Goal Orientation

Another interesting area of research on motivation is the idea of goal orientation (Dweck & Leggett, 1988; Pintrich, 2000). It's hard to say whether this concept is related more to value or expectancy, but it appears to be very influential in determining learner behavior, so I'm putting it here by itself to emphasize its importance and unique nature. This research says that there are different general types of goals that lead to different learner behaviors. When originally proposed, this theory divided goal orientations into two types: learning goals and performance goals. (There are actually several different manifestations of this theory using different terms, but these are my preferences.) When an individual is oriented toward learning goals, he or she wants to learn a new skill or content no matter what has to be done to reach the goal. The purpose is to master the skill eventually, even if there are wrong turns on the road. When an individual is oriented toward performance goals, he or she is interested in demonstrating competency in comparison to others. The purpose is to show how well you can perform the skill rather than how much more you can learn about it. These two orientations have been shown to lead to very different behavior patterns.

Individuals who are operating with learning goals are focused on improvement. They are willing to take risks and try new strategies if there is a chance that those changes will lead to better learning. They interpret mistakes as learning opportunities, and they are interested in getting as much feedback as possible so they can improve. On the other hand, individuals who are operating with performance goals are focused on demonstrating competence. They are not willing to take risks because risk taking could lead to failure, which they want to avoid. They will practice in private so that others don't see their mistakes and only make their performance public when they know it will be better than everyone else's. They are interested in monitoring what others are doing, but not sharing what they themselves are doing.

When this theory was initially suggested, these two types of orientations were essentially thought to be related to some personality variables and somewhat particular to the individual. That proved not to be a good representation of the data. Instead, the theory has changed to say that individuals can have both learning and performance goals even within the same task. For example, back to the tennis court. I can have two goals when I step on to the court. I can want to get better (a learning goal), and I can want to avoid looking foolish (a performance goal). The former would encourage me to try new shots and to be adventurous. The latter would encourage me to stick to what I know best. These warring tendencies will be balanced against one another and go more to one side or the other probably depending on how the match is going. If I'm winning or doing well, I might be encouraged to try new things. If I'm struggling, it's back to basics—just get the ball over the net and into the court. This is probably a realistic description of what learners do all the time. But in classes, where learning is supposed to be key, we should be encouraging students to adopt learning goals because that's what they need to do in order to learn.

How do we as instructors encourage students to adopt learning goals? Carol and Richard Ames (1991), two prominent researchers, have studied this question with younger students, but I think their ideas hold for college-level students as well. The first admonition is to make the classroom a safe place to take risks. If students know that they will be supported if they try new things, they are more likely to do so. Instructors who berate students for making mistakes are pushing them toward performance goals; instructors who accept mistakes as a part of learning are making it possible for students to adopt learning goals. One way to decrease risk is to provide alternative ways of achieving the same goal and allowing or even assisting students to choose the alternative that best fits their strengths.

Instructors also can make a class less risky by not pitting students against one another in terms of performance. Rather than competing with the other students in the class for the highest grade, students should be competing with themselves, with their previous performance, or with an absolute standard that is achievable. Researchers recommend downplaying public comparisons and emphasizing self-reflection as ways of encouraging learning goal orientation.

The instructor can model the kinds of behaviors that are associated with learning goals. For example, if instructors welcome new ideas and are open to working problems out in front of the class, mistakes and all, they show the students the kind of attitude that supports a learning orientation.

Synthesis

To guide your thinking, I've summarized below the ideas about motivation presented in this chapter. I'm not guaranteeing that if you follow them all your students will never experience a lagging motivation again, but I think these suggestions have a sound basis in the literature and are not difficult to implement.

Svinicki's Seven Strategies for Enhancing Student Motivation

1) Be a good role model of appropriate motivation.
2) Choose learning tasks with utility, challenge, and interest value.
3) Encourage accurate student self-efficacy about the course.
4) Base evaluation on progress or absolute level achieved to produce a mastery goal orientation.
5) Encourage attributing success to effort and interpreting mistakes as learning opportunities.
6) Provide choice and/or control over goals or strategies to the learner.
7) Communicate high expectations that are in line with student capabilities.

Other Attempts at Theory Synthesis

The above discussion has been focused very tightly on cognitive models of motivation, which I think are most useful for faculty in higher education. They offer fairly straightforward ways for instructors to look at their students' motivation and do something about it. There are, however, other really excellent syntheses of the literature that are aimed at higher education environments. I mention them here to point you toward further reading on this very complex topic.

One motivational model that has found much of support in the realm of technology-enhanced learning is the ARCS model proposed by John Keller (1999). In this model, instructors are encouraged to consider four aspects of learning represented by the four letters in ARCS: 1) attention, 2) relevance, 3) confidence, and 4) satisfaction. Note the relationship between this model and the amalgamated model described in this chapter. Both deal with value (attention, relevance, and satisfaction) and expectancy (confidence). Keller has primarily worked in distance learning and other technology areas, but the principles are very much the same across the board. An interesting tangent in the research using this model was the development of a motivationally adaptive approach to instruction (Song as reported in Keller, 1999), in which learners' motivation levels were sampled periodically during learning, and the amount of motivational intervention by the instruction varied according to their current levels. The theory was that if you already had a motivated learner, it would be either unnecessary or even counterproductive to interrupt learning to motivate them further. Instead, learners received motivational intervention during learning only when their intrinsic motivation appeared to be diminishing. Keller reported that, under these adaptive conditions, learners' levels of motivation and performance were much higher than those who received continuous motivational support and those who received none. This one study fits with the notions of self-determination and the negative influence of outside interference.

Wlodkowski and Ginsberg (1995) have proposed the Motivational Framework for Culturally Responsive Teaching as a synthesis of theory and research on motivation across cultures. Their model lists four motivation-enhancing conditions that need to be present to enable students to do their best work:

1. Inclusion—students and teachers must feel respected and connected.
2. Favorable attitude toward learning—students experience personal relevance and choice.
3. Meaningfulness—learning experiences are challenging and thought provoking and are based on learners' perspectives and values.
4. Competence—students feel they can succeed.

As you can see, these elements are very consistent with the model proposed in this chapter.

A synthesis of motivational models was presented by Michael Theall and Jennifer Franklin (1999). This contribution summarizes the ideas of 13 authors writing about motivation in higher education. When all the terms, constructs, and research results were compared, Theall and Franklin settled on six key motivation terms that all the theories had in common:

1. Inclusion
2. Attitude
3. Meaning
4. Competence
5. Leadership
6. Satisfaction

The first four terms came primarily from an initial model of motivated learning proposed by Wlodkowski and Ginsberg, and the meanings attributed to them were similar to those proposed by Wlodkowski and Ginsberg. The other two terms were drawn from the remaining theorists represented in the book and are described as follows:

1. Leadership—high expectations (from the authority), structure, feedback, and support
2. Satisfaction—rewards

These terms also seem to be in tune with the amalgamated model proposed in this chapter, although the additional aspect of inclusion goes somewhat beyond self-determination to include others, and leadership speaks to the role of the instructor more than the learner. Nevertheless, the synthesis presented by Theall and Franklin affirms the importance of value and efficacy in motivating learners.

The theory you choose to make motivational decisions is a matter of personal conviction, because so many of the same constructs occur in each version. The important point of this chapter is to recognize that, in cooperation with your learners, you can create an environment in which students will value what they are learning and believe that they can be successful at it, which will be the cornerstones of their motivation.

For Those Who Want to Go Beyond the Basics

As I have in other chapters, I'll devote the last part of the chapter to some of the more speculative or less well documented ideas that may play an interesting role in instructional concerns in the future.

The first of these is emotion or affect and its relationship to learning. This is not a new area, but it has revived recently as new findings from physiology are raising interesting possibilities in explaining some previous findings. First, however, I should say that the more standard discussions of the role of emotions in learning center around anxiety. This is a fairly well-researched area (Ormrod, 1999), and so some pretty safe statements can be made about how anxiety and performance are related. Although there's some question about the way a particularly prominent description of this phenomenon, called the Yerkes-Dodson curve, has been expanded beyond its origins, it does have a lot of face validity for anyone in education. The Yerkes-Dodson curve (Figure 26.2) relates an individual's level of arousal by a situation to his or her measured level of performance. In general, at low levels of stimulation or arousal, an individual will not perform well in terms of quantity or quality. As the level of arousal increases, the quality and quantity of the performance increases until it hits an optimum. From then on, increases in arousal or stimulation are accompanied by a decrease in performance. The hypothesized cause for this bell curve is interference with performance at high levels of arousal. This essentially means that some tension or arousal is good, but too much is bad. For example, this is frequently seen in students in the form of test anxiety. Students who under practice conditions (which are not especially anxiety arousing) perform quite well will fall apart when the actual test is given. Their minds go blank and they have trouble concentrating. One proposed explanation is that they use up working memory and attention capacity by dwelling more on what is going wrong than on actually addressing the task at hand. Eventually, their capacity is exceeded and they shut down. Allegedly, this relationship would hold with positive arousal as well, but I expect that we will seldom see that level of arousal in the classroom.

Can we as instructors do anything about this problem? Most institutions that have student study help centers have programs to teach students how to cope with test anxiety. Although we're often not capable of intervening with an individual student, there are things we can do for a class in general. For example, providing a lot of information about the test situation, its format, the type of questions, the time limits, acceptable behavior, and so on well before the test can alleviate some of the unknowns that are often sources of the anxiety. Practice tests which make the question formats familiar are really appreciated by students. Try to avoid high stakes testing in which the students' grades depend on only one or two test scores. More measures of student learning are not only better for their test anxiety, but also make for more accurate measurement. Students especially appreciate the opportunity to drop a low test score, and I appreciate it because I don't have to allow and arrange makeup tests or listen to all the reasons why a student couldn't take the test.

During the test itself, keeping interruptions or disruptions to a minimum is important so as not to damage student concentration. Be sure that you've proofread the test and had someone else do it

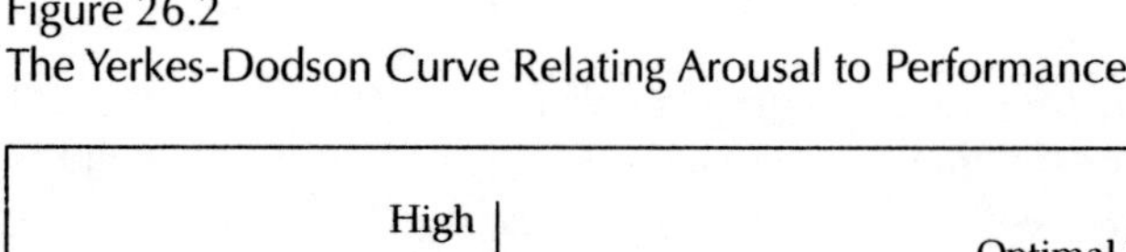

Figure 26.2
The Yerkes-Dodson Curve Relating Arousal to Performance

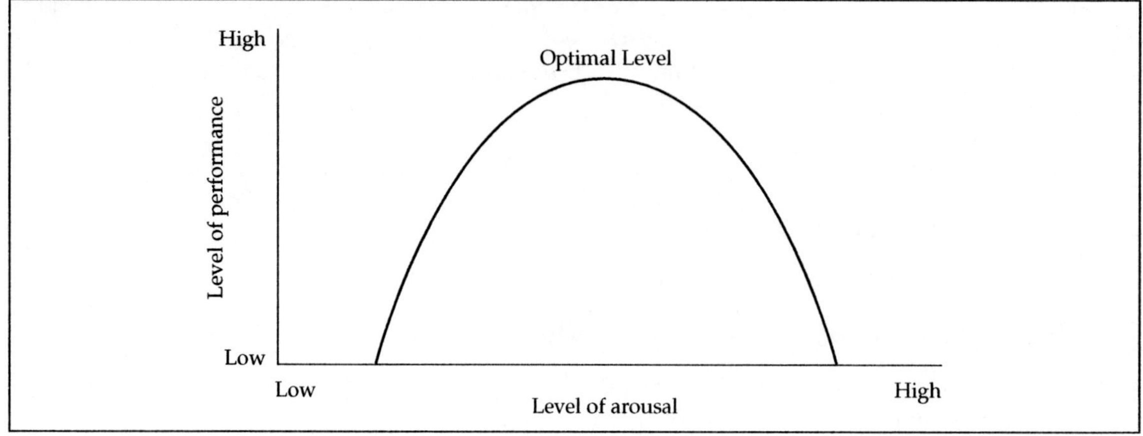

as well, so you don't have to make corrections during the exam. If you can, give students a lifeline in case they get confused. For example, with my multiple choice tests, students are allowed to write an explanation of their answer on a special page if they are struggling over a particular question. Not all students take advantage of this, but it does make them feel less anxious. Another similar anxiety reducing strategy that also influences learning is to allow students to earn back a portion of the points they have missed on a test by redoing or reflecting on those items. The first time I instituted this practice, a student said to me afterward, "Gosh, I guess you really do care whether we learn this or not." I was pleased to be able to tell her that I did and to have my policies and procedures back it up.

There are other aspects of emotion and learning that are a little bit farther out on the cutting edge. There is a lot of speculation and some research being conducted around the impact on memory of emotion at the time of learning (Haskell, 2001). One proposal is that memories have an emotional tag attached to them reflecting their importance at the time of learning (LeDoux, 2002). During recall, that emotional tag serves as part of the retrieval process along with the memories. This had been suggested earlier in the form of state-dependent learning. The research at the time indicated that returning to the state you were in when first experiencing some event will increase your chances of remembering its details. I like to think of an example of this in the context of having a fight with your significant other. As tempers flair, all the things that that person has ever done to irritate you come flooding back and are interjected into the argument, thereby escalating it further. What does this say to us as instructors? It might be telling us that emotion in the classroom has a positive function and can support learning and memory. For example, humor evokes emotion, thereby possibly tagging the content of the joke as something worth remembering. Conversely, negative emotions could be tagged to particularly painful learning episodes, causing them to be avoided and repressed. There is some indication in the literature that "happy" or positive emotions facilitate interconnections and integration of material, a strong component of learning (Isen & Daubman, 1984).

Recent advances in our ability to understand brain structure and function have given a tantalizing hint about a physical reason for the close tie between emotion and memory. The structures in the brain associated with emotion lie very close to those associated with the formation of memories (LeDoux, 2002). And the neural processes connecting these two areas suggest that information passes through the emotion center before going on to the site of long-term memory, the neocortex. It is safe to say that the emotional tone present during learning and performance have a definite impact on the learning that takes place.

A related area has been explored by Antonio Damasio (1994) in *Descartes' Error: Emotion, Reason, and the Human Brain.* This time emotion is related to decision-making. Damasio gives some very convincing evidence about the importance of emotion in the rational decision-making process by showing how individuals with damage to emotional centers of the brain frequently have difficulty making decisions.

This is also related to the area of conceptual change and hot cognition. A lot of original theories about concept formation and change portrayed the learner as a cool and rational evaluator of the evidence—like a scientist who takes in new information, evaluates it carefully, and makes changes based on the evidence. This implies that when we are trying to change a student's mind about some misconception he or she has, all we need do is produce the facts, and the student will adopt the new ideas. However, plenty of research evidence and personal anecdotes say that people frequently hold on to misconceptions in the face of data. I recommend *How We Know What Isn't So* by Thomas Gilovich (1991) or Carl Sagan's *The Demon-Haunted World* (1995) for wonderful discussions of why even intelligent people persist in their beliefs.

This impact of motivation on cognition and conceptual change suggests to instructors that we need to be aware of how different aspects of motivation might assist or inhibit learning. A comprehensive article by Pintrich, Marx, and Boyle (1993) lists seven areas of motivation that have been shown to impact conceptual change. We've discussed many of them already, but they include such things as whether a learner has mastery goals versus performance goals. Obviously, mastery goals make a learner more open to conceptual change. The sources of task value such as personal interest and utility influence the degree to which a learner will expose himself or herself to data that might cause conceptual change. Self-efficacy beliefs and epistemic beliefs about the nature of knowing influence a learner's assessment of the difficulty of changing. And from the conceptual change literature, Pintrich et al. point to the need for a learner to experience disaffection with his or her current beliefs before change is considered.

Another area of advanced interest is the differentiation between motivational behaviors, like goal setting, and volitional behaviors, like persisting in the face of difficulty. One of the first to suggest the multiple nature of motivation was Kuhl (1985), who proposed two distinct stages of motivation. The first was predecisional and was involved in making the decision to engage in some action. This is what we generally think of as motivation, the force that impels us forward toward a goal. The second was post-decisional and was focused on keeping the momentum in the face of obstacles. This is now what we generally think of as volition. Once the learner has crossed the Rubicon between decision and action, the behaviors required are different; this is now thought of as the Rubicon model of motivation/volition (Heckhausen & Kuhl, 1985). On the decision side are such things as the intrinsic motivation or extrinsic motivation associated with the goal plus the tendencies for action. These are the kinds of things that I've been discussing in this chapter. On the implementation side are things like those discussed in the chapter on self-regulation. They have more to do with actions that allocate resources, adaptive strategy use, and emotional control. There is some evidence that learners are susceptible to different influences depending on which side of the decision they're currently on (Corno, 1993). For example, prior to making the decision to engage in a task, learners can be easily influenced by arguments about its usefulness. Once they cross over to implementation, they become much more focused and less susceptible to arguments from others. However, they are susceptible to the conditions they find on the other side, like unanticipated difficulties.

Corno (1993) provides interesting examples of the kinds of volitional control strategies that students use. For example, under motivational control she lists things like setting contingencies for performance, meaning establishing rewards and punishments to implement depending on how the learning goes. She also lists "visualize doing the work successfully," a sort of mental cheer leading for yourself. Under emotional control, she lists "count to ten in your head," a common technique to avoid reacting too quickly in an emotional situation. She also lists "visualize doing the work successfully and feeling good about that." Notice how this differs from the motivational version; here the point is the feeling/emotion associated with success.

Why is volition important? For one thing, procrastination is a major problem in academic life, and the desire to find a solution for it impels a lot of research. Some researchers have pointed to volition as the source of procrastination for a lot of students (DeWitte & Lens, 2000). In studying procrastinators and non-procrastinators, these researchers have found no differences in intentions or abilities, but they do show a difference in the strategies associated with volition. For example, procrastinators have difficulties remembering their initial intentions to achieve a certain goal (Oettingen, Honig & Gollwitzer, 2000). If the learner formulated a plan for a goal, fantasized himself or herself following that plan and achieving that goal, and, perhaps most important, having contingency plans in case something went wrong, the learner was more likely to follow through on the plan later. Oettingen and her colleagues said this was particularly true for naïve students, although more advanced students also benefited from imagining future successes. The skill here seems to be the ability to mentally contrast the current situation with future possibilities. This ability to imagine a possible future self may be one of the important developmental steps in moving toward better volitional strategies.

This issue of volitional strategy use is an important step forward in helping students progress. I've made quite a point of saying that we have to help students over the initial hump of making the decision to learn our content, and I still think that's crucial. If they never make that step (over the Rubicon), they won't need anything else. But once we do convince them to tackle the learning involved in our course, we should perhaps help them develop some strategies for coping with the obstacles they might face.

I said earlier that one possible strategy for helping students learn is to provide a coping model, an example of someone who runs into difficulty and overcomes it. This is one of the ways we can teach volitional strategies to our students. When they see how we cope with uncertainty or how other students react to failure, they are being exposed to volitional control ideas. However, just seeing the model may not be enough. Just as I suggested in Chapter 4 that learning a skill by watching a master needs to be accompanied by an articulation of the thought processes behind the skill, I believe the same applies here. When modeling coping or volitional strategies, an instructor should be very explicit about what he or she is doing. Including comments about affective states in the midst of a cognitive demonstration might help students see that it is normal to feel frustrated or irritated when things go wrong. It doesn't mean that they are inadequate to the task; everyone feels that way now and again. It's what they do in the face of those feelings that counts. The combination of being told that it's normal to feel frustrated (or excited or angry or whatever) and suggestions about how to deal with those feelings (take a deep breath, count to ten) and obstacles (take a break, take a different perspective, brainstorm without editing) could be just as valuable to the learners as specific suggestions about learning the content itself.

This area of volition is very close in feeling to the self-regulation strategies that I discussed in Chapter 6. The research and theories in these two areas overlap, as you might have noticed. In general we might think about these two areas as metacognition dealing with content learning and metaconation (conation is the technical term for the affective aspects of learning) as dealing with motivation/emotion. They are almost inseparable in terms of producing success in learning. But as instructors we tend to favor working only with the cognitive issues and leaving the conative issues to the touchy-feely disciplines. That would be a very short sighted and unproductive stance to take. Perhaps this discussion about helping students take strategic control of the conative side of their learning will inspire you to move from the decision/planning side of the Rubicon of motivational teaching to the implementation side.

Part V—Shared Expectations: Creating Supportive Learning Environments

Recommended Readings

Astin, A. W. (1993). *What matters in college: Four critical years revisited.* San Francisco, CA: Jossey-Bass.

Astin, A. (1999). Student involvement: A developmental theory for higher education. *Journal of College Student Development, 40*(5), 518–529.

Barab, S. A., & Duffy, T. M. (2000). From practice fields to communities of practice. In D. Jonassen and S. Land (Eds.), *Theoretical foundation of learning environments* (pp. 25–49). Mahwah, NJ: Lawrence Erlbaum Associates.

Barnett, R., & Coate, K. (2005). *Engaging the curriculum in higher education.* Maidenhead, UK: McGraw Hill/Open University Press/SRHE.

Blum, Susan D. (2009). *My word!: Plagiarism and college culture.* Ithaca, NY: Cornell University Press.

Border, L. B., & Chism, N. (Eds.). (1992). *New Directions for Teaching and Learning: No.49, Teaching for diversity.* San Francisco, CA: Jossey-Bass.

Bradley, D. F., Pauley, J. A., & Pauley, J. F. (2006). *Effective classroom management: Six keys to success.* Lanham, MD: Rowman & Littlefield Education.

Branche, J., Mullennix, J., & Cohn, E. R. (Eds.). (2007). *Diversity across the curriculum: A guide for faculty in higher education.* San Francisco, CA: Jossey-Bass.

Breaux, A. L., & Whitaker, T. (2006). *Seven simple secrets: What the best teachers know and do.* Larchmont, NY: Eye On Education.

Brockett, R.G. (Ed.). (1998). *Ethical issues in adult education.* New York: Teachers College, Columbia University.

Bronstein, P. & Quina, K. (Eds.). (2003). *Teaching gender and multicultural awareness.* Washington, DC: American Psychological Association.

Burgstahler, S. (2003). Accommodating students with disabilities: Professional development needs of faculty. In C. Wehlburg & S. Chadwick-Blossey (Eds.), *To Improve the Academy: Vol. 21, Resources for Faculty, Instructional, and Organizational Development* (pp. 179–195). Bolton, MA: Anker.

Burman, M. E., & Kleinsasser, A. (2004). Ethical guidelines for use of student work: Moving from teaching's invisibility to inquiry's visibility in the scholarship of teaching and learning. *The Journal of General Education, 53,* 59–79.

Casey, J. G. (2005 (July-August)). Diversity, discourse, and the working-class student. *Academe, 91*(4).

Center for Research on Teaching and Learning (2001). *Guidance for UM instructors leading class discussion on the tragedy of September 11, 2001.* Ann Arbor, MI: The University of Michigan.

Chism, N. (1994). Taking student diversity into account. In W. J. McKeachie (Ed.), *Teaching tips: Strategies, research, and theory for college and university teachers* (9th ed.). (pp. 223–37). Lexington, MA: D. C. Heath.

Clair, J. A., Maclean, T. L., & Greenberg, D. N. (2002). Teaching through traumatic events: Uncovering the choices of management educators as they responded to September 11th. *Academy of Management Learning and Education, 1,* 38–54.

Cook, C. E., & Sorcinelli, M. D. (2005). Building multiculturalism into teaching development programs. In M. Ouellett (Ed.), *Teaching inclusively* (pp. 74–83). Centerville, MA: New Forum Press.

Cowdery, J. R. (2007). *Building on student diversity: Profiles and activities.* Thousand Oaks, CA: Sage Publications.

Cox, M. (2004). Introduction to faculty learning communities. In M. Cox & L. Richlin, *New Directions for Teaching and Learning: No. 97, Faculty learning communities* (pp. 5–23). San Francisco, CA: Jossey-Bass.

Crone, I. (2007, Winter). Motivating today's college students. *Peer Review, 9*(1).

Davis, B. M. (2006). *How to teach students who don't look like you.* Thousand Oaks, CA: Corwin Press.

Decker Lardner, E. (2004). Approaching diversity through learning communities. In J. L. Laufgraben, N. Shapiro, and Associates (Eds.), *Sustaining and improving learning communities.* San Francisco, CA: Jossey-Bass.

DiPietro, M. (2003). The day after: Faculty behavior in post-September 11, 2001, classes. In C. Wehlburg and S. Chadwick-Blossey (Eds.), *To Improve the Academy: Vol. 21, Resources for Faculty, Instructional, and Organizational Development* (pp. 21–39). Bolton, MA: Anker.

Farrell, E. F. (2001, December 21). Hedging against disaster. *The Chronicle of Higher Education,* A40.

Fallows, S., & Ahmet, K. (Eds.). (1999). *Inspiring students: Case studies in motivating the learner.* London, UK: Kogan Page.

Frederick, P. (1981). The dreaded discussion: Ten ways to start. *Improving College and University Teaching, 29,* 109–114.

Ginsberg, M. B., & Wlodkowski, R. J. (2009). *Diversity and motivation: Culturally responsive teaching in college* (2nd ed.). San Francisco, CA: Jossey-Bass.

Grant, A. C., & Sleeter, C. E. (2003). *Turning on learning: Five approaches to multicultural teaching plans for race, class, gender, and disability.* Hoboken, NJ: John Wiley & Sons.

Gurin, P., Dey, E., Hurtado, S., & Gurin, G. (Fall 2002). Diversity and higher education: Theory and impact on educational outcomes. *Harvard Educational Review, 72*(3), 330–366.

Hofer, B. (2006). Motivation in the college classroom. In W. J. McKeachie & M. Svinicki (Eds.), *McKeachie's teaching tips: Strategies, research, and theory for college and university teachers* (12th ed.). (pp. 140–150). Boston, MA: Houghton Mifflin.

Howard, D. L. (2001, September 20). Teaching through tragedy. *The Chronicle of Higher Education.*

Howell, A., & Tuitt, F. (2003). *Race and higher education rethinking pedagogy in diverse college classrooms.* Cambridge, MA: Harvard Graduate School of Education.

Hurst, J. C. (1999). The Matthew Shepard tragedy: Management of a crisis. *About Campus, 4*(3), 5–11.

Hurtado, S. (2001). Linking diversity and educational purpose: How diversity affects the classroom environment and student development. In G. Orfield (Ed.), *Diversity challenged: Evidence on the impact of affirmative action* (pp. 187–203). Cambridge, MD: Harvard Publishing Group.

Kardia, D., Bierwert, C., Cook, C., Miller, A. T., & Kaplan, M. (2002). Discussing the unfathomable: Classroom-based responses to tragedy. *Change Management, 34,* 18–23.

Karumanchery, L. L. (2005). *Engaging equity: New perspectives on anti-racist education.* Calgary: Detselig Enterprises.

Kaufman, L. R., & Stock, E. (Eds.). (2004). *Reinvigorating the undergraduate experience: Successful models supported by NSF's AIRE/RAIRE program.* Washington: Centre for Undergraduate Research. http://www.cur.org/publications/AIRE_RAIRE/toc.asp

Kitano, M. (1997). *What a course will look like after multicultural change.* In A. Morey & M. Kitano (Eds.), *Multicultural course transformation in higher education: A broader truth* (pp. 18–34). Needham Heights, MA: Allyn & Bacon.

Kramer, G. L., & Gardner, J. N. (2007). *Fostering student success in the campus community.* San Francisco, CA: Jossey-Bass.

Kuh, G. D. (2001). Assessing what really matters to student learning: Inside the national survey of engagement. *Change, 33*(3) 10–17.

Kuh, G., Kinzie, J., Schuh, J. H., Whitt, E. J., & Associates. (2005). *Student success in college: Creating conditions that matter.* San Francisco: Jossey-Bass.

Landsman, J., & Lewis, C. W. (2006). *White teachers, diverse classrooms: A guide to building inclusive schools, promoting high expectations, and eliminating racism* (1st ed.). Sterling, VA: Stylus.

Larson, W. A. (Ed.). (1994). *When crisis strikes on campus.* Washington, DC: Council for Advancement and Support of Education.

Laubscher, L., & Powell, S. (2003). Skinning the drum: Teaching about diversity as "other." *Harvard Educational Review, 73*(2), 203–222.

Leamnson, Robert. (1999). *Thinking about teaching and learning: Developing habits of learning with first year college and university students.* Sterling, VA: Stylus Publishing.

Liverant, G. I., Hofmann, S. G., & Litz, B. T. (2004). Coping and anxiety in college students after the September 11th terrorist attacks. *Anxiety, Stress & Coping: An International Journal, 17*(2), 127–139.

MacFarlane, B. (2004). *Teaching with integrity: The ethics of higher education practice.* New York, NY: Routledge Falmer.

Manning, M. L., & Bucher, K. T. (2006). *Classroom management: Models, applications, and cases* (2nd ed.). Upper Saddle River, NJ: Pearson Education/Prentice Hall.

May, W. (Ed.). (1990). *Ethics and higher education.* New York, NY: Macmillan.

McDonald, W. (Ed). (2002). *Creating campus community: In search of Ernest Boyer's legacy.* San Francisco, CA: Jossey-Bass.

Meyers, S. (2003). Strategies to prevent and reduce conflict in college classrooms. *College Teaching, 51,* 94–98.

Moore, S. L. (Ed.). *Practical approaches to ethics for colleges and universities: New directions for higher education.* San Francisco, CA: Jossey-Bass.

Oppenheimer, R. J. (2001). Increasing student motivation and facilitating learning. *College Teaching, 49*(3), 96–98.

Pace, J. L., & Hemmings, A. B. (2006). *Classroom authority: Theory, research, and practice.* Mahwah, NJ: L. Erlbaum Associates.

Palloff, R. M., & Pratt, K. (1999). *Building learning communities in cyberspace: Effective strategies for the online classroom.* San Francisco, CA: Jossey-Bass.

Pascarella, E. & Terenzini, P. (2005). *How college affects students (Vol. II): A third decade of research.* San Francisco, CA: Jossey-Bass.

Pascarella, E., Wolniak, G., Seifert, T., Cruce, T., & Blaich, C. (2005). *Liberal arts colleges and liberal arts education: New evidence on impacts.* San Francisco, CA: Jossey-Bass and the Association for the Study of Higher Education (ASHE).

Paulsen, M. B., & Feldman, K. A. (2005, November). The conditional and interactional effects of epistemological beliefs on the self-regulated learning of college students: Motivational strategies. *Research in Higher Education, 46,* 7, 731–768.

Pratt, D. D. (2002). Good teaching: One size fits all? In J. Ross-Gordon (Ed.), *An update on teaching theory.* San Francisco, CA: Jossey-Bass.

Sandeen, A. (2003). *Enhancing student engagement on campus.* New York, NY: Rowan & Littlefield.

Siegel, D. (1994). *Campuses respond to violent tragedy.* Phoenix, AZ: Oryx Press.

Stanley, C. (2006). Coloring the academic landscape: Faculty of color breaking the silence in predominantly white colleges and universities. *American Educational Research Journal, 43*(4), 701–736

Sweener, K., Kundert, D., May, D., & Quinn, K. (2002). Comfort with accommodations at the community college. *Journal of Developmental Education, 25*(3), 6.

Tatum, B. D. (1992, Spring). Talking about race, learning about racism: The application of racial identity development theory in the classroom. *Harvard Educational Review, 62,* 1–24.

Tisdell, E. J. (2000). Feminist pedagogies. In E. Hayes, D. Flannery, & Associates (Eds.), *Women as learners* (pp. 155–184). San Francisco, CA: Jossey-Bass.

Turner, C. S., Gonzalez, J. C., & Wood, J. L. (2008). Faculty of color in academe: What 20 years of literature tells us. *Journal of Diversity in Higher Education, 1*(3), 139–168.

Warren, L. (2005). Strategic action in hot moments. In M. Ouellett (Ed.), *Teaching inclusively: Resources for course, department & institutional change in higher education* (pp. 620–630). Stillwater, OK: New Forums Press.

Wlodkowski, R. J., & Ginsberg, M. B. (2003). *Diversity and motivation: Culturally responsive teaching.* San Francisco, CA: Jossey-Bass.

Zhao, C., & Kuh, G. (2004). Adding value: Learning communities and student engagement. *Research in Higher Education, 45*(2), 115–138.

Web Resources

AAC&U Diversity Web: An Interactive Resource Hub for Higher Education
http://www.diversityweb.org/

American Association of University Professors (AAUP): Professional Ethics
http://www.aaup.org/AAUP/issues/ethics/

American Psychological Association: Resources on Coping with Traumatic Events http://www.apa.org/practice/ptresources.html

Ethics Resource Center (ERC)
http://www.ethics.org/

National Study of Living-Learning Programs
http://www.livelearnstudy.net/home.html

National Survey of Student Engagement
http://nsse.iub.edu/

Washington Center for Improving the Quality of Undergraduate Education
http://www.evergreen.edu/washcenter/home.asp

General Readings on Teaching and Learning

Association of American Colleges and Universities. (2002). *Greater expectations: A new vision for learning as a nation goes to college.* Washington, DC: Association of American Colleges and Universities.

Banner, J.M. Jr., & Cannon, H.C. (1997). *The elements of teaching.* New Haven, CT: Yale University.

Beaty, L. (2005). Towards professional teaching in higher education: the role of accreditation. In P. Ashwin (Ed.), *Changing higher education* (pp. 99–112). London, UK: Routledge.

Bess, J. (Ed.). (1997). *Teaching well and liking it: Motivating faculty to teach effectively.* Baltimore, MD: The Johns Hopkins University Press.

Biggs, J. (2003). *Teaching for quality learning* (2nd ed.) Buckingham, UK: Society for Research into Higher Education and Open University Press.

Blythe, T., & Associates. (1998). *The teaching for understanding guide.* San Francisco, CA: Jossey-Bass.

Braxton, J.M., Luckey, W., & Helland, P. (2002). *Institutionalizing a broader view of scholarship through Boyer's Four Domains.* ASHE-ERIC higher education report: No. 29. San Francisco, CA: Jossey-Bass.

Brew, A. (2003). Teaching and research: new relationships and their implications for inquiry-based teaching and learning in higher education. *Higher Education Research and Development, 22*(1), 3–18.

Brew, A. (2006). *Research and teaching: beyond the divide.* London, UK: Palgrave Macmillan.

Brookfield, S.D. (2006). *The skillful teacher: On technique, trust, and responsiveness in the classroom.* San Francisco: Jossey-Bass.

Brown, S. & Race, P. (2002). *Lecturing: A practical guide.* London, UK: Kogan Page.

Chen, A. & Maanen, J.V. (1999). *The reflective spin: Case studies of teachers in higher education transforming action.* Singapore: World Scientific Publishing Co. Pte. Ltd.

Christensen, C.M., Horn, M.B. & Johnson, C.W. (2008). *Disrupting class: How disruptive innovation will change the way the world learns.* New York, NY: McGraw-Hill.

Clark, B.R. (1997). The modern integration of research activities with teaching and learning. *Journal of Higher Education, 68,* 241–256.

Colbeck, C.L. & Wharton-Michael, P. (2006). The public scholarship: Reintegrating Boyer's four domains. In J. Braxton (Ed.), *New directions for institutional Research: No. 129, Analyzing faculty work and rewards: Using Boyer's four domains of scholarship* (pp. 7–19). San Francisco, CA: Jossey-Bass.

Collins, R. & Palmer, A. (2004). *Perceptions of rewarding excellence in teaching: Carrots or sticks?* York, UK: The Higher Academy. http://www.headcademy.ac.uk/resources/detail/id394_perceptions_of_rewarding_excellence

Cousin, G. (2009). *Strategies for researching learning in higher education: An introduction to contemporary methods and approaches.* London, UK: Routledge.

Cox, M.D. (2001). Faculty learning communities: Change agents for transforming institutions into learning organizations. In D. Lieberman and C. Wehlberg (Eds.), *To Improve the Academy: Vol. 19, Resources for Faculty, Instructional and Organizational Development* (pp. 69–93). Stillwater, OK: New Forums Press.

Cox, M.D. & Richlin, L. (2004). Building faculty learning communities. In M.D. Cox & L. Richlin (Eds.), *New Directions for Teaching and Learning: No. 97, Building faculty learning communities* (pp. 127–136). San Francisco, CA: Jossey-Bass.

Cox, R., Huber, J.T., & Hutchings, P. (2004). *Survey of CASTL scholars.* Stanford, CA: The Carnegie Foundation for the Advancement of Teaching.

D'Andrea, V., & Gosling, D. (2005). *Improving teaching and learning in higher education: A whole institution approach.* Buckingham, UK: Open University Press, McGraw-Hill.

Dart, B. & Boulton-Lewis, G. (1998). *Teaching and learning in higher education.* Camberwell, Victoria: The Australian Counsel for Education Research Ltd.

Diamond, R.M. (2002). Defining scholarship for the twenty-first century. In K.J. Zaborski (Ed.), *New Directions for Teaching and Learning, No. 90, Scholarship in the Postmodern Era: New Venues, New Values, New Visions* (pp. 73–80). San Francisco, CA: Jossey-Bass.

Donald, J. (2002). *Learning to think: Disciplinary perspectives.* San Francisco, CA: Jossey-Bass.

Gibbs, G. & Habeshaw, T. (2003). *Recognising and rewarding excellent teaching* (2nd ed.). Milton Keynes: TQEF National Co-ordination Team, Centre for Higher Education Practice, Open University.

Gibbs, P., Angelides, P. & Michaelides, P. (2004). Preliminary thoughts on praxis of higher education teaching. *Teaching in Higher Education, 9,* 1983–194.

Glassick, C.E. (2000). Boyer's expanded definition of scholarship, the standards for assessing scholarship, and elusiveness of the scholarship of teaching. *Academic Medicine, 75,* 877–880.

Gunn, V. (2003). Transforming subject boundaries: The interface between higher education teaching and learning theories and subject-specific knowledge. *Arts and Humanities in Higher Education, 2*(3), 265–280.

Hattie, J. & Marsh, H.W. (1996, Winter). The relationship between teaching and research: A meta-analysis. *Review of Educational Research,* 507–542.

Huber, M.T. (2006). Disciplines, pedagogy, and inquiry-based learning about teaching. In C. Kreber (Ed.), *New Directions for Teaching and Learning: No. 107, Exploring research-based teaching* (pp. 69–77). San Francisco, CA: Jossey-Bass.

Jarvis, P., Holdford, J. & Griffin, C. (2003). *The theory & practice of learning.* London; Sterling, VA: Kogan Page.

Jenkins, A., Healey, M. & Zetter, R. (2007). *Linking teaching and research in departments and disciplines.* York, UK: The Higher Education Academy.

Kane, R., Sandretto, S. & Heath, C. (2004). An investigation into excellent tertiary teaching: Emphasizing reflective practice. *Higher Education, 47*(3), 283–310.

Kelly-Kleese, C. (2003). Community college scholarship. *Journal on Excellence in College Teaching, 14,* 69–84.

Kreber, C. (Ed.). *The university and its disciplines: Teaching and Learning within and beyond disciplinary boundaries.* New York: NY: Routledge.

Leamnson, R. (1999). *Thinking about teaching and learning.* Sterling, VA: Stylus.

Lee, V.S. (Ed.). (2004). *Teaching & learning through inquiry: A guidebook for institutions and instructors.* Sterling, VA: Stylus.

Light, R. (2001). *Making the most of college: Students speak their minds.* Cambridge, Harvard University Press.

Lucas, A. (Ed.). (2000). *Leading academic change: essential roles for department chairs.* San Francisco, CA: Jossey-Bass.

Lueddeke, G. (2003). Professionalizing teaching practice in higher education: A study of disciplinary variation and teaching-scholarship. *Studies in Higher Education, 28*(2), 213–228.

Lyons, N. (2006). Reflective engagement as professional development in the lives of university teachers. *Teachers and Teaching, 12*(2), 151–168.

Major, C.H. & Palmer, B. (2006). Reshaping teaching and learning: the transformation of faculty pedagogical content knowledge. *Higher Education, 51*(4), 619–647. http://dx.doi.org/DOI10.1007/s10734-004-1391-2

McAlpine, L. (2004). Designing learning as well as teaching: A research-based model for instruction that emphasizes learning practice. *Active Learning in Higher Education, 5*(2), 119–134.

McKeachie, W.J. (Ed.). (2002). *McKeachie's teaching tips: Strategies, research, and theory for college and university teachers* (11th ed.). Boston, MA: Houghton Mifflin.

McKeachie, W.J. & Svinicki, M. (Eds.). (2011). *McKeachie's teaching tips: Strategies, research, and theory for college and university teachers* (13th ed.). Boston, MA: Houghton Mifflin.

Mentkowski, M. & Associates. (2000, April). *Learning that lasts: Integrating learning, development, and performance in college and beyond.* San Francisco, CA: Jossey-Bass.

Morrison, G.R., Ross, S.M. & Kemp, J.E. (2004). *Designing effective instruction.* San Francisco, CA: Jossey-Bass.

Palmer, P.J. (1998). *The courage to teach: Exploring the inner landscape of a teacher's life.* San Francisco, CA: Jossey-Bass.

Pescosolido, B.A. & Aminzade, R. (Eds.). (1999). *The social worlds of higher education: Handbook for teaching in a new century.* Thousand Oaks, CA: Pine Forge.

Pratt, D.D. (2005). *Five perspectives on the teaching in adult and higher education.* Malabar, FL: Krieger Publishing Company.

Rice, R.E. (1996). *Making a place for the new American scholar. New pathways: faculty careers and employment for the 21st* century project. Washington, DC: American Association for Higher Education.

Rice, R.E. (2002). Beyond "scholarship reconsidered": Toward an enlarged vision of scholarly work of faculty members. In K. Zahorski (Ed.), *New Directions for Teaching and Learning: No. 90,Scholarship in the postmodern era* (pp. 7–17). San Francisco, CA: Jossey-Bass.

Rice, R.E. (2003). *Rethinking scholarship and new practice: a central AAHE priority, New Directions: Special Report 4.* Washington, DC: American Association for Higher Education.

Richlin, L. (Ed.). (1993). Preparing faculty for the new conception of scholarship. *New Directions for Teaching and Learning: No. 54, Preparing faculty for the new conceptions of scholarship.* San Francisco, CA: Jossey-Bass.

Richlin, L. (2006). *Blueprint for learning: Constructing college courses to facilitate, assess, and document learning.* Sterling, VA: Stylus.

Riordan, T. (2008). Disciplinary expertise revisited. *Arts and Humanities in Higher Education, 7*(3), 262–275.

Riordan, T. and Roth, J. (Eds.). (2004). *Disciplines as frameworks for student learning: Teaching the practice of the disciplines.* Sterling, VA: Stylus.

Roth, J.K. (Ed.). (1997). *Inspiring teaching: Carnegie professors of the year speak.* Boston, MA: Anker Publishing.

Royse, D. (2001). *Teaching tips for college and university instructors: A practical guide.* Needham Heights, MA: Allyn & Bacon.

Schon, D. (1983). *The reflective practitioner.* New York, NY: Basic Books.

Shor, I. (1992). *Empowering education: Critical teaching for social change.* Chicago: University of Chicago Press.

Shor, I. (1996). *When students have power: Negotiating authority in a critical pedagogy.* Chicago: University of Chicago Press.

Shulman, L.S. (1999). Taking learning seriously. *Change, 31*(4), 10–17.

Skelton, A. (2005). *Understanding teaching excellence in higher education: Towards a critical approach.* Abingdon, Oxon: Routledge.

Umback, P.D. & Wawrzynski, M.R. (2005). Faculty do matter: The role of college faculty in student learning and engagement. *Research in Higher Education, 46*(2), 1530–184.

Wilson, S.M. (Ed.). (2004). *The wisdom of practice: Essays on teaching, learning, and learning to teach by Lee S. Shulman.* San Francisco, CA: Jossey-Bass.

Young, P. (2006). Out of balance: Lecturers' perceptions of differential status and rewards in relation to teaching and research. *Teaching in Higher Education, 11*(2), 191–202.

Zahorski, K.J. (Ed.). (2002). *New Directions in Teaching and Learning: No. 90, Scholarship in the postmodern era: New venues, new values, new visions.* San Francisco, CA: Jossey-Bass.

Zamorski, B. (2002). Research-led teaching and learning in higher education: A case. *Teaching in Higher Education, 7,* 411–427.

About the Editors

Michele M. Welkener, Ph.D., is an Assistant Professor in the Higher Education and College Student Personnel programs within the Department of Counselor Education and Human Services, and Coordinator of the Ph.D. program in Higher Education Administration at the University of Dayton. She teaches Master's and doctoral-level courses such as *Student Development Theory, Student Cultures in the University Environment, The Professoriate, Critical Reflection in Higher Education Leadership,* and *Building Learning Communities in Higher Education.*

Dr. Welkener has served as an administrator of nationally recognized living learning community, faculty development, and academic programs in higher education, in addition to teaching as an adjunct or full-time faculty member in higher education and student affairs graduate programs. Her professional affiliations include ASHE, American Educational Research Association (AERA) Division J (Higher Education), American College Personnel Association (ACPA), and Association of American Colleges and Universities (AAC&U). She was honored with two "Bright Idea" Recognition Awards from the Professional and Organizational Development Network in Higher Education (POD) for her work with TA/graduate student development.

Her major research interests include teaching and learning in higher education, college student development, creativity, and learning-centered partnerships in academe.

Address:

School of Education and Allied Professions
The University of Dayton
202-D Chaminade Hall
300 College Park
Dayton, OH 45469–0530
(937) 229–3620
< Michele.Welkener@notes.udayton.edu >

Alan Kalish, Ph.D., is Director of the University Center for the Advancement of Teaching and an adjunct Assistant Professor of Educational Policy & Leadership at The Ohio State University.

In addition to his work at Ohio State, Dr. Kalish was a co-founder of the Ohio Teaching Enhancement Programs coalition and has served on the Core Committee (Board of Directors) of the Professional and Organizational Development Network in Higher Education (POD).

His research includes qualitative and quantitative studies of transitions from graduate school to faculty life and on teaching and learning in higher education. A national leader on peer review of teaching, preparing future faculty, scholarship of teaching and learning, and assessment of academic support units, he has been Principal Investigator or Co-PI on grants from the U.S. Department of Education Fund for Improvement of Post-Secondary Education, Ohio Board of Regents, and Ohio Learning Network.

Address:
The Ohio State University
260 Younkin Success Center
1640 Neil Avenue
Columbus, Ohio 43201–2333
(614) 292–3644
< Kalish.3@osu.edu >

Heather M. Bandeen, Ph.D., is the Professional Development Coordinator at the state-wide WIIN Center for Washington's Office of the Superintendent of Public Instruction.

Dr. Bandeen has developed, analyzed, and managed professional development models in three states across K-12 and university systems. These include initiatives with Project Zero at Harvard University, Michigan State University, Western Michigan University, the Connected Mathematics Project, and North Central Regional Laboratory (NCREL). After teaching and coordinating curriculum in Arizona and Michigan, Dr. Bandeen was recruited to develop a regional teacher education program in Northern Michigan. She has taught mathematics, literacy, service-learning, policy, and technology courses at several universities and community colleges.

She earned her doctoral degree in Educational Administration from The Ohio State University with an emphasis in policy. In addition to receiving several scholarships, she was selected for the first professional development internship offered through The University Center for the Advancement of Teaching (UCAT) which funded the final years of her doctoral work. She completed a Master of Arts in Higher Education at The University of Michigan.

Address:
District and School Improvement and Accountability
Office of the Superintendent of Public Instruction (OSPI)
6501 North 23rd Street
Tacoma, Washington 98406
(253) 571–3547
<heather.bandeen@k12.wa.us>